Edwin T. Atkinson

Statistical Descriptive and Historical Account of the North-Western

Provinces of India

Vol. II

Edwin T. Atkinson

Statistical Descriptive and Historical Account of the North-Western Provinces of India
Vol. II

ISBN/EAN: 9783348014694

Printed in Europe, USA, Canada, Australia, Japan

Cover: Foto ©ninafisch / pixelio.de

More available books at **www.hansebooks.com**

STATISTICAL,

DESCRIPTIVE AND HISTORICAL ACCOUNT

OF THE

NORTH-WESTERN PROVINCES OF INDIA.

PREPARED, UNDER ORDERS OF THE GOVT. OF INDIA,

BY

EDWIN T. ATKINSON, B.A.,

BENGAL CIVIL SERVICE.

VOL. II.

MEERUT DIVISION:
PART I.

ALLAHABAD:

NORTH-WESTERN PROVINCES GOVERNMENT PRESS.

1875.

CONTENTS.

PREFACE.

THE preface to the first volume sufficiently explains the origin and object of the present work. Since its publication the position of the Gazetteer has been defined by a Resolution of the Government of these Provinces (No. 724A., dated April 21st, 1875), which runs as follows :—

READ—

(1.) Resolution, Government, North-Western Provinces, No. 2799, dated 23rd June, 1868, laying down a scheme for District Memoirs.

(2.) Report of Officer in charge of the Provincial Gazetteer, No. 1569, dated 29th June, 1874.

(3.) Memorandum by Mr. Atkinson on the difference between the Gazetteer and the District Memoir.

(4.) The first volume of the Gazetteer (Bundelkhand).

OBSERVATIONS.—The general design of the Gazetteer, as originally intended, can be gathered from the series of queries issued with the authority of this Government in 1871, and those subsequently circulated by the Government of India for the guidance of Editors of Gazetteers. In these Provinces, however, the common plan has been somewhat modified by the adoption of a scheme for the preparation of District Memoirs ; and in consequence of this arrangement the Editor of the Gazetteer has not hitherto dwelt on certain classes of subjects which, had it not been intended that they should have formed the main portion of the District Memoir, would have been treated more at length. The first volume of the Gazetteer is thus in some respects incomplete. The plan of a series of District Memoirs, originated by Mr. Thomason, and revived by Sir William Muir, is unquestionably good, but from various causes, and chiefly from the want of leisure on the part of officers competent to undertake the work, the District Memoir scheme has not succeeded. Memoirs have as yet been completed for only three out of the thirty-five districts in these Provinces, and His Honor sees no reason for believing that in future the progress will be greater. He is thus led to consider whether the restrictions as to form and character imposed on the Gazetteer should be maintained.

In view of the training and experience of the present Editor, the Lieutenant-Governor thinks it desirable that the Gazetteer should be more complete in itself, and that the gaps caused by the non-existence of the Memoirs should in future be supplied. The Editor should collect and exhibit all information on public affairs on the points noted in paragraphs 2 to 13 of his memorandum dated November 2nd, 1874, which it may be considered expedient to publish, and should include it in the Gazetteer, whether the information forms a portion of the plan of the District Memoir or not. The work will thus aim at a position differing from and somewhat higher than that of ordinary Gazetteers. It will be complete in itself, and contain an account of all matters of interest connected with each district, or, at least, where a detailed description is not considered necessary, a reference to them.

Whilst signifying approval of the scheme sketched out in the memorandum drawn up by Mr. Atkinson, with the modifications necessary in view of the slow progress of the District Memoirs, His Honor desires his attention to the following instructions. The arrangement adopted in distributing the information in the Gazetteer is approved of, and should be adhered to for every district. As to settlement reports, rent-rate reports, and the like, as a rule it will be sufficient to give the results only of the settlement operations and a short sketch of the fiscal history, omitting details of a purely executive character, such as the reasons for adopting certain classifications of soils in particular localities, the details of the survey demarcation of boundaries, preparation of records, distribution of judicial work, adjustment of circle rates and rent-rates, and other similar matters. At the same time, where possible, a description and history of each fiscal subdivision should be given, sufficient to place officers new to the district charge in possession of such general knowledge of the physical capabilities of the tract, its fiscal history and its inhabitants, as may enable them at once to exercise an intelligent control over its administration. The labour necessary to procure a correct balance-sheet of each fiscal subdivision, from the conquest or cession, would be very great; and as the information, when obtained, is more curious than useful, its compilation need not be attempted. Changes in the Judicial, Magisterial, and Revenue jurisdictions, lists of district officers, lists of villages and their assessment, the reproduction of settlement reports, and other similar matters involving much original research, and the preparation of large tabular statements cannot be attempted with the present establishment. Matters of Imperial policy will not be discussed, the Gazetteer being confined to the record of facts. It is difficult to lay down a hard and fast rule as to what shall be excluded, and in this matter great discretion must be allowed to the Editor, who will, as directed, submit the proofs before final printing for the approval of this Government.

With these remarks the Lieutenant-Governor leaves the work in Mr. Atkinson's hands, with the assurance that no avoidable delay will be allowed in its completion.

The system of transliteration followed is that laid down in the *North-Western Provinces Gazette* for October 3, 1874 (pages 1732-33), and for convenience of reference is reproduced here:—

Transliteration.

RULES FOR TRANSLITERATION.

Every letter in the vernacular must be uniformly represented by a certain letter in the Roman character as follows :—

Vowels.

PERSIAN.		DEVANAGARI.		ROMAN.	PRONUNCIATION.
Initial.	Non-initial.	Initial.	Non-initial.		
ا	´ (zabar)	अ	not expressed.	a	As in woman.
آ	ا	आ	ा	á	„ father.
ا	ِ (zer)	इ	ि	i	„ bit.
ای	ِ or ی	ई	ी	í	„ machine.
ا	ُ (pesh)	उ	ु	u	„ pull.
او	ُ	ऊ	ू	ú	„ rude.
اے	ِ or ے	ऎ	े	e	„ grey.
اے	ِ or ے	ऐ	ै	ai	„ aisle.
او	ُ	ओ	ो	o	„ hole.
او	ُ	औ	ौ	au	As *ou* in house (nearly, being a combination of the a and u above.

Consonants:·

PERSIAN.	DEVANAGARI.	ROMAN.
ب	ब	b
بھ	भ	bh
چ	च	ch
چھ	छ	chh
د or ڎ	द or ड	d
دھ or ڎھ	ध or ढ	dh
ف	wanting	f
گ	ग	g
گھ or غ	घ	gh
ج	ज	j
جھ	झ	jh
ق or ک	क	k
ک or خ	ख	kh
	क्ष	ksh
ل	ल	l
م	म	m
ن	न, ञ, ङ, ण or anuswara	n
پ	प	p
پھ	फ	ph
ز or ر	र or ड़	r
رھ	ढ़	rh
ص or س , ث	स	s
ش	श	sh
ط or ت , ت	य or प	t
تھ or ٹھ	त or ट	th
ر	ध br ठ	w.or v
ی	ब	y
ط or ض , ز , ذ	य	z
ژ	wanting	zh
ع	ditto	ditto
	ditto	omitted, the accompanying vowel only being expressed.
———	ज्ञ	gy

In the present volume my acknowledgments are due to Mr. G. R.
Williams, C.S., for notes on the Saháranpur District. For the Aligarh
District I have depended almost entirely on the statistics given by
Mr. Hutchinson for the pre-mutiny period, and on Mr. W. H. Smith's
valuable reports for the period since the mutiny.   Without Mr.
Smith's assistance I should not have been able to give so complete
an account of the Aligarh District as I have attempted. Mr. Smith,
too, kindly examined the sheets relating to Aligarh whilst passing
through the Press, and similar service has been rendered me for Saháranpur by Mr. E. G. Jenkinson, C.S. Throughout I have consulted with much advantage the valuable records of the Board of Revenue, the numerous settlement reports, and the records of the Government Secretariat. I cannot do better than quote here the remarks
of the late Mr. G. Edmonstone whilst engaged on a similar work:—

" It is, I believe, generally allowed that there are few undertakings
more difficult of successful accomplishment than the detailed
account of a tract of country, a description of its natural resources,
of the improvements which art and civilization have introduced, and
the further amelioration of which it is capable; of the extent and
nature of its population, and, in short, of all the points which have
any relation to agricultural prosperity. Although I have endeavoured to place such a picture before you, I cannot flatter myself
that I have succeeded, and I shall only be too happy if my labours
meet with the indulgent consideration which the zeal and perseverance with which they have been prosecuted deserve." If my progress has been slow, it has been due to no fault of mine, for the care
and labour required in verifying and collecting even the statistics
of the present volume have been such as to take up a great portion
of my time. As it is, however, I trust that the labour has not been
lost, and that the present volume will be found to contain an accurate
and full account as far as my materials would allow, of the various
subjects it professes to treat of. I have not ventured to recompile
authorised statistics such as those relating to the census, settlements, the collection of the land-revenue, excise, stamps, and
education, and give them as I find them on the authority of the
departments concerned.

NAINI TAL :   }   E. T. ATKINSON.
  The 1st July, 1875.   }

STATISTICAL AND DESCRIPTIVE ACCOUNT

OF THE

NORTH-WESTERN PROVINCES.

MEERUT DIVISION.

INTRODUCTION.

CONTENTS:

PART I.

THE MEERUT DIVISION proper comprises the Districts of Dehra Dún, Sabáranpur, Muzaffarnagar, Meerut, Bulandshahr, and Aligarh, but for the purposes of this notice the Dehra Dún District is omitted, as its description comes

Boundaries.

more correctly into the volume devoted to the hill districts. The Meerut Division, as thus restricted, occupies the upper portion of the Duáb between north latitude 27°-29'-0" and 30°-21'-30", and east longitude 77°-3'-45" and 78°-42'-30". It is bounded on the north by the Siwálik (Shiwálak) hills; on the south by the Muttra and Eta Districts of the Agra Division; on the east by the Ganges; and on the west by the Jumna. The area in 1872 comprised 10,110 square miles and 308 acres, occupied by 7,508 villages. The population during the same year numbered 4,860,228 souls, of whom 3,810,321 were Hindús, 1,045,780 were Musalmúns, and 1,378 were Christians and others neither Hindu nor Musalmán. The Hindús comprise about 78 per cent. of the total population, the provincial percentage being 86·3 per cent. The Meerut Division has, next to Rohilkhand, a greater number and proportion of Muhammadan inhabitants than any other division in these provinces.

The Ganges and the Jumna, which include between them the Duáb, issue from the Siwálik hills in nearly the same latitude, and flow southwards in an almost parallel line. For a short distance after leaving the hills they traverse a formation of boulders superposed on shingle, which extends as the gradual denudation of the hills is effected. The boulder beds of the rivers sustain with impunity the great velocity which is a natural result of the considerable fall of the country close to the hills; but when the line of boulder formation is passed, some eight or ten miles below the foot of the hills, they enter on a sandy soil no longer able to withstand a rapid current. The consequence of this is, that the rivers hitherto flowing in channels of moderate width expand into broad valleys, which they have worn out for themselves in the friable soil that they here encounter. Within the limits of these valleys, the great rivers adopt an ever varying course, and within a few miles after leaving the boulder formation, the surface of the water in these rivers is found to be as much as sixty feet below the level of the country, and this difference in level is maintained until the united streams of the Ganges and the Jumna pass out of these provinces in their progress to the sea. The alluvial lands which are formed in the wide valleys or troughs of the rivers are called the *khádirs* of those rivers, and the high and dry plateau of the Duáb which lies between them is called the *bángar* or uplands. The declivity of the country rapidly decreases as the distance from the Himálayas becomes greater. Percolation on a vast scale is continually at work in the shingle and boulder portions of the courses of the rivers, and it is observed that the river Jumna in the latitude of Saháranpur is only fordable at favourable points, even when embankments are made quite across the river near Faizabad, just below the Siwálik gorge, for the purpose of diverting the whole of the available supply of the river into the Eastern and Western Jumna Canals. The great central plateau or uplands touches the hills near the Sháhjahánpur pass to the north of the Saháranpur District. From this point, a well-defined bank runs south-east to the high bank of the Ganges, which it joins near Bhúkarheri in the Muzaffarnagar District, and this high bank thence throughout the Duáb forms the eastern boundary of the central plateau. The western boundary of the uplands runs close to the bed of the Jumna river. The lowlands or khádir here are much narrower than they are on the east, and seldom average more than four miles in width. The soil in these uplands, close to the hills, consists of a clay of a dark chocolate colour, producing fair crops in years of ordinary moisture. Further south loam and sand or sand alone predominates.

The central plateau is drained by the Hindan and its tributaries, which eventually flow into the Jumna, and the East Káli Nadí and its tributaries, which join the Ganges. The Hindan rises in the north of the Saháranpur District, and flowing southwards, receives on the left bank the West Káli Nadí at Rauli, in Parganah Burhána of the Muzaffarnagar District ; and further south, on the right bank, the Karsuni or Krishní Nadí at Barnáwa, in the Meerut District. Thence it bends to the west, and after a total course of 108 miles falls into the Jumna in Parganah Loni of the same district. Both the Karsuni and the West Kálí Nadí take their rise in the Saháranpur District, and themselves receive the waters of numerous drainage lines. To the east of the Ganges Canal the head-waters of the East Kálí Nadí collect in the Muzaffarnagar District, and, uniting further south, flow in a well-defined channel through the District of Bulandshahr, and join the Ganges near Kanauj in the Farrukhabad District. The Sangar rises in the Aligarh District, and flowing southwards joins the Jumna. Besides these main drainage lines of the central plateau there are numerous water-courses, which either join the larger streams, or make a way for themselves into the depressions occupied by the great rivers which form the main arterial lines of drainage. Such are the Kátha, which rises in the Saháranpur District, between the Krishní and the Jumna, and after a course of 32 miles joins the latter river near Kairána, in the Muzaffarnagar District ; the Síla Khála, an important drainage line of the Saháranpur District, joins the West Kálí Nadí ; the Ním and Chhoiya, lines of drainages which collect together in a defined channel in the Bulandshahr District and join the East Kálí Nadí south of Aligarh. The Karon, also rising in the same district, flows through Aligarh and Muttra, and joins the Jumna in the Agra District. These streams are described at length in the notices of the districts through which they flow.

CANALS.

The most important feature in the Upper Duáb is the great canal system

Canals.

which has its origin there, and sends out its ferti-lising streams in every direction. There are two main canals, the Eastern Jumna Canal, which waters the western portions of the Saháranpur, Muzaffarnagar, and Meerut Districts, and the Ganges Canal, of which the main branch, starting from Hardwár at the foot of the Siwáliks, terminates at Cawnpore in the Ganges, and a second branch runs, known as the Etáwa branch, and joins the Jumna. The general history of these canals, as a whole, will be noticed here, reserving the local description and details for the district notices.[1]

The failure from time to time of the periodical rains, and the arid nature of

History of irrigation.

the climate of these provinces during some months of the year, has rendered the practice of artificial irriga-tion a necessity from the earliest ages, and each section of the country possesses its own primitive, and often ingenious, method for raising water for this pur-pose. In a small portion of Bundelkhand[2] a few large reservoirs of water were formed by damming up the narrow outlets of the valleys. These works, after

---

[1] The authorities for this portion of the work are the annual Irrigation Reports ; the Ganges Canal, by Sir Proby T. Cautley : London, 1860 ; Notes on the Eastern Jumna Canal Levels ; and the records of the Board of Revenue of these Provinces.   [2] Gazetteer, I., 147

the lapse of seven to nine centuries, still exist as monuments of the energy and skill of their constructors. Throughout the Tarái, Bareilly, Sháhjahánpur, and Gorakhpur Districts, permanent dams were not attempted, but an indifferent substitute was found in the use of temporary dams thrown across the numerous small perennial streams which intersect those districts, whereby the drainage of the country was impeded and the malarious character of the climate of those districts was very much intensified. In the Duáb and the Benares Division irrigation was effected partly from natural reservoirs known as *jhíls*, and formed in the shallow depressions which abound there, and partly from wells.

All these methods, however, were strictly local in their influence, and the sources on which they depended for their supply of water were generally limited, and liable to total failure in seasons of drought, just when their assistance was most urgently needed, and they have ever proved insufficient to guard the country against the inroads of famine. The absence of a strong central authority, and the parcelling out of the country amongst tribes and clans hostile to each other by religion, birth or tradition, have ever prevented any combined efforts of the people and the Government in carrying out extended schemes of irrigation. Here and there some local governor has made his name remembered by some attempts to provide water for the people of the town in which he resided ; but, with the exception of the canals known as those of Ali Mardán Khán, which have been utilised for portions of the course of the Eastern Jumna Canal, and the Abú Nálá line of drainage in the Meerut District, no remains have come down to us that have been designed to provide for more than the wants of a very limited local area. At present there are seven canal systems at work in these provinces : the great Ganges Canal, opened in 1851 ; the Eastern Jumna Canal, opened in 1830 ; the canals of Dehra Dún, commenced in 1837 ; the Rohilkhand Canals, opened at various times since 1854 ; the small canals of the Bijnaur District ; the Agra Canal, opened in 1874 ; and the Bundelkhand Irrigation Works of the Hamírpur and Jhansi Districts. The works in progress are the Lower Ganges Canal, intended to water the country between the East Kálí Nadí and the Ganges, several projects of irrigation from small rivers in the north of the Bareilly District, and the Bundelkhand works, for utilising the waters of the Ken, Betwa, and Dhasán.

Each of these canals will be described in the volume to which the districts within which it is situated belong. In the present volume I take up the Eastern Jumna Canal and the Ganges Canal, each as a whole, reserving the district details for the district notices.

The original lines of the Eastern Jumna Canal[1] were laid by the celebrated

Canal of Ali Mardán Khán.

Ali Mardán Khán in the reign of Shahjahán. The excessive slope of the country between the Naugang and

---

[1] For a full description of each work on this canal see Captain P. T. Cautley's report : Calcutta, 1845 ; and Colonel Morton's Notes ; Agra, 1852.

Maskara rivers, which would have led to a retrogression of levels fatal to the direction which the former stream now holds, shows that at no time could this canal have contained much water, whilst the absence of distributary channels shows that it afforded little or no irrigation. It would appear that the difficulty caused by the torrents crossed in its course led to the project being abandoned. It is said that the water, at one time, travelled as far as Ranap, a royal hunting preserve on the left bank of the Jumna, nearly opposite Dehli ; and the old hunting seat of Bádsháh Mahál, situated in the forests north of Nayashahr, was undoubtedly built either on an old branch of the Jumna, through which the canal stream was brought, or on an excavated channel made for the purposes of the canal. Zábita Khán, too, succeeded in bringing a stream of water from the Jumna to Ghausgarh, one of his fortified posts in Parganah Thána Bhawan of the Muzaffarnagar District. Tradition has it that in doing so great loss was occasioned to the towns of Bahat and Sahár.anpur.

Another canal project executed by the native Government was that known as
Other canals. the Abú Nála, or canal of Muhammad Abú Khán, the remains of which still exist in the vicinity of Meerut. It consisted of a cut made from the West Kálí Nadí, near the village of Rámpur, to the head of a small tributary of the East Kálí Nadí, called the Khodara Nálá, which rises near the village of Daurála. The length of this cut did not exceed 12½ miles, and its width, judging from the present remains, could not have exceeded 15 feet. The water after reaching Daurála must have passed down the Khodara Nálá to Meerut to irrigate the gardens and orchards around the town. There is no tradition of it as a running stream, though for a season it must have had a supply of water. The bed of the canal was formed by throwing an embankment across the head of the West Kálí Nadí, which checked the floods in the river, and must have given rise to extensive inundations. For these reasons, and the difficulties encountered in keeping the bed clear of silt, the project was abandoned. The present Ganges Canal crosses the Abú Nálá near Jawálágarh, and that portion of the nálá which approaches the canal from the West Kálí Nadí is now converted into an escape for throwing the waste water from the canal into the valley of the river. A similar work was executed by Ghulám Kádir by means of an embankment thrown across the Karsuni or Krishní, which runs westward and parallel to West Kálí Nadí, close by the towns of Jalálabad and Thána Bhawan. Captain Debude, in 1825, proposed to carry out the original design of Muhammad Abú's canal, but the project was found to be unsuited for the objects proposed.

EASTERN JUMNA CANAL.

During the short period of thirty-five years in the beginning of the present
Eastern Jumna Canal. century no less than eight famines occurred; the evident failure of all the ordinary sources and methods

of irrigation gave rise to the conviction that more extended schemes were required, and during this period the foundations were laid of the system of canals, by which in the course of a few years almost the entire area of the North-Western Provinces will be commanded. In 1809, on the 7th of October, the first step was taken by the British Government towards this object. The Board of Commissioners, actuated probably by the disastrous results of the famine of 1803-04, one of the severest on record in the annals of these provinces, recommended that a survey should be undertaken of the Duáb Canal line, now known as the Eastern Jumna Canal, and Lieutenant Todd, of the Bengal Army, was deputed to the work. Lieutenant Todd followed a line taken by Colonel Kyd in the early part of the same year, and appears to have completed his survey in the following year, 1810 ; but the passing interest in the subject had been replaced by State considerations of even more pressing urgency. Years passed by in inaction. The terrible famine in Agra, Cawnpore, and Bundelkhand in 1813-14 failed to induce any exertions beyond the deputation of Major Hodgson, who minutely examined the line between Saháranpur and the Jumna ; and the great scarcity which prevailed in 1819 throughout the lower districts of the Duáb passed by, without any further steps towards the security of the harvests being carried out.

Three years later the subject was again brought forward, and in 1822 Lieutenant Debude, of the Engineers, was appointed to survey and report upon the practicability of re-opening the Duáb Canal. In 1823, Captain R. Smith, of the same corps, was appointed Superintendent, and drew up a rough estimate of the cost of opening the whole line from a proposed new head near Faizabad to its re-union with the Jumna near Loni, amounting to Rs. 2,03,633. Excavation was commenced at the close of 1823. The line taken up by Ali Mardán Khán, the original projector of the canal, passed centrically over the high land between the Hindan and its tributaries and the Jumna, and showed much skill in selecting a course most favourable to the purposes of irrigation. The head was most probably taken from Khara opposite Kalesar; the canal flowed thence through the Bádsháh Mahál by Arfpur to Fatehpur, and entering the bed of the Budhi Jumna above Tánda, followed this bed to Nayashahr. From this point there is a cut to the Raipur river, down the course of which the stream was carried for two miles. Thence it crossed south-east over the high land, passing the Játon-wúla drainage line and Naugang river, beyond which, at the distance of half a mile, it terminated in a depression known as the Bahat Khála. Along this the canal took its course to its junction with the Maskara, in which it ran for 4,000 feet to the village of Kalsiya. Here the excavation commenced again upon high land passing to the west of Saháranpur, and terminating at the head of the Shámli Nála, immediately north of the village of Abba. It followed this nála for twenty-four miles to Bhainswál, where the excavation took a southerly direction, passing west of Shámli, east of Kándhla, and west of Baraut. After passing Baraut the line inclined south-east to Deola, and about twelve miles below the canal terminated in the Sikráni Nálá, down which it was conducted to Ranap and the Jumna.

Captain Smith followed the same line, but made its head much further south, between Fatehpur and Tánda, known as the Faizabad head ; and instead of allowing the Sikráni to carry off all the water, turned it into an escape, making a short canal between Gokalpur and Salímpur the main outlet. Cuts were also made to form an escape for the waters of the Maskara during time of flood. The year 1824-25 was one of famine in the Upper Duáb, and in the following year scarcity was general throughout these provinces. The works were in the meantime pushed on as rapidly as the limited means at the disposal of the engineers would allow, and the canal was opened in January, 1830. Captain P. T. Cautley was appointed to succeed Colonel Smith during the same year. In 1834 it was found necessary to utilise the old Khara head as well, and some slight alterations brought it into use as an alternative source of supply. Numerous works, rendered necessary by the actual experience of the water requirements of the districts through which the canal passed, were subsequently undertaken, and roads, bridges, and embankments were constructed. One feature of this canal, afterwards adopted on the Ganges Canal, was the formation of large plantations of *sál*, *sisú*, teak, and *tún*. Numerous chaukís (or rest-houses for the establishment) were also built. But all these matters, though increasing the cost of construction, were found, on the whole, to result in a very moderate outlay, when compared with the advantages derived from the canal, both in insuring a crop in seasons of drought, as well as in inducing the people to bring under cultivation the lands hitherto lying waste for want of water.

The bed of the canal from the Jumna head to a point opposite Alampur, on the Raipur Nálá, is composed of shingle or stone boulders decreasing in size on the approach to Alampur. From Alampur to Sarkari it consists of sand, with beds of clay here and there, but the sand predominates. From Sarkari to Jauli, clay in some places mixes with the kunkur, and from there to the tail of the canal at Salímpur the bed is sand. On the sandy sections of the canal erosion early set in, owing to the rapid fall in level, and rapids were formed which destroyed several bridges. These difficulties were got over by the construction of falls at Belka, Randaul, and Gúna in the first place, where the injury was most felt, and subsequently at Nagla, Babail, Sukulpur, Jauli, Salímpur, Sikráni, Sarkari, Halálpur, Mekchhapár, Ríri, and Bálpur. In 1852 Colonel Morton carried out the suggestions of Captain Cautley by constructing other falls and cuts, which materially improved the position of the canal as a means of irrigation, not of inundation, as it had on several occasions come to be. He also abandoned the tortuous course of the canal along the Shámli Nálá between Bálpur and Bhainswál, giving a perfectly straight line between Bálpur and the outlet, and thus saved the cost of maintaining 7·5 miles.

The circumstance of the canal lying at right angles to the line of drainage running across the Maskara, Naugang, and Játonwála torrents from west to east, was taken advantage of to relieve the dam at Kalsiya, by leading the surplus waters of the Maskara into the Chaicha, Nágúdeo and Dumaula, the three eastern heads of the Hindan. The result of this was to reduce the Maskara at its contact with the dam at Kalsiya to a moderate torrent. Similarly, the Játonwála drainage was turned into the Naugang stream, which was frequently relieved by permitting it to flow down the canal channel to the Maskara itself. Navigation was a secondary object in the construction, and can now only take place between Sarnauli, in Parganah Loni, and the outlet. As will be seen hereafter, none of the canals are as yet of much value as navigation lines, whilst as irrigation channels they have been perfectly successful.

At the end of the year 1830, the canal was opened with a debit against its
Fiscal history. capital account of Rs. 4,37,996. The following tables show the financial results of the management of the Eastern Jumna Canal for a series of years. These figures differ considerably from the results shown in the annual reports, and represent the latest returns of the office of Controller of Accounts. In regard to the capital accounts both of the Eastern Jumna Canal and the Ganges Canal, the differences between the results now shown and those given in the annual accounts may be set down as due (1) to the addition now made of the balances of stock in 1861-62 and to its fluctuations since then; (2) to the addition of the other suspense balances in 1871-72; (3) to a share of the Controller's office establishment charges from 1863-64 to 1868-69, and (4) to petty adjustments, discrepancies arising from various causes having crept in formerly when the office of the Joint Secretary to Government in the Irrigation Department and the Controller were apart. In the revenue accounts of both canals, the last two sources of difference, and a transfer from the revenue to the capital account of the survey charges for remodelling the works, sufficiently explain the differences in charges; whilst the exhibition of receipts, instead of assessments, accounts for the differences under "revenue." The charges for interest have been altered to suit the revised capital accounts, and altogether the figures now given must be taken as superseding all accounts hitherto published relating to both canals. Five per cent. has been charged on the capital outlay on canals up to 1870-71, and after that the charge is four and a half per cent. Ten per cent. of the outlay on establishments has been charged to the capital account, and the balance has been apportioned rateably

over maintenance and revenue, and the expenditure on works not chargeable to either revenue or capital :—

Capital Account.

Year.	OUTLAY DURING THE YEAR.			OUTLAY TO END OF THE YEAR.		
	Ordinary.	Extraordinary.	Total.	Ordinary.	Extraordinary.	Total.
	Rs.	Rs.	Rs.	Rs.	Rs.	Rs.
1834-35 ...	. 44,282	...	44,282	5,29,079	...	5,29,079
1840-41 ...	27,685	...	27,685	6,73,666	...	6,73,666
1845-46 ...	12,570	...	12,570	9,58,363	...	9,58,363
1850-51 ...	3,344	...	3,344	10,70,798	...	10,70,798
1855-56 ...	1,43,288	...	1,43,288	15,19,940	...	15,19,940
1860-61 ...	11,140	...	11,140	16,36,238	...	16,36,238
1865-66 ...	44,881	...	44,881	17,94,688	...	17,94,688
1866-67 ...	51,132	...	51,132	18,45,820	...	18,45,820
1867-68 ...	67,463	...	67,463	19,13,283	...	19,13,283
1868-69 ...	39,699	21,805	61,504	19,52,982	21,805	19,74,787
1869-70 ...	19,342	11,264	30,606	19,72,324	33,069	20,05,393
1870-71 ...	10,675	15,595	26,270	19,82,999	48,664	20,31,663
1871-72 ...	3,903	13,787	17,690	19,86,902	62,451	20,49,353
1872-73 ...	9,863	2,557	12,420	19,96,765	65,008	20,61,773

Revenue Account, A.

Year.	DURING THE YEAR.			TO END OF THE YEAR.			WORKING EXPENSES.	
	Direct income.	Increased land-revenue.	Total.	Direct income.	Increased land-revenue.	Total.	During the year.	To end of year.
	Rs.	Rs.	Rs.	Rs.	Rs.	Rs.	Rs.	Rs.
1834-35 ...	53,813	...	53,813	1,24,399	...	1,24,399	51,269	2,24,099
1840-41 ...	87,437	...	87,437	5,57,991	...	5,57,991	66,605	6,04,391
1845-46 ...	1,11,491	...	1,11,491	10,78,272	...	10,78,272	66,812	9,02,467
1850-51 ...	1,59,139	...	1,59,139	178,6,307	...	17,86,507	73,924	12,58,775
1855-56 ...	96,878	...	96,878	24,81,939	...	24,81,939	81,677	16,85,075
1860-61 ...	2,84,910	...	2,84,910	32,97,350	...	32,97,350	1,13,765	22,09,441
1865-66 ...	4,14,633	60,000	4,74,633	47,95,238	2,18,000	50,13,238	1,30,613	27,71,460
1866-67 ...	4,31,315	1,77,689	6,09,004	52,26,553	3,95,689	56,22,242	1,22,474	28,93,934
1867-68 ..	5,65,602	1,77,689	7,43,291	57,92,155	5,73,378	63,65,533	1,42,085	30,36,019
1868-69 ...	5,06,245	1,77,689	6,83,934	62,98,400	7,51,067	70,49,467	1,54,881	31,90,900
1869-70 ...	6,57,279	1,77,689	8,34,968	69,55,679	9,28,756	78,84,435	1,65,076	33,55,976
1870-71 ...	6,01,040	1,77,689	7,78,729	75,56,719	11,06,445	86,63,164	1,80,955	35,36,931
1871-72 ...	5,10,263	1,77,689	6,87,952	80,66,982	12,84,134	93,51,116	1,98,801	37,35,732
1872-73 ...	5,62,535	1,23,075	6,85,610	86,29,517	14,07,209	1,00,36,726	2,49,181	39,54,913

Revenue Account, B.

Year.	NET REVENUE TO END OF YEAR.		Charges for interest to the end of the year.	DIFFERENCE BETWEEN NET REVENUE AND CHARGES FOR INTEREST TO END OF YEAR.		PERCENTAGE OF NET REVENUE ON CAPITAL OUTLAY.	
	Exclusive of land-revenue.	Inclusive of land-revenue.		Excluding land-revenue.	Including land-revenue.	Excluding land-revenue.	Including land-revenue.
	Rs.	Rs.	Rs.	Rs.	Rs.	Rs.	Rs.
1834-35 ...	—99,700	—99,700	1,13,775	—2,13,475	...	·52	...
1840-41 ...	—46,400	—46,400	2,93,569	—3,39,969	...	3·22	...
1845-46 ...	1,75,805	1,75,805	4,99,738	—3,23,933	...	4·72	...
1850-51 ...	5,17,352	5,17,352	7,51,070	—2,33,538	...	7·98	...
1855-56 ...	7,96,864	7,96,864	10,44,569	—2,47,705	...	1·08	...
1860-61 ...	10,87,909	10,87,909	14,41,490	—3,53,581	...	10·53	...
1865-66 ...	20,23,778	2 ,41,778	18,64 251	1,59 527	3,77,527	16 23	19·66
1866-67 ...	23,32,619	27,28,308	19,53,985	3,78,634	7,74,323	17·20	27·10
1867-68 ...	27,56,136	31,29,514	20,46,276	7,09,860	12,83,288	22 94	32 58
1868-69 ...	31 07,500	38,58,567	21,41,940	9,65,560	17 16,627	18·36	27·65
1869-70 ...	35,99,703	45,28,459	22,40,679	13,59,024	22,67,780	24 92	33·92
1870-71 ...	40,19,788	51,26,233	23,40,948	16,78,840	27,85,285	20·94	29 80
1871-72 ...	43,31,250	56,15,384	24,32,719	18,98,531	31,82,665	15·33	24 07
1872-73	46,74,604	60,81,813	25,25,883	21,48,781	35,55,990	16 75	22·75

The following table gives the receipts for each year under each item of demand :—

Detail of direct income.

Year.	WATER-RATE.			Mill rents.	Canal plantations.	Navigation.	Miscellaneous.	Total actual receipts.
	Assessment.	Balances.	Realized.					
	Rs.	Rs.	Rs.	Rs.	Rs.	Rs.	Rs.	Rs.
1834-35 ...	37,918	32,018	48,310	3,335	801	...	1,367	53,813
1840-41 ...	89,136	42,564	77,249	3,298	1,505	938	4,347	87,437
1845-46 ...	96,534	55,797	98,039	8,122	1,706	416	3,209	1,11,491
1850-51 ...	1,18,302	65,306	1,34,608	14,178	3,487	750	6,116	1,59,139
1855-56 ...	1,32,315	25,720	80,884	6,770	5,255	224	3,745	96,878
1860-61 ..	2,61,196	1,42,764	27,009	5,953	3,128	60	5,760	2,84,910
1865-66 ...	4,13,760	1,21,283	3,83,141	7,305	10,569	39	13,579	4,14,633
1866-67 ...	5,32,464	1,51,902	4,06,411	7,715	11,791	2	5,393	4,31,315
1867-68 ...	4,61,698	2,77,955	5,44,153	8,853	9,817	26	2,753	5,65,602
1868-69 ...	5,99,560	1,95,500	4,80,375	9,048	5,181	38	11,603	5,06,245
1869-70 ...	5,83,642	3 14,705	6,28,487	6,896	13,569	...	8,627	6,57,279
1870-71 ...	5,44,377	2,70,060	5,78,895	7,597	11,651	13	2,984	6,01,040
1871-72 ...	4,97,838	2,35,542	4,79,942	9,708	18,153	123	2,337	5,10 263
1872-73 ...	4,91,643	2,53,438	5,23,722	8,366	26,124	118	4,205	5,62,535

The canal plantations in 1872-73 numbered 368,774 trees and 835,892 seedlings, and are gradually forming an important portion of the miscellaneous sources of revenue.

The following statement gives all the particulars connected with the supply
from the main canal (130 miles) and distributaries, the
duty it performs, and the area irrigated by the whole
canal from the year 1860-61 to 1872-73 :—

1863-64 to 1872-73.

Year.	Average supply in cubic feet at Kalsiya.	Area irrigated in acres.	Area irrigated per cubic foot of supply in acres.	Length of distributaries open in miles.	Area irrigated per mile of distributary in acres.	Water-rate assessments.	Water-rate.		
							Per mile of distributary.	Per cubic foot of supply.	Per acre irrigated.
						Rs.	Rs.	Rs.	Rs.
1860-61 ...	1,000	2,61,327	296	602	...	2,61,196	...	...	...
1863-64 ...	932	1,81,331	194	602	301	2,53,004	420	271	1·39
1864-65 ...	1,025	2,25,266	220	602	374	3,21,791	·534	314	1·43
1865-66 ...	1,106	1,60,355	145	596	269	4,13,760	694	374	2·58
1866-67 ...	1,068	2,39,555	224	596	402	5,32,464	893	498	2·22
1867-68 ...	911	1,82,544	196	596	306	4,61,698	774	496	2·53
1868-69—									
Kharif ...	1·095	1,02,141	63·0		169·4	2,80,761	·465	256·4	2·75
Rabi ...	792	1,71,960	217·5		285·1	3,18,819	529	402·5	6·85
Total ...	...	2,74,101	280·5	603	454·5	5,99,580	994		
1869-70—									
Kharif ...	1,305	1,19,163	91·3		196·6	3,11,592	514	238·8	2·61
Rabi ...	735	1,31,904	179·5		217·7	2,72,250	449	370·4	2·06
Total ...	...	2,51,067	270·8	606	414·3	5,83,842	963		
1870-71—									
Kharif ...	1,134	98,112	86·3		161·3	3,06,096	503	269	3·12
Rabi ...	778	1,14,603	148·6		183·4	2,38,281	392	306	2·08
Total ...	...	2,12,715	234·9	608	349·7	5,44,377	895		
1871-72—									
Kharif ...	993	72,404	72·9		116·1	2,43,534	400	245	3·36
Rabi ...	970	1,20,345	124·0		194·5	2,54,304	411	262	2·11
Total ...	...	1,92,749	196·9	610	310·6	4,97,838	811		
1872-73—									
Kharif ...	1,058	79,699	75·3		127·5	2,72,146	435	257·1	3·41
Rabi ...	1,043	1,04,455	100·1		167·1	2,09,497	351	210·4	2·10
Total ...	...	1,84,154	175·4	625	294·t	4,91,643	786		

The area irrigated in 1873-74 amounted to 168,048 acres.

The water-rate was increased on the 1st May, 1865, to the following rates :—

| Class. | Nature of crop. | Per acre irrigated by | | Per |
		Natural flow.	Lift.	
		Rs. a. p.	Rs. a. p.	
I.	Sugar cane	5 0 0	3 5 4	Year.
II.	Rice, tobacco, opium, vegetables, gardens, orchards, and water-nuts.	3 0 0	2 0 0	Crop.
III.	All rabí crops, indigo, cotton ...	2 4 0	1 8 0	Ditto.
IV.	All kharíf crops and those not specified above.	1 10 8	1 0 0	Ditto.

Taking these classes, the proportion of irrigation which reaches each class is as follows :—

| Year. | Class I. | | | Class II. | | | Class III. | | | Class IV. | | |
	Flow.	Lift.	Total.	Flow.	Lift.	Total.	Flow.	Lift.	Total.	Flow.	Lift.	Total.
1865-66 ...	15·58	3·06	18·64	24·73	0·171	24·90	42·02	10·12	52 15	3·120	1·170	4·29
1966-67 ...	7·634	1·554	9·189	15·95	0·262	16·21	54·85	14·25	69·11	3·714	1·761	5·47
1867-68 ...	12·45	2 34	14·70	23·52	0 52	24·04	47 62	11·26	58·88	1·73	0·56	2·29
1868-69 ...	9·58	2·0	11·58	13·74	0·34	14·08	50·73	14·17	64·91	7·26	2·17	9·41
1869-70 ...	8·75	2·12	10·87	19·07	0·40	19·47	45 67	12·72	48·39	7·89	2 84	10·73
1870-71 ...	10·52	2·06	12·58	22·26	0·44	22·70	46·79	13·31	60·10	3·54	1·08	4·62
1871-72 ...	10·85	2·38	13·23	17·68	0 33	18 01	54·31	13·54	67·85	0·83	0·08	0·91
1872-73 ...	12·33	2 56	14·89	22·01	0·36	22·37	48·62	11·86	60·48	1·89	0·37	2·26

The number of times and days that the canal has been without water is shown below :—

Year.			Number of times closed.	Number of days closed.	Year.			Number of times closed.	Number of days closed.
1836-40	...	...	58	203	1856-60	...	...	36	267
1841-45	...	...	53	356	1861-65	...	...	31	240
1846-50	...	...	48	194	1866-70	...	...	14	216
1851-55	...	...	47	265					
					Total	...		287	1,741

GANGES CANAL

The example of the success attained on the Jumna Canals, and the necessity

Ganges Canal.

for the adoption of some great scheme of irrigation to meet the periodical occurrence of droughts, led to attention being directed to the Ganges as affording the most constant and sufficient supply of water for a canal that was designed to irrigate the Duáb from the Siwálik hills to Cawnpore. Captain Debude's scheme, drawn up in 1827, for utilising the waters of the West Káli Nadí along the line of the Abu Nálá, for the irrigation of the Meerut, Aligarh, and Bulandshahr Districts, was shown to be deficient in supply and certainty. The united streams of the Hindan and West Káli Nadí were found not to be able to give more than 180 days' supply during the dry months, and during the rains the works would be subject to excessive flood action. Colonel John Colvin, C.B., recommended an examination of the Ganges above and below Hardwár, and on his departure from India in 1836, a series of levels was taken. The Bánganga is connected with the Ganges in the same manner that the Budhi Jumna is with the Jumna, and it was thought possible to utilise the Bánganga for the headworks of the proposed canal in the same manner in which the Budhi Jumna had been used for the Eastern Jumna Canal. The levels showed that this plan was not feasible, owing to the sudden rise of the uplands on the west of the Soláni river, which effectually prevented the taking of water from a place so low down as the proposed site at Bádsháhpur on the Bánganga. Inquiries were still further urged in consequence of the sufferings of the inhabitants of the Lower Duáb during the great famine year (1837-38), when, notwithstanding a loss by remission and otherwise of revenue to the amount of over one and a quarter millions sterling, the people perished in hundreds of thousands from starvation, the loss of cattle was equally great, the fields remained untilled, and a total stagnation of trade and manufactures ensued.

Early in December, 1839, Major P. T. Cautley proceeded to Hardwár and

Cautley's survey.

commenced a close examination of the *khádir* or lowlands of the Ganges in its vicinity. He first attempted to connect the Bánganga project with Debude's proposal for a dam on the west Káli Nadí at Ránípur, the head of the Abú Nála. He, however, found that from the surface of the water at Bádsháhpur, on the Bánganga, to the surface of the water of the West Káli Nadí at Ránípur, a distance of forty miles, there was only a fall of 12¾ feet whilst the high lands on the banks of the latter river near Ránípur were thirty feet higher than the initial level at Bádsháhpur. For the first ten miles from Bádsháhpur to the edge of the upland cliff, the land for nine miles is tolerably level, but it then suddenly rises until it gains an elevation of 83·225 feet near the village of Kumbhera, from which place there is a slope towards Ránípur of about 2½ feet in the mile. Thus a second and closer examination of the proposed site entirely removed this project from the list of those to be attempted. Major Cautley next examined the triangular patch of *khádir* lying between Rúrki and Hardwár, and discovered two lines through which a canal might be taken. The first had a very extended circuit stretching far to the west, and much interrupted by forest and drainage lines ; the second was more direct, but necessitated the construction of an aqueduct across the Soláni. He gave in an estimate for a canal on a minimum scale amounting to 26 lakhs of rupees and providing for 256 miles of main canal and 73 miles of branches, with the necessary appliances for converting the main canal into a navigable line.

The Board of Directors, in their despatch of the 1st September, 1841, warmly took up the subject, and wrote that, " apart from the consideration of financial results, which we are far from contemplating with indifference, there are few measures connected with our revenue administration in India more calculated to contribute to the general improvement of the country, the amelioration of the condition of the people, and to raise the character of the Government, than those of the nature now under our consideration. We concur in opinion with the Government of Agra that a higher ground for advocating these works is found in the security which they afford against famine and its attendant horrors." On receipt of this sanction, a committee was appointed to report on the efficiency of the proposed works, the probable success of the undertaking, the scale on which it should in the first instance be carried on, and the precise measures to be recommended for adoption, the probable effects of the abstraction of the maximum supply of water on the navigation of the Ganges, the probable cost of the extension of the canal to Allahabad, and the probable return from the work. The committee recommended the adoption of the straight line with an aqueduct across the Soláni, and that 6,750 cubic feet per second should be drawn from the Ganges to provide for one main line of navigable canal from Hardwár to Cawnpore, and to supply irrigation to the whole district bounded by the Ganges on the one side and by the Hindan and the Jumna on the other. On the subject of returns, the committee calculated that irrigation would be provided for 2,303 square miles of 1,024 *bíghas* each, which at ten annas a *bígha* would give Rs. 14,86,420, independently of mill-rents, navigation dues, and the sales of miscellaneous canal produce.

The works were commenced on the 16th April, 1842, by opening the excavation between Kankhal and Hardwár, but were stopped in the following July, owing to certain doubts entertained by the Supreme Government as to the propriety of proceeding with the works. These orders were subsequently withdrawn, and permission given to expend up to two lakhs of rupees per annum. The principal objection urged

Project sanctioned.

Works commence.

against the scheme was one based on a clerical error in placing the point of a decimal, by which the proportion of surface of the Duáb which would derive benefit from the canal was much exaggerated, but this was soon cleared up. The probable effect of earthquakes was brought to bear against the construction of the Solúni aqueduct. The injury to the navigation of the upper Ganges and the probable dissemination of malarious diseases were also urged against the canal. " The works, however, had proceeded too far to be violently stopped, and under the restrictions pointed out above, they steadily proceeded with the cordial support of the Agra Government, but with little countenance from other quarters." Major Cautley was the leading spirit of the whole scheme, and under him Lieutenant Strachey, R.E., for some time assumed the executive direction of the northern division of the canal. Early in 1843-44 the levels of the Duáb were completed as far as Allahabad, and reported on in 1845.

Previous to undertaking this survey, the Supreme Government had decided upon a total modification of the original design, and had ordered that the canal " should be in the first place a canal of navigation, and all the water not required for that purpose may be distributed for the purposes of irrigation." The main line was then directed upon Allahabad instead of Cawnpore, and Major Cautley placed, in connection with it, three projects before Government, with estimates of the cost of each appended to them. The first for a main line ending at Allahabad, with a slope of 24 and 12 inches per mile, falls and locks to overcome the superfluous slopes in the northern parts, and ascents and descents into the Jumna. Efficient means of irrigation on the main line were provided as far as the boundary of the Cawnpore and Fatehpur Districts, and, in addition, projects for a branch line of 160 miles to Fatehgarh ; of 70 miles to Bulandshahr ; of 172 miles to Etáwa ; and of 43½ miles to Cawnpore were submitted, at a cost of Rs. 1,02,36,644. The second scheme differed from the first by continuing the main line from Cawnpore to Allahabad by a system of reservoirs and locks to the Jumna, and extending the irrigation to the neighbourhood of the town of Cawnpore, the tail water to be discharged into a ravine of the Pándu Nadí. This was estimated to cost Rs. 97,03,558. By the third scheme, the navigable channel turned off at Jár to the south and joined the Jumna opposite its confluence with the Ken. The Cawnpore line was also designed to be navigable and locked into the Ganges, with a branch for irrigation towards the junction of that river and the Pándu. This plan was estimated to cost Rs. 93,39,747.

Plans of 1845.

Several changes occurred at this time in the administration of these provinces ; Mr. T. C. Robertson was succeeded by Mr. George Clerk, who was followed by Mr. Thomason, and in the middle of 1844 Lord Ellenborough became Governor-

Changes in the administration.

General. Major Cautley went on furlough to England and was succeeded
by Major W: Baker, B.E., in 1845, who with his assistants were obliged to
abandon their work to take part in the Sikh war. A committee appointed to
report on the influence of the canal on navigation and climate presented the
results of their investigations early in 1847 with such a favourable view of the
scheme that Government directed the vigorous prosecution of the work. Again
irrigation became the primary object of the canal, and it was directed, as far as
possible, to lead the channel along the natural level of the country, following
the watershed and interfering as little as possible with existing lines of drainage.
The falls were to be made available as motive power for machinery, and arrangements were to be taken in hand for the formation of reservoirs and plantations
as on the Jumna canals. It was determined, therefore, to push on the Soláni
aqueduct and other masonry works as a first measure, as without them the full
supply could not be utilised, The whole line and its branches was mapped out
into divisions, and the principal works commenced with vigour, whilst the
detailed surveys were carried on during 1847-48. Lieutenant-Colonel Cautley
returned and assumed charge of the canal in January, 1848.

Up to this period the works had been proceeding on the third plan suggested

Final modifications.

by Colonel Cautley in 1845 and noted above. Difficulties were encountered in the character of the sub-stra-
tum, which was found to be sandy and to underlie the clayey surface soil at
depths varying only from three to ten feet. The alignment of the canal had,
at this period, been devised so as to best economise the water and to deliver it
over to the southern districts, where, from the difficulty of sinking wells and
the lowness of the water levels, its benefits would be most appreciated. The main
line was carried on according to the original estimate for 180 miles, throwing off from the left, at the 50th mile near Jauli, a branch intended to proceed
to Fatehgarh, but stopping at Anúpshahr, and on the right, at the 110th mile
near Nidhauli, the Bulandshahr branch. Between the latter and the 180th
mile a branch was thrown off to irrigate the country lying to the left of the
Karon river and to the right of Kol, which is also at present unused. At the
180th mile a few miles below Kol, the main line divided into two channels, one
on the left bearing directly on the Ganges at Cawnpore, and the other on the
right, known as the Etáwa branch, debouching into the Jumna near the boundary
of the Fatehpur and Cawnpore Districts. The latter kept to the right of the Rind
river, watering the Jumna parganahs. These modifications led, with a few
exceptions, to the total re-projection, not only of the masonry works, but of the
capacity of the canal channel itself. The cuttings were deepened, superfluous
slopes were disposed of, and arrangements made for the supply of water to the
new branches in the southern division. The cold-weather rains of 1850-51
seriously impeded the manufacture of bricks, but the delay then caused was made

up in the two following years, which were marked by an uninterrupted and steady advance in the northern division, on a scale that could not be exceeded. The canal was opened on the 8th April, 1854.

At the time of opening the canal, the condition of the works was generally as follows. Above the northern terminus of the Soláni aqueduct the canal was competent to receive and retain safely whatever supply might be admitted. Below the southern terminus to Nánú, a distance of 180 miles from the head, the channel was also good, as well as to Gihror, 57½ miles from Nánú, on the Etáwa branch, and as far as the 81st mile on the Cawnpore terminal branch. Between the northern and southern termini of the Soláni aqueduct lay the works, which rendered the maintenance of a continuous supply impracticable. The masonry aqueduct and the left embankment were quite safe, but the right embankment of the earthen aqueduct was throughout incapable of retaining a full supply. The canal was accordingly closed again on the 12th April, and preparations were at once made for completing the earthwork. A light railway and boats were employed to carry the earth to the spot, but in August alarming signs of failure showed themselves in the masonry revetments of the right bank. At a point about 1,000 feet above the masonry aqueduct, the rear wall of the revetment bowed out to a maximun of 2·62 feet over a section of 300 feet. The result of this was that the arches bearing the steps of the revetment fell in, and on examination the cone of the embankment was found to consist of a semi-fluid mass. The engineers went to work vigorously, so that the canal was re-opened on the 6th November, 1854. At the same time the precaution was observed of admitting the water very slowly. At first only two feet of water was allowed to flow, but from January, 1855, the volume was increased, and by the 2nd of February the water reached Cawnpore. This second trial led to the discovery that the brick-on-edge floorings of several of the falls had been disturbed, and the masonry aqueduct on the Soláni was not water-tight, so that a second closing of the canal for one month was found necessary in March, 1855. It was again opened on the 1st of April, and in one week the water this time reached Cawnpore, and from the 1st May, 1855, irrigation commenced throughout the upper sections of the canal. The knowledge derived from the actual experience in the management of such a large body of water during the next ten years showed that there were several points in which the existing system of construction might be improved. Suggestions were frequently thrown out on isolated subjects, and these were gathered into a formal plan by Major Crofton, whose proposals became the subject of much minuting and correspondence.

The result of these discussions was, in 1866, the appointment of a committee by the Governor-General to decide upon the propriety of proceeding, as previously deter-

Condition of the canal in 1854.

The committee of 1866.

mined, with Major Crofton's project for remodelling the canal, or of stopping
its progress pending the preparation of a detailed project according to the
views of Major-General Sir A. Cotton, with a comparison of the cost and
advantages of the two plans. The committee was composed of Colonel E.
Lawford, R.E., Lieutenant-Colonel J. C. Anderson, R.E., Lieutenant-Colonel J. G. Fife, R.E., George Sibley, C.E., and Hugh Leonard, C.E. The
committee assembled at Cawnpore and examined the Jumna at Agra, the
confluence with the Hindan at Ali, the canal works as far as the Dabauli
falls, the Ganges at Rájghát, and from Garhmuktesar to the Solúni. The
result of their deliberations was that the construction of a weir across the
Ganges below its confluence with the Solúni was not recommended. The project for opening an additional canal head near Rájghát on the Ganges, for
bringing under irrigation lands then not watered by the canal, was considered feasible, but was recommended to be kept in abeyance " until the probable returns appear more proportionate to the outlay than at present." Major
Crofton's plan for remodelling the canal was to be proceeded with, subject to
certain modifications. The construction of a permanent weir across the Ganges
at Hardwár was judged absolutely necessary if it were intended to maintain
a flow of 7,000 cubic feet per second without interruption. Sir A. Cotton
contended that it would have been far better to open the canal heads below
Shukartár in the Muzaffarnagar District, and that even then, instead of
expending large sums on the improvement of the existing line, it would be
preferable to open a new head above Shukartár. The committee found the
valley of the Ganges there four miles wide, most of which comprised a low
bed continually encroached upon by the river, and lying at such a depth
below the high bank as to preclude the possibility of carrying the water on
to the central tracts of the Duáb unless at a very great sacrifice. Garhmuktesar, too, had the same drawbacks. The great breadth of the river
bed, the unfavourable nature of the banks, combined with the scarcity of good
material, rendered it a most objectionable position for a canal head. The committee then recommended the neighbourhood of Rájghát, where the Morádabad
and Aligarh line now crosses the Ganges, as the point from which the main line
might be supplemented or a new line drawn. The remodelling project embraced
the construction of additional falls and the removal of the evils caused by the
excessive velocity of the current at the existing falls, besides rendering the main
line capable of carrying 7,000 cubic feet of water per second. The headway
under the bridges in many cases was found insufficient to admit of the passage of
laden boats, and all these matters are now obtaining their full share of attention.
The only accidents of late years were the injuries caused to the Jauli falls and
Kánípur lock, both of which have been repaired. The remodelling project, with
certain modifications, has been actively carried out since 1868 as opportunities

occurred by the temporary closing of the canal. The whole of the falls of the canal have been made secure, with the exception of those at Jauli, which is to be relieved of half the present pressure of head-water upon it by the construction of a second fall above the existing works. The history of the next ten years will show the effect of these improvements on the efficiency of the canal.

A short sketch of the physical peculiarities of the country through which the canal flows is necessary to complete this notice.

The Khádir.

The *khádir* or low-lying tract in the north-east of the Sahárunpur District is separated from the uplands by a ridge running in a south-easterly direction from the Shahjahánpur and Kunjnáwar passes in the Siwáliks, to the Ganges at Shukartár. The drainage to the west of this line falls into the Jumna by the West Kálí Nadí, and that on the east falls into the Ganges. The towns of Bhagwánpur, Rúrkí, Jaurási, Landhaura, and Núr-nagar are situated on this ridge, and overlook the deep depression of the *khádir* on the east. This *khádir* is bounded on the east by the Ganges, and is alter-nately flooded or drained by the Soláni, Pathari, and Ratmau rivers. The Gan-ges at Hardwár is about a mile in breadth at its narrowest point, and divides into several channels separated by islands. One of these channels or branches leaves the main stream about 2¼ miles above Hardwár, with a considerable volume of its own, and passes down close to the town, rejoining the present stream below Kankhal. It was from a place on this stream, known as Ganesh Ghát, in the village of Mayapur, that the canal was drawn off, as it was found that this branch carried away more than one-third of the total volume of the river, and thus gave a supply amply sufficient for the whole canal. The heads were fur-ther strengthened by the construction of a spur dam and escape cuts. A great portion of the *khádir* tract here consists of the débris of the *bángar* or uplands, which has been swept down towards the Ganges by the mountain torrents which run through it. In addition to this slope to the east, this tract has a slope also parallel to the line of the Ganges itself. Taking advantage of this circumstance, Colonel Cautley so arranged his line that, after obtaining the levels he required, and disposing of the superfluous slope by the construction of masonry falls on the canal, he was enabled to enter the high bank in a moderate cutting. Thus the point at which the Soláni is crossed, though 80 feet below the head at Hardwár, it is 70 feet above the surface water of the Ganges to the east. Between the Mayapur regulating bridge and Rúrki, one of the first obstacles encountered was the Ránípur torrent system at a distance of about 5½ miles from the regulator. The water of this drainage line spreads so over the whole face of the country as to leave hardly any trace of a defined chan-nel. A dam was at first made, with an inlet and outlet on the system that had been followed in the upper works on the Eastern Jumna Canal, but the floods of 1849 showed that this plan was attended with such a deposit of silt

as to completely interfere with the canal itself. A superpassage for the conveyance of the torrent over the canal was accordingly constructed with a
waterway of 200 feet. The advantages of this method of crossing the drainage were soon apparent, resulting in the utter freedom from silt and the evils
arising from the contact of two streams meeting each other at right angles,
freedom from all wear and tear of channel necessary on the admission of
the torrent into the canal bed, freedom from the anxiety of opening and
shutting sluices, and regulating the escapes at the dams, freedom from all
establishment for working the dams, and a consequent reduction of a large permanent establishment necessary for their maintenance. The passage of the
Ránípur torrent over the canal is obtained by throwing arches over the lower
levels of the falls, the waterway of which was divided into eight parallel
descents of 25 feet in width, with a passage of 19 feet in width on the left for the
navigable channel. All arrangements were made for securing the ingress and
egress of the torrent from the superpassage. Between Mayapur and the Ránipur torrent the principal works are two bridges for cross-communication at
Kankhal and Jawálápur, an outlet on the left bank at Kankhal, and three
inlets on the right bank at Launda Laniwála, Kankhal and Jawálápur, giving
an inlet of 200 feet waterway and an escape of 20 feet.

Between the Ránípur superpassage, with its falls and locks, and the Rat-

Ránípur to the Ratmau.

mau torrent, the principal works are the falls No. 2, with
a drop of nine feet; falls No. 3, with a similar drop; the
Salímpur inlet, with a 150 feet opening; the Pathari superpassage, with a water-
way of 300 feet in width, connected with the Dhanauri falls No. 4, having a
drop of nine feet into the bed of the canal; the Bádsháhpur inlet, with an opening of fifty feet; the Ratmau dam and inlet, with an escape of 800 feet and a
bridge for the purpose of regulating the canal supply and of cutting off the
canal stream from its passage onwards towards the Píran Kaliyar excavation
and the Soláni aqueduct, together with a bridge for cross communication north
of the works, and a line of navigable canal from the Jawálápur bridge to the
tail of the Pathari superpassage. From the success attending the Ránípur
superpassage, a similar plan was adopted with the Pathari. The Ratmau torrent, that was next met with, was, owing to its considerably lower level, somewhat more difficult to manage than the others. The valley here was a mile in
width, bounded on the right by the steep bank of Píran Kaliyar, and having a
slope from the point where its main branch left the hill to the intersection of the
canal of 39·18 feet per mile. The effective slope at the point of intersection
was 8·23 feet. The works constructed here consisted of a dam, of which the bed
was flush with the river bed, and masonry sluices on the left for an escape, and
an open branch through the right for admitting flood-water. From the Ratmau
regulating bridge to the high land of the Duáb the canal runs in an uninter-

rupted straight line, reaching the high land to the east of the town of Rúrkí.
Then by a curve to the left, which commences at the terminal point of the Soláni
aqueduct, the channel proceeds in a straight line to the Asafnagar falls. The
slope from the flooring of the Ratmau regulator to the Rúrkí bridge was fixed
in 1854 at 1·25 feet per mile, and from the latter place to the falls at 1·095 feet
per mile. On leaving the Ratmau regulator, the canal channel passes for 5,000
feet through the low land of the Ratmau river. It then enters the Píran
Kaliyar ridge. Through this ridge it has a course of 10,700 feet, with a mean
depth of excavation of 31 feet and a maximum of 37 feet.

At a point opposite the village of Píran Kaliyar, a masonry bridge, with a
The Soláni aqueduct. waterway of 165 feet, has been constructed to connect
the village with the temple tombs, and reservoir at the
Dargáh on the opposite side. On the approach of the channel to the villages of
Bajuheri and Mahewar the line crosses a hollow connected with a ravine which
drains this portion of the ridge. An artificial cut made from the hollow on the
right of the canal, diverted the drainage to the west of the Mahewar village.
From this point the works of the Soláni aqueduct commence. The Mahewar
hollow has, on both sides of the canal, channels of escape built in connection with
the aqueduct and carried under the embankments. From these escapes, the down-
stream bank of which rests on the upper terminus, the canal passes the Soláni
valley in a channel whose base is 150 feet in width, formed on a massive earthen
embankment which was constructed from the excavation of the Píran Kaliyar
ridge. The channel is revetted throughout its length with masonry disposed in
the form of continuous steps resting on arches. The river itself is passed by a
series of fifteen archways of fifty feet in width each. The level of the flooring of
the aqueduct is 24 feet above the bed of the Soláni, and this may be considered
the maximum difference of level between the bed of the canal and the surface
profile of the valley on the whole length upon which the aqueduct passes. The
great advantage derivable from the adoption of this plan is, that the canal was
thus enabled to enter the *bángar* or uplands at Rúrkí with a moderate cutting.
The total length between the extremities of the termini is 15,687 feet, or 2 miles,
7 furlongs and 507 feet, of which 932 feet is masonry and the remainder earth-
work.[1] Cattle gháts and bridges were erected at either end. From the Rúrkí
terminus, the canal passes to Asafnagar by an abrupt curve protected by a
masonry revetment on its right or concave side for 3,200 feet.

Between Rúrkí and Nánú, a distance of 160 miles, the country through which
Rúrkí to Nánú. the canal passes is marked by great declivity of surface,
and by its connection with *bhúr* or tracts of sand-hills.
After leaving Rúrkí the canal turns to the left, and continues on a bearing

[1] Full details of the work on the Soláni will be found in Cautley's Ganges Canal, II., pp.
411—537, from which this notice is taken.

almost due south for about 20 miles, until it reaches the neighbourhood of Belra. On this line it runs parallel to and between the high bank overlooking the *khádir* and the Síla Khála, a shallow depression forming a tributary of the West Káli Nadí. Throughout the whole of this tract the surface is marked by undulating ridges of sand, either skirting the edges of rivers or throwing out ramifications transversely. The line of canal crosses three of these ridges. Beyond Belra the canal makes a slight turn to the right, increasing the curve near Khátauli, where it passes the heads of the East Káli Nadi, which henceforth separates the canal from the Ganges. The distance between the East and West Káli at this point is about eight miles, and through the centre of this tract the canal passes. From a point on the 50th mile a channel is given off to water the tract between the East Káli and the Ganges, known as the Anúpshahr branch and having a length of 83 miles. The other works of importance are those at the 110th mile, where the Bulandshahr branch is thrown off, of which ten miles is regarded as a branch and the remainder as a distributary. The main line proceeds to Nánú, in the Aligarh District, where it divides into two branches, each 170 miles long; that on the right falls into the Jumna in the Etáwa District, and that on the left into the Ganges at Cawnpore. The distance from Mayapur to Nánú is 181 miles; thus we have. 614 miles of main canal, and 3,111 miles of minor distributary channels branching off from the main canal throughout its course, and which are more particularly noticed under each district.

The mode in which the accounts have been prepared is sufficiently explained under the notice of the Eastern Jumna Canal. The following tables show the revenue and capital charges and receipts as recently adjusted in the public accounts:—

Capital Account.

Year.	Outlay during the year.			Outlay to the end of the year.		
	Ordinary.	Extraordinary.	Total.	Ordinary.	Extraordinary.	Total.
	Rs.	Rs.	Rs.	Rs.	Rs.	Rs.
1854-55	...	...	...	1,51,45,277	...	1,51,45,277
1860-61	5,45,433	...	5,45,433	1,91,02,610	...	1,91,02,610
1861-62	19,70,419	...	19,70,419	2,10,73,029	...	2,10,73,029
1862-63	4,86,945	...	4,86,945	2,15,59,974	...	2,15,59,974
1863-64	3,21,609	...	3,21,609	2,18,81,583	...	2,18,81,583
1864-65	5,10,078	...	5,10,078	2,23,91,661	...	2,23,91,661
1865-66	3,24,752	...	3,24,752	2,27,16,413	...	2,27,16,413
1866-67	4,19,767	...	4,19,767	2,31,36,180	...	2,31,36,180
1867-68	1,58,377	6,78,692	7,37,069	2,32,94,557	5,78,692	2,38,73,249
1868-69	1,87,490	5,13,340	7,00,830	2,34,82,047	10,92,032	2,45,74,079
1869-70	21,122	5,35,808	5,56,930	2,35,03,169	16,27,840	2,51,31,009
1870-71	38,664	2,24,860	2,63,524	2,35,41,833	18,52,700	2,53,94,533
1871-72	44,924	3,27,847	3,72,771	2,35,86,757	21,80,547	2,57,67,304
1872-73	1,21,625	4,06,103	2,84,478	2,34,65,132	25,86,650	2,60,51,782

Revenue Account, A.

Year.	DURING THE YEAR.			TO END OF THE YEAR.			WORKING EXPENSES.	
	Direct income.	Increased land-revenue.	Total.	Direct income.	Increased land-revenue.	Total.	During the year.	To end of the year.
	Rs.	Rs.	Rs.	Rs.	Rs.	Rs.	Rs.	Rs.
1855-56	17,215	...	17,215	17,215	...	17,215	2,79,934	2,79,934
1860-61	4,30,868	7,994	4,38,862	10,08,988	15,988	10,24,976	3,59,165	18,62,880
1861-62	6,83,096	11,887	6,94,983	16,92,084	27,875	17,19,959	3,86,856	22,49,236
1862-63	7,57,759	16,887	7,74,646	24,49,843	44,762	24,94,605	6,15,538	28,64,774
1863-64	4,79,511	59,887	5,39,398	29,29,354	1,04,649	30,34,003	5,67,476	34,32,250
1864-65	7,66,975	72,315	8,39,290	36,96,329	1,76,964	38,73,293	8,17,355	42,49,605
1865-66	11,79,896	72,315	12,52,211	48,76,225	2,49,279	51,25,504	7,53,754	5,03,359
1866-67	14,60,136	1,79,639	16,39,715	63,36,361	4,28,918	67,65,279	7,65,103	57,68,462
1867-68	16,15,516	1,80,776	17,96,292	79,51,877	6,09,694	85,61,571	7,95,716	65,65,178
1868-69	15,66,040	1,82,164	17,48,204	95,17,917	7,91,85-	1,03,09,775	7,99,622	73,64,800
1869-70	25,69,536	1,83,481	27,53,020	1,20,87,453	9,75,342	1,30,62,795	9,23,765	82,88,565
1870-71	17,78,153	2,02,980	19,81,133	1,38,65,606	11,78,322	1,50,43,928	8,68,716	91,57,281
1871-72	18,29,075	2,29,341	20,58,416	1,56,94,68-	14,07,663	1,71,02,344	9,13,683	1,00,70,964
1872-73	15,89,919	2,6,68-	18,66,600	1,72,84,600	16,84,344	1,89,68,944	9,88,713	1,10,59,677

The *kharíf* of 1855 showed only 225 miles of *rájbahas* or distributaries in
actual work over 450 miles of main canal, into which the
water had been admitted, whilst 633 miles of distributaries
were under preparation. The mileage opened at the close of the year was 436.
The area irrigated during the year amounted to 98,000 canal *bíghas*, or 54,734
acres, whilst about 166,000 acres in 1,134 villages were placed beyond the
risk of serious damage by drought. The system of collecting the value of the
rájbaha works from the villages through which they were constructed led
apparently to such a check upon the demand for water, that on Colonel Baird
Smith's representation the charge was postponed for some years. The canal
was divided into five divisions: the northern, upper central, lower central,
Cawnpore terminal, and Etáwa terminal divisions, whilst the Navigation
Department was placed under a superintendent resident at Rúrkí. In spite
of all the disturbing influences of the year 1856-57, the area under irrigation
trebled during 1858-59; the water-rate on the *rabí* increased by 12 per cent., and
on the *kharíf* by 93 per cent. The following statement shows the total area (in
acres) irrigated by the Ganges Canal from the year 1859-60 to the year 1863-64,
the details of which are given under each district :—

Year.	Kharíf.	Rabí.	Total.	Year.	Kharíf.	Rabí.	Total.
1859-60 ...	33,292	95,431	128,723	1862-63 ...	90,693	114,912	205,605
1860-61 ...	69,361	273,549	342,910	1863-64 ...	97,538	352,250	449,788
1861-62 ...	77,522	294,800	372,322				

The length of main canal since 1859-60 is 519 miles. The length of the Fatehgarh and Bulandshahr branches from 1862-63 to 1867-68 was 127 miles; from that date to the end of 1871-72 they measured 135 miles, and in 1872-73 the returns show 96 miles. The irrigating capacity of the canal is equal to 1,205,000 acres. From 1855 to 1860 the canal was closed three times, for in all 27 days: from 1861 to 1865 there were ten closures, which lasted for 156 days; and from 1866 to 1870 the canal was without water for 160 days, distributed over seven closures.

Revenue Account, B.

Year.	NET REVENUE TO END OF YEAR.		Charge for Interest to the end of the year.	DIFFERENCE BETWEEN THE NET REVENUE AND CHARGE FOR INTEREST TO END OF YEAR.		PERCENTAGE OF NET REVENUE ON CAPITAL OUTLAY.	
	Exclusive of land-revenue.	Inclusive of land-revenue.		Excluding land-revenue.	Including land-revenue.	Excluding land-revenue.	Including land-revenue.
	Rs.	Rs.	Rs.	Rs.	Rs.	Rs.	Rs.
1855-56 ...	—2,62,719	—2,62,719	25,73,609	—28,36,328	...	—1·73	...
1860-61 ...	—8,53,892	—8,37,904	69,96,914	—78.50,806	—78,34,818	0·34	0·42
1861-62 ...	—5,57,152	—5,29,277	79,52,044	—85,'9,196	—84,81.321	1·55	1·61
1862-63 ...	4,14,931	3,70,169	90,05,695	94,20,626	93,75,864	0·67	·75
1863-64 ...	5,02,896	3,98,247	1,00 83,693	1,05,86,589	1,04,81,940	—·40	—·13
1864-65 ...	6,53,276	3,76,312	1,11,77,772	1,17,31,048	1,15,54,084	—·23	·10
1865 66 ...	1,27,134	1,22,145	1,22,97,355	1,24,24,489	1,21,75,210	1·90	2·22
1866-67 ...	5,67,899	9,96,817	1,34,33,175	1,28,65,276	1,24,56,358	3·05	3·85
1867-68 ...	13,46,699	19,96,393	1,45,89,984	1,32,03,285	1,25,93,591	3·53	4·32
1868-69 ...	21,53,117	29,44,975	1,57,83,646	1,36,30,529	1,28,38,671	3 21	3·97
1869-70 ...	37,98,888	47,74 230	1,70,12,349	1,32,18,461	1,22,38,119	6 69	7·44
1870-71 ...	47,08,325	58,86,647	1,82,66,899	1,35,60 574	·,23,82 252	3 61	4·42
1871-72 ...	56,23,717	70,31,380	1,94,16,698	1,37,92,981	1,23,85,318	3·60	4·50
1872-73 ...	62,24,923	79,09,267	2,05,43,302	1,43,58,379	1,26,74,035	2·32	3·40

The following statement gives the returns of receipts for each year under each item of demand:—

Details of direct income.

Year.	WATER-RATE.			Navigation.	Mill rents.	Plantations.	Miscellaneous.	Actual receipts.
	Balances.	Assessments during the year.	Realized.					
	Rs.	Rs.	Rs.	Rs.	Rs.	Rs.	Rs.	Rs.
1855-56 ...	...	34,648	3,258	2,644	4,274	6,614	425	17,215
1860-61 ...	1,37,682	4,91,819	2,77,572	1,12,757	16,920	11,118	12,501	4,30,868
1861-62 ...	3,51,929	5,99,370	5,76,665	55,725	18,832	17,789	14,085	6,83,096
1862-63 ...	3,74,634	4,51,361	6,76,842	46,834	16,770	14,473	6,664	7,57,759
1863-64 ...	1,49,153	6,93,134	3,99,255	35,376	16,770	15,976	12,134	4 79,511
1864-65 ...	4,43,032	8,95,042	6,73,565	41 246	15,096	26,051	11,015	7,66,975
1865-66 ...	6,64,509	12,69,748	10,85,140	20,949	23,884	34,456	15,467	11,79,896
1866-67 ...	8,49,117	14,06,030	13,32,437	38,919	25,603	45,983	17,994	14,60,136
1867-68 ...	9,22,710	12,38,490	14,90,482	35,218	26,909	45,721	17,187	16, 5,516
1868-69 ...	6,70,718	22,65,320	13,89,801	38,784	25,793	88,910	21,752	15,66,040
1869-70 ...	15,46,237	17,57,573	24,16,804	33,593	20,771	66,590	31,778	25,69,536
1870-71 ...	8,87,006	17,80,176	16,47,055	30,890	30,000	38,084	33 124	17,78,153
1871-72 ...	10,20,127	14,25,875	16,75,240	59,306	36,395	38,005	20,126	18 29,075
1872-73 ...	7,70,762	15,72,198	14,58,561	29,815	19,510	58,294	23,689	15,89,919

The following statement gives the irrigation statistics from the year 1864-65 to the year 1872-73 :—

Year.	Average supply at Rúrkí in cubic feet.	Area irrigated in acres.	Area irrigated per cubic foot of supply in acres.	Length of distributaries opened in miles.	Area irrigated per mile of distributary.	Water-rate in rupees.	Water-rate in rupees. Per mile of distributary.	Per cubic foot of supply at head.	Per acre irrigated.
1864-65... ...	4,026	566,517	140	2,440	232	5,95,042	367	222	1·58
1865-66... ...	4,314	573,129	133	2,777	206	12,69,748	457	294	2·21
1866-67.									
Kharíf	4,391	181,658	41·37	3,039	60	5,12,373	168	117	2·82
Rabí	4,781	453,076	103·55	...	149	8,93,660	294	187	1·87
Total ...	...	634,734	144·92	...	209	14,06,033	...	...	...
1867-68.									
Kharíf	4,340	185,137	42·66	3,040	60	5,62,926	185	129	3·04
Rabí	3,540	348,319	98·39	...	114	6,75,564	222	198	1·91
Total ...	...	533,456	141·05	...	174	12,38,490	...	...	...
1868-69.									
Kharíf	4,944	344,267	69·63	3,112	110	8,14,631	261	165	2·37
Rabí	4,960	734,132	148·01	...	236	14 50,639	463	290	1·97
Total ...	...	1,078,399	217·64	...	346	22,65,320	...	...	...
1869-70.									
Kharíf	4,504	341,846	75·9	3,069	111	8,77,886	286	195	2·57
Rabí	4,797	438,560	91·4	..	143	8,79,687	287	183	2·01
Total ...	..	780,406	167·3	...	254	17,57,573	...	...	...
1870-71.									
Kharíf	3,981	266,683	67·0	3,071	87	7,70,396	251	194	2·85
Rabí	4,618	499,931	108·2	...	163	1,008,971	329	218	2·02
Total ...	...	766,614	175·2	...	250	1,779,367	...	...	...
1871-72.									
Kharíf	4,180	232,688	55·7	3,078	76	6,66,082	216	159	2·86
Rabí	4,203	373,867	89·0	...	121	7,59,793	247	181	2·03
Total ...	...	606,555	144·7	...	197	14,25,875	...	...	...
1872-73.									
Kharíf	5,164	247,191	47·8	3,228	79	7,06,060	227	136	2·85
Rabí	4,575	437,979	95·7	...	141	8,68,379	279	190	1·93
Total ...	...	685,170	143·5	...	220	15,74,439	...	...	...

The total area irrigated in 1873-74 amounted to 177,241 acres.

In the canal accounts, as now revised, a new item appears to the credit of the canal under the head of "increased land-revenue," and it will be well to give here the departmental expla-

Enhancement of land-revenue.

nation of the term.[1] " When the settlement of a district is revised, and it is found
that the land-revenue has been enhanced by the action of the canal, whether by
increasing the irrigated area over that irrigated at the previous settlement, or
by enabling waste land to be cultivated, the amount of the enhancement is
credited to the canal, but only as a book transaction, and not by regular transfer.
It will be understood that this indirect revenue can only be credited from the
time at which the assessment under the new settlement comes in force, and it
cannot be increased until the agreements under that settlement terminate, and
another settlement is made.   It follows that the rate of enhanced revenue will
be very unequal in different districts.   When the settlement of a district is completed before the canal system has become fully developed, the amount of
enhancement due to the canals is very small compared with that obtained in a
district over which the canal-irrigation has had time to spread; and what is of
more importance than the mere paper credit to canals, the actual loss to Government in the postponement of the increased land-revenue till a future revision of settlement, is often very great in the former case.   This is well exemplified by the cases of the portion of the Saháranpur District watered by the old
established Eastern Jumna Canal, and the Bulandshahr District, where the settlement was completed just after the opening of the Bulandshahr Branch,
when the canal-irrigated area was about one-fourth of its present average.   In
the former tract the rate of enhancement, calculated on the area irrigated in
1870-71 (taken as being an average year), was 15 annas per acre, in the latter
only 4·3 annas."

The mode and nature of the assessments under this head vary with the peculiarities of each district, and will be found in the settlement reports; they are
too technical and too incomplete for reproduction here.   Up to the end of 1872-
73 the assessments in six districts had been completed, those for Muzaffarnagar, Eta and Etáwa were partially complete, and those for Agra and Cawnpore
had not been commenced.   The following table shows the amount of enhancement due to the action of the two great canals, as far as has been ascertained,
to the end of 1872-73:—

District.	Amount of enhancement.			Remarks.	District.	Enhancement credited to Ganges Canal.	Remarks.
	Ganges Canal.	Eastern Jumna Canal.	Total.				
	Rs.	Rs.	Rs.			Rs,	
Saháranpur ...	15,263	64,106	79,369	Complete.	Aligarh ...	88,066	Complete.
Muzaffarnagar,	53,500	60,000	1,13,500	Incomplete.	Farrukhabad,	10,410	Ditto.
Meerut ...	79,458	45,781	1,25,239	Complete.	Eta ...	12,439	Incomplete.
Bulandshahr,	33,418	...	33,418	Ditto.	Etáwa ...	27,751	Ditto.
					Mainpuri ...	23,965	Complete.

[1] Irrigation Report 1871-72, p. 23.

These figures would show a credit of Rs. 3,44,270 to the Ganges Canal and Rs. 1,69,867 to the Eastern Jumna Canal for the year 1872-73 under the head of " increased land-revenue." The amounts actually credited in the Controller's accounts are Rs. 2,76,681 and Rs. 1,23,075 respectively. Some years must elapse before the credits under this head can be finally adjusted.

During the year 1866-67 the whole available stream of the Ganges at Hard-
1866-67.
wár was turned into the canal from November until March, and but for the exertions of Major Forbes much difficulty would have been experienced in providing the supply required for irrigation. The average discharges during the same year were 4,391, 4,781 and 4,582 cubic feet, giving respectively returns per cubic foot per second of supply of 42·35, 93·86 and 138·52 acres irrigated for water carried in the canal. When the mean volumes passing through the terminal escapes are deducted from the volumes of supply, the results are 47·56, 115·73, and 155·19 acres per cubic foot per second of supply delivered into distribution channels. The same discharges applied to the water-rate give returns per cubic foot per second of Rs. 116·68 for the *kharif*, and Rs. 186·92 for the *rabí* of 1866-67, and Rs. 306·86 for the year, taken on gross volumes, and Rs. 131·0, 208·9, and 343·7 on the net volumes after deduction of the escape water. The canal ran for 308 days in 1866-67, being closed for 27 days in August for repairs. The following table, prepared from the results of two observations made on the 1st March, 1864, with the gauge at 6·83 (D = 4, 346), and in the 27th April, 1864, with the gauge at 7·25(D = 4,720), shows the discharges at the Rúrkí bridge gauge, on which the calculations of the canal department are based :—

Gauge reading.	Discharge, cubic feet per second.	Gauge reading.	Discharge, cubic feet per second.	Gauge reading.	Discharge, cubic feet per second.	Gauge reading.	Discharge, cubic feet per second.
Feet.		Feet.		Feet.		Feet.	
8·0	5,387	7·1	4,607	6·2	3,873	5·3	3,183
7·9	5,301	7·0	4,522	6 1	3,795	5·2	3,109
7·8	5,216	6·9	4,438	6·0	3,717	5·1	3,035
7·7	5,130	6·8	4,355	5·9	3,639	5·0	2,961
7·6	5,045	6·7	4,273	5·8	3,562	4·9	2,887
7·5	4,957	6·6	4,192	5·7	3,486	4·8	2,815
7·4	4,869	6·5	4,112	5·6	3,410	4·7	2,743
7·3	4,781	6·4	4,032	5·5	3,334	4·6	2,673
7·2	4,693	6·3	3,952	5·4	3,258		

In 1867-68 an alteration was made in the water-rates, by the trans-
1867-68.
fer of gardens and orchards from the first to the second class, whereby they became chargeable twice

a year if watered in each harvest. The following water-rates were then in force :—

Class.	Nature of crop.	Per acre irrigated by		Per
		Natural flow (tor).	By lift (dál).	
		Rs. a. p.	Rs. a. p.	
I. ...	Sugar-cane	5 0 0	3 5 4	Year.
II. ...	Rice, tobacco, opium, vegetables, gardens, orchards, and water-nuts	3 0 0	2 0 0	Crop.
III. ...	All rabí crops, indigo, cotton,	2 4 0	1 8 0	Ditto.
IV. ...	All kharíf crops not specified above	1 10 8	1 0 0	Ditto.

Taking these classes, it will be useful to show the influence of the canal in promoting the cultivation of the better class of crops. The following table gives the proportion of each class to the total area irrigated :—

Year.	Class I.	Class II.	Class III.	Class IV.
1664-65 ...	9·20	5·05	84·08	1·67
1865-66 ...	10·50	5·35	78·15	6·00
1866-67 ...	7·30	6·54	83 38	2·78
1867-68 ...	10·36	8·94	78·29	2·41
1868-69 ...	5·63	5·45	77·71	11·21
1869-70 ...	8·70	7·25	76·64	7·41
1870-71 ...	9·82	5 15	·82·13	2·90
1871-72 ...	10·24	6·44	82·08	1·24
1872-73 ...	9·98	6·55	81·90	1·57

Taking the principal crops for each year the acreage was as follows :—

Season.	Crop.	1865-66.	1866-67.	1867-68.	1868-69.	1869-70.	1870-71.	871-72.	1872-73.
Annual kharif.	Sugar-cane ...	58,416	46,338	55,232	60,664	67,867	75,288	62,125	68,421
	Cotton ...	10,198	19,084	5,617	44,213	40,531	21,394	13,605	7,961
	Indian-corn ...	18,628	9,518	1,754	31,209	23,550	509	476	579
	Indigo ...	47,713	70,487	75,684	75,506	128,496	116,979	118,366	129,780
	Rice ...	23,134	30,539	36,305	43,355	41,754	28,459	24,398	26,762
	Miscellaneous ...	18,254	10,002	10,486	89,321	39,718	24,045	13,743	14,713
Rabí ...	Barley ...	110,257	121,126	88,156	242,354	123,144	125,635	92,990	152,661
	Gram ...	19,844	26,397	13,274	39,985	25,961	15,725	11,039	17,198
	Wheat ...	252,422	279,318	231,559	418,228	264,371	133,511	149,169	242,489
	Miscellaneous ...	14,061	19,912	15,329	33,566	25,024	25,009	20,644	25,607
Total ..	Annual ...	58,416	46,338	55,232	60,664	67,867	75,288	62,125	68,421
	Kharif ...	118,128	139,642	129,906	293,604	274,039	191,446	170,588	178,794
	Rabi ...	396,595	448,753	449,319	734,132	438,500	499,880	473,842	437,955
	Year ...	573,129	634,734	333,457	1,079,400	780,406	766,614	606,555	685,170

The great increase in water-rate during the year 1868-69 was due to the excessive drought of that year, to the increase in the volume of water sent into the canal, and to an improvement in the duty done by the water. Much attention was devoted during this and successive years to the calculation of the volumes of water passing certain points on the canal. The loss by absorption and gain by percolation are two disturbing elements in the estimate which no amount of accurate measurement at the points of entry and exit will eliminate. The information, therefore, given in a previous table must be considered as barely approximate. It is useful in showing, as far as can be ascertained, what duty is being obtained from canal water in each year, and any marked deviation ought to be capable of explanation.

Increase in 1868-69.

The following table shows the mode of irrigation, whether by lift or flow, for crops remaining all the year on the ground (annual), rain-crops (kharíf), and spring crops (rabi):—

Flow (tor) and lift (dál) irrigation.

Year.	Crops.				Year.	Crops.			
	Annual.	Kharif.	Rabi.	Total.		Annual.	Kharif.	Rabi.	Total.
1865-66.					1869-70.				
Lift	2·8	4·85	29·02	36·67	Lift	2·46	8·45	19·08	29·99
Flow	7·4	15·76	40·17	63·33	Flow	6·21	26·66	37·11	70·01
Total	10·2	20·61	69·19	100	Total	8·67	35·11	56·19	100
1866-67.					1870-71.				
Lift	1·92	4·43	25·75	32·1	Lift	2·12	5·35	20·94	28·41
Flow	5·38	17·57	44·95	67·9	Flow	7·70	19·62	44·27	71·59
Total	7·30	22·00	70·70	100	Total	9·82	24·97	65·21	100
1867-68.					1871-72.				
Lift	2·46	3·92	25·39	31·77	Lift	2·17	5·52	18·97	26·66
Flow	7·90	20·43	39·90	68·23	Flow	8·07	22·60	42·67	73·34
Total	10·36	24·35	65·29	100	Total	10·24	28·12	61·64	100
1868-69.					1872-73.				
Lift	1·56	8·36	24·09	34·01	Lift	2·46	5·60	23·78	31·84
Flow	4·07	17·93	43·99	65·99	Flow	7·52	20·50	40·14	68·16
Total	5·63	26·29	68·08	100	Total	9·98	26·10	63·92	100

At the commencement, the falls were utilised as a motive power for mills for grinding corn. The Kankhal mills, with twenty sets of stones, and those at Asafnagar, Chhataura, Salú-

Mill rents.

war and Bhúpa, with four sets each, were opened in 1855; and in the early part of
1856, Bahádurabad, with eight sets of stones, and the mills at Belra, Mahmúdpur,
Jauli, Dásna, Palra, and Semra, each with four sets of stones, were put up for
public competition.   During the first two years the mills were worked under
the direct management of the canal officers, as a temporary necessity, to exhibit
their working capacities; but afterwards, as was usual on other canals, they were
put up to auction to the highest bidder.   In the early part of 1857 a rumour
was circulated that the flour ground at these mills had been mixed with bone-dust
by the orders of Government, and all work was at once stopped on them.   The
revenue in 1867-68 amounted to Rs. 26,908, or nearly two per cent. on
the total income of the year, but even this is very small, when one considers
that at the time the motive power available on the Ganges Canal was equal to
the power of one million horses.

In the earlier years of the canal the transit dues were chiefly collected from
boats working for the canal itself or the contractors
employed on it.   The principle on which the dues were
finally established was that the whole private carrying trade of the canal should
be placed in the hands of private individuals, under a system of licenses graduated
according to tonnage.   In addition to the actual dues brought forward to credit
during 1855-56, the canal authorities claim Rs. 15,461 as savings to the cost
of the works by the use of the canal for transit during that year.   The development of navigation dates from November, 1856, when stations were established at Sardhana, Bulandshahr, Barauta, Dannahar, and Cawnpore.   In the
early part of 1857, a brisk trade was carried on, but towards the end of April
navigation began to decline.   At the breaking out of the mutiny there were 144
boats on the canal; the greater portion of these were either sunk by the rebels
after plundering the goods they carried, or allowed to drift away.   During 1857-58
navigation almost ceased, but in the following year it rapidly improved, and numbers of boats were built, both for the carriage of passengers and for merchandise.
There are three serious impediments to canal navigation : the first is due to the
great velocity of the current, which renders towing up-stream a serious work;
the second is the silting up of the locks in places, and the third is the periodical
closing of the canal for repairs, during which time both the boat and the boat's
crew must remain idle.   The navigation trade consists of either rafting timber or carrying merchandise in boats.   The rafting is almost entirely confined to
the upper portion of the canal, the timber being seldom carried farther down
than the point nearest to Meerut, through occasionally it sometimes goes as far
as Barauta, in the Aligarh District, and even Cawnpore.   The direction of the
grain traffic varies with the market rates.   The metals and building materials
are chiefly carried for the Rúrki Workshop or other Government works.
Cawnpore, Barauta, Nánú, Tátarpur, Rúrki and Jawálápur are the principal

landing and shipping ghâts. Mandakhera, Murádnagar, and Sikandra Rao are of less though growing importance. The following table gives the traffic réturns for four years, all that are necessary to show its character :—

Goods.	1867-68.		1868-69.		1869-70.		1870-71.	
	Number.	Muns.	Number.	Muns	Number	Muns.	Number.	Muns.
Grains ...	...	37,581	...	3,26,148	...	105,039	...	75,160
Cotton ...	...	1,36,662	...	96,027	...	115,756	...	129,365
Oil-seeds ...	...	12,439	...	4,523	...	24,415	...	10,768
Salt ...	...	28,666	...	22,620	...	9,477	...	23,310
Metals ...	...	51,470	...	54,248	...	37 212	...	73,809
Building materials.	...	1,91,466	...	5,07,557	...	2,46,149	...	98,123
Other goods ...	245,949	68,909	243,047	81,982	...	79,837	...	76,490
Bamboos ...	2,039,675	...	4,021,273	...	1,893,772	...	2,556,870	...
Small timber ...	108,244	...	202,806	...	1,96,540	...	159,417	...
Firewood ...	...	226,297	...	183,910	...	2,70,204	...	210,511
Logs ...	2,954	...	2,669	...	2,525	...	1,840	...
Other timber ...	16,158	249	22,378	...	18,832	...	6,174	...
Passengers ...	10,147	...	979	...	3,004	...	2,139	...
Total ...	2,450,427	758,739	4,493,162	1,277,015	31,042	...	40,860	...
Revenue ...	33,227	...	35,484	...	...	...	31,042	...
Expenditure ...	12,169	...	12,881	...	30,670	...	9,318	...
Net income ...	23,049	...	25,903	...	372	...	...	...

The expenses attending the repairs of the nineteen locks on the canal were first debited to the revenue from navigation in 1869-70, reducing it so much that this branch of the canal, though supporting 487 boats, barely covered its expensés during that year. In 1861-62 there were 616 boats on the canal, but these fell to one-half on the opening of the railway in 1863, and since then, though there have been some fluctuations, the numbers have never risen so high. The following table gives the revenue, less refunds, and the numbers of boats plying on the canal for a series of years :—

Year.	Revenue.	No. of boats.	Year.	Revenue.	No. of boats.	Year.	Revenue	No. of boats.
	Rs.			Rs.			Rs.	
1861-62 ...	55,725	616	1865-66 ...	20,949	256	1869-70 ...	33,593	329
1862-63 ...	46,834	313	1866-67 ...	38,119	597	1870-71 ...	30,890	282
1863-64 ...	35,376	285	1867-68 ...	33,218	450	1871-72 ...	59,306	233
1864-65 ...	41,248	243	1868-69 ...	38,784	487	1872-73 ...	29,815	239

The returns under the head of " miscellaneous" consist of the sale of grass and fuel and the rent of small portions of canal lands, besides fines and similar items. At an early period canal plantations were made, which in a few years began to form an

Miscellaneous revenue.

important feature in the miscellaneous revenue. In 1866-67 the income from this source amounted to Rs. 45,983 and the expenditure to Rs. 29,980. The number of trees alive at the close of the year (31st March) 1866-67 was 1,222,726, of which 785,294 were on the canal banks, 325,795 on rájbaha banks, and 111,637 in separate plantations; there were also 159,745 seedlings in nurseries. In 1868-69 large sales were effected in the Meerut Division to the Dehli railway and Meerut Division of the Public Works Department, whilst the felled timber was replaced by young saplings from the nurseries. · The canal banks have an area of about 15,000 acres capable of being utilised for this purpose, and now bear nearly two and a half millions of trees and seedlings. The greatest number is found in the Meerut Division of the canal, and next to this come the Bulandshahr, Aligarh and northern portions of the first circle of superintendence. Strange to say, the luxuriant grass on the banks of the canal brings in nearly as large a revenue as the timber. The receipts from all sources during 1872-73 shows :—From grass, Rs. 21,760; firewood and timber, Rs. 30,404; fruit, Rs. 3,708 ; plants, Rs. 106; and land rent, Rs. 3,312,—or a total of Rs. 58,294.

The whole of the canal plantations have for some years been placed under the superintendence of an officer, called the Inspector of Canal Plantations, who reports yearly on their management. Systematic forestry is practised with much success, and the plantations are being gradually fenced in with agave and other similar plants, whilst increased attention is devoted to the production of trees of rapid growth producing timber useful for firewood and general purposes, such as *siras, shisham, kikar, sirsi, paphri,* and the beef-wood tree. The seeds are usually sown in drills, or, where wanted, about five feet apart, and subsequently thinned out. Some efforts are, however, now being made to plant out the more valuable though slow-growing timbers, such as mahogany, teak, *tún, bákli, &c. Sál* has been tried, but with little success, and it is proposed to confine operations in this direction to the left bank of the canal, leaving the right for the quick-growing acacias. Very much yet remains to be done, and activity in the direction of planting trees deserves every encouragement, even if the plantations supplied the wants of Government works alone. The great increase in the price of firewood and timber of every description presses heavily on the people, and leads them to cut down the groves around their villages, and thus in a measure assist in the denudation of the face of the country, which already has had a serious effect upon the rain-fall.

FAMINES.

A brief summary of the accounts that we possess regarding the famines and droughts that have visited these provinces will form a fitting pendant to the irrigation chapter, and an introduction to the local history of the famines to be found in each district notice. It will also save much repetition hereafter.[1]

Famines.

·One of the earliest famines of which we have any record is that noted by the pious Zíá-ud-dín Barani,[2] which occurred in the reign of Fíruz Sháh Khiljí. The dearth was due to the scarcity of rain, and grain rose to one *jital* per·*ser*. In the Sewálik country the scarcity was very much felt.

1291 A.D.

"The Hindús of that country came into Dehli with their families, twenty or thirty of them together, and in the extremity of hunger drowned themselves in the Jumna. The Sultán and his nobles did all they could to help them. ·In the following year there was abundant rain." This calamity and a storm that occurred about the same time are attributed by the chronicler to the Sultán having caused the execution of one Sídí Maula, a religious fanatic, an event which occurred in 690 *Hijrí* (1291-92 A.D.) The price of grain as fixed by Alá-ud-dín Khiljí about 1300 A.D. was wheat 72 *jítals* per *maund*; barley, 4 ; rice, 5 ; *másh*, 5 ; *moth*, 3; and *nukhud*, 5 per *maund*. I cannot say what the weight of the *ser* and *maund* of either time expressed in our weights would be, but the purchasing power of the *jítal* fell, if we calculate 20 *sers* to the *maund*, from four *sers* to one *ser;* or if the *maund* contained forty *sers* as at present, from eight *sers* to two *sers*.

We next have the long continued distress of Sultán Muhammad bin Tughlik's reign. He ascended the throne in 1325 A. D., and one of his first acts was to increase the revenue by from five to ten per cent. He invented oppressive *abwábs* (cesses), which were collected so rigorously that the cultivators (*raiyats*) were reduced to beggary.[3]

Circa 1327-35 A.D.

The rich turned rebels, the lands fell out of cultivation, and even the inhabitants of distant districts, hearing of the fate of the cultivators in the Duáb, betook themselves to the jungle. A fatal famine took place in Dehli and the Duáb. Grain became dear, and a scarcity of rain made the suffering general. "It continued for some years, and thousands upon thousands of people perished of want. Communities were broken up and families were reduced to distress." · The Emperor was then at Multán, and on his return to Dehli found the famine so· severe that man ate man. "The Sultán strove to restore cultivation and had wells dug, but the people could do nothing. No words issued from their mouths, and they continued inactive and negligent. This brought many to punishment." Shams-i-Siráj, writing some time after,[4] says :—" In the reign of

---

[1] The authorities are Girdlestone and Henvey's Reports, the Native Histories, Board's Records, and Colonel Baird Smith's report. [2] Dowson's Elliot, III. 146, 591. [3] Elliot, *ibid*, III., 238, 245, 619. [4] *Ibid*, 345. Ibn Batuta was an eye-witness of this famine. He says the *maund* of wheat rose to sixty *dirhams* and more. " One day 1 went out of the city to meet the *vazír*, and I saw three women who were cutting in pieces and eating the skin of a horse which had been dead some months. Skins were cooked and sold in the markets. When bullocks were slaughtered, crowds rushed forward to catch the blood and consumed it for their sustenance. Provisions were supplied to every one for half a year at the rate of one pound and a half, Mughribi weight, each."

Alá-ud-dín the necessaries of life were abundant through excellent management ; but, through the favour of God, graincontinued

1351-58 A.D.

cheap throughout the reign of Fírúz Shah (1351 to
1388 A.D.), without any effort on his part." Wheat sold in Dehli at eight *jitals*
per *maund* and gram and barley at half that price. A camp-follower would give
his horse ten *sers* for one *jital*. " If, occasionally, prices rose from bad seasons
or from scarcity of rain, and reached one *tanka* per *maund*, it was only for a short
time. The good fortune of the Sultán prevailed, so that no dearth occurred.
Such was the prosperity that, throughout the Duáb, from the hill of Sakrúdih
and Kharla tô Kol, not one village remained waste, even in name, nor one span
of land uncultivated. In the Duáb there were fifty-two pergunnahs flourishing,
and a similar state of prosperity prevailed elsewhere. The like prosperity
prevailed in every fief (*ikta*) and district (*shikk*). Thus, in the District of
Sámána, there were four prosperous villages within one *kos*, and the inhabitants
were happy and free from care."

In 1398-99, A.D. after the departure of Tímúr, the neighbourhood of Dehli
and all those territories over which his army had passed

1398 to 1661 A. D.

was visited by famine and pestilence. Many died of
sickness and many perished with hunger, and for two months Dehli was desolate.[1] In 1424 A.D., Yahya bin Ahmad[2] relates that the royal army was in
Katehir, and was about to cross the Ganges towards Kanauj, " but there
was a terrible famine in the cities of Hindustán, and consequently the army
advanced no farther." In 1471, owing to the wars between the Lodi Sultáns
of Dehli and the Sultáns of Jaunpur, the lower Duáb and Bundelkhand, which
suffered most from the contending armies, were the scene of much suffering
and want. In 1631 a famine[3] arose from a similar cause in the Dakhin,
where the armies of Shahjahán were employed during the two previous years ;
but in this case scarcity of rain, added to the destruction caused by war, produced a state of things where money could not purchase bread, and "disease
followed famine, and death ravaged every corner of India." During the reign
of Aurangzeb in 1661, famine,[4] caused by extraordinary drought, ravaged the
environs of Dehli and the upper Duáb.

The year 1739 is marked by scarcity caused by the irruption of the Afgháns
from Kábul, and here it may be said that a similar result

1739-83-84 A.D.

followed all their subsequent invasions. The Sikh inva-
sions, too, produced an artificial scarcity hardly less severe than that caused by
a failure of the periodical rains. The famine of 1770 was chiefly confined
to lower Bengal, though from a letter of the commandant of the Allahabad
Fort it would appear that there was a considerable rise of prices in the lower
Duáb. To a demand for a supply of grain for the famine districts below Patna

1 Dowson's Elliot, IV., 36.   2 *Ibid*, 61.   3 Elphinstone, 507.   4 *Ibid*.

he replies : —" I am sorry it is not in my power to comply with your directions. The quantity I have been able to collect to the present time would be barely sufficient to support the garrison a month in case of necessity, and the prospects of getting more are very distant. Though the inhabitants are not in such distress here as in the provinces, yet grains of all sorts are immoderately dear." The North-West, however, felt the full force of the next great famine, the *chalisa* (fortieth), so called from the *Sanvat* year 1840 (1783-84 A.D.,) in which it took place. For the two previous years the rains were unfavourable, and the third year opened with an entire absence of rain in *Asárh* and *Sáwan* (June-July). The next month passed with clouds, but no rain. The fields remained untilled, and the full force of the calamity fell at once upon the tracts removed from artificial irrigation. Towards the end of September the rains began, and with such an equal and regular fall that it is said that grain which had lain in the ground and had not germinated for the previous two years, then came to the surface. Agra first gave signs of distress, and crowds emigrated towards Oudh. "Death left its mark freely along the road.[1] Such was the general apathy that the bodies were not removed from the spot where they lay, even in towns or villages. No relief was held out to the sick or dying. Every man's hand was against his neighbour, and the strong ruthlessly seized the portion of the weak, for the struggle to maintain life overcame all scruples." The famine was severely felt in Benares, where Warren Hastings was himself an eye-witness of its effects. He writes : —"The distresses which were produced by the long-continued drought unavoidably tended to heighten the general discontent * * *. From Buxar to the opposite boundary I have seen nothing but traces of complete devastation in every village." Mr. Rose, of Cawnpore, says that, comparatively with the duration of each, the devastations of the *chalisa* famine were not so dreadful as those of 1837-38. Colonel Baird Smith held a different opinion, and Mr. Keene[2] quotes an old follower of the Gosháin leader, Himmat Bahádur, as saying that wheat sold in 1783-84 for eight *sers* for the rupee ; " which, allowing for the subsequent fall in the value of money, is equivalent to a rate of three *sers* for our present rupee." This famine was undoubtedly very severely felt in the middle Duáb as far as Meerut ; in Etáwa, Aligarh, and Bulandshahr many mounds are still shown which once formed the sites of villages devastated during the *chalisa*.

Turning to the Board's records we find mention of a famine in 1803-04. This

Famine of 1803-04.

was most severely felt in the Duáb, though at the same time it caused an extensive rise in prices from the Benares Division on the south to Rohilkhand on the north. This famine, like most others, was mainly due to a failure of the periodical rains, and partly to the disturbing influence of the political changes that then occurred. The *rabí* or

---

[1] Girdlestone's report, 8. [2] Moghul Empire, 140.

spring crops in the middle Duáb were injured by hail storms in the early part of 1803 ; the rains, too, were scanty in the beginning, and failed about the middle of August. Up to the middle of September the rain-crops had more or less failed, and there was considerable anxiety felt about the spring harvest of 1804-5. These fears were partially realised, for the cold-weather rains also failed. The Government lost by suspensions during this famine alone upwards of thirty lakhs of rupees, most of which Mr. Girdlestone thinks, with justice, must be due to the famine alone.[1] The crops in the upper Duáb yielded an average outturn in 1805-6, but in the following year, the rains, though at first favourable, broke off on the 21st August, and the rain-crops proved generally light, and in many parts which had not the advantage of well water totally unproductive. Similar disasters from like causes took place in the years 1810 and 1812.

In 1813-14, however, a scarcity deserving the name of famine took place

1813-14.

throughout the middle and lower Duáb and Bundelkhand. In Agra the rain crop of 1812 was bad, and the spring crop of 1813 was still more scanty. The rains of 1813, also, were late ; and though large advances for the purchase of grain for seed were made, numbers of people deserted the district for other parts of the country. " Many died from hunger, and others were glad to sell their women and children for a few rupees, and even for a single meal." Though the Board of Revenue had offered to remit as much of the revenue as was thought necessary, the Collector hoped that the rainy season might turn out more favourable than it did, and the result was heavy balances in 1814. In Cawnpore, also, the drought was severely felt, grain selling at prices that it had not reached in 1803-4. Aligarh and Etáwa showed a considerable increase in the prices of necessaries, though whether this was due to the drought or to the export of the home stocks one can hardly say. It was in Bundelkhand, however, that the calamity was most felt. The western parganahs of Hamírpur had, in addition to the drought, to bear the raids of the free-booters who at that time harassed the border districts; and though this tract of country for a short time had some rest, it had never entirely recovered from the years of suffering it had previously passed through. Remissions were granted here as elsewhere, and altogether, amongst the minor famines, that of 1813-14 must be regarded as a costly one. Bundelkhand suffered exceedingly in the scarcity of 1819, and though this time relieved from the attacks of professed bandits, it suffered equally at the hands of the revenue authorities. Mr. Waring's settlements and the drought combined, reduced the people to great distress, and compelled again a sacrifice of revenue, which some supervision and foresight might have rendered unnecessary.

In 1824-25 drought was severely felt over the upper Duáb, and in the following year both Rohilkhand and the middle Duáb as far as Agra felt its effects. It

---

[1] Report, 22.

is the same story of inquiries, grants of advances to stave off the present distress,
and total inability to grasp the real remedy of a catholic
system of canals, which took many years and the
sacrifice of hundreds of thousands in men and money to impress upon Government. 1833-34 repeated the scenes of previous years, and Bundelkhand again
felt a real famine. Mr. Pidcock, writing of the British Districts says:—" The
season of 1241 *fasli* (1833-34) was one of unparalleled distress to the people
of this district (Hamírpur) and of loss to Government. The miseries of famine,
pestilence, and exile which denuded this district of nearly one-half its inhabitants are too well known to the world to need recapitulation here; but it is
not equally well known that, in addition to all this, the avarice and corruption
of the native officers of this district were employed in frustrating the charitable
intentions of Government." By far the greater portion of the remissions were
collected and embezzled by the native Sub-Collectors. The balances amounted
to about sixty-six lakhs of rupees and the remissions to nearly two lakhs during
this famine. Between this and the disastrous year 1837-38 nearly sixteen lakhs
of revenue were remitted on account of bad seasons.

1824-26 and 1833-34.

The year of famine best remembered, and of which we have authentic records,
is the year 1837-38. As this is one of the important
famines, the district details will be given at length in
the district notices, and here it is merely necessary to present a general view
of its influence on the province. In July, 1837, the premonitory signs of the
approaching storm were shown from Saháranpur on the north to Behar in the
south, and from Lucknow to Gwaliar. Baniyas closed their shops, the peasantry
took to plunder, the cattle starved and died, violence to person and property was
rife, and there was a general move amongst the population, each one thinking
any other place must be in better circumstances than his own. Notwithstanding
every effort on the part of the local authorities, disorganisation increased and
the land remained in a state of chaos. Wells dried up, grass perished, the very
trees were despoiled of their leaves to feed the remnant of the cattle. Lord
Auckland, then Governor-General, left Calcutta, and assumed charge of the
Local Government from Sir Charles Metcalfe in the beginning of 1838, and
sanctioned the employment of the starving poor on relief works. Still hundreds
of thousands perished from pure starvation, the roads were strewed with the
dead and dying, and pestilence followed in the wake of famine. Mr. Rose's
account of Cawnpore will be found at some length under the notice of that district, and will serve to show what the general suffering must have been. Between
the months of January and July, 1838, his relief works were attended by
nearly a million of people; burglaries and thefts were double the number
that were before recorded; the receipts from excise fell to nearly one-half;
and the balances of the land-revenue amounted to more than the collections.

1837-38.

Between the years 1837 and 1839 Government remitted close upon forty-nine lakhs of rupees on account of this drought, and balances still remained amounting to nearly thirty lakhs, most of which was subsequently written off. The loss of life was estimated by Colonel Baird Smith at 800,000 souls by hunger and pestilence; the loss of cattle, equally great, crippled the resources of the survivors. Mr. Girdlestone estimates the direct remission of revenue at ninety lakhs of rupees, besides over five lakhs of rupees expended by Government in gratuitous relief, and two lakhs of rupees supplied by private benevolence. So great was the prostration that followed this calamity that more than twenty years elapsed before the revenue regained its former standard, and the loss thus entailed is calculated at 133 lakhs of rupees, or, if all be added together, over two millions sterling in these provinces alone.

The famine of 1860-61 comes next on the long list of famines caused

1860-61.

by droughts in these provinces. From 1858 there had been nothing but a series of bad seasons and more or less failures of the crops until, in 1860-61, the crisis came. Up to the middle of July, 1860, no rain had fallen, the people were driven to the use of wild fruits and grass seeds for sustenance. Between the 15th and 20th of July rain fell, but held off again, and with the exception of the week from the 11th to the 17th of August, and a few days in September, no more fell. Relief works were opened all through the upper Duáb and Rohilkhand, subscriptions were collected, and, as usual, efforts were made to relieve the distressed. By the end of July, 1861, nearly ten millions of souls had received food at poor-houses at a cost of over 4¼ lakhs of rupees, giving a daily average of 63,245 persons fed, and a daily expenditure of Rs. 3,102. Large numbers died, and the loss of cattle also was severely felt. Sir A. Cotton estimated the deaths from starvation and pestilence at 200,000, and Colonel Baird Smith estimated the deaths of cattle in the poorer districts to amount to one-half of those in existence. The balances amounted to 13½ lakhs of rupees, of which about two and a half lakhs were remitted, but to this must be added as dead loss the sums expended in the distribution of food, in the purchase of seed and cattle, and in relief works, swelling the minimum actual tangible loss to over 20½ lakhs of rupees. It is unnecessary to gave further details of this famine, as it will be carefully noticed under each district.

The last famine that I have to record is that of 1868-69, which was felt

1868-70.

throughout Rohilkhand, the Duáb, and more especially in the Jhansi Division. The immediate cause of the scarcity was the failure of the rain crops of 1868. There was a heavy fall of rain in June, succeeded by a month of dry weather, and again in July another heavy fall, succeeded by a similar interval of dryness. The result was, that the crops were destroyed where beyond the influence of artificial irrigation. The *rabi* (or spring) crops of 1869 suffered to a great extent both from drought and hail-storms, and hardly yielded two-thirds of an average season. Prices consequently rose, and much distress was felt all over the country. Relief measures were promptly organised, and the poor-house system of administering assistance to the weak and aged was adopted. Benefiting by the experience of previous years, the principles and details of the arrangements to be adopted were sketched out beforehand, and when it was found necessary to commence operations every one knew exactly what he had to do. The black districts were mapped out into convenient circles and placed under special superinten-dence. Works of permanent utility, such as roads and tanks, were commenced, to find employment for the able-bodied poor, and poor-houses afforded shelter to the aged and infirm. Women who, by the custom of the country, were not used to appear in public received yarn for weaving, or cotton to spin into yarn, and were thus made, in some measure, to contribute to their own support. Each large gang was further subdivided and separately hutted near the places where their services were required. Native medical officers were told off to inspect each circle and prevent, as far as possible, any loss of life by the out-break of epidemics. The principles on which the relief operations were based commend themselves in that they have been found successful in actual practice, and give a test as to how far the pressure of a scarcity exists. Those found capable of labour were obliged to labour, and received wages in money some-what below the average, but sufficient when exchanged for food to support life. Where poor-house relief was asked for, residence within its walls was enforced, and rations were distributed in cooked grain, whilst a light kind of work was demanded from each one that was pronounced fit for it. It is manifest that no able-bodied man would willingly work for famine wages unless real scarcity existed, nor would a residence in a poor-house be endured for the mere sake of escaping work elsewhere. The records, too, show that the numbers on the relief works and in the poor-houses increased with the pressure of the distress, rising with bad weather and high prices, and falling with the commencement of agricultural operations, that gave hopes of a favourable harvest.

To carry out the scheme of charitable relief, the public were called upon to subscribe, and a committee was formed in Allahabad to regulate the collection and the distribution of the funds. Rs. 2,30,295 passed through their hands, but, subsequently, Government took upon itself the whole care of the really helpless, and the functions of the committee ceased. Altogether over four and a half lakhs of rupees were expended in charitable relief, of which about two and a half lakhs were furnished by Government. Balances amounting to over thirteen lakhs accrued, and of this sum about two and a quarter lakhs were remitted altogether. Again, over eighteen lakhs were expended on works of public utility in connection with the relief of the able-bodied poor, and over ten lakhs in advances for the construction of wells and the purchase of seed-grain and cattle. The total cost in actual cash of this famine may be approximately shown thus :—

Total expended on—	Rs.		*Government Share.* Rs.
Labour relief ...	... 18,61,020	..	... 13,37,621
Charitable relief	... 4,50,381	...	... 2,48,946
Loss by remission	... 2,20,000	...	... 2,20,000
Agricultural advances	... 10,16,202	...	... 10,16,202
	35,47,603		28,22,769
Add compensation to lessees of ferries and East Indian Railway for losses			... 3,50,086
		Rs.	... 31,72,855

These figures do not show the loss caused by the check given to the progressive increase in the material prosperity of the districts attacked, or that caused by the abandonment of the claim to a share in the increased profits from the land which would otherwise have been made. These matters are mentioned in the district notices, where further details are given. One thing can be learned even from the very short sketch of the famine history that I have given, and that is, that a famine is an expensive luxury for an Indian Government to indulge in, quite independent of moral and humanitarian considerations; in fact, from the lowest standpoint, it is a thing to be, at all risks, avoided. Accordingly, whatever measures are found useful in preventing, or at least mitigating, the evil effects of a season of drought should be adopted: these are, briefly, the extension of the canal system; the more liberal grant of advances for the construction of wells and reservoirs in places where canal irrigation is at present impracticable ; and the provision of efficient means of communication between every district that is likely to be attacked and the great grain depôts of these provinces. Of the inestimable advantages of the canals in mitigating the effects of a season of drought the history of the year 1868-69 is a proof. Double the acreage irrigated in 1861 then received water, whilst 1861 was itself more than four times ahead of 1837-38. At the same time, the chapter on sanitation will show that if in years of famine the canals have saved life, their evil effects on the drainage system have been so prejudicial to the public health that it may be fairly asked whether the account is not balanced.

METEOROLOGY.

The suggestion of taking meteorological observations[1] of a systematic and
connected kind seems to have been due to Mr. Edmon-
stone, when he was Lieutenant-Governor of these pro-
vinces. The plan of taking the observations was partly drawn up by Colonel
(now Major-General) Cunningham, R.E., who was the Secretary to Government
in the Public Works Department, and Captain (now Colonel) Maclagan, R.E.,
who was then Principal of the Thomason College in Rúrkí. Mr. Edmonstone
had proposed that these observations should be taken as early as April, 1859,
but it was not until September, 1862, that observations began to be recorded,
and towards the close of the same year their publication was commenced as a
weekly supplement to the *Government Gazette*. The number of observatories
at first established was six, and they were at the following places:—Naini Tál,
Rúrkí, Agra, Beawar (in Rajputána), Jhansi, and Benares. In 1865 the
instruments at Beawar were transferred to Ajmer, and those at Naini Tál
were, in 1870, sent to Ráníkhet.

About the beginning of 1865 Government called on the Principal of the
Thomason College for a report on these observations, and as Dr. Murray Thomson was in charge of the observatory at Rúrkí, the duty of drawing up this
report devolved upon him. A first report was published in August, 1865, in
which all the observations made in 1863 were brought together and abstracts of
them tabulated. A second report followed in January, 1866 ; in this the observations of 1864 were treated, and those of 1865 were the subject of a third report
published in April, 1866. In February, 1866, Dr. Thomson was appointed
Reporter on Meteorology for the North-Western Provinces. This was the
first appointment of the kind made, but it was followed immediately by the
appointment of Assistant Surgeon Neill as Reporter for the Panjáb, and in
1867, Mr. H. T. Blanford was made Reporter for Bengal. These appointments
were the result of suggestions made by the Asiatic Society of Bengal. In their
proposal a more extensive scheme of meteorological observation was sketched
out than has as yet been sanctioned. The scheme in its present form was
approved of by the Government of India on the proposal of the Sanitary Commissioners of Bengal, to whom the subject had been referred for consideration and report.

After Dr. Thomson's appointment as Reporter, he obtained authority from
the Government of India to ask for copies of the registers kept in regimental
hospitals and civil dispensaries, and in reply received registers containing the observations made from the beginning of 1866 from twelve stations,
and afterwards five more stations sent registers from the beginning of June,
1866. There were, thus, twenty-three stations at which observations were

_____

[1] From notes by Dr. Murray Thomson.

made : twenty of these were in the North-Western Provinces and three in
the Province of Oudh.   Ultimately this number was reduced to fourteen, one
of which is in Lucknow, and the other thirteen are in the North-Western
Provinces.   In all these stations there is a proper observatory shed for the
reception and exposure of the instruments, and a staff consisting of a superintendent, who is in many cases the civil surgeon of the station, and a native
observer.   Both of these now draw pay, the superintendent having an allowance of Rs. 30 a month, and the observer Rs. 25, with an increase of Rs. 5 every
year until a maximum of Rs. 40 a month is reached.   This improved scale
of pay came into operation in 1873.

The following are the observatory stations at present in existence in these
provinces :—Chakráta, Ráníkhet, Dehra, Rúrkí, Meerut, Bareilly, Fatehgarh
Agra, Allahabad, Gorakhpur, Benares, and Jhansi.   The North-Western Provinces Government bears the expense of all these observatories except Dehra,
which is maintained by the Great Trigonometrical Survey.   The instruments
kept at each observatory are at least a mercurial barometer, dry and wet
bulb hygrometer, maximum and minimum thermometer for use in shade,
maximum solar and terrestrial radiation minimum thermometers, and a rain-
gauge.   A few have, in addition to these, anemometers and other instruments.
It is intended, however, that all should in time be equally well equipped.

From each of these observatories a register is sent to the Reporter every
month, and the register embraces the state of the pressure, humidity and temperature of the air, as ascertained by the reading of the barometer, hygrometer,
and thermometer at 4 and 10 A. M. and 4 and 10 P. M. every day.   The amount of
cloud in the sky, direction of the wind, and general state of the weather are
also noted at these periods.   The self-registering thermometers, rain-gauge, and
anemometer are read once a day.   Mean air-pressure, temperatures, &c., are
taken, as a rule, from the average of the four readings as described above, and
are not the average of the maxima and minima only.   It is the duty of the
Reporter to prepare an abstract of these observations every month, and to
accompany this abstract with notes on the course of the pressure, temperature,
&c., of the air during the month, with comparisons as to previous years.
These abstracts and notes are published in the *Government Gazette* generally
in the last week of the month succeeding that to which the observations refer.
An annual report is also prepared, in which much of the monthly reports are
reproduced and published along with tables of comparative air-pressure and
temperatures, and the weather and meteorological phenomena are fully discussed.   But no report which embraces only a tract like the North-Western
Provinces of India will ever illustrate fully the causes of such important matters as deficient or excessive rain-fall, for the periodical rains of India proceed
from causes which operate over a much larger part of the earth's surface, and no

adequate explanation will ever be given of these until places over the whole continent furnish their quota of observations, and those be discussed by one writer.

As the office of Reporter on Meteorology is but of recent origin, it possesses no records of meteorological occurrences in far back years. And since the office has been in existence there has been very little to record of a more than usually remarkable kind. The following are all that appear worth mention here :—On the night of the 6th of June, 1867, a very severe dust-storm passed over Agra, which did some damage to trees and buildings. Besides this there has been several storms of minor magnitude, but none approached any way near to what might be called a cyclone. On the 28th of June of the same year a fall of muddy rain took place. It was noticed on the same day in Rúrkí and in Naini Tál, and a short account of it was published in the report for 1867. The year 1868 was remarkable for the deficient rain-fall. It was not only in the North-Western Provinces that the rain was short of the average, but likewise over a great part of the Panjáb and Rajputána. The details of the observations made will be found under the notices of the observing stations.

COMMUNICATIONS.

The East Indian Railway runs through the Aligarh, Bulandshahr, and Meerut Districts, and branches off from Gháziabad to Dehli. From Gháziabad the Sindh, Panjáb, and Dehli Railway runs through the remainder of the Meerut District northwards, and on through Muzaffarnagar and Saháranpur to the Panjáb. The Oudh and Rohilkhand Railway communicates with the Duáb lines at Aligarh. The water communication by the Ganges Canal and the navigable rivers, the Jumna and Ganges, is fairly complete. The principal trade-routes commencing on the north are the lines by the Mohand pass to Mussooree (Mansúri), and by the Timli pass to Chakráta. By Hardwár a line follows the left bank of the Ganges to the great shrines of Kedárnáth and Badrínáth in British Garhwál, and, by the Níti and Mána passes, communicates with Tibet. On the east, arterial lines connect Bijnor with Saháranpur and Muzaffarnagar ; Morádabad with Meerut, and by Anúpshahr with Bulandshahr ; whilst Bareilly is in direct communication with Aligarh. Through the centre of the Duáb, the Grand Trunk Road runs through Háthras, Aligarh and Bulandshahr to Dehli. Main lines connect all the principal towns with each other and the lines on either side of the Duáb. To the west, Umballa (Ambála) is connected by Jagádri with Saháranpur, and again by Karnál and Shámli with Muzaffarnagar. Pánipat and Rohtak are each in direct communication with the Duáb, and further south, lines converge upon Dehli from all parts of the Duáb, and through Khair and Tappal upon Palwal. The means of communication are, therefore, nearly complete, and, with the exception of isolated portions of the Saháranpur, Bulandshahr, and Aligarh Districts bordering upon the low lands of the great rivers, are amply sufficient for all purposes of trade and the conveyance of grain in seasons of scarcity. In fact, there is, perhaps, no portion of British India better supplied with the means of communication than the five districts noticed in this volume. The existence of extensive kunkur beds renders the metalling of roads here an easier and far less expensive task than in other less favoured districts. ·

POPULATION.

Amongst the 4,860,228 souls comprising the population of the five districts
Population. noticed in the present volume, it has been already stated that 3,840,321 are Hindús, 1,045,780 are Musalmáns, and 1,378 are Christians. Some further brief remarks are necessary as an introduction to the local details given under the district notices. Commencing with the Hindús, I find that 442,787 persons are entered as Brahmans,
Hindús. and of these 281,009, or more than one-half, belong to the great Gaur subdivision, and next to them in numbers come the Saraswats and Sanádhs. Though a numerous and powerful body, none of the Brahman clans possess much political influence. The Gaurs are equally numerous in the Bijnor, Morádabad, and Muttra Districts, but further south are replaced by the great Kanaujiya subdivision. Rajpúts number 261,970 souls. In Sahárunpur, the characteristic clans are the Pundírs, numbering 14,843 souls, and the spurious Chauhán Rajpúts. In the neighbouring district of Muzaffarnagar the same clans show the largest numbers, and next to them comes the Chhotiyána clan. In Meerut the Chauháns number 17,207 souls, and next to them come the Tuár, Gahlot and Bhál clans, whilst in Bulandshahr the Badgújars (13,116), Jádons and Chauháns form the characteristic elements of the Rajpút population. Bais, Bhál, Gahlot, Chandel, Bagola, Jaiswár, and Jaromiya Thákurs are also tolerably numerous in Bulandshahr. In Aligarh the Jádons predominate, numbering 36,423 souls, or nearly one-half the entire Rajpút population. Chauháns here, too, are numerous (15,408), and with Kirárs, Pundírs, Badgújars, Gahlots, and Jangháras make up the majority of the remainder of the Rajpút population.

Baniyas number 247,345 souls, of whom 145,579 belong to the Agarwál division alone. The remainder are chiefly Saraugis or Jainas, Gindauriyas, Bishnois, Chausainis, Dásas, and Bárahsainis. They are a wealthy, money-getting class, and have during the British rule attained to positions as land-holders, which may at some time be the cause of grave political anxiety. The great mass of the population, entered in the census returns as "other castes," number 2,858,219 souls. To these belong the Aheriyas, who number over 7,000 souls in Aligarh. The Ahirs, so numerous from Meerut southwards, number 64,507 souls. Then come the Banjáras, chiefly to be found in Sahárunpur, Muzaffarnagar, and Aligarh. The Barhais, or carpenters, number over 67,000 souls, and similarly numerous are the great castes following domestic service or trades, such as the Lohárs or blacksmiths, (20,594); Dhobís or washermen (25,957); Darzís or tailors (13,729); Chhípís or cloth-printers (12,722); Hajjáms or barbers (73328); Málís or gardeners (58,504); and Sonárs (53,883). The characteristic class amongst the labouring population is the Chamárs, who number 777,308 souls, or more than one-fifth of the entire Hindu population. Garariyas or shepherds form an important element in the same class, and number 84,060 souls. Gújars, Tagas, and Játs, described more at length under the Sahárunpur, Muzaffarnagar, and Meerut Districts, respectively, form the characteristic elements amongst the cultivating village communities. The Gújars number 188,251 souls, the Tagas 76,979; and the Játs 370,361. Other important castes are the Juláhas or weavers (29,932); Káchhís (22,060); Kahárs (162,593); Kaláls (20,379); Kayaths (18,907); Khákrobs or sweepers (156,321); Khatíks (46,156); Kolis (72,023); Kumhárs (75,434); Lodhas (101,483); Orhs (26,360); and Sainis or Sánis in the three northern districts (51,995). The mendicant classes are fairly represented by the Bairágis, who number over 13,000 souls; the Gosháins (15,289), many of whom have taken to agricultural pursuits; and the Jogis (39,976).

The Musalmán population presents some difficulties in the way of classification.

Musalmáns. So many converts from Hindúism are entered under the head of Shaikhs that it may be considered, at least in the upper Duáb, as a generic term for all who profess Muhammadanism, and do not belong to the well-known classes of Mughal, Pathán, or Sayyid. The returns show 410,267 persons as Shaikhs, and to these may be added the 483,635 Musalmáns entered without other specification than religion. Sayyids number 35,984 souls, or more than any other division except Rohilkhand, doubtless due to their presence so long and in such numbers in the Bárha tract of the Muzaffarnagar District. Mughals number 9,030 souls, chiefly in Meerut and Muzaffarnagar, and Patháns give 71,686 persons, pretty evenly distributed over all the five districts. In no part of these provinces have the Musalmán missionaries been so successful in making converts. There are few classes of Hindús, whether Brahman, Baniya, Rajpút, Gújar, Taga, or other caste, that are not divided into a Hindu and Musalmán branch. Much of this is, no doubt, due to the fact of the proximity of this portion of the Duáb to Dehli, and the attractions of the court. In Sahárunpur alone the returns show 9,395 Musalmán Gújars, and over 12,000 Musalmán Rajpúts. In Bulandshahr the Musalmán Badgújar and other Rajpúts number 7,811 souls. In Sahárunpur again Musalmán Tagas are numerous, and in Bulandshahr and Aligarh Musalmán Mewátis are found. It is under the unspecified and classes entered as Shaikhs that the majority of the Hindu converts are found, and, on the whole, they cannot be

put down at less than from one-half to two-thirds of the entire Musalmán population, a remarkable proof of the success of unscrupulous propagandism in India.

The population is distributed amongst 7,508 villages, containing 1,015,037
houses, or a number of houses to the square mile ranging from 88 in Sahárunpur to 114 in Meerut, and inhabitants to each house ranging from 4·4 in
Muzaffarnagar to 5·1 in Bulandshahr. About nine per cent. of the population
occupy houses built by skilled labour ; the remainder are satisfied with the
ordinary mud-built huts. About forty per cent. of the entire population, or
2,019,011 souls, are engaged in occupations connected with agriculture, and keep
under cultivation 6,830 square miles of land. The land-revenue amounts to
Rs. 76,87,398, or with cesses Rs. 85,65,190; the former falling at the rate of
about Re. 1-14-0 per cultivated acre. The cultivated area distributed amongst
the male adult (above fifteen years of age) agriculturists would give an average
holding of about six and a half acres to each person, for which he pays close
upon Rs. 3-8-0 an acre, and has to support about three persons by his exertions.
It is not to be argued from this that the peasantry of the upper Duáb are badly
off; they are wealthy when compared with the southern districts and the Benares
Division, but still they have, like all their brethren, to live from hand to mouth,
and, with the exception of the industrious Játs, Gáras, and Tagas, there are few
that have or indeed are able to lay by anything for times of distress.

GEOLOGY.

The geology of the North-Western Provinces is separable [1] into three divisions, corresponding to three distinct geographical regions. Twenty-three of
the thirty-five revenue districts are entirely on the Gangetic plains. On the
north, three districts (Dehra Dún, Garhwál, and Kumaon) belong altogether
to the Himálayan region. Out of nine districts on the south, seven are in
a very large proportion covered by the plains-deposits ; three only being in
whole or in great part within the rock-area of the Peninsula of Hindustan.
It is at once apparent that these geographical divisions are also strictly geological ; and it may be here stated that no identification or relation has as yet
been made out between the rocks on the north and on the south of the plains.

The middle region naturally claims first attention. It is often spoken of
as " the alluvial plains of the Ganges," or such like
The plains.
expressions. In a general sense these terms are
admissible ; there is no doubt that the materials forming the plains were conveyed
by the Ganges and its tributaries. But in this range of meaning the Siwálik
deposits might claim to be included, for it has been shown that they, too, were
accumulated through the existing Himálayan drainage system. Confining the
word alluvium to its strict geological meaning—to ground subject to flooding
from the very elements that now exist, the alluvial ground of the North-Western

---

[1] By Professor H. B. Medlicott, Geological Surveyor.

Provinces becomes very small. It is necessary to specify still further to bring out the distinction to be made in the area under notice; the word "alluvium" is scarcely understood unless as applied to fine deposits from tranquil inundation, —and it applies to such indiscriminately; whereas the point to be indicated is, what ground is undergoing increase from any form of deposition, and on what ground abrasion is in permanent action, or in other words, where river action is formative and where it is destructive. A very large proportion of the plains-area is permanently undergoing denudation : the main rivers run through it in confined and fixed channels, the flood-waters being well below the general level of the country. Several considerable streams, as the Hindan, take their rise within this area, and though subject to local overflow, with deposition of alluvium, must on the whole carry away annually a large quantity of earth. The fixed channels of the great rivers are of very variable width, and are generally bounded by steep high banks. The deep course of the river oscillates within the larger channel ; the whole of the latter being liable to inundation from the floods.

"*Khádir Matti*" is as near as possible the native equivalent for the English 'alluvial land.' But though there is always a large

The Khádir.

total area of alluvial land in the *khádirs* of the great rivers, it is possible that, on the whole, these *khádirs* are undergoing denudation—that the new alluvial land formed by the changes of the river may be progressing lower than the older patches removed by the same process. There are no data for settling the point : it can only be stated that the fall of the rivers through this province is greater than that at which silt-carrying rivers become on a large scale depositing rivers, that the current here seems able within the year to carry off all the silt it receives. Below Ghazipur, on the border of the provinces, the fall of the Ganges lessens, and the river becomes on a large scale formative, great tracts of country being subject to inundation from it. It has not yet been defined how much of the eastern districts come under this or that condition of fluviatile action. The whole of the Province of Oudh would come under one or other of them.

Independently of such tracts as come within the sub-deltaic region of the great rivers, there is a considerable stretch of country

Recent deposits.

where the drainage is formative. The minor streams from the outer skirt of the mountains do not run on into the plains in deep channels, but through the deposits of earlier times, and flow, at least for many miles, in broad shallow and ever-shifting beds formed of their own deposits. The load of shingle, gravel, sand, and earth washed into these torrents by the heavy rain-fall off the precipitous sides formed of the soft conglomerates, sandstones, and clays of the Siwálik hills, is far more than the current can carry into the great rivers. Something of the same kind no doubt takes place in these rivers also: the quantity of large shingle brought by them to the mouth of their gorges is certainly not carried much further; but for the rest, the clear water issuing for the greater part of the year from the gorges seems to carry off any excess deposited thereabouts in time of flood. The clear water becomes quite muddy soon after entering the *khádir*. There is thus along the northern margin of the plains a broad belt of ground, the formation of which is strictly recent. The upper portion of it, having a steeper slope than the rest, is chiefly composed of shingle and gravel with a filling up of sand and earth. This is the forest-bearing zone known as the "*bhábar*." Except in the rainy season the

The Bhábar.

bhábar is devoid of water, streams of considerable volume soon sinking into the porous ground, to reappear (at least in part) along the lower fringe of the coarse deposits. From the cause just mentioned, this outer zone, though having on the whole a considerable slope (greater than the general slope of the plains) is especially watery and swampy: it is well known as the Tarái. In the Jumna-Ganges

The Tarái.

Duáb the formation process is especially active owing to the greater development here of the soft upper Siwálik rocks, which are the most abundant sources of detritus. The Tarái in this Duáb is scarcely a noticeable feature, owing probably to the good natural drainage; the watershed being here 400 feet above the Ganges at Hardwár. Eastwards from the Ganges the Tarái becomes more and more distinct; and in the same direction remnants of an ancient bhábar deposit become frequent and of increasing elevation, till in the far east, at the base of the Sikhim Himálaya, they stand at 1,000 feet over the actual torrents. To the south of the plains some analogous cases of recent deposits may be found, but they are altogether insignificant, the large rivers there also running in channels which they do not overflow to any extent. The phenomena under notice have been only incidentally examined, so that the sketch here given is very incomplete and open to correction.

It having been shown that the great mass of the plains-deposits belong

Pliocene deposits.

to a bygone phase of formation, it devolves upon the geologist to ascertain the age and nature of that same. Very little progress has as yet been made to that end, the systematic study of the question not having been taken up. Some have maintained that the deposits are marine or estuarine; others, as seems more likely, that they are purely fluviatile, by a process precisely like what is now going on in the Lower Provinces. No trace of marine organism has been discovered in them. But some bones of terrestrial mammalia were found in a hard bed of calcareous gravel in the bed of the Jumna near Etáwa, and which seem to belong to species or varieties now extinct, so that these deposits will probably take rank among the later tertiaries. From observations made in sinking wells along the line of railway, one of the engineers has stated the ground section in the Duáb to be as follows, viz., loam 35 feet, blue silt 30 feet, strong clay 20 feet, resting on a water-bed of reddish sand, from which the water rises some 30 feet. The appearance of salts to a very deleterious extent in the water and as an efflorescence in many parts of the country has been an object of anxious enquiry, especially as it seems on the increase. The source of the mischief has not yet been determined : it. may be altogether due to the great evaporation with insufficient surface drainage.

There is more variety for the geologist in the rocky regions north and south of the plains. In Kumaon and Garhwál the boundary of the province extends up to the great snowy range, the frontier of Tibet. West of the Ganges, the District of Dehra Dún (including Jaunsár) comprises only a small portion of the Lower Himálaya. There is much uniformity in the arrangement of the Himálayan rocks, of which one may make three great divisions. The youngest of these includes the tertiary epoch, ranging from the nummulitic age to the Miocene Siwáliks. It has been named the Sub-Himálayan series, as principally forming the lower ranges flanking the mountains.

Himálayan region.

Sub-Himálayan series.

In it, again, three well-marked physical stages have been described. In point of elevation the order of sequence of these has been reversed, the oldest being highest, and the youngest lowest. This has not taken place by inversion nor yet (it has been argued) by upheaval in steps, through faulting. Appearances are best explained by the supposition that, during successive periods of elevation, an irregular scarped line of erosion was weathered out along the newly-raised strata (like the present cliffed face of the Siwálik hills), and that against this as a boundary the newer groups of deposits were accumulated, just as we see the *bhábar* slopes of the present day. As would result from such a process, the oldest group has been most exposed and has suffered most from denudation; only remnants of it are left along the flanks of the higher hills. The typical area, in which all the sub-divisions of this group are seen, lies to the west of the Jumna; the hill stations of Kasauli, Dagshai, and Subáthu are on these rocks. The lowest member of the series consists at its base of brown clays with limestone and fine sandstone, passing up into thick red clays and strong sandstones. The age of the lower portion is well characterised by abundant nummulitic fossils. Only a very small remnant of those beds has been noticed in the North-Western Provinces; it occurs on a gap of the ridges bounding the eastern Dún, close above Rikhikesh and just north of the village of Bhawan. The middle group of the series is largely developed in the hills immediately at the base of the mountain range, as spurs of which they might be hastily described; but their distinctness as a range is well marked by a line

Lower group.

Middle group.

of low gaps and of open longitudinal valleys along the geological boundary, the drainage passing through the range by narrow gorges. These features may be well seen under Mussooree. From Rájpur to the Ganges this flanking range has been removed, but east of the Ganges it appears again in great force, continuing so up to the Nepál frontier. The strata are well exposed along both roads up to Naini Tál. They consist principally of very massive grey sandstone (very like the molasse of Switzerland), with subordinate bands of clay. The small nests of lignite found at many places in the sandstone have more than once given rise to exaggerated hopes, and even to confident statements, as to the existence of coal. The fine hematite iron ore of Dehchauri, near Kálidhúngi, is only a local concentration of the iron oxide which occurs so finely disseminated as an ingredient of the clays. This middle member of the series has been called the Náhan group, from the chief town of Sirmor.

The youngest member of the sub-Himálayan series is the Siwálik group, so

Upper group.

called from the name given to the outermost range of hills by the authors of the well-known Fauna Siva-lensis. These hills are much lower than those of the middle group, from which they are generally separated by the broad longitudinal valleys known as "dúns." These are structural features, not mere valleys of denudation; the form of dis-turbance of the strata is very regular, broad "normal" anticlinal flexures, the axis-plane sloping towards the mountains: the hills have been weathered out along the axis of the flexure, and the dúns lie on the flat northern slope. The original Siwálik hills are that well-defined portion of the range between the Ganges and the Jumna, separating Dehra Dún from the plains. From a short distance east of the Ganges the range is broken and scarcely recogniz-able, having probably been denuded off and covered up, if indeed it had ever been so prominent as to the west: the bhábar deposits often reach up to the base of the minor range. The Pátli Dún is an irregular valley of denudation in these hills of the Náhan group. The lower part of the Siwálik group is very like the Náhan group in composition, save that the sandstone is softer and fresher. At the top there is great thickness of conglomerate, both earthy and sandy. The physical separation between the Siwálik and the Náhan groups' has recently been clearly made out; but the distinction was, unfortunately, not observed in the collection or the description of the great series of fossils fomerly procured from this region. The vast majority, if not all, of the large mamma-lian remains were obtained from the younger group: some vertebrate fossils were found in the Náhan rocks, but were confounded with the rest. A very interesting point—the comparison of the two faunas—was thus lost.

The second great rock system to be noticed consists of an unknown thick-

The slate series.

ness of slates, limestones, and sandstones forming the first range of the mountains from end to end.

The stations of Chakráta, Mussooree, and Naini Tál are on this range. The strata are greatly contorted, although preserving a strike approximately parallel to the mountain range ; and the order of the several bands of rock has only been vaguely suggested. The only fossils certainly known to have been procured from them were some casts of indeterminate bivalves from a band of limestone in the gorge of the Tál river, at the east end of the Dehra Dún. The lead mines of Sirmor and Subáthu are in these rocks Trappean intrusions occur in many places.

The remaining rock system is that of the metamorphic and crystalline rocks

The metamorphic series. with intrusive granite, forming the greater part of the broad zone of the outer or lower Himálaya, up to the snowy range. The junction of these rocks with the slate series is well marked in the valley north of Naini Tál. There is a large mass of intrusive granite near Almora. Copper ores occur at many places and are worked by the natives. They have not been favourably reported on by European mineral-viewers. There are many fine bands of rich iron ore, but the inaccessibility of the ground prevents their being extensively used. Impure graphite is found in several places.

The boundaries of the plains on the south are on the whole irregular

Southern region. although the arrangement and relations of the rocks are very simple. There are here but two rock systems deserving more than mere mention, the great Vindhyan series and a

The Vindhyans. crystalline series. The Vindhyans represent a whole epoch in the geology of Hindústan, and are divided into an upper and lower series, each having several groups. Both of these series are fairly represented in the Mirzapur District. The plateau between the Ganges and the Són is formed of upper Vindhyan rocks, principally of the Kaimúr group ; and in the Són valley the lower Vindhyans are well seen. From the eastern edge of the provinces, in Mirzapur, the upper Vindhyans are continuous right away to Agra, but in great part through Native States ; the northern scarp forming approximately the boundary of the North-Western Provinces throughout the Districts of Allahabad, Bánda, Lalitpur, and Jhansi. There is a break here, Sindia's territories running up, to the Jumna, but further to the north-west, a ridge of Vindhyan sandstone, of the Bhaurer group, on which stands the famous ruins of Fatehpur Síkri, runs to within a few miles of Agra city. The upper Vindhyans consist of strong bands of sandstone alternating with strong bands of shales, in some of which limestone occurs. Along the boundary in Bánda, Lalitpur, and Jhansi, the bottom beds rest undisturbed upon the crystalline, having for the most part completely over-lapped the lower Vindhyans, of which only a narrow and broken strip is exposed between Kirsir and the Dhasán. The lower Vindhyans are made up of limestones, sandstones and shales, a characteristic variety of which has porcellanic and trappoid aspects.

Throughout their immense area in this part of India the Vindhyan strata are quite undisturbed, except along the south margin, as in the Són valley, and again along the north-west boundary, as in the ridge of Fatehpur Síkri. The direction of disturbances in this latter position is parallel to that of the Aravali system, of which it is probably only a secondary and reflex effect. The Vindhyan rocks have given great disappointment to geologists in not having as yet yielded any fossil remains. It is only known through their stratigraphical relations to the Indian coal-bearing rocks that they can be at latest of middle palæogoic age. The sandstones of the Vindhyans afford everywhere admirable building stones.

The crystalline rocks only appear to any extent in lower Bundelkhand, in the wide bay formed by the Vindhyan scarps; principally in the Districts of Lalitpur and Jhansi, occupying the head of the bay, and to a less extent in Jalaun, Hamírpur, and Bánda, where the outcrops through the plains-deposits become less and less frequent. The rock is chiefly gneiss, often granitoid. The strike of the foliation and bedding, when observable, is generally east and west. Greenstone dykes are of frequent occurrence, with a prevailing north-west to south-east direction. But the most remarkable feature of this area is the number of great quartz-reefs. They have a prevailing north-easterly run, but exceptions are frequent. They stand up in abrupt wall-like ridges, sometimes over 300 feet high, many yards wide, and running perfectly straight for several miles continuously or appearing again on the same strike. They seem to be of earlier date than all the trap-dykes, and are often highly impregnated with steatite, and otherwise displaying metamorphic characters. It might be thought that gold should be found in or about these great quartz-reefs, but there is no trace or tradition of its occurrence.

The crystallines of Bundelkhand.

The other rocks, of which more mention may be made, occupy a few square miles in British Singrauli, the southern division of the Mirzapur District. On the entrance south there is gneiss, part of the great gneiss area of Behar and Bengal. Between this and the lower Vindhyans there is a band of sub-metamorphic rocks, principally clay-slates. South of this band, and resting on the gneiss, there is a small patch of this coal-bearing rock, the eastern extremity of the south Ríwá basin. From the Kota mine in Singrauli was derived all the coal that for many years used to be taken on pack-bullocks across the Vindhyan plateau to Mirzapur.

Singrauli.

FISH.

Attention was directed to the fisheries of India in 1867, and Dr. Day was appointed to report on the fish of these provinces as well as the rest of India. His report was published

Fish-economy.

in 1873. He divides the fish into those of the hills and those of the plains. Amongst the more important of the plains species is the *maháser* (or carp), which lives in the rivers of the plains during the cold months, when the hill-streams are too small and too cold to afford proper sustenance. During the rains the maháser migrates to the hills, and ascending some distance up the colder waters of the larger rivers, turns aside for breeding purposes into their warm side-streams. These side-streams, unreplenished by snow-water, are the natural breeding-places of most of the more valuable fish of the carp family residing near such places, and anything that interferes with them whilst there, must materially injure the fisheries. A large majority of the young fish remain in the hill-streams until the next rains. The local non-migratory fishes pass up small water-courses and channels, depositing their eggs in irrigated fields, flooded plains, temporarily formed tanks, on the grassy sides of rivers and lakes.

Much destruction is caused by the canals through which large quantities of fish find their way from the hills, but having once entered them, they are unable to return again for breeding, and multitudes perish when the canals are allowed to run dry for repairs. Again, the existence of fixed weirs across the hill-streams, up which large carp proceed to breed, is a fertile source of destruction. These are constructed in Kumaon and Garhwál at the close of the rains, and remain until the next floods. They are placed usually at the tail of each pool, or at the junction of two rivers, and effectually prevent the escape of any fish that has once got above them. Similar contrivances exist on all the small streams within the hills, and the dams made to draw off a supply of water for the small flour-mills are utilised for the same purpose. In the plains, engines, fixed and movable, are also used in the most wasteful way. Some account of the nets and other implements in use will be found in the description of each district, and here it will be useful to give the opinions of the district officials on the question of the necessity for Government interference in the preservation of fish in the Meerut Division.

Causes of the destruction of fish.

The Commissioner writes :—" I think it may safely be concluded that the proportion of the population who live by fishing as a trade is not large ; the proportion of persons who have no other occupation than fishing is small, but it is increased by others who resort to fishing at odd times, probably in times when they have nothing better to do. So far, then, as the fisherman class is concerned, I do not think there is much to fear of their efforts making any appreciable impression on the fish-supply. But there is a fear that, unless the reckless system of wholesale destruction is stopped, the fish-supply may become scant. There seem to be two main causes which lead to this wanton destruction of fish : the first is by

Fish-preserving in the Meerut Division.

reason of the facilities afforded for doing so in the canals and distributary channels, and the second is the absence of any check in respect of rivers." He continues that nets or gratings at the head of canals will be liable to be carried away in heavy floods, so proposes fish-ladders at each fall. "The main points for consideration would be : *first*, to prevent damming streams for the purpose of catching fish ; *second*, a limit to the size of the mesh in nets ; *third*, a close season, say from first July to first October, seems to be essentially necessary, and catching fish within these dates should be prohibited. The close season need not apply to every kind of fish, but to those more generally used for food. The limit to the size of the mesh of nets would only stop the fry being caught, but the prohibition to damming or diverting streams would also prevent the wholesale destruction which now takes place." "There is no doubt that the most wanton destruction of fish does take place, and that fish are disappearing from the sub-streams of the Ganges and Jumna. Where twenty or thirty years ago fish of ten or fifteen pounds could be caught, none are now to be seen except fry, and such fry the native fishermen net and snare in every way at all seasons.

The Collector of Saháranpur "has no remarks to offer on the subject."

Opinions of Collectors.

The Collector of Meerut (February 22nd, 1872) observed that "there is no question that considerable damage is done to the young fish, by the indiscriminate use of nets with extremely small meshes, without any regard to the spawning season, and in the smaller streams, by the practice freely resorted to by the fishermen and others of damming up the streams, drying off the portion below, and then taking out the larger fish, while the smaller are left to perish. I do not think the establishment of a close season would meet with any opposition. At the spawning season, fish are considered impure and scarcely fit for food, and it is only the very poorest part of the population that makes use of fish at that season. There would be little difficulty in the introduction of a fixed close season, and this would greatly protect the fishing interests. I think a close season from 15th June to 1st November would give a fair time for spawning and the growth of the young fry. The mesh I would recommend should be one inch and a half from knot to knot, or perhaps even two inches. Small rewards for crocodiles' eggs would aid in the extermination of those reptiles, and this could be easily arranged for." The Assistant Collector of Meerut reported that "as little fishing is carried on in the rains, the destruction of breeding fish and fry is not very great. No doubt there is considerable destruction, for all fish, breeding or not, are, when caught, killed without distinction." Difficulties would exist in regulating the minimum size of the mesh of nets, and he is "opposed to Government doing anything, especially as regards fry, because the subordinate native officers and the police being high-caste men among the

Hindu population, it would rest with persons quite unacquainted with distinctions in classes of fish to decide as to what is fry and what is not; while we may be sure that considerable oppression would be exercised." The Collector of Muzaffarnagar (March 29th, 1872) reported, *first*, that there is no limit to the size of mesh employed, but that nets having very small meshes are used mainly for fishing in *jhíls* and ponds, and nets with larger meshes for river-fishing; *second*, that nature practically provides a close season for fish during the monsoon; *third*, that the consumption of fish in the district is not excessive, and consequently the destruction of small fry does not appear to take place systematically. "Except occasionally, when fields are flooded in the rains, there does not seem anywhere, or at any time, to be any wholesale destruction of small fry;" he sees no practical difficulty in regulating the minimum size of the meshes of nets, or prescribing a close season, but does not consider such necessary in his district.

Nothing, that I am aware of, has been done to carry out any of these suggestions, or to interfere in any way with the present wanton and wholesale destruction of fish. I give the names of the more common description of fish found in these provinces, with a reference to the page of Dr. Day's report,[1] where they are described at some length. The mammalia, birds, and insects will be found in the next volume, and thus a complete list will be given illustrating the natural history of these provinces.

Sub-fam. TELEOSTEI.

Order ACANTHOPTERYGII.

Family PERCIDÆ, *Cuv.*

Ambassis baculis, Ham. Buch. *Kunggi*, H. Scales minute. Day, 249.

Ambassis nama, Ham. Buch. *Bhakra, pompiya*, H. Small. Day, 249.

Ambassis lala, Ham. Buch. *Chandi*, H. Scales minute; lateral line absent. Orange, with four or five vertical bands; first dorsal nearly black. Only a few inches long. Day, 249.

Family MUGILIDÆ, *Rich.*

Mugil cascasia, Ham. Buch. *Kakse, bua*, H. Silvery; uncovered space on chin, eye, base of pectoral, and centre of base of caudal gamboge yellow. Found in Ganges and Jumna. Day, 252.

Mugil corsula, Ham. Buch. *Anwdri* of the Ken. D. 4⅓, A. ⅜, L. l. 50, L. tr. 15.

Family GOBIIDÆ.

Gobius giuris, Ham. Buch. *Gulú*, H. Blotched and spotted with rusty-brown. Attains a foot and a half in length. Day, 253.

Family NANDIDÆ, *Günther.*

Badis Buchanani, Bleeker. *Chiri, kála pútiya*, H. Purplish black, banded. Day, 254. Small.

Badis dario, Ham Buch. Lateral line absent. Colours and size as in last species. Day, 254.

Nandus marmoratus. Cuv. *Gadha, húlsa, badhal*, H. No pseudobranchiæ. Day, 255.

Family LABYRINTHICI, *Cuv.*

Trichogaster fasciatus, Bl. Schn. *Kangi*, H. Greenish, banded, and some of the fins red-spotted. Day, 256. Small.

T. lalius, Ham. Buch. Banded, owing to every scale being half light blue and half scarlet; fins spotted red.

[1] Calcutta, Government Press, 1873.

Family OPHIOCEPHALIDÆ, *Bleeker.*

Ophiocephalus marulius, Ham. Buch. *Saul, daula, kabra, H.* Orange, with vertical bands and white spots. Sometimes as long as four feet. Day, 257.

O. striatus, Lacép. *Chota saul, maral,* H. Grey above, whitish beneath, striated with black. Day, 257.

O. gachua, Ham. Buch. *Chabu, dheri dhok,* H Greenish; pectoral barred; the other fins with orange edgings. Attains a foot in length. Day, 258.

O. punctatus, Bloch. *Gari, phúl dhok,* H. Dirty green, banded, and sometimes with numerous black dots over the body. Same size as preceding. Day, 258.

Family RHYNCHOBDELLIDÆ, *Bl.*

Mastacemblus, pancalus, Ham. Buch. *Gúrchi, jugar,* H. Attains a length of about six inches. Day, 259.

M. armatus, Lacép, *Bahm,* H. Marbled and striped, sometimes with round spots. Found throughout India, even to the Himálaya, attaining two feet and upwards in length. Day, 259.

Order ANACANTHINI.

Sub-order *Anacanthini-pleuronectoidei.*

Family PLEURONECTIDÆ.

Synaptura pan, Ham. Buch. A species of sole found in the Ganges high above tidal influence. Day, 260.

ORDER PHYSOSTOMI.

Family SILURIDÆ.

Macrones aor, Ham. Buch. *Singhári,* H. Maxillary barbels extend to the end of the caudal fin. Adipose dorsal with a black spot at its posterior extremity. Large cat-fish, attaining several feet in length. Day, 261.

M. Lamarri, Cuv. *Tengara,* H. Maxillary barbels extend to the end of the first dorsal fin. A black spot at the posterior end of the adipose dorsal. Found in the upper portions of the Ganges and Jumna, attaining several feet in length. Day, 251.

M. chrysnus, Day. *Ptla katarni,* H. Barbel scarcely longer than the head. No separate inter-neural shield on the nape. Body golden, a black blotch behind the opercles. Day, 262.

M. carcio, Ham. Buch. *Kagar, katahra,* H. Maxillary barbels reach the caudal fin. Dorsal spine serrated on both sides: adipose fin short. Banded, and having a shoulder mark a few inches long. Day, 262.

M. nangra, Ham. Buch. Maxillary barbels reach the vent. Dorsal spine entire; adipose fin short. Mud coloured, with three vertical green bands. Ganges and Jumna, to two inches long. Day, 262.

M. botius, Ham. Buch Barbels shorter than the head. Dorsal spine entire. Brown. Length up to six inches. Day, 262.

M. tengara, Ham Buch. *Tingara,* H. Maxillary barbels reach the caudal. Dorsal spine entire; adipose fin long. Longitudinal bands and a dark shoulder mark. Upper portions of Jumna and Ganges; grows to six inches. Day, 263.

M. cavia, Ham Buch. *Kanya tengara,* H. Maxillary barbels as long as the head. Dorsal spine entire; adipose fin short. Brownish, with two transverse bands across the tail. Grows to six inches. Day, 263.

Pseudeutropius atherinoides, Bl. *Pathal, patahri,* H. Maxillary barbels reach the base of the anal fin. Three or four longitudinal lateral bands. Attains to four inches in length. Day, 265.

P. murius, Ham. Buch. *Bachúa,* H. Maxillary barbels reach the base of the anal fin. Attains to eight inches. Day, 265.

P. garua, Ham. Buch. *Bachúa, karúd,* H. Maxillary barbels reach the ventral fin. Adipose dorsal fin becomes absorbed in the adults. Silvery. Attains a length of one foot. Day, 265.

Callichrous bimaculatus, Bl. *Gángwári, paphta,* H. Four barbels, the maxillary reach the middle of the fish. Anal not confluent with the caudal; pectoral spine internally denticulated near its end. A round black spot above the middle pectoral fin. Day, 266.

C. pabda, Ham. Buch. Four barbels, the maxillary reaching to the second third of the anal fin, and not confluent with the caudal; pectoral spine smooth. A black blotch behind the gill-opening. Ganges.

C. Egertonii, Day. *Palawa, palu,* H. Four barbels, the maxillary extend slightly beyond the base of the pectoral fin. Anal not confluent with the caudal; pectoral spine denticulated internally. Numerous brownish blotches cover the body, and a large one exists over the posterior half of the pectoral fin. Day, 257.

Wallago attu, Bl. *Malli, boalli,* H. A voracious feeder; sometimes known as the fresh-water shark. Attains to several feet; is good eating. Day, 267.

Clarius magur, Ham. Buch. *Kagga, magúr*, H. Maxillary barbels reach nearly to the end of the pectoral fin; vertical fins not united. Dirty brown colour. Attains to 18 inches, and is considered good eating. Day, 259.

Saccobranchus fossilis, Bloch. *Singi*, H. Maxillary barbels reach the middle of pectoral, or even the commencement of the ventral fins. Leaden, sometimes with two longitudinal yellow bands. Day, 269.

Ailia Bengalensis, Gray. *Paphta*, Panj. Grows to seven inches. Silvery; some of the fins frequently stained with grey on the edges. The barbels extend to nearly the middle of the length of the fish. Day, 270.

Ailiichthys punctata, Day. *Patási, patuwa*, H. Barbels extend to the middle of the fish. Silvery; upper surface of the head nearly black; a large black spot on the base of the caudal fin. Attains to four inches in upper portions of the Jumna. Day, 270.

Eutropiichthys vacha, Ham. Buch. *Nimach*, H. Barbels about as long as the head. Silvery; greyish along the back. Grows to a foot. Day, 270.

Hemipimelodus cenia, Ham. Buch. *Paduwa, chetuwa*, H. Six barbels; no nasal pair. Attains to five inches. Day, 272.

H. viridescens, Ham. Buch. *Hadda*, H. Greenish brown, with two light green bands; a dark mark on the dorsal fin and each lobe with a similar blotch. Jumna. Day, 272.

Glyptosternum striatum, McClelland. *Nawa, japa*, H. Breadth of head nearly equals the length. Maxillary barbels extend beyond the root of the pectoral. Lips not fringed. Occipital process three times as long as broad. Caudal peduncle nearly twice as long as high. Dorsal spine more than half as long as head. Brown; fins yellow stained with black. Rivers along the base of the Himálayas. Day, 273.

G. telchitta, Ham. Buch. *Tiliya*, H. Head longer than broad. Maxillary barbels extend to the posterior edge of the orbit. Lips roughened, but not fringed. Occipital process three times as long as broad. Caudal peduncle twice as long as high. Fin rays not plaited inferiorly. Dorsal spine two-thirds as long as the head. Blackish brown; fins yellow with black bands. Caudal black, with a yellow edge. Day, 273.

G. modestum, Day. Breadth of the head equals its length. Lips not fringed. Occipital process slightly longer than broad at its base. Caudal peduncle two-thirds as high as long. Fin rays not plaited inferiorly. Dorsal spine half as long as the head. Uniform brown. Attains to three inches. Day, 274.

Amblyceps mangois, Ham. Buch. *Sukhse, billi, suddí*, H. Head as wide as long. Maxillary barbels reach the end of the pectoral spine. Occipital process rudimentary. Caudal peduncle as deep as long. Olive brown, with a dark line commencing opposite the opercles and dividing into two, one proceeding to the centre of the caudal, the inferior to the base of the anal.

Family. SCOMBRESOCIDÆ.

Belone cancila Ham. Buch. the pike. *Kanga*, H. Lateral line not keeled. Four or five dark blotches between the bases of the pectoral and anal fins.

Family. CYPRINIDÆ.

Mayoa modesta, Day. Greenish brown; a blotch below dorsal fin and another at the base of the caudal. Probably from the Himálayas. Day, 277.

Discognathus lamta, Ham. Buch. *Pathar chata*, H. Four barbels. A dark spot behind the gill-opening, and generally a band along the side. Attains to six inches. Day, 277.

Oreinus sinuatus, Heckel. *Gúl-guli, saul*, H. Silvery and spotted; sometimes a few of the spots are red. Attains to two feet in the Himálayas, where it is sometimes called a trout. Day, 278.

Schizothorax Hodgsonii, Günther. *Dinawa*, H. Attains to 18 inches in Himálayas and head of the Ganges. Day, 278.

Labeo nancar, Ham. Buch. Four barbels. Obtained in Gorakhpur.

L. calbasu, Ham. Buch. *Kalabáns* or *kalabains* H. Four barbels. Attains to four feet.

L. curchius, Ham. Buch *Kursa, kurchi*, H. Attains to five feet. Day, 279.

L rohita, Ham. Buch. *Rohu*, H. Four barbels, the rostral sometimes absent. Day, 279.

L. morala, Ham. Buch. Four barbels, Ganges. Attains a length of six inches. Day, 279.

L. ricnorhynchus, McClell. *Gidh*, H. One pair of maxillary barbels. Himálayas. Day, 279.

L. bicolor, McClell. *Gidha, mucheli, gaiwa*, H. One pair of maxillary barbels. Himálayas.

Cirrhina mrigala, Ham. Buch. *Naim*, H. Two barbels: upper lip entire. Attains to three feet or more.

C. gohama, Ham. Buch. *Bahra, tilári*, Panj. Two rostral barbels; upper lip fringed Attains a length of eight inches.

C. latia, Ham. Buch. Four barbels ; upper lip fringed. Small.

C. reba, Ham. Buch. *Riwa,* H. One pair of short rostral barbels; upper lip fringed or entire. About a foot. Day, 282.

Cutla Buchanani, Cuv. *Bawása, katla,* H. Attains to several feet in length, and is good eating. Day, 283.

Barbus immaculatus, McClell. No pores or snout. Day, 284.

B. sarana, Ham. Buch. *Gidhi, kauli, derhi,pota,* H. Attains a length of two feet.

B. tor, Ham. Buch. *Mahaser,* H. Lips lobed. Day, 285.

B. chilinoides, McClell. Grows to eight inches. Day, 285.

B. chola, Ham. Buch. *Kuchcha karawa,* H. Six inches in length.

B. conchonius, Ham. Buch. *Kanchon pangti,* H. A black spot on side over anal fin. Day,286.

B. ticto, Ham. Buch. *Kauli, kotri,* H. Rarely exceeds four inches in length. Day, 287.

B. stigma, Cuv *fatiya,* H. A dark spot near posterior end of lateral line, another across the base of middle dorsal rays.

B. chrysopterus, McClell. *Bawári,* H. Fins black tipped.

Nuria danrica, Ham. Buch. *Sumara, mola, mahwa,* H. A black lateral band. Day, 288.

Rasbora daniconius, Ham. Buch. *Millaoa,* H. No barbels ; mostly a black lateral stripe.

Aspidoparia morar, Ham. Buch. *Chilwa,* H. Attains up to six inches in length. Day, 289.

A. jaya, Ham. Buch. *Pahrua,* H.

Rohtee cotio, Ham. Buch. *Gúrdha, chandálu makni,* H.

Barilius piscatorius, Ham. Buch. *Lohári,* H. Ten vertical bars. Attains to five inches.

B. modestus. Day. Back dark ; sides silvery. Four inches in length. Day, 290.

B. shacra, Ham. Buch. *Gúrha,* H. Twelve vertical bars. Five inches. Day, 290.

B. vagra, Ham. Buch. Indistinct vertical bars.

B. barila, Ham. Buch. *Persi,* H. Fourteen or fifteen vertical bars.

B. bola, Ham. Buch. *Gúla,* H. Two rows of blotches. Day, 291.

B. hoalius, Ham. Buch. *Hayali,* H. To six inches in length.

Danio devario, Ham. Buch. *Daba, dahriya,* H. No barbels.

Perilampus atpar, Ham. Buch. *Moriya,* H. Greenish, with a silvery lateral band. Day, 292.

P. laubuca, Ham. Buch. *Kuncheliya,* H. A black mark above base of pectoral fin. Day, 293.

Chela bacaila, Ham. Buch. *Cheliya,* H. Attains to six inches.

C. gora, Ham. Buch. *Cheliya* H. Attains to eight inches in length.

Botia dario, Ham. Buch. *Baktiya,* H. Barbels eight.

B. Almorhæ, Gray. Barbels eight.

Nemacheilus botia, Ham. Buch. *Gúluwa,* H. Body irregularly blotched. Caudal emarginate. Day, 296.

N. rupicola, McClell. *Chítal,* H. Eleven to seventeen bands, brown, and wider than the ground colour. Caudal forked. Length 3¼ inches. Day, 296.

N. zonata, McClell. Eleven to thirteen dark zones encircle the body. not half the width of the ground colour. Caudal forked.

N. montanus, McClell. *Lál machhli,* H. Twelve vertical brown bands, Caudal forked. Himálayas.

N. spilopterus, Cuv. Eleven to fifteen irregular bands. Caudals slightly emarginate. Himálayas.

Family CLUPEIDÆ.

Engraulis telara, Ham. Buch. *Pencha,* Ben. Found in the Ganges. Day, 299,

Family NOTOPTERIDÆ.

Notopterus kapirat, Bonn. *Moh,* H. Attains to two feet or more.

Order PLAGIOSTOMATA.

Sub-order *Selachoidei.*

Family CARCHARIIDÆ.

Carcharias gangeticus, Müll. Of a grey colour. This savage ground shark attains a length of five feet. Day, 305.

Sub-order BATOIDEI or Rays.

Trygon uarnak, Forsk., and *T. sephen,* Forsk. Both found in the Ganges.

HISTORY.

THE earliest settlement of the Aryan race within the confines of India was in that portion of the Panjáb lying between the Drishadwati (Khagar) and Sára-

Vaidik period.

swati (Sarsúti) rivers, to the west of and adjoining the upper Duáb, the Brahmávarta of Manu. It was here that the principal personages mentioned in the Vedas lived, and, under the auspices of Saraswati, the goddess of learning, the Vedas and Puránas were compiled. The Vedas show us a colony of fair-complexioned strangers settled amongst dark-skinned, rude and uncivilised aborigines. The mode of life of these colonists was simple in the extreme. The head of the family combined in himself the office of priest and chief, and the members devoted themselves chiefly to cultivating the ground and tending cattle. Hence they spread into the Duáb and eastern India. The Solar race gave kings to Ajudhiya in southern Oudh, and colonies to a great part of these provinces. One branch settled in Tirhút and founded the family of the Maithila kings, and another occupied southern Tirhút or Vaisáli (Sáran). The Lunar race sprung from the same stock, and occasionally intermarrying with the Solar line, gave princes to Pratishthána, a city to the south of Ajudhiya (Ayodhya), to Káshi (Benares), Magadha and Behar ; to the Vindhya hills, and across them to Berar (Vidarbha). The earliest princes of Kusasthali, on the Narbada, Dwárka in Gujrát, Hastinápur and Muttra, belong to the same race. Though there are hints of settlement in the peninsula, yet these are so indistinct, that it is difficult to say whether they belong to the original works in which they are mentioned or are interpolations of later times.[1]

The earliest traditions regarding these provinces are connected with the upper Duáb, and there centre in Hastinápur, the ancient city of the Pándavas, situated in the parganah of Hastinápur in the Meerut District. Few traces of the old city now remain to show what its extent may have been, but universal report points

The Mahábhárata.

out the existing shapeless *kheras* or mounds as the residence of the moon-descended princes of the house of Bhárata, from whom came the actors in the great war mentioned in the pages of the Mahábhárata. With the exception, perhaps, of the Ramáyana, devoted to the achievements of the Solar race, there is no work in India which has had such influence on the Hindu mind as the Mahábhárata. Its legends are as household words, and are used as commonly and naturally in the conversation and writings of the people as the mythical history of Greece and Rome and the narratives of the Sacred Scriptures are quoted in the west. And this is no decaying influence, for up to the present day, the belief is universal that

---

[1] For a popular and accurate resumé of the facts known concerning the Vaidik and Brahmanic ages, I would refer the reader to Mrs. Manning's (Mrs. Speir) "Ancient India," and for the literature and its history to Max Müller's works.

the perusal, or even listening to the perusal, of the Mahábhárata cleanses from all sin. It is impossible to understand almost any modern popular work written by Hindús for Hindu readers without at least an acquaintance with the outlines of the story of the Lunar race ; so that apart from its historical interest, the records of this great family would appear to demand some notice in the present volume.

Setting aside the miraculous events, which in common with the Iliad and Æneid surround, as with a halo, the births and exploits of the principal heroes, Historical value of these legends. the residue of the narrative may be accepted as founded on facts. There is nothing unnatural in the circumstances of the dispute between the rival branches of the family of Kuru, and no reason appears for considering the whole as a gigantic fraud perpetrated by the nation at large and permitted to pervade the entire post-Vedic literature of the different Hindu communities throughout India for the purpose of deception. This is not the place for entering into a critical examination of the Mahábhárata, as to whether it is the work of one hand or of many, or what portions have been written soon after the events they record, and what may be considered the interpolations of successive editors. Professor H. H. Wilson places the compilation at no later date than the thirteenth or fourteenth century before Christ, whilst General Cunningham fixes on the end of the fifteenth century before Christ, making the birth of Parikshit to have occurred in 1430 before Christ, six years before the great war.[1]

---

[1] V. P. IV, 232. General Cunningham in Arch. Rep. I., 125. The grounds on which this opinion has been adopted are, (1) Bentley's statement that certain positions of the planets recorded in the Mahábhárata took place in 1824-5 B. C., and there is no year either before or since that period in which they were so situated. (2) The Vishnu Purána (V. P. IV. 232,) declares that at the birth of Parikshit the seven Rishis (the great Bear) were in Mágha, and the Káli age then commenced. The Rishis pass through each lunar asterism in 100 years (*Ibid* p. 233, note) and this gives an interval between Nanda and Parikshit of 1,000 years. All the copies of the Vishnu Purána give 1,015 years; the Matsya Purána has 1,050 years, and the Bhágavata 1,115 years. The items, however, recorded in the Bhágavata make up 1,590 years. Professor Wilson considers the shorter period is best proportioned to the number of kings ; for reckoning from Sahadeva, who was a contemporary of Parikshit, there were forty-seven kings, which as the divisor of 1050 (Matsya), gives rather more than twenty-two years to each reign. The duration of the reigns of the nine Nandas will place the birth of Parikshit, according to the Vishnu Purána, 1,115 years before the accession of Chandragupta (Sandrakottus) in 315 B. C., or 1430 B. C., that is, six years before the great war in 1424 B. C. According to the Matsya chronology the date of Parikshit's birth will be 1465 B. C., and according to the Bhágavata, 1530 B. C. Colonel Wilford (As. Res. IX., 116) places the conclusion of the great war in 1370 B. C., and Hamilton (Buchanan) conjectures it to have occurred in the thirteenth century before Christ. Colebrooke (I. Misc. Ess., 109, 200) infers from astronomical data that the arrangement of the Vedas by Vyása, the substituted husband of the widows of Vichitravírya, took place in the fourteenth century before Christ. Mr. Bentley (Hindú Astronomy, p. 67) brings the date of Yudhishthira to 575 B. C., but the weight of authority, according to Professor H. H. Wilson, "is in favour of the thirteenth or fourteenth century, B. C., for the war of the Mahábhárata, and the reputed commencement of the Káli age." The popular date for its commencement is 3101 B. C., or the date of Noah's deluge (Mill).

The account given in the Mahábhárata may be supplemented from the genealogical portions of the Puránas, which substantially agree with the facts recorded in the great epic.

The Puránas.

The Puránas are eighteen in number, compiled at different times and by various hands. The Vishnu Purána, which has been translated by Professor Wilson[1] and edited by Dr. Hall, is the principal, and next to the Bhágavata is still regarded as the great authority on matters connected with their religion by large sections of the Hindu community. Professor Wilson attributes its compilation to some time before the twelfth century of our era. According to Amara Sinha, who flourished fifty-six years before Christ, a Purána should contain five books, one relating to primary creation or cosmogony; the next to secondary creation, or the destruction and renovation of worlds, including chronology; thirdly, the genealogy of gods and patriarchs; fourthly, the reigns of the Manus, or periods called *manwantaras;* and lastly, history, giving an account of the Lunar and Solar races, and of their descendants, to modern times. None of the Puránas come up to this standard, and the Vishnu Purána only in part; but so much more so than the others, that " it is one of the circumstances which give to this work a more authentic character than most of its fellows can pretend to." Imperfect as they are, and disfigured by absurd stories and interpolations of later times, the Puránas, with the great epic poems, are the chief amongst the few historical records we possess of any antiquity to assist us in compiling an account of the heroic age.[2]

The Lunar race in the Puránas are descended from Brahma, who sprang from the lotus forming the navel of Naráyana. From Brahma came Atri, and from Atri, Soma or the moon, whom

The Lunar race.

---

[1] Collected works, Vols. VI. to X.: London, 1862-71. [2] Professor Wilson writes:—"The different works known by the name of Puránas are evidently derived from the same religious system as the Ramáyana and Mahábhárata, or from the mytho-heroic stage of Hindu belief. They present, however, peculiarities which designate their belonging to a later period, and to an important modification in the progress of opinion. They repeat the theoretical cosmogony of the two great poems; they expand and systematize the chronological computations; and they give a more definite and connected representation of the mythological fictions and the historical traditions. But, besides these and other particulars, which may be derivable from an old, if not from a primitive era, they offer characteristic peculiarities of a more modern description, in the paramount importance which they assign to individual divinities, in the variety and purport of the rites and observances addressed to them, and in the invention of new legends illustrative of the power and graciousness of those deities, and of the efficacy of implicit devotion to them. Siva and Vishnu, under one or other form, are almost the sole objects that claim the homage of the Hindús in the Puránas, departing from the domestic and elemental ritual of the Vedas, and exhibiting a sectarial fervour and exclusiveness not traceable in the Ramáyana, and only to a qualified extent in the Mahábhárata. They are no longer authorities for Hindu belief, as a whole: they are special guides for separate and sometimes conflicting branches of it; compiled for the evident purpose of promoting the preferential, or, in some cases, the sole worship of Vishnu or of Siva." (V. P. I, v.)

Brahma installed as the sovereign of Brahmans, plants and the stars. Soma, by an intrigue with Tárá, the wife of Brihaspati, preceptor of the gods, had a son named Budha, who married Ila, a daughter of the sun. To him was born Pururuvas who, by the nymph Urvasi, had six sons, the eldest of whom was named Ayus. Yayáti, the son of Ayus, had five sons, to whom he severally applied to remove the premature decay under which he suffered owing to the curse of his father-in-law. All refused to undergo the privations of old age except Puru, the youngest, who willingly gave his youth to his father and became an aged man. Yayáti, touched with the piety of his youngest son, subsequently determined to resume his decrepitude. He called all his sons before him and restored to Puru his youth, and distributed amongst them all his kingdom. To Turvasu he gave the south-east of his kingdom, and his posterity ended with Marutta, who adopted Dushyantu of the race of Puru. Druhyu[1] was made prince of the west, Anu of the north, and Yádu of the south. All were directed to govern as viceroys of Puru, who was declared monarch of the whole earth.

Yádu had several sons, and amongst his descendants were Krishna and Báláráma, the allies of the Pándavas. In the line of Puru

The Pauravas.

came Dushyantu, who was adopted by his cousin Marutta, and had by Sakuntala,[2] the mighty king Bhárata, the emperor of the entire earth. He is the first great king of the race, and to this day India is known amongst Hindús as Bháratavarsha, or the country of Bhárata. Amongst his descendants come Sahotra, the father of Hastin, who founded Hastinápura. Hastin had three sons, the eldest of whom was named Ajamírha. The sovereignty of Hastinápura itself remained in the hands of his son Rikshu, who was succeeded by Samvarana. Haryaswa, the fifth in descent from Nila, the brother of Rikshu, had five sons, of whom their father said—"These my five (pancha) sons are able (alam) to protect the countries," and hence they were termed Panchálas. Even thus early dissensions existed in the family, for we find from the Mahábárata that the Panchálas expelled their cousin Samvarana from Hastinápur, which was again recovered by his son Kuru, who gave his name to the holy district of Kurukshetra.[3] In the Puránas the possessions of the Kauravas and the Panchálas form the middle districts of Bháratavarsha. To the

---

[1] The sons of Prachetas, the eighth in descent from Druhyu, are subsequently said (V. P. IV., 119) to have been the "princes of the lawless Mlechchas of the north," while the Mahábhárata calls them "Vaibhojas, a people unacquainted with the use of carts or beasts of burthen, and who travel on rafts ; they have no kings." As king of the south-east he should rule over Arakan and Ava, but many authorities derive the nations of the peninsula also from him (Ibid, 117.) [2] The legend of Dushyantu and Sakuntala has been dramatised by Kálidasa in his beautiful poem of Sakuntala, or "Sakuntala recognized by the ring," the scene of which is laid in the Bijnor District. (Ed. Williams: Hertford, 1855.) [3] Near Thanesar.—Cunningham. Anc. Geogh. 331.

Panchála. Panchála family belonged Drupada, in whose reign their possessions were divided. Drona,[1] with the assistance of the Pándavas, conquered the entire kingdom, and then ceded the southern portion to Drupada. Panchála at this time would seem to include the entire tract of country to tho north and west of Dehli, from the Siwalik (Shiwálak) hills to the Chambal. In the southern portion, the principal cities were Makandí on the Ganges, and Kámpilya or Kampil in the Farukhabad District; Ahichhatra in the Bareilly (Bareli) District was the chief city of northern Panchála.

From Jahnu, the son of Kuru, was descended the Rája Sántanu, who had, by the river goddess Ganga, the great Sántanava. Sántanu in his old age desired a young wife, and Sántanava procured him such a one in Satyávatí, but the girl's parents refused to give their consent, on the ground that Sántanava would succeed to the throne before their daughter's son. On hearing this, Sántanava, to please his father, vowed a life of celibacy, and gave up his right to the throne to the offspring of Satyávati. Henceforward he went by the name of Bhíshma or "the dreadful," on account of his dreadful vow. Satyávati bore two sons, Chitrángada and Vichitravírya. The first was killed in conflict with the Gandharvas or inhabitants of the hilly tracts to the north, and the latter married the two daughters of the king of Káshí (Benares). Vichitravírya died without issue, and his mother thereupon applied to his half-brother Bhíshma to raise up sons to continue the line. Bhíshma's vow of celibacy precluded him from undertaking the task. The Rání Dowager[2] then ordered her son Vyása to take to wife his half brother's widows. The offspring of this marriage was Dhritarashtra, the blind, Pándu the pale, and, by a slave-girl, Vidura.

Rája Sántanu.

The three boys were brought up by their uncle Bhíshma, who on their coming of age set aside Dhritaráshtra, because he was blind, and Vidura because of his lowly birth, and elevated Pándu to the ráj of Bhárata. Amongst the Sátwatas descended from Kroshtu son of Yádu was a prince named Súra, who gave his daughter Pritha to Bhoja or Kuntí-bhoja, a rája who dwelt on the Vindhya mountains. She married Pándu and bore to him Yudhishthira, Bhíma and Arjuna, who, owing to Pándu, from a curse pronounced on him, being unable to procreate children, were in reality the offspring of the deities Dharma, Váyu (the air), and Indra. Before her marriage with Pándu, Pritha or Kunti had a son (Karna) by the divine

Pándu.

[1] Satya dhriti, a Panchála prince, had a daughter by Urvasí, whom he abandoned. She was found by Raja Sántanu, who brought her up and gave her in marriage to Drona; she bore to him Aswatthama.—V. P. IV., 146.   [2] Satyávati is said to have borne Vyása or Krishna-dwaipayána, the relator of the Vishnu Purána to Parásara, before her marriage with Santánu. He also was therefore a half brother of Vichitravírya, and as such was then legally entitled to marry his deceased brother's widows.

Aditya (the sun,) whom she exposed, while still an infant, on the banks of the Jumna. He was found there by Adiratha, the *súta* or charioteer of king Súra, who brought him up as his own son.[1] Pándu had a second wife named Mádri, who bore him, by the twin sons of Aditya (Násatya and Dasra), the brothers Nákula and Sáhadeva. Pándu died soon afterwards, and was succeeded in the *ráj* by Dhritaráshtra, who married a daughter of the Rája of Gándhára (Peshawar). She bore him Duryodhana, Duhsásana, and other sons to the number of one hundred, known henceforth as the Kauravas, from their progenitor, Kuru, to distinguish them from the Pándavas, the five sons of Pándu.[2]

The youths of both families were brought up together in Hastinápur, and were

Early life of the Pándavas and Kauravas.

instructed in the use of arms by Drona, who had quarrelled with the Panchála Rája Drupada, and taken up his residence with Bhíshma. Drona made one condition with them, that on their acquiring a thorough knowledge of their weapons, his pupils should assist him in fighting against Drupada.[3] Yudhishthira became a proficient in the use of the spear; Arjuna was the most famous archer of his time; Bhíma learned the use of the club;[4] Nákula, the management of horses, and Sáhadeva became an expert swordsman. Arjuna and Bhíma were the favourite pupils of Drona, and on this account excited the jealousy of Duryodhana and his brethren the Kauravas. The military school soon became famous, and many sons of Rájas flocked for instruction to Drona, and amongst them the son of the Rája of the Bhíls, whom, as a barbarian, Drona refused to instruct. Nothing daunted, the Bhíl prince set up an image of clay to represent Drona, and learned archery by practising before the image. On seeing this Drona permitted the Bhíl to continue the practice, but bound him by an oath to use the middle finger alone in drawing the string, hence this custom is said to have descended amongst the Bhíls to the present day. Continuous public assaults of arms were held by the pupils of Drona, with whom many strangers[5] tried their strength.

The Kauravas, according to the compact with Drona, first attempted the

Feuds arise.

reduction of Panchála, but were unsuccessful. The Pándavas however succeeded, and this added to the jealousy with which they were regarded by their cousins. This was further

---

[1] See Wheeler's History, I., 93. [2] For a fuller account of the Mahábhárata, see Wheeler's History of India, Vol. I.: London, 1867; and for a translation of the entire poem, see Fauche; Paris, 1863-70. [3] Drona was the son of the preceptor Bharadwaja, and was brought up by his father with Drupada, son of Priehata, the Rája of Panchála. When both grew up, Drupada treated Drona with disrespect and continually taunted him with his inferiority, as a mendicant Brahman, to the position of himself as a Kshatriya Rája. On this account Drona sought revenge. [4] Hence the monoliths bearing Asoká's edicts are popularly known as *Bhím Sen ke gadá,* or ‘Bhím Sen's club.’ [5] Karna, the charioteer, first appears in public at one of these assemblies.

heightened by the contest for the post of heir-apparent or Yuvarája, which was conferred on Yudhishthira by Dhritaráshtra. But to such a height did their contentions go, that the Mahárája recommended the Pándavas to proceed for a time to Váranávata (Allahabad), until matters could be arranged.[1] There Duryodhana caused them to be lodged in a house smeared with lac and other combustible materials, with the intention of burning the Pándavas and their mother Kunti in it.[2] From this fate they were delivered by digging an underground passage, at the suggestion of Vidura, through which they escaped unnoticed to the great jungle. Here they met with many adventures: Bhíma subdued the Rakshasa Hidimba, whose daughter he married, and the cannibal Asura Váka, who used to devour daily one of the inhabitants of the city of Ekachakra, identified with the modern Ara (Arrah).

On their departure from Ekachakra, the Pándavas heard of the approaching *swayamvara*[3] of Draupadi, the beautiful daughter of the Panchála king Drupada. They proceeded to Kámpilya, the residence of the Rája, and there Draupadi was won by the prowess of Arjuna, who struck the eye of the golden fish through the *chakrá* at the first discharge from his bow. The catalogue of the Rájas attending the assembly is of some interest, as showing the principal kingdoms of those days. From Dwárka came Krishna and Báláráma; from the north-west the Rája of Sindhu (Indus), and the sons of the Rája of Gándhára (Peshawar); from the east came Vatsarája, the Rája of Kosala (Berar), Járasandha, Rája of Magadha (Bahar), and the Rája of Paundra (Bengal proper); from the south came the Rája of Chhedí (on the Narbada), the Rája of Viráta (Matsya),[4] and the Rája of Madra (Panjáb). Draupadi married the five brothers, and returning to Hastinápur it was resolved to divide the *ráj*. The Pándavas took the western half known as Khándava-prastha, and founded the city of Indra-prastha on the bank of the Jumna. They then burned the forest and drove out the Nágas and their Rája Takshaka from the neighbourhood, and built separate houses for themselves. Draupadí lived in turn with each of the brethren, and it was agreed amongst

Marriage with Draupadi.

Arjuna's exile.

them that "if a brother entered the house of another brother while Draupadi was dwelling there, he should depart into exile for twelve years." Arjuna broke this rule first, and in consequence set out from Indra-prastha to visit other countries. Amongst the places visited by him are Hardwár on the Ganges, where he had an intrigue with Ulúpí, the daughter of Vásukí, the Rája of the Nágas. He then went to Mahendra or Malabar, where he visited Parasurám;[5] and next to Manipura

---

[1] There is good reason for believing that this episode of the exile to Váranávata is an interpolation of later times. [2] See V. P. IV., 80. [3] The *swayamvara* gave the woman, as the prize of skill and valour, to the most distinguished of the competitors, or allowed her to choose from amongst the suitors for her hand. [4] A kingdom to the west of Muttra in Gwaliar. [5] See Vishnu Puráṇa, IV., 24.

where he married Chitrángadá, the daughter of the Rája. We then find him at Dwárka in the Yádava country, where he met Krishna and Bálaráma, and espoused their sister Subhadra, with whom he returned to Indra-prastha.

In the meantime the new settlement prospered so much, that Yudhish-thira resolved to celebrate the royal sacrifice[1] (ra-jasúya), intended as an assertion of sovereignty as well as a sacrifice to the gods. Yudhishthira had previously subdued many of the neighbouring Rájas, and it is even said that Bhíma and Arjuna had visited Magadha and slain Járasandha. To complete the preparations, Yudhishthira sent his four brethren to the four quarters of the earth to collect tribute from all countries for the space of a year. On their return all assembled at a great feast in the council hall, including representatives of the four castes,[2] when the argha[3] was presented to Krishna as the most important personage present. In return for this Krishna slew Sisupála, Rája of Chhedi, for presuming to interfere with the sacrifice. The success of the inauguration of the new ráj induced Duryo-dhana to plan fresh schemes whereby he might dispossess the Pándavas. For this purpose he induced his father to invite the Pándavas to Hastinápur, and there inveigled them into a gambling match with his uncle Sakuni. In the game Yudhishthira lost his kingdom, his brethren, himself, and finally his wife Draupadi. A terrible scene then ensued. Draupadi was insulted by Duryodhana, and at length released by his father, who arranged that there should be another game, at which whoever lost should give up his ráj and depart into exile for twelve years in a jungle, and one year in a city in disguise. If discovered dur-ing the year they lived in disguise they were again to go through their exile. The Pándavas again lost the game, and leaving their mother Kuntí under the care of Vidura, set out into exile.

Condition of Indra-prastha

For twelve years they wandered through the forest with Draupadi,[4] occa-sionally visiting holy places and living on the game they shot on the way. Arjuna visited the Himálayas,

Exile of the Pándavas.

---

[1] These sacrifices, as observed by Mr. Wheeler, underwent several modifications. The original type, or the coronation banquet, was subsequently converted into sacrificial sessions of a purely religious character; then came the Buddhists, who substituted ower offerings for animals; and finally the *homa* (clarified butter), and *páyasa* (rice and milk) came in with the Brahmanical revival in the ninth century.   [2] "All Brahmans and Kshatriyas, and all the respectable Vaisyas and Sudras."   [3] The *argha* is an offering of flowers, milk or honey still made to idols, or a Brahman, or a bridegroom on his wedding day.   [4] Draupadi bore five sons, one to each of the Pándavas : the son of Yudhishthira was Prativindhya ; of Bhímasena was Srutasoma ; of Arjuna, Srutakírtti ; Nákula begot Satánika; and Sáhadeva, Srutakarman. In his notes on the history of Kashmír (As. Res. XV., II.) Prof. Wilson alludes to the traditions which make Kashmír the native seat of the Pándavas. Besides the history of Kashmír, which positively asserts that 52 kings of the Kaurava family ruled there, Wilford shows, from Hindu authorities, that the city of the Pándavas was in the valley ; and even the Mahábhárata makes " the holy mountain of Himavat" the birthplace of the five sons of Pandu.

where, by propitiating Siva, he became possessed of powerful weapons. Whilst in the jungles the Pándavas heard that the Kauravas had been captured by the Gandharvas of the hills, and returning good for evil rescued them from their enemies. This was not the only adventure that befel them, for the Rája of Sindhu, passing by the hermitage of the Pándavas during their absence, saw Draupadi, and falling in love with her, carried her off, when she was with difficulty rescued by Yudhishthira. For the year of exile in disguise the Pándavas chose the city of Rája Viráta (Matsya), and entered into his service under assumed names. They remained there for the year, and defeated an attack of the Kauravas and the Rája of Trigarta (Hill State of Kotoch). The Pándavas then disclosed their real origin and made an alliance with the Rája, confirmed by the marriage of his daughter Uttara with Abhimanyu, the son of Arjuna by Subhadra. At a council held immediately after the marriage feast, it was resolved to send an embassy to Hastinápur to demand the restoration of Indra-prastha. Drupada despatched his family priest on behalf of the Pándavas, and Dhritaráshtra and Bhíshma lent a favourable ear to their application ; but Karna[1] and Duryodhana were intractable, urging that they had discovered the Pándavas before the expiration of the thirteenth year. Sanjaya, the charioteer of the Mahárája, was, however, despatched to the Pándavas, but the negotiations ended in disappointment, nor did Krishna fare better in his efforts at mediation.

War was resolved on by both sides, forces were collected, and every preparation made. Both Kauravas and Pándavas marched

The great war.

to the plain of Kurakshetra near Pánípat, and there intrenched themselves. Bhíshma was appointed generalissimo of the Kauravas, and Dhrishtadyumna, son of Rája Drupada, filled the same office on the side of the Pándavas. Every precaution was observed. A lake lay between the Pándavas and their enemies, on one side was the Saraswati river, and on the other a deep trench was dug, while sentries were posted, and signs and passwords were appointed by which they might recognize their own people. A challenge[2] was then sent by Duryodhana to the Pándavas, filled with the most insulting references to the events that had taken place, and this was replied to by Arjuna. The next step was the formation of a code of rules by the commanders of each army for ameliorating the horrors of war, which, however disregarded during the war in individual instances, were generally adhered to.[3]

---

[1] Karna owed Arjuna a grudge on account of Draupadi's objecting to his candidature at her *swayamvara* because of his suspicious parentage. [2] The herald charged with the message recapitulates all the wrongs the Pándavas had suffered at the hands of their cousins, and dares them to take revenge; in fact the harangue is something of the nature of the speeches Fenimore Cooper puts in the mouths of his American Indian heroes. [3] These 'Geneva' rules deserve reproduction. They are—(1) We agree not to make war by stratagem or treachery. (2) When fighting we will fight to death, but when we leave off we may visit each other, hold conference together, or mess

The battle opened with the usual shouting and clangour of drums and conch

The battle. shells, and lasted for eighteen days[1] The Pándava commander remained to the last, but on the tenth day the Kauravas lost Bhíshma, slain by Arjuna. Bhíshma was succeeded by Drona for five days; on his death Karna assumed the command for two days only, when he also was slain. Sálya was the Kaurava commander on the last day. The narrative of the battle during the first ten days is little more than a description of a succession of charges, and the conversations of the principal actors on the day's events. On the twelfth day some curious tactics were displayed. The Kauravas were drawn up as a spider's web and entirely surrounded their enemies until relieved by Abhimanyu, who charged them repeatedly, and while doing so lost his life. The battle was then renewed by torchlight, and on the fourteenth day Drona fell at the hands of Drishtadyumna. The principal events of the two days during which Karna commanded are the fight between Bhíma and Duhsásana, when Bhíma fulfilled his vow of drinking the blood of Duhsásana, on account of an insult offered by him to Draupadi; and the fight between Arjuna and Karna, in which the latter was slain. Sálya, Rája of Madra, who commanded on the last day, was slain by Yudhishthira, and but three warriors were left to the Kauravas. On seeing this, Duryodhana concealed himself amid the bulrushes in the lake, but was discovered and compelled to fight with Bhíma. Both were wounded in the encounter, and the conflict ceased. The Pándavas then proceeded to plunder the camp of the Kauravas, but during their absence Aswatthama, the son of Drona, one of the surviving Kaurava warriors, entered the Pándava camp and slew not only their general Drishtadyumna, but also the five sons of Draupadi. Duryodhana died of his wounds on the field. The next scene represents the reconciliation of the Pándavas with Dhritaráshtra, the visit of the wives and families of the deceased warriors to the field of battle, and the cremation ceremonies.

After the funeral ceremonies were completed, Yudhishthira proceeded to

Installation of Yudhishthira. Hastinápur, where he was installed as Rája, under Dhritaráshtra, and attempted the celebration of the great

together. (3) We will spare all drummers, charioteers, those that run away and those that lay down their arms. (4) Horsemen alone shall fight with horsemen, elephant riders with the same class, footmen with footmen, and those in chariots with warriors in chariots. (5) When warriors are only abusing each other they shall not also use arms. (6) No man shall take up arms against another without giving him warning. (7) When two combatants are engaged together, no third person shall interfere. These unique rules need no comment, and even here the chronicler is forced to say very often "they fought fairly for an hour or two, and then like drunken Asuras, they forgot all the laws of fair fighting, and fell to in great confusion."

[1] Before commencing, Yudhishthira piously asked permission of his preceptors Bhíshma and Drona to attack them.

aswamedha or horse-sacrifice.[1]   Arjuna led the army which followed the horse with many adventures for one year, and returned successfully to Hastinápur, where the great sacrifice was made with *homa* of curds, milk and clarified butter.   For some time after this all lived in peace, until Dhritaráshtra, mindful of the death of his sons at the hands of Bhíma, determined to separate from the Pándavas, and with his family retired to the jungles on the banks of the Ganges, where they all perished in a jungle fire.   From Dwárka, too, news came of the death of Krishna and Bálaráma, and the destruction of the city by a cyclone.   Oppressed by these disasters, the Pándavas resolved to abandon worldly affairs, and gave the *ráj* of Hastinápur to Parikshit, the son of Abhimanyu by Uttara, and grandson of Arjun, and the *ráj* of Indra-prastha to Yuyutsu, the only surviving son of Dhritaráshtra.   Then, assuming the garb of devotees, they passed forth from the city towards the rising sun, and reached the Himálaya mountains, where they died.

The preceding story gives us the history of the fortunes of the first great outpost of the Aryan immigrants after they passed the Saraswati to Brahmarshi-desa, or the land of the *Rishis* or Sages.   It also marks the commencement of the Brahmanical period, when the Brahmans first began to assume the exclusive direction of religious ceremonies, and the permanent distinctions of caste began to be established. The Puránas make mention of Brahmans being descended from several of the ancestors of the Pándavas; of others it is said that they were progenitors of

State of society.

---

[1] The *aswamedha* seems to have been of a more important character than the *rajasúya*. In the former the mere proposal to sacrifice carries with it the idea of universal sovereignty, while the latter seems to consist for the most part of the mere inauguration ceremonies of a new State.   In the *aswamedha*, a horse was taken of a black colour or 'of a pure white colour like the moon, with a yellow tail and a black ear,' and was allowed to run loose wherever he willed for the space of one year.   The Rája and his army followed the horse into every country, and wherever it went the Rájas were obliged either to fight or submit.   At the expiration of the year, if always victorious, the Rája and his army, accompanied by the other Rájas whom he had subdued, returned to his city, where a grand sacrifice was made, at which the horse was killed and eaten by the guests.   Before the sacrifice the principal actor and his wife bathed, and then the ground was measured off by the Rája and ploughed by him, while the Ráni sowed a portion of each kind of seed, and the Brahmans and women prayed.   The ground was then paved with golden bricks, and eight pillars and a canopy were erected of the same material.   Then eight large pits were dug and eight ladles made for the *homa* of curds, milk and clarified butter, in which skins stuffed with every edible vegetable were placed.   Water was brought from the Ganges by the principal guests and their wives, on whom the Rája in return bestowed garlands of jewels, and gave them betel-nut to eat, and at last a fire was lighted in each pit, and the various ingredients for the *homa* were presented to it.   The Rája was then bathed in the Ganges water as well as the horse; the horse was then decapitated and opened for the discovery of omens, after which portions of his flesh were added to the *homa*, and the remainder was distributed among the guests.   The assembly closed with the ceremony of bathing the Rája and his wife with Ganges water by the assembled guests and their wives.

representatives of the four castes. The sage Vyása himself, the compiler of
the Vedas and the Mahábhárata, was the reputed father of the Kshatriya Pándavas. All through the Vaidik records the Brahman is held to be inferior to the
Kshatriya, and even here we see it in the treatment Drona received at the
hands of Drupada. At the same time the gradual reversal of the position of
the two classes may be traced, and the gradual submission of brute force to
intellect. The legends also show the processes of early colonization. When the
settlement at Hastinápur became overpopulated, a colony was formed on the
Jumna, whose first care was to burn down the forest and drive out the aboriginal tribes known as Nágas, Daityas, Asuras and Bhíls. The conquerors frequently took to themselves wives from these peoples, or were adopted into their
families. The form of government was a patriarchal despotism, the connecting link between the family rule of the Vaidik age and the monarchical institutions of later times. Submission to the head of the family and the preceptor was regarded as a sacred duty. Polyandry[1] was practised, as well as the
custom still existing among semi-aboriginal tribes such as Játs, Gújars, Ahírs,
Pásís, Chamárs, &c., of marrying the widow of a deceased kinsman. The
only instance of *satí*, or the burning of wives with their deceased husbands,
is clearly a modern interpolation. Hunting and athletic sports were the
principal amusements, while all engaged in agriculture, the chief himself marking
its dignity by ploughing the ground with a golden plough at the great sacrifice.
Cattle, too, formed a great portion of their wealth, and every third year there
was an expedition to the forests to brand all the calves that had been born.
The weapons in use were the sling, lasso, spear, club, bow and sword. Horsemanship was considered an accomplishment, and driving the chariot of the
Rája was an office of high rank, and only held by a confidential servant. The
uprohit and the charioteer frequently appear as the advisers, ministers and
ambassadors of the Rája. The women of the family showed themselves in public,
and were present at the great feasts, where wine and flesh were freely partaken
of. At the *swayamvara*, women were allowed to choose their husbands among the
suitors, and even where given away as a prize to the victor in the tournament,
had a right to exclude an unwelcome suitor from the trial. They also presided
over the distribution of food and all the household arrangements, but even here
the mother-in-law was the head of the spindle-side.[2] The most popular vice
of the Kshatriyas was gambling, while the aboriginal tribes seem to have been
addicted to drunkenness. Altogether the picture still presented to us is that

---

[1] At the same time Pándu had two wives and Dhritaráshtra had only one.   [2] Witness
the story of the mother of the Rája of Badravati, who, when invited to accompany her son to the
aswamedha, replied " I will never quit this house ; for if I stir, all the goods and chattels here
will be used up. My maids and servants will be every day plundering milk and grain and
butter, so that when I return half my property will be wasted or stolen."

of a family of fair-complexioned immigrants, with their dependants and followers, settling down in a land clothed with forest and inhabited by dark-skinned wandering tribes. Their chief wealth lay in their cattle, but they brought with them also the arts of agriculture. Increasing numbers and a settled life carried with them new wants and modified the form of government. Each colony from the parent stock in course of time assumed independence, and became mindful of its own interests alone. Hence numerous petty states arose, which, in the natural course of events, sought each to aggrandise itself at the expense of the others, until one became paramount; and, whilst permitting a certain amount of independence, assumed a general control. Instead of the great council, where all Brahmans and Kshatriyas and even respectable Vaisyas and Sudras were present and gave their opinions, the power gradually centred in the Rája alone, who was assisted by a minister and a commander of the forces. When the numbers were small, every one who might be called upon to assist in the defence of the State had a voice in its deliberations; with increasing civilisation the privilege became confined to the Brahmans and the Kshatriyas, until the former became supreme as the spiritual counsellors and trusted advisers of the king.[1]

The Vishnu Purána continues the history given in the Mahábhárata, and
Subsequent history of Hastinápur. from it we learn that Parikshit had four sons, Janamejaya, Srutasena, Ugrasena and Bhímasena. From Janamejaya came Sátanika, whose son was Aswamedhadatta or 'he who was given by reason of a horse-sacrifice.' To him succeeded Adhisima Krishna, whose son was named Níchakru. In his reign the capital was transferred from Hastinápur to Kausámbi, in consequence of the former city having been swept away by the Ganges.[2] After him came twenty-one princes, ending with Kshemaka. Giving a reign of 18 years each to these princes, their dynasty would end in the tenth century before Christ.

No traces of the ancient Indraprastha now remain, with, perhaps, the
Subsequent history of Indraprastha. exception of the Nigambodh Ghát immediately outside the northern wall of the city of Sháhjahánabad. This is celebrated as the place where Yudhishthira caused the eight pits to be dug for the reception of the homa at his great horse-sacrifice.[3] The site of the ancient city is traditionally connected with the space between the kotila of Fírúz Shah and the tomb of Humáyun, within which lies the fort of Indarpat or Purána Kila. The old bed of the Jumna, lying one mile to the westward of its present

---

[1] I can merely give a most meagre outline of the story contained in this wonderful poem, but feel convinced that in the apparently most puerile and absurd of its legends there must be some germ of fact, which a careful study of the poem as a whole, and the different works bearing upon it, would discover, and afford materials for a genuine 'History of India' during the Hindu period.   [2] Kausámbi has been identified with Kosim on the Jumna, near Allahabad. See the volume relating to the Allahabad Division.   [3] Wheeler's History, I., 128.

course, is easily traced beneath the walls of the old fort.[1] The Rájávali and Bhágavata Purána make the Indraprastha line of princes continue in the family of Arjuna. Kshemaka of Hastinápur was deposed by his minister Visarwa, a contemporary of Sisunága of Magadha. Taking the birth of Parikshit in 1430 B.C., and his accession to the throne in 1400 B.C., and giving 18 years each to the reigns of the thirty princes of his line, this would bring the revolution of Visarwa to 860 B.C. Again, adding the reigns of the Nandas (100 years) and those of the Saisunágas (362 years) to the date of the accession of Chandragupta (315 B.C.), we have the date 777 B.C., or a difference of about 89 years, which, in this arbitrary mode of calculating the duration of reigns, is not to be considered conclusive of the existence of any substantial error. Visarwa was succeeded by thirteen other princes of the same family, ending with Madpál, who was slain by his Rajpút minister Maháráj or Mahraje, of the Gautam clan.

Mahraje, who is probably the Mahúraje of Firishta, was followed by four-teen princes of the same family, ending with Antinai, who resigned his kingdom to his minister, the founder of the Mayura dynasty.[2] The last of these princes, Rájápála, is said to have been attacked and killed by the Rája of Kumaon, called Súkáditya or 'lord of the Sákas.' Colonel Tod states that Rájápála invaded Kumaon and was killed by Sakwanti, who seized on Indraprastha, whence he was expelled by Vikramáditya. Regarding the identity of this Vikramáditya, the authorities are conflicting. "The Hindu accounts of Vikramáditya are not to be found in the regular Pauránik histories, but only in separate legends, such as the Vikrama-charitra and others mentioned by Wilford,[3] all teeming with confusion, contradictions and absurdities in an unusual degree. The genealogical tables of the Solar and the Lunar lines contain no such name; neither does it occur[4] among the few notices of embassies to and from India to Syria and Rome, in the authors of the west." It has even been hinted that the name of Vikramáditya and the Bactrian Greek Eukratides "bear a close resemblance both in sound and in signification; while the epoch and the 'scene of their martial exploits are nearly identical." Following up this train of reasoning, General Cunningham has identified the Vikramáditya of 57 B.C. with the Hima Kadphises of the coins, an Indo-Scythian prince.

Other dynasties.

---

[1] Arch. Rep. I., 136. Dehli is now beyond the limits of these Provinces, and its history can only be very briefly given here, and only so far as it illustrates the local history of the Duáb. Mr. Beglar's survey of the antiquities of Dehli and its environs will be found in Arch. Rep. Vol. IV. [2] Colonel Tod's list, Ward's list (I., 24), and General Cunningham's list (J. A. S. Ben. VII.) of this dynasty are given in Prinsep's Essays, II., 239. Tieffenthaler (Bernoulli, I., 152) continues the list through Vikramáditya's descendants, through the Bais Rája Tilokchand and a Bengal dynasty, to the dynasty founded by the lord of Badordes, who was succeeded by the Chauháns. [3] As. Res. IX., 117. [4] Prinsep, I., 187; II., 249, 250.

Dehli.

With the advent of the Sákas the name of Dilli first appears, which, according to one tradition, was given to it by a Rája Dilli or Dhilu, its founder[1]. Firishta adopts this account, and makes Rája Dhilu reign for some time and succumb to the arms of Rája Phor or Porus of Kumaon, who is identified by General Cunningham with the Sákáditya of the Rájávali. The overthrow of the Sákas is commonly attributed to the Vikramáditya, who assumed the title of Sákári, and established the era dating from 57 B.C., which is still in common use throughout Northern Hindustan. It is, however, more probable that the defeat of the Sáka conqueror of Dilli should be placed in 78 A.D., the initial date of the Sáke-era of Sálivána, and the foundation by Rája Dhilu in 57 B.C., who was displaced immediately after by an Indo-Scythian prince. Tradition declares that Dehli was deserted from the time of its conquest by Vikramáditya to its being rebuilt by Anang Pál, the first Tomar prince. The existence of the iron pillar set up by a Rája Dhava during the fourth century, and, if correct, the identification of the Daidala and Indabara of Ptolemy with Dehli and Indarpat, would, however, at least show that it was inhabited during this period.[2]

Some slight light is thrown on the early history of the Upper Duáb from the chronicles of the Buddhist rulers and travellers.

Buddhist chronicles.

Amongst the ancient remains still existing at Dehli are two stone pillars, bearing the edicts of the great king Asoka. One of these was brought[3] by Fíruz Shah Tughlak from a place called Topur, Tobra, Tamera or Nahera, on the banks of the Jumna, in the district of Sálaura, not far from Khizrabad, "which is at the foot of the mountains, ninety *kos* from Dehli" in the Sahárunpur District. The second pillar, recently restored and standing near Hindu Rao's house, was brought by the same ruler from Meerut. Both of them contain inscriptions in the Páli language, written by order of Asoka or Priyadarsin, who reigned in Magadha or Behar from 263 B.C. to 223 B.C. Similar inscriptions are found on the Allahabad stone pillar (*lát*), and on the rocks at Girnar in Káthiwár; at Kapurdigiri near Peshawar; at Dhauli in Orissa, and at Kálsi on the Jumna, in the Dehra Dún, a short distance north of Khizrabad. These are

---

[1] See on this point Arch. Rep. I., 140. Tieffenthaler (Bernoulli, I., 125) has the same story, but gives the name Ráseo. [2] Prinsep has translated this inscription (Ess. I., 320). It records the erection of the pillar in commemoration of the victorious prowess of Dhava, who seems to have deceased prior to its completion. Dhava's forces subdued the Vahlikas on the Sindhu, so that even at the time of the inscription, his army " and defence on the south of the river are sacredly respected by them." Though it is not necessary that Dehli must have been either the original site of the pillar, or, if it were erected there, that Dhava had his residence in Dehli, yet its presence shows that there must have been some inhabitants in the place. Mr. Prinsep connects the Vahlikas here mentioned with the Bactrian Greeks of Balkh, who receded before the Scythians to the south of the Paropamisan range. [3] In A. H., 752 to 790; Prinsep, Ess. I., 324; A. H., 757, or A. D. 1356; Cunningham, Arch. Rep. I., 161.

undoubtedly authentic records showing the supremacy of the Buddhist sovereign of Magadha all over Hindustan, from Orissa to Peshawar. Local tradition makes the Kálsi stone the boundary between the Húnas on the north and the Emperors of Hindustan on the south. The subject of the extent and character of Asoka's rule will be more fully considered under the notice of Allahabad.

Fa Hian, the Chinese Buddhist traveller[1] who visited India from 399 to 413 A.D., does not mention any place between Muttra and Taxila. Hwen Thsang, however, in 634 A.D., passed through Sthâneswara (Thanesar) on his way from Muttra to Srughna, and may have passed close to Dehli if proceeding by the direct road along the Jumna or by Meerut, which, owing to its being a station of one of Asoka's pillars, must have been of some interest to a Buddhist. Neither of these places are noticed by him, a fact which would, at all events, show their small importance in the middle of the seventh century. At the time of his visit to Thanesar, that city was the capital of a kingdom tributary to Harsha Vardhana of Kanauj, bounded on the north by the principality of Srughna; on the east by the Ganges, which separated it from Mandáwar in the Bijnor District; on the west by the Satlaj river; and on the south by an irregular line drawn from near Pákpatan on the Satlaj, by Bhatner and Nárnol to Anúpshahr on the Ganges.[2] It therefore included the southern portion of the Muzaffarnagar District, the entire district of Meerut, and the northern half of Bulandshahr. At the time of his visit, Hwen Thsang found only three Buddhist monasteries in Thanesar, while the Brahmanical temples numbered one hundred.

Hwen Thsang proceeded from Thanesar by the Gokantha monastery to Srughna,[3] the capital of the kingdom of the same name, which was bounded on the north by the mountains; on the east by the Ganges; on the south by an irregular line passing through Muzaffarnagar; while the Jumna flowed through the middle of it. The capital has been identified by General Cunningham with the village of Sugh, situated in a bend of the old bed of the Jumna, which surrounds it on three sides, on the old road from Jagádri to Saháranpur, close to a bungalow belonging to the Western Jumna Canal. This agrees with the pilgrim's account, who places it on the west bank of the Jumna. The greater part was then in ruins, but the foundations still remained, and showed the circumference of the city to have been something more than three miles. It possessed fine monasteries, containing one thousand monks, and one hundred Brahmanical temples, besides numerous stupas or topes containing relics of Buddha and other holy men. The site would appear to have been known as Mandal, from the adjoining village of Mandalpur, as early as the reign of Firúz Tughlak.

The Chinese pilgrims.

Srughna.

---

[1] Translated by the Rev. S. Beal: Lond., 1869. Arch Rep. II., 221.　　[2] See Cunningham's Anc. Geogh., 329; Arch, Rep. II., 226.　　[3] Arch, Rep. II., 226.

In 1834, Captain Cautley communicated[1] the discovery of an old town while
Old town near Bahat. clearing out the canal bed south of the Belka falls,
near Bahat or Behat, in the Saháranpur District. The
site was found to be seventeen feet below the general surface of the country,
and twenty-five feet below that of the modern town near it. Coins and other
remains were discovered in the shingle laid bare by the action of the canal
water. The coins were numerous, and some of them were of Indo-Scythic origin,
containing inscriptions in Arian or Bactro-Páli, of Semitic origin, also transli-
terated into Indian Páli of a type little subsequent to the characters on Asoka's
pillars. The remains, on the whole, stamp the place as decidedly Buddhist, but
" it would be hazardous to attribute to them any greater antiquity than the
early part of the Christian era." The discovery is further useful in showing
the existence of towns boasting a considerable degree of civilization at this
early period, in what may be called the wilder parts of the Upper Duáb. The
soil on the site contained numerous specimens of pottery; bricks of a large
size and an unusual shape appearing as if they had been made to suit the circular form of wells; pieces of the slag of iron, smelting furnaces, arrow-heads,
ornaments and beads. The extent of the deposit, too, would seem to denote a
town of considerable extent ; and without accepting Bahat either as the centre
or positive capital of the kingdom[2] for whose currency the coins discovered
there " were designed to provide, its boundaries might be conjectured as extending down the Duáb below Hastinápur, and westward beyond the latter river
to some distance along the foot of the Himálayas into the Panjáb."

Returning to the chronicles of Dehli, we find it universally acknowledged
Tomars. by all authorities that Dehli owes its re-existence as a
capital city to Anang Pál, the first prince of the
Tomar dynasty.[3] This event took place, according to tradition, in 736 A.D.,
and, on independent evidence, General Cunningham considers this date " as

---

[1] J. A. S., Ben., (Jan. 1834) ; Prinsep's Ess. Vol. I., 73, 76, 112, 200. [2] Mr. Thomas,
Prinsep's Ess. I., 204. [3] Chand Bardai, the celebrated bard, recounts the founding of Dehli
by Anang Pál, who, guided by a happy omen, struck an iron column so deeply into the ground
that its point entered the head of Seshnág, the king of the Nágas or Indo-Scythians. Upon the
stability of this pillar was to rest the fortunes of the Tomar dynasty; yet, deceived by Takshak,
the brother of Seshnág, Anang Pál was weak enough to allow it to be moved. Anang Pál then
sought counsel of the sage Vyása, who related to him the fortunes of his house. (J. A. S., Ben.,
XXXVII, 119: XXXVIII, 1, 145, 161). May not this legend have a foundation in fact, that
the Indo-Scythian rulers of the north had still considerable influence so far south as Dehli, and
were able to impede the colonizing projects of the Tomar prince. Kumaon traditions place
the Katyúras about this period, whose connection with the Katora of Chitrál and the Indo-
Scythian princes of Kábul will be noticed in the volume devoted to the Hill Districts. I will
only remark here that it is a curious coincidence that Vásudeva, the successor of Kanishka and
Huvishka, the Indo-Scythian rulers of Káshmír, bears the same name as the eponymous founder
of the Katyúra line in Kumaon, known there as Básdeo.

being established on grounds that are more than usually firm for early Indian history." It is probable also that shortly afterwards the Tomars transferred their capital to Kanauj, which, owing to the pressure of the Musalmáns, they abandoned for Bári in Oudh (1021 to 1051 A. D.); and subsequently, under Anang Pál the Second, returned to Dehli in 1052 A. D., where he built Lálkot or the red fort near the Kutb Minár. Tradition ascribes the building of Táragarh near Ajmer, Indragarh, Tejora between Gúrgaon and Alwar, Achhnera between Bharatpur (Bhurtpoor) and Agra, and Sirsa, to the sons of Anang Pál, which would show that his dominions extended from Hánsi on the north to Agra on the south, and from Ajmer on the west to the Ganges on the east,—the entire tract beyond the Ganges being at this time held by the Katehriya Rajpúts. Anang Pál II. was succeeded by three other princes of the same family, the last of whom, Anang Pál III., was conquered by the Chauhán Prince, Bisal De or Vísala Deva.

The conquest of Dehli by the Chauháns under Vísala Deva took place about 1151 A.D. The Fíruz Shah pillar, or golden lát, already mentioned as containing the edicts of Asoka, has an inscription of this prince, which has been translated by Mr. Colebrooke.[1] This was written in 1164 A.D., to commemorate the fortunate Vísala Deva, the son of Vella Deva, Rája of Sákambhari, who had reduced under his sway the entire country from the Vindhya to the Himádri. In this inscription he urges on his descendants not to permit their " minds to be void of exertion to subdue the remainder." The conqueror appears, however, to have left Anang Pál in possession of a portion of the Dehli territory. Someswara, son of Vísala, received in marriage the daughter of Anang Pál. The issue of this union was the famous Prithivi of Prithiráj, also known as Rai Pithaura.

Prithiráj was adopted by Anáng Pál in 1169 A.D., and succeeded him in the following year as king of Dehli, where he reigned for 22 years. For his history we have fortunately the voluminous poem by Chand, known as the Prithvi Ráj Ráesa already alluded to. It is divided into several books. Mr. Beames has translated a portion relating to the seizure of Padmávati in the fort of Samud Sikhar by Prithiráj, and the fight between him and Shiháb-ud-dín, and the entire work is now being printed. The Chandel-Chauhán war has been mentioned under the notice of Mahoba,[2] and the chapter on Kanauj will be found under Kanauj. Dehli was captured by the Musalmáns in 1193 A.D., and with this date commences the Musalmán occupation of Eastern India; and as it is not my purpose to trespass upon the work so well done by Elphinstone and others, this sketch of the early history of the districts of the Upper Duáb will close here where the Musalmán historian Firishta and his editors commence their histories. I will merely add

Chauháns.

Prithiráj.

---

[1] Prinsep's Essays by Thomas I., 325 ; As. Res., VIII., 130.   [2] Gazetteer, I., 526.

what I have been able to glean from local traditions, and leave the general history up to the eighteenth century to be gathered from the pages of Elphinstone and Elliot.

Connected with the Muhammadan invasion of India, there is no one of
Sálár Masaúd. whom more wild legends are recorded than Sipáh Sálár Masaúd, the prince of martyrs. He is the popular hero of the Musalmán romances, occupying in them the position of the Pándava Arjuna in the Hindu poems. Sálár Masaúd was the son of Sálár Sáhu,[1] brother of Mahmúd, and was born in Ajmer[2] in 1014 A.D., while his father was living there. When he was only twelve years of age he led an expedition against Rawál, in which he was successful. Throughout his life he acted on the principle that "no faith should be kept with unbelievers." When Mahmúd permitted the ransom of the idol of Somnáth, though the money was paid by the Hindús, the youthful fanatic persuaded Mahmúd to break his word, and broke the idol into pieces. To such a degree was his influence felt, that several of the old servants of Mahmúd retired from the court in disgust, so that Mahmúd was reluctantly obliged to exile his favourite by sending him on an expedition to Hindustan. Masaúd's force captured Multán, where he remained during the rains, and then advanced to Ajudhiya. Delighted with the climate and the sport, he remained there until the end of the following rains, and then proceeded to Dehli. Here he was reduced to great straits in his contest with Rája Mahípál, but was relieved by the unexpected arrival of reinforcements from Ghazni, by whose aid he entirely defeated the Hindús. Leaving a garrison in Dehli, Sálár Masaúd proceeded to Meerut, where the princes of that place acknowledged his supremacy, and received again their possessions as tributaries of the Musalmáns. Rai Ajípál of Kanauj in the same manner is said to have done homage to the Musalmán leader. From Kanauj he made a ten days' march to Satrakh,[3] which is described as lying in the centre of India; "it had, moreover, good hunting grounds, and was a sacred shrine of the Hindús." Hence he made expeditions to Benares, Muttra and Gopamau, and eventually 'suffered martyrdom' at the hands of the Hindús at Bahráich in 1033 A.D. Within the next three centuries the tomb of this warrior had become a place of pilgrimage, as we read of Sultán Muhammad-bin-Tughlik proceeding to Bahráich to make offerings at the shrine in 1343 A.D., so that there may be some foundation in fact for the popular legends regarding this pioneer of Muhammadan conquest in Eastern India.

---

[1] It may well be doubted whether he ever existed, or, if so much must be conceded, whether his exploits are founded on historical facts. In the *Mir-át-i-Masúdi*, which gives an account of his life, facts and fiction are strangely combined, and the great actions of other men are unscrupulously appropriated to the hero of the tale (Dowson's Elliott, II., 514). [2] Sunday, 21st Shabán, 405 A.H. [3] Identified by General Cunningham with Besákh, a name of Sáhet or Ajudhiya.

Some further information regarding the distribution of power amongst the
Local tradition. Hindu inhabitants of the Upper Duáb during the Musalmán occupation may be gathered from local traditions.
In the three upper districts of the Duáb, Pundírs, Gautams, Gaurs, Gahlots
and Tagas were amongst the earliest inhabitants ; subsequently, large immigra-
tions of Játs and Gújars took place from the west. The Tagas received their
lands for the aid rendered by them to Rája Janamejaya in his great snake sacrifice. Here again we have local confirmation of the contests between the Aryan
colonists and the Indo-Scythic tribes. Rája Ahibaran (the snake coloured)
founded Baran in the Bulandshahr District. His dynasty was succeeded by
that of the Dors, who, under their leader Hardatta, occupied the Duáb from Kol
to Meerut, where he constructed forts to guard the boundaries of his territory.
The Dors were followed by the Mewatís, and they again by the Bargújars in the
southern districts, and these latter now form the characteristic element amongst
the Rajpút population of Bulandshahr. The Dors fell with the advent of the
Musalmáns and the pressure of immigrant races from the west. In the Aligarh
District they have been replaced by Chauháns, Pundírs, Jádons and Porachs.
It would be useless repetition to give any further details here, as they belong
properly to the local history of each district.

From the Jesuit traveller Tieffenthaler we learn that in the middle of the
The Upper Duáb in the last century the Súbah of Dehli contained the Sirkárs
eighteenth century. of Dehli, Budaon, Sambhal, Kumaon, Saháranpur,
Rewari, Sarhind and Hissar Fíroza. In the Sirkár of Dehli were Baran with
a brick fortress, Bhagpath (Bágpat) situated between two rivers, Barnauva
(Barnáwa), Pouth (Púth), Dancor (Dankaur), Schacarpour (Shikárpur),
Tánda Bhágban (Tánda), Tilbegampour (Tilbegampur), Zaharsa (Jharcha) with
a brick fort, Djevar (Jewar), Zazhana (Jhanjhána), Djelalabad (Jalálabad)
lying between two rivers, Djelalpour Serot (Jalálpur Sarwat) between two
rivers, Dassna (Dásna), Dadaritaha (Dádri), Sikandarabad, Saráva (Saráwa)
with a brick fort, Gharmuctessor (Garhmuktesar) with a fort built of bricks,
Cotána (Kutána), Cándela (Kándhla), Cassna (Kásna), Karkhád (Karkho-
da), Kikar Khera (Kankar khera), Louni (Loni) with a brick fort, Merath
(Meerut) with a fort constructed of the same material, Haschtnapour (Hastinápur), and Hapour (Hápur). In the list under Sirkár Saháranpur, the
names of the parganahs are alone given, and these are identified in the
district notice. Passing from the country to the people, I shall now give
a sketch of the history of the Upper Duáb during the decline and fall
of the Mughal Empire, and will thus show the predisposing influences which
led to the intrusion of a foreign power into the heart of India, as well as
give the general history necessary to understand the local annals of each
district.

The decline of the Mughal Empire may be said to commence from the death of Aurangzeb, for, though the seeds of dissolution were sown during his reign, the plants had not yet appeared, and the fruit was not gathered for some half a century afterwards.[1]

Decline of the Mughals.

It was during this period that the British merchants commenced the formation of their settlements in Bengal ; the Persian trader, Saadat Khan, founded the hereditary vazírship of Oudh ; the Sayyids of Bárha in the Muzaffarnagar District came into prominent notice ; the Bangash family obtained possession of Farukhabad ; the Marhattas of the Dakhin began to interfere in the affairs of Hindustan ; and the Rohillas and other adventurers flourished and fell. Aurangzeb died at Ahmadnagar in February, 1707, without making any provision for a successor; and, perhaps animated by his example, his sons at once commenced to fight amongst themselves for the possession of the throne. Their names and those of their descendants are given below :—

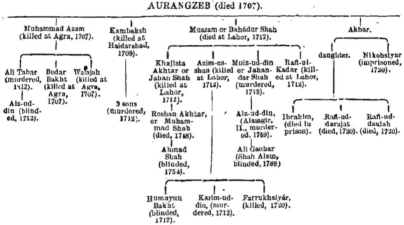

AURANGZEB (died 1707).

This catalogue of the descendants of Aurangzeb and the fates that befel them is in itself a sufficient commentary on the disorder and anarchy of these troubled times.

---

[1] As it is impossible, in a work like the present, to do more than give an outline of the principal events of local importance, the reader is referred to the following works for further information on the general history of these Provinces during the eighteenth century:— *Siyár-ul-Mutakherin*, of which one volume was translated by Colonel J. Briggs : London, O. T. F. 1832 ; and two volumes by a French renegado named Mustafa ; *Tarikh-i-Muzafari*; *Aamad-us-Saadat*; *Shah Alamnamah*, a work by S. Raza Khan and Muhammad Hashim, known as Kháfí Khan, all as yet in manuscript ; Francklin's Shah Aulum : London, 1798 ; Grant Duff's Mahrattas, 3 vols.: London, 1824 ; Jonathan Scott's Hindustan; Fraser's Life of Skinner ; Francklin's Life of George Thomas : London, 1805 ; Hamilton's Rohillas : London, 1787 ; Keene's Mogul Empire : London, 1866 ; Prinsep's Ameer Khan : Calcutta, 1832 ; Sleeman's Rambles and Recollections of an Indian Official : London, 1837 ; L. F. Smith's Sketch of the Rise of the Regular Corps, commanded by European Officers, in the service of Native Princes : Calcutta, *circa* 1801.

Muhammad Azam, who was nearest to the Emperor's camp, took possession

Accession of Bahádur
Shah, 1707 A. D. of the treasure and marched upon Agra. He was, however, anticipated by Azim-us-shan, the son of Prince Muazam, who invested the city on his father's behalf during the absence of the latter in Kábul. Muazam by forced marches joined his son, and the rival armies met on the plain of Ajaju close to Agra, where a desperate battle was fought on the last day of May, 1707, in which Prince Azam and his sons Bedar Bakht and Walajah, were slain, and Muazam assumed the imperial power with the title of Bahádur Shah. Kámbaksh, who set up for himself in the Dakhin, fell in the battle of Haidarabad in 1709, and with him ended all opposition to the new Emperor. Bahádur Shah was not slow to reward those who had exerted themselves in his cause. The battle of Agra was won, in a great measure, by the energy displayed by a contingent of Bárha Sayyids from the Muzaffarnagar District, who had taken service with Azim-us-shan in Bengal ; and when the latter was confirmed in his government, he made S. Abdullah Khan, one of the principal Sayyid leaders, his deputy at Allahabad, while S. Husain Ali, a younger brother, was made vice-governor of Patna. These men were sons of S. Abdullah Khan, so much renowned in Ajmer under the name of Miyán Khan.

Bahádur Shah died at Lahor in 1712 A.D. For a few days Azim-us-shan

Jahándár Shah 1712—13
A. D. attempted to retain in his own hand the considerable power he exercised during his father's life-time, but perished in the attempt. Again, Khajista Akhtar, with the title of Jahán Shah, reigned for a few days, but both he and his brother, Rafi-ul-Kadr, were slain by the adherents of their brother Muiz-ud-din, who eventually succeeded to the throne with the title of Jahándár Shah. His first care was to remove all possible competitors for the throne out of his way, and for this purpose he put to death the children of Prince Azam and Prince Kámbaksh, and demanded the person of Farrukhsiyár, the youngst son of Azim-us-shan, from S. Husain Ali, then at Patna. The Sayyid, who owed so much to the father, was reluctant to obey the order ; and learning the state of affairs at court, where Jahándár Shah was alienating all his supporters by the cruelty of his acts and the devotion that he showed to his Hindu mistress Lál Kuar, Husain Ali resolved to make one bold attempt at power for himself and the family of his former benefactor. He levied a large force in Bengal and communicated his designs to his brother at Allahabad. The latter at first attempted to dissuade his brother from such a rash undertaking, but seeing that Husain Ali was resolved to persevere, at length threw his whole energy into the conspiracy. S. Abdullah intercepted the revenues of Bengal as they passed through Allahabad to Dehli, and thus supplied with the sinews of war, equipped a considerable force, and converted the artillery of the fort into a powerful field battery.

In the meantime, Jahándár Shah despatched an army of twelve thousand cavalry, with a complement of artillery, to attack the Sayyid forces at Allahabad before they could be joined by the Bengal rebels. Abdullah knowing his own weakness shut himself up in the fort of Allahabad with one half of his force, whilst he sent the remainder under his younger brothers to harass and distress the enemy, and thus give time for the arrival of reinforcements. The imperial army contrived to elude their opponents, and invested the fort, but had hardly begun their preparations for the assault when they were attacked in the rear by the Duáb flying columns, whilst a sally was made from the fort, which ended in their total rout. Alarmed at this victory, Jahándár Shah tried to detach Abdullah from the service of Farrukhsiyár ; but, unfortunately for the success of this movement, the young prince had already arrived at Allahabad with S. Husain Ali and a numerous following, including some of the most distinguished generals of his father. Jahándár Shah then despatched his son, Aiz-ud-dín, with another army, to oppose the progress of the Sayyids. Aiz-ud-dín advanced as far as Kadjuwa on the Ganges ; but although he possessed a vastly superior force, he did not consider himself a match for the enemy, and on their first attack, abandoned his camp and baggage into their hands. Early in November the Emperor advanced in person towards Agra, and met the Sayyid forces close to the city, where he was totally defeated, and fled to Dehli. On the accession of Farrukhsiyár to the throne, S. Abdullah was honoured with the title of Kutb-ul-Mulk, and received the command of 7,000 horse, with the office of Vazír, whilst his brother, S. Husain Ali, was named Ihtimam-ul-Mulk, and was given a similar command, with the offices of Amír-ul-Umara and Commander-in-Chief. S. Husain Ali, after some successes in Udepur, received the viceroyalty of the Dakhin, whilst his brother remained at Dehli to watch over their mutual interests.

The Sayyids, anxious to strengthen their faction, obtained for their master the hand of a Hindu princess, and it was for his services in enabling Farrukhsiyár to consummate this marriage that Gabriel Hamilton, a physician in the employ of the English settlement on the Húgli, procured a grant of the 24-parganahs for his employers. The Sayyids became all powerful, but quarrels soon arose at court, and a coalition was formed against them, in which the Emperor joined, forgetful of their services and jealous of their power. When this become known, the younger brother came from the Dakhin ; and, uniting their forces, the Sayyids deposed Jahándár Shah (1720 A. D.) and raised Rafi-ud-darajat, the son of Rafi-ul-Kadr, to the throne. Rafi-úd-darajat died after a short reign of three months, and was succeeded by his brother Rafi-ud-daulah, who also died within the year. The Sayyids then raised to the throne Prince Roshan Akhtar, with the

title of Muhammad Shah.   He soon gave signs of a vigour which, had it been
                 foreseen, would assuredly have consigned him for ever

Muhammad Shah.

to the obscurity from which he had been raised.
Intriguing with Nizám-ul-mulk, Muhammad Amír Khan and others, he tacitly
approved of the removal of the Sayyids.   Husain Ali Khan was assassinated in
the Emperor's camp in the year 1720 A.D., while his personal troops were
defeated and scattered.   On hearing of these events, Abdullah raised a brother
of Rafi-ud-daulah to the throne, under the title of Sultán Ibrahím, and exerted
his utmost vigour to collect an army and supplies from all quarters.   In the
meantime the old landholders of the Upper Duáb, whose villages he had seized,
rose on all sides and expelled his agents; and finding there was no one to oppose
them or restore order, the Gújars and Játs fought amongst themselves and plundered their neighbours.   By the lavish expenditure of money, Abdullah was able
in a fortnight to march against Muhammad Shah, and being joined on his way by
Churáman, the leader of the Ját colony who settled in the Agra súbah in the

1721 A. D.

reign of Aurangzeb, he gave battle to the imperial
forces near Hasanpur, between Agra and Dehli, on the
20th October, 1721.   The Sayyid forces were here completely routed.   Abdullah
was taken prisoner, and died by poison three years afterwards, and with him
ended the power of this remarkable family.

Beyond the rise of the Játs, who murdered the Deputy-Governor of Agra,
and the intrigues of the now independent Viceroy of the Dakhin with the
Marhattas, there are few events of local importance to detain us during the

1722—1736 A. D.

remainder of Muhammad Shah's reign.   The Marhattas took part as mercenaries in the wars between
the more powerful nobles, and acquired such influence, that Nizám-ul-mulk
conceived it to be of advantage to him to employ them against the provinces
that remained faithful to the Emperor.   They invaded Málwa and expelled
the imperial governor ; and advancing thence by Bundelkhand (see BUNDEL-
KHAND, Gazetteer, Volume I.), they threatened Allahabad, and routed the
governor, Muhammad Khan Bangash, in several encounters.   Emboldened by
their successes, and finding the plan hitherto pursued by their enemies, of purchasing their forbearance, attended with little danger and much profit, the Marhattas in 1732 extended their ravages as far as Agra ; and in the two following
years so harassed the Duáb, that the Emperor bribed them with the gift of Málwa
and Gujarát, territories they had conquered with the sword and still held in

1736 A. D.

their grasp.   Saádat Khan's slight success near Sadabad, in the Muttra District, served for a time to stem
the tide of Marhatta invasion ; but not until the Marhattas had an opportunity of
sacking the environs of the capital itself.   Notwithstanding the necessity that
existed for union, the councils of the Emperor were distracted by the private

quarrels of his nobles, and, in consequence, Kumr-ud-dín Khan, the Vazír, was permitted to wreak his long-cherished vengeance on the Sayyids of Bárha by sacking Jánsath in 1737, with the aid of the Rohillas.

The next important event is the sack of Dehli and the surrounding villages by Nádir Shah in 1738, and the general massacre and plunder of the inhabitants. On the departure of the Persians, the state of society in the Upper Duáb was merely a reflection of the anarchy and confusion existing at Dehli. The army was disorganised, the treasury was empty, and the only districts spared by the Marhattas were now visited with fire and sword by the Persians. The Marhattas on the south, the Játs, Sikhs, and wandering Afghán bands on the west, and the Rohillas on the east, all agreed in considering the Duáb an enemy's country,—a fit object for spoliation. The death of the Marhatta leader, Báji Rao, in 1740, promised for a time to relieve the empire from those troublesome invaders, but Báláji Rao had scarcely secured his position as Báji Rao's successor than he applied himself to the affairs of Hindustán. He began at once to organise an expedition against the Duáb, from which he was only prevented by an insurrection in his rear. Málwa was again granted as a sop to the Marhattas, whilst Nizám-ul-mulk became absolutely independent in the Dakhin, with his son, Ghází-ud-dín, now son-in-law of the Vazír, holding the chief power at Dehli. The Rohillas, too, under Ali Muhammad threw off all pretence at allegiance; and, to crown all, Dehli was again attacked from the north by Ahmad, the leader of the Abdáli or Duráni tribe of Afgháns, who was, however, obliged to retire. Muhammad Shah died in 1748, and was succeeded by his son, Ahmad Shah.

Ahmad Shah made Ghází-ud-dín Khan Commander-in-Chief, and Abul Mansúr Safdar Jang, the Governor of Oudh, his Vazír, and calling in the Játs and Marhattas, and a large contingent under Káyam Khan Bangash of Farukhabad, repelled an invasion of the Rohillas. Ghází-ud-dín retired to the Dakhin, and died at Aurangabad. He was succeeded in his high office by his nephew, Shaháb-ud-dín, son of Fíroz Jang, the fourth son of the Nizám. Shaháb-ud-dín, on his uncle's death, assumed the name of Ghází-ud-dín and the title Aamad-ul-mulk, and commenced the quarrel with Safdar Jang which ended in the latter being deprived of the office of Vazír, which was conferred upon Azíz-ud-dín, son of the late Kumr-ud-dín, and uncle by the mother's side of Ghází-ud-dín. He is, however, better known by the name Intizám-ud-daulah Khan Khánán. Ghází-ud-dín shortly afterwards proceeded by Agra and Muttra, and attacked the Játs of Bhartpur who had befrien... Safdar Jang in his distress. The Emperor and his Vazír conceiving this to be a good opportunity for ridding themselves of their over-active and overbearing Commander-in-Chief, intrigued with the Játs; but their treachery being discovered, Ghází-ud-dín marched upon Dehli, seized and blinded

1738—43 A D.

Ahmad Shah, 1748—1754 A.D.

the Emperor, and raised Prince Azíz-ud-dín, son of Muiz-ud-dín and grandson
of Bahádur Shah, to the throne, under the title of Alamgír II. This happened
in the month of July, 1754.

Safdar Jang died soon afterwards, and was succeeded by his son, Shújah-
ud-daulah. In 1756, Ahmad Shah Abdáli again invaded Hindustán and sacked
Dehli. He removed Ghází-ud-dín from the vizárat, and
appointed the young prince, Ali Gauhar, to succeed him.
At the same time he marched against the Játs; where Ghází-ud-dín so distinguished himself that the Abdáli restored him to the vizárat before his departure. The sack of Muttra and the plunder of Agra are the two most noteworthy
events connected with this year's history of these provinces. Ghází-ud-dín,
on the departure of the Afgháns, became once more supreme at Dehli, and
Najíb Khan was ousted from his appointment of Commander-in-Chief, which
was conferred upon Ahmad Khan Bangash of Farukhabad. Several attempts
were now made to unite the Rohillas, the Oudh chief, and the Játs in a league
against the Vazír, for the purpose of redressing the cause of Ali Gauhar and freeing the Emperor from the tyranny of Ghází-ud-dín; but the dread of the
Marhatta allies of the Vazír obliged them to decline engaging in such a dangerous enterprise. Ali Gauhar fled to Lucknow, and the Marhattas invoded
the Duáb, driving Najíb Khán to take refuge in his fort at Shukartár,
near the confluence of the Soláni and the Ganges, and eventually overran
the whole of Rohilkhand. Alarmed at these successes, Shujah-ud-daulah
joined with the Rohillas in repellling the Marhattas, and defeated them at
the fords of the Ganges. During this time Ali Gauhar had proceeded to
Bengal, with the intention of driving out Jafar Ali
Khan, who had been raised to power by the British,
and establishing himself there. He crossed the Karmnása in 1759 A.D., but,
repulsed in his attacks upon Patna, retired to Allahabad, where he remained
until intelligence of his father's death reached him. Ghází-ud-dín, on hearing
of the repulse of his Marhatta allies and the approach of the Afgháns, had
caused the Emperor to be assassinated. The Abdális in the mean time surprised and cut to pieces one half the Marhatta army under Dátájí, and utterly
dispersed the remainder under Malhar Rao Holkár, after which they retired
to Anúpshahr, where they encamped for the remainder of the year. Both sides
now prepared to contest the sovereignty of Hindustán. Ali Gauhar was written to and installed as Emperor, under the title of Shah Alam. The vizárat
was conferred upon Shújah-ud-daulah, and the Rohillas and Najíb Khan were
urged to assist the great Musalmán confederacy. On the other hand, the Hindús
and their allies were not idle: Ghází-ud-dín roused the Játs of Bhartpur, and
the entire resources of the Marhatta nation were placed at the disposal of
Sadásheo Bhau as Commander-in-Chief. Before the close of the rains the

Marginal notes:

Alamgír, II. 1754–59 A.D.

Ali Gauhar in Bengal.

Marhattas had not only occupied Dehli, but had driven in the Afghán outposts along the Jumna, and between it and the hills, destroying the entire garrison of Kúnjpura and other fortified towns. This success was shortlived, for when the rains ceased, Ahmad Shah crossed the Jumna, and, on the 6th January, 1761, completely routed the Marhattas at Pánipat, where two hundred thousand of the enemy are said to have perished. The Marhattas retired from Hindustán, Najíb Khan was made Amír-ul-Umara, Shújah-ud-daulah continued as Vazír, and Prince Mirza Jawán Bakht represented his father at Dehli.

We left Shah Alam at Allahabad in 1759, where he had retired after his

Shah Alam, 1760–1788 first unsuccessful attempt upon Bengal. Collecting
A.D.   •   another army in the following year, he again invaded Bengal, and though worsted in two engagments, laid siege to Patna. In this attack he was assisted by a party of French under the Chevalier Law. The siege was raised by the efforts of Captain Knox, and all subsequent attempts were repulsed. Shah Alam again took the field in 1761, but met with no better success, and at length agreed to a compromise by which he received the province of Allahabad and Korah, and an annual subsidy of £260,000 a year from the revenues of Bengal. In return for this the Diwáni of Bengal, Behar and Orissa was conferred on the English. Shah Alam fixed his residence at Allahabad, but here fell into the hands of Shujah-ud-daulah, Nawwáb of Oudh, who kept him for two years in a sort-of honourable confinement, sometimes at Lucknow, sometimes at Allahabad, and sometimes at Benares. The Nawwáb, under the name of the Emperor, again attacked the British in 1765 at the Karmnása, where he was utterly routed, and further negotiations were entered into, which can be more correctly detailed with the history of the Benares Province.

Enough has been said by way of introduction to connect the general history

Najíb Khán. of the Upper Duáb in the first half of the last century with the local history of the latter half, which alone is the object of the remainder of this notice. The portions of the Upper Duáb comprising the present districts of Sahárunpur, Muzaffarnagur, Meerut and the northern parganahs of Bulandshahr, were known as the Báwani or Baoni Mahál, from its containing 52 (báwan) parganahs or fiscal sub-divisions. This tract, in the middle of the last century, formed the jágír of Intizám-ud-daula Khan Khánán, the minister of Ahmad Shah. When Gházi-ud-dín resolved to depose Ahmad Shah, he despatched Najíb Khán, who had already distinguished himself as a partisan leader in Rohilkhand, with a body of Mughal troops to occupy the country about Sahárunpur. Najíb Khan was an Afghán of the Kumrkhel tribe, who had in his early youth come from the mountains of Kandahar to seek his fortunes under his uncle Bishárath Khan. With him he entered the service of Ali Muhammud, of the tribe of Roh, who was then

settled in Katehir, and received, in reward for his services, a small *jágír* in the
north-west of Rohilkhand, in the district now known as Bijnor. Here he
became independent, and received the daughter of Dúndi Khán, another Rohilla
leader, in marriage. On the outbreak of the quarrel between Safdar Jang and the
Emperor, when the former called upon Háfiz Rahmat Khán, the Rohilla leader,
to fulfil the terms of an offensive and defensive alliance that had been agreed
upon between them, and the latter conceived it to be his duty to simply withdraw
his forces, the Emperor's agents offered large sums of money to induce the
Rohilla Sardárs to enter his service. Najíb Khán, who then commanded one
hundred horse, was the only one who accepted the bribe ; but when the private
soldiers saw that large rewards were bestowed on those who adopted the Emperor's cause, they flocked to the standard of Najíb, who soon found himself
in command of two thousand men.[1] In the battle of Kotila (or Kohtala),
which shortly afterwards took place, Najíb Khán behaved with great gallantry,
and slew with his own hand Indargír Gosháin, the leader of Safdar Jang's
forces. In reward for this exploit, he received Saháranpur, Búrhána, and all the
villages of the Sayyids of Bárhá, in *jágír*. It was on this account that Gházi-
ud-dín chose Najíb to represent him in the Duáb ; and to still further attach him
to his interests, promised him the remainder of the districts bordering on his
jágír, then held by Intizám-ud-daulah.

Najíb Khán, after the downfal of Ahmad Sháh, repaired to the court of the
new Emperor, and so ingratiated himself with those
1754 A. D.   in power, that when Ahmad Shah Abdáli invaded Dehli
and permitted Alamgír to choose his own ministers, Najíb Khán was made
Bakshi of the empire, with the duty of collecting the revenues. It is said that
Najíb Khán, on taking possession of his new office, expelled the females of
Gházi-ud-dín's household from their home ; and this act so enraged the Vazír that,
on the departure of Ahmad Shah, he invited the Marhatta leaders Raghunáth
Rao and Malhar Rao Holkár from the Dakhin, and joining them with his own
forces from Farukhabad, attacked the royal army. For five and twenty days
repeated actions took place, the result of which was that Najíb Khán was confirmed in his *jágír*, whilst Gházi-ud-dín remained at Dehli. This was a hollow
truce, and each of the combatants eagerly waited for an opportunity to crush
the other. It was to Sikandarabad, then in the possession of Najíb Khán, that
the Prince Ali Gauhar, afterwards known as the Em-
1759 A. D.   peror Shah Alam, fled when he escaped from the hands

---

[1] This act of Najíb Khán led to a misunderstanding between Dúndi Khán and Háfiz Rah-
mat Khán, which nearly broke out into open war. The latter accused the former of conniving at
Najíb Khán's practical contravention of the terms of the treaty made between Safdar Jang and the
Rohillas, and led a force against Bisauli, a *jágír* belonging to Dúndi Khán ; but friends inter-
vening, it was shown that Dúndi Khán, though father-in-law, was not to be held responsible for
Najíb Khán's acts.

of Ghází-ud-dín. Najíb Khan allotted the young prince a monthly income of £5,000 for his expenses, and treated him with every respect, and endeavoured in every way to induce the Rohillas and others to assist him. Hearing of these intrigues, Ghází-ud-dín again called in the Marhattas to assist him in destroying his hated rival and resuming the *jágír;* and these formidable allies, under Jankojí and Dátájí, arrived at Dehli in 1759. Najíb Khan intrenched himself on the Ganges at Shukartár, and, in his turn, solicited aid from the Rohillas and the Viceroy of Oudh, whose combined forces marched from Bareilly in November, 1759, and, on reaching Hasanpur, heard that the Marhattas had made preparations for crossing the river. Bakshi Sardár Khan was at once despatched to oppose them, and others were directed to follow. On his arrival at Sabalgarh the Bakshi found that a large body of the enemy had already crossed, and throwing himself into a fort, awaited the arrival of the reinforcements. [1] On their approach the enemy retreated; and, hearing of the advance of Ahmad Shah from Kábul, consented to execute a treaty of peace, which was of no long

Ahmad Shah. continuance. Ahmad Sháh, marching along the foot of the hills, crossed the Jumna opposite Saháranpur and entered the Duáb, where he was joined by Najíb Khan and the other Rohilla chiefs, and, crossing the Jumna at Bágpat, defeated the Marhattas and proceeded to Dehli. Najíb Khan was again appointed Bakshi of the Empire and guardian of the Prince Mirza Jawan Bakht, who then represented Sháh Alam at Dehli. We next hear of Najíb Khan intriguing with Shúja-ud-daulah against the Afgháns of Farukhabad; and again, in 1746, defending the Duáb against the Bhartpur Játs, who had advanced as far as Tappal

The Játs in the Duáb. in the Aligarh District. The Játs had previously been in possession of these districts, but had been expelled by Ahmad Sháh, who parcelled out the Duáb amongst his Rohilla allies. The fief of Sikandra was conferred on Najíb Khan, and thus his possessions became nearly conterminous with the present Meerut Division. The Játs now sought to recover their authority in the Duáb; and in the campaign against them, Najíb Khan, from the smallness of his force, thought it best to retire northwards. Súraj Mal followed with a small force as far as Shahdara on the Hindan, in the Meerut District, where there was an old hunting seat of the Emperor, and the main body, under his son Jawáhir, occupied Sikandra. Whilst enjoying the pleasures of the chase at Shahdara, Súraj Mal and his party were surprised by a squadron of Mughal horse, who succeeded in killing the whole party, including their leader. The head of Súraj Mal, displayed as a standard, struck such terror amongst the Játs in the battle that followed, that they were thoroughly routed and driven back to their own country. Six months afterwards

---

[1] The Siyár-ul-Mutakheim states that the Marhattas crossed the Ganges, destroyed 1,300 villages, and obliged the Rohillas to fly to the hills of Kumaon.

Jawáhir Mal renewed his attacks on Dehli with the aid of Malhar Rao Holkár, and, surrounding the city, cut off all supplies of grain. Najíb-ud-daulah fortified the city as well as he could, called in his Duáb levies and his allies the Rohillas, and wrote to Ahmad Shah, at Kandahár,,for assistance. At the same time the Sikhs took advantage of Najíb's absence to invade Saháranpur ; and as they even threatened the Rohilla country, the Rohilla leaders despatched at once a force of 6,000 horse to expel the Sikhs, and with the main body marched towards Dehli. Jawáhir Mal and Malhar Rao, on hearing of the approach of the Rohillas on the one side and of Ahmad Shah on the other, at first redoubled their attacks on Najíb Khan's small force ; but when the reinforcements approached nearer, Malhar Rao marched off to his own country, and the Játs to Díg. Relieved from these enemies, Najíb Khan again devoted his attention towards organising an expedition against the Farukhabad Patháns, and for this purpose invited a large Marhatta force under Madhojí Sindhia, Túkají Holkar, and Ramchandra Ganesh, to invade the Central Duáb. Zábita Khan, the son of Najíb, was sent as his representative to the Marhatta camp ; but before anything could be accomplished, Najíb Khan died at Hápur in the Meerut District, and his remains were carried to Najíbabad, and deposited in a mausoleum erected to his memory.

1767.

1770.

Zábita Khan escaped from the Marhatta army and joined his father's forces, then encamped near Farukhabad, by whom he was received and acknowledged as chief, to the exclusion of his half brothers Malu and Kalu. The Farukhabad Patháns now joined with the Marhattas, and induced Shah Alam to leave Allahabad and proceed to Dehli (December, 1771,) under their joint protection ; and at the same time every effort was made to prevent Zábita Khan from assuming the power and influence which his father had so long enjoyed. Faizullah Khan, Rohilla, whose sister had married Zábita Khan, was employed to dissuade the latter from attempting to oppose the wishes of the Emperor and the Pathán-Marhatta confederacy; but disregarding advice and threats alike, Zábita Khan proceeded towards Dehli, and encamped at Shukartár. The royal army now approached, the Marhattas in the van and the imperial troops under Mirza Najf Khan in the rear. Zábita Khan drew out his forces a few miles in advance of his entrenchments and offered battle to the Emperor's troops. The combat was bloody, the Rohilla leaders, Saádat Khan and Sayyid Khán, behaved with great gallantry, but the former being killed by a cannon ball, his troops gave way, and the defeat of the entire Rohilla force was followed by the plunder of their artillery, baggage, stores and military chest. The Marhattas appropriated the spoil to their own use, and crossing the Ganges, captured Najíbabad and Najfgarh, while the royal army marched

Zábita Khan.

1772 A. D.

upwards though the Duáb, and expelled all the Rohilla garrisons excepting Ghausgarh. The family of Zábita Khan fell into the Emperor's hands, and amongst them his eldest son, named Ghulám Kádir, who is said to have been transmuted into a haram page by the Emperor's order, and who lived to exact a fearful revenge for the injury done him. In the meantime, Zábita Khan intrigued with the Marhattas, who agreed to restore him to his former dignities in consideration of his advancing them a large sum of money. The money having been paid, the Marhattas proceeded to Dehli, and after a bloody contest with the troops of the Emperor, took possession of the city. Zábita Khan was pardoned and presented with a dress of honour, and was not only reinstated in his government at Saháranpur, but was officially confirmed in the appointments of Bakshi of the empire and Amír-ul-Umara so long held by his father. Najf Khan, however, still remained nominally Commander-in-Chief.

1772 A. D.

Zábita Khan remained for some time at his forts of Ghausgarh, Shukartár and Pathargarh, reducing the country to order, and establishing his authority amongst the villages occupied by the Gújars and Pundírs, who during the recent troubles had assumed an independent attitude. The Sikhs from the west, too, engaged much of his attention; but having once brought his affairs into order, he conceived himself at liberty to withhold the stipulated tribute from the royal treasury, and prepared to resist any attempts to levy it by force of arms. Abdul Kásim Khán was sent against him; and Zábita Khan, then posted in Ghausgarh, marched out and offered the imperial troops battle. A desperate fight took place, in which the Emperor's army was on the point of proving victorious, when a body of Pathán horse, which had been planted in an ambuscade, rushed out, and attacking Abdul Kásim's forces in the rear, utterly discomfited them. The commander himself was slain, and but few of his troops escaped.

1776 A.D.

Inflamed by his success, Zábita Khán now took large bodies of Sikhs[1] into his pay; and resolving to persist in his rebellion, actually threatened Dehli itself with a siege. The imperial troops under Mirza Najf Khán were then engaged in the Ját country, from which they were recalled, and the Emperor himself prepared to lead them against the rebel; but first resolving to see what could be effected by diplomacy, he sent an embassy, consisting of Raja Dya Rám; the Gosháin leader, Hímmat Bahádur; and the Oudh envoy, Latáfat Khán; in advance of the imperial army to Ghausgarh. Though they failed to induce Zábita Khán to abate one whit of his pretensions, yet the Emperor was so unwilling to come to an open rupture, that on the

1777 A.D.

---

[1] It is said that Zábita Khan not only formed alliances with the principal Sikh chiefs, but even embraced the tenets of the Sikh religion, and became a convert to their faith. (Francklin's Shah Aulum, 71.)

mere semblance of submission he pardoned the rebel and confirmed him in his government. In addition to this, Mirza Najf Khán took the Pathán's sister to wife, and his follower, Najf Kúli Khan (a converted Rajpút), married Zábita's daughter.

It was at this time (1778) that Walter Reinhard, also known as Sumru

1778-79 A.D. or Sombre, was placed in charge of the country adjoining Zábita Khan's lands, and fixed his head-quarters at Sardhana in the Meerut District. The Kashmíri Abdúl Ahíd Khán, known by his title of Nawwáb Majad-ud-daulah, is said to have been privy to Zábita Khán's alliance with the Sikhs; but so well did he keep his connivance secret, that he was chosen to command the imperial army raised to expel the Sikhs from Sirhind in the following year (1778-79). The Prince Imperial, Jawán Bakht, accompanied the army, which was at first successful, but subsequently, owing to the treachery of Majad-ud-daulah, was surprised by a Sikh force at Patiyála, and driven back to Pánipat. The Sikhs then divided into several parties, and, crossing the Jumna, entered the Upper Duáb, where they committed everywhere acts of cruelty, devastation and death. Mirza Najf Khán was again sent for to take the place of Majad-ud-daulah, now disgraced and imprisoned, and with the titles of Zulfakár-ud-daulah and Vakíl-i-Matlak, became absolute director of all affairs at Dehli.

At the commencement of 1780, preparations were made to take the field

1780 A.D. against the Sikhs, who now for some months had remained in possession of the Duáb. A large force under Mirza Shafi, a young nobleman of great promise, and nephew of the Captain-General, crossed the Jumna in quest of the enemy. After several ineffectual skirmishes and much desultory fighting, he succeeded, about the middle of August, in bringing them to a decisive action before Meerut. The imperial troops, eager to wipe of the disgrace of their defeat in the previous year, exerted themselves to such good effect, that the Sikh forces were completely routed, with the loss of their leader and 5,000 men, and at once evacuated the country. Mirza Shafi's next care was to settle the country, and finding the people utterly unable to pay up the taxes for the year during which the Duáb was occupied by the Sikhs, he remitted them in the Emperor's name.

Mirza Najf Khán died in the month of April 1782, and amongst the competi-

Afrasyáb Khán, tors for the vacant post of head of the adminstration, the **1782 A.D.** principal were Afrasyáb Khán and Mirza Shafi. The former was the adopted son of the deceased minister, and the latter was his nephew, and held command of the Panjáb. Each prepared to support his respective pretensions by force of arms, but Afrasyáb Khán first succeeded in obtaining for a time the insignia of Amír-ul-Umara. He then released the Kashmíri ex-minister Majad-ud-daulah, and placed him and Najf Kúli Khan in charge of the citadel.

Afrasyáb Khan then proceeded to Agra, where Muhammad Beg Hamadáni had attempted to make himself independent. Whilst on his way news arrived that Mirza Shafi had entered Dehli, seized the citadel, and confined the officers who had been left in charge. Afrasyáb thereupon resolved to make peace with Muhammad Beg, and uniting their forces both marched towards Dehli. In the meantime a counter-revolution took place there, which totally changed the complexion of affairs. The Prince Jawán Bakht aspired to the office of Captain-General, and finding himself supported by M. Paoli, the commandant of Begam Sumru's brigade, Yákúb Khán, Latáfat Khán and other nobles, he induced the Emperor to take the field against Mirza Shafi. The latter, finding himself unable to meet the imperial forces, released Majad-ud-daulah, and with him proceeded to the camp of his whilom inveterate foe Afrasyáb Khán. These strangely assorted allies met at Muttra, and there agreed that the effects of the late Najf Khan should be equally divided between Mirza Shafi and Afrasyáb Khan; that the former should be reinstated in the post of Vazír; and that the latter and Muhammad Beg should be left in possession of the Duáb from Koil southwards. Their united forces then marched towards Dehli, and Majad-ud-daulah was sent to the Emperor with their ultimatum. The Emperor appointed Prince Jawán Bakht, Latáfat Khán, and M. Paoli to negotiate on his part; but the unfortunate ambassadors fared ill: M. Paoli was assassinated by command of Muhammad Beg, and Latáfat Khan was taken prisoner, deprived of his sight, and thrown into prison. The Prince alone escaped, but found himself obliged to accompany the conspirators, as if a voluntary actor, in their triumphal entry into Dehli.

The next scene in this real drama[1] of the "Reward of treachery, or the unscrupulous Mogul" rises on a quarrel which broke out between Muhammad Beg and Mirza Shafi. By the convention of Muttra, the former was entitled to a share of the southern Duáb: but Mirza Shafi refused to carry out this portion of the compact, and further incensed the entire body of the Mughal nobles by avowing his intention of resuming the lands held by them on condition of military service. Dissembling his resentment for a time, Muhammad Beg joined the camp of Afrasyáb Khán, and induced the latter to invite the Mirza to a conference to settle all their difficulties. Mirza Shafi, attended by a few followers, came on his elephant, and whilst embracing Muhammad Beg, was stabbed from behind by Ismáil Beg, the Hamadáni's nephew. Afrasyáb Khán was at once promoted to the office of Amír-ul-Umara, whilst Zain-ul-abdín Khán, the brother of the murdered nobleman, was ordered to give up the Governorship of Meerut, which he then held. Afrasyáb Khan advanced to Meerut to enforce these orders, but by

1783 A.D.

---

[1] The name actually given to a piece in which the principal events of this period were dramatised.

the advice of his principal officers first tried the effect of negotiations, with the result that Zain-ul-abdín was induced to throw himself on the Emperor's clemency, and give up the Meerut command, which was then bestowed on Kutb-ud-daulah. Zain-ul-abdín then proceeded to Dehli, where he was formally pardoned, but at the same time kept in a sort of honourable confinement in his own house.

Early in 1784, Mr. Hastings, the British Governor, arrived at Lucknow, and sent Major Brown as his agent to the Dehli Court.

1784 A.D.

Mirza Jawán Bakht, considering this a good opportunity for attempting to induce the British to interfere on behalf of his father, succeeded, with the aid of a body of Gújars, in making his escape to Lucknow. The presence of the British agent at Dehli was partly due to the natural desire of Mr. Hastings to procure more accurate information regarding Dehli politics than the confused and contradictory rumours that reached him afforded, and partly to his wish to arouse the Dehli Court to make some exertions to stem the tide of Sikh invasion which now threatened to involve the whole Duáb in one common destruction. Afrasyáb Khan induced the Emperor to order the return of the Prince, and determined, if he once again got hold of the heir to the throne, to effectually prevent his ever after giving any trouble. Muhammad Beg, too, felt the minister's resentment, and went into open rebellion; whilst Majad-ud-daulah, notwithstanding his great services, was imprisoned in the fort of Meerut. Under these circumstances, Shah Alam, finding himself a mere puppet in the hands of whichever faction chose for the moment to assume the direction of affairs, commenced to intrigue with Sindhia, and in this course of action he was encouraged by Afrasyáb Khan, who hoped by means of the Marhattas to rid himself of his rival Muhammad Beg.

Early in 1784, the Emperor, accompanied by Afrasyáb Khan, marched to Agra, whilst the Marhattas, advancing from the west,

Sindhia arrives at Agra.

encamped at Fathepur, and, opposed to both, lay the forces of Muhammad Beg Hamadáni, some forty miles off. Sindhia now found himself appealed to by all three. To Muhammad Beg he granted an interview; and appearing to be satisfied with the explanations which were made, he promised his good offices in procuring the Emperor's pardon for the offender. A few days later, in November, at an interview with Afrasyáb Khán, Sindhia laidd own a plan for a combined attack on Muhammad Beg. Zain-ul-abdín, the ex-commandant of Meerut, had been released from confinement through the influence of Sindhia, and burning to avenge his brother's death and his own disgrace, hung about the imperial camp. He accompanied the chiefs to the interview with Sindhia, and after the ceremony was over, and Sindhia and the other officers had taken leave, there remained no one in the tent except Afrasyáb Khán and Zain-ul-abdín. The latter entered into conversation with the minister, and professed his strong

desire to live in future on a more amicable footing, that all past differences
Assassination of Afrasyáb Khán. should be forgotten, and that each should consider the
interest of the other to be the same as his own; Afras-
yáb Khán, puzzled at this sudden reconciliation, remained for sometime absorbed
in silence. When about to reply, Zain-ul-abdín rose up from his seat, and,
at this signal, one Mahdi Beg rushed in and stabbed the minister in the breast.
Afrasyáb Khán expired on the spot, and his assassins found refuge in Sindhia's
camp, whilst Himmat Bahádur, the Goshain leader, and other Mughal officers,
repaired to Sindhia's tent, and offered him their congratulations as if he had
already been appointed Vazír.

While these events occurred at Fatehpur, the Emperor was at Agra, and
The Emperor flies to Dehli. was there joined by Majad-ud-daulah, who found
means, not only to effect his own release from prison,
but to induce Kutb-ud-daulah, his jailor, to accompany him to Agra. Shah
Alam received his old friend with great kindness, and would most probably
have taken him into favour and restored him to his former office again, had
not both Raja Daya Rám, and Shuja Dil Khán, the Governor of Agra,
endeavoured to arouse suspicions of the Kashmíri's fidelity in the Emperor's
mind. The insolent manner in which they urged their remonstrances showed
that they, as the partisans of Afrasyáb Khan, believed that the Emperor was
entirely in the power of their faction, and this not a little contributed
to the desire Shah Alam showed to escape from their hands. In order
to blind his keepers, the Emperor ordered a great portion of his family to remain
behind, and, taking Majad-ud-daulah with him, proceeded to Dehli. Sindhia entered Agra, and sent for Muhammad Beg, on whom he conferred a *jágír*
of Rs. 16,000 a month from the revenues of Shikohabad, and, further, gave him
employment in the Dakhin. Sindhia proceeded from Agra to Dehli, where, in
January, 1785, he was invested in full darbár with the office of Amír-ul-Umara,
whilst the Peshwa, for whom he professed to act, was honoured with the title of
Vakíl-i-Matlak, or plenipotentiary of the Empire. As may be supposed, during
the late troubles the administration had fallen into the utmost disorder, and the
first care of the new minister was given to the improvement of the finances.
The collection of the revenue had for several years been in the hands of Raja
Daya Rám; but his behaviour towards the Emperor at Agra determined Sindhia
to remove him from that office, which was accordingly bestowed upon Naráyan
Dás, a person of great capacity and of some skill as a financier. Sindhia next
reduced Agra and Aligarh, and with the capture of the latter fortress acquired
the immense accumulations of specie and jewels that a long course of plunder
had allowed Afrasyáb Khán to make. At the close of the year 1785, Zábita
Khán died, and was succeeded by his eldest son, Ghulám Kádir Khán. Sindhia
was master of the whole of the Central and Southern Duáb. Muhammad Beg

was powerless, and, deserted by his troops, was only too glad to accept anything that the new Amír might give him. Mr. James Anderson was the British envoy with Sindhia, and Colonel Harper filled a similar office at the court of the Nawáb of Oudh, who was still titular Vazír of the Empire. Sháh Nizám-ud-dín was appointed superintendent of the royal household, for which a provision of £120,000 a year was allotted.

We must now return to Saháranpur affairs. Zábita Khán, after a long life

Ghulám Kádir Khán.

of alternate success and misfortune, marked by the evils resulting from an ill-tempered judgment and a naturally restless disposition, died unnoticed and uncared for in the year 1785. He was succeeded by his eldest son, Ghulám Kádir Khán, the same who is said to have received such unpardonable injuries at the hands of the Emperor during the Shukartár campaign in 1772. He was a youth of a proud, cruel and ferocious disposition, and at once showed his true character by dispossessing Afzal Khán, brother of Zábita Khán, of the lands that had long been in his possession, and by seizing upon his effects. Ghulám Kádir then proceeded to assume all the insignia of independence, and proclaimed himself ruler of the Upper Duáb under the name of Najíb-ud-daulah Hoshyár Jang. Affairs to the west of the Jumna so occupied the attention of Sindhia, that Ghulám Kadir was allowed to consolidate his power and act as he pleased. The Jaipur prince, assisted by Ismaíl Beg, the nephew of Muhammad Beg, defeated Sindhia himself and laid siege to Agra. At the same time Raja Daya Rám fomented the discords that prevailed amongst the Mughal nobles, and detached them from the Marhatta cause; but falling into the hands of Sháh Nizám-ud-dín, Sindhia's Deputy at Dehli, the intriguer was trodden to death by elephants in the royal presence. Dehli was placed in a state of siege, and every preparation made to meet the storm which the Marhatta party felt must sooner or later fall upon them.

The need of these precautions was soon shown. Ghulám Kádir having,

Ghulám Kádir attacks Dehli; 1787 A.D.

during the last two years, raised and disciplined a considerable force, resolved to make the Empire at large pay for their support, and, marching down the Duáb, encamped opposite Dehli towards the close of the year 1787. He was encouraged in this step by letters received from Mansúr Ali Khán, Názir of the household and a confidant of the Emperor, which urged him to come and demand the vacant office of Amír-ul-Umara. Shah Nizám-ud-dín and the Desmukh, a son-in-law of Sindhia, in command of the Marhatta force, were inclined to under-estimate the importance of the crisis. They contented themselves with sending small detachments across the river, with orders to attack the force of Ghulám Kádir. The result was, that their troops were defeated with great slaughter, and both the leaders fled to Gwaliar. Ghulám Kádir at once crossed the Jumna, and was introduced into the palace by the treacherous Názir. He then demanded the appointment he sought, and the wretched Emperor, seeing himself without resource, was obliged to confer on this arch-rebel an office which now seems to have belonged to any one bold enough to attempt to secure the Emperor's person. Amongst those who, at this time, preferred the existing state of affairs, and had some regard for the Emperor's dignity, was the Begam Sumru, who, on the death of her husband, the infamous Sumru, had succeeded to the command of the disciplined battalions he had raised, and to the possession of the lands granted for their maintenance.

The adventurer known by the name of Sumru or Sombre[1] was a butcher by profession, a native of Salzburg, or some say Trèves, in the Duchy of Luxemburg. His real name was Walter Renard or Reinhard. He came to this country as a soldier in the French army, and deserting that service took employment with the British, where he attained to the rank of sergeant. Deserting again, he joined the French party at Chandernagore, and, on the surrender of that settlement, accompanied M. Law in his wanderings throughout India from 1757 to 1760. In the latter year Law's party joined the army of Shah Alam in Bengal, and remained with the Emperor until his defeat in 1761, when M. Law was taken prisoner and his European troops were dispersed. We next find Sumru in the service of Mír Kásim, by whom he was employed to murder the English prisoners at Patna, in October, 1763. He then escaped into Oudh, and after some time took service in Bundelkhand. We next find him in the Ját country, where he served Mirza Najf Khán. Deserting him, Sumru entered the service of Súraj Mal, the Ját leader, with a battalion of disciplined infantry, a detail of artillery, and some three hundred Europeans, the dross of all countries and nationalities. From the Játs he went to the Marhattas, whom he served for several years, but deserted to the Imperial army after the battle of Barsána in 1775.

In 1777, Mirza Najf Khan again took Sumru into his service, and, in addition to his own battalions, gave him command of a body of Mughal horse. For the support of the whole he assigned him the parganah of Sardhana and the adjacent lands, then valued at six lakhs of rupees a year. On the death of Reinhard, in 1778 A.D., his force was maintained by his widow. This remarkable woman was the daughter, by a concubine, of Asad Khán, a Musalmán of Arab descent, settled in the town of Kutána in the Meerut District. She was born about the year 1753 A.D. On the death of her father, she and her mother became subject to ill-treatment from her half-brother, the legitimate heir, and they consequently removed to

Early history of Sumru.

Settles in Sardhana.

---

[1] The name Sombre is said to have been given to him from his gloomy disposition; whilst others say it arose from his assuming the name of Walter Summers. The latter account gives the more probable origin of the name.

Dehli about 1760. There she entered the service of Sumru, and accompanied him through all his campaigns. Sumru, on retiring to Sardhana, found himself relieved of all the cares and troubles of war, and gave himself entirely up to a life of ease and pleasure, and so completely fell into the hands of the Begam, that she had no difficulty in inducing him to exchange the title of mistress for that of wife. Having attained to this dignity, she perseveringly exercised the rights thereby attained, to raise herself to the actual enjoyment of all the powers derived from Sumru's political position. Sumru died in 1778, and was buried in the Roman Catholic cemetery at Agra, where his tomb still exists.[1]

Sumru left a son, Zafaryáb Khan, by a concubine named Baha Begam, but his widow assumed the management of the estate and the command of the troops, which now numbered five battalions of sepoys, about 300 European officers and gunners, with forty pieces of cannon, and a body of irregular horse. In 1781 the Begam was baptised, according to the ritual of the Roman Catholic Church, under the name of Johanna. Her troops were at this time commanded by a German named Paoli, who intrigued with the Prince Mirza Jawán Bakht against the Shafi and Rohilla faction, to raise the Prince to the dignity of Amír-ul-Umara, and, as we have seen, was assassinated by order of Muhammad Beg Hamadáni in 1783 A.D. After the murder of Paoli, Messrs. Baours, Evans, and Dudrenec successively commanded the Begam's forces, which were principally occupied in opposing the inroads of the Sikhs. In 1787 George Thomas entered the Begam's service at Dehli. Sumru's party was never famed for their military achievements. They never gained a gun and never lost one until they were defeated by the British at Ajanta Ghát. Sumru was distinguished for his excellent retreats. He was accustomed to draw up his men in line, fire a few shots, form a square, and retreat, so that if his corps gained no laurels, they preserved their reputation. His troops were the most mutinous in India, and are said to have frequently attacked their own officers and beaten them with clubs, whilst on more than one occasion Sumru was tied astride a gun, and exposed to the mid-day heat, to compel him to obey their wishes.

Having brought the history of the Sardhana fief down to the year 1787, I shall proceed with the main story. Ghulám Kádir, on obtaining his patent of

Ghulám Kádir made Amír-Ul-umara.

office, opened communications with the Begam, then operating against the cis-Satlaj Sikhs. He offered her,

---

[1] The inscription on it runs thus—

AQUIIAZ.	EO AOS 4.
OWALT.	DE MAYO.
ERREINHA.	NO ANNO.
RD MORR.	DE 1778.

not only an extension of her *jágír*, but even an equal share in the administration of affairs, if she would support his authority. Well versed in eastern politics, and well acquainted with the Afghán character for treachery, the Begam repulsed these offers with scorn, and advanced with her troops to the capital. Here she was received as the saviour of the imperial cause, and so intimidated the rebels that they withdrew across the Jumna. From thence Ghulám Kádir demanded the dismissal of the Begam and her troops; and on this not being granted, opened fire upon the palace itself. For some time desultory skirmishes took place, and though Najf Kuli Khan came to the assistance of the Emperor, little impression was made on the rebel's force. Marching down the Duáb, Ghulám Kádir possessed himself of Aligarh, and, uniting his forces with those of Ismaíl Beg, defeated Rána Khán, the Marhatta General, at Cháksú. Mansúr Ali Khán, faithful to his friend Ghulám Kádir, refused to supply the Emperor's purse, and conveyed intimation to the enemy that the Prince Jawáu Bakht was approaching, with a large force, to relieve the city. He further advised that Ghulám Kádir should embrace this opportunity to make terms whilst he was still able. Profiting by this counsel, the Rohilla signified his sorrow for his late conduct, and offered to restore the lands in the Duáb that he had lately usurped. These offers, backed by a handsome present in ready money, of which the imperial treasury stood in much need, were accepted, and the rebel marched back to Sahárunpur, with the confirmation of his appointment as "first of the nobles" in his hand.

The conduct of Sindhia during this time needs explanation, and the materials available do not afford anything that can be considered satisfactory. On establishing his authority in Upper India, Sindhia found that the greater portion of the State lands was parcelled out amongst the Mughal nobles on condition of military service, and resolved to carry out the project attempted by Mirza Shafi and others, and resume these grants, paying those employed in the army from the public funds, and devoting the revenues of the resumed lands to this purpose, and to the support of a standing army raised and disciplined in the European fashion. The design was carried out, but not without considerable murmurs, which nothing but the presence of an overwhelming Marhatta force prevented from breaking out into open rebellion. Naráyan Dás, too, was removed from the superintendence of the revenue, which was conferred upon Shah Nizám-ud-dín, whilom superintendent of the imperial household. In this critical time of doubt and uncertainty, matters were brought to a crisis by the action of the Jaipur Prince, who induced Muhammad Beg to join him, and, on his death in battle, Ismaíl Beg, his nephew, became the head of the malcontent Mughals. In the war between Sindhia and the Raja of Jaipur, small bodies of Mughal troops, led by men whose lands Sindhia had resumed, continually deserted to the enemy,

Causes of Sindhia's in-action.

and in the end he had none but his own countrymen to rely upon. Numbers proving too much for him, Sindhia retired to Gwaliar to await reinforcements, and for a time was powerless to prevent the advance of the Rohilla adventurer. These facts, we may fairly infer, were the causes which led to the inaction of the Marhattas during the eventful year 1787.

In the beginning of 1788, Sindhia prepared to cross the Chambal, whilst the Emperor himself also awoke to new life, and com-

1788 A.D.

menced a royal progress throughout the territories close to the capital. The Raja of Jaipur was compelled to yield the usual tribute, and Najf Kuli Khán was invested in his strong fortress of Gokalgarh. The latter had the presumption to demand the office of Amir-ul-Umara

Siege of Gokalgarh.

as a condition of his submission; and were it not for the urgent representations of some of the few faithful friends of the court that still remained, the Emperor would have consented to the arrangement, especially as the proposition was coupled with the offer of £60,000 in ready cash as the fine on investiture. The imperial troops comprised, at this time, several battalions of half disciplined levies known as *najíbs*, the body-guard called the red battalion, a considerable force of irregular horse, and three battalions of disciplined infantry from the Sardhana fief, under the command of George Thomas, with a respectable train of artillery. Najf Kuli Khán himself lay in an intrenched post at about a mile from the fort. The Gosháin Raja, Himmat Bahádur, commanded the force opposed to Najf Kuli, and the Emperor himself invested the fort with the main portion of the army. The Gosháin's forces were, for the most part, a rabble composed of the dregs of the armies of all the nations of India. He had only two disciplined battalions under a Danish leader, Colonel Meiselback, that did good service both here and in Bundelkhand.[1] The officers of his force, accustomed to riot and debauchery, could not bear the unwonted labour of the trenches, and, forgetful of the danger of their situation, continued to indulge themselves to excess. The soldiers soon followed the example of their leaders. Najf Kuli being informed of this state of things by his spies, selected a strong detachment of cavalry, and made a night attack on the Gosháin's quarter. The lines were instantly carried, and such a general slaughter took place that any possibility of a rally was prevented. The terror caused by this sudden attack communicated itself to the main body, who began to prepare for flight, and for this they were the more ready when they found that Mansúr Khan, who commanded in Gokalgarh, had, by an arrangement preconcerted with Najf Kuli, slipped out of the fort, and attacked the imperial camp in the rear.

Shah Alam and his family were now in the greatest danger. Their tents were struck and removed to the advanced guard com-

Gallantry of the Begam.

manded by Shah Mír Khán, who endeavoured to rally

---

[1] See Gazetteer Index, Vol. I, under 'Meiselback'.

the flying troops. The Sardhana brigade, under the command of George Thomas, and with the Begam in person present, now greatly distinguished itself. At the first alarm they drew up as if on parade, and the Begam sent a respectful message to Shah Alam, desiring him to repair to her quarters, and she would punish the rebel or die in defence of the imperial cause. At the same time she wrote to Najf Kuli, upbraiding him for his conduct, and threatening him with exemplary punishment should he persist. She then placed herself in her palanquin at the head of one hundred men, who, led by George Thomas, repeatedly charged the troops of Mansúr Khán, and drove them back to the fort. The imperial leaders had now time to collect their men, and Himmat Bahádur and Shah Mír Khán led the attack against Najf Kuli, who was eventually obliged to retire with heavy loss. The brave Shah Mír Khán was killed on the Emperor's side. Najf Kuli Khán submitted, and in the darbár held for this purpose, the Begam was invested with a dress of honour, and received the title of "daughter of the Emperor" and "Ornament of her sex" (*zeb-un-nissa*), with the parganah of Badshábpur in *jágír*.

Sindhia, on advancing into the Duáb, sent Ráná Khán to relieve the fort of Agra, which was still besieged by Ismaíl Beg. The latter had previously made engagements with Ghulám Kádir for their mutual support, but the faithless Rohilla had no intention of carrying out his part of the treaty. The consequence of this conduct was, that Ismaíl Beg was defeated and obliged to fly to the Rohilla camp, then at Aligarh. The united forces proceeded northward, and, after expelling Sindhia's troops from the Duáb, marched upon Dehli, with the intention of plundering the imperial palace. The immediate cause for this step was the alleged discovery of a letter addressed to Síndhia by Shah Alam, in which he called on the Marhatta for assistance. The Názir, Mansúr Ali Khan, still held the first place in Shah Alam's counsels, and still kept up a traitorous correspondence with the Rohillas. By his influence, Himmat Bahádur and the few Mughal nobles then at court abandoned the palace and city, and left the Emperor in the hands of the rebels. Ghulám Kádir and Ismaíl Beg, with two thousand Rohillas, took possession of the palace, and forced themselves into the hall of audience, where they found the Emperor, and standing on each side of the throne, obliged him to approve of all their acts. They then dismissed him to the inner apartments, and consulted on their future course of action.

The Názir was admitted to their counsels, and by his advice one Sítal Dás, a sub-treasurer, was sent to Shah Alam, with a message that one of the young princes should be sent to accompany the army against the Marhattas, whilst the citadel and garrison should be immediately delivered up to the Rohillas. To strengthen this proposal, Ghulám Kádir, with his own hand, drew up an agreement, in

Sindhia relieves Agra.

Weakness of the Emperor.

which he solemnly swore to defend the person and interests of Shah Álam
against all comers. Though Sítal Dás used his utmost endeavours to dissuade
the Emperor from accepting these proposals, he was sent back with the agreement ratified by the sign manual, and sealed with the imperial seal. In the
meantime the Rohilla troops kept pouring in, and in a short time occupied both
palace and fort. The imperial troops were disarmed and expelled, and their officers were placed in confinement. Ghulám Kádir then insolently demanded the
keys of the imperial treasury, and when informed that the coffers were empty,
prepared to offer the last indignities to the aged Emperor.

Early the next morning, Ghulám Kádir, accompanied by a numerous band
of followers, entered the audience chamber, and expelled
all the inmates except Shah Alam. He then sent for
Bedar Bakht, a son of the late Emperor Ahmad Shah, from Salímgarh, and placed
him on the throne under the name of Jahán Shah. Shah Alam and his family
were transferred to Salímgarh, and his quarters in the palace were occupied by
Jahán Shah. The next step was the plunder of the ladies of the haram. Mali-
kah Zamána and Sahiba Mahál, the widows of Mahmúd Shah, first felt the
rebel's cruelty. They were ordered to appear, and to them was committed the
invidious task of removing the jewellery from the persons of the inmates of the
seraglio. The spoil produced did not satisfy the inhuman tyrant, who then
ordered that those ladies themselves should be plundered of all they possessed,
and be expelled from the palace. Jahán Shah himself was next sent on a similar
errand, and by menaces and entreaties succeeded in procuring a large amount
of jewellery, which he sent on trays to the Rohilla. Dissatisfied with this also,
Ghulám Kádir sent for the Emperor and all his family, and sternly demanded the
imperial treasures. In vain did the Emperor plead his
utter poverty and the emptiness of his coffers. Inflamed
by a protracted debauch, which had thrown him into a paroxysm of rage, the
tyrant threatened his sovereign with instant loss of sight. "What!" exclaimed
the suffering prince, "what! will you destroy these eyes, which for a period
of sixty years have been assiduously employed in perusing the sacred Korán?"
Regardless of this appeal, the Rohilla caused the Emperor to be thrown down,
and planting himself on the bosom of the prostrate prince, transfixed his eyes
with a poignard, and expelled him, with every mark of indignity, pale and
bleeding, from the audience chamber. This occurred on the 10th August, 1788.

The next to feel what the barbarity of a degraded Afghán could do and
dare was the Názir, Mansúr Ali, the treacherous confederate of Ghulám Kádir. Perhaps some compunc-
tions visited even him for his conduct towards his master. On the occasion of
the installation of Jahán Shah, when the deposed Emperor cried out in his
agony—"Better will it be for Ghulám Kádir to plunge his dagger in my bosom

Shah Alam deposed.

The Emperor deprived
of his sight.

The Názir also spoiled.

than load me with such indignity," the Rohilla put his hand on his sword; and had not the Názir restrained him, would then and there have put an end to the Emperor's sufferings. However this may be, the Názir rendered himself an object of suspicion to Ghulám Kádir, who put him into close confinement, and plundered him of all his effects, to the amount of £70,000. In all these acts Ismaíl Beg was a passive participator; but when he asked for a share of the spoil, the Rohilla refused to acknowledge him. Incensed at this, Ismaíl Beg offered his services to the Marhattas, who, under Ráná Khan, advanced on Dehli.

Ghulám Kádir, hearing of the approach of the avenging army, collected all his spoil, and, taking with him the imperial family and the Názir, fled to Meerut. The Marhattas occupied Dehli, Ismaíl Beg was despatched to act against Gokalgarh, and Ráná Khán and Appákhandi Rao, with Ali Bahádur from Bundelkhand, invested Meerut. Ghulám Kádir cut his way through the besieging army, and fled towards Sahá-ranpur, but was captured on the way, and handed over to the Marhattas. On refusing to discover the place where he had deposited the spoils of the palace, he was confined in an iron cage constructed for the purpose, and carried in front of the army. Day by day he lost a hand, an ear, or a foot, until death put an end to his sufferings. His confederate, the Názir, was trodden to death by ele-phants,—both thus dreadfully atoning for their great and many crimes. The Marhattas next reduced the whole of the Upper Duáb, and in their hands it remained until it was conquered by the British.

Capture and death of Ghulám Kádir.

Shah Alam was again restored to the throne of his ancestors, with an allow-ance of £90,000 per annum for the support of his household, which was again placed under the control of Shah Nizám-ud-dín. Ismaíl Beg, who had been sent against Najf Kuli Khán, found that in the meantime his opponent had died, and that his widow was in command of the troops. She induced him to take her side against the Mar-hattas, and for some time their combined forces maintained their ground, until the death of the widow in battle induced her troops to abandon Ismaíl Beg. He then surrendered himself to the Marhattas, and was conveyed a prisoner to Agra, where he died in 1799. Sindhia's next enemy was Holkar, whose forces were almost annihilated in the bloody action of Lakhairi, near Kánúnd, in 1792. In this battle the disciplined troops of Sindhia, under M. deBoigne, greatly distinguished themselves, so that the Marhatta directed their increase to 24,000 infantry and 130 pieces of artillery, and assigned for their support fifty-two dis-tricts in the Duáb. Towards the middle of 1793, Sindhia returned to his own country, leaving Gopál Rao as his representative in the north, and M. deBoigne in command in the centre of his new possessions. Sindhia died in Febru-ary, 1794, at Wanauli, near Poona, and was succeeded by his nephew Daulat Rao. The remainder of the general history of the Upper Duáb may be divided

Sindhia supreme at Dehli.

into a few sections,—the rise of George Thomas, the continuation of the
account of the Sardhana fief, the Marhatta administration, and the arrival of the
British.

The short and brilliant career of George Thomas distinguishes him amidst
the crowd of European adventurers in the Marhatta

George Thomas.

service who at this time sought their fortunes in
upper India. He was a native of Tipperary in Ireland, and came to Madras
as a sailor in a man-of-war about 1782. In Madras he deserted his ship to
join the forces of some Poligár chief; and in 1787 made his way to Dehli, where
he entered the service of Begam Sumru. Here he distinguished himself at the
siege of Gokalgarh, and remained at Sardhana until 1792, when LeVaisseau,
the commandant of the Begam's artillery, who had always been the rival and
bitter enemy of Thomas, succeeded in supplanting him in the Begam's confidence. Thomas, ill-brooking his disgrace, resigned his employment, and betook
himself, to the town of Anúpshahr, then a frontier-station of Britis htroops. He
had not been long here, when overtures were made to him on the part of Appákandi Rao, the Marhatta Governor of the trans-Jumna territory, who, at this
time, sought to establish his authority in Ismail Beg's former *jágír* of Mewat.
Thomas accepted the Marhatta service, and in a short time so distinguished
himself, that his employer presented him with several parganahs in *jágír* as a
reward for good and faithful service,—the latter a novelty in Marhatta politics.

The gift, however, was not so valuable as might have been expected. These
parganahs were inhabited by a wild and warlike race,

Thomas at Jájbar.

living in fortified villages, and accustomed to oppose
all comers, whether with cause or without cause. It took Thomas many months
and much hard marching and fighting to reduce them to even a semblance of
submission, and this only lasted whilst he was within recall. Though an un-
profitable field as a source of revenue, his *jágír* gave Thomas an excuse for keeping up a large force, who, by discipline and experience, soon became a body of
men that could be relied upon in the field against any of the surrounding
tribes. His fame increased, and with it his power, for soldiers of fortune from
the Duáb and Rohilkhand continually flocked to his standard, and in a few years
he found himself at the head of two well-drilled battalions of infantry, with a
complement of irregular horse and cavalry, and a park of field artillery. Begam Sumru, instigated by LeVaisseau, now her husband, sought in every way
to injure Thomas, and urged on his Marhatta employers the danger of allowing
a man of his character to assume a position of *quasi*-independence. She even
marched against him with the entire force of the Sardhana *jágír*; but before
reaching his territory, a mutiny amongst her troops and the death of LeVaisseau put an end to the expedition. Whether worked on by the Begam's
remonstrances, or actuated by selfish motives of his own, even Appákandi Rao,

Made Warden of the Marches. whose life Thomas, on more than one occasion, had saved, was induced to plot his destruction ; but twice the hired assassins failed in their attempts. Notwithstanding that Thomas was well aware of all this treachery, he took no notice of its authors, and was always ready to carry out the orders he received, though frequently their execution was both difficult and dangerous. One of his principal duties was to oppose the invasions of the Sikhs from the west; and in this he was so successful, that Lakwa Dáda, who had succeeded Gopal Rao as the Marhatta commander in the north of the Duáb, assigned him a second *jágír*, and gave him charge of the entire frontier of the present Meerut Division. Whilst thus employed, he returned good for evil by reinstating the Begam at Sardhana, whence she had been driven by a mutiny of her troops ; and he also distinguished himself at the sieges of Shámli and Lakhnauti. About this time Appákandi Rao, whilst suffering from an incurable disease, performed the *samádh* by drowning himself in the Jumna, and was succeeded by his nephew, Váman Rao, whose first desire was to resume the *jágírs* held by Thomas.

Breaks with the Marhattas. Thomas, on hearing of this, retired to his own country, and strengthened himself there by raising more troops and building small forts, to which he might retire, or which might serve as depôts for stores and ammunition. He, at the same time, continued his operations against the Sikhs, whose forces he frequently repulsed. Whilst thus engaged, Váman Rao attacked Jájhar, but retired on hearing of Thomas's approach ; and the latter took the opportunity of invading and plundering parganah Dádri, now in the Bulandshahr District, and then held by one Kashmíri Boli, who was justly suspected of being the instigator of Váman Rao's treacherous attack. The breach was further widened by some misunderstanding with Bápú Sindhia, the successor of Lakwá Dádá at Saháranpur, whose troops Thomas defeated in two successive actions. Thomas was now considered dangerous enough to be left alone; and having no money to pay his troops, he led them into the Jaipur and other neighbouring States, where he levied contributions sufficient to satisfy their present wants. This state of things could not continue for long, and he looked about for means whereby he might place his affairs on a more stable foundation.

Thomas becomes Independent. In 1798, Thomas first formed the design of carving out an independent kingdom for himself, and for this purpose selected the tract known as Hariána, which, from the troubled state of the times, had for some years acknowledged no master. His first efforts against Kanhori were unsuccessful, but persevering in his attacks, he eventually reduced it to submission, and with it the south of the province fell into his hands. In the north the Raja of Patiyála and the Bhatís held out for some time ; but by the close of the cold weather, Thomas had extended his authority as far as the river Sarsúti, and included the important towns of Hánsi, Hissár, Mahím and Tuhána amongst his possessions. He selected Hánsi as the capital of his State, rebuilt the walls and fort, established a mint, cannon foundry, and a manufactory of powder and small arms. To attach his soldiers to his service he granted pensions to the wounded, and to the families of those who perished in battle he allowed half the pay drawn by the deceased. It was his desire to put himself in a capacity, when a favourable opportunity should offer, of attempting the conquest of the Panjáb, and he aspired to the honour of planting the British standard " on the banks of the Attock (Indus)." One of his first expeditions was in conjunction with Váman Rao, the Marhatta Sub-Governor of Bulandshahr, against the Raja of Jaipur. The combined forces were at first successful, and captured the important town of Fatehpur; but the Raja, advancing against them with a levy *en masse*, compelled the Marhattas to retire, and eventually to make peace. Thomas was not much more successful in an attack on Bikanír. Towards the close of 1799, he joined with Ambají Inglia in an expedition against the territories of the Ráná of Udepur, one of the most powerful and important of the Rajpút States. Their object was to expel Lakwá Dádá, the Marhatta commander there, who had joined the Ráná, and acted in opposition to Sindhia's orders in regard to his predecessor's widows, the Báís. In this expedition, chiefly through Thomas's skill, they were successful.

Whilst engaged in Udepur, the enemies of Thomas were not slow to take **Combination against him.** advantage of his absence to invade Hariána; and, with the usual duplicity evinced by those in power, especially amongst the Marhattas, the foremost amongst his assailants was Ambájí, his own colleague, and General Perron, the Marhatta commander in the Duáb. Both concluded that as Lakwá Dáda had fallen in battle, and Holkar's force was completely defeated at Indúr, there was no further need for Thomas's services, and that his growing power would make him a formidable enemy in the event of his interests ever clashing with theirs. Thomas, however, proceeded on his way as if nothing had happened, and the invasion of the Sikhs, and other matters requiring prompt attention on the part of Perron, becoming more pressing, Thomas and his possessions were for a time saved. During this interval of rest, Thomas employed himself in arranging the affairs of Bikanír and Jodhpur, and at the same time he made occasional excursions into the Duáb. His own towns, too, often occupied his whole attention, and more than once he was obliged to sit down and regularly invest Bhawáni, Jamálpur, and others places.

Perron at length took the field against Thomas, with a force of ten battalions of infantry, six thousand horse, a body of Rohillas, and sixty pieces of heavy artillery. **Perron attacks him.** A portion of this force, under Captain Smith, invested Georgegarh, a small fort built by Thomas near Jájhar, and another, under a Mr. Lewis, advanced on Mahím. Thomas succeeded in raising the siege of Georgegarh, and defeated Captain Smith, with the loss of his ammunition and baggage ; and again, in a battle fought near Bairi, he routed the combined forces of Perron, Smith and Lewis, with a loss to the enemy of 2,000 men and thirty pieces of artillery, and a loss on his own side of 700 men, and twenty pieces of artillery rendered unfit for future service.   Perron, dismayed at this defeat, made every effort to collect reinforcements from all sides.   From Sahâranpur came the forces of Bápú Sindhia ; from the west a number of Sikh chieftains who had long felt the power of Thomas to be a bar to their plundering expeditions ; Meerut furnished a contingent under the Gújar Rajas Ramdayál and Nain Singh ; from Aligarh came the Háthras and Mursán Rajas ; Colonel Hessing came from Agra ; and from the south the Ját ruler of Bhartpur joined the confederate camp-with a large following.   Thirty thousand men, and a train of one hundred and ten pieces of artillery, now surrounded Thomas on all sides, and so overawed the peasantry of the neighbourhood, that they ceased to bring him in supplies.   Many of his own officers, whose families resided within the districts in the occupation of the enemy, were bought over, and carried with them the troops under their command. Conspicuous amongst these were Shitáb Khán, the commandant of Georgegarh, and Khairát Khán, the subahdár of his first

Defeat and death.   matchlock regiment.   Unable to meet the enemy in the field, Thomas cut his way through their midst, and succeeded in reaching Hánsi ; but here, too, treachery was rife, and he was eventually compelled to yield up the fort, and, with the escort of one battalion of sepoys, crossed the English frontier in January, 1802, and proceeded thence towards Calcutta.   He only reached as far as Bahrámpur, where he died on the 22nd August, and was buried in the English cemetery.

Thus closed the career of one of the most remarkable men amongst the many

His character.   that appeared during the troublous times preceding the advent of the British.   It was his fixed intention, after consolidating his possessions about Hánsi, to invade the Panjáb and plant his standard on the Indus.   This he resolved to accomplish by a fleet of boats, constructed from timber procured in the forests near Firozpur on the Satlaj, by means of which, proceeding down the river with his army, and settling the districts he might subdue on his way, he hoped to reduce the whole country within one or two years.   At the same time he offered his services, his territory, and his army to the British, detailing his plans, and declaring that he had nothing in view but " the welfare of his king and country."   In the words of his biographer[1] and friend—" Upon the whole, however, we may be justified in remarking that, on a review of the life and actions of this very extraordinary man, it is difficult which most to admire, whether the intrepidity of spirit by which he was incited to the performance of actions which, by their effect,

[1] Francklin's Memoir of George Thomas, London, 1805, p. 338.

raised him from the condition of a private subject to rank and distinction among princes, or the wonderful and uncommon attachment generally exhibited towards his person by natives of every description, who fought and conquered with him in his long and arduous career, and whose assistance exalted him for a time to a height of respectability and consequence that seldom falls to the lot of an individual."

I have already brought down the history of the Sardhana fief to the year *Further history of the* 1787 A.D. In that year the Begam was joined by *Sardhana fief.* George Thomas, who remained in her service until the year 1792. During this time the Begam obtained great influence in the imperial councils ; and, endowed by nature with masculine intrepidity and a correct judgment, she was able to hold her own country and preserve her authority unimpaired under the successive administrations of Najf Khan, Mirza Shafi and Afrásyab Khan. When Sindhia in 1785 became supreme, he added to her possessions certain parganahs on the western bank of the Jumna ; and such confidence had he in her ability and integrity, that in the war with Jaipur he committed to her charge the important station of Pánipat. When Ghulám Kádir invested Dehli, in 1787, the Begam at once marched to the assistance of the Emperor, and, declining all overtures from the rebel, resolutely compelled him to withdraw across the Jumna. Here a reconciliation was patched up between Shah Alam and Ghulám Kádir, and the Rohilla departed to his own country. In 1788, the Begam's troops, as we have already seen, distinguished themselves at the siege of Gokalgarh and in the capture of Meerut. Early in 1792, the Begam began to show a partiality for M. LeVaisseau, or LeVassont as he is also called, a young Frenchman of birth, talents and great pride of character, who had been for some time in her service, which ended in his marrying[1] the Begam privately, in order to bring the corps under his own command. George Thomas at once sent in his resignation and entered the Marhatta service, whilst *LeVaisseau.* LeVaisseau set about to reform his turbulent troops. But not content with the work he had to do at home, he must needs intrigue against Thomas, who was then employed in reducing the districts contiguous to the Begam's trans-Jumna possessions. Thomas retaliated by plundering the Begam's parganahs. In 1793 the Begam, in concert with the Marhatta Governor of Dehli, sent a force to watch Thomas, who retired to Tijára. The Begam then went so far as to bribe the Marhatta officers to advise his dismissal ; and a body of Marhattas having joined her army, she marched from Sardhana to Thomas's new district of Jhájhar. Her force then consisted of four battalions of infantry, 20 pieces of artillery, and about 400 cavalry, whilst Thomas had only 2,000 men, with ten guns and 700 cavalry. It was no secret that the expedition was intended to act against Thomas ;

---

[1] The Begam then added the name of Nobilis to Johanna.

but events now took place, which not only induced the Begam to relinquish her intention of attacking Thomas, but ended in the total subversion of her authority for the time.

There was at this time in the Begam's employ a native of Liege, only known

The Liegeois' revolt.

by his nick name of Liegeois, who had been for many years an intimate friend of Thomas, and on the present occasion used all his endeavours to bring about a reconciliation. His conduct was highly displeasing to LeVaisseau, who used his influence with the Begam to procure the Liegeois' degradation; and to make his disgrace more mortifying, the place was given to a junior officer, a creature of LeVaisseau's. The soldiers, ever ready for mutiny, sided with the Liegeois, and resolved to effect the downfal of both the Begam and LeVaisseau, who, owing to the privacy with which the marriage ceremony was performed, was looked upon as her paramour. They invited Zafaryáb Khán, the son of the late Sumru, from Dehli, to become their commander. This young man, who has been characterised by a contemporary as " a compound of ignorance, cruelty and debauchery," consented to join the conspiracy, on condition that the deputation sent by the army to invite him should take an oath of fidelity to him on the spot. Having sworn allegiance to their new leader, the rebel troops, with Zafaryáb Khán at their head, proceeded, in May, 1795, towards Sardhana, to which place the Begam and her husband had fled on hearing of the negotiations at Dehli.

Whether from jealousy, satiety, or some other cause, the Begam herself

Death of LeVaisseau.

now became as anxious to get rid of her husband as she had formerly been to obtain the sanction of the Church to her passion for him. The rational explanation of her conduct on this occasion would, however, appear to be the discovery that LeVaisseau was unfitted by temperament to manage the unruly body of troops that she was obliged to entertain. To accomplish her purpose, she is said to have got up the revolution that we have just noticed, representing to her husband that a plan had been laid for murdering both herself and him, and seizing on the *jáyír;* and urged him, thereupon, to collect all the treasure that could readily be transported, and by flight save both their lives and a portion of their wealth. Having thus far succeeded, she extorted from her intended victim a vow, in which she joined, to the effect that, in case of her flight being intercepted, each party should, by death, secure escape from the probable consequences; and to enable her to effect this, should it become necessary, the lady, as well as her husband, carried arms. All arrangements being perfected, the fugitives, with their treasure, departed under the cover of night; but scarcely had they passed the boundary of her own *jágír,* than they encountered a party of troops, placed in the position which they occupied by order of the Begam. Resistance and recourse to flight seemed alike hopeless, and the report of a pistol from the Begam's *pálki,* followed by loud cries from her attendants, assured the husband that his wife had performed her share in their mutual agreement. Portions of her garments, stained with blood, were exhibited to confirm the impression, and, under the influence of terror, more probably than of conscientious regard for his pledge, the entrapped victim followed the supposed example of his wife, and with a pistol terminated his life.

Of the actual occurrence of this catastrophe there is no reason to doubt; but the circumstances attending it are so differently related, that there is much difficulty in ascertaining the real facts. The story, as told by Mundy and Bacon, is given above.[1] George Thomas's biographer[2] relates that the Begam and her husband were cut off in their intended flight into British territory at the village of Karwa, close to Sardhana, and that the troops who were with her were promised a free pardon and their arrears of pay on condition of their laying down their arms and giving up the Begam and her husband. In the confusion that arose, and before any resolution could be taken, some shots were fired and a few men were slightly wounded. The soldiers, perceiving they had nothing to hope from the Begam, openly declared themselves for Sumru's son. The infantry then surrounded her palanquin, and demanded her surrender: the cavalry at the same time surrounded her husband who was on horseback. The Begam at that instant drew a poniard from her side, and running the point of it across her breast, drew a little blood, but with no intention of killing herself. Her attendants called for assistance, and LeVaisseau hearing the tumult, demanded to know what had happened. He was answered that the Begam had killed herself. Twice he put the same question, and twice he received the same answer, on which he deliberately shot himself in the mouth.

Thomas's account.

Sleeman, who had particularly good opportunities for ascertaining the real facts of the case, whilst repeating the story of the compact between the husband and wife ",that neither should survive the other," describes the actual occurrence as follows :—" They had got three miles on the road to Meerut, when they found the battalions gaining fast upon the palanquin. LeVaisseau drew a pistol from his holster, and urged on the bearers. He could easily have galloped off and saved himself, but he would not quit his wife's side. At last the soldiers came up close behind them. The female attendants on the Begam began to scream, and, looking into the litter, LeVaisseau saw the white cloth covered with blood. The Begam had stabbed herself, but the dagger had struck against one of the bones of her chest, and she had not courage to repeat the blow. Her husband put the pistol to his temple and fired. The ball passed through his head, and he fell dead to the

Sleeman's account.

---

[1] Bacon's First Impressions, II, 41; Mundy's Sketches, I, 371, as quoted by Thornton.
[2] Francklin's life of Thomas, 59.

ground." On the evidence, as a whole, this may be accepted as the most correct account; and subsequent events would seem to corroborate the opinion that the Begam was not in league with the mutineers. Thomas's account gives no support to the contrary opinion; and had he believed the Begam guilty, he would probably have mentioned his belief to his biographer.

On the death of LeVaisseau, "the villains," says Thomas, "who, the preceding day, had styled themselves his slaves, now committed every act of insult and indignity upon his corpse." For three days it lay exposed to the insults of the rabble, and was at length thrown into a ditch. The Begam herself was carried back to the fort, and stripped of all her property and tied to a gun, and would here have perished of starvation and exposure had she not been attended to by a faithful servant, who supplied all her wants. Released from her terrible position by the good offices of M. Saleur, a gentleman of her army, the Begam was still kept in confinement. Here she found means to communicate with George Thomas, and implored him to assist in her release, promising any sum that the Marhattas would demand if again reinstated in her *jágír*. On receipt of these letters, Thomas, by an offer of £12,000, prevailed on Bápú Sindhia, the Marhatta Governor of the Upper Duáb, to march towards Sardhana; and in the meantime Thomas himself intrigued with the mutineers, and finding a party amongst them favourable to the restoration, advanced to within a few miles of Sardhana with his own troops. To assist him in his negotiations, he sent a message, proclaiming that he was come by order of the Marhatta chief to reinstate the Begam. This proceeding had the desired effect. A portion of the troops mutinied, and confined Zafaryáb Khán; but before Thomas could arrive he was again released. Thomas, ignorant of this change in affairs, advanced with a slender escort of only fifty horse, directing his infantry to follow. Zafaryáb Khán, perceiving his opportunity, ordered an attack upon Thomas; but before this could be carried out, the infantry arrived, and the mutineers, thinking the whole Marhatta army was upon them, broke and fled. The Begam was then brought out from her confinement and restored to power, whilst Zafaryáb Khán, stripped of all his property, was reconducted as a prisoner to Dehli, where he died in 1803, and was buried beside his father in the Agra grave-yard.

The Begam paid a portion of the sum stipulated for her release to Bápú Sindhia, and promised the remainder. With the aid of George Thomas she arranged her affairs once more, and gave the command of the troops to M. Saleur, an old Frenchman, who had been in the corps since its first formation. Thomas describes the Begam at this time as small in stature, but inclined to be plump. Her complexion was fair; eyes—black, large, and animated. She adopted the Hindústáni costume made of the most costly materials. She spoke both Persian and Urdú, and in

The Begam restored by Thomas.

The Begam at home.

her conversation was engaging, sensible, and spirited. Her house was well built, and furnished partly in the European and partly in the Hindústáni style ; but she always followed the customs of the country, and never appeared out of doors or in her public darbár unveiled. Her officers presented themselves in front of the place where she sat, which was separated from the public rooms by a screen, and here she gave audience and transacted business of all kinds. She frequently admitted to her table the higher ranks of European officers, but natives never came within the enclosure. On dinner being announced, twenty or thirty of her female attendants, most of whom were Christians, carried in the plates and dishes, and waited on the guests during the repast.

The darker side of the Begam's character is shown by the story of the slave

      Murder of the slave girl's murder. By some it is said that the girl's crime
      girl.   consisted in her having attracted the favourable notice of one of the Begam's husbands. Whatever may have been the offence, her barbarous mistress visited it by causing the girl to be buried alive. The time chosen for the execution was the evening, the place the tent of the Begam ; who caused her bed to be arranged immediately over the grave, and occupied it until the morning, to prevent any attempt to rescue the miserable girl beneath. By acts like this the Begam inspired such terror, that she was never afterwards troubled with domestic dissensions. She augmented her troops to six battalions in 1797-98, and we next find them fighting on Sindhia's side against the English in 1802. Five battalions marched to the Dakhin, and one remained at Sardhana. At the battle of Asái, the Sardhana troops, under M. Saleur, lost one battalion and four guns. After the fall of Dehli, the Begam made submission to the British Government, and to the end of her life remained faithful to their interests. In 1825 she showed her loyalty by leading her troops in person to assist the British at Bhartpur (Bhurtpore). She died in the early part of 1836. The description of the Begam's possessions and their history being purely local, will be found under the Meerut District.

Mention has been made of the disciplined corps entertained by Sindhia ; and

      DeBoigne.   as the subjugation of the Duáb was principally due to their presence in the Marhatta army, this seems the proper place to give some account of the regular corps in the service of the native princes that have been employed in the Duáb. Sumru's brigade has already been noticed at length, from its having been connected for so many years with the Meerut District, but it never had the preponderating influence or the notoriety of DeBoigne's brigade.[1] Benoit DeBoigne was by birth a Savoyard, and at an early age entered the Sardinian army. This he exchanged

---

[1] Captain Lewis Ferdinand Smith, a Major in DeBoigne's corps, Captain Francklin and Captain Duff, who were all personally acquainted with DeBoigne, are the principal authorities for these notes.

for the Irish Brigade in France, and finally for the Russian service. He was taken prisoner in the war between Turkey and Russia, and sold as a slave by his Turkish captor. His parents procured his ransom, and he again visited Russia, where he obtained a command in the Greek archipelago. Here he met an English nobleman (Lord Percy), who gave him letters of introduction to Lord Macartney, then Governor of Madras, and Mr. Hastings, then in Bengal. In 1780 A.D. De Boigne came to Madras, and after some service there, proceeded to Bengal, where he was cordially received by Mr. Hastings, and obtained letters of introduction to the Resident at Lucknow. In 1783, De Boigne arrived in Lucknow, where he received a considerable present from the Nawáb. He then went to Agra, and entered the Raja of Jaipur's service. This came to the ears of Mr. Hastings, who immediately ordered DeBoigne to return to Calcutta. De-Boigne obeyed with alacrity, and so ingratiated himself with the Governor, that he was allowed to return to Lucknow, where he set up as a cloth merchant, with considerable success.

From Lucknow DeBoigne again went to Agra in 1784, with Major Browne,
DeBoigne enters Sindhia's service. the British envoy to the Dehli court, and there began to turn his attention to military affairs. He found that the Ráná of Gohad was at this time closely besieged by the Marhattas under Madhojí Sindhia, and communicated a plan to the Ráná for the relief of the fort of Gohad, which evinced much military skill, and which might eventually have been successful had not the correspondence been discovered by Sindhia. DeBoigne, disappointed at this untoward circumstance, was in despair ; but what seemed to be so prejudicial to him was in reality the foundation of all his subsequent fortunes. Sindhia was so pleased with the talent and boldness shown in the plan formed by DeBoigne, that he consulted Mr. Anderson, the British Resident at his Court, in regard to taking DeBoigne into his service. The result of this was that DeBoigne obtained the command of two battalions in Sindhia's service, to be raised by himself and to be disciplined according to European tactics. These troops were attached to the force commanded by Appákandi Rao, the Marhatta chief who subsequently gave George Thomas his first command. DeBoigne's battalions participated in all the early conquests of Madhují Sindhia in Hindustán and were chiefly instrumental in gaining the battles of Chaksána and Agra in 1785 and 1786, and the battle of Lálsot in 1788.[1] Sindhia was so pleased with this success, that he ordered DeBoigne to increase his battalions, first to ten, and subsequently to sixteen, with a train of one hundred guns. This was completed in 1790; and shortly afterwards the newly-raised force was engaged in the bloody battle of Pátan Tanwar in the

---

[1] The Marhattas under DeBoigne, and the Játs under M. Lestonneaux, were defeated by the Mughals, under Ismaíl Beg, and the Rohillas, under Ghulám Kádir, at Cháksu, about five kos from Bhartpur, April 24, 1788.

Shaikháwáti country (20th June), fought against the Rahtors of Jaudhpur, who had been joined by Ismail Beg. The battle was a long and bloody one, and the enemy lost seventy pieces of cannon. They fled thence to Pípar in Jaudhpur, where another force of Rahtors were collected, and here again DeBoigne's forces were victorious (September 12th), in the equally severe battle of Mairtha.

In 1792, at Lákhairi Ghát, in the Búndi country, DeBoigne's sepoys met a similar force, raised and disciplined by the Chevalier Dudrenec, then in the service of Takúji Holkar.

Services of the brigades.

DeBoigne's troops were again successful, and Dudrenec was obliged to retreat, with the loss of nearly all his officers. The result of this battle was that Sindhia became supreme in Hindústán. At Kánand, in the Mewati country, DeBoigne's brigades defeated the combined forces of Najf Kuli Khán's widow and of Ismail Beg. In 1793 DeBoigne received an assignment of lands valued at £160,000 a year, for the support of his troops, and he then formed the third brigade. By this act he made many enemies, and when his old master died, Daulut Rao Sindhia, who succeeded to power, no longer gave him the cordial support that he had hitherto received. In addition to this, his health began to fail, and he was anxious to return to his own country. He accordingly made arrangements to leave the Duáb in December, 1795, and reached Calcutta, whence he embarked for Europe. He settled down at Chamberi, in his native country, and lived there a long and useful life. Tod, Duff, Francklin, and others of our old writers on Indian history, visited him in his retreat, and there learned, from his own mouth, the particulars of his eventful life which have come down to us.

DeBoigne's description of his brigades is worth transcribing :—" Each consisted of ten battalions of 750 men each, seven of which were regulars, known as *talingas*, clothed and armed like the troops in the service of the East India Company. The remaining three were Patháns, armed with matchlocks manufactured at Agra. The whole brigade was manœuvred by word of command. To each brigade was attached a force of 500 Mewatís for camp duties, 500 cavalry for patrols, and sixty well-mounted field pieces from 3 to 6 and 9-pounders. A supplementary force of 1,000 Rohillas was subsequently added to lead storming parties." According to his friend and comrade, Smith, De Boigne was a fair Latin scholar, and read and wrote English, French and Italian with ease and fluency. He had a good knowledge of the current literature of the day, and in conversation was polite, affable, pleasant, humorous and vivacious. "He was elegant in his manners, resolute in his determinations, and firm in his measures." To the subtlety of the Italian he added experience gained in every school of life, and proved himself more than an equal match for Eastern politicians. He approached power in disguise, and only showed his real designs when too strong to be resisted. In the Duáb he was dreaded and idolised, feared and respected, admired and beloved. His name was enough to put down armed resistance; and from the time of his assumption of authority there were no more revolts in the portion of the Duáb under his charge. It is said that Najf Kuli Khán, on his deathbed, gave this parting advice to his courageous wife — " Resist, but if DeBoigne attacks you, yield.".

His administration of justice was a fair medium between relaxation and severity, and in the conduct of business he was indefa-

His daily life.

tigable. A writer[1] in the *Telegraph* newspaper, in a letter, dated Agra, January 2, 1797, says of him— " I have seen him (DeBoigne) daily and monthly rise with the sun, survey his *kárkhána*, review his troops, enlist recruits, direct the vast movements of three brigades, raise resources, and encourage manufactures for their arms, ammunition and stores, harangue in the darbár, give audience to ambassadors, administer justice, regulate the civil and revenue affairs of a *jágir* of twenty lakhs of rupees, listen to a multitude of letters from various parts, on various important matters, dictate replies, carry on an intricate system of intrigue in different courts, superintend a private trade of lakhs of rupees, keep his accounts, his private and public correspondence, and direct and move forward a most complex political machine. All this he did without an European assistant, for he is very diffident in placing his confidence, and extremely cautious in bestowing his trust. He used to say that any ambitious person who reposes confidence in another, risks the destruction of his views. Such was his laborious occupation from sunrise until past midnight, and this was not the fortuitous avocation of a day, but the unremitting employment of nine or ten years. To this exhausting and unceasing toil he sacrificed one of the firmest and most robust constitutions which ever nature formed to bless mankind. He left his station with accumulated diseases, extinguished health, and a debilitated frame, but with the poor comparative recompence of uncommon fame, and a splendid fortune of £400,000. In his person he was above six feet high, giant-boned, large-limbed, strong-featured, and with piercing eyes. There was something in his countenance which depicts the hero, and compels us to yield implicit obedience. In his deportment he was commanding, and he trod with the majestic step of conscious greatness. DeBoigne, luminous as he was, had his shades ; and great as he appears, had his foibles and little weaknesses ;—he was avaricious to a degree verging on contempt, exceedingly tenacious of power, greedy of authority, meanly jealous of merit in those under him, and unworthily envious; but where is perfection ? Every officer and soldier when wounded received a certain present, in proportion to his wound, from fifteen days' to three or four months' pay, without any stoppage of pay during the time of his cure. The disabled of his army had a pension for life to the amount of half

---

[1] Captain L. F. Smith, of the Marhatta service.

their pay, and lands besides ; and the relations of the killed and of those who died of their wounds, got the property of the deceased."

At the departure of DeBoigne there were three brigades,—one at Poona, under the command of M. Perron ; one at Koil, under M. Pedrons ; and one at Muttra, under Major Sutherland. DeBoigne neither nominated nor recommended a successor, but Perron, being at Poona, obtained the command for himself. It is said that DeBoigne's parting advice to Sindhia was never to give the control of all these brigades to one person ; and that to his successor was embodied in the clause that he introduced into his own written agreement with Sindhia—" never to fight with the English." Perron came out to India in the *Sardine*, a French frigate, in 1774, as a common sailor. Deserting thence he entered the service of several of the partisan leaders in different parts of India, and in 1789 received a commission from DeBoigne. Perron was a man of great courage, activity and industry. His attention to his duty and his personal bravery at Kanond, in 1792, induced DeBoigne to promote him to a majority ; and in 1793 he was sent in charge of the first brigade to the Dakhin. He returned to Koil as Commander-in-Chief of the Duáb forces in February, 1797.

M. Perron.

The revenue of De Boigne's districts in the Duáb had risen under his care from sixteen to over twenty lakhs of rupees a year. Perron not only received these, but added to them on all sides. He arranged and pursued a systematic plan for the aggrandisement of his possessions and fortune, and in this was so successful, that in a short time the entire country from Lahor to Kota, and from Jaudhpur to Koil, acknowledged his authority. The principal obstacles to his attaining undivided influence in the Marhatta empire were Tantia Pagnavís, Lakhwa Dáda and George Thomas. The first was taken prisoner and died by poison ; Lakhwa Dáda fell in 1801, after the fight at Datiya ; and George Thomas, as we have seen, succumbed to the united battalions of all Perron's contingents, now raised to four brigades, at the close of the same year. Perron's revenues at the beginning of 1802 amounted to more than forty-one lakhs of rupees a year, from sixty-eight parganahs. At the same time a cloud began to gather in the west, and at the risk of the safety of his power, and even of his life, Perron was obliged to visit the Marhatta camp at Ujain, where he arranged matters for the time by a liberal use of money. Sindhia in the meantime was preparing to assist the Peshwa and attack Holkar, and asked for a second brigade from Perron, who, though he risked the independence, and even the existence of the Marhatta empire, delayed for his own sake for three months to send the reinforcement asked for, and then only despatched his newly-raised fourth brigade. Even this force arrived too late, as the British had already stepped in and restored the Peshwa, who had thrown himself into

Perron's administration.

Perron retires.

their hands. This so alarmed the Marhattas, that, laying aside their mutual jealousies, the Berar Raja, Holkar and Sindhia, united for a time against the English, and resolved to carry out a plan of campaign drawn up by Perron, who advised their active alliance for this purpose. But before anything could be done in pursuance of their agreement, quarrels again broke out. Holkar withdrew himself from the confederacy, and Sindhia, resolving to supersede Perron, bestowed the command of the Duáb on Ambáji. Perron found his fourth brigade, under Dudrenec, ready to desert him. Bourquien had induced the second and third brigades to revolt, and had even written to the commanders of the irregular horse at Koil to encompass the death of Perron. Knowing all this, Perron only made a half-hearted resistance at Koil, and fled by Háthras to Muttra, where he surrendered to Lord Lake, and proceeded thence by Calcutta to Europe.

Bourquien, who commanded at Dehli, was put under restraint by his own troops, who met the British on the road between Aligarh and Dehli, where the Marhattas were completely defeated on the 11th September, 1803. The Prince Akbar, who had succeeded to the position of heir-apparent since the death of his eldest brother Jawán Bakht at Benares, in 1788, came out to meet the British Commander-in-Chief, and conducted him into the city, where he was received by the blind and aged emperor. The treaty with Sindhia, dated Surje Anjangaum, 30th December, 1803, ceded to the British all the forts, territories and rights held by the Marhattas in the Duáb and the countries to the north of the territories of the Rajas of Jaipur and Jaudhpur, and the Rana of Gohad.

Though the war with Sindhia was thus brought to a successful termination in 1803, Holkar, in the following year, renewed hostilities; and, having been joined by the Játs of Bhartpur, sent a considerable force to invest Dehli, which was then in possession of a British garrison under the celebrated General Ochterlony. In 1804, Lord Lake collected stores and supplies, and set out by Muttra for Dehli. On his way he drove out Ghulámi Khán, who had been plundering the Aligarh District; and Holkar retired from Muttra at the approach of the British force. Holkar's light troops accompanied the army, and hovered on the flanks all day, cutting off stragglers, whilst at night they always encamped out of reach.

Near Dehli, Holkar branched off and crossed into the Duáb near Bágpat; thence he proceeded northwards by Sardhana and Shámli; but on being pursued by Lord Lake, left the latter place on the 3rd November, and presented himself before Fatehgarh. The civil officers retired into the fort, which, with the old cantonments, were preserved; but the cavalry lines and new cantonments, which lay beyond the ravines, and were therefore beyond the line of defence taken up by the troops, were burned by

War with Holkar.

Holkar's raid.

Holkar. Here he was surprised by General Lake on the 17th of November, and, in the words of his own historian, " was totally defeated, with great slaughter," and retreated across the Jumna into Bhartpur territory, where he was joined by Amír Khán, the Pindara leader.

On the 7th February, 1805, Amír Khán crossed the Jumna at the Mahában ghát, with a body of horse lightly equipped, intending to create a diversion in the British rear. He plundered Gokal and relieved Kamona in the Aligarh District, then held by Dúndi Khan. Thence he passed up the Duáb by Púth in the Meerut District, and crossing the Ganges at Kumr-ud-dínnagar, caused some disturbance in Rohilkhand. Driven thence by General Smith and Skinner's horse, he re-entered the Duáb at the same point, and rejoined Holkar's force before Bhartpur on the 21st March, 1805, after an absence of six weeks. General Smith followed two days afterwards. The peace of this tract was never again seriously disturbed until the outbreak of the mutiny in 1857.

The mutiny narratives of the Meerut Division abound with instances of firm devotion and unflinching bravery. As they are given in some detail under each district, it will be necessary here to make only some few general remarks on the mutiny in this division as a whole, and this cannot be better done than by giving Mr. Fleetwood Williams' summary of the origin and progress of the rebellion in the Meerut Division.[1] He writes—" That the rebellion had been planned by the Musalmáns, I have no doubt. It is not the province of a local officer to trace this, but one or two indications may be mentioned. Though there was no apparent sympathy, the idea of the restoration of the Musalmán religion to power has been repeatedly kept alive. Invitations to join in a war against infidels, emanating from the Swát country, have circulated through the upper part of Hindústán. The anxiety of the Rohilkhand Patháns, particularly the members of the family of Háfiz Rahmat Kháu, that Government should not suffer anarchy and oppression to continue in Oudh, but should interfere and introduce the just administration with which they were blessed, seemed at the time to be the loyal desires of enlightened men. Late events show that they anticipated the long-hoped-for opportunity which the cry of annexation and the decreased importance of the native soldiers in Oudh, under British rule, afforded. The march of the mutineers from Meerut to the arrival at Dehli might be the policy of soldiers, but the re-exaltation of the Múghal king, and the immediate submission of the Hindu sepoys to the head of the Musalmáns, had a deeper source. The recorded conversation, in March, 1857, of the Bijnaur Nawáb and his friends— 'Is there any security now for Islám?' and that ' Islám was form-

Amír Khán's raid.

Mutiny.

---

[1] Narrative of Events, 406 of 1858, dated November 16, 1858, paras. 425, et seq., by F. Williams, C.S.I., of the Civil Service, Commissioner of Meerut.

erly the dominant religion,' is a specimen of the movement among the Muhammadans. An earlier conversation than this could be traced, I believe, between one of the family of Háfiz Rahmat Khán and a Rajpút in Rohilkhand, in or about December, 1856, when the Pathán ·recommended the Thákur to · look to his weapons, as he would be wanting them soon.

· "The tone of the Muhammadan portion of the native press, and the readiness with which, not the impoverished and discontented only, but the well-to-do Muhammadans in every rank and station staked their all upon the issue, and, with few exceptions, joined in rebellion ; their extraordinary association with ' idolators' to exterminate ' the children of the book,' in opposition to the laws of their prophets, and the *fatwahs* of the few Maulvís who dared to speak out ; even the exceptional loyalty of that portion of the Muhammadans whose views on the matter of proselytism· differ from those of the majority ; the happily unavailing endeavours of ·the Muhammadan leaders to make the mass of the population join them ; and the bitter complaints of the Hindu mutineers, that they had been deeply deceived ; all these indicate that, though a spirit of mutiny may have prepared the native army, the real movers were·Muhammadans. Even at Meerut the first move was made by Muhammadans. A

Outbreak at Meerut.

Hindu said he had fired off the new cartridges, and that all would have to do it. But two Muhammadans spread the story about cow's and pig's fat being used in greasing the cartridges, saying that all would be polluted ; that it did not so much matter for the Muhammadans, since they could · remove the pollution, but the Hindús would irrecoverably lose caste ; and at the instigation of these Muhammadans, the troopers of both sects bound themselves by an oath not to use them. There is no doubt that all the native soldiers retired from the parade when their comrades were disgraced, muttering ' mutiny.' The rumours that the Europeans were coming to seize the magazine, which issued from the Suddur Bazar, and on which the sepoys rushed to arms, may have been an accident or mistake. But that there were secret agents, and those Muhammadans, watching, if not guiding events, it seems impossible in this part of the country to doubt.

" The mutiny was apparently unpremeditated, yet the Suddur Bazar people

General disloyalty of the Musalmáns.

were ready before a shot was fired in Cantonments. The outbreak immediately assumed a Muhammadan character ; a holy war against the infidels (the Europeans and Christians) was proclaimed ; and eventually, in the Upper Duáb and in Rohilkhand, the mass of the Muhammadan population rose against Government. I believe that in Rohilkhand the Nawáb of Rámpur, and a few of his own trusted friends, and the Nawáb's own trusted personal attendants ; in Bijnaur, the Deputy Collector and Sadr Amín ; Wiláyat Husain Khán in Moradabad ; the family of Hakím

Khán and Bashír Khán in Pilibhít; Muhammad Nur Khán in Sháhjahánpur, and a few Governmemt officials, were the only Musalmáns who from the first stood out for Government.

In Saháranpur it was remarked that the extensive risings were attributed entirely to the influential Muhammadans. In Muzaffarnagar is a class of Sayyids who do not go the lengths Muhammadans generally do in matters of proselytism by the sword. These Sayyids even were warned, but their loyalty was happily fixed by remonstrances conveyed to them by some of their headmen; and though in this district the Muhammadans were late in rising against Government, eventually a vast multitude gathered under the ' green flag,' and displayed the bitterest animosity,—massacreing in their mosque men of their own religion, after the most solemn promises of safety, because they were faithful to their rulers. In Meerut, though there were some good exceptions, Muhammadans were generally ill-disposed, and most joined in the rebellion. In the whole district of Bulandshahr, I can only bring to mind one exception, that of the family[1] of Murád Ali Khán, of Chatári and Pahásu, who took the side they had taken in Lord Lake's time,—that of the British Government. Everywhere in this part of the North-Western Provinces, as a general rule, the antagonsim of the Musalmáns showed itself in every place, from the open rebellion of multitudes, to the scowling impertinence of individuals; from the public proclamations of rebel leaders, to the muttered imprecations of bigots in the mosques. The very fact that the few who shone out as loyal subjects or merciful men were stigmatized as Christians, infidels, apostates from the true faith, should show what the belief and feeling of the Indian Musalmán is. There was a marked difference between the conduct of Muhammadans and other rebels in this part of India. The first warred against Government and Europeans, the others plundered. The first, from the beginning and throughout, abstained from injuring the inhabitants of the country, assured them in order to win them to Muhammadan rule, and urged them to join against Government. The plundering tribes, almost the only Hindús who in these parts decidedly and thoroughly misbehaved, turned their hands against every one that had property, —their enemies and creditors first. The Mawai Játs of the Baraut parganah, in the Meerut District, were almost the only Hindús who showed unmitigated disloyalty, and they were urged to it by a notorious bad character, Sáh Mal. The Gújars even were in some instances against us, and sometimes took the side of Government. Vast numbers even of these plundering tribes, who bear Hindu names—Gújars, Rajpúts, Tagas, &c.—are Muhammadans, forced proselytes when the power was paramount in Dehli, and, like all such proselytes, intensely bigoted. It was not a national movement against Government.

---

[1] Converted Hindús of the Badgújar clan.

" With the exception of the immediate neighbourhood of Meerut, it was
generally sometime before Government offices and
Government property were attacked. In Saháranpur,
the towns of Deoband and Nakúr were plundered, and of course the Government offices in them were not exempted. A mob collected to attack the treasury at Saháranpur, but was easily dispersed. These were the only instances in which extensive plundering assumed the type of rebellion. Muzaffarnagar must be treated as an exception. The best disposed populace in this world have been tempted to let loose the innate wickedness of human nature by disappearance of all authority. In Meerut the widely-spread report that all the Europeans had been destroyed (which was not contradicted, as it should have been by their appearance in every direction) ; the uninterrupted passage of the Bareilly mutineer brigade ; the total surrender of the Bulandshahr District to Walidád Khán, who should have been seized by a small force, and hung within three days of his breaking out into open rebellion ; the propinquity of Dehli, and the constant hope of assistance from the mutineer force there ; by which concatenation of circumstances every bad character in the district was encouraged to evil, induced a tendency to rebellion, which was favoured by the retention in the lines of the troops who ought to have been enforcing order and checking insurrection. But even in this and in the Bulandshahr District, till, in the latter, the refusal of aid from Meerut, the approach of mutineers from below, and the hope of rescuing the prisoners that the district officers had made, incited the people to it, the outbreak was characterized by aggressions of the lawless part of the population on the better conditioned,—the prevalence of crime, in consequence of a conviction that authority had ceased, rather than by rebellion against the State. The last offence, as a general rule, spread among the people slowly, as delay at Dehli brought conviction that the British power was passing away, and even then only broke out here and there, when notorious bad characters, flushed by success in plundering, led their followers to greater enterprizes.

Progress of the mutiny.

" The normal state of the ordinary mass of the people, i. e., those not
either Muhammadans or thieves, was waiting events ;
and their conduct depended on the amount of their
good sense or their credulity. There were some who from the first felt that, though the few Englishmen in India might be crushed for the time, an overwhelming British force would come out to reconquer the country and take vengeance on the traitors. These were the few. There were some who believed the false or exaggerated rumours circulated by the rebels, and hastened to separate from the foreigners, and secure favour from the native rulers. These were more in numbers than the first class considerably ; but still the many wavered between the two extremes. But all feared,—all were employed in an anxious

Feelings of the people.

endeavour to ascertain what would be their own individual interest; the unfailing consideration of the natives of Hindústán. This their sole consideration, and cowardice, both moral and physical, made mutineers of half the native army, and a percentage of the population, (the said percentage fluctuating according to circumstances, but never very large,) rebels. Had there been European soldiers and non-commissioned and commissioned officers to the extent of ten per cent. in each native regiment, a nucleus for good men to fall back upon, with a firm front to face the fire of mutineers, half the men of the mutinous regiments would not have gone, and half the regiments in the service would have stood staunch to their duty; but bodily fear and mental weakness, the absence of all principles of the all-controlling sense of duty, and a dastardly dread of being killed, made well-intentioned men follow the majority of their comrades, and peaceable subjects seek safety in disaffection. Those who have lived in the midst of it, and who should be the best judges, cannot but feel that the theory that it was a purely military revolt; and the other, it was a national effort to shake off tyrants, are equally far from the truth. Had not the mass of the people awaited the issue, had any large proportion of them joined, what would have become of the small but gallant bands that in differents part of the country stood out against their active enemies, may be concluded from

		Population.	Troops.
Saháranpur	...	801,325	800
Muzaffarnagar	...	672,661	500
Meerut	...	1,135,072	1,500

Bulandshahr was abandoned, but when the Málágarh rebel was ousted, was held by less than 500, the population being 778,342.

the marginal table, showing in round numbers the population of the districts of this division, and the strength of the troops which maintained Government authority. Neither can people on the spot be persuaded to believe that efforts to Christianize the natives led to rebellion. Had this been the case, how is it that Benares, the largest city in India, to Hindús the holiest, and where Muhammadan bigotry is sharpened by its peculiar position, the place where missionaries have worked more extensively than in any part of India, where the Bible is openly studied and read by hundreds of students in many schools, did not send some of its 180,000 to save the mutineer brigade from the 200 British soldiers.

"Beyond all doubt the secret movers of the revolt disseminated widely the wildest and most false reports that Government was going forcibly to convert the people; and during the outbreak these rumours were spread abroad to such an extent, that many ignorant men believed them, and, when peace was restored, some have stated their readiness to become Christians, and were astonished when told that no man could make another a Christian. But here, round Meerut, where the mutiny commenced, missionaries have been more successful in one year than they had ever been; and I have been told by a native deserving of all confidence, that in Bareilly, Muhammadans and Hindús agreed that to be all of one, and that the

Causes of the mutiny.

Christian religion, would be better than to be exposed to the tyranny of Khán
Bahádur Khán, and his following of miscreants: It is difficult to believe that
the efforts of Government to give education to the people can have caused the
mutiny and rebellion, when in some districts, the only public institutions
maintained during the anarchy, where doctors were driven out, and dispensaries were distroyed, were village schools ; the only public buildings saved were
village school-rooms ; and the people, when asked to account for this, stated their
intentions to have maintained their schools, even if the rule of India had changed
hands. During the outbreak, as far as experience goes, the most loyal,
the most trustworthy, were young men who had received an advanced English
education in the Government institutions. I have known such, of the writer
class, not a fighting race generally, become brave, soldierly men ; I have seen
English letters from such men, the matter and composition of which would
have done credit to any Englishman, written from the midst of fanatic rebels,
conveying full and useful information, openly and boldly given, though the
writer stated he knew he was suspected and watched, and immediate death
would be the certain result of discovery. The only approach to the sense of
duty which has animated Anglo-Saxons through this struggle was to be found
among such educated men.'' I have nothing to add to this account, and the
district narratives will speak for themselves.

The medical history of the division shows a steady increase in sickness of late

Medical history. years, much of which has been traced to preventible
causes, such as bad drainage, bad sanitation, and inat-
tention to the most ordinary precautions for the preservation of health. Taking
the three principal diseases—cholera, small-pox and fever, the following facts
may be gathered from the reports[1] in regard to the frequency and virulence of
their attacks. Cholera broke out in 1867 amongst the pilgrims returning from the
Hardwar fair, and, strange to say, seems to have very generally restricted itself
to those who had been at the fair, and not to have shown itself out of the line of
march of the pilgrims. Though deaths from cholera occur at all times of the
year in almost every district, yet cholera seldom becomes epidemic in the Upper
Duáb. During the epidemic of 1869, the deaths hardly reached more than 0·2
per thousand, whilst in Allahabad and the Benares Divisions, they rose from 2·1
per thousand in Allahabad, up to 10·9 per thousand in Lalitpur. During
this year cholera was absent in the hill districts altogether, and little prevalent
in those lying immediataly under the hills, increasing in intensity to the south.
The actual number of deaths attributed to cholera during 1869, in the five
districts noticed in the present volume, was 1497 ; in 1870 and in 1871 the
numbers were merely nominal ; and in 1872 there was a slight outbreak of cholera

---

[1] Dr. Cutcliffe's report on the sanitation of the Meerut Division, II ; Sel. Rec. Government,
North-Western Provinces, 13 ; Dr. Planck on the same, Reports for 1869—72.

in the Sahāranpur District; but the full force of the epidemic was felt, as before, chiefly in the southern districts.

Small-pox, amongst preventible diseases, carries off more victims than all the

Small-pox.

rest put together, except fever. The deaths recorded from this cause for some years are shown below. In 1868 it can hardly be said to have existed in an epidemic form, though the mortality was so great; but there is no contagion so strong and sure, or so far reaching, as that of small-pox, and perhaps no disease is more fatal. In 1869, the disease was epidemic in several districts, and prevalent in almost all. It seems to commence as an epidemic during the cold-weather, and rages with intensity during March, April and May, after which it gradually subsides with the seting in of the rains. The Upper Duāb and Rohilkhand, in exchange for their practical immunity from cholera, have, by comparison, almost a monopoly of small-pox, which is not nearly so prevalent in the cholera districts of the Lower Duāb and the Benares Division. From 1870 to 1872, the upper districts suffered excessively when compared with any other district except Basti. The vaccination statistics and details are shown under the district notices.

It is to fever, however, that the greatest mortality is due, and inquiries

Fevers.

go to show that the deaths from fevers have gone on in an increasing ratio for several years. In 1867 the attention of Government was called to the abnormal proportion of deaths attributed to this disease in the Meerut Division, and Dr. Cutcliffe was appointed as Sanitary Commissioner to inquire into the causes, and propose a remedy. Doctor Planck was employed on similar duty during subsequent years. Before making use of their remarks, I will give a comparative table, for all five districts, of the causes of death for the years for which any statistics exist.

District.	Population in 1865.	DEATHS IN											
		1867 from			1868 from			1869 from			1870 from		
		Small-pox.	Fevers.	All other causes.	Small-pox.	Fevers.	All other causes.	Small-pox.	Fevers.	All other causes.	Small-pox.	Fevers.	All other causes.
Sahāranpur ...	866,483	1,136	5,853	6,463	3,174	7,210	5,316	1,106	11,189	6,004	1,977	19,906	21,883
Muzaffarnagar	682,189	965	5,104	7,697	2,345	4,131	4,174	1,074	10,541	6,475	2,966	16,855	19,821
Meerut ...	1,199,593	914	10,287	8,552	894	8,425	6,035	4,984	9,626	4,611	2,218	20,263	22,481
Bulandshahr	800,481	2,356	4,654	2,877	1,339	5,769	3,064	6,340	6,650	4,095	1,585	11,464	13,049
Aligarh ...	925,538	426	6,086	4,092	1,933	5,662	2,641	6,449	6,668	3,848	518	8,603	9,121
Total ...	4,474,284	5,797	31,984	29,681	10,090	31,197	22,130	19,953	44,676	25,024	9,264	77,091	86,355

District.	Population in 1872.	DEATHS IN 1871 from			1872 from			RATIO OF DEATHS PER 1,000 OF THE POPULATION IN					
								1870.		1871.		1872.	
		Small-pox.	Fevers.	All other causes.	Small-pox.	Fevers.	All other causes.	Fevers.	All other causes.	Fevers.	All other causes.	Fevers.	All other causes.
Saháranpur	890,669	4,441	21,184	4,261	5,296	14,839	6,080	22·97	10·54	24·41	10·05	16·84	12·92
Muzaffarnagar	793,000	4,332	15,507	2,529	1,097	13,794	1,966	24·70	11·75	22·73	10·05	19·59	4·35
Meerut	1,221,454	1,307	28,823	4,773	826	38,209	6,171	16·89	6·52	23·86	5·21	30·04	5·51
Bulandshahr	987,733	444	15,944	4,018	1,048	23,208	5,902	14·32	6·59	19·91	6·33	34·77	7·42
Aligarh	1,057,939	701	12,954	3,683	593	15,307	5,127	9·29	4·31	13·99	4·74	14·47	5·40
Total	4,950,789	11,225	94,412	19,858	8,860	1,05,357	25,246	...	...	...	..	...	...

These figures show conclusively the extent and gravity of the epidemic.

Dr. Kirton, of Muzaffarnagar, pronounces the fever prevalent in the Upper
Duáb to be "a true malarious fever of intermittent
Character of the fever. type,—such a fever, indeed, as is generally attributed
to effluvia arising from alluvial soil saturated by moisture. The attacks were
characterised by distinct paroxysms, consisting of a cold and hot stage, followed
by periods of intermission. The paroxysms mostly occurred daily, but frequently every other day." Dr. J. P. Walker, writing of Rúrki in 1867, calls it
"intermittent fever." Dr. Drysdale, of Her Majesty's 79th Highlanders,
describes the fever that prevailed in his regiment at Rúrki as "intermittent
fever in a spurious form." Dr. Metcalfe, of Saháranpur, says of the fever that
it was "undoubtedly malarious in its character, subject to relapses, but not
often when quinine had been given sufficiently early and in sufficiently large
doses." The fever, as a rule, commences in July-August, and ends about
December. In many cases the protracted fever brought on diarrhœa, which
accompanied nearly all the fatal cases, and might possibly lead to the supposition that typhoid fever either co-existed with malarious fever in some of the
towns, or that the prevailing fever was a hybrid variety between malarious
and typhoid fever. Dr. Cutcliffe,[1] however, thought that all his inquiries pointed
"to a common local cause of origin of the disease, and led strongly to the belief
that the cases which occurred were varieties of one and the same endemic
disease,—malarious fever." Dr. Planck, in 1869-72, gives it the same character.

Besides the deaths due to fever and the utter prostration occasioned by
continuous attacks of the disease, one of its most remarkable effects is the
causing of impotency. Dr. Cutcliffe first pointed this
Impotency and spleen as out in 1867, and expressed his opinion "that impotency
sequelæ. is extraordinarily frequent in the most malarious tracts;"

[1] See his observations on the true character of malaria and effluvia in Sel. Rec. Gov., N.-W. P.
II., N. S. 65.

and, again, " of this fact I convinced myself, by the frequent applications that were made to me, that the men inhabiting the very malarious tracts which I have described are suffering from impotency, to an extent which I have never known or heard of elsewhere." Dr. Planck's attention was specially drawn to the same subject, and he writes—" Concerning the general prevalence of impotency, I am of opinion that that condition is more than usually common in some places of the Saháranpur District, as a result of the general debility arising from repeated fever attacks ; but I do not think it is a condition so common as to threaten to lead to a depopulation of the country. I think this condition exists principally in those who are about to succumb to fever disease, and whose spleens are much enlarged ; but I do not think that, as a rule, it affects men in the prime of life for many years before they die." Still, in 51 villages examined by him in the Saháranpur District alone, he found in four villages that enlargement of the spleen was very common ; that in four villages it was rather common ; in fifteen villages it was common ; and in the remaining villages, thirty-one cases were seen, and this too by an observer marching continuously throughout, and unable to examine others than those voluntarily brought to him, and who happened to be present when he visited their villages. These include both irrigated and unirrigated villages. In eighteen irrigated villages in the Muzaffarnagar District he found enlargement of the spleen—very common, in four villages ; common, in the same number ; uncommon in six : and non-existent in two, in one of which the site was raised and sandy, and in the other the site was low, but here the spring-level was 24 feet from the surface. It is very strange to see that in places where the site was clean there was more mortality than where it was very filthy ; but I frequently notice this remark added—" much stagnant water near." In fifteen unirrigated villages in the same district the returns show—in two cases, no spleen enlargement ; in one case it was very uncommon ; in nine cases, uncommon ; and in only three cases common ; and these three lie within the Nágal khádir, with a spring-level varying from only six to eight feet from the surface. It has been a painful task to go through the records of these fever-stricken villages, and read the constant remarks " many persons afflicted with spleen, especially children ; coughs and ophthalmia common ; a general complaint of sickness was heard here"—" people very unhealthy looking"—" fourteen houses, only two children left, used to have many, now dead"—" paralysis, a result of fever, much complained of, and some cases of it seen"—" one-half the people down with fever in the rains"—" an earnest cry for remedies"—" people in low spirits and despondent." Enough has been said to show that this fever is a serious matter, which, though it carries off only three in every hundred every year, yet so wastes the energies of the survivors, as to render them unable to carry on their work of life as cultivators of the ground. The sub-division of the soil yields little enough to the labour of the man who can work his full tide, but if to this be added the utter prostration of the bread-winner of the family, it needs no words of mine to paint the distress which must ensue in thousands of families amongst the inhabitants of the northern districts of the Upper Duáb.

The fever being of a malarious type is undoubtedly due to the miasma evolved from over-saturation of the soil. In proportion to the intensity of the miasma we have the disease " in the formidable remittent type, and from the slight ague and fever, which scarcely shakes a strong man, to the pukka jungle fever which, if it should not kill outright, will necessitate a prolonged change of climate for the recovery of a body impaired for the remainder of its existence." To the north of the Saháranpur District fever prevailed to a much greater extent in former times,·especially about Kheri and Sakrauda, and along the line to Mohand. The improvement here is undoubtedly due to the clearing of jungle and the extension of cultivation. Lower south the disease may be traced along those places where the drainage lines are naturally slow, or have been impeded by artificial obstructions, such as the canal lines and the railway embankments. The towns and villages along the Ganges Canal, from Manglaur southwards, suffered very much, but many of these, such as Manglaur, Libarheri, Púr, Bhainswál and Jauli, are so filthy, that it is no wonder that they have been frequently attacked by fevers. Dr. Cutcliffe describes them as " reeking with human excrement and filth of every description." Rúrki, too, was unhealthy in 1867, and so also were the tracts along the Kalandar Nadi, Kátha Nadi, Khála, Síla, and Krishni Nadís, all slow streams, running through swampy, ill-drained depressions. The same may be said of parts of the West Kali Nadi, the old bed of the Jumna, the Eastern Jumna Canal, and in the vicinity of these streams and the khádir of the Ganges. All these places, covered with swamp and stagnant water, are prolific sources of malaria, which they must disengage in large quantities. Drainage, and the enforcement of a greater economy in the use of canal water, could to a great extent prevent the evolution of malaria in these tracts. For the khádir of the Ganges and Jumna rivers it has been proposed to plant a belt of trees along the high bank separating them from the uplands, in order to intercept the malaria borne from them by the easterly and westerly winds,—a plan which experience elsewhere has shown to be valuable and feasible. These means, with the supply of the only reliable antidote, quinine, and more attention to conservancy, are the principal remedial measures recommended by Dr. Cutcliffe. The canals form so important a feature in the hydrography of the Duáb, that their influence on the public health demands a separate and more detailed notice.

In 1845 a committee was appointed to report upon the sanitary effects of the canal. The sittings were interrupted by the Sikh war, but were renewed in 1846, and their report was sub-

Causes of the fever.

Influence of the canals on the public health.

mitted to the Governor-General at Rúrki in March, 1847.   In writing on this
subject, Major P. T. Cautley remarks :—" In referring to the low tracts of the
Duáb, and especially to those situated in the Fatehpur District, my attention
has been drawn, during the last two years especially, to an opinion which has
been prevalent, that wherever lines of canal exist in these provinces the germs
of malaria and sickness hold undisputed authority.   Without producing proofs,
that are numerous, that the epidemics which have shown themselves in towns
and villages near the canals have been equally felt at others far removed from
the influence of either canals or of irrigation, it is natural to infer that the
introduction of moisture and excess of vegetation on the surface of countries
which had been comparatively dry before, must necessarily lead to a change of
climate. That change must necessarily demand an alteration in the habits of the
people subjected to its influence."   This alteration has not taken place,—the
same light clothing is worn, the same habit of sleeping on the ground and working in the night air is continued, and to this Major Cautley attributed much of
the illness.   In 1843, Rámpur, Saháraupur and Shámli were afflicted with
malarious fevers, whilst the notoriously unhealtly jungle tracts to the north were
left untouched.   Similarly, sickness supposed to be due to the presence of
canals was found to be prevalent in places where there were no canals and no
irrigation.[1]   A report from the Meerut District, in calling for medical aid for
the population on the canal banks, shows the feeling of the district officers.
At that time the only canal in the district was the Eastern Jumna Canal, which
irrigated a small strip of land between the Karsuni and the Jumna.   In
1843 there was sickness in this tract as well as all over the district.   It was as
rife at Begamabad, 23 miles east of the canal, as in parganah Loni on its banks.
Murádnagar, and other large towns which had no connection with the canal,
suffered in a precisely similar way, yet aid was only asked for the canal tract,
based on the foregone conclusion of a connection between the sickness and the
canals.

The results arrived at by the Sanitary Committee of 1843 show that there
was an epidemic in 1843, which was generally, though not universally, more
severely felt in the canal tracts than elsewhere.   In places totally unconnected
with the canal, fevers prevailed to an extent and with an intensity as great
as in the worst canal villages.   Much of the evils complained of were due to
bad drainage, the natural drainage being checked and impeded, and the
soils being stiff and retentive of moisture.   The Committee recommended
the stoppage of irrigation within five miles of large towns, and that certain
sanitary arrangements should be carried out in the villages, as, on the whole, the
influence of irrigation was very local.   They found that the Eastern Jumna
Canal furnished some of the best and worst results of canal irrigation !—sick-

---

[1] Ganges Canal, I., 57.

ness where the drainage had been obstructed and where the soil was clayey, as in the centre division; health where the drainage was perfect and the soil light, as in the northern and southern divisions. Or, in other words, the Committee of 1843 found that the salubrity or otherwise of the canal depended on the nature of the soil and the efficiency of the surface drainage. The Committee summed up their recommendations as follows :—1. That the canal should be kept, as far as possible, to the ordinary level of the country ; 2, that earth, when required for embankments, should never be obtained from excavations made outside the canal without proper precautions being taken for drainage ; 3; that the canal should be taken along the watershed, so as to interfere as little as possible with natural drainage lines, which, when intercepted, should be relieved; 4, masonry drains should be constructed under distributary channels and bridge ramps, where these cross natural lines of drainage ; 5, no private water-courses should be allowed ; 6, irrigation should be prohibited within five miles of large towns ; 7, grass and weeds should not be allowed to lie and rot, but should be burned ; and 8, irrigation should be altogether prohibited in localities which appear naturally to possess a malarious character.

Dr. Cutcliffe pursued the same line of inquiry in his researches into the causes of the epidemic of 1867. He found that the water-level all round had been greatly raised by the introduction of canal-irrigation, and that this had been effected as well by the increase to the natural water-resources caused by the volume of water thrown over the country by the canal, as by the supercession of wells in irrigation, which carried up the water from the sub-soil and distributed it over the surface of the ground, where much was lost by evaporation. In addition, this raising of the spring-level had made the water in many of the wells unfit for use, as well by the liquefaction of the salts that lie in such abundance at no great distance from the surface of the ground, as by coming sooner in contact with the animal and vegetable impurities which an absence of any attempt at sanitation allows to accumulate within the site of every village, and often close to the wells used for drinking water. At the same time that sickness was general along the Ganges Canal from Manglaur to Meerut, and along the Jumna Canal as far as Baraut, it was noticed again that the attacks were more frequent and virulent in the neighbourhood of swamps; and where these occurred at a distance from the canals the sickness was equally felt. In villages, whether close to the canal, or even in the beds of streams where there was proper and efficient natural or artificial drainage, fever was unknown. In Meerut, Sardhana alone showed any unusual sickness, and in Bulandshahr, the town of Galauthi suffered severely. In the latter place the sickness was correctly attributed to the undue collection of stagnant water around the village site, and with proper drainage arrangements the fever disappeared.

Dr. Cutcliffe's opinion in 1868.

Dr. Planck in 1869-70 travelled over the greater portion of the Muzaffarnagar

Dr. Planck in 1869-72.

District, and in 1871 examined the Sahâranpur District ; the results of his investigations are the same as those already arrived at by his predecessors ;—excessive irrigation raising the spring-level in canal-irrigated tracts, and no means taken to improve existing lines of drainage ; or, where the natural lines were impeded by the canal works, no new ones were formed, hence excessive moisture, the destruction of the wells, and the defilement of the drinking water. In tracts removed from the direct influence of the canal, the same cause—bad drainage —was at work. It would be unduly lengthening this notice to recapitulate the details given by Dr. Planck. He corroborates the opinion of the Committee of 1845, that the epidemics which now annually desolate the Upper Duáb are due to insufficient drainage, enhanced in canal-irrigated tracts by the action of the canal in raising the spring-level, and yet to the present time very little has been done to remedy this evil ; and, as I have shown, of late years it has been increasing in a ratio which bids fair to assume gigantic proportions. Whilst money is being liberally expended to meet the possible chances of a famine in Bengal, men are dying in thousands from a disease which is preventible by the exercise of more careful supervision in the expenditure of canal-water, and the construction of drainage lines to carry off excessive moisture.

One result certainly followed upon the reports of the Sanitary Commissioners,

Measures of relief undertaken.

and this was the assembling of a conference of canal officers at Meerut in November, 1870, when it was resolved " that a survey of the districts concerned should be undertaken by the Engineers of the Department, working in conjunction with the civil authorities, for the express purpose of determining how the natural drainage channels of the country could be made more efficient. That wherever, in the districts concerned, the spring-level of the sub-soil water was at any time of the year less than ten or twelve feet from the surface, there canal-irrigation should cease or be checked." The survey was carried out during the cold-weather, but the same facts of the existence of fever far away from canal-irrigated tracts led the canal officers to doubt whether the fever had anything to do with canal irrigation. Dr. Planck again visited the Muzaffarnagar District, and found, as before, that the fever prevails in tracts unirrigated by the canal as well as in canal-irrigated tracts. He writes—" Second.—This fact appeared, that the form of fever with which we have to deal is more persistent in its prevalence, more virulent, and therefore more fatal in its results, in the canal-irrigated country than in the country not irrigated by the canal, unless the latter should be naturally a very moist country. Third.—This fact appears, that filthiness is common to all the villages, and cannot, therefore, be the cause of the prevalence of ague ; otherwise it should prevail equally in all the places inspected, and the people should all have the same unhealthy aspect. *Fourth.*—This fact appears, that the most unhealthy people of all are those who live in places naturally moist, the moisture of which has been increased by canal-irrigation,—in low land irrigated from the Jumna Canal, and in the Nágal *khádir.* Considering these facts, one may justly arrive at the opinion that ague has not been introduced as a new thing into the canal-irrigated country, but that its area and period of prevalence, and its intensity of attack, have very greatly increased since irrigation from the canals was introduced ;—this prevalence and intensity being very fairly measurable by the increased moisture of the soil, and consequently of the atmosphere, denoted by the height of permanent rise in the spring-level at any given place,—a rise which no man can doubt must be due to canal-irrigation." Having ascertained by repeated inquiries the connection between bad drainage, whether directly connected with canals or not, and malaria, the canal officers and the district authorities have, at last, prepared large schemes for the improvement of the drainage of the Upper Duáb. Amongst these may be mentioned the drainage of the town of Saháranpur, the improvement of the drainage of the Pándhoi and Dumaula rivers, the deepening and straightening of the cut on the Síla Khála, and the removal of the impediments to the drainage passing down by the Krishni and Kátha nadís. The Chief Engineer informs me that, altogether, the sum of one lakh of rupees a year has been set aside to improve drainage lines of the canal-irrigated tracts. Several of these projects have been taken in hand, and have already had a marked effect in improving the health of the people ; but much remains to be done ; and before the Irrigation Department can really take credit for the saving of lives in seasons of drought, this annual waste of life from bad drainage must be met and remedied.

SAHARANPUR DISTRICT.

CONTENTS.

SAHÁRANPUR, the most northerly district of the Duáb, has somewhat the form
of a great triangle, with its apex to the north-west. It
is bounded on the north-east and east by the Siwálik
hills and the Ganges ; on the north-west and west by the Jumna; and on the
south by an irregular line separating it from the district of Muzaffarnagar, the
whole of which formerly lay within what was then known as the Sahúranpur

Boundaries, area.

District.[1] The district, as at present constituted, lies between north latitude 29° 34′ 45″ and 30° 21′ 30″, and east longitude 77° 9′ and 78° 14′ 45″, with an area of 1,420,194 acres, or 2,219·05 square miles,[2] and a population in 1872 numbering 883,782 souls, or 399 to the square mile. Its extreme length from north to south is about 54 miles, and its extreme breadth 63 miles.

The following table gives the administrative divisions at present existing,

Administrative divisions. and their statistics, with the revenue and police jurisdictions.

Present Tahsíl.	Parganah.	Entered in the Aín-i-Akbarí in	Number of villages.	Land revenue in 1872-73, in rupees.	Area in acres, 1872.	Population in 1872.	In the Police jurisdiction of the station of
Sahāranpur.	Sahāranpur,	Haveli ...	140	1,18,033	82,677	109,767	Sahāranpur, Bahat, Nāgal and Rāmpur.
	Faizabad ...	Raipur, Tātárpur.	129	65,745	116,675	42,882	Raipur, Bahat and Chilkāna.
	Muzaffarabad.	Muzaffarabad...	136	64,465	129,625	46,278	Muzaffarabad, Bahat, Mohand and Fatehpur.
	Haraura ...	Various ...	118	83 275	67,232	54,444	Fatehpur, Manglaur, Bahat, Nāgal and Sahāranpur.
		Total ...	523	3,31,518	396,209	253,371	
Deoband.	Deoband ...	Deoband ...	85	94,452	86,552	69,430	Deoband and Badgaon.
	Rámpur ...	Rámpur ...	115	1,15,892	82,493	74,726	Rámpur, Nánauta, Nāgal and Badgaon.
	Nágal ...	Various ...	110	91,713	77,845	54,537	Nágal, Manglaur, Deoband, Badgaon and Rámpur.
		Total ...	310	3,02,057	246,890	198,693	

[1] The authorities for this notice are notes by Mr. G. R. C. Williams, C.S.; the Settlement Reports of Messrs. VansAgnew, Robertson, Wynne and Webster; Cautley's Ganges Canal; the Sanitary Reports of Doctors Cutcliffe and Planck; and the records of the Board of Revenue in Allahabad. [2] The census of 1848 gives a total area of 2,165·45 square miles; that of 1853 gives 2,162·9; Mr. Plowden, in 1865, gives 2,227 square miles; and the last census shows 2,217 square miles. The Settlement Reports give 2219·05 square miles, and this estimate has been followed here. In fact, from the inclusion in some accounts, and the exclusion in others, of the jungle tracts, it is impossible to give the total area correctly. The total area in 1866, as shown by the Board's review of the Sahāranpur Settlement, amounts to 1,081,763 acres, or 1,690·2 square miles, for the revenue-paying area. The total area is elsewhere given at 2,227 square miles, without details.

Present Tahsíl.	Parganah.	Entered in the Aín-i-Akbari in	Number of villages.	Land revenue in 1872-73 in rupees.	Area in acres, 1872.	Population in 1872.	In the Police jurisdiction of the station of
Roorkee. (Rúrki.)	Roorkee. (Rúrki) ...	Rúrki ...	107	53,034	127,096	54,854	Rúrki, Manglaur, Fatehpur and Jawálápur.
	Manglaur ...	Manglaur ...	115	93,215	77,580	66,742	Manglaur, Rúrki, Sultánpur, Kanári.
	Jawálápur ...	Bhogpur ...	133	50,686	144,846	57,330	Rúrki, Jawálápur, Sultánpur, and Kanári.
	Bhagwánpur,	Various ...	143	79,653	156,558	63,770	Manglaur, Rúrki, Fatehpur, and Nágal.
		Total ...	498	2,76,588	506,080	242,696	· ·
Nakúr.	Nakúr ...	Nakúr ...	103	66,119	69,780	50,590	Rámpur, Gangoh, Nakúr.
	Sarsáwa ...	Sarsáwa ...	93	63,463	60,588	38,306	Sarsáwa, Nakúr, Saháranpur.
	Gangoh ...	Gangoh ...	107	72,109	83,783	54,748	Gangoh, Nánauta, Rámpur.
	Sultánpur ...	Bahat Kanjáwar.	102	61,097	56,864	45,378	Chilkána and Sarsáwa.
		Total ...	405	2,62,787	271,015	189,022	
		GRAND TOTAL,	1736	11,72,950	1,420,194	883,782	

Under the Dehli Emperors, Sirkár Saháranpur contained thirty-six maháls, divided into four dastúrs, viz., Deoband, Kairána, Sardhana and Indri, and included the Duáb from the Siwálik hills to the middle of the Meerut District, as well as portions of the tract to the west of the Jumna, now included in the Panjáb. Nineteen of these maháls lay within the modern district of Saháranpur. These were increased to twenty-four at the time of the settlement under Regulation VII. of 1822, in the year 1839-40. The revision of Mr. Edgeworth in 1842 absorbed nine parganahs, and that of Mr. A. Ross, in 1855, absorbed three more, whilst three others were created, leaving fifteen parganahs, as at present, distributed amongst the four tahsíls of Saháranpur, Deoband, Rúrki and Nakúr. The relative area of these tahsíls is 25·1, 22·8, 26·8 and 25·3 per cent. of the total area respectively.

To understand references to Saháranpur local history, it is necessary to give *Akbari parganahs.* some account of each of these changes. The following table traces the history of the nineteen maháls existing in the time of Akbar : the changes in their distribution were effected for the most part during the usurpation of the Rohillas and the Gújars in the last century.[1] .

Parganahs as known in the Ain-i Akbari.	Included in modern parganah of	In tahsíldari of	Notes.
2 Ambahta ...	Nakúr ...	Nakúr ...	Absorbed before 1842.
5 Bahat Kanjáwar,	Bahat and Sultánpur.	Sahâranpur ...	This parganah became Bahat Sultánpur in Shahjahán's time. Najíb Khán separated the two parganahs. The village of Kanjáwar is in Muzaffarabad.
6 Bhogpur ...	Jawálápur ...	Rúrki ...	The town is near Hardwár.
11 Thána Bhím ...	...	...	Subsequently Thána Bhawan, which was absorbed in 1842 in the neighbouring parganahs, and the Muzaffarnagar District.
13 Jaurásí ...	Rúrki ...	Ditto ...	Absorbed in 1855, in Rúrki, Manglaur, Jawálápur, Haraura and Bhagwánpur.
16 Haveli ...	Sahâranpur ...	Sahâranpur.	
17 Deoband ...	Deoband ...	Deoband.	
18 Rámpur ...	Rámpur ...	Ditto.	
19 Rúrki ...	Rúrki ...	Rúrki.	
20 Raipur Tátár ...	Faizabad Bahat...	Sahâranpur ...	The old name of Faizabad, which was given after the building of the Bádshah Mahal by Shahjahán.
22 Sarsáwa ...	Sarsáwa ...	Nakúr.	
30 Gangoh ...	Gangoh ...	Ditto.	
31 Lakhnauti ...	Ditto ...	Ditto ...	Portion absorbed in Gangoh ; remainder in Muzaffarnagar.
32 Muzaffarabad ...	Muzaffarabad ...	Sahâranpur.	
33 Manglaur ...	Manglaur ...	Rúrki.	
34 Malhaipur ...	...	Sahâranpur ...	Absorbed in neighbouring parganahs in 1842.
35 Nakúr ...	Nakúr ...	Nakúr.	
36 Nánauta ...	...	...	Absorbed in 1842 in Rámpur, Gangoh and Muzaffarnagar.

[1] The numbers refer to the list of Akbari maháls given in Beames' Elliot, II., 128. Tieffenthaler gives a precisely similar list—Bernoulli, I, 134.

At the same time that these changes occurred, a number of new parganahs
was created from the old ones, by the successive
rulers of this district.

New parganahs.

Parganah.	Now included in parganah.	Note.
Kheri ...	Muzaffarabad ...	This parganah was separated from Rúrki in the time of Zábita Khán, and absorbed in the neighbouring parganahs in 1842.
Sakrauda ...	Various ...	Was separated from Jaurási by Ráo Kutb-uddín in the time of Zábita Khán, and absorbed in 1842.
Jamálgarh ...	Nakúr ...	Formed from Gangoh, by Jamál Khán in the time of Najíb Khán, and absorbed in Nakúr in 1842.
Jawálápur ...	Jawálápur ...	From new capital of the old Bhogpur parganah.
Faizabad ...	Faizabad ...	New name of Raipur Tátár.
Patehar ...	Faizabad and Sultánpur.	Formed from Bahat Kanjáwar, in Najíb Khán's time, by Anwar Khan, absorbed in 1842.
Jahángírabad ...	Do. and Jawálápur,	Originally in Raipur Tátár. Absorbed in 1842.
Sultánpur ...	Sultánpur ...	Formed from Bahat Kanjáwar, in the time of Shahjahán.
Kátha ...	Rámpur, Deoband and Nágal.	Absorbed in 1855 in neighbouring parganahs.
Tháná Bhawan ...	Ditto ...	Absorbed in 1842 in neighbouring parganahs.

The size of these parganahs varied with the power and influence of their
possessors, and they remained, in name at least, up to
1842, when the changes proposed by Mr. M. P. Edgeworth were sanctioned. These were briefly as follows[1] :—

Changes in 1842.

Parganah.	Nature of change.	Parganah.	Nature of change.	Parganah.	Nature of change.
Saháranpur ...	Retained ...	Rámpur ...	Retained ...	Sarsáwa ...	Retained.
Malhaipur ...	Among neighbouring parganahs.	Kátha ...	...	Sultánpur ...	...
Faizabad ...	Retained ...	Manglaur ...	...	Nakúr ...	...
Bahat ...	...	Jawálápur ...	...	Gangoh ...	...
Muzaffarabad,	...	Jaurási ...	...	Jamálgarh ...	Nakúr.
Patehar ...	Faizabad and Sultánpur.	Rúrki ...	...	Tháná Bhawan.	In neighbouring parganahs.
Jahángírabad	Ditto and Jawálápur.	Sakrauda ...	Jaurási and Muzaffarabad.	Nánauta ...	Rámpur, Gangoh and Muzaffarnagar.
Deoband ...	Retained ...	Kheri ...	Muzaffarabad,	Chausat Kheri,	Ditto ditto.

[1] Sanctioned by G. O. No. 796, 11th of January, 1842, which gives the transfer of revenue
and area in each case. (See parganah notices)

The above table gives the state of the district sub-divisions at and after the thirty years' settlement under Regulation VII. of 1822. The alterations of boundaries that then took place so completely mixed up the greater number of the parganahs, that it would be difficult to attempt to follow out their individual or fiscal history, even if no further changes had been made. Not only were interchanges of villages between neighbouring parganahs effected, but large transfers were made between Saháranpur and the neighbouring district of Muzaffarnagar,—134 estates, yielding a land revenue of Rs. 1,06,092, and

Exchanges with Muzaffarnagar. the Thána Bhawan tahsíli were transferred from Saháranpur to Muzaffarnagar, and 95 estates, yielding a revenue of Rs. 78,048, were received in exchange. The next series of changes were made by Mr A. Ross, and received the sanction of Government in 1855. This completed the breaking up of all the parganahs to such a degree, that it is now impossible to recognize any of the old sub-divisions. For example, the parganah of Saháranpur gave up 48 villages in 1855 to five parganahs, and received 21 villages from six parganahs in exchange; and similarly all through the whole district. The present parganahs, therefore, only resemble the old ones in name. Three parganahs—Kátha, Bahat and Jaurási—were absorbed, and three new parganahs were created,—Haraura, Nágal and Bhagwánpur.[1] These were distributed amongst four tahsíls as at present.[2]

The tahsíls of Saháranpur and Nakúr are within the civil jurisdiction of the

Civil jurisdiction. Munsif of Saháranpur, and the remainder of the district is under the Munsif of Deoband, from both of whom appeals lie to the Judge of Saháranpur. There are at present (1874) ten stipendiary and three Honorary Magistrates within the district, subordinate to the same Judge, who has also appellate criminal jurisdiction. Similarly, the Magistrate has revenue jurisdiction as Collector, and most of the other stipendiary officers have dual powers.

The following table gives the number of Courts in existence at different periods :—

Class of Court.	1840.	1850.	1860.	1870.
Magisterial Courts ...	1	3	4	4
Civil Courts, including Revenue Courts.	8	11	10	10
Covenanted officers at work ...	2	4	5	5

[1] Haraura from Saháranpur (23); Rúrki (28); Jaurási (1); Muzaffarabad (63); Deoband (21); and Bahat (1): Nágal, from Deoband (113), and Kátha (9): Bhagwánpur, from Rúrki (69); Manglaur (19); Muzaffarabad (17); Jaurási (22); and Deoband (1). See further the parganah notices. [2] Sanctioned by G. O. No. 2050 of 14th May, 1855, which gives the number of villages, area and population in each transfer.

There are 29 police-stations, including eight outposts, in the district, supervised by a District Superintendent of Police. The jail is in charge of the Civil Surgeon. The other local officers are the Superintendent of the Botanical Gardens, the Superintendent of the Stud, the District Engineer, Canal-Engineers and their Assistants, Deputy Inspector of Schools, and the Opium Agent, besides the large European staff at Rúrki.

The scenery of the Saháranpur District presents much more variety of feature than that of any other of the Duáb districts:

General appearance.

on the north lie the Siwáliks, and below them the country presents, on a small scale, the same features of bhábar and tarái that are met with further east, under Garhwál and Kumaon. Next comes the great alluvial *khádir* land in the north-east corner of the district, through which one-half the mountain drainage finds its way to the Ganges; then the great basins of the Ganges and Jumna; lastly we have the *bangar* or uplands, a great part of which is also, on a smaller scale, divided into lowland and upland, marked by the basins and watersheds of the rivers which flow through it southwards.

The Siwáliks run parallel to the Himálayas, having the same direction, from north-west to south-east. The length between the

The Siwáliks.

Ganges and the Jumna is 46 miles; the breadth averages from six to eight miles; and the highest peak attains an elevation of 3,140 feet above the level of the sea. The range is pierced by numerous passes, the principal of which are the Mohand and Kheri or Lál Darwáza, almost bisecting the chain, and the Timli, about seven miles east of the Jumna. The road to Masúri (Mussooree) passes through the Mohand pass, and that to the military station of Chakráta passes through the Timli pass. The other gorges are difficult of access, and have in a great measure never been explored. The whole range appears to be a mass of close-lying hills, with jagged and narrow tops worn into the most fantastic shapes, and clothed with *sain*, *sál*, and various species of *Bauhinia*. Extensive forests of the *pinus longifolia* (*chír*) cover the northern slopes. The Siwáliks are abrupt and rugged on the southern side, and slope gently towards the Himálayas on the north. They may be roughly described as a series of right-angled triangles, with bases resting on the passes, perpendiculars facing the south-west, and hypotheneuses sloping towards the north-east. Hence the serrated outline which strikes the traveller, a feature which is constantly exaggerated, owing to the destructibility of the material of which the hills are composed.

The geology of the Siwáliks has been the subject of much discussion, and will be more fully noticed in the description of the

Geology.

neighbouring district of Dehra Dún. The sandstones of which the rocks are composed appear to belong to the newer tertiary or upper miocene period ; and Dr. Falconer regards them as débris swept down from the Himálayas, overlying an upheaved portion of the plains at the foot of the higher range. Major Herbert also, in his mineralogical survey of the Himálayas, adopts a simlar theory.[1] Professor Medlicott, in a recent paper on the Náhan rocks, describes the Siwáliks as formed for the most part on the northern side of a great anticlinal flexure.

According to him, the local dip " varies very considerably, but there is a line along the south base of the chain, inside which the dip is invariably to some point between east and north. Near the axis the dip often amounts to 40° and 50°; but in all the sections it lowers gradually to where it passes into the more or less horizontal strata of the Dún. At almost every point along the southern base we find the beginning of the reverse southerly dip; and in two places, one on the right bank of the Jumna, and the other on the right bank of the Ganges, the section of the rocks on the south of the anticlinal is nearly complete; and in both we observe the very opposite tendency to that described in the north, namely, in a direction from the axis the dip increases rapidly almost to the vertical."

" At each of the great transverse river gorges there is a complete break in the continuity of the anticlinal flexure, no doubt involving transverse faulting. In approaching Hardwár from the south, the structural conditions of the rocks are discernible from a distance. As far as the eye can reach to the west, the face of the Siwálik range presents a very broken series of bare cliffs, formed by the scarped edges of the

The river beds.

---

[1] The following list gives the principal local papers that have hitherto been published on the subject :—

Dr. Gerard's Fossil Shells and Chelonian Fragments. Everest's As. Res. XVIII., Part II., 107.

Dr. H. Falconer and P. J. Cautley on Sivatherium Giganteum, Fossil crocodile, Fossil gharial, Fossil hippopotamus, Fossil camel, tiger (Felis cristata), bear (ursus sivalensis), from the Siwáliks, As. Res. XIX, 1, 25, 32, 39, 115, 135, 193.

H. M. Durand on hippopotamus and other Fossil Genera of the Sub-Himálayas in the Dadúpur collection, Sus and Cheirotherium, in a note, Ibid, 54,59.

Duncan and Leslie on fossil bones of elephants, Glean I., 23.

Gerard's Organic Remains in the Himálayas, Glean I., 109.

Herbert's Ammonites of the Himálaya, Glean III., 269.

Everest's Himálayan Fossils, Glean III., 30.

Falconer and Cautley on Fossil Remains of Anoplotherium and Giraffe from Siwáliks. Cal. J. N. H. V. 577.

Fauna Antiqua Sivalensis, Lon. 1845, 6 parts.

Owen's Palæontology, Edin., 1860.

Palæontologica Indica, 6 volumes, published by the Geological Survey, Calcutta.

Catalogue of the Fossil Remains of Vertebrata from the Siwáliks, &c. in the museum, A. S., Cal., by H. Falconer.

Medlicott in Records, Geological Survey, Vol. III., (Part 2.)

massive strata of clear gray sandstones which lie on the north of the anticlinal, and all of which dip to the north. For some miles, near the Ganges
valley, the hills rise less abruptly, and are covered with jungle. The strata
here dip southwards, on the south of the anticlinal, which strikes the Ganges
near Bhímghora, to the north of the main mass of the range. Eastwards,
across the Ganges, the usual structure of the range is restored: in the grey
cliffs of the Chándi hill we see the scarped edges of strata dipping northwards.
This contrast is most observable in the gorge at Hardwár, where the strata on
the two sides of the river are seen dipping in opposite directions." " The alteration in the features of the range to the west of the Ganges is not caused by
any sudden turn in the direction of the anticlinal line of flexure; the curving
is in the range itself : nor, on the other hand, is the change purely a caprice
of denudation, for, together with the passage of the range to the south of the
line of flexure, the strata on the north of the line are let down by a fault along
the axis. Hence at Bhímghora we find the topmost beds of clay and gravel
in contact with the base of the cliffs of sandstone, and inclining gently northwards. About the Motichor Rao (torrent) there is a flat synclinal ; the Motichor ridge being formed of about the same beds of clay, gravel and boulders
inclined to the south-west. These contrary slopes merge into the uniform
northerly inclination west of Kánsrao.'

"This Bhímghora fault must have a throw of many thousand feet, estimated
by the thickness of the continuous section of the strata

Hardwár.

to the south ; and these clay and gravel beds on the
north of the fault are probably even higher in the series than any beds in the
section to the south. The northern contact beds are certainly associated with
those of the Motichor ridge, which are certainly upper Siwálik, and, though
here so little disturbed, have been in fact subject to the full effects of the
disturbing forces. In proof of this assertion, we find a very rare and important
section in the precipitous bank of the Ganges at Raiwála. Through the
greater part of the cliff the stiff clays and the gravels have a steady south-
westerly inclination, evidently the continuation of the arrangement in the
Motichor hill ; but at the north end of the cliff the same beds are seen to curve
rapidly over to a high north-easterly underlie. On the east of the Ganges
we again find the mode of arrangement that usually obtains in the Siwálik
range : the lower beds on the south have a moderately high dip, and pass
into the slightly disturbed upper beds on the north or Dún side. Along the
south base an anticlinal is readily detected continuously from the Ganges to
Paili Parao in the Bijnaur District. The Bhímghora fault makes no appearance on the east side of the river, the upper conglomerates being quite unbroken
in front of it. The interruption of direct continuity, within so short a space, of
so great a fault as that at Bhímghora, necessitates the existence of some oblique

fracture along which the upheaval may die out. The abrupt change of dip on the two river banks points to this as the position of such a fracture. From the resemblance of the general sections on each side, one is inclined at first to suppose the features to have been once continuous, namely, the Chándi hill anticlinal with that at Bhímghora, and to have been so separated by a subsequent cross fault. This is not, on the whole, the most satisfactory view; unless it keeps strictly in the bed of the river, there can be no such fracture, and general appearances are against it. The strata of the Motichor synclinal seem to correspond with those facing them to the east of the Ganges. The Chándi anticlinal is certainly representative of that in the main Siwálik range; and it is supposed that all these features of disturbance have been contemporaneously produced.

"In the gorge of the Jumna, we find, again, a northerly dip on the east side
Jumna.
confronted by a southerly dip on the west, and on the same strike. The dislocation does not appear to be so great as in the Ganges, and, the river course being more winding, the opportunities for studying the details of structure are better. The anticlinal axis is easily traced along the base of the Siwálik range. North of it, near the Jumna, the north-easterly dip of the sandstones and conglomerates is very steady; but along a narrow north-and-south band close to the river, the beds curve rapidly round to a north-westerly dip. Against this narrow transition dip the strata strike steadily from the north-west, and with a high south-westerly underlie. About half-way through the gorge the river takes a sweep to westwards, leaving on its left bank a terrace of these western rocks. Along this terrace the contrasting dips can be seen almost in contact. Towards the Dún this line of fracture bends off, and seems to identify itself with an anticlinal line traceable along the southern edge of the Kayárda Dún, as far as Kolar. The section on the right bank of the Jumna is a good deal more complicated than the Hardwár section. The anticlinal of the Kayárda Dún is obscurely seen in the Bhatta, just at its confluence with the Jumna. There appears to be more or less of faulting too; yellow boulder clays on the north are in crushed contact with sandstone and sandstone conglomerate on the south. A south-westerly dip soon becomes steady in these latter rocks, and continues so for four miles, to Kalesar, in the coarser conglomerates. In the ridge south of Kalesar these same beds rise by a sharp uniclinal curve to a high north-easterly dip, thus forming the most prominent ridge of the range. It is this ridge which bends-round in continuation with the crest of the range south of Kalesar, thus cutting off the wedge-shaped area of the south-westerly dip. Orographically, and to some extent structurally, this area occupies a very analogous position to that of the Motichor Rao at the Ganges. At the south-east angle of these hills, next the Jumna, we have another change

in the section : for a mile or more the conglomerates and sandstones dip at 80°
to the southward, the strike thus converging to that of the ridge. A culmina-
tion of this convergence seems to be reached before we lose sight of the rocks ;
since in the river bank below Faizpur the sáme beds dip at 80° to the south-
east. Here also, as at the Ganges, we observe a maximum of disturbance in the
external portions of the range. In the case of the Jumna there is nothing to
interfere with the suggestion, that the irregularities in the actual state of disturbance in the region of the gorge may be, in a great measure, owing to the
unequal accumulation of deposits at the former river's mouth ; and it may at
least be asked if the river may not have had a more direct influence if, in the
early stages of upheavement and contortion, the special erosion in the river
course may not have had some influence in determining the position of these
irregularities. Whatever view is adopted for the Jumna must be allowed its full
force in the case of the gorge at Hardwár." [1]

The portion of the district lying along the base of the Siwálik hills is still

Sub-montane tract.

for the most part covered with forest and jungle. This
tract is intersected by numerous torrents, dry during
the hot weather, but carrying a considerable volume of water in the rains. These
torrents flow into the Jumna on the west and the Ganges on the east. The
watershed throughout is clearly defined, and may be traced to the Sháhjahánpur and Kúnjnáwar passes into the Siwáliks. These passes adjoin each other,
and on their east the water trickles down to feed the most western tributary of
the Soláni, an affluent of the Ganges ; whilst on the west, and within a few hundred yards, the drainage unites with the head-waters of the Hindan, an affluent of the Jumna. From the utmost north-western point of the eastern watershed, a well-defined bank runs in a south-eastern direction towards the Ganges,
inclosing between it and the Siwáliks an ever-widening expanse of low-lying
lands, intersected by numerous torrents and continued through the midst of the
Manglaur parganah into the adjoining district of Muzaffarnagar, where it joins
the high bank of the Ganges at Shukartár. To the west, however, the case is
different : the highlands or raised central plateau there extend to the border of
the Búdhi Jumna, the old course of the Jumna, within a few miles of the
existing river, and the *khádir* is small in extent. The broad tract of lowlying
land mentioned above deserves particular notice for itself, and as being the
site of the head-works and principal engineering triumphs of the great Ganges
Canal.

This tract is of a triangular form ; its apex lies at the Sháhjahánpur pass, its
northern side is formed by the Siwáliks, its southern side by the upland ridge
already mentioned, and its base is the lowlands or *khádir* proper of the Ganges.

---

[1] From Professor Medlicott's notice in the Rec., Geol. Sur., Vol. III. (Part. 2), p. 121.

The surface, besides having a slope from north to south, has also a slope to the south-east, perceptible in the direction of the drainage lines. Within it, to the westward, there is a tract of upland on which the villages of Kheri and Júdi are built. This tract is intersected by channels, into which the drainage collects, from not only the main plateau, but also from numerous lesser plateaus or mounds which have been chosen as the sites of villages in those parts. The most westerly of these channels drains all the country lying to the north of Kheri and Shah Mansúr, including the drainage from mountain torrents for a distance of eight miles from the pass which forms the eastern watershed. The waters thus collected unite to form the Soláni river. Next we have the central lines of drainage in the Ratmau river ; and further to the north-east the system known as the Patharinadí. Between the latter and the base of the hills there is a good deal of scattered drainage, which depends very much on the rain-fall for its character, and which is carried off by numerous small channels into the Ganges. The soil in this sub-montane tract is of a dark-chocolate colour, and rests on a stratum of boulders. In the immediate vicinity of the hills, the water rises to the surface, and exhibits itself in pools or streams and rills, which flow for a short distance and then disappear in the sand and shingle. Parallel to and south of this line is a belt (bhábar), varying from five to ten miles in width, in which water can only be found at depths varying from 100 to 150 feet. This belt consists of a layer of boulders resting on an impervious bed of indurated gravel and clay, along which the percolation-water runs, until the bed again crops up at the surface to form the southern boundary of the waterless tract, and the northern boundary of the tarái or moist tract. Here the streams again appear at the surface, and unite together to form rivers. In consequence of this absence of surface water, and the difficulty in constructing wells, there is little cultivation in this tract, which is in a great measure abandoned to primeval jungle. The lowlands on the west of the sub-montane tract are confined to the old or existing bed of the Jumna, and require no separate notice.

The remainder of the district may be roughly divided into *khádir* or lowland, and *bangar* or upland. The *khádir* comprises the valley of the Jumna on the west, and that of the Ganges on the east. The western *khádir* consists of a strip of land bordering the left bank of the Jumna, and having an average breadth of four miles. The rise from this *khádir* to the uplands is marked by a very steep bank, which is sometimes cut up into ravines, but is more often sufficiently sloping to be cultivated. This bank rises in the Faizabad parganah, and from thence to Patna just below Chilkána is single. It there bends suddenly inland towards the east, and encircles the depression in which the Síkri jhíl lies. It finally disappears as a marked bank in Pilkhana, but reappears to the south in Rajdhán

Division into uplands and lowlands.

of Sarsáwa, and after touching the Dhaulápra jhíl, gradually trends to the east and again to the south, so as to form the lip of the Kumbárhera jhíl, until it finally disappears at Jagahta Gújar, in the central plateau on the road from Saháranpur to Ambahta. Immediately south of Patna a second bank becomes visible, which, though at first low, soon increases in height until it reaches Sarsáwa, where it too becomes double. The true *khádir* is marked off by a bank, that incloses the tract from Kalyánpur which adjoins Sarsáwa on the west, to Júdí on the north of Sarúrpur, whilst this again is separated by an inner bank from the true uplands of Sarsáwa. At Júdí the two banks join and continue single through the whole of parganahs Nakúr and Gangoh, with the exception of a break at Aghiána and at the extreme south of the district, caused by an outlying projection from the main line. On this bank are situated the important towns of Sultánpur, Chilkána, Sarsáwa, Nakúr, Gangoh and Lakhnauti. On the whole, the Jumna *khádir* is more compact and less swampy than that of the Ganges, and is therefore more highly cultivated.

The *khádir* proper or lowland of the Ganges imperceptibly amalgamates with the north-eastern tract already noticed. The upland bank forming the south-eastern boundary of this tract is much broken up by ravines near Jaurási in parganah Rúrki. These ravines in many places are annually cutting further back into the cultivated lands, from want of care on the part of the people. To the east of the bank which separates the lowlands of the Ganges from the uplands of the central plateau, and nearly parallel to it, there is a sandy ridge which runs through parganah Manglaur. To the west of this there is a more marked ridge, which rises near Ganeshpur in parganah Rúrki, and intersecting parganah Manglaur, runs first on one side, and then on the other, of the Síla Khála, and passing through Deoband, enters the Muzaffarnagar district. The plateau itself consists of a series of broad belts of high lands separated from each other by the depressions which contain the drainage lines known as the west Káli Nadí, the Hindan, the Karsuni or Krishní, and the Kátha. All of these lines have a course for the most part from north to south, and present few marked peculiarities.

Ganges khádir and uplands.

The patches of waste land called *úsar* further south, caused by the efflorescence of *reh*, are much more rarely met with in Saháranpur than in the districts further south, but in the tract watered by the Eastern Jumna Canal, from Nánauta southwards, the presence of *reh* is a well marked and distinguishing feature of the soils. The ridges between the torrents of the sub-montane tracts are in most places covered with jungle, which, though now rapidly giving way to cultivation, is still extensive. These forests were left in the possession of the Rajpút zamíndárs of the neigh-

Waste.

bouring villages until the year 1839, when they were excluded from the area under settlement, and measured together under the general heading of forest in the revenue survey, as follows:—Kheri forest, 84,377 acres ; Kánsrao forest, 18,794 ; Pathari Nadi forest, 39,249—total 142,420 acres. Soon after, sanction was received to the waste lands being given away to grantees under the usual conditions. The plan has been upon the whole successful. The original number of the grants was fixed at 114, and by the year 1856, tenders for 107 were accepted. Since then, several have been included in the assessed area, others have been resumed, and the number actually in the possession of grantees in 1870 was 79, viz., 63 in the Rúrki Tahsíl, and 16 in Saháranpur.[1] Although agriculture has made extraordinary progress in Saháranpur during the last 30 years, the amount of land which is either barren, or culturable yet not cultivated, appears to be considerable.

The soils throughout the district are known as to quality under the terms

Soils. *mísan, rauslí, dákar, bhúr* and *bhúda. Mísan* consists of the highly manured and carefully cultivated lands lying near the village site. The *dákar* and *rauslí* are next, and are of equal value ; the first is described as a stiff clay soil, and the latter as a light rich clay ; both yield valuable winter and rain crops. The *bhúr* is a light sandy soil, in some places rising into ridges, as in the Manglaur and Deoband parganahs, where it is called *ghúr*, and which, without irrigation, only affords a rain crop. *Bhúda* or *bhúa* is the name given to the worst description of soil. The artificial classification adopted at the recent revision of settlement was into —(1) canal-irrigated ; (2) *khádir* or lowlands ; (3) *bangar* or uplands ; (4) a mixture of both ; and (5) the waste and other jungle tracts beneath the Siwáliks. This arrangement sufficiently indicates the physical peculiarities of the district. The first comprises the tracts through which the Eastern Jumna Canal and the Ganges Canal, or their off-shoots, pass, and includes the whole of parganahs Saháranpur and Rámpur, and portions of Nágal and the parganahs bordering on the Jumna.

The second class includes the tracts lying in the valley of the Jumna and the north-eastern half of Tahsíl Rúrki. The third class is formed from the parganahs occupying the centre of the district, from Faizabad to Deoband, and includes the eastern half of the Jumna parganahs. In the fourth class those villages are placed which, lying on the borders of the highland ridge, possess both upland and lowland cultivation, and those which occupy the *khádir* of the Hindan, Soláni, and other streams. The fifth class contains the shingle tracts immediately under the Siwáliks, the jungle wastes of Jawálápur, Bhagwánpur and Manglaur, and the greater portion of the lands adjoining the Káli Nadí in the Deoband and Nágal parganahs. The following statement gives the

---

[1] See further under Jungle Grants.

area and character of each class of soil throughout the district, as ascertained by Mr. VansAgnew in 1864 :—

Classes.		Number of villages.	Total area in acres.	Assessable area.	Cultivated.	Irrigated.
I.	Canal-irrigated ...	433	226,554	199,211	168,463	84,404
II.	Khádir, lowlands ...	299	161,555	139,877	102,555	4,411
III.	Bangar, uplands ...	611	322,519	281,336	233,678	39,533
IV.	Upland and lowlands ...	96	74,896	61,120	46,540	7,318
V.	Sub-montane and jungle tracts.	353	284,998	247,275	185,637	26,651
	Total ...	1,792	1,070,522	928,819	736,873	162,317

In parganah Sah*á*ranpur the soil varies from a light soft clay (*raus*lí),
Parganah character- corresponding to that found in Har*a*ura and Muzaffar-
istics. abad, to a hard stiff clay, which more nearly approaches that prevailing in R*á*mpur. Both varieties are found in the central portion of the parganah more or less mixed together, so that they appear to pass insensibly from one into the other. In Har*a*ura the soil is generally of a light soft character, which in low situations becomes indurated by continued submersion. In the northern parts of this parganah, the soil is occasionally more sandy, and there is therefore less cultivation. In Faizabad the soil is still lighter and more easily worked. Along the foot of the Siw*á*liks, wherever the ground is not cut up by hill streams, as also on the strip of land between the B*ú*dhi Jumna and the main bed of that river, a dark-chocolate soil is found, which, when of any depth, is extremely valuable and productive. This soil is found under the same conditions throughout one-third of parganah Muzaffarabad, the remaining two-thirds to the south, known as Raotala, with perhaps the exception of a few estates in the lowland of the Sol*á*ni, are covered with a soft light clay, which varies in value as it is more or less mixed with sand.

In the Jumna parganahs, comprising Tahs*í*l Nak*ú*r, the boundary between
Jumna parganahs. the uplands and the lowlands is sharply defined. In Sult*á*npur the lowlands, consisting of a sandy loam covered with silt deposits, is found the best for rice ; on the *bangar*, a ridge of poor red sand, taking its rise at Mahesri, is seen, which reappears at intervals in the villages to the south. East of this line there is a continuous strip of fine *d*á*kar* soil. In Sars*á*wa the soil varies from a stiff hard clay to a loose porous sandy soil, that is little retentive of moisture. In Gangoh and Nak*ú*r the soil is of a mixed description, due to the undulating character of the surface, but on the whole rich and highly cultivated.

In Tahsíl Deoband the soil consists of a rich clay, occasionally interspersed with sandy ridges. This tahsíl is made up of a series of duábs between the Kátha, the Hindan and the heads of the Káli Nadi, and therefore contains strips of land comprising every kind of soil. Tahsíl Rúrki is more varied still, containing as it does a large amount of the lands touching the foot of the Siwáliks. In Bhagwánpur the uplands are tolerably level, and in the lowlands the soil is excellent, changing from a rich loam to a rich clay. In Rúrki, with the exception of a few sandy ridges, the soil is good and fertile. Jawálápur from its proximity to the hills, varies in character throughout its entire area. The south-western portions of Manglaur and Bhagwánpur differ little from the adjoining parganahs of Tahsíl Deoband. The main characteristic of the soils in the midland and southern portions of the district is the presence of kunkár, or impure carbonate of lime, occurring in spongy cavernous nodules of varying texture, in the sub-soil ; lime-stone tufa, too, is occasionally found. To the north the substratum consists of shingle and boulders, gradually giving place to sandstone, which at Mohand appears at the surface.

The surface of the country has a general slope from north to south, and in the

Elevation.

north-east of the Saháranpur district, this is combined with a slope towards the south-east. The bench-mark of the Trigonometrical Survey at Mohand shows 1,489 feet above the level of the sea. Following the road southwards, we have Bhatpura, 954 feet; Saháranpur, 902 feet ; Deoband, 831·9 feet ; Muzaffarnagar, 790 feet; Khátauli, 789·8 feet; Meerut, 735·4 feet ; Hápur, 692·7 feet ; Bulandshahr, 667 feet ; Khúrja, 647·7, and Aligarh, 610 feet. The fall is gradual throughout when once the raised land immediately under the hills is passed. The slope to the south-east, in the north-eastern portion of the district is shown by the course of the Solání and other torrents which intersect that tract and flow into the Ganges on the right bank. The inclination of the plain to the west is shown by the barometrical heights of Bádshah Mahál, 25 miles north of Saháranpur, near the debouch of the Jumna from the hills, which is said to be 1,210 feet above the level of the sea. The fall from Saháranpur to Bhainswál, 125 miles lower down, on the Eastern Jumna Canal, is only 125 feet ; whilst from Hardwár to Belra, on the Ganges Canal, in the same parallel, it is 136 feet.

The only large rivers are the Ganges on the east and the Jumna on the west.

The Ganges.

The main stream of the Ganges enters the Saháranpur district 180 miles from its source, by a well-marked gorge formed in the rock at Hardwár. The town of Hardwár lies at the foot of a high hill on the right, and the Chándni Pahár, 1,930 feet above the level of the sea, lies on the left; the main stream, known as the Níldhara, flows under the Chándni hill. The width of the gorge at its narrowest point is about one mile. Throughout it is divided into several channels, separated from each other by islands, many of which, are wooded with. *sisú*, and are high enough to be beyond the reach of high-flood ·water. One of these branches, passing directly under the town of Hardwár, joins the parent river at Kankhal, about two miles down. It is from a spot known as Ganesh Ghát, on this branch, that the waters of the great Ganges Canal have been drawn. One of the first feeders of the Ganges is the Ránípur torrent, having a catchment basin of about 45 square miles. It is crossed by the canal at about 2¾ miles from its debouch from the mountains. Next to this comes the Pathari drainage system, divided into two parts, one called the Pathari or Patharo proper, connected with the mountains, and another, extending over the country lying to the east of Salímpur, and confined to a tract separated by a band of grass and jungle land from the mountains. The catchment basin here extends to about 80 square miles, and, from its source to where it is intersected by the canal, the Pathari has a course of about five miles. Next comes the Ratmau, with a catchment basin of about 126 square miles, of which 36 lie within, and 90 at the foot of the mountains. It carries off the whole of the drainage of the Kánsráo and Sakrauda forests. Its watershed on the east separates it from the Pathari valley, and on the west from the Soláni. And, lastly, we have the Soláni, which is noticed hereafter.

The drainage area of the Ganges is about 11,200 square miles. From the

The volume of the Ganges.

middle of October the waters diminish rapidly, until, by the middle of January, they attain their minimum. By March this volume is doubled, and increases during the summer months by the melting of the snow along its catchment basin within the Himálayas, until it reaches its maximum·during the rains. Colonel Cautley, in his survey prior to the execution of ·the Ganges Canal, ascertained that the discharge of the Ganges at Hardwár in December and January was 8,000 cubic feet per second. The results of experiments made in 1842 gave the discharge at Hardwár on the 1st March at 7,166·1891 cubic feet per second, whilst at Garhmuktesar, on the same date, the gauges showed 8,685·2194 cubic feet per second ; and on the 2nd of March, the discharge was 8,883·195 cubic feet, and on the 25th February, 8,681·894 cubic feet per second. The latter returns exhibit the increase due to the drainage of the *khádir* for a distance of 95 miles from Hardwár, and the waters of the Soláni, Pathari, and other streams.

On the promulgation of the scheme for the Ganges Canal, for which it was proposed to take away 6,750 cubic feet of water, and leave only 1,250 cubic

The navigation controversy.

feet, one of the first objections urged by its opponents was the injury that would thereby be caused to navigation. Colonel Cautley clearly showed that the conditions of the tract lying along the upper course of the Ganges was in every respect similar to those of the upper course of the Jumna, and that both showed the same peculiarities of bhábar and tarái as are found in Rohilkhand, with this exception, that whereas in Rohilkhand the northern boundary of the tarái is marked by the visible rise of springs and rills from the surface, in the Duáb it is shown by a decrease in the depth from the surface of water in wells. The river beds, as well as the uplands, have their bhábar and tarái belts. In the river beds a deep impervious stratum exists, which is conterminous with the rise, near the foot of the hills, of the same stratum in the uplands, and crops out again at the northern limit of the tarái belt. The intermediate space is dry and filled with boulders, beneath which the river water runs, and passing over-the indurated stratum which underlies the boulders, again collects at the surface lower down; consequently embankments thrown across river beds in a bhábar tract can only to a moderate extent interfere with the supply. Percolation will still go on, and the water will collect again when it arrives at the Tarái portions. This was shown to be the case with the Jumna, which, though deprived of all its visible volume to feed the Eastern and Western Jumna Canals, still remained navigable at Agra, 250 miles below. Between the canal embankments on the Jumna and Agra, the only considerable feeder is the Hindan. Arguing from these premises, Major Cautley showed the fallacy of the objections raised by his opponents, and the results have fully justified his conclusions. Before the introduction of the canal, a few boats used to pass up to Garhmuktesar and Shukartár; but the trade was unimportant, and is now fully provided for by the canal itself, which is navigable from end to end of the main line, and along the Cawnpore terminal branch to the Ganges.

From the report of the Committee of 1866, the flood discharge of the Ganges at Hardwár would appear to be from 180,000 to 190,000 cubic feet per second in the rains, without including the quantity discharged by the Mayapur dam and the canal, which would probably amount to 20,000 feet more. The discharge of the Soláni in time of flood has been estimated at 84,000 cubic feet, and the discharge of other drainage systems between Hardwár and Shukartár at least at as much more. The Committee estimated that a rise of $13\frac{1}{2}$ feet above the ordinary low level at Shukartár would give a flood discharge there of 516,000 cubic feet per second, but that this would seldom happen. According to the registers kept at Cawnpore and Fatehgarh from 1843 to 1853, the highest flood at the former was 13 feet 8 inches, and at the latter was 10 feet 8 inches. Taking eleven feet as the normal rise between Hardwár and Fatehgarh, this would give 279,000 cubic feet as the flood discharge per second at Shukartár. In the dry season the depth in mid-channel still remains at from nine to ten feet. In April, 1866, the discharge was shown to be 5,300 cubic feet per second, whilst 5,000 cubic feet was passing down the canal.

Further inquiries as to the volume.

The bed of the river in the upper part of its course is composed of stones and
boulders, for the most part limestone, which have formed
for a long time an article of trade. These disappear
from twelve to sixteen miles from Hardwár, and are replaced by a quartzose
sand intermingled with mica, which becomes less abundant lower down. The
slope in the upper portion of the stream is excessive, but disappears gradually
with the substances of which the bed is composed. The banks, too, vary very
much. Near the hills they are low on one side and very high on the other, whilst
the depression through which the river wanders, stretches out to a great extent,
and again contracts, until, at its confluence with the Soláni, it is barely two to
three miles wide.

Bed of the river.

The Jumna debouches into the plains at a place, about 123 miles from its
source, called Khára, with a discharge of about 4,000
feet per second in March. The character of the bed is
the same as that of the Ganges—at first boulders, then quartzose sand interspersed with mica, then sand alone, and finally mud. It passes through a gorge
somewhat resembling that of the Ganges at Hardwár, but bolder and more
varied in scenery. Presently the valley expands, and the river separates into
several channels, one of which, the Búdhi Jumna, cuts off a large piece of the
Ambála District, and rejoins the main stream eighteen miles lower down ; whilst
another of the same name branches off to the east. The *khádir* is more uniform
in its width than that of the Ganges, neither expanding nor contracting to any
great extent, except to the south of the Faizabad parganah, where it makes a bend
for a short distance, which gives a maximum width of twelve miles, the average
throughout being not more than four miles. The Jumna receives only the
torrents passing through the north-western parganahs during its course through
this district.

1 The Jumna.

Proximity to the Dún and the hills has given the northern portion of the
district a character of its own. The rain-fall averages
sixty inches a year over the belt of land lying at the
foot of the Siwáliks. In addition, this tract receives the entire drainage of
the Siwáliks themselves, from their watershed, which lies at a depth of seven
or eight miles towards the Dún, to their southern base. Owing to the steep-
ness and rocky character of these hills, and the non-retentive properties of the
soil through which the water flows, the ' raos ' or hill torrents carry with them,
with little diminution, nearly the entire rain-fall, and are the sources of almost
all the considerable streams in this and the districts further south. Commencing at the north-west, the Búdhi or Búrhi Jumna, already mentioned, diverges
from the Jumna at Murtí, just below the lower head of
the Eastern Jumna Canal, and, after having run a mile
or two through dense jungle, is arrested by a dam and turned into the canal.

Hill streams.

Búdhi Jumna.

This river originally served for the irrigation of the considerable tract lying between it and the Jumna, and the loss caused to the proprietors of the estates along its banks, by the appropriation of its water by the canal authorities, was brought to the notice of Government by Mr. E. Thornton in his report[1] on the settlement, in 1839. A.D. Mr. Thornton proposed that a cut should be made a little below Murtí, which should pass through 21 cultivated villages, and be sufficient to supply wholesome drinking water, and, for those who chose to pay for it, water for irrigation purposes also. This application, as yet, has had no effect; and a subsequent attempt, by the proprietors of certain estates, at their own expense, to make a cut in another place, has only resulted in failure. As observed elsewhere, the soil of this tract is of the deep chocolate colour, resting on a boulder formation, which does not admit of the construction of earthen wells; and, owing to the great depth at which water is found, a brick-built well is entirely beyond the means of the inhabitants.

East of the Búdhi Jumna, the Raipur, Jatonwála, Naugang and Maskhara

Other torrents.

torrents intersect the Faizabad parganah. The Jatonwála drainage has been turned into the Naugang, whilst the latter, in its turn, has been relieved by permitting a portion of its waters in time of flood to enter the Eastern Jumna Canal. The Naugang eventually joins the Maskhara, and through it the Jumna. The Raipur torrent flows into the Búdhi Jumna. Parganah Muzaffarabad is also intersected by four hill torrents, two of which, the Barkala and Sahnsrao, after joining the Duáb Canal, fall into the Maskhara; a third joins the Hindan, and a fourth flows into the Soláni.

The northern portion of the *bangar* of Tahsíl Nakúr is drained by a small

Búdhi Nála.

stream which joins the Maskhara near Badgaon, and the middle portion of the tahsíl forms the reservoir whence the Búdhi Nála is fed. This stream rises near Patna, where the drainage of the Abdullahpur and Chílkána basins finds its way into the *khádir*, and, after closely skirting the upland bank as far as Gokalpur in Sarsáwa, thence crosses the *khádir*, and finally falls into the Jumna just below Fatehpur in Nakúr. On its way it receives the drainage of the Síkrí jhíl by a channel which, Mr. Wynne considers, might easily be deepened so as to completely drain the more swampy portions of that marsh. The Dhaulápra jhíl occupies the next great depression to the south, but has at present only an imperfect outlet, which it is intended to improve towards the Búdhi Nála. Close to it is the Kumhárhera jhíl, which appears to have two outlets,—one to the west, passing through Birwi, and eventually entering the Saindli Nadi near Meghan Mazra on the borders of the district, and another to the east, which forms the head of the tortuous Kátha Nadi.

---

[1] Set. Rep., I., 114.

The Kátha pursues a slow winding course until it falls into the Jumna
near Nagla Rai, of parganah Kairána, in the Muzaffarnagar district. The bed is dry for three-fourths of
the year between Harpál and Mirzapur. Thence, as far as Nágal in Gangoh,
the water collects, and often overflows its banks and forms swamps on either
side. From Nágal to Radaur the bed only contains water during the rainy
seasons. Thence the swamps recommence, and these have been increased by
the injudicious admission of the drainage from near the old canal bed in
western Rámpur, and that of the Andauli swamp, by means of cuts constructed
by the canal officers. The water heads back in the Kátha to such an extent
as to check the flow in the cuts, and consequently the Rámpur cut often bursts
its banks during the rains, while the other is of little use in draining the
marsh. Mr. Wynne estimated the loss in revenue from the want of proper
drainage at Rs. 4,000 a year. The drainage of western Nakúr is effected
by the Saindli Nadi, which takes its rise in a large crescent-shaped jhíl in
the Jumna *khádir* near Kalheri, which appears to have been the remains of
a former bend in the old bed of the river. It assumes the character of a
stream first at Sirsli, and receiving at Meghan Mazra
the drainage from the western outlet of the Kumhár-
hera jhíl, flows in a fairly straight course close to the upland bank in Gangoh,
and finally debouches in the Jumna below Kúuda.

Passing hence to the south of the central tract, the drainage of the west of
Rámpur is carried off in the bed of the old canal until it collects near Anantmau,
whence it is taken by the Andauli cut into the Kátha. The drainage of the tract
south of this and about Núnauta is carried off by another cut into the Krishni
on the east, while in the extreme south-west another cut leads the drainage
through Titron into the Kátha. The heads of the Krishni are in the old canal
and in an off-shoot of the Hindan, having its origin in the Saháranpur parganah. It flows down the centre of Rámpur in a well-defined course, and eventually joins the Hindan. To the west a small rivulet carries off the superfluous
moisture of a long strip of *dákar* land, from Chakní southward.

The central drainage, however, chiefly passes off through the Hindan. This
river, also known as the Chhaja, has its rise in parganah
Muzaffarabad. It takes thence a direction slightly
south-west until it enters the Saháranpur parganah, where it receives on the
right bank the Nágádeo Nadi, and seven and a half miles below Saháranpur,
the united streams of the Pandhoi, a rivulet rising near the village of Sanklapuri,
a little north of the city, and of the Dumaula, a small river draining the country further north-east, and meeting the Pandhoi at Saháranpur. From
Ahmadpur the Hindan communicates, by a cross channel, with the Krishni or
Karsuni Nadi, and again near Niámu, in the Muzaffarnagar District. It is

Kátha Nadi.

Saindli Nadi.

Hindan.

everywhere fordable in Saháranpur, except after rain, and, indeed, generally either altogether or nearly dry. It is not used for irrigation. It is crossed by the road from Saháranpur to Dehra, that from Karnál to Meerut, and Karnál to Muzaffarnagar. At the southern extremity of the Muzaffarnagar district, it receives the west Káli Nadi, which rises in the same latitude on the east, and below this the Krishni on the opposite side, and eventually joins the Jumna in parganah Dankaur of the Bulandshahr district.

East of the Hindan the West Káli Nadi rises about sixteen miles south of
West Káli Nadí.
the Siwáliks, and passing through parganahs Haraura and Nágal, flows southward through Deoband into the Muzaffarnagar district. It receives on its left bank the Kalandra, Síla, Khála and Kalandar streams. The last flows inside the upland sandy ridge of the Manglaur parganah, and joins the Káli on the border of the district. The great drainage line of the east, however, is formed by the Soláni, called near
Soláni.
its source the Kandúr. This river issues from the Mohand pass, having its source at the summit, near Shorepur, and then skirting the uplands of Kheri cuts across, the *khádir*, and follows the upland bank until it finally debouches into the Ganges through the Gordhanpur jhíl in the Muzaffarnagar district, near Shukartár, after a course of about 55 miles. The Soláni is joined in its course, first, by the Háljaura, itself the recipient of many 'raos' or hill torrents; and second, by the Ratmau. The latter takes its rise in a pass of the same name, and receives the drainage of the several 'raos' from its source to Kánsrao. It passes across the Ganges Canal at Dhanauri, where it is used as an escape for the canal. The volume of water is so much increased by this, that when it joins the Soláni it contains a greater volume than its recipient, and frequently causes injury to the neighbouring estates by diluvion and inundation.

Proceeding eastward, the next stream is the Pathari Nadi, which also takes its rise in the Siwáliks, and is carried over the Ganges Canal near Bichpurí. A few hundred yards beyond, the distinct channel ceases, and the water finds its way as it can to the *khádir* land below, covering the upper lands with silt, and cutting up the lower lands on the slope with ravines. As soon as the *khádir* is reached, the several scattered channels again collect into one, and the Pathari flows through swampy ground till it joins the Bánganga. This river issues from the Ganges just above Ajítpur, in parganah Jawálapur, and flows through the thickly wooded wastes of the centre, and the open but scantily cultivated plains in the south of the parganah. Of late the Ganges has begun to pour more and more of its waters into the Bánganga, which has led to considerable damage being done to the villages affected by jt in the Muzaffarnagar district. Mr. S. Martin has suggested that something might be done to avert, or at least control, this excessive flow, especially as those interested were willing to bear the cost, and the remedy has been pronounced by Captain Forbes quite feasible, and not expensive.

To prevent repetition of facts and figures which should otherwise be given

Canals.

under many districts, the general history of the two great systems of canals in the Upper Duáb has been given once for all in the introduction. The Eastern Jumna Canal was opened in the year 1830, and the Ganges Canal commenced to distribute water for irrigation in 1855. The amount of land irrigated in this district by both the canals will be found under the head of "Irrigation" in Part II. of this notice.

The highest point on the river Ganges which boats have ever reached is

Navigation.

Shukartár. Above that point, the navigation is entirely restricted to timber-rafts, or now and then a boat built in the Dún and floated empty down the river, but there is a brisk traffic up and down the Ganges Canal, which was opened for navigation in 1856. Mr. W. Connor has given some calculations, showing the amount of canal traffic to and from and passing Rúrki, from the 1st January, 1870, to the 31st December, 1872. It may be noted here that the principal exports (in maunds) during that period were—cotton, 12,477 ; iron, 13,246; and hemp, 2,745. The principal imports were—iron for the Rúrki workshops, 27,229 maunds ; firewood, 148,344 ; limestone boulders, 138,144 ; earth, 117,800 ; kunkur, 12,150 ; squared timber, 10,351 pieces ; timber in logs, 1,463 ; bambús, 345,516 ; unsquared timber, 14,028 ; and bricks 87,683. Hardly anything passes up by way of Rúrki except stone, 5,000 maunds ; and the principal commodities passing down by Rúrki seem to be timber, grass, firewood, bambús, lime, boulders, in fact forest produce of various descriptions, and bricks. The average tonnage of the boats plying on the canal is 400 maunds, and right-of-way is levied quarterly on each, at the rate of Rs. 13-8, without reference to distance or locality.

There is no navigation on the Jumna Canal, and that on the Jumna river is

Jumna.

naturally even more limited than that on the Ganges, though it appears that boats averaging 52 feet long at top, 32 feet at bottom, 16 feet wide at top, 13 feet at bottom, 4 feet in depth, and drawing 2¼ feet of water when laden, of 600 maunds burden, used to be built at Rámpur Mandi, opposite Rajghát in the Dún, and floated down the river for sale. It is also stated that from 300 to 350 such boats, laden with karts and logs, used annually to leave for Dehli and Agra ; while the amount of bhang yearly despatched from Rajghát amounted to 3,000 or 4,000 maunds, besides the same quantity of stone-lime. This traffic was chiefly carried on in the hot weather and rains, and some return traffic in Agra stone, millstones, iron and drugs also existed. Little or no trace of either traffic is now to be found in this District.

The principal jhíls in the district have already been noticed. The old

Sultánpur jhíl had increased (1860) to such an extent to swallow up quite the bulk of the formerly cultias vated lands, so that the revenue of several villages had been largely reduced, while others were held under direct management. Owing to the successful operations of the canal officers, the swamp has been drained, and all but a few isolated patches reclaimed; and the improvement has been so steady, that these patches, too, will also become culturable. Other projects for the reclamation of lands swamped by excessive percolation from the canal, and by bad drainage, have been undertaken by the same department with the happiest results.

The main line of communication is the Dehli and Panjáb Railway, opened in 1869. The first station is Deoband, five miles from the border of the

Muzaffarnagar district; the next is Saháranpur, 21 miles further on ; and the last is Sarsáwa, 10 miles from Saháranpur and five miles from the Jumna. The railway follows the road that has been the highway from the Duáb to the Panjáb from the earliest times. A project for a branch line from the Dehli line at Deoband *viá* Rúrki and Hardwár to Dehra, was prepared by Mr. A. Campbell, Superintendent of the Rúrki Workshops, in the year 1868, but nothing came of his proposals. A detailed account of his design, based upon the narrow gauge system and the theory that the Ganges Canal works might be utilised for railway purposes, has been printed at the Thomason Civil Engineering College Press. His estimate of the probable cost was Rs. 13,70,000. Surveys have also been undertaken in connection with the Oudh and Rohilkhand Railway which is to join the Panjáb line at Saháranpur.

Amongst the principal roads of the first class and metalled is that from Saháranpur to the tunnel in the Mohand pass leading to Dehra,

$34\frac{3}{4}$ miles. The traffic to the Dún and the large hill stations of Landour and Mussooree (Masúri) follows this road, which is passable for wheeled carriages on to Rájpur, at the foot of the Landour hills. Another route to the Dún, formerly much used, was a road branching off from the old trunk road a little above the town of Muzaffarnagar, and thence to Rúrki, 22 miles east of Saháranpur, and on to Fatehpur, 13 miles from Mohand and 15 miles from Saháranpur. This line also is metalled throughout. An unmetalled road runs from the Muzaffarnagar boundary through Deoband and Nágal to Saháranpur, which is metalled from 6 miles on the Deoband side of Saháranpur through Sarsáwa to the Jumna. The metalled road from Rúrki to Fatehpur is joined to that from Mohand to Saháranpur by a raised earthen road from Bhagwánpur, $6\frac{1}{2}$ miles beyond Rúrki, to Gágalheri, 7 miles from Saháranpur, for a distance of $8\frac{1}{2}$ miles.

The second-class raised and bridged unmetalled roads, and the third-class raised unbridged and unmetalled roads within the district, are as follow :—

Second-class Roads.

From		To		Length.		From		To		Length.	
				M.	F.					M.	F.
Saháranpur	...	Jalálabad	...	23	7	Rúrki	...	Bahádurabad	...	9	2
"	...	Karnál	...	29	4	"	...	Bijnaur	...	22	2
"	...	Chilkána	...	9	0	Gágalheri	...	Nágal	...	10	0
Gangoh	...	Badgaon	...	17	0	Lakhnaur	...	Manglaur	...	16	4
Deoband	...	Manglaur	...	10	6	Títron	...	Jalálabad	...	3	0
Sarsáwa	...	Nakúr	...	8	6	Rúrki	...	Lúksár	...	11	2
Nakúr	...	Títron	...	18	6	Nakúr	...	Rahmanpur	...	5	2
Saháranpur	"	Muzaffarnagar	...	21	1	"	...	Deoband	...	26	4

Third class Roads.

From		To		Length.		From		To		Length.	
Bahádurabad	...	Hardwár	...	8	0	Hardwár	...	Khára	...	43	0
Muzaffarabad	...	Kandúr Nadí	...	6	2	Bhagwánpur	...	Bahádurabad	...	13	0
Deoband	...	Bijnaur	...	6	2	Manglaur	...	Lúksár	...	11	0

Bridges and ferries.

The river Hindan is crossed by a good bridge at Gágalheri, and there used to be another bridge across the same river at the village of Lakhnaur, six miles from Saháranpur, on the road to Deoband ; but it was carried away by a flood some years ago, and has never since been repaired. From Rúrki to Hardwár, the left bank of the Ganges Canal affords an excellent path, nineteen miles long, for foot passengers ; but country carts are forced to take a more difficult, though shorter route, through the Ganges *khádir.*

Ferries.

The ferries on the Ganges are at Shíshamghát Báláwáli, and Nágal ; those on the Jumna are at Begi, Fatehpur Ját, Rájghát and Maudhapur. The former are under the Collector of Bijnaur, and the latter under the Deputy Commissioner of Umballa (Ambála). The only ferries under the Collector of Saháranpur are those at Ránípur and Dargáhipur on the Bánganga ; and these are only required during the rains. There is also a bridge-of-boats across the Ganges opposite Kankhal.

Meteorology and climate.

The climate of Saháranpur is that of the North-West Provinces in general, modified by a northern position and proximity to the hills. It is at one season tropical, at another partially European. The cold weather commences earlier and lasts longer than in the districts further south-east, but the heat in May and June is considerable. Another peculiarity of the climate is, that although the severity of the hot season is, at its commencement, sometimes mitigated by local thunderstorms and showers, evidently due to the neighbourhood of the hills, the regular rains (or summer monsoon) are later in their arrival here than in the Lower Provinces, and the rain-fall is less. The minimum temperature observed by Dr. Royle was 37° in January, the maximum 105° or 107°, as compared with 111° at Ghazipur and 114° at Benares. The mean temperature of the cold weather months, November, December, January and February, is 64°, 55°, 52°, and 55° respectively. The temperature rises rapidly from the beginning of March, and by the middle of June the maximum is attained. The rains usually set in towards the close of that month, and last till the middle of September; but they have been known to continue a month later. Irregularities in their occurrence are surely followed or accompanied by disease, generally in the form of fever.

The following table gives the mean monthly temperature in the shade, and the mean monthly range at Rúrki, in the north-east of the district :—

			January.	February.	March.	April.	May.	June.	July.	August.	September.	October.	November.	December.	Annual mean.
1870	Mean	...	57	64	70	80	92	91	85	83	81	77	64	58	75
	Range	...	32	26	27	31	33	21	14	14	18	27	35	32	
1871	Mean	...	56	65	71	82	85	85	82	83	83	76	65	58	74
	Range	...	28	25	34	32	24	16	11	12	17	31	36	28	
1872	Mean	...	57	59	73	81	88	90	83	83	81	75	66	59	73
	Range	...	37	43	45	24	48	42	23	28	30	40	48	41	

For 1872 the range shows the difference between the highest and lowest reading of the maxima and minima in the shade. The general mean is that of the standard thermometer. See ROORKEE for details.

The average total rain-fall, according to seasons, for the whole district, has been as follows from 1860-61 to 1870-71 :—

Period.		1860-61.	1861-62.	1862-63.	1863-64.	1864-65.	1865-66.	1866-67.	1867-68.	1868-69.	1869-70.	1870-71.
1st June to 30th September	...	16·7	34·2	42·6	38·4	30·7	26·9	25·1	40·6	12·5	15·6	33·6
1st October to 31st January	...	0·2	0·5	2·1	3·3	...	4·7	1.2	2·8	2·2	2·3	1·8
1st February to 31st May ...	...	2·0	2·4	11·9	2·7	9·8	2·4	3·4	6·0	5·5	3·2	4·7
Total	...	18·9	37·1	56·6	44·4	40·5	34·0	29·7	49·4	20·2	21·6	40·1

The actual total rain-fall for the principal towns in the district for a series of years, and irrespective of season, is given below from records existing in the office of the Board of Revenue :—

Name of Station.	1844-45.	1845-46.	1846-47.	1847-48.	1848-49.	1849-50.	Average.
Sadr Station	45·81	30·30	35·10	48·74	20·07	28·31	34·72
Deoband	40·02	28·25	48·90	41·88	24·66	68·06	41·96
Manglaur	37·86	23·26	36·51	49·01	20·16	39·27	34·51

Name of Station.	1848-49.	1849-50.	Name of Station	1848-49.	1849-50.	Name of Station.	1848-49.	1849-50.
Nakúr ...	31·22	47·59	Jawálapur ...	21·35	52·34	Gangoh ...	27·19	44·98
Rúrki ...	30·87	58·25	Hardwár ...	49·58	50·47	Kheri ...	32·47	52·93
Nágal ...	24·30	54·14	Sultánpur ...	38·02	50·85	Bahat ...	26·58	53·72
Badgaon ...	17·04	40·21	Bhagwánpur ...	26·92	53·64	Raipur ...	23·15	54·12
Rámpur ...	31·19	47·79	Chilkána ...	24·36	44·14	Mohand ...	31·01	60·14

PART II.

PRODUCTIONS OF THE DISTRICT.

The *fauna* of the district is abundant and varied. Tigers (*sher dárhidár*) are

Animal kingdom.

still numerous in the forest belt along the foot of the Siwáliks, and also in the khádir of the Ganges. According to Hamilton the lion existed in vast numbers in this district in the early part of the present century, but Dr. Royle, whose means of information were of the best description for the same period, speaks of the lion as only having been found "to the west of the Jumna, especially on the edge of the

Lion.

desert near Hánsi." It is stated by Bernier, as quoted by Thornton, that the country about Agra and Dehli and along the upper course of the Jumna had extensive waste tracts abounding in wild beasts, and that, among others, the lion was frequently hunted and slain by the rulers of Dehli. There is, however, no well authenticated tradition of

Panther.

lions ever having been found in this district. Leopards are common, and Mr. H. B. Webster, C. S., describes three varieties. The first and largest kind is the leopard proper or panther, locally called the *sher guldár*, a powerful animal capable of killing a bullock. The second is smaller and of a darker colour; it is known as the *lakhabagha*, or tree-tiger, and seeks inferior prey; and the third variety, named *tendúa*, is not much larger than a small sized setter, and not so high. Wild cats of all sorts are numerous, some of them are not larger than the domestic cat, and others approach the *tendúa* in size.

The lynx is also found as well as the hyena, and wolves are numerous. The sloth-bear *(jhábar)* inhabits the Siwáliks, and the wild-boar is found all over the district, and is especially abundant in the khádir. In the rains wild elephants frequently descend from the Siwáliks to feed, and often come as far as the Ganges valley, ten miles south of the hills, where they cause much destruction amongst the rice fields. The most common species of deer are the *sámbar* otherwise called the *mahá* or *jarau*, the *chítal* or spotted deer, the *khákar* or barking deer, and the *párá* or hog deer. Antelopes *(hiran)*, the four horned antelope *(chausínga)*, and the *gúral* or Himálayan chamois are also found, but the two latter do not venture into the lowlands, and the black buck is comparatively rare. The *nílgái* (Portax pictus) is found in the river basins and small jungles to the north. The *langúr* (Presbytis schistaceus) so common at Mussooree descends as far as the very edge of the Siwáliks, a fact which is the more remarkable as the *langúr* is also found at elevations of from 11,000 to 12,000 feet in Kumaon. The smaller mammalia, as jackals, foxes, porcupines may be passed over. The animals inhabiting the Dún will be found under the notice of that district, and those common to all the Duáb districts will be given under the Farukhabad district. There are not many poisonous snakes; the *karait* and the *kobra* are those best known. Of those not poisonous, the Siwálik python, a sort of boa-constrictor, which grows to an immense size, is the best known, but, notwithstanding that it often attains a length of twenty-five feet, it appears to be harmless, and confines its depredations to the smaller mammalia. The deaths from snake bites and the attacks of wild animals are not numerous, considering the character of the district. In 1869 the deaths from these causes were given at 45, of which 44 were due to snake bites and only one to wild animals. In 1872, the deaths from snake bites and wild animals were as follow :—

Month.	Males.	Month.	Males.	Females	Month.	Males.	Females.	Month.	Males.	Females.
January ...	1	April ...	...	...	July ...	4	4	October ...	2	1
February ...	...	May ...	1	1	August ...	5	4	November...	1	...
March ...	1	June ...	1	1	September ...	3	2	December...	2	...

As observed in other districts, the deaths from snake bites are more frequent during the rains. No rewards are given for their destruction, but for that of other wild animals, the following scale is allowed:—Tigers and full-grown bears, Rs. 5 ; hyena or female wolf, Rs. 3 ; tiger cub, Rs. 2-8 ; male wolf, Rs. 2-2 ; female wolf-whelp 12 annas ; male-whelp 8 annas.

There is no local breed of cattle in the district. Cows fetch from
Domestic cattle.
Rs. 10 to Rs. 40 a head, according to their milch qualities. The bullocks in common use for agricultural purposes cost from Rs. 15 to Rs. 50 each. The average is about Rs. 30. The price of buffaloes varies from Rs. 20 to Rs. 40. The breed of horses in
Horses.
the southern part of the district called the Kátha is considered very good, and it was partly on that account that a stud depôt was established at Saháranpur in the year 1842. Stud stallions have been located for breeding purposes in Bhaila, Simlána and others of the Kátha villages, as well as at Bhagwánpur, Chandanpur, and Bhalewa Gaj in the Rúrki Tahsíl, and the foals produced from the zamíndári mares are purchased on account of Government. It would be very hard to calculate the cost of a horse thus procured before it is fit for use. Each can hardly cost Government less than from Rs. 1,000 to Rs. 1,200, if not more. Casters, which used to be sold by auction at the Hardwár fair every year, fetch from Rs. 50 to Rs. 300 each, the average being from Rs. 100 to Rs. 150. A fair country-bred can be had for about Rs. 200 in the district, but at Hardwár, prices are much higher, and a good horse can rarely be purchased for less than Rs. 400 or Rs. 500. The best horses are generally picked up by the agents from the Irregular Cavalry regiments, before the caravans of horse dealers from Afghánistán or elsewhere actually reach the fair itself, and are in this way bought at more reasonable prices. A private speculator is fortunate if he can get a really good animal for Rs. 400. At Saháranpur, oats have been used instead of gram for feeding horses, with much advantage, though natives are, through habit, prejudiced against its use. The Rájpút zamíndárs have been, from time immemorial, the principal horse breeders in the district.[1]

There are three systems of breeding in the farms. First the *asámi* system, under which the Government lend mares to the farmers and supply stallions ; second,

---

[1] A Parliamentary return recently issued on the state of the breeding studs in India, shows that the system has not been successful after the experiment has been tried for 76 years. The Bombay and Madras armies are supplied with horses, from the open market, the former paying £55, and the latter £57 10s. per horse though the Madras horse is raised to £91 by the unwise retention of the animals in depôt. The Government cost of breeding horses is stated by the Controller of Military Accounts at £148, and by the latest Stud Committee at £219 ; the difference arises from the modes of debiting to the Department. This enormous discrepancy is rendered all the more glaring by a statement of the Committee to the effect that strings of northern horses from Kabul are brought to the market at £40 each.

the *zamíndári* system, under which Government supply the stallions to the farmers' mares and buy the foals ; and thirdly, the home system, under which Government owns both stallions and mares. It is believed that the Government of India propose to abolish the *asámi* system and to some extent the *zamíndári* system, and to establish a new breeding farm in the Panjáb in order to maintain a reserve of one thousand horses. The Duke of Argyll objected to both these proposals. While, however, granting that studs cannot immediately be abolished, he proposed that Government should gradually withdraw from horse-breeding and liberally encourage private enterprise in that direction by prizes, giving good prices for foals and importing stallions. The report shows that at present horse-breeding is a decaying pursuit.

The *magar* or snub-nosed alligator, which attacks both cattle and men, and the *gariyál*, an alligator provided with a long snout, which lives on fish, are found in the Ganges, the Jumna, the canals, and sometimes in the smaller streams. The larger rivers harbour a repulsive looking kind of fish called a *gúnchi*, a regular fresh-water shark, of which specimens have been caught weighing over one hundred pounds. The character of the fisheries in the Meerut Division has already been noticed in the introduction, and a list of the principal species found in these provinces has been given there. The most valuable of the edible fish found in this district are the *rohu, maháser, anwári, sol*, and *chilwa.*

Fish.

Though not so plentiful as formerly, fish are still found in the larger rivers in considerable quantities, and in the small streams after rain ; but measures are sadly needed to prevent the wholesale destruction of fish of all sizes near the canal heads, more particularly on the Jumna Canal. Fish is used as an article of food by the Muhammadans, which form so important an element in the population, by the lower orders of Hindús, and even by certain clans of Rájpúts. The Meos, both Hindú and Musalmán, are the principal fishermen, and come into this district chiefly from Bijnaur. The price of fish is generally from one to two annas a ser, but the *anwári* is dearer.

The forest produce will be described under the Dún District and in the supplementary volume on the vegetable products of these provinces. It is sufficient to notice here the food grains and products under cultivation in the district. The *rabí* or spring crop is sown in October and reaped in March to April. Its staples are wheat, barley, oats, millet, peas, beans, carrots, vegetables, linseed and the different species of mustard seed, both of which last are cultivated for the oil obtained by expression. The *kharíf* or rain crop is sown in June and gathered in October, and consists of rice, joár, Indian corn, *bájrá*, cotton, melons and vegetables. Indigo and cotton are also grown to a considerable extent since the introduction of canal irrigation has rendered the growth of the former crop

Vegetable kingdom.

a certainty. The following tables, submitted to the Board of Revenue in 1869-70 and 1871-72, show the distribution and produce of the principal crops:

Kharif.	Area in acres in 1869-70.	Area in acres in 1871-72.	Weight in maunds in 1871-72.	Rabi.	Area in acres in 1869-70.	Area in acres in 1871-72.	Weight in maunds in 1871-72.	Two season crops.	Area in acres in 1869-70.	Area in acres in 1871-72.
Rice ...	72,644	86,731	943,834	Wheat and barley.	262,652	284,309	2,120,617	Sugar ...	24,421	28,143
Cotton ..	64,992	46,178	57,626	Pulse ...	4?,329	59,055	4,95,189	Vegetable,	8,988	8,072
Joar and Bajra.	63,316	71,447	287,466	Oil-seeds ...	2,885	49,064	...	Fruit trees,	11,095	6,538
Oilseeds ...	4,017	6,480	31,417	Others ...	60,440	...	1,247,133	...	...	...
Other crops,	211,578	154,147	...	...	...	...	...	Total ...	44,504	...
Total ...	398,547	364,983	1,299,843	Total ...	369,606	392,528	3,662,939	Grand Total	812,657	43,753

Of the total area in 1869-70, 33,940 acres were cropped in both harvests, leaving an actually cultivated area amounting to 778,717 acres. Of the grain recorded by weight, it was estimated that in 1871-72 the exports amounted to 800,650 maunds, and the grain kept for home consumption to 4,362,131 maunds of 82 ℔s. each.

The following table gives the local estimate of the cost of production per acre

Cost of production per acre.

of the principal crops, with their outturn and value for two tahsíls. The average is struck on the outturn from superior grain and land, and inferior grain and land.

	Tahsíl Deoband.			Tahsíl Nakúr.			Tahsíl Rúrki.		
	Cost of production.	Outturn.	Value.	Cost of production.	Outturn.	Value.	Cost of production.	Outturn.	Value.
	R. a.	M. s.	R. a.	R. a.	M. s.	R. a	R. a.	M. s.	R. a.
Wheat	14 3	9 0	12 11	5 12	18 20	15 0	10 8	24 0	19 3
Barley ... a.	12 3	18 0	18 0	5 8	20 0	10 0	9 8	30 0	20 0
Rice	13 7	15 0	15 0	6 8	36 0	18 0	10 0	24 0	16 0
Peas	8 3	12 0	15 0	...	...	...	...	...	...
Joar ...	6 13	4 20	5 10	...	...	...	9 0	...	21 0
Gram	12 1	9 0	5 10	3 6	12 0	8 0	8 8	36 0	28 0
Linseed ...	8 8	4 20	13 8	...	...	...	...	...	...
Cotton	14 12	4 20	18 0	10 0	12 0	24 0	13 0	4 20	18 0
Til	5 2	4 20	9 0	...	...	...	...	...	...
Mustard ...	9 13	12 0	24 0	...	...	...	...	...	...
Indigo ...	38 9	0 32	64 0	...	...	...	...	...	...
Safflower ...	6 12	0 15	7 8	...	...	...	...	...	...
Indian corn ...	6 9	12 0	12 12	5 0	15 0	9 0	10 3	24 0	16 0
Bajra	5 2	4 20	5 10	1 12	9 10	6 0	7 8	12 0	10 0
Vegetables ...	6 12	...	16 0	...	...	...	...	...	...
Sugar-cane ...	44 0	18 0	54 0	13 4	21 24	36 0	50 4	24 0	72 0
Poppy ...	25 8	0 12	60 0	...	...	...	...	...	...

These tables show such curious discrepancies, that there can be no doubt but that the proper mode of collecting this description of agricultural statistics is at present but very imperfectly understood. Mr. Thornton's produce tables will be found at p. 23 of the Appendix to the Settlement Report (1864).

The mode of husbandry does not differ from that practised in Meerut and other districts of this division. The local estimate of the extent of land which can be cultivated by a single plough depends upon the number of bullocks used. One plough usually takes two pair of oxen, and is called a *pukka hal,* while a plough with only one pair is known as an *ádhá hal.* By means of the former, from 80 to 100 *kuchcha* bíghas (13 to 16 acres) may be tilled in the year, and by the latter from 40 to 50. Sometimes three pair of bullocks are used in one plough; in which case 150 bíghas *kuchcha*[1] and upwards may be kept under cultivation between the two harvests. One plough represents a capital of from Rs. 71 to Rs. 137, as noted below.[2] The rotation of crops is guided by the season, and land is seldom intentionally left fallow for any length of time, except in such places as the wilder parts of the Ganges *khádir.*

Agriculture.

Irrigation is carried on extensively in this district from wells, tanks, and canals. According to Mr. Court's return of 1870, out of a total cultivated area amounting to 736,873 acres, 162,317 acres were irrigated, and of these more than one-half, or 84,404 acres, were irrigated from canals alone. In parganah Saháranpur the irrigation is almost exclusively from canals, with a small amount from wells and tanks, and none from the Hindan, Dumaula and Pandhoi, which intersect the parganah. In Haraura, Muzaffarabad and the greater portion of Faizabad, again, we have only well-irrigation, and in the northern portions of the two latter parganahs only from *pukka* wells, owing to the great depth at which water is found. In the Nakúr Tahsíl the uplands beyond the reach of canal irrigation, as a rule, afford facilities for the excavation of earthen wells which last from one season to two or three years according to the nature of the subsoil. In the country about the head-waters of the Kátha, Hindan and west Kálí Nadí, the earthen wells require to be strengthened by a circular framework of roughly-hewn short flat planks, or rather plates of *dhák (Butea frondosa)* wood, loosely fitted together; above this, again, is a wattling of *bájrá* stalks to within a few feet of the top, when the soil is usually stiff enough to require no further protection. But even this somewhat elaborate arrangement will seldom last more than four years. In portions of Bhagwánpur, the timber lining has often to be carried

Irrigation.

---

[1] The *pukka* bígha is 0·5062 of an acre, and three *kuchcha* bíghas are equivalent to one *pukka* bígha. [2] One or two pair of bullocks, Rs. 60 to Rs. 120 ; plough and appurtenances, Rs. 2-8 to Rs. 3-8 ; harrow, Rs. 1-8 ; *úd* or *kolhu,* Rs. 5 to Rs. 10, and sundries about Rs. 2. As this calculation differs according to the insertion or absence of petty items, it might be safer to say that the capital invested in one plough varies from Rs. 81 to Rs. 150.

to the very tip of the well. These protected wells are usually known as *kathkúls*.

In writing of parganah Bhagwánpur, Mr. Wynne remarks—"Considering the nearness of water to the surface, I was at first incredulous as to the impossibility of using kuchcha wells far more extensively, but by digging two experimental wells in different places, I found that after irrigating about one-fourth of a bígha the lower portion became quicksand, in which sand and water were mixed inseparably, and that almost immediately afterwards the whole fell in. Indeed, I must here remark that, as a general rule, there is in this respect (the adaptability of the soil for the digging of *kuchcha* wells) a very great difference between the lands west and those east of the Hindan. In the former, the facility is practically only limited by the number of cattle and the labour available ; nearer to the Hindan the well is more expensive, but can still be dug with advantage ; but across the Hindan to the east there is, speaking broadly, only one tract (that down the centre of Nágal and north of Deoband) where *kuchcha* wells can be used freely, and to the east of Tahsíl Rúrki they are unknown in the uplands. I may here mention another striking difference between the methods of irrigation east and west of the Hindan. To the east, the use of the leathern bag is universal, to the west that of the Persian wheel. I have never seen a Persian wheel east, and have rarely seen a leather bag used west of the Hindan. The cause assigned in answer to my enquiries was that it required relays of three men, all hard tasked, to work the '*charas*' (leather bag) ; and only a man and a boy (the latter hardly tasked at all) to work the '*harat*' (Persian wheel). The inference which I was told to draw, was that labour was more scanty to the west. This however is not the case, but rather the reverse, as will be seen by looking over the percentages of agricultural population. The true inference is, I think, that the people are (as is, indeed, the fact) more indolent in the tract to the west. There can be no doubt that the *charas* does more work than the other. " *Ogals* or mere water-holes are used in the khádir.

In 1870 we have seen that more than one-half of the irrigated area was watered by canals, comprising the greater portion of parganahs Sahâranpur and Râmpur, and considerable areas in parganahs Faizabad, Sultánpur, Sarsáwa, Nakúr, Gangoh and Nágal. The area irrigated by the Eastern Jumna Canal is much more extensive than that supplied with water by the Ganges Canal, which has a comparatively short irrigating course in this district.

During the exceptional year of drought, 1860-61, the area irrigated by the Ganges Canal in this district was, for the *kharif* of 1861, 6 470 acres, and for the *rabi* of 1862, 12,627 acres ; from the Eastern Jumna Canal the returns show—*kharif* of 1861, 28,368 acres, and *rabí* of 1862, 52,635 acres. On the Ganges Canal, the kharíf of 1862 gives 7,677 acres ; rabí of 1863, 2,793 acres ; kharíf of 1863, 3,904 acres ; and *rabí* of 1864, 8,180 acres. A similar falling off is shown on the Jumna Canal,—the *rabí* of 1863 fell to 21,488 acres, and in 1864 the irrigated area during the same season only amounted to 14,149 acres. There was, again, a great increase during the drought of 1868-69, when the total average area irrigated reached its maximum, and a corresponding decrease in the following years of ordinary and abundant rainfall.

The following table gives the irrigated area for each season in the parganahs watered by the Ganges Canal in this district :—

Year.			Parganah.					
			Jawálápur.	Rúrki.	Manglaur.	Deoband.	Bhagwán-pur.	Total.
1866-67.			Acres.	Acres.	Acres.	Acres.	Acres.	Acres.
Kharíf	...	...	1,186	38	5,113	1,518	84	7,939
Rabí	...	...	2,907	140	7,790	3,283	130	14,250
	Total	...	4,093	178	12,903	4,801	214	22,189
1867-68.								
Kharíf	...	...	1,727	61	6,899	2,518	124	11,329
Rabí	...	...	2,442	27	4,113	2,108	59	8,749
	Total	...	4,169	88	11,012	4,626	183	20,078
1868-69.								
Kharíf	...	...	2,310	50	5,776	2,288	92	10,516
Rabí	...	...	10,890	2,097	15,825	5,477	401	34,690
	Total	...	13,200	2,147	21,601	7,765	493	45,206
1869-70.								
Kharíf	...	...	3,926	258	7,605	2,289	175	14,253
Rabí	...	...	2,148	26	2,547	1,799	19	6,539
	Total	...	6,074	284	10,152	4,088	194	20,792
1870-71.								
Kharíf	...	...	3,107	103	5,143	1,681	104	10,138
Rabí	...	...	2,043	21	5,086	2,536	37	9,723
	Total	...	5,150	124	10,229	4,217	141	19,861
1871-72.								
Kharíf	...	...	1,372	34	4,475	1,551	113	7,545
Rabí	...	...	1,422	61	4,276	2,348	51	8,158
	Total	...	2,794	95	8,751	3,899	164	15,703
1872-73.								
Kharíf	...	...	1,403	69	5,236	1,734	108	8,550
Rabí	...	...	840	30	2,542	1,405	21	4,838
	Total	..	2,243	99	7,778	3,139	129	13,388

As early as 1856-57, the area irrigated by the Eastern Jumna Canal amounted to 17,470 acres in this district. Its work during the last seven years is shown below. It may, however, be remarked here that, owing to defects in construction and the difficulties presented by the natural obstacles which pass its line, the Jumna Canal has undoubtedly, in some places, been the means of producing prejudicial effects upon the health of the people :—

Eastern Jumna Canal.

Year.	Faizabad.	Muzaffarabad.	Saháranpur.	Sultánpur.	Sarsáwa.	Nakúr.	Rámpur.	Gangoh.	Deoband.	Total.
	Acres.	Acres.	Acres.	Acres.	Acres.	Acres.	Acres.	Acres.	Acres.	Acres.
1866-67.										
Kharíf ...	335	46	7,786	1,429	409	1,479	11,760	2,482	630	26,356
Rabí ...	1,301	50	13,187	2,372	1,306	2,931	19,966	5,463	920	47,496
Total ...	1,636	96	20,973	3,801	1,715	4,410	31,726	7,945	1,550	73,852
1867-68.										
Kharíf ...	618	57	11,148	1,802	607	1,844	13,454	3,184	818	33,532
Rabí ...	1,081	67	10,742	2,144	1,318	2,229	13,894	3,320	494	35,289
Total ...	1,699	124	21,890	3,946	1,925	4,073	27,348	6,504	1,312	68,821
1868-69.										
Kharíf ...	1,869	84	12,066	2,002	763	1,885	15,650	3,512	895	38,726
Rabí ...	4,218	277	21,716	3,442	1,747	4,125	27,253	6,181	982	69,941
Total ...	6,087	361	33,772	5,444	2,510	6,010	42,903	9,693	1,877	108,667
1869-70.										
Kharíf ...	1,366	71	14,634	1,930	1,056	2,428	17,642	4,258	818	44,203
Rabí ...	1,175	...	9,881	1,987	1,593	3,083	19,223	4,636	737	42,315
Total ...	2,541	71	24,515	3,917	2,649	5,511	36,865	8,894	1,555	86,518
1870-71.										
Kharíf ...	1,016	30	11,490	1,594	770	2,064	16,111	3,827	862	37,764
Rabí ...	1,117	9	7,986	1,582	770	1,890	12,938	3,620	457	30,369
Total ...	2,133	39	19,476	3,176	1,540	3,954	29,049	7,447	1,319	66,133
1871-72.										
Kharíf ...	613	46	6,249	1,083	482	1,424	11,993	2,672	724	25,286
Rabí ...	404	...	6,946	1,524	607	1,986	11,364	3,326	730	26,887
Total ...	1,017	46	13,195	2,607	1,089	3,410	23,357	5,998	1,454	52,173
1872-73.										
Kharíf ...	594	88	8,553	1,616	634	1,548	13,499	3,258	758	30,548
Rabí ...	667	11	8,230	1,741	783	1,852	11,544	2,910	840	28,578
Total ...	1,261	99	16,783	3,357	1,417	3,800	25,043	6,168	1,598	59,126

In 1836-37 A. D., 126 out of 204 villages traversed by the Duáb Canal, and only 24 villages not immediately on its banks, received

Progress of irrigation.

water. Some of these were either held free of revenue or were not then under settlement. In 81 villages which Mr. Thornton examined, only 5,030 acres were irrigated by the Duáb Canal, and the Ganges Canal was not then in existence. In 1854-58, the measurement papers. show 164,911 acres, or 21·9 per cent. of the total cultivated area received water from all sources, most of which was from wells. In 1865-66, the canal irrigation reached 48,546 acres, which rose to 96,041 acres in 1866-67 ; 88,899 acres in 1867-68 ; 153,873 acres in 1868-69 ; 107,310 acres in 1869-70 ; 87,994 acres in 1870-71 ; 67,876 acres in 1871-72, and 72,514 acres in 1872-73. The increase from 1867-68 to 1869-70 is due to the drought of those years. How much of this was given to lands previously dry, and how much has superseded well-irrigation has not been ascertained, but freshly irrigated land may be put down at more than one-half the total area irrigated by canals. The proportion of well irrigation to canal irrigation may also be estimated at two-thirds.

In 1838 Mr. Thornton estimated the increase of revenue due to canal irri-

Increase of revenue due to canal irrigation.

gation on the 5,030 acres he examined at Rs. 1,177 or 3 annas 8·9 pie per acre. In the Sahâranpur Tahsíl, Mr. Robertson attributed Rs. 19,505 of his assessment to the action of canals on 28,071 acres, giving an influence of 11 annas 1·4 pie per acre. He does not explain the method by which he arrived at this result. Mr. Wynne in the remaining three tahsíls claims Rs. 59,864 as due to canal irrigation on 68,652 acres, which thus gives an increase of 13 annas 11·4 pie per acre. This result was obtained by deducting the rates assessed upon unirrigated land with similar capabilities in the neighbouring villages from that assessed upon the canal-irrigated land. " This calculation can only be correct if it were assumed that all the irrigation is from canals, and that there was no well-irrigation previously which canals have susperseded. No information is given on these points.' The canal department calculates the increase of land revenue due to canal irrigation during 1872-73 at Rs. 79,369 in this district, and credit Rs. 64,106 to the Eastern Jumna Canal, and Rs. 15,263 to the Ganges Canal. The influence of the canal has been exercised to more advantage even than causing an increase in the land-revenue. Its civilising effects on the hitherto unruly and singularly uncontrollable Gújar clans has been mentioned in the notice of parganahs Gangoh and Rámpur. The same beneficial results are generally observable throughout the canal irrigated tracts in other parganahs. As a rule, the people have become more thrifty and more industrious in view of the certain return for labour now insured to them, whether the season be unfavourable or not. Similarly, in the adjoining district of Muzaffarnagar, the settlement officer writes :—" The chief caste in the trans-Hindan villages are Gújars, wonderfully transformed by the canal, and in some degree respectable themselves, though not the cause of respectability in others. They find agriculture more profitable than thieving ; but they harbour Kahárs and others who live by roguery, and are always ready to pass on a stolen buffalo, or foil the inquiries of a police officer."

The cultivated area has steadily increased in the last twenty-five years, and

Cultivated area.

continues to progress, more especially towards the north of the district. The following table gives the statistics at different periods :—

| Year. | Total area in acres. | ASSESSED AREA | | UNASSESSED AREA. | | Revenue demand in rupees. | RATE PER ACRE. | | |
		Cultivated.	Culturable.	Revenue-free.	Barren		On total area.	On assessed area.	On cultivated area.
							Rs. a. p.	Rs. a. p	Rs. a p
1848	1,385,899	681,117	341,812	30,407	332,563	1846-47 10,67,434	0 12 6	1 0 8	1 9 1
1853	1,383,898	774,253	211,449	54,597	343,599	1851-52. 10,64,513	0 12 4	1 1 3	1 6 0
1865	1,425,825	781,867	202,922	219,651	221,385	1863-64. 10,93,950	0 12 3	1 1 9	1 6 5
1866	1,081,763	745,178	194,320	12,788	129,477	1866-67 12,47,951	1 2 8	1 5 7	1 11 1
1872	1,420,194	797,675	205,937	109,729	306,853	1872-73. 13,54,655	0 15 3	1 5 7	1 11 2

The figures for 1866 [1] exclude from the total area the Siwálik tract. In 1838 the cultivated area started with 606,847 acres under cultivation. There have been modifications of boundaries since then, so that comparison until 1853 is impossible. Of the whole culturable area, 79 per cent. is now under cultivation; 21·9 per cent. of the cultivated area of revenue-paying estates is irrigated, and 31·7 per cent. of revenue-free estates. In 1872, 395,174 acres were under spring crops, and 402,501 acres under rain crops. It is remarkable that, as early as 1842, 314 estates had attained to such a state of cultivation that a pledge was given that the assessment should not be raised until the revenue-rate on· the contiguous villages exceeded the incidence of the revenue-rate in these estates. This pledge was observed at the recent settlement.

[1] From Settlement Report, 1870, which does not give the total area, or materials from which it can be discovered. The area there given is 1,078,511 acres, of which 13,682 are revenue-free, 142,037 barren, and 923,674 assessed. The totals of three statements relating to the same areas do not agree.

In 1806-7 there were 30,093 bighas, or about 15,000 acres under cotton as the district then stood. In 1838 the cotton area was three per cent. of the total cultivated area; and in 1866, in three tahsíls it had risen to 8·1 per cent., owing to the high prices during the American war. It has since fallen considerably. Wheat and barley are, how-

Cotton.

ever, the most important crops of all; in 1806-7 A.D., they occupied 320,300 bighas, or about 160,200 acres, and yielded 28 per cent. of the revenue. In 1838 the area cultivated for these cereals amounted to 30 per cent. of the total cultivated area; and in 1866 in three tahsíls to 31·7 per cent. In 1869-70 there were 262,652 acres under wheat and barley, or 33·7 per cent. of the total cultivated area of the whole district.

Wheat and barley.

The rice area in 1866 in the Nakúr, Deoband and Rúrkí Tahsíls amounted to 12·05 per cent. of the total area. In the *dákar* tracts of Sultánpur, and in the villages lying along the old bed of the Jumna, *chahora* rice, known by its long drooping ears, is grown. The rice grown from Dása Mazra to Manoharpur, in the same parganah, is very good, but inferior to that produced along the Kátha in Nakúr, and near Títron in Gangoh, which, next to the *chahora*, is the best in the district. Oil-seeds occupy a comparatively unimportant position amongst the agricultural products, showing under 7,000 acres in 1869-70.

Rice.

Mr. Guthrie estimated the export of sugar in 1805-6 to be 53,151 maunds, which rose to 88,883 maunds in the following year. Taking 12 maunds of gúr to the local bigha, his cal-

Sugar-cane.

culation gives 7,407 bighas, or 3,700 acres, as under cane cultivation in 1806-7, exclusive of the considerable area of which the produce was consumed in the district. Taking the local consumption at one-third of the gross produce, the total area under cane amounted to 11,110 bighas, or about 6,000 acres and esti-mating a maund of *gúr* to be then worth Rs. 2-4, the value of the produce exported is somewhat less than two lakhs of rupees, or one-eighth of the revenue. Mr. Guthrie subsequently gives the number of bighas under cultivation in revenue-paying estates in 1214 *fasli* (1806-7 A.D.) as 22,291, or 11,200 acres, yielding 266,500 maunds of *gúr*, valued at Rs. 6,01,875, or 18·7 per cent. of the revenue. The proportion of the total cultivated area under cane was 1·5. At Mr. Thornton's settlement the proportion was 5·0, and in 1866 it was 4·8. The sugar-cane grown in the villages watered by the Eastern Jumna Canal in Parganah Sultánpur is of a very fine description, but inferior to the species known as *menthi*, grown near Títron in Gangoh, and Libarheri in Parganah Manglaur.

The capricious nature of the rain-fall in the mountains above often produces sudden floods in the Ganges and Jumna, and 13·21 inches of rain have been known to fall within the 24

Floods.

hours at Dhanauri, a canal post five miles from the foot of the Siwáliks. In spite of this, nothing approaching an inundation has ever occurred; but along the Jumna, villages, or portions of them, have been frequently transferred from one side of the river to the other. In all such cases the rule observed is that of *machcha sím*, i. e., the deep stream of the river is the invariable boundary line whatever course the river may take. This is also the rule generally observed on the banks of minor streams. The number of villages liable to fluvial action is said to be —on the Jumna, 97 ; Ganges, 32 ; other streams, 201,—total 330. Throughout the west of Gangoh and Nakúr, and (to a less degree) of Sarsáwa, the crops, in former years, were exposed to consider-

Wild animals.

able injury from herds of antelope, but these have, in a great measure, disappeared. Throughout the Pathari Nadi forest in Parganah Jawálapur, and in the forests along the foot of the Siwáliks, herds of wild elephants are met with; and great damage is done by wild pigs both here and in the Ganges khádir.

An outline of the general history of the famines in these provinces has been given in the introduction, and here it will only be neces-

Famines.

sary to give the local history of the three great famines of late years—1837-38, 1860-61 and 1868-69. During the hot weather of 1837, the first symptoms of the approaching scarcity were shown by the prolongation of the hot westerly winds, which continued to blow on into July and August. There were some few showers in September, and the land remained dry and untilled, except where the Eastern Jumna Canal supplied water for a few acres and the low-lying lands in the khádirs of the great rivers possessed some natural moisture. From Meerut downwards the famine was most severely felt; but were it not that a copious shower fell in this district in February 1838, it would have suffered equally severely with the more southern districts. As it was, the remissions for 1245-46 *fasli* (1837-38 to 1838-39) amounted to Rs. 1,03,264 in this district alone.

The famine of 1860-61, however, fell with much more force on this district. Up to the 13th of July, 1860, scarcely a drop of rain

1860-61.

had fallen in the Duáb, and in a few days afterwards, instructions were issued for the organisation of relief works should the anti- cipations of scarcity be fulfilled. In this district the principal work undertaken by the relief committee was the construction of a road from Rúrki to Dehra, through the Mohand pass. About the middle of December 1860, the first batches of labourers came to the works, principally from Saháranpur. " Wretchedly wan and hunger-stricken were these poor creatures, who would have died on the road had it not been for the gratuitous support which Government officials were ordered to afford them. When they arrived at the rendezvous, many were in the last stage of exhaustion, and could do but little at first to earn a livelihood. For the first month the engineers reported that the price at which the work was done was very high. Earth-work, which, under ordinary circumstances, was accomplished at the rate of Rs. 1-6 per 1,000 cubic feet, cost treble that sum, and the most sanguine person did not expect that the value would ever be less than Rs. 2 per 1,000 cubic feet, whilst the Lieutenant-Governor acknowledged that he should be satisfied if an average of Rs. 3 per 1,000 cubic feet was maintained. When once the fact was generally known that employment was to be had, the people flocked rapidly to the scene of labour."

By the end of January their numbers had increased to 10,000. Besides these able-bodied poor, 17,640 persons, including the old, infirm, and children of tender years, were relieved during January, 1861. The distress went on increasing in intensity until July, 1861, and up to that period 231,066 persons had been relieved, at a cost of Rs. 15,248, giving a daily average of 1,540 persons in receipt of poor-house relief, and an average daily expenditure of Rs. 437. Of the sum expended, Rs. 7,959 were supplied by local donations and subscriptions. The Rúrki and Dehra road during the same period supported 2,951,424 souls, at an expenditure of Rs. 2,50,686. After July the people were busied with the rain-crops, and the number of paupers at once began to diminish. The people set to work to restore the cultivation, and in this they were assisted by a grant of Rs. 20,000 to purchase seed-grain, implements, and plough-cattle. The loss in life and cattle must have been very severe, for Sahá-ranpur felt the drought intensely. Balances amounting to Rs. 2,19,300 accrued, and of this portion, the realisation of Rs. 1,39,842 was postponed indefinitely. Up to 1865, the sum of Rs. 37,149 had been remitted altogether on account of 1860-61. The influence of the great canals had a great effect in mitigating the intensity of the scarcity in this district, so that in two-fifths of the district there was an average spring crop in 1861. The total receipts for relief opera-tions amounted to Rs. 58,550, of which Rs. 29,822 were expended in general relief, Rs. 20,000 in purchasing seed-grain and implements, and Rs. 5,000 on minor works.[1]

The drought of 1868-69 was severely felt in the district. "Plentiful rain

1868-69.

fell in July, 1868, and land was extensively sown, but during August there were only a few showers in the central parganahs of Saháranpur, Rúrki, and Nakúr." In September a hot wind blew, the air was filled with dust, and the weather was such as might have been looked for in April and May. The storm which spread over so large a portion of the Duáb did not reach Saháranpur, but a few showers here and there improved whatever remained of the kharíf crops, and enabled farmers to prepare for the rabí sowings. Speaking generally, but little of the autumn

[1] See Girdlestone and Henvey's Famine Reports, from which this account has been compiled.

sowings came to maturity, except in the neighbourhood of the canals, and the rabí area was greatly restricted. On this point some details have been given by the Collector. The decrease of cultivation compared with the average is estimated at nearly 200,000 acres, or about 25 per cent., but this decrease was entirely on dry land, for the irrigated area was increased by 40,995 acres. The cold-weather rains came late, but in time to be of great benefit to the crops. Mr. Webster, the Collector, in an official report, states :—" The spring harvest had been sown almost exclusively in such lands as possessed means of irrigation, or, from their nature, or conformation, or situation, retained a supply of moisture sufficient to warrant a reasonable hope of successful sowing. The higher and sandy tracts, where irrigation was absent, remained for the most part unsown, or, if they were sown, the seed did not germinate. In irrigated tracts the crops were fair, and when, in the latter half of January, heavy rain, followed by repeated genial showers, fell all over the district, the crops which were alive were so invigorated that there was quite an average outturn per acre in the land sown in which the seed germinated. " The official estimate of the spring harvest put " barley at an average crop ; wheat, two-thirds ; and gram, a total failure. With the rains of 1869, which were timely and abundant, all anxiety for agricultural prospects ceased."

As soon as the Sindh, Panjáb and Dehli Railway was opened, a trade in grain commenced with the Panjáb on the west, and the Lower Duáb on the south. Up to July, 1869, 162,300 maunds of wheat and barley were exported from Saháranpur, against an import of 147,700 maunds of gram, Indian-corn and wheat. Mr. Henvey writes—" The markets were unsteady and sensitive. It was some time before the low level of other districts was attained, but the effect of this drought is visible in the price-currents of December, when wheat was at 10¾ sers. There was a marked fall in January, and the rain of February kept prices moderately low until the harvest. But in July the prevailing scarcity made itself severely felt : wheat rose to 12½ sers. Again, in August, 1869, a temporary apprehension of a second season of drought sufficed to send wheat up to 10½ sers, and the closing prices of the year were extremely high. The coarser grains were as dear as wheat and barley. For a short time, immediately after the kharíf harvest, joár and bájrá were fairly cheap, but in November and December, 1868, these grains were scarcely procurable ; and although the opening of the railway encouraged considerable importations, the prices of joár and bájrá quoted during July, August, and September, 1869, —eight sers for the rupee—denote exhaustion of stocks."

Scarcity brought on distress with the beginning of 1869. Poor-houses were opened, and relief works commenced, so that by the middle of January, 2,400 people were employed near Saháranpur on the roads and streets ; 29 miles of road from Manglaur to

Relief operations.

Ránipur were also commenced, besides a road by the Timli pass to Kálsi and Chakráta. The daily average on the famine works for 77 days, from January to March, 1869, gave 2,948 souls, at a cost of Rs. 23,925, of which Government gave Rs. 3,941, the remainder being defrayed from the Municipal and Local Funds. At the same time the average number supported by gratuitous relief between the 13th January and the 31st May (138 days), was 161, at a cost of Rs. 2,795. These figures show that there was no wide-spread distress; and when the rains came down, the numbers on the famine works fell to nothing. Some Rs. 60,343 were also given as advances for the construction of wells in tracts to which canal-irrigation could not be brought, and for the purchase of seed-grain and plough-cattle. The following table gives the prices of the principal food-grains during the seasons of scarcity:—

Months.	Wheat.	Barley.	Gram.	Bájra.	Joár.	Rice.	Dal.
	S. C.	S. C.	S. C.	S. C.	S. C.	S. C	S. C.
1861, January ...	8 8	10 12	9 12	10 4	10 4	8 0	7 8
,, February ...	8 4	11 4	10 12	10 12	9 12	7 8	7 8
,, March ...	10 2	12 14	10 12	11 12	11 4	7 8	9 12
,, April ...	14 8	18 4	12 14	10 12	15 8	10 8	10 4
,, May ...	14 8	17 0	11 4	12 12	11 12	9 12	11 4
,, August ...	15 0	16 0	14 12	11 12	11 12	8 0	9 0
,, September ...	15 0	16 8	13 0	25 12	21 8	8 8	9 12
,, October ...	16 0	20 0	18 12	26 12	21 8	9 0	11 4
,, November ...	16 0	19 4	18 8	25 2	25 12	15 0	10 12
,, December ...	9 12	12 12	11 4	12 14	12 6	8 8	7 8
1862, January ...	15 8	22 8	17 0	26 12	25 4	13 12	13 12
,, February ...	14 6	23 2	17 0	22 8	22 8	13 12	12 12
,, March ...	15 0	32 4	16 12	22 0	25 12	13 8	20 0
,, April ...	23 8	30 0	24 0	22 0	21 0	16 8	24 0
,, May ...	27 0	35 0	24 0	21 8	21 8	17 12	22 8
,, June ...	31 0	43 0	21 12	21 8	32 4	17 8	28 12
1868, July ...	22 10	35 9	25 7	21 4	19 6	15 0	19 6
,, August ...	17 0	23 6	19 4	10 12	19 6	9 11	15 0
,, September ...	11 4	17 4	12 15	10 12	15 1	11 13	11 13
,, October ...	12 6	15 1	14 4	14 0	14 0	7 8	11 13
,, November ...	11 12	14 0	12 1	11 13	11 13	9 11	10 12
,, December ...	24 2	31 4	22 0	26 12	26 13	...	19 6
1869, January ...	26 0	42 0	45 0	35 0	33 0	20 0	30 0
,, February ...	26 0	40 0	47 0	34 0	33 0	18 0	30 0
,, March ...	28 0	47 0	48 8	33 0	33 0	18 0	32 0
,, May ...	30 8	44 0	42 0	28 0	...	18 0	30 0
,, July ...	29 8	...	38 8	26 0	30 0	17 0	30 0
,, August ...	30 0	35 0	37 8	28 0	34 0	17 0	30 0
,, September ...	29 0	37 0	37 0	28 0	38 0	17 0	31 0
,, October ...	25 0	28 0	31 0	26 0	28 0	15 0	27 0
,, November ...	24 0	29 0	28 8	25 0	28 0	15 0	25 0
,, December. ...	34 0	34 0	39 0	31 0	30 0	17 0	30 0

The great range of temperature, which extends from the freezing-point to 100°, combined with the influence of the periodical rains,

Botanical gardens.

produces a variety of vegetation, which early pointed out Saháranpur as a suitable place for the establishment of a botanical garden; and since the experiments made there are directly connected with the question of agriculture, this seems the proper place to introduce an account of that

institution. Its origin is principally due to the efforts of Doctor Govan, Civil
Surgeon of the station, who suggested the advisability of utilising an old garden called the Farhatbaksh, laid out under the Rohilla Government, by devoting it to scientific subjects. The Marquis of Hastings was then (1816) Governor-
General; and, whilst making a tour in the upper provinces, was informed of the
design, and not only approved of it, but sanctioned an establishment being entertained for its support. Accordingly the Farhatbaksh garden was transformed
into the botanical garden in 1817. Doctor Govan was appointed the first
Superintendent, and was succeeded by Doctor Royle in 1823. Doctor Felconer
took the latter's place in 1831, and was followed by the present Superintendent
Doctor Jameson.

The gardens, exclusive of the farm, are as nearly as possible 3,000 feet long
by 2,000 feet broad; the whole being laid out with many fine walks and car-
riage-roads. Doctor Royle described the choice of situation as showing much
judgment, Saháranpur being nearly the northern limit of the flora of India,
and southern border of that which is called the Oriental or Persian region.
The tropical situation of the Calcutta garden considerably limited its use for
economical purposes, whilst the proximity of the Himálayas rendered Saháranpur peculiarly fitted for the acclimatization and cultivation of the plants of
other countries; and in a short time Doctor Royle was able to report—"We have
collected in one place, and naturalised in the open air, various fruit-trees of
very different countries, as of India, China, Kabul, Europe and America."
In 1826 a medical garden was added, and a nursery in connection with it was
formed in Mussooree. A few years afterwards the charge for the medical garden
was abolished, and sundry other reductions enforced by the minute frugality of
Lord William Bentinck. The effect of this cutting down was subsequently
found to be a diminution of the utility of the establishment. Lord Auckland
manifested great anxiety for the success of the institution, and a strong desire
to restore its efficiency, deeming this important, as well because the garden
was an object of great interest to the inhabitants, as on the ground of its
obvious tendency to the extension of knowledge, and to the promotion of the
benefit both of Asia and Europe. Steam navigation was at this period beginning to display its advantages as a connecting link between Great Britain and
her possessions in India; and thus were opened facilities, previously unknown,
for the interchnge of the seeds, plants and trees of the two quarters of the
world, to the advancement of agricultural, horticultural, and botanical science,
and to the probable increase of the comforts and gratification of the tastes of
the inhabitants of countries widely separated by distance, thus making them
mutually contributary to the wants of each other, and co-labourers in diffusing
the elements of enjoyment, physical and intellectual. To effect the necessary
improvement involved a small additional expense, but the representations of •

the Governor-General were effectual ; and in 1840 the Court of Directors gave their sanction to measures for placing the establishment of the garden in such a state as should insure its efficiency for the purposes for which it was maintained. The total cost of all the gardens, including Saháranpur, Dehra, Mussooree, Hawalbagh, Chajauri and Ayártoli, during 1872-73, amounted to Rs. 45,127, against a cash income of Rs. 4,961, leaving a balance of Rs. 40,166 to represent the net cost of the gardens to the State.

The gardens have been eminently successful under their superintendents, and have fully answered the expectations of the founder. Not to speak of purely scientific botany, remarkable results have been obtained in the naturalization of useful plants, fruit trees and timber trees collected from all quarters of the globe. The effect is one palpable to the most casual observer who visits this charming locality. In the department of agriculture proper, so much has not been done as might have been expected ; but then a more liberal allowance of space, which means also money, would be indispensable to progress in this line.

During 1872-73, 37,393 fruit trees, 156,766 flowering shrubs, and 5,530 parcels of seeds were distributed. The Canal Department, the Calcutta gardens, cantonments, cemeteries, soldiers' gardens, the Kew gardens, and public gardens

Work of the garden.

like those at Dehli, Jaipur, Bangalor, Sattara, &c., all participated in the distribution. The Medical Department was supplied with 207℔s. of extract of *hyoscyamus*, 224℔s. of the dried leaves of the same plant, 1,409℔s. of the tubers of *Aconitum heterophyllum (atís)*, 148℔s. of oak bark, and 64℔s. of *Kamela (Rottlera tinctoria)* powder. For the purposes of experiment, 35 acres were sown with the rhea grass, and much of this was used in the trial of the machines entered to compete for Lord Mayo's

Rhea.

prize for the best fibre-cleaning machine. Only two machines were exhibited, and one of these was withdrawn as quite unfitted for properly cleaning the fibre. The second machine, entered by Mr. J. Greig of Edinburgh, was tried for eleven days on 3½ tons of rhea stems in the presence of Colonel Hyde. The machine weighs 1½ tons, the fly-wheel alone weighing 4 cwt. Attached to the machine is a scutcher (of the ordinary kind used in flax mills), five feet in diameter, having five blades, and making 260 revolutions a minute. All the fibre, after passing through the machine, has also to be cleaned by the scutcher, to remove the small portions of the stalk and green bark not taken off by the first process, and found adhering to the fibre after it has left the first machine. The fibre is turned out very wet from the machine, and it is necessary to dry it in a free current of air. If the fibre is scutched wet, a second scutching becomes necessary when it is dried. In the work of producing 2 cwt. of fibre, 207℔s. were turned out in 37 hours, which gives 5¼℔s. per hour. This trial gave 63℔s. per ton of stems, or 138℔s. of fibre per acre, the outturn by hand being

about 200℔s. per ton. In summing up the working of the machine, Colonel
Hyde states :—"The machine is a *bonâ fide* meritorious attempt to meet the
want that the Government has set forth as existing. I do not think the machine
is successful, or that it will continue in its present shape; but I believe that its
construction and working cannot fail to advance the question, and to prove a
considerable step towards solving the difficulty of producing a machine that
will prepare the rhea fibre." An American machine (Rœzl's patent), belonging
to Government, is of a much simpler construction, but it is also very defective,
and does not turn out the fibre in a properly cleaned state. To grow the plant
is a very easy matter. Dr. Jameson writes :—" It requires rich, well-drained,
and manured land, and, occasionally, irrigation. It yields four crops annually,
and each crop may be estimated at about two-and-half tons of green stems, or
ten tons per acre per annum ; and estimating the yield per ton of fibre at 112℔s.,
we would thus have half a ton of fibre per acre, which, at £45 per ton, would
yield £22-10 per acre, and thus afford a considerable profit to both grower and
preparer." Though no machine has as yet been made to properly clean the
fibre, it can easily be prepared by hand with a blunt knife, and in this manner
can still be utilised.

The other experiments in economic botany carried on through the gardens,
are the cultivation of cinchona, potatoes, Carolina rice, black Tartary oats,
mulberries for silk-worms, fruit-trees, vegetables, and tea. The cinchona plants
were distributed over Kumaun, Garhwál, and the Dehra Dún, in the Govern-
Cinchona. ment plantations, and a private company established
gardens in the Kangra valley of the Panjáb. The
results were all unfavourable,—the plants were completely destroyed by frost.
Dr. Jameson writes :—" The cultivation has now received a fair, patient,
attentive, and prolonged trial by experienced and practical hands, and the results
fully show that cinchona cultivation can never become of any practical value, in
an economical point of view, in the dúns or hills of these provinces or the
Panjáb, and in no locality where frost exists during the cold weather will it
succeed. In the plains the hot moist weather met with during the rains is
equally hostile to this genus of plants." The Kangra and Government planta-
tations have since been abandoned. Potatoe cultivation has of late years
spread rapidly all over these provinces, and the Saháranpur gardens assisted by
the introduction of fresh seed and new varieties. Experiments with Carolina
rice have proved successful, giving a return of 27 maunds per acre, or 39 bushels
of 56℔s. each. Black Tartary oats do not seem to be adapted to this country,
and hitherto the experiments show little signs of success. Large numbers of
mulberry trees of the *Morus multicaulis* and *Morus Chinensis* varieties have been
planted out in the Dehra Dún with great success, and some efforts have recently
been made there to establish sericulture on a sound basis. Various kinds of

vines, apples, pears, quinces, peaches, apricots, nectarines, cherries, figs, rasp-
berries and gooseberries, sweet chesnuts, timber trees, and vegetables, have been
extensively propagated and distributed.

Tea.

The subject of tea will be taken up with the hill districts; but as it is intimately connected with the Saháranpur gardens, some
notice of it is required here. Dr. Jameson, in his report
for 1872-73, writes:—" Tea cultivation progresses, but it is no longer carried
on by Government, as private enterprise now fully occupies the field. A fine
trade is now springing up with Central Asia. Panjáb and Afghán merchants
now visit the different plantations in the hills and dúns, and offer good paying
prices for tea at the factories, and at the same time make their own arrangements for packing and transmitting the teas to the Panjáb. To make the tea
plantations of Kumaun, Garhwál, Dehra Dún, and the Panjáb pay, good markets
alone were wanting, as the teas there grown will always compete favourably
with those grown in the much moister climate of Assam, Cachar, and Darjee-
ling, where green teas are prepared with difficulty. For these reasons the tea
factories of the North-West Provinces and Panjáb will aiways be able to command the markets of Central Asia, as green teas are the only ones in demand
by the Panjáb and Kabul traders. It, too, is a significant fact, that Indian téas
have attracted the attention of the Russian Government, and favourable transit
duties promised. For this part of India we may, therefore, expect to see a
more rapid extension of the cultivation. To open up the Central Asian tea
trade we have long made strenuous efforts, and urged for years two of the
largest tea firms of Amritsar to direct their attention to these markets. By
them, for years, many thousands of pounds of teas manufactured in the Government factories have been purchased. The advance of the Russians, too, in
Central Asia has, no doubt, tended to develop this market, the limits of which
are not bound by tens of millions of pounds. The time, therefore, is not far
distant when the produce of the hill districts will become as important to
the State as those of the plains, and India a powerful rival to China in the
markets."

Mineral kingdom.

The mineral products of the Síwálik hills are insignificant, viz., carbonate
of lime cementing the sandstone, a little selenite, and
pyrites. The tufaceous limestone of the plains has been
already mentioned. Stone hard enough to be used for building purposes is

Building materials.

scarce; pieces of sufficiently strong consistency to be
thus utilised may here and there be picked out of the
Siwálik sandstone stratum; but although most of the houses in Hardwár and
Kankhal are built of materials so procured, the quantity extracted is not large
enough to repay the expense of carriage to a long distance. Stone for building
is obtained from Agra, at an average cost of 24 annas per 100 cubic feet,

and carriage by rail at three annas per 100 maunds per mile. Stone for road metal is found in the beds of the Soláni (Kandúr), Hindan, and Sukhrao streams.

Large bricks, burned in flame kilns as at Shaikhpura, cost from eight to ten rupees per 1,000 ; and in ordinary *pajáwas*, from six to eight rupees. Small native bricks cost one rupee per 1,000. All these prices vary with the quality. Fresh lime from Dehra, brought to Saháranpur and slaked there, fetches Rs. 27 per 100 cubic feet. Excellent lime is procurable from the boulders covering the beds of the hill torrents ; and amongst the kunkur pits noted for their good quality may be mentioned those at Kumhárhera, Dhúláhera (parganah Sarsáwa), Zainpur, Raghunáthpur (parganah Nakúr), Mánikpur, Telipura (parganah Sultánpur), Tikraul (parganah Rámpur), and Bájúheri. The quarry at Belra, in parganah Rúrki, is a bad one.

Sál logs cost Rs. 4 per cubic foot landed at Saháranpur, —an excessively high rate considering its nearness to the base of supply in Garhwál and the Dún. One hundred cubic feet of kunkur cost, for digging and breaking to from 1 to 2½ inch cubes and stacking on the road, Rs. 2 ; carriage per mile, 10 annas; and consolidation, one rupee; or total Rs. 3-10. As an average, stone metalling costs Rs. 4-8,—for collection of boulders for one hundred cubic feet of metal, 2 annas ; carriage, 10 annas per mile ; breaking, Rs. 2-8 ; consolidation, Rs. 1-4. For some roads boulders are brought by the Ganges Canal from Hardwár at 5 annas per 100 cubic feet per mile, and stone is now used on the three main roads, to Chakráta, to Dehra, and from Rúrki to Dehra. Stone metalled roads are, however, inferior to those made with kunkur.

PART III.

INHABITANTS OF THE DISTRICT.

Population.

.The earliest enumeration of which records remain is that of 1848, which gives the population at 547,353 souls, distributed as follows:—Hindús: agricultural, 273,543, non-agricultural, 62,971, including 3,708 labourers employed on the Ganges Canal, who may not have been residents of the district; Muhammadans: agricultural, 139,907, non-agricultural, 70,932 ; the total giving 253 souls to the square mile. There were 1,447 inhabited, and 449 uninhabited villages. Of the former, 1,370 had less than 1,000 inhabitants ; 72 had between 1,000 and 5,000 inhabitants ; and those above 5,000 were Jawálápur with 8,862 ; Manglaur, 5,959 ; Gangoh, 6,260 ; Deoband, 11,634 ; and Saháranpur, 34,294 inhabitants.[1]

---

[1] Shakespear's Memoir on the Statistics, N.-W. P., p. 42. The changes in 1852 should be remembered in connection with this census.

The total population according to the census of 1853 was 801,325, giving 370
souls to the square mile. The distribution according
to sex and religion is shown in the following table[1] :—

Census of 1853.

	HINDÚS.			MUHAMMADANS AND OTHERS, NOT HINDU.			
Agricultural.		Non-Agricultural.		Agricultural.		Non-Agricultural.	
Male.	Female.	Male.	Female.	Male.	Female.	Male.	Female.
155,176	109,146	165,789	125,829	53,281	44,833	79,840	67,431

There were 1,481 villages, of which 1,328 had a population under 1,000 ; 144
had a population between 1,000 and 5,000; and nine towns had a population
exceeding 5,000, viz., Kankhal, 6,275; Rámpur, 5,566; Rúrkí, 8,592 ; Landhaura,
5,197 ; Ambahta, 6,311 ; Saháranpur, 37,968 ; Manglaur, 10,322 ; Jawálápur,
12,162 ; and Deoband, 18,638.

The census of 1865 shows[2] a total population numbering 869,176 souls, of
whom 1,126 were Europeans, and 108 were Eura-
sians, giving 389 inhabitants to the square mile. With
the distribution of the population according to sex, age, and religion, the statistics of 1872 may be given for the purpose of comparison :—

Census of 1865.

CLASS.		AGRICULTURAL.					NON-AGRICULTURAL.					GRAND TOTAL.
		MALES.		FEMALES.		Total.	MALES.		FEMALES.		Total.	
		Adults.	Boys.	Adults.	Girls.		Adults.	Boys.	Adults.	Girls.		
Hindús ...	1872 ...	123,871	...	84,945	...	208,816	212,123	...	183,483	...	395,606	604,432
	1865 ...	79,905	47,003	58,439	31,369	216,716	125,928	77,174	110,298	61,922	375,322	592,038
Musalmans	1872 ...	56,383	...	47,647	...	104,030	92,131	...	83,199	...	175,330	279,360
and others	1865 ...	32,752	19,232	27,211	16,437	95,632	57,302	36,545	54,545	30,421	178,813	274,445
Total ...	1872 ...	180,254	...	132,592	...	312,346	304,254	...	266,692	...	570,936	883,782
	1865 ...	112,657	66,235	85,650	47,800	312,348	183,230	113,719	164,843	92,343	554,135	866,483

The figures for 1872 give the total number of each sex according to occupation, without distinction of age. The number of villages recorded amounted to
1,514, of which 1,340 had a population less than 1,000 ; 165 had a population
between 1,000 and 5,000 ; and the remainder, having more than 5,000 inhabitants, were—Landhaura, 5,118; Ambahta, 6,336 ; Rúrkí, 7,588 ; Rámpur,
8,464 ; Jawálápur, 9,665 ; Manglaur, 10,206 ; Gangoh, 10,899 ; Deoband,
21,714; and Saháranpur, 44,119. In 1863 Mr. Vans Agnew states that there
were 1,904 estates ; to these were subsequently added 27 grants, one village

[1] Christian's Report on the Census, N.-W. P., p. 98.   [2] Plowden's Census Report, vol. I.

(Láljíwála) received through Bijnor from Garhwúl, and one village by partition—total 1,933. Three villages were subsequently taken up by Government,
leaving 1,930 estates in 1863.

The census of 1872 gives a total population of 884,017 souls, or 399 to the
square mile.   Of these, 604,422 were Hindús ; 279,015
were Musalmáns ; and 345 were Christians, and others
not included in the first two classes.   There were 1,736 villages, giving an
average of 0·8 villages to each square mile, and 509 inhabitants to each village.
The actual classification of villages shows 627 with less than 200 inhabitants ;
579 with from 200 to 500 ; 363 with from 500 to 1,000 ; 128 with from
1,000 to 2,000 ; and 30 with from 3,000 to 5,000 inhabitants.   The towns
having a population exceeding 5,000 were the same as in 1865.   The next
table gives the parganah details according to religion, sex and age :—

Census of 1874.

Pargana.	Hindús.				Muhammadans and others, not Hindu.				Total.	
	Up to 15 years.		Adults.		Up to 15 years.		Adults.			
	Male.	Female.	Male.	Female.	Male.	Female.	Male.	Female.	Male.	Female.
Sahá ranpur ...	13,211	9,966	19,925	17,118	10,279	8,633	15,527	15,108	58,942	50,825
Haraura ...	8,831	6,820	11,789	10,246	3,845	3,180	8,845	7,913	29,465	24,979
Faizabad ...	6,063	4,684	8,035	6,848	4,042	3,298	5,206	4,706	23,346	19,535
Muzaffarabad,	8,130	6,290	10,457	8,932	2,887	2,469	3,784	3,329	25,258	21,020
Deoband ...	11,153	7,062	16,262	13,121	4,534	3,588	7,023	6,687	38,972	30,458
Nágal ...	10,237	7,431	14,313	11,873	2,412	1,930	3,416	2,925	30,378	24,159
Rámpur ...	13,689	10,075	19,125	16,312	3,301	2,687	4,890	4,644	41,008	33,718
Jawálápur ...	9,746	7,687	15,755	12,210	2,686	2,213	3,610	3,223	31,997	25,333
Nakúr ...	8,180	5,886	12,129	9,717	3,150	2,513	4,495	4,520	27,954	22,636
Sarsáwa ...	6,815	5,100	9,246	7,544	2,142	1,756	2,946	2,757	21,149	17,157
Bhagwánpur...	9,750	7,539	13,534	11,251	5,065	4,014	6,643	5,974	34,992	28,778
Rúrkí ...	7,544	6,218	11,507	9,388	4,498	3,596	6,558	5,545	30,107	24,747
Manglaur ...	11,293	8,259	15,481	13,239	4,006	3,319	5,810	5,335	36,590	30,152
Gangoh ...	8,276	6,291	11,772	9,823	3,972	3,313	5,870	5,43.	29,890	24,868
Sultánpur ...	5,748	4,636	7,998	6,861	4,590	3,650	6,124	5,770	24,460	20,918
Total ...	138,666	103,944	197,328	164,484	61,412	50,159	90,947	83,867	484,508	399,274

This table shows that the number of Hindu males in 1872 was 335,944,
or 55·6 per cent. of the entire Hindu population ; Hindu females number
218,428, or 44·4 per cent., whilst Musalmán males number 148,322, or 53·2
per cent., and Musalmán females 130,693, or 46·8 per cent. of the total Musalmán population.   The percentage of Hindús on the total population is 68·4,
and of Musalmáns is 31·6, or about one Musalmán to every two Hindús.   The
percentage of males on the total population is 54·8, and of females, is 45·2, whilst
the divisional percentages are 54·0, and 46·0, respectively.

The statistics relating to infirmities were collected for the first time in 1872.
Infirmities.

The result for this district is that there are 31 insane persons (12 females), or 0·3 per 10,000 inhabitants; 8 idiots (one female); 83 deaf and dumb (25 females), or 0·9 per 10,000; 1,013 blind (460 females), or 11·4 per 10,000; and 95 lepers (20 females), or 1·1 per '10,000. The statistics relating to age were also collected for the first time in 1872, and exhibit the following results for this district. The table gives the
Ages.

number of Hindús and Musalmáns according to sex at different ages, with the percentage on the total population of the same religion. The columns referring to the total population discard the difference of religion, but retain the sex distinction.

Ages.	Hindús.				Musalmáns.				Total population.			
	Males.	Percentage on total Hindús.	Females.	Percentage on total Hindús.	Males.	Percentage on total Musalmáns.	Females.	Percentage on total Musalmáns.	Males.	Percentage on total population.	Females.	Percentage on total population.
Up to 1 year ...	14,149	4·2	12,273	4·5	6,592	4·4	6,101	4·6	20,747	4·2	18,385	4·6
Between 1 and 6 ...	46,086	13·7	38,640	14·3	20,131	13·5	18,377	14·0	66,244	13·6	57,044	14·3
„ 6 „ 12 ...	57,501	17·1	39,977	14·8	25,735	17·3	19,366	14·8	83,267	17·1	59,367	14·9
„ 12 „ 20 ...	56,410	16·7	40,475	15·0	23,471	15·8	19,978	15·2	19,913	16·4	60,479	15·1
„ 20 „ 30 ...	67,288	20·0	55,317	20·6	29,083	19·6	26,543	20·3	96,412	19·8	81,897	20·5
„ 30 „ 40 ...	47,061	14·0	38,734	14·4	20,652	13·9	18,427	14·0	67,746	13·9	57,177	14·3
„ 40 „ 50 ...	27,217	8·1	23,509	8·7	12,718	8·5	11,918	9·1	39,946	8·2	35,433	8·9
„ 50 „ 60 ...	13,548	4·0	12,284	4·5	6,461	4·3	6,077	4·6	20,016	4·1	18,362	4·6
Above 60 years ...	6,734	2·0	7,219	2·6	3,479	2·3	3,906	2·9	10,217	2·1	11,130	2·8

The proportion of Hindu males under twelve to the total Hindu population is 35·0 per cent., and of Hindu females is 35·4 per cent.; amongst Musalmáns the percentages are 33·9 and 33·6 per cent. respectively. Taking the quinquennial periods up to 15 years of age, or 0 to 5, 5 to 10 and 10 to 15 years, the percentage of both sexes to the total population is 15·7, 13·5 and 10·9 respectively; or, taking females alone, the numbers are 16·2, 13·0, and 9·3 per cent. Here, as in other districts of this division, females are slightly in excess in the first period, and considerably below the males in the third period, the figures for which are—males 12·3 per cent., and females, 10·2. Again, taking the whole population of the same sex and religion only, the proportion of Hindu males of the ages of 10 to 13 to all the Hindu males is 7·0, and of Hindu females is 5·3; whilst Musalmáns show 8·0 and 5·0 per cent. respectively. The proportion of Hindu males between 13 and 20 years of age to the total number of the same sex and religion is 16·8 per cent., and of Hindu females is 14·2; the Musalmáns for these ages show 13·9 and 14·8 per cent. Taking the proportion of ages for the quinquennial periods in Austria, both sexes show 13·0 per cent. from 0 to 5, 10·8 from 5 to 10, and 9·9 from 10 to 15 years of age, whilst the proportion of females to the entire population gives 12·8, 10·7, and 9·7 per cent. respectively. In Saháranpur the females are in excess of the Austrian standard in the first two periods, and slightly below it in the third. For the reasons given under the head of population in the Meerut district, the life statistics of these provinces more nearly approach the Austro-Italian than the English standard, and the higher we go in the scale, the more close is the resemblance.

Distributing the Hindús amongst the four great classes into which they are commonly divided, the census of 1872 shows 45,148

Castes.

Brahmans, of whom 20,283 are females ; 27,420 Rajpúts (10,564 females) ; 36,694 Baniyas (16,396 females); and, as in the other districts of these provinces, the great mass of the population is included amongst ' the other castes' of the census returns, who show 495,160 persons, of whom 221,185 are females. The Brahmans belong for the most part to the great

Brahmans.

Gaur sub-division, who number 41,023 souls. The Gaurs trace their origin to the old kingdom of Gaur ; and, in common with the older inhabitants of this district, say that they settled here in the fourteenth or fifteenth century. They hold a fair proportion of land in the district. Other sub-divisions are the Aoháraj (951), Sarasút (424), Bhát (257), Gujráti (225), Kanaujiya (194), Dakaut (170), Bharadwáj (145), and Sanádh (55). The Bangáli, Gata, Mahárást, Sarwariya, Tilang, and Sangaldwipa sub-divisions number less than 50 souls each, and 1,653 are returned without specification. At the recent settlement, Brahmans held two entire villages in each of the parganahs of Saháranpur, Haraura, and Muzaffarabad, besides shares in other villages, and 18,899 acres in other parts of the district.

The most numerous clan of Rajpúts in Saháranpur is the Pundír, who num-

Rajpúts.

ber 14,843 souls. They own a cluster of thirty-six villages in the tract known as the Kátha, once a separate parganah, and now distributed amongst parganahs Deoband, Nágal and Rámpur. In their midst there is one small colony of Mawúls. The term Rángar, a word of doubtful meaning, which is sometimes incorrectly stated to be

Pundírs.

the term applied to converts to Islám, is here usually given to the Pundírs of the Kátha. They are a fine hardy race, and in former times were much given to help themselves from the property of their neighbours. In this respect they were worse than the Gújars, and, like them, were powerful by reason of their union amongst themselves. Whilst other clans have fallen a prey to the usurer, the Pundírs have comparatively escaped scot-free. Mr. Wynne writes—"Confident in their power of combination, the Pundírs used to resist the police and revenue authorities by open force. A steadily-continued course of the severest punishment at last broke their stiffneckedness, and also reduced them to a state of destitution, from which they are now, however, gradually recovering. They are still notorious cattle-lifters, and protect many Sansiyas[1] and other professional thieves." These men, moreover, are equally distinguished by their pride. In the famine of 1860-61 they preferred to die in their homes rather than seek aid at the central station only 20 miles off. Infanticide, too, is very common amongst them. The Pundírs intermarry with the Jangháras. Their more ancient settlements were to the north, in the tract known as Raotala, the country of the Raos or Ráwats, i. e., the relatives of the Ráná or chief. This extends from the uplands to the Jumna, running along the skirts of the town of Sahárapur. There is a tradition of a chaurási[2] in this direction, which is probably the same as the Ráugar chaurási which Sir H. M. Elliot places in the Kátha.[3] In the town of Jaurási, which the same writer connects with chaurási, the Pundírs are still the principal residents. In the Rámpur parganah they are, next to the Gújars, the most important race, and once held a cluster of twelve villages, still named the Náthábárûh. Mr. Williams considers that the Mawáls are the only other pure Rajpúts in the district.

The other tribes entered as Rajpúts in the district census are the Bargújars (88), Bais (187), Banáphar (57), Bargoti (149), Chandrabansi (78), Gahlot (149), Gaur (95), Jaiswár (75), Jander (135), Jhotiyána (133), Kachhwáha (69), Nágbansi (71), Narauliya (287), Panwár (74), Rahtor (92), Solankhi (65), Tuár (119), and Vashisht (409). The following clans have less than fifty members each in this district, viz., Bhál, Bharadwáj, Bhanwag, Chandel, Chhonkar, Dahima, Gaharwár, Gautam, Gohil, Janghára, Jádon, Jadiyána, Jhála, Kinwar, Kathariya, Karanwál, Kharag, Kasyáp, Mohil Pahári, Raikwár, Rawat, Rorh, Ronakhet, Raghubansi, Surajbansi, Sawant, and Tanak, while 1,175 are unspecified. At the recent settlement, Rajpúts held three entire villages in parganah Sahárapur, 13 in Haraura, 21 in Faizabad, and 10 in Muzaffarabad, besides shares in other villages, and 67,645 acres in other parganahs of the district.

The mercantile classes consist chiefly of Agarwáls, who number 25,560; next
Baniyas. to them come the Saraugís or Jains (2,864), and next the Bishnoi sect (1,271). The other sub-divisions found

---

[1] A caste whose profession is burglary.   [2] Cluster of eight-four villages.   [3] Beames' Elliot, II., 51.

in this district are the Chhoti Saran (382), Dhúsar (18), Dasa (402), Gindauriya (60), Gata (601), Garg (532), Goyel (670), Mahesri (36), Mithal (201), Sangal (639), and Sutal (212), whilst 3,246 are unspecified. The Mahájans, thanks to the British rule, now form an important body amongst the landowners in this district ;—at the recent settlement they held nine entire villages in parganah Saháranpur, ten in Haraura, seventeen in Faizabad, and twenty-two in Muzaffarabad, besides 87,376 acres in other parts of the district. The Agarwáls settled here from Agaroha, on the borders of Hariána, about 1400 A.D., and the Dhúsars, from Riwari in Gúrgaon about 1840 A.D.

The following list gives the names and numbers of the other castes found in the district in 1872. Many of these names are the names of trades rather than castes, the members whereof, however, comprise separate communities, having in many respects distinctions similar to those observed amongst the acknowledged castes. Chamárs, when forsaking their hereditary occupation as curriers or cultivators, frequently change their caste name, becoming Mochís when working as shoe-makers, Beldárs when skilled excavators, Bandhanís when removing stones from quarries, Ráj Mistries when masons, &c. :—

Other castes.

Name		Number	Name		Number	Name		Number
Aheriya	...	1,147	Kahár	...	39,794	Raín	..	1
Ahír	...	6,139	Kalál	...	2,148	Ramaia	...	116
Banjára	...	2,932	Kambo	...	2,534	Rángar	...	5
Bánsphor	...	39	Kanjar	...	362	Rangrez	...	26
Baranwar	...	10	Kanpri	...	152	Rawa	...	128
Larhai	...	15,216	Kaiasth	...	1,466	Keshamgar	...	19
Bari	...	71	Khági	...	2	Hiwarí	...	2
Beldár	...	305	Khákrob	...	25,155	Sánsi	...	2,197
Bhaddri	...	256	Khatík	...	1,966	Saini	...	29,637
Bharbhúnja	..	1,728	Khattri	...	2,516	Shoragar	..	1
Bhát	...	1,798	Kisán	...	2	Sikh	...	20
Bhartia	...	77	Koli	...	6,982	Singhariya	...	23
Bisati	...	44	Kumhár	...	14,700	Sunár	...	4,719
Bohra	...	923	Kúrmí	...	453	Taga	...	15,208
Chamár	...	1,58,859	Kuzabgar	...	101	Tamboli	...	129
Chhípi	...	3,504	Lodha	...	3,169	Tawáif	...	8
Chauhán	...	10,076	Lohár	...	7,762	Teli	...	211
Dabgar	...	14	Maimár	...	1,122	Thathera	...	49
Darzi	...	2,062	Mali	...	16,275	Vaishnu	...	94
Dhanak	...	6	Malláh	. ...	178	Bairági	...	1,171
Dhobi	...	3,5.7	Manihár	...	18	Barwa	..	99
Dhúna	...	573	Mewafarosh	...	638	Brahmachári	...	5
Dom	...	70	Mochí	...	496	Charandasi	...	6
Gadaria	...	10,555	Nat	...	236	Fakír	...	487
Ghosi	...	3	Niariya	...	4	Gosháin	...	1,611
Gújar	...	53,576	Nunera	...	1,002	Jogi	...	8,761
Hajjám	...	8,068	Orh	...	2,690	Kabírpanthi	...	25
Jaiswár	...	80	Padahá	...	228	Udási	...	135
Ját	...	12,583	Pási	...	366	Sádh	...	279
Juláhah	...	9,191	Patwa	...	504	Saniási	...	16
Káchhi	...	216	Puj	...	40	Pahári	...	41
						Purabiya	...	25

The Aheriyas are a jungle-living clan who practise fowling and hunting. The Ahírs possess five villages in Haraura, and 2,367 acres in other parganahs. They are amongst the oldest inhabitants, and trace their origin to Muttra and

Rewari in Gúrgaon. The Banjáras or Branjáras say they settled here some 400 years ago.[1] Bánsphors, or workers in bambú, are natives of the district, who assumed the name of their trade as a caste name some 150 years ago. Barhais are carpenters, and Beldárs are expert labourers. Bisátis came here from Kairána in the neighbouring district of Muzaffarnagar; Bharbhúnjas or grain-parchers derive their origin from Bhatner in Sarsa; Bohras came from Márwár 90 years ago, and Bairágís from Ujain about 500 years ago. These last hold over 5,000 acres of land, whilst the Bháts, who came here at the same time, have 186 acres as proprietors. Chamárs, who comprise the great mass of the rural labouring population, possess a few acres as landholders. The Chauháns belong to the nondescript clan noticed under the Meerut district who follow the practice of *karao*, like the Játs and Gújars, and are never considered as true Rajpúts, though they bear the name of Chauháns and have adopted many of the usages of that clan. They are commonly called Khagis here, and their principal *gots* are the Janu and Tabákchandi. The Chhípís are cloth-printers, who came from the Panjáb. The Darzi is a tailor, and the Dhobi a washerman, many of whom came from Jodhpur. The Gadariyás are shepherds, who came from the Panjáb.

The Gújars and the Tagas form the characteristic element amongst the Hindu population of the Upper Duáb. In this district the Gújars number 53,576 souls; in Meerut,

Gújars.

60,350; in Muzaffarnagar, 24,899; in Búlandshahr, 48,786; and in Aligarh, 640. In the Rohilkhand Division they number 39,488 souls; in the Agra Division, 19,835; in the Jhánsi Division, 6,956; and further south their numbers are insignificant, except in the wilds of Mirzapur, where we find a colony of 2,698 souls. Altogether there are, according to the 1872 census, 258,855 Gújars in these Provinces. The Gújars as a clan bear a bad character for turbulence and cattle-lifting. Sir H. M. Elliot mentions that a great part of the present district of Saháranpur was called Gujrát during the last century. The Gújars themselves divide the district into three parts, and use these divisions in common conversation. The first, known as Ghar, comprises the tract of lowlands from the *bangar* or uplands to the Ganges on the east. The second, from the uplands to the Jumna on the west, is known as Raotala. The remainder of the district, with the exception of the tract known as the Kátha and inhabited by the Pundírs, is known as Gujrát. Gujrát extends down to Kairána and Jhanjána in the Muzaffarnagar district, and comprises Gangoh and the old parganahs of Lakhnauti, Nánauta and Títron, now included in Rámpur, Nakúr, Gangoh and the neighbouring parganahs of Muzaffarnagar. A part

---

[1] These proximate dates are the results of inquiries made by the late Mr. H. D. Robertson, C. S., whilst Collector of the district in 1866. The Banjáras, though often passing through the district as carriers in olden times, have only settled here very recently.

of this tract, occupied by the Khúbar *got,* to which Raja Ramdayál of Landhaura belonged, is known as Badanon, " a name," says Elliot,[1] "affixed by themselves, in order to feed their vanity of being reputed men of either lofty stature or eminent in war or council." The same writer adds, the Gújar " estimate of 125,000 subordinate villages within Gujrát alone must vanish when it comes to be examined. Three thousand is the utmost they could have possessed. They might, perhaps, have doubled that, had they included the tract called Taliáyin, which extended from Hastinápur and Bahsuma in a semi-circle to the south of Meerut up to Bágpat. The Gújars of this tract were despised, chiefly because they shaved, and did not live in such a lordly fashion. The tract opposite Dehli, from Loni to Kásna, was called Bhatner, from the prevalence of the Bhatti Gújars."

The principal *gots* of the Chhonkar sub-division of the Gújars are the Líkar, Basíla, and Chhaori. They hold twelve villages near Títron on the Muzaffar-

Sub-divisions.

nagar border still nearly intact, and known as the *bárah Chhonkaron ka.* They say that they are descended from a Jádon Rajpút and a woman of inferior lineage. The chief *gots* of the great Kosas sub-division of the Gújars in this district are the Khúbar, Básla or Básila, Batár, Chahumán, Kalsán, Mardsa, Dholi, Gori, Kathán, Ráwal, Deora, Kutúna, Chhaori, Lodhi, Bágri, Chábni, Chahchak, Dublák, Nurála, Bahrána, Khala, Kota, Ghugla, Bijbirána, Choána, Nún, Káns, Dápa, Rahtor, Chauhán, Paswál, Jangal, Kabári, Sakhún, Dharwál, Khúri, Chamchi, Múswál, Shagli, and Bhárkala. The Batárs held a *baoni* or cluster of fifty-two villages in Gangoh and Lakhnauti. The Pundír and other *gots* contain quite as large a number of subdivisions in this district. Nearly all intermarry with each other, the only prohibited *gots* being those of the father, mother, and paternal and maternal grandmothers. The Gújars are the principal landowners in Saháranpur, and hold five entire villages and shares in others in each of the parganahs of Saháranpur and Muzaffarabad, besides 138,896 acres in other parganahs, especially Rámpur, Sarsáwa, Sultánpur, Nakúr and Gangoh. They are still bad cultivators ; but, as in the Meerut District, they seem to improve when living near the industrious Játs, and when brought under the civilising influence of canal irrigation.

Gújars are numerous in the Dehli and adjacent districts of the Panjáb and

History.

as far west as the Indus. In the Duáb they say that they came from the west some 500 years ago, and almost universally claim descent as a mixed race from Rajpút fathers and women of other tribes. The Játs, too, assert for themselves a similar origin in the west, and both are coupled together in the well-known proverb :—

" *Ját, Gadariya, Gújar, Gola,*
 In charon ke hela mela,"

---

[1] Beames' Elliot, I, 100.

which ascribes a commonalty of interest, custom and origin to the four tribes mentioned. Together these tribes form one-half the population of the Panjáb. General Cunningham[1] identifies the Gújars with the Yuchi or Yuetchi, a branch of the Tungnu or Eastern Tártars, who, several centuries before the Christian era, founded an extensive empire in Western Tartary, now comprised in Tangut, West Kansu, and Thiangshan. About 200 B. C., the Yuchi were defeated by Mothe, chief of the Hiungnu, who became paramount between the Volga and the frontier of China. During the first half of the second century before Christ, the Hiungnu continued their career of progress and drove before them the Yuchi. The latter divided into two hordes; the little Yuchi occupied Tibet, and the great Yuchi the country along the Jaxartes, until further pressed they moved west and south upon Kashgár, Yárkand and Khoten. Hence they went further to the south and west to Sogdiana and Tahia, or the country of the Dahæ. In the beginning of the first century before Christ, Khieu-tsiu-ki, king of the Kuei-shwáng tribe of the great Yuchi, united all the five tribes of the nation together, and conquered the country from Gándhára (Peshawar) on the east to the borders of Persia on the west, and from the Hindúkush on the north to Bilúchistán on the south. He took Kaofu and Kipin from the Sakas and Hantha. The power of the Yuchi remained unimpaired until their overthrow by the Ephthalites or white Huns, in 222 A. D. The last king of the Yuchi mentioned in history is Kitolo, whose son made Peshawar the capital of their kingdom.

So far the history of the Yuchi from Chinese sources. Lassen identifies the Tochari and Asiani of Strabo with the Yuchi and Kuei-shwang above-mentioned; and General Cunningham identifies the latter with the Kushán and Khushán of coins, and the Gushán of inscriptions. The medallic form of the name often appears as Korsou, Korsea, Khoransu and Korano; the first three exclusively on the coins of Kadaphes or Kadphizes, the successor of Hermœus, and the last on the series minted by Kanerki and his successors. General Cunningham thinks it probable that the name which is intended in the first three readings may still be found in Khorásán; and if this view be correct, the original name of the tribe must have been Kors or Khorans, which was afterwards softened to Kor and Kush, or Korano and Kushan. He adds—"In all these names, I think that we may recognize, without much straining, the original form of the Sanskrit Gurjjara and the Hindi Gújar or Guzar." The statement of the Chinese, that the Yuchi or Tochari occupied the country of the Dahœ, is confirmed by Justin with the date 123 B. C., and this would bring their aggrandisement under Khieu-tsiu-ki, or Kujula, or Kujulaka, or Kadphizes, to about 70 B. C. Lassen discusses this identification at greater length. The Tochari were taken into the employment

---

[1] See Archæ. Sur. II., 61. The remainder of this notice is taken from Cunningham, Prinsep (Ind. Ant.), Elliot (Hist. Ind.) and Lassen (Bactrian coins).

of Phrahates of Parthia in his expedition against Antiochus of Sida. They arrived too late, and received no compensation, so they plundered the Parthian country and slew Phrahates in 126 B. C. He was succeeded by his uncle Artabanus II. (Arsaces VIII.), who fell in conflict with the Thogarí (Tochari) in 123 B. C. Next came the great Mithridates, who again fought the Scythians, but most of his time was taken up by the wars with the Romans, so that the Scythians had then an opportunity to extend their conquests. Lassen places the war of Phrahates IV. with Tiridates, whom he expelled with the aid of the Scythians, in 40 B. C., and the succession of a son of Khieu-tsiu-ki in 20 to 25 A. D. According to Ptolemy, the Indo-Scythian empire comprised the country on both sides of the Indus, from Attak to its mouth, and the peninsula of Suráshtra or Gujrát. This must be the Yuchi colony founded by Kadphizes or Khieu-tsiu-ki on the ruin of the Sakœ, who were destroyed by Vikramáditya in 57 B. C.

Some slight assistance is obtained from the Persian historians. The *Tarikh-ul-Hind* of Abú Rihan al Birúni mentions that Kábul was formerly governed by princes of Turki (or Tochari) lineage for sixty[1] generations. "The last of them was Katormán, and his minister was Kalar, a Brahman" who usurped the throne.[2] As it would be beyond the object of this notice to follow out these investigations any further, the reader is referred to the authorities quoted below for the history of the Kábulian kingdoms. This much may be gathered from all the authorities, that a great Scythian tribe, known as the Yuchi, Yuetchi, or Tochari, occupied the country of the Sákœ in the latter half of the first century before Christ. They invaded India and established themselves along the Indus and in Sauráshtra, and in the time of Fa Hian (400 A. D.) their power had greatly declined. With the exception of the Játs, hereafter identified with the Sáka,[3] there is no other tribe of presumably foreign origin that are numerous enough to represent the Yuchi. The Kaira copper-plates[4] mention three princes of a Gurjjara race, the last of whom reigned in 380 Sáka, or 458 A. D. General Cunningham identifies them with the princes of the Gurjjara kingdom mentioned by Hwen Thsang, of which the capital was at Balmer, half-way between Amrkot and Jodhpur. They were expelled by the Bhálas about 505 A. D., and shortly afterwards are found in Gujrát. In the Baroda inscription, Indra, Raja of Sauráshtra, is said to have conquered the king of Gurjjara just one generation before 812 A. D., or between 775 and 800 A. D. These instances show that a powerful colony remained in the countries that we know were once subjected to the Yuchi. We next find traces of a Gújar kingdom in the district of the Chaj Duáb in the Panjáb still called Gujardes. This country was attacked by Sankara Varmma, king of Kashmír in A. D. 883, when the Gújar

[1] Dowson's Elliot, II., 403-429.   [2] The founder was Barhtigin, and amongst his successors Kank or Kanishka : Prinsep by Thomas 1, 38, 41, 144, &c.   [3] See Meerut District.
[4] Thomas's Prinsep I 269.

Raja Alakhana was defeated. This Gurjjara lay between Trigartta or Kangra and the country of Sahi, amongst the mountains to the west of the Jhílam.

Then, pressed eastward by the continual advances of the Musalmáns, we find the northern Gújars all along the foot of the hills, and, crossing into the Duáb, they percolated southward as far as Agra; crossing the Jumna at Muttra they keep to the hilly country, and own the native State of Samthar to the west of Jálaun. Across the Ganges they are found in considerable numbers in the wilder parts of Bijnaur, Murádabad and Bareilly, still close to the hills. Whatever value may be attached to these conjectures, the identification of the Gújars with a foreign invading race is at least plausible, and may stand until future investigations show that the theory is ill-founded. As early as 1540 A.D. the Gújars of the Duáb were powerful enough to interfere with Sher Sháh whilst building his fort [1] and mosque at Dehli. Sher Sháh himself marched against Páli and Páhal and reduced the Gújars to subjection. "He left orders that they should be expelled from that country; consequently, not a vestige of their habitations was left." They however did not attain to any political influence until the middle of the last century, when the foundations of the great *mukararis* of Rajas Ramdayúl Singh and Nain Singh were laid in the Saháranpur and Meerut Districts.

The next numerous cultivating tribe is the Játs, of whom the clans settled in this district are the most northern off-shoots. The

Játs.

great Ját country lies further south in the Muzaffarnagar and Meerut Districts, and the colonies settled here are comparatively of recent origin. Hajjáms are barbers and Juláhas are weavers; Kaláls possess two villages in parganah Saháranpur, and Kayaths have one village, besides 4,442 acres elsewhere. The Musalmán Kaláls came from Dehli in the last century, whilst the Hindu Kaláls came from the Panjáb about 1400 A. D. The Kambos came here from Kamúdnagar, 300 years ago. Kanjars are a very low caste usually appearing as vegetable-sellers, and are the same as the Mewa-farosh. Many members of this caste in this district are addicted to thieving, and are found wandering about in gangs, both here and in Muzaffarnagar. Khákrobs or Bhangís are sweepers, and Khatíks are another low caste chiefly given to rearing fowls. Kolís, Kumhárs and Kúrmís came here some centuries ago from the Lower Duáb and Oudh; Kanpris and Kazahgars came from Rohilkhand 400 years ago; and Kahárs from Dehli. Very many Lodhas came here from Gúrgaon in the Panjáb as labourers when the canal works commenced, and most of these afterwards settled down in the district. The Musalmán Málís came from Dehli. Mochi is synonymous with Chamár. The Nats are a gipsy tribe, Nuneras are salt-makers, and Manihárs are workers in glass. The Patwás say they came from the Agra district. The Rains came from Ghar Ghazni, and

---

[1] *Taríkhi-Dáudi*; Dowsons' Elliot, IV., 477.

Sarsáwa in Afghanistán. Rawas are numerous in Meerut. Reshamgar is a trade name meaning silk-worker, Shoragar a saltpetre-maker, Singharia a water-caltrop planter, and Tawáif a prostitute. The Sainís, a division of the Máli or gardener caste, trace their origin to Dehli; they hold one village in parganah Saháranpur, and 7,569 acres elsewhere. Sunárs, or goldsmiths, also from Dehli, hold 196 acres; and Rorhs have 6,625 acres in different parganahs, and three whole villages in Haraura.

The more common *gots* of Tagas in this district are the Bharadwáj, Pachas and Kalsigán. The Bichhu, Kadha, Mahtáb and Búgarwála *gots* are also

Tagas. tolerably numerous. Tagas, besides numerous shares, possess five entire villages in the Saháranpur parganah, four in Haraura, and 36,068 acres in other parts of the district. The same legend is told about them here as in Meerut, that they were Brahmans invited to be present at the great snake-sacrifice proclaimed by Raja Janamejaya, and were rewarded with grants of land, for the sake of which they abandoned their priestly character (*tyág dena*) and became cultivators of the soil. The Herís or Hírís say that they came from the Lower Provinces, and the Mahras ascribe their origin to Central India, whence they emigrated to this district. Both are jungle-loving tribes, who inhabit the country at the foot of the Siwálik hills to the north of the district, and are found again in the Dún. Though, in common with most other tribes, they claim a Rajpút descent, there is no evidence forthcoming in support of their pretension. The Tambolís or *pán*-sellers, Telís or oil-makers, and Thatheras or brass-workers, are all immigrants from the Panjáb. The Vaishnus or Bishnois are more fully noticed under the Meerut district.

The Musalmán population consists both of followers of the different invaders

Musalmáns. of Northern India and a considerable number of converted Hindús. In the former class are the Sayyids (5,878), who possess four entire villages in parganah Saháranpur and three in Haraura, besides 11,689 acres in other parganahs. Mughals (1,721) hold 1,400 acres in the south and east of the district, and Patháus (15,263) hold 22,117 acres in the same portions of the district. Shaikhs, who include amongst them many Hindu converts, have nine entire villages in the Saháranpur parganah, four in Haraura, and one in Faizabad, besides 11,689 acres in other parts of the district. All the abovementioned sub-divisions say that they have settled in this district for the last 500 years. The Musalmán Gújars number 9,395 souls, and possess nearly 20,000 acres in Tahsíls Nakúr, Deoband and Rúrki; Musalmán Rajpúts (12,010) hold 26,619 acres in the same tracts; Musalmán Tagas (1,594) hold 2,659 acres. There are also Fakírs (348), Musalmán Játs (73), Meos (17), Hajjáms, Malláhs and Bilúches amongst the Musalmán community. 207,516 Musalmáns are unclassified in the census returns.

Amongst them the Jojhas and Gáras deserve a passing notice. The former declare that they assumed the apellation 500 years since; they have two villages in Haraura, and possess 5,339 acres in the southern and eastern tahsíls. Some of the Gáras call themselves Mughals, whilst others say that they are descendants of converted Sombansi Rajpúts located here by Akbar. They preserve the names of different Rajpút tribes amongst their clans, and are probably the result of the first great proselytising efforts of the Musalmáns amongst the mass of the Hindu population. The name Gára is probably derived from the new custom adopted by the converts of burying their dead (garna). They usually marry amongst themselves, but one clan is known as the Sayyid Gára from the fact that the daughters of these Gáras are received in marriage by Sayyids. The Pírzádas of Bahat and Ambahta are a distinguished family, and the former still possess one village in Saháranpur and four in Faizabad. Many of the Musalmán inhabitants are known by the trades they follow; such as Kamángars or bow-makers, Tírgars or arrow-makers, Pajáwahgars or lime-burners, converted Kanjaras known as Mewa-faroshan or fruit-sellers, Sabúngars or soap-makers, Kághazís or paper-makers, Miumárs or masons, Kangigars or comb-makers, Juláhas or weavers, also called Safed-báf and Núr-báf; Kasais or butchers, Khairádis or turners, Atashbáz or firework-makers, Sikalgars or cutlers, and Bhatiyáras or inn-keepers. From the example of the Hindús, these trades are gradually assuming the character of castes, even amongst the Musalmáns, and especially amongst those who are descendants of converted Hindús, who in a great measure retain the customs and prejudices of the clans from which they are derived. The question of caste will be noticed hereafter; here it is sufficient to say that the castes of the present day appear to be a complex, artificial system of very modern growth, and that the celebrated division into four great classes, though adopted for convenience, has no foundation in fact, if the accounts given by each caste of their origin can be relied upon.

Christians are few in number, but hold one entire village in Saháranpur and three in Faizabad, besides 7,538 acres in other parganahs.

The distribution of the population into the two great divisions of those engaged in cultivating the soil and those following other occupations has been sufficiently noticed. The agriculturists, as a body, will be described hereafter. The whole population was divided into six classes for the purposes of the recent census, each of which was further sub-divided, and included all the male adults (not less than fifteen years of age) employed in the occupations it represented. The first, or professional class, embraces all Government servants and persons following the learned professions, literature, the arts and sciences, and numbered 8,768 male adults, amongst whom are included 7,184 purohits or family priests, 229 pandits, 89 muazzins or reciters of the call to prayer, 30 druggists, 362 musicians, &c. The

Occupations.

second class numbers 38,107 members, and comprised all males engaged in domestic service, such as washermen, personal servants, water-carriers, barbers, sweepers and inn-keepers. The third class represents commerce, and numbered 19,531 males, amongst whom are all persons who buy or sell, keep or lend money and goods of various kinds, as shop-keepers (13,961), money-lenders (1,871), bankers (141), and brokers (83), and all persons engaged in the conveyance of men and animals or goods, as pack-carriers (549), ekka and cart drivers (317), and coolies (359). The fourth class includes persons possessing or working the land as proprietors (16,856), cultivators (94,170), ploughmen (879), and gardeners (210), and every one engaged about animals, as shepherds (706) and herdsmen (990). The fourth class numbers 114,118 male adults. The fifth class, containing 47,417 members, includes all persons engaged in the industrial arts and mechanics, such as pat-wás or necklace-makers (69), masons (379), carpenters (4,270), and perfumers (55); those engaged in the manufacture of textile fabrics, as cloth-printers (492), weavers (17,806), tailors (2,289), and cotton cleaners (1,033); and those engaged in preparing articles of food or drink, as grain-parchers (675) and confectioners (223), as well as all dealers in animal, vegetable or mineral substances. The sixth class contains 71,112 members, including labourers (62,842), persons of independent means (92), and 8,177 persons supported by the community, and of no specified occupation. Altogether there are 299,053 male adults classified according to occupation in this district, of which nearly one-half are engaged in cultivating the soil.

The description given of the houses, clothing, customs and food of the people under the Meerut district will apply equally well to Sahárunpur. It is only necessary to note here any local peculiarities. The census of 1872 show that there were then 79,734 enclosures in the district, of which 49,836 were occupied by Hindús, 29,382 by Musalmáns, and 66 by Christians. This shows 35 enclosures to the square mile, and eleven persons to each enclosure. The separate houses numbered 197,235, distributed as follows :—

Houses.

Class of house.	Hindús.	Muhammadans.	Christians.	Total.	Number of inhabitants.
Houses built by skilled labour	11,763	7,434	103	19,300	94,863
„ „ unskilled labour	121,597	56,332	6	177,935	788,919
Total	133,360	63,766	109	197,235	883,782

This return gives 88 houses to the square mile, and 4·4 inhabitants to each house. The proportion of persons inhabiting the better class of houses is only 10·8 per cent. on the total population, which, while higher than the provincial average, is below Muzaffarnagar and Aligarh. The district averages range from 60·1 in Gurhwal to 0 in the Tarái, or, taking the Duáb districts alone, from 21·9 in Cawnpore to 2·9 in Mainpuri. The town houses are of the usual fashion, constructed according to the means of the owner. In villages there are few *pukka* houses, and in the north of the district, under the Siwálik hills, the huts are exclusively made of grass, as mud of a sufficiently tenacious character to withstand the heavy rains of that tract is not procurable. The only buildings devoted to public worship with any pretensions to architectural beauty are the new mosques at Saháranpur and Deoband and a few temples at Hardwár. The lower classes, as a rule, consume Indian-corn, *bájra, joár,* and barley, and those better off eat wheaten unleavened cakes, seasoned with split pulses *(dál)* and various condiments.

Although a remarkably fine mosque in the town of Saháranpur, recently commenced by public subscription, attests the zeal of the Musalmán community, and a few Wahábis are undoubtedly found in the city, Muhammadanism does not seem to be making any progress amongst the people; but, on the other hand, Hindúism has received a severe shock, and even the popularity of Hardwár and the Himálayan *tírthas,* or places of pilgrimage, is not so great as before. Christianity, however, has not made its influence felt, and, in fact, the great mass of the people is without any religion of any kind. Civilization, whilst it has sapped the foundations of the old systems of belief, has not given the people anything which can supply their place. This is perhaps a necessary consequence of all progress, but still it is one to be deprecated as containing the germs of some political and social difficulty for the next generation.

The Ludhiána Mission, organised under the care and supervision of the General Assembly of the Presbyterian Church in the United States of America,[1] extended its operations to Saháranpur as early as the year 1835, when the Reverend J. R. Campbell settled in this station, and laboured conscientiously for many years. He opened an English school in connection with the Mission in 1837. This institution was at first naturally regarded with grave suspicion, and the number of the pupils did not exceed 40; now there are 345.[2] They receive a good sound education, and so alive are the people generally to its advantages, that many of the Múnshis in the Collector's office have been educated there. An orphanage was

Religion.

Christian Mission.

[1] From an interesting little book called Missions in Hindústan, by the late Reverend J. R. Campbell, page 160. [2] Forty-five boarders and 300 day-scholars.

established in the year 1838. For a long time the average number of orphans was not more than 20 ; now there are 50. In the year 1863, Mrs. Calderwood, the wife of the present Missionary, set up a girls' school, of which there are at present three, with an attendance of from 60 to 70 pupils. In 1849, the members of the Native Church were only eight; there are now 25 or 29, and the whole Native Christian community numbers 302 souls. The Mission premises are commodious, and include an excellent church, with an average congregation of 100. In 1871-72, four converts were gained, and the Reverend A. P. Kelso, while acting for Mr. Calderwood, lately introduced an excellent practice of sending some of the orphans to Rúrki, and apprenticing them to the workshops there for the purpose of learning trades. The S. P. G. F. P. Mission commenced operations at Rúrki in 1862, and has continued them with varying success up to the present time. The school has done much for the town and neighbourhood; and in 1872 the Reverend J. Gavin, Chaplain of Rúrki, who manages the institution with the assistance of a native pastor, baptized six converts from Hindúism. There is no native charitable or literary association in the district.

There are no dialects peculiar to the district which demand special attention.

Language. The inhabitants generally speak remarkably good Urdú, a language with which even most of the peasantry are fairly acquainted, and speak with a degree of purity only to be accounted for by their early intercourse with the Muhammadans. The Banjárás and Sánsís, who are professional thieves, have a dialect of their own, but that cannot be considered peculiar to the district.

Education in this district is under the supervision of the Inspector of the first or Meerut Circle, in concert with the local committee, of which the Magistrate is president. The zila school was opened in 1867, and has a boarding-house attached for the accommodation of boys from the interior of the district. The tahsílí schools were opened in 1851-54, the halkahbandi village schools in 1860, and the female schools in 1866. The aided schools are under the management of the American Presbyterian Mission already noticed. The towns of Deoband and Saháranpur are noted for their large Arabic and Persian schools, which are included under the head "indigenous." In 1850 these schools numbered 133, with 1,367 pupils, and 32 of them had then been in existence for more than ten years. The Sanskrit and Hindi schools at the same time numbered 90, with 1,336 pupils, and of these 35 had been in existence more than ten years. The number of male children under instruction in 1850 was 2,733, or 5·9 per cent. of those between the ages of four and fourteen. The number of pupils under instruction in 1871-72 was 7,934, or 6·2 per cent. of those between the same ages. The following table gives the statistics for 1860-61 and 1871-72 :—

Class of School.	1860-61.			1871-72.							
	No. of Schools.	No. of pupils.	Cost.	No. of Schools.	No of pupils.			Average daily attendance.	Cost per head.	Proportion borne by State.	Total charges.
					Hindús.	Musalmáns.	Others.				
Government. { Zila (inferior),	...	...	...	1	63	9	2	69	50 14	37 10	3,513
Tahsíli. ...	6	341	1,492	4	135	91	...	172	6 9	6 1	1,254
Halkahbandi ...	29	511	1,331	109	2,322	1,112	...	...	3 10	1 13	11,345
Female ...	...	...	...	15	34	227	...	183	3 15	3 15	825
Anglo-vernacular (aided) ...	1	15	291	7	198	127	59	304	17 6	7 0	5,286
Female (aided),	...	...	...	2	...	60	...	57	10 5	4 0	624
Indigenous (unaided). ...	363	4,772	12,476	243	1,633	1,862	...	2,601	5 0	...	13,899
Total ...	399	5,639	15,590	381	4,385	3,488	61	6,001	...	...	36,746

In 1872 an attempt was made to collect the statistics of education amongst

Educational statistics —the census.

the people generally. Though confessedly imperfect, the results may be received as a fair indication of the state of education in the district. The statement given below shows the number of Hindús, Christians and Musalmáns of each sex at different ages, and the number who can read and write (literate), with the percentage of the same to the total population of the same religion, sex and age.

Ages.	HINDÚS.					MUSALMÁNS.					CHRISTIANS.			
	Males.			Females.		Males.			Females.		Males.		Females.	
	Number.	Literate.	Percentage.	Number.	Literate.	Number.	Literate.	Percentage.	Number.	Literate	Number.	Literate.	Number.	Literate.
1 to 12 years,	117,736	537	0·4	90,890	*Nil.*	52,459	208	0·3	43,844	*Nil.*	64	2	62	*Nil.*
12 to 20 „ ...	56,410	795	1·4	40,475		23,471	230	0·9	19,978		32	25	26	
Above 20 „ ...	161,848	3,44:	2·1	137,063		72,093	905	1·2	66,871		96	65	65	

The girls' schools must have been able to turn out some of their pupils with the elements of primary education during these years, so that in regard to female education the returns are evidently very imperfect. The total number of males recorded as able to read and write is 6,211, or less than the number under instruction in the previous year. We may, however, gather that there is great room for the increase of schools, and that the activity shown in the matter of education during Sir William Muir's administration was directed towards supplying a want which was really felt. Even if we double the number of persons returned as literate in the district, still this will only give seven in every hundred inhabitants. There is but one native lithographic press in the district, and one English press, at the Thomason College.

Post-office.　　　　　The Post-office statistics for three years in the last decade are shown in the following table :—

Year.	Receipts.						Charges.					
	Miscellaneous, savings, fines.	Passengers and parcels.	Deposits, guarantee funds, family funds.	Remittances.	Postage.	Total receipts.	Charges, fixed and contingent, salaries, &c.	Mail service.	Remittances.	Other charges, refunds, advances, printing.	Cash balance.	Total charges.
1861-62,	106	...	100	5,398	6,575	12,179	4,209	...	9,139	55	25	13,428
1865-66,	98	...	...	8,189	10,009	18,296	5,240	2,895	10,055	...	106	18,296
1870-71,	1,531	...	11,179	21,890	11,286	45,886	11,598	9,171	20,587	4,552	178	45,886

In addition to the above, receipts in 1860-61 from staging bungalows amounted to Rs. 2,362, and the expenditure to Rs. 1,113; the receipts for service postage to Rs. 14,376, and the expenditure to the same amount, making a total receipts of Rs. 28,917. The following table gives the number of letters, newspapers, parcels and books received and despatched during 1861-62, 1865-66, and 1870-71:—

	1861-62.				1865-66.				1870-71.			
	Letters.	Newspapers.	Parcels.	Books.	Letters.	Newspapers.	Parcels.	Books.	Letters.	Newspapers.	Parcels.	Books.
Received ...	120,888	7,121	914	738	157,831	10,111	1,955	1,273	278,464	14,430	2,112	3,076
Despatched,	117,536	1,826	1,673	200	142,211	2,269	1,926	399	195,519	3,741	697	878

There are twelve Imperial Post-offices in the district, viz., Saháranpur, Ambahta, Bahat, Deoband, Gangoh, Hardwár, Jawálápur, Manglaur, Nakúr, Rámpur, Rúrkí and Sarsáwa; and twelve District Post-offices, viz., Badgaon, Chilkána, Fatehpur, Landhaura, Lakhnauti, Mohand, Muzaffarabad, Nágal, Nánauta, Raipur, Sultánpur and Titraun or Títron.

There is but one jail in the district, the statistics of which are as follow :—

Jails.

The average number of prisoners in jail in 1850 was 406, in 1860 was 131, and in 1870 was 216 ; the ratio per cent. of this average number to the population, as shown in the census of 1865 (866,483), was in 1850, ·047 ; in 1860, ·015 ; in 1870, ·025. The number of prisoners admitted in 1860 was 1,251 and 1870 was 785, of whom 15 were females. The number of persons discharged in 1870 was 493. In 1870 there were 444 admissions into hospital, giving a ratio of admissions to average strength of 205·55. Of these 31 died, or 14·35 of the total strength. The cost per prisoner per annum in 1870 was for rations Rs. 17-0-3; clothing Rs. 2-1-8 ; fixed establishment Rs. 11-15-8 ; contingent guards Rs. 5-12-0 ; police guards, Rs. 2-6-10; and additions and repairs Rs. 6-6-10, or a total of Rs. 46-3-9. The total manufactures during the same year amounted to Rs. 1,539, and the average earning of each prisoner to Rs. 7-1-11. In 1870 the Muhammadan prisoners numbered 231, and the Hindús 447. There were four prisoners under 16 years of age, 494 between 16 and 40, 147 between 40 and 60, and 38 above 60. The occupations of the majority of the male prisoners were - agriculturists, 225, labourers, 273, and shop-keepers, 38.

The chaukídárs or village watchmen numbered 1,624 in 1873, or one to each 447 inhabitants. They have recently been reorganised under the provi-

Police.

sions of Act XVI. of 1873, and their cost is now defrayed from the municipal cesses at about the rate of Rs. 3 a month for each man. This, with the re-allocation of the regular police, leaves little to be done for the watch and ward of the district. The regular police during 1873 numbered 843 men of all grades, costing Rs. 95,372 per annum, of which Rs. 71,390 were chargeable to the Provincial Revenue. The proportion of police to area is one to 2·64 square miles, and to the total population is one to every 1,048 inhabitants. The following table shows the statistics of crime for several years, and the mode in which the police have dealt with cases cognizable by them :—

Year.	Cases cognizable by the police.					Value of Property.		Cases.			Persons.			
	Murder.	Dacoity.	Robbery.	Burglary, and attempts.	Theft, &c.	Stolen.	Recovered.	Total cognizable.	Under inquiry.	Prosecuted to conviction.	Brought to trial.	Convicted and committed.	Acquitted.	Proportion of convictions to persons tried.
1865...	4	1	8	513	971	39,622	12,566	1,900	461	306	720	400	300	55·5
1867...	6	...	2	434	954	31 175	8,733	1,798	774	375	860	629	238	41·4
1868...	4	2	5	721	1,115	46,826	13,313	2,303	1,648	375	815	577	178	70 7
1870...	5	1	11	596	561	46,255	7,473	1,860	1,054	568	1,102	849	253	77·0
1871...	3	1	9	790	560	36,087	8,891	2,098	1,356	742	1,390	1,251	139	90·0
1872...	5	1	4	852	551	31,797	14,319	2,228	2,036	789	1,700	1,309	191	77·0
1873...	3	...	8	933	613	34,728	18,797	2,420	2,336	1,012	1,906	1,483	187	77·8

In the more heinous offences the police have been successful in their convictions, but in petty burglaries and thefts, especially cattle thefts, the returns for the last ten years show some inability to grapple with these offences on the part of the police that contrasts unfavourably with other districts. Undoubtedly the presence of a large Gújar community, whose profession is cattle lifting, has much to do with this state of affairs. The scarcity of 1868-69 led to some increase in the number of petty offences during its prevalence, but on the whole there is little abnormal in the crime calendar of this district. There are first-class police-stations at Saháranpur, Gangoh, Roorkee, Fatehpur, Jawálápur, Deoband, and Rámpur; second-class stations at Nakúr, Bahat, Chilkána, and Manglaur; and third-class stations at Sarsáwa, Nágal, Mohand, Sultánpur, Kunári, Badgaon, Nánauta, Bhagwánpur, Muzaffarabad, Mirzapur, Basi, and Dausni. There are also outposts at Gágalhera, Mandáoli, Phandpuri (Rahmánpur), Mán Singh ke Tánda, Kankhal, and Hardwár.

As early as 1853 the question of the existence of the practice of killing female
Infanticide. infants amongst the Rajpút tribes attracted the attention of the authorities in this district. Mr. Craigie, the Magistrate, set inquiries on foot; but as the Tahsildárs reported that the practice had died out, the matter was allowed to drop. In 1862, the Inspector-General of Police recommended the adoption of the rules for repression which had been found so successful in Agra and Mainpuri, and these were introduced with some success into 171 villages amongst the Gújar, Rajpút and the Kálikánthawála (those wearing a black necklace) Játs. One result of the inquiries that were now set on foot was the discovery that the Játs were not so universally guilty as had been supposed. A regular census of the suspected clans was then taken in hand, and the provisions of Act VIII. of 1870 were enforced against the Pundír Rajpúts in 64 villages, other Rajpúts in 17, Gújars in 136, Játs in 18, Tagas in six and Kolís in one village. Five of these villages recur twice, so that the true number of villages proclaimed in 1871-72 is 237. The special census of the same year gave a total population of 52,375 souls, of whom 11,721 were boys and 5,222 were girls, the percentage of girls to children being only 30·8. The percentage varied from 23 amongst the six villages of the Tagas to 31·8 amongst the Gújars. The returns of 1872-73 show 239 villages on the proclaimed list, inhabited by 52,996 souls. The births during the year were 1,328 boys and 1,273 girls, or 50 per mille of the total population. The deaths of infants under one year recorded during the same period showed 252 boys and 235 girls. The rules drawn up under the Infanticide Act were carefully worked, with the result of the conviction of 49 persons for evasion, whilst 118 inquests were held, and *post-mortem* examinations were made on the bodies of 21 infants.

In 1873 the standard of exemption was lowered to 35 per cent. of female children in a village instead of 40 per cent. as before, and the result of the revision of the records in accordance with these orders was found to give 118 Gújar, 50 Pundír (Rajpúts), 12 Rajpút of other tribes, 19 Taga, 26 Ját, 10 Kolí, and 2 Musalmán villages. In June, 1873, 44 villages were added to the list, giving a total of 277, with a population of 51,838 souls, of whom 21,604 were male adults, 13,420 were women; there were 11,396 boys and only 5,418 girls, or 32·2 per cent. of the minor population. These figures show conclusively the necessity that existed for some active interference on the part of Government. The cost of the extra establishment employed is defrayed by a cess on the 2,000 "blood-red and suspected" families of one rupee a year, whilst 6,302 families pay one-half that amount. The cess yields Rs. 5,151 per annum, and the expenditure amounts to Rs. 3,960.

As a rule, the soil is owned by the village communities; the old assignees of the Government revenue and talukadárs have disappeared. Besides the money-lenders, there are hardly any men of note amongst the proprietary body at present existing. As Mr. Wynne says, " the list begins and ends with Raja Raghubír Singh of Land-haura, the Messrs. Powell, and Hamullah Khán of Kailáspur." Some account of the families which have exercised considerable influence in the district follows, but, with the exception of the Landhaura Gújars and the Ambahta Shaikhs, none of them claim more than a passing notice.

Old families.

The Pírzádahs of Bahat claim descent from the famous saint Baháuddín Zak-ariyá of Multan, mentioned by Firishta. Their ances-tor, Sháh Abdullah, is said to have settled at Bahat in the reign of Bahlol Lodi, from whom he received several villages in the neigh-bourhood free of revenue, for charitable purposes. A religious assembly (*urs*) is held annually in honour of this personage. At one time the Pírzádahs poss-essed considerable estates as farmers, but for many years they have had barely sufficient to keep up the appearance of respectability. At present the leading man amongst them appears to be Sháh Ghulám Abbás. Some of the descen-dants of Shaikh Abdúl Kaddús mentioned in the historical sketch linger in poverty at Gangoh.

Pírzádahs.

The Ambahta Pírzádahs, descended from Sháh Abúl Máali, also mentioned hereafter, are tolerably well-to-do. They possess twenty-two villages free of revenue, except some patches of resumed land. Their lands yield, in cash alone, a rental of Rs. 7,152 per annum, but they are much in debt. Their principal men are Sháh Ali Ahmad, son of Sháh Sábir Baksh, and Sháh Muhammad Kutb-ud-dín, son of Sháh Ghulám Sharf. The Shaikhs of Rájúpur are a community that once exercised considerable influence in the district. They also claim descent from a famous Musalmán saint, Shaikh Ráju, the founder of the town. One of his descendants, named Shaikh Kalan, is celebrated in the fiscal history of the district as an enterprising farmer, whose operations were conducted on so extensive a scale as to necessitate the interference[1] of higher authority. His grandsons are now in a condition barely removed from poverty.

In the Nawábganj fort at Saháranpur, the same built by Raja Indargír Goshain, lives an extraordinary character, named Nawáb Shaistah Khán, who seldom goes abroad, and spends his time in the study of chemistry, or, as some say, alchymy, his object being the discovery of the philosopher's stone, of which he is indeed sadly in need, although the grandson of one of Perron's *Jágírdárs*, and a relative of the Nawáb of Jhajhar, who had the misfortune of being hanged in the mutiny. When the *jágír* of Jhajhar was confiscated, Shaistah Khán and other loyal members of the family were allowed a small pension, not more than sufficient for them to live upon; and a journey to London, undertaken for the purpose of appealing against the decision of Government, involved him deeply in debt. He returned thence to end his days in poverty at the residence which his grandfather once occupied as commandant of Saháranpur under General Perron.

Nawáb Shaistah Khán.

Amongst the old Musalmán talukas broken up since the British occupation of the district, were the *jaedáds* of Nijábat Ali Khán[2] and Mandal Pathán in 1806, and the mukarari of Murtaza Khán, consisting of thirty-one villages known as Taluka Patehar in 1813-14.

The Turkmán colony at Lakhnauti, all true Shiahs, is said to have been founded by a detachment from Bábar's army. In later days their chief obtained possession of Tappa Kaini, comprising twenty-one villages near Gangoh. This taluka was broken up in 1809, on the death of the last acknowledged chieftain, Bahrmand Ali Khán, who left no male issue, and whose surviving relatives are now in a state of miserable poverty. A colony of Afgháns, under Muhammad Anwar Khán, settled at Patehar in Parganah Sultánpur, during the Rohilla supremacy, and obtained an estate, which ultimately came to include thirty-four villages. The estate was resumed in 1814, and Ali Ahmad Khán, the present head of the family, is now a tahsíldár. Pitambar Singh, Rána of Jusmor, the titular head of the Pundír clan of Rajpúts, manages to subsist at the village of Jusmor in the north of the Raotala. The history of his childhood is a tale of rascality and spoliation, for he was left an orphan in his infancy, and the remainder of what had been once a fine estate, comprising villages in the Dún as well as in this district, was nearly all frittered away by dishonest agents. He, too, has little more than a bare subsistence allowance.

Turkmáns of Lakhnauti.

The Pundír Raja of Jusmor.

On the high land overlooking the left bank of the Soláni river, about nine miles north-west of Rúrkí, stands Sákrauda, once a stronghold of the Musalmán Pundírs who bear the

Raos of Sakrauda and Kheri.

---

[1] See subsequently, under fiscal history.   [2] Comprising Bahat, Jahangírabad, Muzaffarabad and Sarsáwa.

title of Rao. Under the Rohilla Government, in the time of Zábita Khán, the Sakrauda Raos had sufficient influence to have the lands occupied by them separated from the neighbouring parganah of Jaurási under the name of Tappa Sakrauda. This tappa at the settlement in 1839 was found to consist of fifty-five villages, of which only eighteen were cultivated. The remainder was measured off with the large tract included in the Kánsrao and Kheri jungles. Mr. Thornton settled sixteen of the cultivated villages with the zamíndárs, to whom an allowance of ten per cent. on the land revenue was allotted, whilst the málguzárs obtained a hereditary and transferable right in their villages.[1] Rao Muhammad Ali Khán is now the leading man of the community. The Kheri tappa had a similar origin, and was owned by the Raos of that place. It contained thirty-nine villages at the settlement in 1839, of which only nine were cultivated, and of these Kheri and Alawálpur are situated on a high isolated piece of land in the centre of the *khádir*, and the remaining villages lie within the *khádir*. In the early settlements the entire tappa was considered one estate, and assessed at a very moderate land-revenue. At the fourth settlement an enhancement took place, and Bábar Khán, the surety for the payment of the revenue, was admitted as málguzar in the following year. In 1820-21 the zamíndárs recovered their possession, and a settlement for ten years was made with them from 1830-31, after a division was made into four pattís. Mr. Thornton broke up the tappa by distributing the assessment separately over each of the ten villages that he found possessed of cultivated lands, and by including the remainder in the waste tract placed at the disposal of Government. (See WASTES.)

Raja Rámdayál Singh, the Gújar proprietor of a vast estate held at a fixed

The Landhaura *muka-rari.*

revenue (*mukarari*), was the most important personage in the district at the conquest, and since, he and his family have exercised considerable influence on the progress of events in the Saháranpur District, a more detailed account of his family and their possessions will not be out of place.[2] The Landhaura family trace their origin to one Chaudhri Manohar Singh of the Khúbar *got* of Gújars, who received in 1173 *híjri* (1759 A.D.) from Najíb Khán, Rohilla, the grant of some 505 villages and 31 hamlets on a fixed revenue. The Rohilla leader was at that time engaged in consolidating his acquisitions in the Upper Duáb, and was glad to purchase the assistance of such a powerful ally as the head of this great sub-division of the Gújar clan. Manohar Singh was succeeded by Lál Kunwár, and he by Budh Singh, Mohar Singh and Raja Rámdayál, the last of whom was found in possession of 794 villages and 36 hamlets at the British occupation in 1803,

---

[1] Set. Rep. I, 86-91.   [2] Mr. Thornton's report of 1839, I, Set. Rep. 98 ; Sel. Rev. Rec. N.-W. P., 305, and the Board's Records *passim* are the principal authorities. This history is also useful in showing how our statesmen got rid of troublesome mushroom-potentates.

representing the gradual acquisitions of himself and his predecessors in the troubled times of the Rohilla and Marhatta Governments. The Raja then paid a fixed annual revenue amounting to Rs. 1,11,597, which was confirmed to him for life.[1] A list of his villages was obtained from him in 1810 A.D., which showed in the column for proprietors the Raja's own name as proprietor of 496 villages and 31 hamlets; the names of other persons as proprietors of 35 villages and five hamlets; and in the remaining 260 villages this column was left blank, and the villages were therefore known as 'khánakháli.' The estate lay for the most part in the Saháranpur District and the northern portions of the Muzaffarnagar District. Raja Rámdayál died on the 29th March, 1813, and the revenue of the year 1812-13 was collected direct from the cultivators. The arrangement made with the Raja was only for his life, and the estate then came under a regular settlement. Mr. Chamberlain, the Assistant Collector, was despatched from Meerut to make such inquiries on the spot as were considered necessary. He found that the estate comprised 827 villages and 36 hamlets, in which the Raja's heirs claimed 596 villages and all the hamlets as theirs by right as proprietors, and put forward two *farmáns*, one by the Emperor Aurangzeb and the other by the Emperor Jahán Shah, in support of their pretensions. Mr. Chamberlain found that these *farmáns* were forgeries; but that the Raja and his ancestors had been in possession of the 505 villages and 31 hamlets entered in the lease granted by Najíb Khán, for nearly sixty years.

The Board of Commissioners concluded engagements for these villages with
Settlement on Rám-   the Raja's heirs, but only as occupants claiming the
dayál's death.   proprietary right, leaving it to some future period to settle the question between them and those in the villages who claimed the same rights. In those cases where the Raja's heirs acknowledged the proprietary right to be vested in others, the villzage amíndárs were ascertained, and the settlement was made with them. The grounds of this temporary postponement of the complete settlement of the estates were apparently a feeling of consideration for the family of Rámdayál, both on account of the great alteration that must in any case take place in their circumstances, and also because the deceased Raja had always exerted himself to support the measures of Government. In many of the villages settled with the Raja's heirs, claimants appeared, who were acknowledged to be possessors of the proprietary right; but still their position was ignored for the time being, on the plea that the Raja had asserted his claim to the proprietary title in all these villages by the list he furnished in 1810 A.D., and had held the fiscal management of them for a very long period. It was, moreover, considered to be more expedient that the claims in the entire estate should be investigated and decided upon at one and the same time.

_____

[1] Board's Rec., October, 1, 1804, September, 30, 1805.

Amongst the 505 villages and 31 hamlets taken to form the Landhaura estate
Sub-divisions of the in 1815, were five small talukas which the Raja had
mukarari. made over to a similar number of distant relatives.
This distribution was confirmed by the Raja's heirs. Kunwar Siwái Singh, the
eldest son of Raja Rámdayál had predeceased his father, leaving a widow, Ráni
Sada Kunwar, and a son, Badan Singh, by another wife. Disputes arose
between these regarding the disposition of the remaining villages, which, at length,
were settled by the intervention of Nain Singh as arbitrator, who assigned
taluka Thitki to Khushál Singh, the second son, under charge of his mother,
Ráni Dhan Kunwar, whilst the remainder of the villages were divided into two
talukas, and given over to Ráni Sada Kunwar and Badan Singh respectively.
The subsequent fiscal history of these talukas will best be told from Mr. E.
Thornton's accurate and careful report.

Taluka Thitki, held by Khushál Singh, consisted of 239 villages, 17 biswas
and 11 hamlets. The Ráni entered into engagements for the entire estate, at a
Taluka Thitki. revenue for 1221 *fasli* (1813-14 A. D.) amounting to
Rs. 1,90,475, with a progressive increase for the remain-
ing year of the settlement. Mr. Chamberlain, who made this assessment, considered that it would leave the Ráni a net profit of Rs. 16,000 a year ; but though
this was the proportion of the gross assets allowed by the regulations, he considered it insufficient to maintain the rank and situation of the family, and
he estimated the profits derivable from 15½ villages held free of revenue at
Rs. 15,000, and further recorded that the Ráni possessed a large sum in money
and Government securities. In November, 1817, Government directed the
relinquishment of the progressive increase to the revenue, and the deduction
of one-eleventh from the initial assessment, thus leaving the annual charges at
Rs. 1,73,405. In November, 1820, the Government further permitted Khushál
Singh to continue to hold the 15½ revenue-free villages on the same terms
as a mark of favour. The next settlement was made for seven years, 1226 to
1232 *fasli* (1818-19 to 1824-5 A. D.), and was accepted by the Ráni Dhan Kunwar on behalf of her son at the land revenue of 1225 *fasli*, the last year of the
previous settlement. She subsequently refused to abide by the agreement, and
the Collector was directed to form a village settlement. Scarcely had this
been done when the Ráni again applied to be admitted to settlement. Mr.
Ross, the Senior Member of the Board of Revenue, was then (1822) on tour
in the district, and finding that the Ráni had, in the interval between the
settlement with herself and that with the village zamíndárs, successfully used
her influence to cause a decrease of cultivation, and compel a reduction of
revenue, he considered that whilst she had, by her own act, foregone the position to which she had originally no clear right, it was also in every point of
view desirable that the settlement should be made with the village occupants,

who at the same time asserted themselves to be proprietors. He proposed, however, that as it had not yet been decided that Khushál Singh had not any
right in the villages, a sum of five per cent. on the actual collections should be
allowed him in addition to the proceeds of the 15½ villages which he then
enjoyed free of revenue.

The sanction of Government to these arrangements was communicated to
the Board in Mr. Holt Mackenzie's letter of the 18th July, 1822, but it was
also distinctly laid down that the five per cent. allowance on the collections
made to the young Raja Khushál Singh, and his mother the Rání Dhan Kunwar,
was not an acknowledgment of right, and that the circumstances of the family
were among the considerations which induced Government to accede to the
proposal. The error that would have been committed had the taluka of Thitki
again been subjected to the Rání was strongly insisted on. Subsequently
the proprietary right was adjudged to belong to the village zamíndárs, and
not to the *mukararidár ;* the allowance was, however, continued to Khushál Singh
up to his death. On the death of Rání Dhan Kunwar, the question as to the continuance of the allowance to Lád Kunwar, widow of Khushál Singh, was again
brought forward, when it was ruled[1] that the allowance was a personal stipend
which ceased on the death of the grantee. The revenue-free villages, however,
still remained, and were continued to Lád Kunwar for her life.[2] On her death
the proprietary titles were investigated, and settlements were made with the
village zamíndárs.

Taluka Jabarheri fell to Rání Sadá Kunwar, and consisted of 49 villages
and three biswas. She refused to agree to the land revenue on eleven villages,
but accepted the remainder, of which the assessment amounted to Rs. 26,578,

Taluka Jabarheri.

with a progressive enhancement. As in Thitki, the progressive enhancement was relinquished, and a deduction
of one-eleventh made from the revenue by Government in 1817, leaving the
assessment at Rs. 24,162. The second settlement for seven years was made by
Mr. Moore with the Rání on the assessment of the last year of the expired settlement 1225 *fasli* or (1817-18, A.D.). In 1822, Mr. Ross proposed this
arrangement for confirmation, not on the ground that the Rani had been found
to possess a right in the villages, but because, whilst few of the village head-men
had expressed dissatisfaction at being continued under her and she had regularly
discharged the revenue, no sufficient ground was found to exist for taking
the fiscal management out of her hands. Government sanctioned Mr. Ross's
proposals, but at the same time explained the provisions of Regulation VII.
of 1822, and pointed out the propriety of at once commencing the detailed
settlement of the taluka ; the object being the ascertainment and record of

---

[1] Board, 18th November, 1836, 211.   [2] Government to Commissioner of Delhi, September 1st, 1829.

the nature of the rights of the persons admitted to settlement under the claim of being proprietors of the individual villages on the one hand, and of the heirs of the late Raja on the other hand. Mr. Ross had simply stated the position of the parties at the time, without detailing the circumstances which had brought them to this position. On this vague statement the Government were led to imagine, from the presence of acknowledged village proprietors side by side with a settlement made with the late Raja's heirs, that there might be a tenure of the nature of a *talukadári* existing in the estate. It was to clear up this question, and settle all existing rights, that Mr. Thornton, in 1836, undertook the examination of the settlements of these talukas noticed hereafter.

Mr. Turner made the settlement under Regulation VII. of 1822, and assessed a revenue of Rs. 24,000 on the taluka, which took effect from 1241 *fasli* (1833-34 A. D.). An arrangement was made for the payment of the balances that had accrued, but these were remitted at the recommendation of Mr. Thornton. Mr. Turner had recorded the Ráni's inability to undertake the fiscal management of the taluka, and had prevailed on her and Ráni Dhan Kunwar of Thitki, who had previously been on very bad terms with each other, to come to the following arrangement:—Ráni Dhan Kunwar was to be jointly responsible with Ráni Sadá Kunwar for the Government revenue, and to take half the net profits that should remain. " From the gross profits, Ráni Dhan Kunwar was to deduct the usual percentage for standing security for the moiety of revenue due from the other. She was to advance the instalments as they became due, and deduct the interest due on this account; and she was to repay herself for the expenses of collection,—the actual management being to vest in her. After the death of Ráni Dhan Kunwar, her heirs Ráni Lád Kunwar, &c., took her responsibilities and engagements. Ráni Sadá Kunwar was thus free from keeping up any establishment for the management of the taluka, but of course her profits from it were as small as her partners might choose to make them, still she gained by the reconciliation with the other party, for though she became dependent on their bounty, they treated her well ; and besides the resources above mentioned, they still had a large hoard of Raja Rámdayál Singh's accumulations stored in their house at Landhaura.

" The settlement proceedings for this taluka were sent to Mr. Thornton for revision, together with the remainder of the settlements of the estates comprised in the Deoband Tahsíldári. The right of the Ráni had not been investigated, and the amount of her demand on the communities had not been limited, nor even had her actual demand been recorded. Soon after Mr. Grant joined the district as Officiating Collector, the complaints of the village communities led him to call on their representatives for a list of their rentals. In his letters of the 4th and 11th April, 1835, he strongly urged the propriety of a settlement with the

village communities, as did Mr. Lewis in his report of the 9th January, 1836. "
Large balances had accrued for some years, and at length the Board of Revenue
directed the Collector to take the management of the taluka into his own hands.
It was found that most of the villages had been sublet to the village communities, and by collecting according to these leases for the years 1235-38 *fasli*
(1827-28 to 1830-31 A.D.), there was realized in excess of the revenue a sum
of Rs. 4,122. The examination of the rights in the taluka was made by Mr.
Thornton, who found it contained 34 villages. In nine of these the settlement
was made with the resident proprietary community. In four small villages,
where the Ráni's ancestors had located the cultivating community, the settlement was made with the residents as proprietors, whilst a *malikána* or proprietary allowance of ten per cent. on the Government demand was allotted to the
Ráni. In three other cases, where the cultivating community opposed the claim
of the Ráni, the dispute was referred to arbitration. Of the remaining eighteen
villages, four belonged to Núrnagar in the Muzaffarnagar District, and fourteen
were settled with the Ráni in full proprietary right. In most of these villages,
however, the remains of an agricultural brotherhood were found, whose lands
were transmitted hereditarily. In many of these cases the brotherhood were
said to have been originally located by the ancestors of the late Raja Rámdayál,
and to them the position of hereditary cultivator, with a right of occupancy at
a fixed money rate, twenty per cent. above the Government demand, was
granted at the settlement.

Taluka Baledh, assigned to Badan Singh, son of Siwúi and grandson of
Rámdayál, consisted of twenty-four villages, of which

Taluka Baledh.

he accepted the assessments made on twenty. At the
second settlement for 1226 to 1232 *fasli* the taluka was again settled with
Badan Singh, but he failed to fulfil his engagements, and a village settlement
was made from 1819-20 to 1824-25 (1227 to 1232 *fasli*). The only village in
which a proprietary right was declared in his favour was Baledh khás, his residence. The village of Babail, which he had held for some time free of revenue,
was continued to him, but subsequently the proprietary rights in this village
also were found to belong to others.

Taluka Kúnja belonged to Kora Singh, and he entered into arrangements
for all of the 44 villages it comprised. At the second

Taluka Kúnja.

settlement for 1226 *fasli* (1818-19 A.D.), his son,
Biji Singh, was admitted to engagements. It was this Biji Singh who harboured the great gang of dakaits that plundered Bhagwánpur and the treasure
escort from the Jawálápur Tahsíli in 1824. Kúnja was besieged by a party of
the Dehra regiment, under the Hon'ble J. Shore and Colonel Young, and a
party from Saháranpur led by Mr. Grindall, the Magistrate. Biji Singh fell
in the defence with a large number of his followers, and the villages of Taluka

Kúnja were settled with the resident proprietary bodies. Taluka Dádli, held

Taluka Dádli.

by Guláb Singh, consisted of thirty-two villages and two hamlets, and he entered into engagements for all except one village. . The second settlement, from 1818-19 A.D., was made with Mohar Singh, son of Guláb Singh, but he failed to meet his engagements, and a village settlement was made with the resident cultivating communities in 1819-20 A.D. (1227 *fasli*).

Taluka Tálheri was held by Ráni Dayú Kunwar, the widow of Bakht Singh,

Taluka Tálheri.

and consisted of 24 villages and three hamlets, for all of which she engaged at an annually progressive revenue which in 1225 *fasli* amounted to Rs. 16,941. At the second settlement in the following year, the demand was reduced to Rs. 15,000. In 1822 the occupant zamíndárs of 17 out of the 24 villages complained to Mr. Ross of the exactions of a farmer to whom the Ráni had made over the entire taluka, being herself unable to manage it. Mr. Ross cancelled the engagements, and admitted the zamíndárs to settlement. Tálheri khás, the residence of the Ráni, was settled with her in full proprietary right, and an allowance of five per cent. on the revenue of the remaining villages was allowed to her, pending the decision of her claim to the proprietary right. This state of things continued until her death, when the allowance ceased. Taluka Játaul was held by Kúra Singh, and

Talukas Játaul and Chaundaheri.

consisted of 49 villages and 13 hamlets, which, owing to the refusal of Kúra Singh to accept the terms offered, were settled with the village zamíndárs. Taluka Chaundaheri consisted of 42 villages and two hamlets, held by Basáwan Singh, who also refused to engage for the revenue assessed. A similar course was adopted in his case.[1] Thus the great Gújar estate was broken up.

[1] The following table summarises the history of the whole *mukarari*, consisting in 1813-14 of 827 villages and 36 hamlets :—

Name of taluka.	With whom settled in 1813-14.	When settled with the village proprietors.	Number of	
			Villages.	Hamlets.
...	Village proprietors ...	1813-14	323	5
Thítki ...	Ráni Dhan Kunwar and Khushál Singh.	1821	239$\frac{11}{15}$	11
Jabarheri ...	Badan Singh ...	11 villages in 1813-14, remainder in 1836	49$\frac{3}{20}$	...
Baledh ...	Ráni Sada Kunwar ...	4 villages in 1813-14, 20 ditto in 1819-02	24	...
Kúnja ...	Kora Singh ...	1821	44	...
Dádli ...	Guláb Singh ...	1819-20	32	2
Tálheri ...	Daya Kunwar ...	1822	24	3
Játaul ...	Kúra Singh ...	1813-14	49	13
Chaundaheri ...	Basáwan Singh ...	1813-14	42	2
			827	36

Fortunately for the owner of Landhaura khás, he came into possession as a minor, and his estates fell under the administration of the Court of Wards. Arrangements were made in 1853 for the household expenses of the minor Raja Raghubír Singh and his mother, and the management of the estates in their respective districts was vested in the Collectors of Saháranpur and Meerut. In 1854 these comprised 38 villages or portions of villages, yielding in the Saháranpur District a revenue of Rs. 26,000 a year. Subsequently the Raja received eleven villages in reward for good conduct during the mutiny and two by purchase. Before the mutiny his profits amounted to Rs. 4,992 besides six villages held in direct management. In 1863 the profits rose to Rs. 7,748 on the villages which were sublet, besides 16 villages paying Rs. 7,872 held under direct management. Raghubír Singh died in 1868, some say from poison, and his widow has adopted one Nathu Singh, a relative of her husband's mother. By this adoption the headship of the Gújar clan has passed away from the Khúbar got, and has, therefore, been the cause of much irritation amongst the members of the family. This year (1874), a person claiming to be Raghubír Singh appeared at Naini Tal, and demanded to be recognized and put in possession of the Landhaura estates. His history runs that he was half-poisoned and half-burned, and was then thrown into the Ganges river, whence he was rescued by a mendicant, with whom he has remained from 1868 until now.

On the 2nd of October, 1803, immediately after the capture of Aligarh, the Governor-General appointed the Collectors of the border districts to take charge of the country conquered from Sindhia, and provide for its administration, subject to the orders of the Commander-in-Chief. They were further directed to divide the districts into three divisions, to be attached to Etáwa, Murádabad and Fatehgarh, respectively. The Commissioners met at Koil on the 28th October, 1803, and proposed the distribution of the conquered territory into four divisions. The first portion comprised the present districts of Saháranpur, Muzaffarnagar and a part of Meerut, altogether fifty-three maháls or parganahs. The second portion included Khúrja, Sikandarabad, Bulandshahr, Shikárpur, Dádri, Dásna, Kásna, Dankaur, Gháziud-dín-nagar (Gháziabad), Begamabad, Malakpur, Garhmuktesar, and some other neighbouring parganahs, altogether thirty in number. The third portion, to be attached to the Fatehgarh District, contained Koil, Kanka, Atrauli, Dibhái, Chhara, Bamauri, Pindráwal, Khair, Noh, Chandaus, Barauli, Murthal, and Pítampur, altogether twelve maháls. The fourth portion, to be attached to Etáwa, contained fifteen maháls,—Firuzabad, Sahpu, Sadabad, Kandauli, Raya, Jiwar, Mursán, Mát, Mahúban, Hasangarh, Gorai, Husain, Tuksán, Háthras, Jalesar, Khalílganj, Sonai, Moheriya and Daryápur. The Commander-in-Chief, on the 4th November of the same

Early fiscal history.

1850-1866.

year, gave orders that the first division or district of Sahâranpur should be divided[1] into two portions, the northern and southern, and that the latter should be placed under the Collector of Morádabad, Mr. Leycester, whilst the northern portion of the district remained under Dehli. The settlement of the second division was entrusted to Colonel Ochterlony, the Resident at Dehli. The third division was entrusted to Mr. Claude Russell, the Governor-General's Agent at Fatehgarh; and the fourth was placed under Mr. R. Cunyngham, the Collector of Etáwa.

In August, 1804, Aligarh was formed by the union of the second, third.
1803-4. and fourth divisions, with the addition of parganahs Sikandra Rao from Etáwa, and Anúpshahr from Murádabad. The subsequent fiscal history of these divisions will be found under the Aligarh District. The northern division of Sahâranpur was placed under charge of Mr. J. D. Guthrie, and instructions were issued to all the new Collectors to make a settlement for one year with the actual proprietors or amils[2] of respectability, or, if it should be found necessary, the collections might be entrusted to tahsíldárs. All large estates were to be settled by the Collector in person, and, where possible, security should be taken for the due payment of the revenue. All arrears due to the Marhattas were to be remitted, and a separation was to be effected between the land revenue proper and the miscellaneous duties and taxes, such as bazar and transit duties, that had been imposed by previous rulers. The Collectors were further instructed that " while fixing a fair and equitable rate, they should remember to impress upon the people the inestimable advantages of the British rule, and conciliate their attachment and confidence." The monopoly of the sale of salt was broken up, and a system of duties on the import of western salt, and the manufacture of salt within British territory, was substituted for it. The year 1804-5 was marked by the raids of the Marhattas and Amír Khán, and military rather than fiscal affairs demanded the entire attention of the District
1804-5 Officers. In November, 1804, a Judge-Magistrate was appointed to both Sahâranpur and Meerut, and their jurisdiction was defined. Both divisions, however, still remained under one Collector, who resided at Meerut,[3] and formed the settlement of both divisions of the district, with the aid of two Assistants. In October, 1804, the Commander-in-Chief issued instructions for the settlement for 1804-5 (1212 fasli). He directed the Collector to cause the Amíns to examine the rent-rolls of each village for the years 1801-2 and 1802-3, and in all possible cases to take engagements from the actual proprietors at an easy revenue. Possession was to be upheld, and in a taluka, if the subordinate proprietors could be discovered, they were

---

[1] The line separating the two divisions ran through the middle of the present district of Muzaffarnagar.   [2] Apparently here a kind of farmer.   [3] 27th November, 1804, Board.

to be admitted to engagements. All cesses were abolished, and the revenue
was assessed on the produce of the land only. Regulation VIII. of 1793 was
quoted for the guidance of the Collector, who was further directed to appoint
tahsíldárs, who were to receive 11½ per cent. on the collections, and be responsible for the police of their respective charges. They were to give security
equal to the largest instalment they had to collect, and were to be assisted by
the kánúngoes.

Though it was evidently the wish of Government to make engagements
with the actual proprietors of the land, yet it was found impossible suddenly to
break up the great estates held on fixed rates, which in this district quite equalled

1805-6 to 1807-8.   in area the lands held under a temporary settlement.
1213 to 1215 fasli.   Raja Rámdayál Singh of Landhaura, Raja Nain Singh,
Rao Ramdhan Singh, Rao Ajít Singh, Zulfakár Ali Khán and Bahrmand
Khán were all confirmed in their holdings, and the first triennial settlement
under Regulation IX. of 1805 was made with them, at the same rates (1805-6 to
1807-8).[1] This farming system had been the practice under the Marhatta
Government, and even in the temporarily settled portion under the British
Government, a system known as the amáni was in force, by which the amíns or
amils received ten per cent. on the collections made by them. In the latter case,
the standard observed was a certain undefined proportion of the crops, which
was collected either in kind or in cash, according to the market rates current
in the neighbourhood. The amount of this proportion depended on the will or
ability of the amil. The natural consequence of this state of affairs was, that
agriculture had been gradually on the decline in the district during the latter
years of the Marhatta rule, the revenues had shown a corresponding decrease,
and the people were sunk in indigence and despondency. Since the annexation of the district, the repeated incursions of the Sikhs, Marhattas and Pin-
dárís had still further caused great loss to the people, so that at the commencement of the first triennial settlement, the Collector had much to encounter before
he could show any improvement in the revenue.

Writing in 1807, Mr. Guthrie, however, notices a gradual improvement
in the state of cultivation, and remarks, that whilst for-
Gradual improvement.
merly 12 to 15,000 bullocks were carried out of the
district annually to carry grain for the armies in the field at Rs. 2-13 per
month, a rate then considered profitable, the charge in 1805 had risen to
Rs. 3-8, and in 1807, not only were these bullocks employed within the district,
but there was a considerable importation of cattle from the trans-Jumna
districts. The Banjára bullock-owners, too, had taken to settled habits, and
were then engaged in pasturage or cultivation in the waste tracts along the

_____
[1] Board's Rec., October 1, 1804; September 30, 1805. The full history of each of these
talukas will be found under the head of "old families" in the district notices.

Jumna and under the hills. The land-revenue of 1211 *fasli* (1803-4) stood at Rs. 12,69,820 ; this rose in 1212 *fasli* to Rs. 13,16,237 ; in 1213 there was an increase of Rs. 44,506 ; in 1214 of Rs. 48,109 ; and in 1215 of Rs. 80,191 ; giving an actual increase in 1215 *fasli* (1807-8) of Rs. 2,08,444, or, if the revenue from lapsed revenue-free lands (Rs. 10,781) be added, of Rs. 2,19,225 over the initial settlement of 1803-4 A.D. The improvement was further shown in the cultivation of the more valuable kinds of produce, such as sugar-cane and wheat.

To illustrate his remarks, Mr. Guthrie prepared an estimate[1] for the year
Mr. Guthrie's produce 1806-7 "in three parganahs selected for the purpose, as
estimate in 1807. being in the middle degree with respect to the fertility
of the soil and improvement." Having ascertained the quantity of each article of produce, and fixed its price according to the average rate of the market for that year, he calculated the proportion the value bore to the assessment, and then, according to the average produce of the lands, computed the extent of cultivation (for each article) necessary to yield a quantity equal to the proportion its value bears to the assessment. The rate at which the assessment was calculated was in general one-half of the produce, or eight annas on the rupee, payable to Government, the other moiety being the proprietor's share. In several places, however, the proprietor's share, according to established local custom, exceeded one-half of the produce ; and the average rate of the assessment upon the different articles of produce would perhaps have been more accurately estimated at the proportions of seven annas on the rupee as the Government share, and nine annas as the share for proprietors. The year was a favourable one, followed by a year of scarcity from drought.

Estimate for the year 1214 fasli *of the produce of the lands in the Saháranpur District paying revenue to Government, showing the extent of the cultivation and of the produce of the different articles, and the proportion which the value of each article respectively is supposed to bear to the assessment.*

Articles.	Produce of one acre in maunds.	No. of acres in cultivation.	Total produce at the average rate of one acre.	Value according to the average rate of the market in 1214 *fasli*.
	M. s. c.	Acres.	Mds.	Rs.
Sugar	21 19 11	12,695	266.500	6,01,875
Uncleaned cotton ...	0 35 1	17,137	15,047	1,00,313
Toriya	1 8 0	21,638	31,348	25,078
Carrots	...	19,041	...	16,719
Manduwa	3 20 7	13,388	47,022	25,078
Manduwi	3 20 7	13,388	47,022	25,078

[1] The figures in the original are in bíghas, and these I have changed into acres for the sake of uniformity ; see Sel. Rev. Rec., N.-W. P., p. 290, Allahabad, 1872.

Articles.	Produce of one acre in maunds.	No. of acres in cultivation.	Total produce at the average rate of one acre.	Value according to the average rate of the market in 1214 *fasli*.
	M. s. c.	Acres.	Mds.	Rs.
Rice, 1st sort	5 34 0	21,434	125,391	1,00,313
„ 2nd „	4 6 13	72,158	300,936	1,50,469
Indian-corn	8 31 3	28,562	250,781	1, 0,312
Joár	7 0 15	17,851	125,391	1,00,313
Chari (fodder)	...	11,870	...	25,078
Bájra	3 32 5	13,170	50,156	33,428
Urd	4 15 12	28,562	125,391	1,00,3.2
Múng	2 25 6	16,661	43,887	50,156
Moth	4 33 2	14 281	68,965	50 156
Lobiya	2 25 6	9 520	25,078	16,719
Kúrjad	0 35 2	16,661	14,629	16,719
Kangni	2 16 9	12,117	29,258	16,719
Sanwak	2 16 9	13,848	33,438	16,719
Kodo	9 37 14	6,924	68,875	33,438
Total ...	...	3,80,906	1,669,115	16,05,003
Tobacco	...	4,760	...	33,438
Onions	...	15,232	...	33,438
Chena	2 16 7	24,255	58,516	33,438
Wheat	7 9 11	1,14,249	827,579	6,01,675
Barley	8 31 1	68,550	601,876	3,00,938
Gram	7 0 2	99 969	702,186	4,01,250
Arhar	4 15 9	6,664	29,258	16,719
Masúr	8 31 3	13,329	117 011	66,875
Sarson	0 8 12	3,04,668	66,875	66,875
Kurr	0 17 8	57,125	25,078	16,719
Miscellaneous	6 12 15	8,924	62,695	23,437
Total ...	...	6,817,725	2,491,096	16.05,002

The table given above is useful in two ways,—it gives the opinion of a more than ordinary intelligent observer as to the general state of cultivation at this early period of British rule, and affords material for comparison with the later statistics of the three districts it refers to as to the amount of produce per acre before the introduction of the canal system. This question is noticed under each district separately, but I would here once again warn the reader that, as far as I can see, we have not, as yet, statistics as to the productive powers of the land of such scientific accuracy as would warrant any but the most general conclusions to be drawn from them. Throughout these volumes I give only the estimates that bear on their face an appearance of some care in their preparation, and carry with them the sanction of a name of established reputation. It would be beyond the scope of this work to add any remarks of my own, or draw those general conclusions which might safely be made even from the imperfect data we possess: these I leave for a second edition, when, perhaps, more carefully prepared statistics, and a more extended experience, may enable me to educe the sound principles which must underlie the present heterogeneous mass of agricultural statistics.[1]

Continuing Mr. Guthrie's description of the general state of the district, he states his opinion that in point of cultivation, whilst superior to the lands adjoin-

General condition of the district.

ing Bareilly and Murádabad, Saháranpur was inferior to the Duáb districts adjoining it on the south. Towards the Ganges, the lands comprised in the great *mukararis*[2] were flourishing, which Mr. Guthrie says "evidently shows the happy effects of giving to the occupiers all the power over, and interest in the soil which is necessary for improvements;" but which may be more correctly attributed to the fact that the holders of these estates were too powerful to be trifled with, and were able, by their local position, their numerous forts and their clan influence, to defy or buy off the Sikh invaders, and compel their Marhatta rulers to accept a moderate revenue. Further westward, towards the centre of the district, the lands showed less improvement, and near the banks of the Jumna the waste land bore an excessive proportion to the cultivated area. Villages were few, and the owners were sunk in indigence, not because the land was less productive, but entirely owing to this tract being constantly exposed to the depredations of the Sikhs. These raiders "not only exacted from every land-holder a tribute, denominated *ráki*, the amount of which was proportioned to his means, but on many occasions reduced the zamíndárs to total ruin by burn-ing their villages and driving off their cattle." The appearance of the villages showed the state of general insecurity; almost every one was surrounded by a wall or ditch, or both, as a means of defence against invasion.

. Exclusive of Begam Sumrú's *jágír*, the district was estimated to contain

The settlement.

about 5,900 square miles, or 6,289,400 local bíghas,[3] which Mr. Guthrie distributes as follows :—

	Cultivated.	Uncultivated.
	Bs.	Bs.
Lands held in *mukarari*, or on a fixed assessment ...	736,000	337,000
Ditto under a temporary assessment ...	924,000	887,000
Ditto free of revenue...	617,000	474,000
Rivers, hills, roads, waste, &c.		2,314,000
Total ...	2,277,000	3,012,000

[1] The great errors at present made are, first and greatest, the entire absence of any explanation as to the mode in which the statements were prepared,—whether allowance was made for the rain-fall, the presence or absence of canal irrigation, the nearness of markets, the pressure of assess-ment, the means of communication, the existence of scarcity elsewhere which had an influence on the price of grain, the character of the cultivators and their landlords, the spring-level of the well water, and other similar matters which affect the amount and value of the produce.   [2] The term applied to estates held on a fixed revenue, such as those of Rajas Ramdayál and Nain Singh.

[3] Giving 1,066 bíghas to the square mile, or 1·665 bíghas to an acre; see further, Sel. Rev. Rec., N.-W. P., 1818-20, p. 43 ; *Ibid*, 1821-27, p. 300.

At the same time, by a rough census, the population was estimated at 703,575, or 119·25 persons to the square mile. Except in the case of revenue-free lands, the amount of cultivation. was computed on the spot village by village by actual measurement or estimate, and in revenue-free villages the total is based on the estimate of the kánúngo. "In every instance where the zamíndár offered objections to enter into engagements for the payment of what was considered a fair and equitable assessment, the amount produced was ascertained by the actual measurement of the crops on the ground, and the extent of the land cultivated." In no case was the settlement in these estates made with a farmer, except where the actual proprietor refused to engage. Excluding the *mukararís* of Rámdayál and Nain Singh, there were no considerable renters in the district, the farms being generally extremely sub-divided, yielding on an average about Rs. 800 a year. Mr. Guthrie's great difficulty in carrying out the orders of Government in this respect was the depressed state of the smaller proprietary bodies, who, from want of stock to perform the business of cultivation, and from want of confidence in the permanency of the new rule, frequently "resigned the probable advantages to be gained by managing their own lands for the certainty of sharing a stipulated part of the produce."

The story of Captain Shaikh Kalan is worth reproduction, as giving what even in 1828 was considered an illustration of the evil "effects produced by summary settlements for the land-revenue of large tracts of country with an intermediate agent, whether designated as zamíndár, talukadár, or revenue-farmer," and which contributed in a small degree to the downfall of the talukadári system. Kalan belonged to an old Shaikh family in Rájúpur, and early sought employment in the military service of the Marhattas. At the conquest in 1803 he joined the irregular corps formed by the British, and retired with the rank of Captain in 1810. In 1817-18, when the Collector had some difficulty in arranging for the villages of Rámdayál's *mukararí* that had then lapsed, Kalan stepped forward and offered to take as many as he could get in farm. He obtained possession of 149 villages, of which 47 were farmed to him with the consent of the proprietary body, 34 were given to him on account of the proprietors not attending to engage, 55, in consequence of a refusal to engage, and in 13 he had acquired the proprietary right by purchase. His mode of management is thus described by Mr. Reade, who was sent to investigate the affairs of this farm :—"It was customary with this farmer to under-farm the villages to the inhabitants, and on each village, in proportion to its size, he raised his under-farming assessment from Rs. 200 to Rs. 600 or Rs. 700 above the Government revenue. At the end of each year, after the accounts had been closed, he made the defaulters execute bonds for the sums due to him on their engagements." Bonds were also taken by the farmer for balances of advances made for carrying on the cultivation.

Shaikh Kalan.

The result of all this was, that the people were thoroughly discontented; and when Mr. Ross came on deputation from the Board of Revenue into this district in 1822, they poured out their complaints before him. Mr. Ross made inquiries, and found that the conduct of Kalan in the management of his estate was both arbitrary and oppressive, and that the lease had never been confirmed by Government. He recommended that the lease should be cancelled, and a settlement be made with the village communities. This was done, and gave rise to Kalan's claim to over 1¼ lakhs of rupees as damages, which was subsequently adjusted by an offer of Rs. 15,000 on the part of Government. His sons, Zámin Ali Khán and Nijábut Ali Khán, followed in the footsteps of their father, and engaged in the sometimes profitable business of buying up speculative parcels of land, and rights and interests in land of private individuals, at the sales by auction which so frequently took place in the earlier days of our rule. By a skilful management of the Civil Courts, they were able to obtain in Roorkee, for a trifling debt against three individuals, the lands owned by seventy-two persons in actual possession of their shares (see ROORKEE.). This was, no doubt, in a great measure due to the imperfect state of the record-of-rights; but it speaks badly for our administration that, though the wrong done was discovered, the only remedy that could be found was to apply to the same Court that wrought the injury by way of appeal against its own judgment.

The second triennial settlement was also under Regulation IX. of 1805, from 1216 to 1218 *fasli* (1808-9 to 1810-11 A.D.), and the assessment was to be framed upon the difference between the actual amount of the previous assess-

Second triennial settlement for 1808-9 to 1810-11.

ment and the actual produce of the land at its termination by adding two-thirds of such difference to the annual revenue of the first settlement. Section V. of the same Regulation further provided that at the expiration of the year 1218 *fasli* a new settlement should be concluded with the same persons (if willing to engage) for a further period of four years, viz., 1219 to 1222 (1811-12 to 1814-15), at a fixed equal annual revenue formed by adding to the annual revenue of the second triennial settlement three-fourths of the net increase of revenue found to have accrued during any one year of that period.[1] The second triennial settlement of this district was formed by Mr. H. Dumbleton, and gave a land revenue for 1218 *fasli* (1810-11 A. D.) of Rs. 18,93,743, exclusive of the great *mukararís*, or Rs. 4,78,632 in excess of the last year of the first triennial settlement. The drought of 1807-8, already noticed, produced serious embarrassments, so that the landholders were unable at once to accede to the terms pro-

[1] It is unnecessary to notice the permanent settlement promised by section 7 of Regulation IX. of 1805 and Regulation X. of 1807, as the controversy on this subject continued to our own days would fill a volume by itself.

posed, and reductions were allowed, amounting to Rs. 82,791 in the first
year, and Rs. 19,480 in the last year of this settlement. The Commissioners,
who then stood in the position of the Board of Revenue, noted the large proportion of estates in many parganahs either still altogether waste or only
partially brought into cultivation, and recommended the exclusion of the
northern division of the Saháranpur District, comprising the present district
of that name and a great part of Muzaffarnagar, from the benefits of a permanent settlement on this account, as well as because of the improvement
in agriculture contemplated from the reopening of the canal. It was also
found that, notwithstanding the anxiety of the Revenue Officers to admit the
proprietors to form engagements, a very extensive recourse to farming still
appeared to be necessary. The following table shows the demand, receipts and
balances, from 1803-4 to 1813-14 in rupees as finally adjusted[1] in the Provincial accounts :—

Year.	Demand.	Receipts.	Balance.	Charges of collection.	Year.	Demand.	Receipts.	Balance.	Charges of collection.
	Rs.	Rs.	Rs.	Rs.		Rs.	Rs.	Rs.	Rs.
1803-4,	12,71,821	12,49,182	22,639	1,41,737	1809-10,	20,05,753	19,90,544	15,209	1,19,148
1804-5,	13,11,929	12,18,264	93,665	2,05,058	1810-11,	21,43,677	21,24,887	18,790	1,15,294
1805-6.	15,00,473	14,96,660	3,813	2,27,976	1811-12,	21,55,600	20,83,181	72,419	1,22,705
1806-7,	16,06,316	16,05,001	1,315	2,68,617	1812-13.	23,29,124	22,88,702	40,422	1,26,791
1807-8,	16,79,610	16,78,637	973	2,30,217	1813-14,	25,79,817	25,53,724	26,093	1,44,438
1808-9,	18,83,243	18,80,798	2,445	1,56,973	Total...	2,04,67,363	2,01,69,580	2,97,763	18,58,984

The balances on the whole were very small when compared with Aligarh
and Agra, showing that the assessment could not have pressed heavily on the
people, whilst the revenue had more than doubled.

The next settlement was for four years, and was made under section V. of
Quartennial settlement   Regulation IX. of 1805, as already noticed. The total
for 1811-12 to 1814-.5 A.D. land-revenue from all sources for 1218 *fasli*, or 1810-11
A.D., amounted to Rs. 21,43,378. The new settlement showed a progressive
enhancement: that for the first year, or 1219 *fasli*, amounted to Rs. 21,56,026 ;
for 1220 *fasli*, to Rs. 21,75,176 ; for 1221 *fasli*, to Rs. 25,79,818, and for 1222
fasli, to Rs. 26,73,904. In 1813-14 the great *mukarari* of Raja Rámdayál
Singh lapsed by his death.[2] From the occupation of the British in 1803 to the
death of the Raja, the assessment amounted only to Rs. 1,11,597. At the first

---

[1] Sel. Rec., N.-W. P., 1818-20, p. 370.   [2] By 1813-14 the greater number of the talukas
combined in the old *mukararis* were broken up, and settlements were made with the village
proprietors, whilst the villages themselves were incorporated with the other villages of the parganah in which they were situated, on a common list; so that from this time the names even of
the old talukas disappear from the public records, and their boundaries can no longer be traced
with any approach to accuracy.

summary settlement for five years the revenue was more than quadrupled, and
showed as follows :—

1813-14.	1814-15.	1815-16.	1816-17.	1817-18.
Rs.	Rs.	Rs.	Rs.	Rs.
4,91,395	5,53,715	5,76,446	4,78,552	5,79,317

Abatements were made in two of the estates, leaving the revenue at the close of
the fifth settlement at Rs. 5,59,561. The next settlement of these estates was
made for seven years, from 1818-19 to 1824-25.

The district settlement was for five years, from 1223 *fasli* to 1227 *fasli* (1815-
16 to 1819-20 A.D.), and was made under Regulation
X. of 1812. This settlement was extended for a second
period of five years, or from 1228 to 1232 *fasli* (1820-
21 to 1824-25 A.D.), by orders of Government in 1818. It was during the
currency of these settlements that Meerut and Muzaffarnagar were formed into
separate charges. The Sikandarabad, Tilbegampur, Ada, Dankaur, Kásna,
Baran, Málagarh and Ahár Malikpur parganahs were taken from the Aligarh district and added to the southern parganahs of the Sahárunpur district to form
the district of Meerut, whilst the midland parganahs of Sabáranpur were placed
under a Joint Magistrate and Deputy Collector resident at Muzaffarnagar. The
subsequent history of these divisions will be found under their respective districts. In the meantime Regulation VII. of 1822 had been passed. The English
copy was distributed in November, 1822, but the Persian copy was not ready
until April, 1824, and in June of the same year the Governor-General in Council passed a resolution postponing the introduction of the procedure prescribed
by the Regulation, as it was judged inexpedient to attempt to carry out its provisions in the short time that would elapse before the expiry of the second
quinquennial settlement. It was therefore ordered that a third settlement for
five years, from 1233 to 1237 *fasli* (1825-6 to 1829-30 A.D.), should be made
at existing rates, until such time as the revision contemplated was completed.

*Three quinquennial set-
tlements, 1815-16 to 1829-
30 A.D.*

Mr. Chamberlain, who had been deputed to assess the lapsed *mukarari* of
Raja Rámdayál, was again sent to make the fourth settlement, or first quinquennial settlement of the whole of the parganahs now forming the district. He
appears to have ascertained the actual out-turn of each estate, including even
profits derived from the cultivation of small revenue-free patches ; and taking
this as his basis, he merely deducted the percentage allowed by the Regulations.
Shortly after concluding the settlement, Mr. Chamberlain died, and was succeeded by Mr. Calvert. The assessment was soon found to be much greater
than the people could pay, and the Board of Commissioners directed Mr. Calvert

to make such remissions as he thought to be necessary. In 1817, Government relinquished in many cases the progressive increase that had been imposed by Mr. Chamberlain. The assessment, however, still remained far too high, and the partial revisions that subsequently took place led to further reductions, so that the revenue of the last year was considerably lower than that of the first year of the new assessment. Similar revisions took place during the second and third quinquennial settlements, with the same results.

The settlement under Regulation VII. of 1822 and IX. of 1833 of parganah Manglaur was made by Mr. Plowden in 1835; that of parganahs Deoband and Rámpur in 1834, by Messrs. Louis and Turner; that of parganahs Jawálapur, Jaurási and Rúrki, and tappas Kheri and Sakrauda by Mr. Grant in 1835; and that of the remainder of the district, and the revision of the whole of his predecessors' work, by Mr. E. Thornton during the years 1836-38. The proceedings were concluded and the records completed by Mr. M. P. Edgworth in 1841.[1]

The district then comprised twenty-one parganahs, two tappas (Kheri and Sakrauda), and two talukas. These sub-divisions were revised in 1841, and the number of parganahs was reduced to fifteen, in which the talukas and tappas were also absorbed. The measurements for the new settlement were commenced in 1833, and were finished in June, 1836, but were materially incorrect. Much land fit for, but not under cultivation, was entered as cultivated, and no uniform system for describing the soils and the land to be recorded as irrigated was adopted. The consequence is, that the statistics relating to both these subjects at this settlement are too untrustworthy for publication. The preceding assessments being found too high, Mr. Thornton proceeded to examine the fiscal history of each estate, and the rates of the different assessments, thus distinguishing those that were found capable of realization from those that were found insupportable. The principal causes of increase were the revenue from resumed revenue-free estates, which in 1838-39 was estimated at Rs. 1,25,000, and the re-settlement of the lapsed talukas of Rámdayál's *mukarari*.

It was Mr. Thornton who took up the settlement of the villages comprised in the *mukarari* estate, and ascertained whether the village communities or the Settlement of rights in the *mukarari*. heirs of Rámdayál were to be considered proprietors. He found that the proprietary right throughout the district almost universally rested in the resident cultivating communities. He found the villages of the *mukarari* were intermingled with others in the district, so that out of a circle including forty or fifty villages, some would be of either kind; and where not included in the *mukarari*, the cultivating community were acknowledged by all to be proprietors. The Rajpút or Gújar inhabitants of

---

[1] The proceedings of Mr. Thornton were sanctioned by G. O. 592, dated April 27th, 1840, and of Mr. Edgworth by G. O. 5263, dated December 19th, 1843.

the whole circle, however, traced their origin to a common ancestor, the head of the common colony, so that the location of the settlements in both cases must have been about the same time, and due to the same cause. If in one case the community were to be considered proprietors, they must be equally regarded as such in the other case, for the only other source of proprietary right, viz., transfer by sale or otherwise, was not pleaded ; and in fact the heirs of the late Raja did not claim for themselves the proprietary right, or to be admitted to settlement, except for such villages as they were themselves in occupancy of as proprietors. This delay in the recognition of the rights of the real proprietors for a period of twenty years was very prejudicial, not only to them, but to the safety of the general revenue. Though they had been under engagements for the revenue, they were unable to transfer their land or borrow money on the security of it. Mr. Thornton writes [1] on this subject, that " the refusal on the part of the revenue authorities to recognize the right has thus, owing to the view the people and the Court have taken of it, put in abeyance the right itself. Really distressing results from this have not unfrequently come under my notice, and I consider that much loss of revenue has ensued, particularly in the parganahs of the Jawálápur tahsíldári, where, the climate being insalubrious, the people require every inducement to connect them with the soil ; and the suspension of their right in it, while it has prevented them from attaining prosperity, has offered a remarkable temptation to bad faith, for as the 'Khána Kháli' villages were never sold for balances, these people might make any terms with Government by a temporary abandonment of their villages, though in balances occasionally. However these desertions were met by the tahsíldár locating new persons in the abandoned villages, and thus has arisen another evil,—the absolute loss of the suspended right, for a community, when dispersed for some years, cannot be re-united at the will of a Settlement Officer, nor be traced ; and in the absence of all latter claimants, I have had, in some cases, to record, as in proprietary possession, persons of very recent occupation." The record-of-rights was drawn up for the first time at this settlement, and the smallest sub-division of the land in each village was entered, with the name of the manager and the amount of land-revenue due from it. Arrangements were made for the appointment of patwárís or village accountants, chaukídárs or village watchmen, and the selection of lambardárs or the representatives of the village communities in their engagements with Government.

For the year 1260 fasli (1852-53 A. D.), the demand amounted to Rs. 10,04,567, giving a net increase on the previous actual receipts of Rs. 13,587. In 1859-60, previous to Mr. VansAgnew's assessment, the land-revenue amounted to Rs. 10,93,946. Mr. VansAgnew assessed the district at Rs. 11,29,442 ; this settlement, however,

New settlement.

---

[1] Set. Rep., I., 150.

was not sanctioned, and orders were issued for its revision. These were carried out by the late Mr. H. D. Robertson, and the late Mr. H. LePoer Wynne, whilst the final report was drawn up in 1870 by Mr. H. B. Webster.[1] Their assessment amounted to Rs. 11,38,580, or with cesses, and exclusive of jungle grants, which were separately assessed, to Rs. 12,47,951, and including these, to Rs. 12,97,313. The orders of Government on the settlement were not issued until April, 1874, or twenty years after the first steps towards the assessment had been taken in hand. In 1854, Mr. Ross commenced the measurements, which were almost completed under the superintendence of Mr. Spankie when the mutiny broke out. They were continued again at the close of 1857, and completed by April, 1858. Early in 1859, Mr. VansAgnew commenced the assessment of the district, and completed it in 1863. He found the measurements fairly correct, and in the whole district only 107 villages had to be re-measured in this and the succeeding operations. The record-of-rights had, however, to be completely remodelled, as well owing to the natural changes caused by lapse of time, as to the effects of the rebellion of 1857-58, and the no less serious disturbances of proprietary right caused by the great famine of 1860-61. Mr. VansAgnew's mode of assessment, whilst satisfying himself, and, as subsequent inquiries showed, resulting in a tolerably fair apportionment of the State demand, was not recorded in writing, and afforded no materials by which the Government could judge of the expediency of confirming his arrangements. As Saháranpur was the first of the old settlements to fall in, great care was taken in drawing up a series of rules for the guidance of the officers employed in revising the assessments. These rules, known as the "Saháranpur instructions," were framed by the late Mr. J. R. Colvin, then Lieutenant-Governor of these Provinces, and form the basis on which all subsequent instructions were drawn up. The main alterations made were—firstly, the reduction of the standard by which the demand of Government was settled from two-thirds to one-half of the calculated assets; and secondly, the adoption of the Panjáb system of plane table survey instead of the cumbrous and inaccurate chain survey previously in use.

In 1864, the instructions for a revision of the entire assessment were issued. The proceedings were to embrace an inquiry into the adequacy and moderation of the assessment in general, and the actual assessment of each village in detail; and were to include the correction of the vernacular records and completion of the English records on the recognized system. The revision of the assessment of the Saháranpur tahsíl

Mode of assessment.

Mr. VansAgnew.

Mr. H. D. Robertson.

---

[1] Report, Allahabad, 1870. The discrepancies as to the total of the assessment and the total of the area in this report are simply irreconcilable, and the figures given above are those finally accepted by the Board of Revenue and by Government.

was accomplished by Mr. H. D. Robertson. His assessment was based upon soil rates. The soils were divided into *rausli, dákar, mísan,* and *bhúda,* but subse-quently *rausli* and *dákar,* comprising two-thirds of the entire area, were thrown together as one soil. These were again sub-divided into irrigated and unirri-gated, and for each of the six classes a set of average rent-rates was drawn up. The rent-rates were based upon (1) cash rents, (2) rates framed on an esti-mate of the average value of the average produce of the crops, and (3) the village rent-rolls giving (where the rent was paid in kind) the value of the zamíndár's share of the crops in a given year. Mr. Robertson depended chiefly upon the cash rates; but his accepted rates are often below the cash rates in *mísan* and *bhúda* soils, and above then in *rausli-dákar.* These discrepancies are left unexplained. The general result, however, of his entire proceedings gave a land-revenue at assumed rates of Rs. 3,07,936, whilst that actually assessed amounted to Rs. 3,19,243, or with cesses, Rs. 3,51,136, or an increase in land-revenue over Mr. Thornton's assessment of Rs. 49,346. Of this sum, Rs. 19,505 are shown as due to canal irrigation over 28,071 acres.

Mr. Wynne revised the assessment of the Deoband, Rúrki and Nakúr tahsíls, for which he submitted a rent-rate report previ-

Mr. Wynne.

ous to assessment. He at first divided the soils of each parganah into a number of circles, and calculated for each of these a series of six percentages relating to the proportion between the cultivated and irrigated areas, cultivated and culturable areas, manured and cultivated areas, sandy and cultivated areas, the number of the agricultural population, and the entire popula-tion to each one hundred acres. These elaborate calculations were, however, entirely disregarded in the actual assessment, which, like Mr. Robertson's final figures, was based upon the cash rates prevailing in each circle. "Having fixed[1] the average rate on all cultivated land in a circle, Mr. Wynne proceeded to select an average village as representative of the circle, and to graduate all other villages above or below this, according to their value. In doing this he must have been guided by the impressions received at the time of inspection, and have formed his own judgment as to the amount to be added to, or deducted from, the standard rate in each case. He then made an addition for old and new fallow (valuing them respectively at one-third and two-thirds of the rate on cul-tivation, after deducting 10 per cent. of the cultivated area for pasturage), and so worked out the assessment of the village. If he thought that assessment, or its rate of incidence, too high as compared with the other villages in the graduated list of the circle, he lowered it summarily, so as to agree with them." The rental estimated on this system amounted to Rs. 16,17,066, of which only Rs. 66,617 was assessed upon fallow land. The revenue, with cesses imposed, amounted to Rs. 8,99,783.

[1] Government review of the Sahâranpur settlement, p. 9.

As already noted, the rental of the last year of the expired settlement is said

The new settlement as a whole. to have been Rs. 10,93,946, and that of the revised settlement to be Rs. 11,38,580, showing a total increase of Rs. 44,634. From the review of the settlement report, it would appear that Mr. Thornton's revenue-rate fell at Rs. 2-6-6 per acre on the cultivated area, and Mr. VansAgnew's assessment at Rs. 1-9-6. The former was calculated at 75 per cent. of the assets, and the latter at 50 per cent. only. "In 1866 the cultivated area of the district was 732,031 acres, the revenue Rs. 11,38,580, or Rs. 1-8-10 per acre; and the rental was Rs. 22,76,155, or Rs. 3-1-9. per acre. The increase in the rental was, therefore, Rs. 7,04,217 ; in the cultivated area, 76,190 acres ; and in the rent-rate, Rs. 0-11-3, or 29 per cent. of the increase of rental. Of the rental increase, Rs. 2,36,904 (Rs. 76,190 × Rs. 3-1-9) is due to enlarged cultivation, leaving Rs. 4,67,313 to be accounted for by other causes. The Settlement Officers attribute Rs. 79,369 of revenue, or Rs. 1,58,738 of rent, to canal irrigation, so that only Rs. 3,08,575, or a rise of Rs. 0-6-9 per acre, or 22·8 per cent., remains as due to the increased competition for land and the rise in prices,—a rise which the Board of Revenue have shown to have been about 18 per cent. Thus, as is natural in a district where so much of the rent is paid in produce, the rent-roll advanced *pari passu* with the heightened price of the produce."

Mr. Thornton expressly stated in his report that the demand then fixed

Board's review. "stopped far short of a fair demand," and wished that "when a really good state of cultivation had been reached, a gradual approach should at each future revision be made to the sum fairly demandable." Mr. Bird, too, remarked that "Sahâranpur had been partially very much over-assessed, and that the measures employed for collecting the revenue had been equally harsh and illegal; some of the communities composed of the most industrious classes had been cruelly depressed. He looked to further equalization of the revenue on revision, and to an increase from extended cultivation." I cannot do better here than quote the Board's review on the settlement as a whole[1] :—"Sahâranpur, in truth, has not been happy in its fiscal history. The first 25 years of British rule were one long struggle on the one side at extracting large revenues, met by a resolute determination on the other to resist payment. The names of Messrs. Chamberlain and Moore are prominently connected with those early days. The efforts of the former to extract what he considered a proper revenue from Raja Ramdayál Singh's tenure ended in depopulating a large part of the district. Mr. Moore's assessments led to innumerable farms, and ultimately to an uprising of the Gújars at Kunja. Immense balances accrued, and the district, noted as one of the richest in the days of the Mughal, deteriorated rapidly. The settlement of 1838 did much to

---

[1] Letter 975, of 18th August, 1871, para. 85.

restore confidence, and to bring emigrants back. But all accounts agree that since the recent revision of settlement, by which the burden of land-revenue has been more equitably adjusted, and since the rapid extension of irrigation, the character of the hitherto unruly communities who inhabit the district is undergoing an extraordinary change, and the increase of prosperity is marked. The demand of the early settlements was, in fact, never collected. The settlement of 1838-58 worked, on the whole, fairly ; but the district made little or no advance. Twenty-six per cent. of the district changed hands at very low rates. In many parts of the district, land could attract little or no capital. Population remained nearly stationary. Cultivation, however, had increased about nine per cent.; irrigation, too, had increased, but the exact amount cannot be ascertained, and prices had risen about 25 per cent. But neither extension of cultivation, nor irrigation, nor, so far as could be seen, any permanent rise in rents, justified the assumption of a larger increase in rental than 39 per cent. To have taken two-thirds of that rental would have enriched the Government revenue at the expense of the tardy progress of the district, and Saháranpur owes its present prosperity to the moderation shown in the revision of the demand. The demand fixed by the Settlement Officers was eventually accepted by all the proprietors, with the exception of one estate."

The demand in each tahsíl for the year 1866-67, and from the year 1883-84

Result of the assessment. to the end of the settlement is distributed as follows (in rupees and omitting fractions of a rupee) :—

Class of estate.	Saháranpur.		Nakúr.		Bárki.		Deoband.		Total.	
	1866-67.	1883-84.	1866-67.	1883-84.	1866-67.	1883-84.	1866-67.	1883-84.	1866-67.	1883-84.
	Rs.	Rs.	Rs.	Rs.	Rs.	Rs.	Rs.	Rs.	Rs.	Rs.
Revenue-paying ...	3,45,066	3,50,374	2,86,154	2,89,700	2,72,645	2,75,597	3,31,399	3,32,966	12,35,164	12,47,657
Revenue-free—										
(a) For life cesses,	2,617	2,617	158	158	...	...	1,686	1,686	4,461	4,461
(b) In perpetuity do.	524	524	1,246	1,246	160	160	736	736	2,666	2,666
Grant ...	13,400	14,408	...	...	23,441	26,120	...	...	36,841	42,528
Total ...	3,61,602	3,67,923	2,87,558	2,90,104	2,96,247	3,03,878	3,33,731	3,35,408	12,79,132	12,97,312

This assessment has been confirmed for thirty years, from July 1st, 1860, to June 30th, 1890. All other details will be found under the parganah notices.

The following table gives the collections, demand, and balance, according

Collections. to the official returns, from 1860-61 to 1871-72. In the latter year there were Rs. 2,346 outstanding at the beginning of the year, of which Rs. 623 were collected, Rs. 976 were remitted and removed from the accounts, leaving a balance of Rs. 747 on account of old outstandings :—

Year.	Demand.	Collections.	Balances.	Particulars of Balance.				Percentage of balance on demand.
				Real.			Nominal.	
				In train of liquidation.	Doubtful.	Irrecoverable.		
	Rs.	Rs.	Rs.	Rs.	Rs.	Rs.	Rs.	
1860-61	10,80,568	8,19,413	2,61,155	60,140	1,47,240	6,630	47,145	24·16
1861-62	10,94,305	10,06,309	87,996	39,034	...	196	48,766	8·04
1862-63	10,97,019	10,45,342	51,677	2,814	...	128	48,735	4·71
1863-64	10,98,023	10,48,138	49,885	1,722	307	1,610	46,246	4·54
1864-65	10,98,210	10,50,237	47,973	932	520	409	46,106	4·37
1865-66	11,00,913	10,43,762	57,151	10,197	45,853	...	1,101	5·19
1866-67	11,02,949	10,06,516	96,433	...	96,433	...	...	8·74
1867-68	11,32,281	10,80,405	51,876	...	...	51,876	...	4·68
1868-69	10,07,358	9,76,082	31,276	30,988	288	...	...	3·10
1869-70	10,07,641	10,02,115	5,526	4,854	672	...	...	0·54
1870-71	10,07,648	10,05,676	1,972	806	...	...	1,166	0·20
1871-72	10,13,867	10,09,673	4,194	2,901	8	181	1,104	0·30

The estates in this district are all either *zamíndári, pattidári* or *bháyachára.*

Proprietors. These may, once for all, be defined here. *Zamíndári* tenures are those in which the whole land is held and managed in common, and the rents and whole profits of the estate are thrown into one common stock and divided amongst the several proprietors, whose rights are estimated according to fractional shares, whether of a rupee, or of the local unit of land measure known as a *bígha. Pattidári* tenures may be divided into perfect and imperfect pattidári or bháyachára. Perfect *pattidári* is that tenure wherein the whole lands are held in severalty by the different proprietors, all of whom are jointly responsible for the Government revenue, though each is theoretically responsible only for the quota represented by the proportion of the land he holds to the whole estate. Imperfect *pattidári* is where portions of the land are held in severalty, and portions in common, with a joint responsibility for the Government demand. In this case the revenue is primarily made up from the rents of the common lands, and the remainder by a *báchh,* or cess, proportioned to the holdings in severalty, and calculated either by custom or on a fixed scale. Mr. Wynne writes that "the habits of proprietors and cultivators alike are simple. Both are ignorant of the extremes of poverty and riches. They all live from hand to mouth; get from the village Baniya an advance when they need it on account of a marriage or funeral, or a bad season, or fine from a Court of law, and repay it with interest, according to the extent of their credit, from 12 to 30 per cent."

The tract of waste jungle and forest land lying along the base of the

Jungle grants.

Siwálik hills remained nominally in the occupation of the estates bordering on it, or anyone who chose to use it, until the settlement in 1838. Mr. Thornton then measured off the superfluous waste, and included it in the large tracts mapped as the Kheri, Kánsráo and Pathari Nadí forests. In 1839 orders were issued by the Board of Revenue to lease these tracts to persons capable of bringing them under cultivation. In 1840 Mr. Edgeworth took engagements from various parties, but his settlement was not sanctioned, and subsequently, under the new grant rules, fresh arrangements were made by Messrs. Davidson, Craigie, and Ross, all of which were sanctioned by Government. The following statement shows the number and locality of the grants, the period for which they were settled, and the initial and full revenue demand, omitting fractions of a rupee.

Number and locality of grant.	Period for which settled.		Demand.		Number and locality of grant.	Period for which settled.		Demand.	
	From	To	Lowest.	Highest.		From	To	Lowest.	Highest.
			Rs.	Rs.				Rs.	Rs.
8 Pathari Nadí	1838-39	1864-85	31	2,838	1 Kheri ...	1846-47	1890-91	7	592
1 „	1841-42	1887-88	3	243	7 „	1847-48	1896-97	518	2,800
2 „	1842-43	1888-89	16	1,269	6 „	1850-51	...	21	1,741
2 „	1843-44	1889-90	9	750	93 Kánsrao ...	...	1879-80	4,952	7,940
3 „	1844-45	1890-91	59	4,824	2 Kheri	1854-55	1904-05	16	1,141
5 Do. & Khari	...	...	81	6,646	5 „	1857-58	...	37	2,993
3 Pathari Nadí	1845-46	1990-91	46	3,767	5 „	...	1903-04	41	3,362
1 „	...	1891-92	2	175	4 „	1859-60	1890-91	40	8,143
10 „	...	1884-85	69	5,617	10 „	...	1905-06	77	6,798
1 „	...	...	6	528	6 Kánsrao ...	1843-44	1889-90	27	2,242
1 Kheri	1844-45	1890-91	28	2,306	1 „	1844-45	1891-92	6	502
6 „	...	...	51	4,145	2 „	...	1890-91	16	1,341
3 „	1845-46	1894-95	437	2,724	Total 104	...	...	6,596	70,446

All of these grants, were in force in 1863 except six grants, which were resumed for nonfulfilment of the conditions on which they were granted. Three of them were subsequently settled,—Nasírpur in the Pathari Nadí forest and the two Kánsrao grants of Lálwála and Mujáhidpur Satiwála. In the beginning of 1863, the remainder of the unlet jungle grants were handed over to the Forest Department. Many of the grants were resumed[1] in 1865, and others were included in the assessed area of the neighbouring parganahs, so that only 79 remained in 1870 on the grant register.

[1] See G. O. 4741, of June 4th, 1866; 4090A., of 30th September, 1872. 18,709—111.

The cultivator with a right of occupancy appears to have been unknown in
the district previous to the enactment of Act X. of
1859. Mr. Thornton in 1838 writes:—" The cul-
tivators who are not zamíndárs are throughout the district, to speak generally,
mere tenants-at-will." In portions of taluka Jabarheri and parganah Jawá
lápur alone did Mr. Thornton find cultivators of this class, and these were the
old zamíndárs who had dropped out of the fiscal management of their villages.[1]
Wherever rent-payers were found, they were invited to advance their claim
to occupancy without the zamíndár being able to eject them at will. The
claim when advanced was merely to occupancy subject to the payment
of a fair rent, and no right was urged to hold at low rates." Again, Mr.
Wynne[2] writes—" There is, as a rule, hardly any distinction between the rent-
paying tenant and the revenue-paying proprietor. The former never claims
the title of zamíndár. He, as well as the mere cultivator, calls himself *Sirkár-
ka-ryat*," the subject of the Government, and he knows the payment of the
tenant (rent), and his own payment (revenue), both by the same name, "*bákí*"
(arrears) ; or, if he is choice in his mode of expression, "*muamla*" (a matter,
the matter, *par excellence*, of importance in his life). The rent which the
tenant pays is often no more than the allotment of the Government demand on
his share, and especially in *bháyachára* communities it is often calculated at an
advance of 25 per cent. (*siwái*), or 50 per cent. (*deorhi*) on that demand. It
is true that this system of regulating rents by custom is gradually disappearing, and has already disappeared very extensively, but the traditional feeling
in which it originated is still shown in the absence of a marked distinction
between the proprietor and cultivator. There is still hardly anywhere any difference in the appearance, dress, houses or mode of living in general of the two
classes. I do not mean to say that in all these respects the proprietors are not,
as a whole, better off than the cultivators, but that it is difficult to pro-
nounce from the circumstances of any particular man in these respects to
which class he belongs. From the absence of social distinctions between the
two classes, the happiest relations prevail, as a rule, between them. Suits
under the rent law are very rarely brought into Court. Indeed, questions regarding rent can hardly arise in a community thus constituted. Nearly all the
suits that have come under my cognizance have arisen in the few villages
where the proprietary right is vested in a single powerful individual, or in the
numerous cases in which the old proprietor has been bought out by a money-
lender."

Since Mr. Wynne wrote, however, the tide has set against the abnormal
status of the non-proprietary cultivator ; the zamíndárs have begun to exercise

Marginal note: Cultivating classes.

---

[1] Set. Rep., L ; see further Coll. 304, dated 20th August, 1874, and Board's 595, dated 28th
October, 1874.   [2] Rep. 186.

their power of enhancement, and he is surely falling to a position where he will have less privileges and pay a higher rent. Strange to say the Játs and Gáras, who are really frugal and industrious, seem to be more in debt than the unthrifty Gújars and Rajpúts. This is said to arise from two causes :—firstly, they can get longer and more extensive credit from the money-lenders; and secondly, these men were for a long series of years singled out for the payment of more than the usual proportional share of the Government demand. Mr. R. Bird noticed this fact in his minute on the settlement. Mr. Thornton perceived it, too, and did as much as he could to equalize taxation. Mr. Vans Agnew and Mr. Wynne both proposed large reductions with the same object of giving industrious classes an opportunity to throw off the load of debt that oppresses them. The labouring population consists chiefly of Chamárs. They are not in such a degraded condition as the men of the same class in the eastern districts of the Benares Division. Mr. Wynne writes:

Labourers.

" They (the labourers) are under a very modified kind of servitude to the proprietors of the particular village in which they reside. That is to say, in return for the protection received, and the skins of all the dead animals, they are bound to provide the families of the proprietor with two pairs of shoes a year, and are in all cases bound to meet any call for labour that may be made on the whole village. They were moreover bound to serve the landlord in the field for wages in grain; but of late, especially since the railway and canal works gave such an impetus to the demand for labour, they have begun to emancipate themselves from even this mark of servitude, and such is the call for labour, that I have met with instances of a high-caste proprietor, even a Rajpút, associating a Chamár in partnership with himself in his seer."

Though the population is dense compared with other districts in these Provinces, it cannot be said that there is any pressure on the resources of the land.[1] Every parganah has a large proportion of culturable waste, or land capable of much higher cultivation, sufficient to meet any normal increase in the population. Mr. Wynne, however, anticipates the possibility of an excessive increase in the canal-irrigated tracts, where the certainty of a return for labour has attracted a large population from without. He instances the villages along the Eastern Jumna Canal as presenting " occasional instances of that simultaneous co-existence of poverty and wealth which is so happily wanting in the rest of the country. When this process is complete, the power of a canal-irrigated tract to supply, in case of drought, a surplus of grain for the famine-stricken districts will be much impaired. The mischief, such as it is, will, however, be considerably held in

---

[1] Mr. Wynne enumerates amongst the checks to improvement the want of wells, not only for irrigation but even for drinking water, experienced in portions of Bhagwánpur, Nágal, Rúrki, Manglaur and Deoband, and the extreme size of many of the villages. His remarks will be found in the Settlement Report, p. 141.

check by the steady rise in the canal water-rates, which I have always advocated—raise your water-rent to the point at which, in point of cheapness, it barely competes with irrigation from wells, and you will at least delay the excessive influx of inhabitants from without." The town population present a painful contrast to the agricultural population. Sub-division of shares has been carried to the extreme, and every man, however small his share, disdains personal labour. Hence the degraded miserable state of the Musalmán inhabitants of the decayed towns of Gangoh, Lakhnauti and Nánauta.

The average holding of cultivators, as given by Mr. Robertson for the Sahá-

Distribution of the cultivated area amongst proprietary and non-proprietary
cultivators.

ranpur tahsíl, shows the seer holding of proprietors as five acres, the average holding of cultivators with rights of occupancy as eight acres, and the holding of tenants-at-will as six acres. Mr. Wynne's figures for the remainder of the district in bíghas, equivalent to 0·5062 of an acre, are as follow :—

	1-6 bíghas.	6-8.	8-10.	10-15.	15-20.	20-25.	25-30.	30-40.	40-50.	50-75.	75-100.	100 upwards.
Proprietary cultivators.	10,419	3,055	2,710	4,845	3,624	2,576	1,885	2,481	1,625	1,883	852	820
Non-proprietary cultivators.	12,697	2,621	2,631	4,748	3,522	2,520	1,867	2,292	1,320	1,247	420	260
Total ...	23,116	5,676	5,341	9,593	7,146	5,096	3,752	4,773	2,945	3,130	1,272	1,080

It will be seen that the majority of the holdings are under six acres. Mr. G. Williams has given me the following table showing Mr. VansAgnew's distribution of the cultivated area in 1862, and the estimates given by the tahsíldárs in 1872 (in acres). [1]

Class of cultivators.	VansAgnew. Whole district.		Tahsíldárs' estimates of the number of each class in each tahsíl.					
	Total area held.	Average by each.	Numbers.	Rúrkí.	Saháranpur.	Nakúr.	Deoband.	Total.
Proprietary cultivators.	357,789	9	37,762	9,201	1,631	40,026	15,345	66,203
Hereditary cultivators.	147,694	7	20,526	6,343	4,380	12,854	5,719	29,246
Non-hereditary cultivators.	212,349	6	36,320	13,250	6,706	5,719	8,280	53,331
Total ...	717,832	...	94,608	28,794	12,667	58,599	29,344	148,780

[1] Mr. Williams obtained another return from the Collector's office which only seems to complicate matters. On the whole, he thinks the tahsíldárs' returns, except Nakúr, are as nearly accurate as can be hoped for.

Mr. Williams writes—" It is useless to attempt to draw inferences from figures which are palpably untrustworthy, for although the difference between the number of hereditary and non-hereditary cultivators in these statements is perhaps susceptible of explanation, none can be offered for the glaring discrepancy between the figures in the first line of the statement. It is incredible that the proprietary cultivators at present holding land in the Nakúr tahsíl alone outnumber those in the whole district ten years ago. The figures are accordingly given for what they are worth. Mr. VansAgnew's calculations tend to show that the average holding is small, and seldom large enough to afford a decent subsistence to one family, for an ordinary cultivator finds it hard to extract a profit of more than Rs. 2 or Rs. 2-8 a month from five acres of land, or say about 30 bíghas *kuchcha*. A proprietary cultivator would, of course, be better off with a farm of that size, but his condition could hardly equal that of a person receiving a salary of eight rupees a month, unless his lands were remarkably good. It will therefore be easily understood that the peasantry (with the exception of the sturdy Rajpúts and Gújars, who have always eked out a subsistence by cattle lifting, and must always continue to do so, so long as the present state of things lasts) are, as elsewhere, in a most miserable condition, being to all intents and purposes merely serfs of the petty money-lenders, who not only exact usurious interest, but also sell with light weights and short measures, and buy according to standards arranged on the opposite principle. Again, if a man borrow twenty rupees to day and pay the equivalent in grain, or otherwise, within 36 hours, inexorable custom compels him to give from six to twelve months' interest, all the same, at the rate usually charged. This practice has evidently been introduced with great ingenuity, for the purpose of discouraging debtors from getting out of debt when they have the means of doing so at hand. Gold or silver ornaments are considered the best security, and on such a pawn money can be borrowed at 12 or sometimes even 6 per cent., but if it be lent on a bond with land as the security, the interest rises to 18 and 24 per cent., and the peasant proprietor is fortunate if he can procure a loan at that rate, for 36 and 38 per cent. is often charged. The hypothetical classification of holdings is—large holding, 150 to 200 bíghas *kuchcha* (25 to 33 acres); middling, 80 to 100 *kuchcha* bíghas. There are certainly not many middling holdings in the district, and still fewer large holdings."

Certain tables were prepared in 1864-65 and 1865-66, to show the annual value and distribution of the agricultural produce of the district. These tables give the results of an examination of the returns framed by the patwáris, and the results of the Settlement Officer's own investigations. Mr. Robertson, in making his estimates for the Sahéranpur tahsíl, divided each parganah into circles, for which he ascertained the quantity of the produce and the zamíndár's share from

Distribution of the value of produce.

the village papers (for the year 1864-65) of four or five representative villages in each circle. The returns were tested by comparing them with the private record *(khasrah kankút)* of the proprietors. The value of the produce was obtained from the village price-current, "and this being divided by the number of bíghas cultivated in each circle, gave the gross produce and the zamíndár's share in each circle." Mr. Wynne also relied upon the proprietors' private papers for the average return of each crop, and with them corrected the village papers throughout the Sultánpur parganah. Taking these as his basis he graduated the other parganahs according to the relation which their productive qualities were known to bear to Sultánpur. Whilst Mr. Wynne's estimate of the value of the produce exceeds that made by the patwáris in four out of eleven parganahs examined by him, Mr. Robertson's estimate is in excess throughout. These estimates, though imperfect, are as near an approach to the actual truth as we are likely to obtain. I accordingly give an abstract of them, referring to the original for details. [1]

Messrs. Wynne and Robertson.

Distribution of produce statistics for 1864-65.

Detail of occupancy.	MR. WYNNE's *estimate for Deoband, Nakúr and Rúrki.*			MR. ROBERTSON's *estimate for Saháranpur Tahsíl.*		
	Cultivated area in bíghas.	Value of produce in rupees.	Zamíndár's share in rupees.	Cultivated area in bíghas.	Value of produce in rupees.	Zamíndár's share in rupees.
Cultivated by proprietors,	566,655	28,03,721	28,03,721	108,031	5,91,517	5,91,517
By tenants paying only their share of the revenue ...	35,139	1,91,995	34,950	6,342	34,077	6,169
By assignees of the land revenue ...	13,084	59,183	...	8,832	49,354	...
By cultivators paying in kind ...	214,898	9,47,368	3,13,761	173,207	8,97,010	2,91,696
By cultivators paying in cash ...	345,559	16,84,683	4,57,225	119,301	6,26,091	1,71,147
Total ...	1,175,338	56,86,950	36,09,687	415,712	2,98,049	10,60,529

[1] Board's Rec., 603, of August 16th, 1867 ; and 606, of September 25th, 1866.

The Government share, or the land revenue with cesses, and omitting the chaukídári cess, amounted to Rs. 11,19,579. Deducting this from the total of the zamíndár's share, as given above, we get Rs. 35,50,637 as the zamíndár's profit; and deducting both of these from the total value of the produce, or Rs. 78,84,999, we obtain Rs. 32,14,783 as the cultivator's share. The statistics for 1865-66 were prepared in the same manner by the same officers, and the details vary so little that it is unnecessary to give them here. The value of the produce is apparently less,—in consequence, probably, of the deficiency in the rain-fall. The value of the total produce in 1865-66 is given at Rs. 76,31,089, of which the Government share amounted to Rs. 11,50,954, the zamíndárs' share to Rs. 34,53,008, and the cultivators' share to Rs. 30,27,127.

The Board of Revenue, in their review of the Saháranpur settlement report,

Board's estimates.

give an estimate of the rental of the district for 1869-70. According to this, the Government share amounts to Rs. 11,65,540, the rental in cash to Rs. 15,70,700, and the rental in kind to Rs. 7,80,518, or a total of Rs. 23,51,218. Deducting from this the Government share, the zamíndár's share in villages cultivated by others than the proprietors amounts to Rs. 11,85,678, as compared with Rs. 12,74,978 in 1864-65, and Rs. 12,48,321 in 1865-66. No account is apparently taken of their profits as proprietors when cultivating their own lands, nor is it shown how the value of the rent paid in kind is calculated, and the proportion between the amount of rent paid in cash and in kind differs considerably from that described to exist in the district notices. The total value of the produce is not given, so the cultivator's share is not ascertainable. The last attempt to settle this question was made at the census of 1872, which puts the rental of the district at Rs. 18,48,971, and the revenue at Rs. 12,94,062, giving the zamíndár's share of the rental as Rs. 5,54,909. Here, again, we have no explanation as to how this result was arrived at, and must reject the figures as misleading. Altogether it would appear that in this district Government gets only one-seventh of the produce of the land, the remainder being pretty evenly divided between the cultivator and the proprietors.

Payment in kind was the rule in this district until very recently. Mr.

Rents.

Thornton writes[1] that " a general opinion has prevailed in the district that rents must naturally be paid in kind, and that the substitution of a money rate is contingent on the consent of the cultivator. The process for ousting cultivators, too, has not been understood. On these accounts bháyachára villages with ill-conditioned owners were unsaleable. It was in vain to buy the proprietary right, as the men remained on the land. If such low rates in kind were not allowed as would leave the purchaser

_____

[1] Set., Sept., I., 112.

no profit, they grew the worst grains and rented land from their neighbours for their best crops." In 1863, Mr. VansAgnew writes :—" In 680 villages the tenants pay their rents in kind ; in 760 villages they pay partly in money and partly in kind, and in 169 villages money-rents only prevail. Besides being so much in a minority, money-rents are clearly abnormal, and it is highly probable that they seldom obtained, excepting under peculiar circumstances, and where the cultivator had some claim to consideration and to easy terms, either from being a kinsman of the zamíndár, or from holding long on easy terms, or, from wherever derived, from some undefined but understood right to a share in the proprietor's dues. One proof of the favourable nature of the money-rents here is the great struggle always going on for them on the part of the tenants, and for payment in kind on that of the zamíndárs. All the tenants in this district wish for the former, and, it appears to me, consider them to convey a *quasi*-proprietary title, and the zamíndárs never concede them." This struggle still goes on, and even now (1875) the landholders always take the earliest possible opportunity of reverting to rents in kind, and the cultivators always resist it. Mr. Vans Agnew does not give any areas. Mr. Robertson found 16,000 acres out of 208,435 acres paying cash rates, and Mr. Wynne found 139,605 out of 558,553 acres, altogether about twenty per cent., under cash rates. In the Nakúr and Saháranpur tahsíls payment in kind seems to be most common, and in Deoband and Rúrki cash rents prevail. The enactment of Act XIV. of 1863 gave a great impetus to the commutation of produce for cash rents. In 1864-65, 221,774 acres were recorded as held by tenants paying in kind, against 251,350 acres held on cash rates. In the following year the numbers were 187,628 and 270,596, respectively. In 1869-70, the returns show that 66 per cent. of the holdings paid rent in cash only, and the remainder in cash and kind. Where rent is paid in kind, the proprietor takes from one-third to one-half the produce, but more commonly one-half (*nisf*). Sugar-cane is charged for at the rate of from one to two rupees per *kuchcha* bíghá, cotton at fourteen annas to one rupee, and *charí* at six to eight annas. These are called *zabti* crops. There are no statistics that can be relied upon to show the influence of the rent laws on rent-rates. In the Nakúr tahsil there has been some enhancement.

Rent-rates are tolerably steady throughout the district, being from fourteen

Rent-rates. to sixteen annas per *kuchcha* bígha (one-sixth of an acre) on the best land, and five or six annas on the worst. The average is about ten or twelve annas, but in the northern parganahs, grant-lands recently brought under cultivation will not fetch more than three annas per *kuchcha* bígha. The small number of cases in which rent in cash was taken up to the end of Mr. VansAgnew's settlement renders any conclusions from his rates misleading. The assumed rent-rates of his successors are equally useless for my purpose, as they made their assessments very considerably in advance of the rents which in many cases were actually paid. As early as 1842, there were 314 estates which had reached a state of cultivation that obtained from Government " a guarantee that the revenue upon them should not be increased until the revenue-rate on the cultivable area of all contiguous villages exceeded the incidence of the revenue-rate in these estates." Certain statements prepared by the Settlement Officers would show that between 1865-66 and 1868-69 the rental of those villages recommended for permanent settlement had increased 29·25 per cent., and where canal-irrigation had come amongst them, to 49·6 per cent. The Board consider that "a further rise in the rent-roll throughout the district will undoubtedly take place, the district being in a transition, and on the whole, in a backward state." The competition for land and the tendency towards cash rents both help to push up the value of land, which is the tendency of the processes now going on.

For a series of years after the conquest, hard seasons and injudicious settle-

Alienations.

ments combined with the action of the Civil Courts to produce extensive alienations of property. Few of the old respectable families retain their estates, which have fallen principally into the hands of the Saháranpur money-lenders. Mr. VansAgnew's report[1] contains a statement from which it appears that, during the twenty years of Mr. Thornton's settlement (1839-40 to 1859-60), 53 whole estates and 725 portions of estates, having an area of 110,390 acres, and yielding a revenue of Rs. 85,979, and valued at Rs. 6,18,895, were transferred by private arrangement: the transfers under decrees of the Civil Court during the same period amounted to 18 entire villages and 895 portions of villages, having an area of 104,356 acres, and giving a revenue of Rs. 1,15,301 and valued at Rs. 4,74,420, and in addition 12 whole estates and 621 parts of estates were mortgaged. The transfers in the Saháranpur parganah amount to 42 per cent., and if mortgages be added, to 60 per cent., the average of the district being 19 and 26 per cent., respectively. The averages for the Saháranpur tahsíl are 32 and 49 against 13 and 3½ for Rúrki, 13 and 4 for Deoband, and 19 and 24 for Nakúr. Transfers were most numerous in the parganahs lightly assessed, and which gave the best return for the investment of money.

The mutiny, too, did something towards increasing the number of transfers.

Confiscation.

Twenty-seven entire villages and 48 portions of villages were confiscated for rebellion in 1857, and of these 24 villages and 19 portions of villages were given away in reward for loyal service. The remaining estates were sold by auction to the highest bidder. That the process of transfer is still in vigorous action, the following table from the Board's

[1] For details see the paraganah notices.

records continuing the alienation returns up to 1871-72 will clearly demonstrate :—

Year.	Under orders of Court.				By private transfer.				
	Sale.		Number of other cases.	Total number of cases.	Sale.		Succession number of cases.	Mortgage number of cases.	Total number cases.
	Number of cases.	Aggregate revenue of property transferred.			Number of cases.	Aggregate revenue of property transferred.			
1860-61 ...	171	8,198	334	505	200	10,139	• 939	128	1,267
1861-62 ...	167	4,590	562	729	334	13,510	1,054	261	1,619
1862-63 ...	149	6,165	327	476	301	10,174	1,412	149	1,862
1863-64 ...	129	3,934	283	412	299	12,729	1,050	181	1,530
1864-65 ...	102	3,102	280	382	269	98,667	1,207	144	1,620
1865-66 ...	112	3,115	299	411	278	22,450	1,236	217	1,731
1866-67 ...	102	2,299	218	320	361	13,205	1,003	283	1,647
1867-68 ...	135	3,186	279	414	370	14,152	1,069	302	2,541
1868-69 ...	160	4,039	225	385	418	15,146	975	521	1,914
1869-70 ...	143	2,713	180	323	479	18,187	1,657	585	2,721
1870-71 ...	195	6,718	203	398	378	10,582	2,354	325	3,057
1871-72 ...	102	2,824	...	102	531	11,457	2,027	356	2,914

The prices brought by the lands transferred during Mr. Thornton's settle-

Selling price of land.   ment give an average of no more than six times the revenue demand, or, taking the assessment at two-thirds the assets, only 4½ times the rental or 18 times the presumed profits. The transfers by private sale for the whole district average nine per cent., and brought an average value of Rs. 6-8-4 per acre, assessed at an average revenue of Rs. 1-0-10 per acre. The transfers by decree of Court amounted to ten per cent. on the total area, and brought in an average value of Rs. 4-5-1 per acre, assessed at an average revenue amounting to Rs. 1-6-8. The mortgage transfers amount to seven per cent. of the total area, and show a value of Rs. 7-8-1 per acre and assessed at Re. 0-15-2. Taking the whole of these transfers for the entire district, the average selling price per acre is Rs. 5-14-6 for land assessed at an average revenue of Re. 1-0-1 per acre. The selling price of land is now Rs. 30 to Rs. 60 per acre. Land near towns, of course, fetches a much higher price.

The most industrious classes as well as the laziest seem to have lost by
transfers. The following table shows the number of
Vendors and vendees.
villages and portions of villages alienated, and the number still remaining to the principal castes in 1863 :—

Caste.			Alienated.		Remaining.		Total.	
			Entire estates.	Parts.	Entire.	Parts.	Entire.	Parts.
Sayyids	...	...	6	55	13	47	19	102
Shaikhs	...	...	4	25	21	18	25	43
PathÁns	...	...	5	50	17	40	22	90
Rajpúts (Hin.)	...	...	15	274	117	194	132	468
Rajpúts (Mus.)	...	...	...	25	12	19	12	44
Brahmans	...	...	5	9	5	11	10	20
Gújars	...	...	14	439	160	379	174	818
Tagas	...	...	8	67	19	64	27	131
Játs	...	...	...	51	22	22	22	73
Sainis	...	...	1	3	10	5	11	8
Gárás	...	...	1	70	19	44	20	114
Others	...	...	15	252	158	249	173	501

So much for those who have lost their lands. The new landlords are nearly in all cases the money-lenders, dwellers in towns, the worst possible class of absentees. Mr. Wynne says of them :—" The power and influence of the money-lending class is rapidly increasing, and is, in my opinion, most mischievous. It is true that they are men of large capital, able, if they cared, to turn the land to the very best account, whereas the dispossessed proprietor must have been deprived of every particle of capital and credit alike before he parted with his ancestral share. But it is no part of the money-lender's scheme to lay out money on his purchase. He will raise the rents, and will, by studiously breaking down all rights that do not emanate from himself, by reducing the favoured and unfavoured tenants alike to one uniform level and then taking all he can from each of them, make the estate pay him far more than it paid before, but this result is attained at a sacrifice of all the comfort and contentment that characterized the village under its former owner. It is no matter of astonishment that the money-lender, transformed into a landlord, should be so bad a landlord. None of the traditions of his caste guide him in his new profession. He understands the art of making money in his own proper line, but does not understand the particular demands of his new profession, or see that his true interest requires that he should undergo some outlay if he wishes to secure a large return. Add to this that the extemely illiberal pursuit, to which his main attention continues to be devoted, unfits him for dealing liberally with anyone, yet seasonable liberality is admittedly the first requisite in the management of a tenantry. Add, finally, the fact that he is invariably an absentee, and manages his estate through an agent. It will be easily imagined how this circumstance tends to keep him dissevered from his tenants and ignorant of what measures their requirements and his own interests alike demand."

Owing to the rise in prices during the last few years and the increased
demand for labour caused by such works as the Ganges
and Jumna Canals, the railway and the Rúrki Work-
shops, wages generally have risen. The wages of bricklayers and carpenters have risen from three and four annas a day to five and six annas ; of blacksmiths from three and four annas to five annas; of well-sinkers *(chahkun)* from twelve annas per lineal foot to one rupee, common labourers from eighteen pie to two and two and a half annas, and women and children in proportion. The approximate number of landless, unskilled labourers in the district is 190,692. Of these a large number, calculated at 51,950, mostly Chamárs, Kahárs, Sainis, Gáras, Jhojhas, &c., work in the fields. Their wages vary according to the season of the year and the nature of the work to be performed ; thus reapers get daily one sheaf supposed to contain from four to five sers *pukka* of grain, a ploughman may get one-eighth of the crop, weeders are paid two annas a day and upwards, or from 5 to 6 sers of grain a day, one *kuchcha* bígha representing 12 hours' work. They are paid better for weeding cotton than for weeding sugar-cane ; the rate of wages in the former case sometimes rising to three annas or seven sers of grain per *kuchcha* bígha. Generally speaking, however, no rules can be laid down about the wages of agricultural labourers, which in a great measure depend upon the terms of the contract made, and probably differ more or less in every village according to local custom. Women and children are also often employed in field labour, the former chiefly in plucking cotton, for which they get sometimes from a tenth to a fourth of the amount plucked, and sometimes one rupee per *kuchcha* bígha of work done, or one and a half annas a day ; for plucking safflower they get as much grain as the flower plucked, or one-half of the original commodity itself. The nominal rate of wages for female labourers is six pice and for children about four pice, but there is reason to believe that the latter are rarely, if ever, paid separately; the work of both seems really to be taken

together and remunerated according to the amount done, not by a system of daily wages.

Prices.

The following table gives the prices of the principal articles of agricultural produce and provisions in the central tahsíl of Saháranpur and the north-eastern tahsíl of Rúrki for the years 1861 to 1870. The figures give the number of sers sold for one rupee, the ser being the standard one of 80 tolas or 2·057lbs. avoirdupois.[1]

Class of crop.	1861.		1862.		1863.		1864.		1865.		1866.		1867.		1868.		1869.		1870.		Average of the ten years.	
	R.	S.	R.	S.	R.	S.	R.	S.	R.	S.	R.	S.	R.	S.	R.	S.	R.	S.	R.	S.	R.	S.
Paddy ...	15¾	18½	27¾	37½	34¾	38¾	30¼	26½	26¼	23	26½	23	26	27½	26	19¼	13	18½	12½	38¼	24	26½
Common paddy (husked) ...	8¼	9	10¾	16	12½	22¼	12½	15¼	11¼	14	11½	14½	11½	16	4¾	11	8	12½	9	13½	10½	14½
Best do. (do.)...	6½	6½	7	13	9	12½	7¾	9¾	5¼	8	6½	8	6¾	9	7	8¼	6	9¾	5¾	10½	6¾	9½
Wheat ...	11	9½	21½	35	28¼	30	21½	24½	17½	22½	18¾	20½	19¾	22¼	17	15	11	11	12	17	17¾	20½
Barley ...	12¾	14½	31¼	38	14¾	37	33⅓	38½	21¾	25½	28¼	27	25¼	30½	25¼	20	14¼	12½	19	25	27	27½
Bájra ...	13	16	27	38½	36	35	24	25½	20½	24	20	20	19¼	22	16½	14½	10½	10½	14½	26½	20	23
Joár ...	13	12½	25½	26½	29½	28	22½	23	19½	23	21¼	25½	18¾	21½	17¼	15½	10	14½	15	30	19	22
Gram ...	10	11½	20	38	30¼	34½	25¼	27½	21	25½	22½	24½	18¼	21½	16½	17½	10	9	20½	20½	19¼	23
Lentils, Masúr	10½	11½	26¾	38½	28½	39	31¼	29¼	22	25½	23¼	26¼	21¼	19½	21	19½	11¼	10½	14	25	21¾	24
Moth ...	11	10½	24½	35½	29¼	37½	22¼	25	20	22½	22	21½	18¼	21½	15¾	14½	10	11½	15¼	34	18¾	23½
Urd ...	10	10½	23¼	15½	16¾	22¼	16	17½	18¾	22¼	21½	22¼	17½	19¾	16½	14	9¾	10¾	14½	20½	16½	17½
Cleaned cotton,	3½	3¼	3¼	2¾	1½	1½	1½	2¼	3	3	2¼	3	3	3¼	2¼	2¼	1¾	1¼	2	1½	2¼	2¼
Sugar (raw) ...	3	4	3	4¼	3	4½	3	4½	3½	5½	3½	4	2¾	4½	3	4½	3	3½	3	3½	3	4½
Do. (refined)...	...	3½	..	4¼	...	2¾	...	3½	...	3¾	...	4½	...	3½	...	3	...	2¾	...	3	...	3½
Salt ...	6	7½	6¼	8	6½	7	6¼	7	6½	7¼	6¾	8¾	6½	7¾	6½	7	6	5½	7	8	6½	7
Ghí ...	2	2¼	1½	2¼	1¾	2½	1¾	2¼	1¾	2½	2	1¼	1½	2	1¼	2	1¼	2	1¼	1½	1¾	2
Milk ...	18	18	19¼	18	20½	16	19½	16	19½	16	17¾	16	16¾	16	16	16	15	18	15	18	17¾	16¾
Tobacco ...	7½	7	8	8	8¾	8	10¼	8	9	8	9¼	9	7¼	11	5¾	10½	6¼	10½	6¼	11	7¾	9
Oil-seeds (sarson)	11¼	9	11	11½	12	14½	15¾	17½	18¼	18	14¾	18½	14½	16½	10	13	10	13½	9½	16	12¾	14¾
Til ...	9¼	10	9½	15½	8¾	11	10	11	12½	13½	12½	14	11¾	13½	9¼	10½	8¾	11½	9½	17	10¼	12¾
Túriya ...	...	10	...	15¼	13	10½	...	10½	...	12½	19¼	14½	17¼	14½	15¼	9¾	12¼	11½	14	18	15	12½
Alsi ...	10½	10½	12¼	13½	12½	14	16	20	12¼	21½	19¼	22½	14	17½	12¾	14¾	11¼	11½	13¼	16	13½	16
Zíra ...	...	10½	...	10	...	10½	.	11½	...	11½	...	13½	...	16	...	10½	...	12½	...	17	..	12¼
Potatoes ...	9	11	11¼	15½	12	13½	15¾	13½	11¼	18	13¼	15¼	13	17½	13½	13	13¼	13½	12	13½	12¼	14½
Spirits (25° below proof) ...	1½	1½	1½	1½	1½	1½	1½	1½	1½	1½	1½	1½	1½	1½	1½	1½	1½	1½	1½	1½	1⅛	1½
Raw materials (gúr) ...	7½	10½	9½	10½	11¼	13½	10	10½	12¼	15½	15¼	15¼	9¼	9¼	8¼	7	6¾	8	10¼	10½	10	10¾
Radishes ...	28½	..	28	...	28	...	28	...	28	...	28	...	28	...	28	...	28	..	28	...	28½	...
Shíra ...	...	20½	...	20½	...	26¾	...	21	...	29	...	26½	...	18	...	13½	...	15¾	...	19¾	...	21

Trade and manufactures.

Saháranpur cannot boast a very large trade, but a great deal of raw produce is exported to other districts, and the opening of the railway has stimulated the traffic immensely. The

[1] Appendix F. of Plowden's "Wages and Prices" gives the prices-current in Saháranpur of the principal grains from 1840 to 1870. R. represents the Rúrki Tahsíl and S. the Saháranpur Tahsíl.

following return shows the outward and inward traffic of each station in the district for the year 1872.

Name of Station.	Outward.		Inward.		Total inward and out-ward.	
	Number of passengers.	Quantity of goods in maunds.	Number of passengers.	Quantity of goods in maunds.	Number of passengers.	Quantity of goods in maunds.
Deoband	21,216	33,264	20,456	6,216	41,672	39,480
Saháranpur ...	62,363	93,464	58,146	146,944	120,509	2,40,408
Sarsáwa	5,267	11,144	4,594	700	9,861	11,844
Total for half-year ending 30th June, 1872 ...	88,846	137,872	83,196	153,860	172 042	291,732
Deoband	15,794	17,621	15,182	5,528	30,976	23,149
Saháranpur	51,465	1,09.611	50,663	113,646	102,128	223,257
Sarsáwa	5,809	43,048	5,517	1,161	11,326	44,209
Total for half-year ending 31st December, 1872...	73,068	170,280	71,362	120,335	144,430	290,615

Mr. Angus Campbell, in connection with his project of a railway to Rúrki and Dehra, estimated the traffic in 1868 across the bridge-of-boats at Kankhal for the first six months of the year at 85,366 maunds of goods, and the passengers going to Hardwár in January at 17,877 and in April at 11,450, and for the different sections of the proposed line he estimated 42,929 maunds of goods and 18,445 passengers.[1] The octroi returns of Saháranpur, Deoband and Hardwár will be found under those towns in the alphabetical arrangement.

The only fair in the district that deserves special notice in connection with trade is that held in April at Hardwár, which, not-withstanding its essentially religious associations, in

Fairs.

[1] The following are the details of the bullock train traffic already in existence :—

Deoband section.	Goods in maunds.	Passengers.	Rúrki and Dehra section.	Goods in maunds.	Passengers.
Meerut and below to Rúrki	10,569	8,004	Rúrki to Dehra ...	2,139	526
Rúrki to Meerut ...	5,057	5,057	Dehra to Rúrki ...	433	375
Saháranpur to Rúrki ...	806	1,747	Rúrki Workshops ...	1,169	...
Rúrki to Saháranpur ...	2,495	2,410	Meerut to Dehra ...	7,215	155
Rúrki Workshops ...	11,057	...	Dehra to Meerut ...	1,990	171
	29,984	17,218		12,945	1,227

Add to this from Rúrki and Mayapur section for charcoal for Rúrki Workshops 37,000 maunds, and firewood from Dadhiya 13,000 maunds.

former days annually became a great mercantile emporium, but now retains little of its commercial character, except as a resort for horse dealers, who come here in great numbers every year from Afghánistan and the Panjáb. Besides horses, trinkets of all sorts and articles of clothing of every kind find a ready market among the pilgrims. The fair is attended by about 400,000 persons, and lasts eight days. Some further remarks about the Hardwár fair will be found under the notice of Hardwár town. A fair, attended by about ten to fifteen thousand people and lasting two days, is held in September for the purpose of bathing in the Ganges at Jagatiwála and at Nánakmau or Mánikmau. Near the city is a small fair, where the people assemble from a radius of from forty to fifty miles. A large fair takes place at Indarpur Bháwan, and lasts for five days in September-October. There are few indigenous manufactures[1] and none of any great note. In all the larger towns the weavers make

Manufactures.

a coarse cloth called *gárá;* Rámpur has been nicknamed Rámpur Manihárán because bracelets *(chúris)* and such like ornaments are there extensively made by the workers in glass ; skilful silversmiths and goldsmiths are to be found almost everywhere, and the capital town is famous for its artists in wood-carving, as well as for the confection of a very popular sweetmeat called *peta.* This is about all that can be said of indigenous manufactures.

The Rúrki Workshops were originally established in connection with the

Rúrki Workshops.

Ganges Canal works in the year 1843, on a very modest scale, being then something between a timber-yard, a smithy, and a carpenter's shop.[2] In 1848, Lieutenant A. Allen, of the 55th Native Infantry, was appointed to take charge of the establishment, which from that date began to develope rapidly. Within a year, the most necessary portion of the buildings, including lathe, model and engine accommodation, was completed ; and in 1851, a supply of machinery, among which was a ten horse-power condensing steam engine, with boilers, was sent out from England by the Court of Directors. Up to this time the shops had been exclusively employed upon the manufacture of articles required for the Ganges Canal Works, and the demand for surveying and mathematical instruments at the Rúrki Civil Engineering College first suggested the advisability of utilising them in other ways. In 1852, the establishment ceased to have any connection with the Ganges Canal, and was placed under the superintendence of Lieutenant Allen, as a self-supporting institution. Its duties were to be three-fold,—the supply of iron and wood for general purposes, the manufacture and repair of mathematical instruments, and iron founding. Until

---

[1] By Mr. G. R. Williams, C. S.   [2] Cuatley's Report on the Ganges Canal, Vol. II., p. 326, and No. 236. of Professional Papers on Indian Engineering, by Mr. A. Campbell, printed at the Thomason College Press.

March, 1864, " the workshops progressed in size and capacity for executing work, but their financial condition was neglected, and the consequence was a loss to Government of Rs. 4,24,455 in a period of 11½ years, without making allowance for the use of capital provided by the State. Since then the profits have been large, and in 1868-69 reached Rs. 1,28,909. In 1870-71, however, the net profits fell to Rs. 59,608. Some useful calculations by Mr. Campbell, are appended :—

Period.	Value of work executed.	Value of capital.	Net profit.	Percentage of profit on capital per annum.
	Rs.	Rs.	Rs.	Rs.
1st March, 1864, to 30th April, 1865, 14 months.	3,35,282	10,82,845	63,166	6
1st May, 1865, to 1st May, 1866, 12 months.	2,80,523	9,73,083	29,270	3
1st May, 1866, to 1st April, 1867, 11 months.	3,28,818	9,53,544	60,199	6
1st April, 1867, to 1st April, 1868, 12 months.	3,82,441	11,03,371	1,00,173	9
1st April, 1868, to 1st April, 1869, 12 months.	4,76,041	11,78,416	1,28,909	11

" The works contain a turning shop worked by a 20 horse-power engine, a foundry with a 12 horse-power engine, a smith's shed with two steam hammers, a scrap furnace for wood fuel, a fitting and boiler-making shop with a steam rivetter, a pattern shop, a carpenter's shop with saw mills driven by a 10 horse-power engine, and lastly a mathematical instrument shop. The range of work executed is very great." Here are made, among other things, steam engines of all sorts, pumps, printing presses, hydraulic presses, planing, slotting and drilling machinery, lathes, levels, prismatic and surveying compasses, and scientific instruments in general ; bridge and girder work of every kind is also executed. The profit derived from the establishment is a very slight consideration compared with the advantages ensuing from the consequent improvement that may be expected in the mechanical skill of native artisans. The Rúrkí Workshops, three years ago, employed no less than 141 Muhammaada nnd 277 Hindu artisans, besides 143 Muhammadan and 508 Hindu labourers ; in all 1,069. The wages of the former in the mathematical instrument department vary from twenty to four annas a day and in other departments from eight to three and a half annas a day. Mr. A. Campbell, a very shrewd observer, bears testimony to the superior activity and intelligence of the Muhammadan workmen, which he justly attributes to their having more ambition than the Hindús, over whom they appear to have a moral ascendancy. A plan of the foundry and workshops will be found in a professional paper by that gentleman, referred to in a preceding footnote.

An institution of still greater local importance is the Thomason Civil Engineering College, so called after its founder the late Lieutenant-Governor of these Provinces. The origin of the
Thomason College was due to the want felt, during the construction of the great
canal-works and roads, of some systematic training for Civil Engineers in this
country. To this was added the professional skill required by the various com-
mittees appointed in each district to administer the funds of the ferry and
road collections, and the demands of the Great Trigonometrical and Revenue
Surveys. The well-educated European required instruction in the native languages, especially in the vernacular terms of science and also in the peculiarities
of materials and construction in this country, whilst the uneducated subordinate
staff required scientific instruction to develope their energy and usefulness.
Efforts were at first made to supply these wants by existing institutions, but
resulted in failure. In January, 1845, Lieutenant Baird Smith, R.E., undertook to conduct an engineering class for native youths at Saháranpur. Certain allowances were made for this purpose, and two of the more advanced
scholars in the Agra and Dehli Colleges were placed under his superintendence,
whilst masters were appointed to those institutions to instruct in architectural
drawing and surveying. The first great impetus to scientific study was given
by the establishment in 1845 of the grade of Sub-Assistant Executive Engineer,
with a special standing and privilege, which afforded a certain reward to
study, and created a superior class of subordinate officials in the Public Works
Department

The determination of Lord Hardinge, in 1847, to commence the Ganges
Canal, again raised the question of the necessity for a
well-trained staff of experienced Civil Engineers who
should be able to face all the difficulties arising in a large undertaking of this
nature. Out of this emergency Rúrki College had its rise. Its establishment
there was due to the presence of the large workshop, and extensive structures in
course of formation for the head-works of the canal with the necessary scientific
appliances where the pupils could practically work out the problems submitted
to them in their daily course of study. Lieutenant Maclagan was appointed the
first Principal in October, 1847, and in January of the following year, the first
pupils were enrolled. It was not, however, until the middle of the year that
the preparations were completed and the institution was in full session. War,
too, came to interrupt its progress. In 1848-49 the second Panjáb War broke
out, and the Principal, Head-master and Military students were obliged to
leave their studies for the field, where they were absent for two months on
active duty. In 1850 the military students were increased from 10 to 15,
and the period of their stay at the college was prolonged to a year, the first
six months being probationary. The stipendiary students, drawing five rupees

a month, whilst kept at the same salary to the number of sixteen, had a higher class granted them, by which eight of their number drew a double allowance. Up to July, 1850, the expenditure amounted to Rs. 35,277. In 1851 there were 50 students, and 42 had already entered the public service. In 1852 proposals were made and sanctioned for an improved building, and the establishment of a press and workshop in connection with the College, whilst a library was formed, and an increase was made to the educational staff.

The original prospectus of the college explains the object of its foundation,

Its progress.

which was to give theoretical and practical instruction in Civil Engineering to Europeans and Natives, with a view to their employment on the public works of the country, according to their several qualifications and the requirements of the service. The rules and regulations of the institution have been considerably modified since the year 1852, but its duties remain the same. The progress which it has made in performing them may be judged from the fact that the list of passed students for 1848 contains only three names—two in the upper subordinate class and one in the lower ; the former of two gunners in the artillery, the latter of one solitary native student from the Dehli College. The list for 1871 gives the names of eighteen gentlemen (officers and others) belonging to the engineering classes, of 54 students (privates, non-commissioned officers, natives and others) belonging to the upper subordinate classes, and of 48 natives belonging to the lower subordinate classes ; so that in that year no less than 112 students qualified for the public service, and to this total should be added the names of nine students belonging to the officers' surveying class. The college calendar gives a full account of the curriculum.[1]

The following statement shows the number of estates on the revenue-roll of

Land-revenue.

the districts, with their land-revenue, and the number of registered proprietors paying revenue direct to Government, at five different periods :—

	1806.	1850-51.	1860-61.	1870-71.	1872-73.
Number of estates ...	1,099	1,761	1,908	1.916	1,916
Number of registered proprietors or coparceners.	1,211	3,887	3,823	3,889	3,875
Total revenue-demand ...	3,35,222	10,58,441	10,93,066	11,63,839	11,72,950
Average demand from each estate...	305	601	573	607	612
Average revenue paid by each proprietor.	277	272	286	299	302
Expenditure on revenue administration.	Not known	Rs. 73,102	74,598	61,842	66,109

[1] The number on the rolls on the 1st Januray, 1873, was—Principal and Assistant Professors, 15 ; Native masters, 11 ; petty establishment, 122 ; total 149. Students of the first year, —engineering classes, 18 ; second year, 27 ; lower year, 112—total 157.

The actual assessment of the income of the district, at six pies in the rupee,

Income-tax.

calculated upon profits exceeding Rs. 500 for the purposes of the income-tax of 1870, during 1870-71 was Rs. 1,08,032. There were 1,184 incomes between Rs. 500, and Rs. 750 per annum, 364 between Rs. 750 and Rs. 1,000, 298 between Rs. 1,000 and Rs. 1,500, 140 between Rs. 1,500 and Rs. 2,000, 399 between Rs. 2,000 and Rs. 10,000, and 27 between Rs. 10,000 and Rs. 1,00,000. The total number of persons assessed was 2,412, and their total income was Rs. 36,54,741.

In 1871-72 there were 4,732 documents registered under the provisions of

Registration.

the Registration Act (VIII. of 1871), on which fees to the amount of Rs. 12,848 were collected. The expense of establishment, &c., during the same period amounted to Rs. 5,530. There were 2,222 registrations affecting immovable property, in which the registration was compulsory under Section 17 of Act VIII. of 1871, and 894 in which the registration was optional. The other registrations effected refer to movable property, wills, &c., and the total aggregate values of all the documents registered amounted to Rs. 13,18,593.

The net receipts on account of excise amounted to Rs. 21,394 in 1862-63, and

Excise.

rose to more than double that amount in 1871-72. At the close of the latter year there were 82 shops for the sale of native liquors, and 15 shops for the sale of English spirituous and fermented liquors in the district. Thirteen licensed stills were at work, and 18,302 gallons of liquor were issued during the year. The receipts and charges on account of excise for ten years were as follows, showing a remarkable increase under almost every head of revenue :—

Year.		License fees for vend of spirits.	Duty on spirits.	Opium.	Madak.	Tari.	Intoxicating drugs.	Fines, &c.	Gross charges.	Net receipts.
		Rs.	Rs.	Rs.	Rs.	Rs.	Rs.	Rs.	Rs.	Rs.
1862-63	...	556	12,174	6.469	...	18	3.435	...	787	21,394
1863-64	...	2,830	7,220	12,240	...	15	3,365	83	892	24,861
1864-65	...	7,592	12,141	13,145	...	...	4,917	68	7,990	29,172
1865-66	...	10,709	12,296	18,179	...	...	3,483	88	11,268	33,488
1866-67	...	14,836	15,825	19,533	...	...	4,510	68	11,975	42,787
1867-68	...	15,885	17,136	23,056	...	...	5,246	50	14,149	47,225
1868-69	...	13,673	12,858	22,480	...	...	6,371	44	13,480	41,946
1869-70	...	921	11,727	27,138	39	75	3,436	369	16,440	27,265
1870-71	...	4,878	17,894	27,200	542	73	5,053	1	15,682	39,959
1871-72	...	10,704	21,108	27,520	719	100	6,810	74	15,424	51,110

Stamp duties are now collected under the General Stamp Act (XVIII. of
1869) and under the Court Fees Act. The following
statement shows the revenue and charges under this
head for a series of years.

Stamps.

Year.	Adhesive stamps and hundis.	Blue-and-black document stamps.	Court fees.	Duties and penalties realized.	Total receipts.	Gross charges.	Net receipts.
	Rs.	Rs.	Rs.	Rs.	Rs.	Rs.	Rs.
1862-63 ...	2,594	50,542	...	238	53,374	4,209	49,166
1863-64 ...	5,059	96,103	...	204	61,365	4,547	56,818
1864-65 ...	6,791	5,,957	...	109	6,285	4,600	58,257
1865-66 ...	7,368	64,535	...	97	71,999	5,524	66,475
1866-67 ...	2,453	68,042	...	209	70,704	5,493	65,011
1867-68 ...	2,907	89,654	...	114	92,675	6,676	85,999
1868-69 ...	2,452	91,786	...	250	94,489	5,525	88,964
1869-70 ...	2,815	98,539	...	367	1,01,720	7,954	93,767
1870-71 ...	2,475	16,457	73,228	794	93,015	5,414	87,601
1871-72 ...	1,996	17,854	64,379	185	84,414	2,673	81,741
1872-73 ...	1,735	22,530	75,816	432	99,562	1,986	97,576

The income from canal irrigation is large. The revenue of the Jumna Canal,
which in 1856-57 was only Rs. 21,586, amounted in
1872-73 to Rs. 1,63,915. This does not include mis-
cellaneous items,[1] which cannot be separated for the different districts. The
following statement shows the revenue accounts of both canals for seven years :—

Canal revenue.

GANGES CANAL.				EASTERN JUMNA CANAL.				
Year.	Collections.	Establishment.	Fees.	Net collections.	Year.	Collections.	Establishment.	Fees.	Net collections.
1866-67...	40,857	235	...	40,622	1866-67...	52,828	472	...	52,356
1867-68...	71,382	261	218	70,903	1867-68...	1,94,965	518	215	1,94,232
1868-69...	53,569	272	522	52,775	1868-69...		Not given.		
1869-70...	1,25,495	296	3,112	1,22,087	1869-70...	2,16,101	532	3,842	2,11,727
1870-71...	49,926	293	2,519	47,114	1870-71...		Not given.		
1871-72...	46,786	307	2,081	44,398	1871-72...	1,95,630	548	6,209	1,88,873
1872-73...	48,845	3,5	2,256	46,374	1872-73...	1,63,915	573	6,232	1,57,091

A portion of the income of the Forest Department must also be credited to
Sahárunpur. In 1862-63, this item amounted to
Rs. 7,168, and in 1869-70 to Rs. 8,499. Before and

Forest revenue.

---

[1] Captain Howe, R.E. On the Ganges Canal there are 20 sets of mills at Kankhal, eight at
Bahádurabad, two at Roorkee, six at Asafnagar, and six at Muhammadpur. On the Jumna
Canal there are altogether seven mills.

after the years in question the Saháranpur accounts cannot be separated from those of Dehra Dún.

The most ancient remains belonging to this district should most probably be some of the ruins about Hardwár[1] and Mayapur on the Ganges, but it is so difficult to assign a specific date to any particular building, that we must take the golden lát of Firuz Shah Tughlak, now at Dehli, as the oldest monument having any connection with this district the history of which is known. Shams-i-Siráj Afíf, in his chronicles of the reign[2] of Firuz Shah, mentions the removal of the mindra-i-zarín or golden lát (obelisk) from the village of Tobra, in the district of Sálaura and Khizrabad at the foot of the hills (Koh-payah), ninety kos from Dehli, to Firuz's new capital of Firuzabad, where it was placed in the palace constructed by Firuz near the Jama Masjid. He describes the mode of the removal of the lát, and its re-erection in Dehli; and, as he says that he was twelve years of age at the time, he was probably also an eye-witness. Firuz Shah reigned from 1351 to 1388 A.D., so that the removal probably took place about 1379 A.D. The chronicler reports the tradition concerning the pillar—that the column had been " the walking-stick of the accursed Bhím, a man of great stature and size. The annals of the infidels record that this Bhím used to devour a thousand maunds of food daily, and no one could compete with him. In his days all this part of Hind was peopled with infidels, who were continually fighting and slaying each other. Bhím was one of five brothers (the Pándavas), but he was the most powerful of them all. He was generally engaged in tending the herds of cattle belonging to his wicked brothers, and he was accustomed to use the stone pillars as sticks to gather the cattle together." The same tradition is universal throughout these Provinces to the present day. This and similar monoliths in Bahar, Gorakhpur, Gházipur, and Allahabad are still called Bhím Sen ke gada (club).

Shams-i-Siráj further notes that " after it was raised, some ornamental fringes of black and white stone were placed around its two capitols, and over these there was raised a gilded copper cupola, called in Hindí kalas (spire or pinnacle)," and hence the name mindra-i-zarín or golden lát. " On the base of the obelisk there were engraved several lines of writing in Hindí characters. Many Brahmans and Hindu devotees were invited to read them, but no one was able. It is said that certain infidel Hindús interpreted them as stating that no one should be able to remove the obelisk from its place till there should arise in the latter days a Muhammadan King named Sultán Firuz, &c." The writing remained undecyphered until 1837-38, when it yielded, to the untiring industry and energy of James Prinsep, the discovery that the older writing on

---

[1] See Hardwár and Mayapur under the Gazetteer list of the district.   [2] Dowson's Elliot, III., 350.

it contained a transcript of the edicts of the great Buddhist Emperor Asoka, who lived in the third century before Christ. Several guesses had already been made as to the characters employed. Thus Edward Terry[1] says that he was told by Tom Coryate that there was a pillar of marble in Dehli with a Greek inscription; whilst Purchas notices that the inscriptions were in Greek and Hebrew, and that "some affirm the pillar was erected by Alexander the Great." The characters are those of the ancient Páli, or spoken language of that day, and are thus described by General Cunningham[2] :— "The alphabetical characters, which are of the oldest form that has yet been found in India, are most clearly and beautifully cut, and there are only a few letters of the whole record lost by the peeling off of the surface of the stone. The inscription ends with a short sentence, in which King Asoka directs the setting up of these monoliths in different parts of India. * * The record consists of four distinct inscriptions on the four sides of the column facing the cardinal points, and of one long inscription immediately below, which goes completely around the pillar. The last ten lines of the eastern face, as well as the whole of the continuous inscription round the shaft, are peculiar to the Dehli pillar," and contain new forms similar to those on the rock inscription at Kálsi in the Dún. A second inscription records the victories of the Chauhán Prince Vísala Deva, which has already been noticed in the introduction. General Cunningham identifies Khizrabad with the present village of that name on the Jumna, just below the spot where the river issues from the hills in parganah Faizabad of this district. Sálaura is clearly Sadhaura, a large place only a few miles west of Khizrabad. The name of the village from whence the obelisk was brought is variously written Topur, Topera, Toparsuk, Tohera, Tawera, Tobra and Nahera, and the same writer identifies it with Paota, on the western bank of the Jumna, about twelve miles north-east of Khizrabad. According to Shams-i-Siráj "the height of the obelisk was thirty-two *gaz*; eight *gaz* were sunk in its pedestal, and twenty-four *gaz* were visible." General Cunningham found it to consist of "a single shaft of pale pinkish sandstone 42' 7" in length, of which the upper portion (35') has received a very high polish, while the remainder is left quite rough. Its upper diameter is 25·3 inches, and its lower

---

[1] " Dillee, which signifies a heart, and is seated in the heart of the Mogul's territories. It was once the city and seat of King Porus, who was conquered about this place by Alexander the Great ; and here he, encountering with huge elephants, as well as with a mighty host of men, said, as Curtius reports—*'tandem par animo meo inveni periculum'*—that he had met with dangers equal to his great mind. I was told by Tom Coryate (who took special notice of this place) that he, being in the city of Dillee, observed a very great pillar of marble with a Greek inscription upon it, which time had almost quite worn out, erected (as he supposed) there and then by Great Alexander, to preserve the memory of that famous victory."—Terry's Voyages (London, 1655) reprinted, 1777, p. 77.   [2] Arch. Sur. I., 161 ; see ALLAHABAD volume for a full account of the Asoka inscriptions.

diameter 38·8 inches, the diminution being 0·39 inches per foot. Its weight is rather more than twenty-seven tons. In its dimensions it is more like the Allahabad pillar than any other, but it tapers much more rapidly towards the top, and is therefore less graceful in its outline."

The next remains of ancient date are the ruins of the old town of Bahat,
Srughna. which have been noticed in the introduction. Then we come to the journeys of the Chinese traveller Hwen Thsang in the middle of the seventh century of our era. In travelling from Thanesar, Hwen Thsang at first proceeded south for some seventeen miles, to the Gokantha monastery, and thence for 67 miles to Srughna. The kingdom of Srughna is described as extending to the hills on the north and the Ganges on the east. The town itself was situated on the west bank of the Jumna, and was 3⅜ miles in circuit. The greater part was even then in ruins, but the foundations still remained. It possessed five monasteries, one hundred temples, and many stupas. General Cunningham[1] identifies Srughna with the village of Sugh, situated on a projecting triangular spur of high land, surrounded on three sides by the old bed of the Jumna, now the western Jumna canal, and opposite to Bahat in the Faizabad parganah. Tradition and the discovery of large bricks and extensive finds of old coins all point out the antiquity of the present site of the village and that of the neighbouring village of Mandalpur. Mahmúd in his twelfth expedition,[2] or that against Kanauj, passed along the foot of the
Sarsáwa. hills under Kashmír, and crossed the Jumna, in 1018 A.D., whence he proceeded down the Duáb to Baran (Bulandshahr). Abu Rihan, who wrote during this time, mentions[3] in his itinerary, that "from Kanauj going north, and turning a little to the west, you come to Sharasháraha, fifty parasangs, then to Pinjor, eighteen parasangs." Elliot identifies this place with Sarsáwa or Sirsáwa, sometimes called Sirsapatan, an old town lying ten miles to the east of Sugh, and on the line of road usually followed by the invaders of India from the west. On his return from Kanauj, Mahmúd is said to have attacked "Chand Rái, one of the greatest men of Hind, who resided in the fort of Sharwa," which General Cunningham identifies with Sarsáwa[4] or perhaps with Sugh, and adds:— "But whichever of the two places is intended, it is certain that the high road from the Gangetic Duáb to the upper Panjáb must have crossed the *ghát* between them." Al Utbi relates that there had been constant war between Chand Rái and Purú Jaipál, the ruler of the Panjáb, and that at last the latter sought a compromise, and sent his son Bhímpál to receive the daughter of Chand Rái in marriage. Chand Rái imprisoned the son, and demanded compensation for the losses which had been inflicted by the father, and war continued between

[1] Arch. Sur., II, 226.   [2] Dowson's Elliot, II., 42, 458.   [3] *Ibid*, I, 61.
[4] Dowson's Elliot, II., 47; Arch. Sur. II., 230.

them as before. This was the state of affairs on the arrival of Mahmúd, who, on his return from Kanauj, determined to reduce the Hindu prince to subjection. In the meantime, by the advice of Bhímpál, his prisoner, Chand Rái abandoned his fort and retreated to the hills, lest he should suffer the fate of the uncles and relations of Bhímpál, who were made Musalmáns " when they demanded quarter in their distress." The Sultán captured the fort and pursued the fugitives to the hills, where in January, 1019 A.D., shortly before midnight, he came upon the enemy in the midst of the forest, and defeated them with great slaughter. The booty amounted in gold, silver, and precious stones to 300,000 dirhams, and " the number of prisoners may be conceived from the fact that each was sold for from two to ten dirhams." It is said that the fifth share due to the Sayyids was 150,000 slaves. However this may be, there can be no doubt but that a great part of the northern portion of this district fell out of cultivation during this period, and that it was not for several centuries afterwards that much improvement took place.

The town of Sahâranpur was not founded until the reign of Muhammad
Tughlak (1325-1351 A.D.), and was named by him
Musalmáns. after Sháh Haran Chishti, a celebrated *pir* or Muhammadan saint, whose shrine still attracts a considerable assemblage of the devout. The progress of colonisation, which had been going on for some years, received some impetus from the invasion of the Mughals under Tarmsharín Khán, who, at this time, crossed the Jumna by the old route under the hills, and marched down the Duáb plundering as they came. The Mughals were only got rid of by the grant of a large contribution in money. They did not, as one would expect, immediately return to India, though, in anticipation of such an event, the imperial posts were pushed northwards, and stations were occupied near the principal ghâts on the Jumna. It was in one of his progresses for the inspection of these posts through this district that Fíruz Tughlak saw the Asoka column at Khizrabad. In 1379 Fíruz Shah passed through[1] Ambála and Shahabad to the hills of Sahâranpur, and after taking tribute from the Ráis of Sirmor and the hills he returned to his capital. In 1384 he again visited the hills and spent two months in hunting the rhinoceros (*kark*) and the elk (*gozan*), and it was here that Muhammad Khán sought refuge when despairing of succeeding his father Fíruz, and occupied the fort of Baktári or Baknári beyond Náhan.

The garrisons along the Jumna proved of little avail against the forces of
the Mughál Emperor Tímúr, who, after the sack of
Tímúr. Dehli in December, 1398 A.D., crossed into the Duáb, and sweeping through the Meerut and a part of the Bijnaur District, recrossed the Ganges near Hardwár : Tímúr himself gives an account in his memoirs[2] of

---

[1] Dowson's Elliot, IV, 14, 16, 17, 19.   [2] Malfúzát-i-Tímúrí in Dowson's Elliot, III., 455, 513.

the fights that took place. When he heard that the *gabrs*, as he calls all that were not followers of Islám, had assembled near Hardwár, he followed them, and ordered his men to charge. "Spurring their horses, shouting their war-cry, and brandishing their swords, they fell upon the forces of the enemy like hungry lions upon a flock of sheep." The enemy broke and fled, and an immense booty was obtained. Tímúr had at this time only one hundred men with him as a personal guard, and was attacked by Malik Shaikha with a larger force. When about a bow-shot remained between the two parties, Tímúr asked a soldier in advance who those approaching, as if to attack, were. The soldier said that they belonged to the party of Shaikh Kúkar, one of Tímúr's officers, and on this Tímúr turned to retire. The enemy rushed on the Mughal troops, and would have annihilated them had not their own leader, Malik Shaikha, been slain in the first onset, when, as is the custom with orientals, his troops dispersed.

A small party of the enemy, with the wives and children of those who had taken part in the first fight, took refuge at Kúpila (Hardwár), about two *kos* off. When Tímúr heard of this, he marched there, and, joined by Prince Pír Muhammad Jahángír, attacked the fugitives. After a slight resistance the enemy took to flight, but many were slain, and the women and children, "the property and goods, gold, money, grain, camels, horses, cows and buffaloes," fell as spoil to the soldiers. Tímúr would then appear to have pursued the remainder along the foot of the hills, where he spent some days plundering and destroying everything that came in his way. On his return he encamped at Bahrah, "a dependency of Bakri well known as the country of Miyápur," and halted the next day at Shikk Sár, a distance of four *kos*, and the next day went to Kandar. On leaving Kandar he crossed the Jumna. The *Zafar-náma* of Sharf-úd-dín Yazdi makes the stages Bahrah, Shikk-Sársáwa and Kandar : where Tímúr gives the name Sár, his chronicler gives the name Sarsáwa. The position and the marches clearly corroborate the identification of Sár with the modern Sarsáwa. Mention is made that Fíruz Shah conducted the stream of Fíruzabad from the mountains of Mandati and Sirmor to Dehli. [1] Firishta calls the place Mandawi, though Briggs has Mandui, Dow has Manduli, and Elliot has Mandir. The canal was drawn from the Jumna opposite Faizabad, and therefore the name may be identified with that of Mandalpur, close to Sugh. Sugh was therefore, so early as the fourteenth century, supplanted by Mandalpur.

We next find the *iktá* and *shikk* of Saháranpur bestowed by Sultán Sayyid Khizr Khán on Sayyid Sálim, the chief of the Sayyids in 1414 A.D. [2] As this was about the date of the settlement of the Sayyids of Bárha in the adjacent district of Muzaffarnagar, it is probable that they went there under the protection of the Sayyid governor,

Sayyid Sálim.

---

[1] Dowson's Elliot, IV, 8 ; Arch Sur. II, 230.   [2] *Táríkh-i-Mubárak Sháhi*, Dowson's Elliot, IV., 46.

Sálim. In 1526 A.D., during his fifth expedition to India, Bábar passed through
Sarsáwa, and one of the skirmishes preceding the invader's victory over Ibrahím
Lodi at Pánipat must have taken place in the neighbourhood of Títron, in parganah Gangoh of this district. The Turkmán colonies of Lakhnauti and the
neighbouring villages trace their origin to this expedition.

In the following year (933 Hijrí) the famous saint Abdul Kaddús, a

Shaikh Abdul Kaddús.   descendant of Abú Hanífah, founded the Saráí, or new
town of Gangoh, where his descendants still reside.
His mission was followed by the conversion of many of the Rajpút, Gújar and
Taga inhabitants, and materially strengthened the Musalmán element in the
population. He was succeeded by his son Shaikh Rukn-ud-dín, who was amongst
the learned men assembled at the court of Akbar at the time of Bairám's fall.
Shaikh Abdun-nabi, son of Shaikh Ahmad, and grandson of Shaikh Abdul

Shaikh Abdun-nabi, Sadr   Kaddús, was several times in Makka, where he studied
of the Empire.   the Hadís. He succeeded the celebrated Mauláná
Abdullah of Sultánpur in the favour of the court, and was at all times a man
of mark at Dehli. He had many enemies, and amongst them was Makhdúm-
ul-mulk, who wrote a pamphlet charging the Shaikh with murder under pretence
of punishing heresy; that it was wrong to say prayers with the Shaikh, who
had been undutiful towards his father, and "was, besides, afflicted with piles!"
Murder, unfilial conduct, and hæmorrhoids were the cumulative charges on
which the Ulamas who sided with Makhdúm demanded the degradation of
the Shaikh, and in this they were successful. The leaders of these factions,
however, soon became friends again, for we find them joining in 1579 A.D. in
a document, which made the order of the Imám in all disputed questions of law
final. From 1564 to 1577 A.D., Shaikh Abdun-nabi had been Sadr of the
empire, during which time he gave much offence by his mode of treating the
holders of State lands.[1] The arbitrary execution of a Brahman led to his
deposal from office; and in 1578 Akbar gave him money for the poor of
Makka, and sent him on a pilgrimage. When he came back he was called to
account for the money, was put into prison, and there murdered in 1584 A.D.

During the reigns of Akbar's successors the district of Saháranpur was the
chosen retreat of the nobles of the court, to whom its cool and comparatively
healthy climate, and the facilities afforded for the amusement of hunting, rendered

Empress Núr Jahán.   it peculiarly attractive. The Empress Núr Jahán[2] or
Núr Mahal, the consort of Jahángír, resided for a
short time in a Gújar village to the north of the Tughlikpur parganah, where
some remains of her mansion are still visible, and her name is perpetuated in

---

[1] Blochmann Aín-i-Akbari, 185, 490 ; Elliot, V, 542.   [2] She was known as Mahr-un-nisa
Khanum whilst the widow of Sher-Afkan, and received the title of Núr Mahal on her marriage
with Jahángír, and was later called Núr Jahán.

that of the village of Núrnagar. Under Shahjahán, the celebrated Alí Mardán

Alí Mardán Khán.

Khán constructed the royal hunting seat still known as Bádsháh Mahal. It lies to the north-west of the Faizabad parganah, on the left bank of the Jumna. The palace was pleasantly situated opposite to where the Dehli canal is drawn off, and its remains are now utilised as a modern house. To the same nobleman is due the construction of the Duáb canal, now known as the Eastern Jumna Canal. This canal was conducted, with a considerable knowledge of hydraulics, along the crest of the high ground between the Jumna and the Hindan, so as to admit of its water being thrown off on both sides for irrigation purposes. From the absence of traces of bridges and lateral off-shoots, it is supposed that the great difficulty experienced in the passage of the torrents which cross the line of canal, in the upper portion of its course, led to its early abandonment. It was realigned, completed and opened in 1830.

The first important inroad of the Sikhs took place during the reign of Bahá-

The Sikhs.

dur Shah in the year 1709. Under their chief, Bandu, they poured in irresistible numbers into Sirhind, murdering, plundering, and burning wherever they came. The Imperial Governor was defeated in a pitched battle, and the Sikhs gathering strength from this, crossed the Jumna and ravaged the Upper Duáb. Though the Musalmáns were the first objects of their attack, the Sikhs were not restrained by any considerations of religion, or by any mercy for age or sex. Whole communities were massacred with wanton barbarity ; and it is said that even the bodies of the dead were dug up and thrown out to the birds and beasts of prey. The Sikhs returned the following year, when the same scenes of outrage and violence were perpetrated, so that the Emperor himself was constrained to lead a force against them in 1710 A.D., which succeeded for a time in driving the enemy into the hills. The Emperor retired to Lahor, leaving a detachment to watch the enemy and prevent their approaching the Duáb. We do not hear much of them again until 1716 A.D., when Bandu, again issuing from his retreat, spread death in every direction, and threatened the Duáb. A force was sent against him under Abd-us-Samad Khán, who captured Bandu and nearly annihilated his followers. For many years after this the Sikhs remained quiet, recruiting their shattered forces, and it was not until the almost entire absence of authority in the Upper Duáb appeared to give them the desired opportunity for repeating their incursions, that we hear of them again.

From 1712 to 1721 A.D., this district, with the neighbouring district of

The Sayyids.

Muzaffarnagar, formed part of the possessions of the Sayyid brothers of Bárha. As their family is more intimately connected with the Muzaffarnagar District, the story of their romantic career will be found in the notice of that district. They belonged to the

Tihanpuri branch of the Sayyid family settled at Jánsath. Husain Ali was assassinated in 1721 A.D., and in the same year his brother, Shaikh Abdullah, lost the battle of Husainpur. Their possessions were conferred upon Muhammad Amín Khán, who succeeded in establishing his authority in this district. He was followed by the Vazír Kumr-ud-dín, the implacable enemy of the Bárha Sáyyids. In 1737 A.D. the Vazír despatched one Marhamat Khán to the Saháranpur District, with orders to expel the Sayyids from their *jágírs*. In carrying out these orders Marhamat Khan acted with such violence, that the Sayyids rose in rebellion and slew him. This was what the Vazír most desired, and assembling an overwhelming force, he despatched it, under command of his own brother, Azimullah, who quickly overran the whole district, and utterly defeated the Sayyids at the memorable capture and sack of Jánsath.

In the reign of Muhammad Shah, the fief of Saháranpur was conferred on
        Zafar Khán, better known by his title of Roshan-ud-
Roshan-ud-daulah. daulah, and as the builder of the mosque which bears
his name in the Chándni Chauk at Dehli. This nobleman bestowed parganah Ambahta, in this district, upon Shah Muhammad Bákir, son of the famous Mír Shah Abdul Maúli, whose descendants are in possession to the present day. Shortly after the accession of Ahmad Shah, in 1748 A.D., quarrels broke out between the Vazír Safdar Jang and Shihab-ud-dín, best known by the family affix
        of Ghází-ud-dín Khán, who had succeeded his uncle
Najíb Khán. Ghazi-ud-din I. in command of the forces. Safdar
Jang sent an army under Iudargír Gosháin, which ravaged the Upper Duáb, and occupied Saháranpur itself. In the battle of Kotila, which shortly afterwards took place, Najíb Khán joined the imperial forces under Ghází-ud-dín, and so distinguished himself that he obtained parganahs Saháranpur, Búrhána, and all the Bárha villages in *jágír*. Chait Singh of Bahsuma attempted for a time to resist his authority, but before the end of 1754, Najíb Khán had reduced his new possessions to obedience. Najíb Khán then devoted all his energies to the extension and consolidation of his power, and before his death, which occurred in 1770 A.D., his *jágír* extended on the north, not only to the Siwálik hills, but across them into the Dún, which he conquered about 1757 A.D.; on the west they were bounded by the Jumna, and contained the fortress of Ghausgarh; on the east they extended into the Bijnaur District, with the fortresses of Pathargarh and Najíbabad; and on the south he held Shámli, in the Muzaffarnagar District, and the lands to the border of the present district of Meerut, which were commanded from his fort of Shukartár.

Towards the close of Najíb Khán's rule, the district suffered severely from
Zábita Khán, 1770—1785 A.D. the inroads of the Sikhs[1] on the west, and the Marhattas on the south. The latter departed for a time on

---

[1] Four distinct Sikh invasions are counted between the years 1761 and 1770.

the advance of the Afgháns under Ahmad Shah Abdali. When Zábita Khán succeeded his father, Najíb Khán, one of his first acts was to refuse the tribute due to the Emperor; and knowing that he was in disfavour with the court, then entirely under Marhatta influence, he set about collecting troops and fortifying the strong places in his district. Amongst these was Shukartár, where he awaited the attack of the royal army, and was completely defeated in 1772. The royal army then advanced through the Duáb, and took possession of Sahāranpur, and all the Rohilla forts except Ghausgarh, where Zábita's family resided; and having appointed a Governor, Shah Alam returned to Dehli. Shortly afterwards Zábita made peace with the Marhattas, and through their instrumentality received back his possessions. The year 1775 is marked by an invasion of the Sikhs, who plundered nearly every considerable town from Sahāranpur to Meerut. Zábita Khán, finding himself powerless to oppose them, took numbers of these men into his employ, and strengthening himself by an alliance with their chiefs, openly rebelled against the Emperor. Abdul Kásim Khán, sent from Dehli against Ghausgarh, was slain in the attack, and until the arrival of Najf Khán, the imperial authority was little regarded in this district. A battle took place between the forces of Najf Khán and the Sahāranpur troops near, Ghausgarh in 1777, which ended in a reconciliation, and the Rohilla chief was again pardoned and confirmed in his possessions.

The cis-Satlaj chiefs, irritated at the defection of the Rohilla, granted him little peace during the remainder of his life. He died in 1785, and was succeeded by his son Ghulám Kádir, a man of bold and determined character, and little likely to yield to his enemies without a struggle. He confiscated the *jágírs* of many of the principal men in his districts, and amongst them that of his own uncle, Afzal Khán. He then re-annexed the entire country possessed by his grandfather, which during the recent troubles had been occupied by the Sikhs, and reconquered the Dún. The Sikhs, too, were held in check, and the country, for the first time for many years, enjoyed peace under a strong Government. On his death, in 1788, the Marhattas took possession of the district, which remained with them until the British conquest. Ghani Bahádur was the first governor, and he was succeeded by Bála Rao.

In 1794 the Sikhs recommenced their inroads into the Duáb, and succeeded, not only in defeating the Marhatta garrison at Sahāranpur, but compelled them to take refuge in the fort of Jalálabad. Lakhwa Dáda, on hearing this, applied for the services of George Thomas, then an adventurer in the service of Apa Khandi Rao in Mewat, to command a force of 2,000 infantry, 200 cavalry, and sixteen pieces of artillery, raised for the protection of the Marhatta possessions in this quarter, and assigned him parganahs Pánipat, Sonpat and Karnál for their pay. Thomas remained

[margin note: Ghulám Kádir, 1785-1788.]

[margin note: George Thomas.]

there for some time and co-operated with Bápu Sindhia, who was named Governor of Saháranpur and the country adjacent, which at this time yielded a revenue of ten lakhs of rupees. Thomas distinguished himself in the reduction of Shámli, then in Gurdat Singh's *jágtr*, and in the siege of Lakhnauti ; but on the death, by suicide in the Jumna, of his patron Apa Khandi Rao he withdrew for some time to his *jágtr* in Mewat, whence he was recalled to meet the Sikhs again. Thomas defeated the Sikhs in four successive actions near Karnál, whilst Bápu Sindhia drove them from the northern parganahs of the Duáb, and even pushed his forces into their own country, which became for a time a scene of the same plunder and devastation with which they had so often laid waste the Duáb. In 1797 Thomas retired from Saháranpur to push his fortunes in Hariána.

In 1799, Sambunáth[1] a grain merchant, was the díwán of Inám Baksh Khán,

Perron.

Governor of Saháranpur, who sided with Lakhwa Dáda in his feud with Sindhia. The díwán took the field against M. Perron, the Marhatta commander of Aligarh; but his troops were corrupted by means of a large sum of money which Perron found means to distribute amongst them, and their leader was obliged to yield up a portion of the districts he held to save the rest. In the following year M. Perron left Dehli with a large force, in order to seize upon the remainder, and after a sharp action at Khátauli in the Muzaffarnagar District, was able to compel Sambunáth to leave the Duáb altogether, and take refuge with the Sikhs. As illustrative of the state of the country, the massacre of the Gosháins near Hardwár by the Sikhs in 1796 may be mentioned. In fact, the greater portion of the Upper Duáb was still divided amongst the Sikh Sirdárs, ostensibly as *jágtr*, but in reality in lieu of black mail. The only portion of the district that enjoyed even the semblance of security was the strip of country on the east, stretching from Jawálápur to Bahsúma in Meerut, in which the Gújar Raja Rámdayál Singh had assumed a semi-independent attitude.

In the year 1801, Rámdayál received the thanks of the Marhatta comman-

Ghulám Kádir, II.

der for crushing an insurrection headed by one Azáz Khán, at Bachaiti near Deoband. This adventurer gave himself out as the true Ghulám Kádir; and the failure of his attempt was in a great measure due to the treachery of the Gújars, who joined him only to have an opportunity of more effectually looting whichever side should prove

The British.

victorious. On the fall of Aligarh and the capture of Dehli in 1803, a British force, under Colonel Burn, started from Dehli for Saháranpur in October, but had hardly reached the civil station, when news arrived of a threatened Sikh invasion, which would have

---

[1] Sambunáth was our first tahsíldár at Saháranpur, and his grandson is now tahsíldár of Bágpat in the Meerut District.

been converted into a real attack but for the arrival of James Skinner with a strong detachment of irregular horse. Presently news came of Colonel Monson's disastrous retreat, and Colonel Ochterlony, finding his position at Dehli precarious, recalled the commandant of Sahâranpur, barely in time to save that city from Holkar's adopted son, Harnáth. But just as General Lake's approach raised the siege of Dehli, intelligence was received of a Marhatta inroad. General Lake in person repulsed the Marhattas, but again a Sikh invasion (the thirteenth : October, 1804)[1] took place. Sher Singh of Buriya was ravaging the district, while the Collector, Mr. Guthrie, remained shut up in the Kila Ahmadabadi, a fort built by Ghulám Kádir, and since converted into a jail. Colonel Burn marched to meet the Sikhs with Mr. Guthrie, who, having managed to escape from the fort with the assistance of the Begam Sumru, had joined the army at Khátauli. Sher Singh awaited the

Battle of Charaon.

attack at Charaon in the Kátha, where a fight, celebrated in local tradition, took place on the 24th November, 1804. The day, however, cannot be considered glorious to either side, for our irregular cavalry displayed such cowardice, that, had the Sikhs shown more determination, the event would have been very doubtful. Fortunately, the enemy dared not face our artillery, an arm with which they were not yet familiar. To this fact, Colonel Burn owed an indecisive victory. A cannon ball carried off Sher Singh's leg during the engagement, and his old uncle, Rai Singh, brought him back to die at Buriya. In spite of this lesson, the district was not yet safe. Intelligence of the fall of Díg alone prevented the Begam Sumru from turning against us, in spite of her professions of fidelity to General Lake ; and Colonel Burn had not got rid of the Sikhs. We find them overrunning the country within a month of their defeat at Charaon.

In February, 1805, Amír Khán's wild Pindáris threatened to swoop across

Amír Khán.

the Ganges opposite Muzaffarnagar, and some actually did venture over. In March, the commandant was summoned into Rohilkhand, but the moment he turned his back, the fifteenth Sikh invasion recalled him to the district. Fruitless negotiations interrupted the campaign which followed. Colonel Burn soon found it necessary to take upon himself the responsibility of breaking them off, and after resuming the last remaining Sikh jágír, Gúrdat Singh's of Jhanjhána, he forded the Jumna and attacked Karnál (April). These energetic measures brought the Sirdárs to their senses, and so ended the last Sikh invasion.

Comparative tranquillity prevailed down to the year 1813, when Raja Rámdayál Singh died, and the settlement operations con-

Disturbances of 1813.

sequent upon the resumption of his enormous estates were attended by a Gújar rising, which was happily quelled before it became

---

[1] Without including the innumerable minor incursions.

serious. In 1814, the Gúrkha war broke out, and the Dún was, after a short interval of non-regulation, annexed temporarily to Saháranpur under Regulation IV. of 1817. A full account of the new subdivision will be found in the volume devoted to the hill districts.

In the year 1824, a variety of circumstances tended to cause a rising of a far more dangerous character than that of 1813. The principal leaders of the disturbance were two Gújars : Kalwá, a famous bandit, and Biji Singh, talukadár of Kúnja near Rúrki, and a relative of Rajá Ramdayál Singh. The rendezvous of the insurgents was at the latter's fort, where they were collecting in rapidly increasing numbers, strange to say, without the knowledge of the authorities, when two daring exploits, the sack of the town of Bhagwánpur and the plunder of a strong treasure escort, bringing in a large sum of money from the Jawálápur tahsíl, led to the disclosure of their movements. Mr. Grindall, the Magistrate of Saháranpur, obtaining a reinforcement of Gúrkhas, under the command of Captain Young of the Sirmor Battalion, at once attacked them, in company with his Joint Magistrate, the Hon'ble Mr. Shore. The fight lasted all day, ending in the total discomfiture of the rebels, who lost nearly two hundred killed and wounded. Among the former were Kalwá and Biji Singh. The enterprise thus nipped in the bud was no petty undertaking of ordinary marauders. It had been planned on a grand scale, and large reinforcements were coming to Biji Singh's assistance from this as well as other districts, when the unexpected fall of Kúnja made the whole confederacy collapse.[1]

The district is happily barren in historical events from 1824 to 1857, when the mutiny[2] broke out at Meerut. Fortunately there was a man in Mr. R. Spankie, the Magistrate, who was equal to the emergency. News of the outbreak was received on the 12th of May, and on the following day the women and children were sent to the hills, and not too soon, for the day after came news of the massacre at Dehli. Extra police were raised, and the Europeans established themselves as a regular garrison in the Magistrate's house. The district soon rose; the Gújars and Rangars especially made themselves notorious for their turbulence, and when the intelligence of the disturbances in Muzaffarnagar arrived, a general outbreak took place. Ancient feuds were renewed ; village plundered village; bankers were robbed of their property, or had to pay black mail for its protection ; and in many cases debtors took advantage of the general anarchy to obtain from the money-lenders

Disturbances of 1824.

The mutiny.

---

[1] The forests under Garhwál and Kumaun were the favourite lurking-place of Kalwá and his followers. The records of the office of the Commissioner of Kumaun show that, in concert with the authorities of Moradabad, frequent and fruitless efforts were made to dislodge him.

[2] From the official narrative, by Mr. R. Spankie, C.S, now the Hon'ble R. Spankie, Judge of the High Court, Allahabad.

their account-books and bonds. Mr. Spankie writes :—" It would appear as if the disturbances in the commencement were less directed against Government than against particular people and castes. When the fall of Dehli ceased to be looked upon as imminent, the agricultural communities began to turn their eyes towards the local treasuries, and did not scruple to oppose themselves to Government officers and troops."

The local officers did their best to put down the disturbances in their earliest

Local efforts.

stage. On the 21st May, the raiders who plundered Malhaipur were punished ; and on the following day a demonstration was made along the Rúrki road as far as Nágal, which resulted in the capture of some men who had refused to pay their revenue. Affairs in the city now assumed a serious phase. The kotwál or head police officer, whilst appearing faithful, was in reality stirring up the people to disaffection. The shopkeepers shut up their shops, and, burying their valuables, prepared for the worst. Confidence was, however, restored for a time by the appearance of Mr. W. C. Plowden, with a party of cavalry and infantry under Captains Wyld and Garstin, from Jagádri. Advantage was taken of their presence to make a raid on Mánikpur, then held by one Amrao Singh, who had set himself up as Raja. The village was taken and burned, but the rebels succeeded in effecting their escape. The late Mr. H. D. Robertson, C. S., was then despatched to Deohand, which was threatened by a rising of the Rajpúts of the Kátha. In the meantime a portion of the native infantry at Saháranpur mutinied, and fired upon their officers (June, 2nd), fortunately without effect; and were it not for the opportune arrival of the Gúrkhas under Major Bagot, it would have fared ill with the small European body at Saháranpur. The Gúrkhas were next employed in dispersing a body of Gújars who had come to attack the treasury, and were again sent to meet a body of the Jalandhar mutineers, 300 strong, in the south of the district.

About this time news arrived of the plunder of Nakúr and Sarsáwa by the Gújars, and on the 9th of July the remainder of the native infantry (29th native infantry) fled from the station. Mr. Robertson did good service in the Ganges khádir, where, in conjunction with Captain Read, he defeated, at Fathúa, the Banjáras who had been committing great excesses in the more unprotected villages, and coming round by Deoband, he inflicted signal punishment on the rabble who had plundered one-third of that town (see DEOBAND). Mr. Robertson was recalled to Saháranpur to defend the city against an attack of Gújars, Kátha Rajpúts and Rangars, who, aided by the lower Musalmán population, proposed an attack upon the European quarters and the jail. The jail guard was disarmed, and the duty was handed over to the Gúrkhas, whilst forty Europeans arrived from Landour, and, with their assistance, the muharram was passed without any disturbance. The people of the towns were occasionally able to do something to protect themselves, thus the Musalmáns of Deoband made a gallant defence on two occasions against the Kátha insurgents, and the people of Kankhal repulsed the attacks of dakaits. Assistance was given to the Muzaffarnagar authorities in their attack upon Tháná Bhawan, where Mr. Lowe, C.S., was severely wounded; and after this the influence of the aid from the Ambála District, the presence of the Gúrkhas, and the energy displayed by the European officers, prevented any further real danger to the safety of the district. Still much uneasiness was caused by the raids of the rebels from Bijnaur, in one of which a police-station was burned, and some horses of the irregular cavalry were carried off. To prevent these raids, Colonel Baird Smith established a movable column, which did good service, and was fortunate enough to defeat a party of one thousand men who crossed at Mayapur below Kankhal, but were not allowed time to do any great mischief.

Mr. Spankie then commenced setting about the testing of re-measurements, in preparation for the ensuing settlement of the district; and in December, 1857, found himself able to move about the district with a slight personal guard. He writes—"The people were civil and respectful. But in point of fact there can be no confidence placed in the demeanour or bearing of the people. They would always be respectful and submissive until it is in their power to be otherwise. The people of this district, and in all other parts of the country, I, suppose, have no sympathy with Government, British or native. Separate castes and communities have separate ends and desires to attain, and the weakness of Government is their strength. Revenge and loot, in the first instance, led the agricultural communities astray. The burning of records, as in tahsíl Nakúr, was the crowning result of a determination to have no obligations towards any one. The common brotherhood of the Muhammadans is a different thing; and I think it would be impossible to deny that they were heart and soul against us. They had everything to gain and little to lose as a general rule. They were in arms against the excesses of the Gújars simply because their own time had not come. These Gújars and others were out for a temporary gain, and to make the best of the present. The moment they found their's a losing game, they stopped it; and they bow to the strong hand as long as it is strong. The Muhammadan population is ever against us." The kotwal of Sahásanpur and the múnsif of Shámli (both Musalmáns) were executed, and, on the whole, exceedingly severe and wholesome punishment was awarded, which, "with the eclipse of the Sudder Court," and thus the prevention of the escape of offenders by appeal to the higher courts, rendered the safety of the district secure. There was never much loss of the Government revenue, and agricultural operations went on much as usual; and though in the Rúrki tahsíl, the Raos (Musalmáns)

Mr. Spankie's opinions.

of Jawálapur and other Muhammadans came under grave suspicion, the disarmament of the inhabitants of Kankhal, Hardwár and Jawálapur removed all cause for uneasiness. On the whole, the wild country in the south of the Jawálapur parganah, the khádirs of the great rivers, the tracts near the Kátha, and the villages lying amid the Gújar colonies, suffered most; and the principal disturbers of the peace were the Gújars, Musalmán Rajpúts, Pundír Rajpúts of the Kátha, Banjáras, and the low Musalmán population of the towns. Since January, 1858, the district has returned to its normal state, and all matters pertaining to its history belong to the different heads under which the district notice has been distributed.

A general sketch of the sanitary operations in this district is given in the introduction. Fever and small-pox are the principal diseases. Fever is especially rife, and belongs to that class known as malarious. Fever epidemics have periodically occurred all over this tract from time immemorial. Over-saturation of the soil combined with bad drainage, is the principal cause of the fever, but to this may be added the drainage of refuse water into the many excavations which are found around every village site, and the great heat that is always present. In 1871 a large amount of quinine was imported from England and a staff of four hospital assistants were sent to travel through the fever-stricken portions of the district and attend the sick at their homes. Over 5,000 cases were treated, but with what result is not known.

The following statement gives the mortuary statistics from 1867 to 1873:—

Year.	Fever.	Small-pox.	Bowel complaint.	Cholera.	Other causes.	Total.	Percentage of deaths to 1,000 of the population.
1867	5,853	1,136	731	887	4,845	13,452	15·5
1868	7,210	3,174	792	138	4,886	16,200	18·6
1869	11,189	1,106	894	182	4,928	18,299	21·1
1870	19,906	1,977	...	113	7,048	29,044	33·51
1871	21,164	4,441	2,385	164	1,712	29,886	34·46
1872	14,839	5,296	2,569	1,351	2,160	26,215	29·74
1873	12,174	3,811	2,137	45	2,691	21,058	23·61

GAZETTEER

OF THE

SAHÁRANPUR DISTRICT.

—

CONTENTS.

—

—

AMBAHTA, or Anbahtah, a town in parganah Nakúr of the Saháranpur district, is distant 16 miles south-west of the town of Saháranpur. The population in 1853 numbered 6,311 souls, and in 1865 was 6,336. In 1872 there were 6,039 inhabitants, of whom 2,767 were Hindús (1,298 females), and 3,272 were Musalmáns (1,722 females). The town site contains 55 acres, giving 110 inhabitants per square acre. Ambahta contains 16 muhallas or wards, amongst which the houses are distributed. There are many good brick-built houses in the town, and the bazár consists of a double roadway, with a centre line of poor-looking shops. The roadways are well made and well drained of late years, and are in places paved with bricks. Gardens and clumps of mango trees make the suburbs look well-wooded. The site as a whole is well raised, so that drainage flows easily away towards the south-east, and there are few places where excessive rainfall can accumulate. The soil is light and porous ; water in the wells is good, and is found at a depth of twenty-four feet from the surface. The Pírzádah family of Sayyids of Ambahta are well known throughout this district. Their ancestors came from Makka some 300 years ago. Shah Abul Maáli, a celebrated personage in the seventeenth century, and belonging to this family, is buried here. The family still hold several revenue-free grants, and one representative resides in the fort, and another near the Shah's tomb. The tomb is a fine domed building with minarets, all in good repair, and situated in the middle of the town. It is the object of a yearly urs to the devout Muhammadans of the district. Ambahta was originally a cantonment for Mughal troops, established by Fírúz Shah; hence the place was known as Firúzabad. The present town is comparatively modern, and contains two masjids built in Humayún's reign. Act XX. of 1856 (the Chaukídárí Act) is in force, and in 1873 supported a village police numbering 13 men, at an annual cost of Rs. 720, defrayed from a housetax. A staff of 13 public sweepers is also enteratained for conservancy purposes. The total income was Rs. 2,456, falling at Re. 0-6-3 per head of the population. Considerable attention to conservancy matters has been shown here of late years, and the only great sickness occurred in 1870, when 730 persons died from fever. The town possesses an outpost of police, a branch post-office, and a well-kept village school. The Musalmáns of this town were suspected of exciting disturbances during the mutiny.

AMBAHTA, an old parganah of the Saháranpur district, is mentioned in the Aín-i-Akbari. It has always been held free of revenue since the British occupation, and of late years has been included in parganah Nakúr.

BAHAT, an old parganah or fiscal sub-division of the Saháranpur district, known in Akbar's time as Bahat Kanjáwar. In the time of Shahjahán the name was changed to Sultánpur Bahat. The village of Kanjáwar is now in Muzaffarabad. Bahat and Sultánpur became separate parganahs under the Rohillas in the last century, and remained separate up to 1842, when several changes took place. The land revenue of Bahat, as it stood in 1840-41, was Rs. 35,556, and of this Rs. 3,639 were transferred, and Rs. 8,976 received in exchange, leaving the revenue at Rs. 40,893. In 1855 the changes made resulted in the absorption of Bahat amongst the neighbouring parganahs. It then contained 91 villages, with an area of 64,918 acres, a land revenue of

Rs. 46,222, and a population numbering 33,980 souls. These were distributed as follows :—

To parganah.	Number of villages.	Area in acres.	Revenue.	Population.	To parganah.	Number of villages.	Area.	Revenue.	Population.
			Rs.					Rs.	
Faizabad ...	25	14,931	14,163	10,598	Sultánpur ...	1	357	285	93
Muzaffarabad, ...	57	44,254	25,557	19,545	Haraura ...	1	644	750	426
Sahâranpur, ...	7	4,732	5,466	3,318	Total ...	91	64,918	46,221	33,980

BHAGWÁNPUR, the chief town of the parganah of the same name in the Sahâranpur district, is distant 18 miles from Sahâranpur and 6½ miles north-west from Rúrki, on the Sahâranpur and Rúrki road. The population in 1872 numbered 2,412 souls. Bhagwánpur is said to have been founded in 1118 sanvat (1061 A.D.) by a colony of Rajpúts and Brahmans. It has a second class police-station, a branch post-office, and a village school. Act XX. of 1856 (the Chaukídári Act) is in force, and in 1873 supported a force of eight men, at an annual cost of Rs. 432, defrayed from a house-tax. The total income for 1872-73 amounted to Rs. 1,118, giving an incidence of Re. 0-7-4 per head of the population and Rs. 2-2-0 per house. Bhagwánpur, though the head of a parganah, is merely a small agricultural village, without any trade or manufacture, and only a good sized market to supply the local wants.

BHAGWÁNPUR, a parganah in tahsíl Rúrkí of the Sahâranpur district, is bounded on the north by the Siwálik (Shiwálak) hills; on the west by parganahs Haraura, Nágal and Muzaffarabad; on the east by parganah Rúrkí; and on the south by parganah Manglaur. According to the census of 1872, parganah Bhagwánpur had a total area of 244 square miles, of which 95 square miles were under cultivation. The area assessed to Government revenue during the same year was 147 square miles, of which 95 square miles were cultivated, 36 square miles were culturable, and 16 square miles were barren. This parganah naturally divides into four tracts. The first tract comprises the villages in the southern uplands owned by a mixed proprietary of Gújars, Gárás, Tagas, Mahájans, Brahmans, Rajpúts, &c. It is, on the whole, tolerably level, and includes the sources of the Káli Nádí, with less inferior land and less bhúda soil than in the corresponding tract in the adjoining parganah of Nágal. Water is found at a depth of about eleven feet from the surface; but, owing to the quicksand in the sub-soil, earthen wells are for the most part impracticable. The people, from over-assessment under the old settlement, could not afford to construct brick-built wells, hence there is

Area.

Natural divisions.

but little irrigation, and even, in places, an insufficiency of water for domestic purposes. The sub-soil is retentive of moisture, and if this were not the case, large tracts must remain uncultivated in seasons of drought. The people here suffered much during the famine of 1860. The second tract includes the villages having mixed uplands and lowlands. The villages immediately on the bank of the Soláni are very poor, and constantly exposed to diluvion by inundation. Those further north grow good kharíf corps and sugar-cane. Here the lands of a few villages on the bank above are poor, but the surface almost at once begins to slope towards the head of the Kálí river, and the soil there is very good. Water is 23 feet from the surface, but earthen wells only last a year and a half, so that irrigation is scanty.

The lowland villages occupying the valley of the Soláni, between Kheri and Sakrauda on the north and the highlands on the south, form the third tract. The valley is narrow towards the north, but opens up towards the south-east. The soil to the north consists of a rich loam, which changes into a rich clay to the south-east; both are good and productive, but the agricultural condition of the several villages varies very much. From Fatehullahpur, near the Mohand Pass, down to Sodíwála, opposite Kheri, the cultivation is scanty, and interspersed amid patches of grass jungle. The Rángar proprietors reside in a mass at Kheri. They formerly owned a large extent of land in this parganah, but owing to their indolence and jealousies many villages were taken from them in 1836, and settled with the resident cultivators. Since then the Rángars have lost much more by private and public sale. On the south-east, where the Sakrauda Rángars are the proprietors, the villages are better off, though the Rángars, as a rule, make hard and exacting landlords. The Powell family, also, have some villages here. In the north, spring crops form the staple; in the centre, autumn crops; and to the south, rice. Irrigation is nowhere necessary. The last tract includes the lands lying on the plateau of Kheri and Sakrauda, which consists of an infinity of mounds and hillocks, separated from each other by ravines with sloping sides covered with brush-wood. On the Kheri side there is some fair timber, but towards Sakrauda the carissa (karaunda) prevails. Mr. Powell reclaimed and brought under cultivation the uplands of two villages, but on the whole there is much waste here. Water is as deep as 36 to 38 feet from the surface, but this is partially counterbalanced by the abundant rain-fall, which gives good bájra and joár crops, and in the small khádir patches wheat is grown.

The last year of Mr. E. Thornton's settlement gave a land revenue amount-

Land revenue.

ing to Rs. 81,456; this was increased by Mr. Vans-Agnew to Rs. 82,063; and Mr. Wynne, on revising the proceedings of Mr. VansAgnew, proposed a land revenue of Rs. 81,863 on an area then comprising 81,678 acres, of which 71,249 acres were assessed to the land revenue, and of these 52,875 acres were under cultivation. The actual land revenue for 1872 amounted to Rs. 79,653 (or with cesses, Rs. 87,598), falling at a rate of Re. 0-8-2 per British acre on the total area ; at Re. 0-13-7 per acre on the area assessed to Government revenue ; and at Re. 1-5-0 per acre on the cultivated area. The sum paid by cultivators to the landowners as rent and cesses during the same year has been estimated at Rs. 1,26,659.

Between the years 1839-40 and 1859-60, five whole villages and 60 portions

Alienations.

of villages, having an area of 8,217 acres, and paying a revenue of Rs. 9,332, and valued at Rs. 52,752, were transferred by private arrangement in this parganah. The transfers by decree of Court comprised one entire village and 61 portions of villages, having an aggregate area of 7,687 acres, and paying a revenue of Rs. 8,196. The value recorded was Rs. 28,495. Out of the 33 whole and 77 portions of villages remaining with the original proprietors, 1,465 acres, bearing a revenue of Rs. 856, valued at Rs. 6,226, of the former, and 4,776 acres, bearing a revenue of Rs. 4,971, valued at Rs. 34,234, of the latter, were under mortgage. These statistics give a percentage of private transfers to the total area of ten per cent., of transfers by decree of Court amounting to nine per cent., and of transfers by mortgage amounting to eight per cent. The average value per acre in each of these cases was Rs. 6-6-8, Rs. 3-11-3, and Rs. 6-7-0, and the land revenue assessed amounted to Re. 1-2-2, Re. 1-1, and Re. 0-15 per acre respectively. The result from the entire parganah on 27 per cent. of the total area, gives an average value of Rs. 5-8-0 per acre, when the average land revenue amounted to Rs. 1-1 per acre. Gújars lost three whole villages, and Shaikhs, Pathán and Rajpúts lost one each.

According to the census of 1872 parganah Bhagwánpur contained 143

Population.

inhabited villages, of which 62 had less than 200 inhabitants ; 37 had between 200 and 500 ; 26 had between 500 and 1,000 ; 15 had between 1,000 and 2,000 ; three had between 2,000 and 3,000. The records show that there were 131 estates at settlement, of which fourteen were jungle grants. The total population in 1872 numbered 63,770 souls (28,778 females), giving 261 to the square mile. Classified according to religion, there were 42,074 Hindús, of whom 18,790 were females ; and 21,696 Musalmáns, amongst whom 9,988 were females. Distributing the Hindu population amongst the four great classes, the census shows 2,667 Brahmans, of whom 1,257 were females ; 900 Rajpúts, including 377 females ; 1,839 Baniyas (815 females) ; whilst the great mass of the population is included in " the other castes" of the census returns, which show a total of 36,668 souls, of whom 16,341 are females. The principal Brahman subdivisions found in this parganah are the Gaur (2,452) and Acháraj. The Rajpúts belong to the

Pundír, Khági and Maudhar clans, and the Baniyas to the Agarwál (1,099), and Saraugi subdivisions. The other castes containing more than one thousand members are the Kahár (2,507), Chamár (13,166), Khákrob (1,442), Gújar (2,901), Barhai (1,177), Sainí (4,291), Taga (1,892), and Banjára (1,679). The Musalmáns are distributed amongst Shaikhs (607), converted Pundírs (107), converted Chauháns (49), other converted Rajpúts (1,483), and Patháns (271) ; the remainder are entered without distinction. The principal land-holders are Musalmán Rángars and Mahájans in the north, and those already mentioned in the first tract on the south.

The occupations of the people are shown in the statistics collected at the

Occupations.

census of 1872. From these it appears that of the male adult population (not less than fifteen years of age) 536 are employed in professional avocations, such as Government servants, priests, doctors, and the like ; 2,244 in domestic service, as personal servants, water-carriers, barbers, sweepers, washermen, &c. ; 1,019 in commerce, in buying, selling, keeping or lending money or goods, or the conveyance of men, animals, or goods ; 8,601 in agricultural operations ; 3,257 in industrial occupations, arts and mechanics, and the preparation of all classes of substances, vegetable, mineral, and animal. There were 4,832 persons returned as labourers, and 727 as of no specified occupation. Taking the total population, irrespective of age or sex, the same returns give 742 as landholders, 23,024 as cultivators, and 40,004 as engaged in occupations unconnected with agriculture. The educational statistics, which are confessedly imperfect, show 270 males as able to read and write out of a total male population numbering 34,992 souls.

Bhagwánpur was formed in 1855, by Messrs. Craigie and Ross, from the parganahs mentioned below :—

Parganah.	Villages.	Area in acres.	Revenue.	Population.	Parganah.	Villages.	Area in acres.	Revenue.	Population.
			Rs.					Rs.	
Rúrki ...	69	43,208	56,803	35,066	Jaurási ...	22	25,624	9,461	5,362
Manglaur ...	19	4,754	9,715	4,601	Deoband ...	1	110	200	113
Muzaffarabad	17	18,274	7,490	6,939	Total ...	128	93,970	83,669	52,081

CHAUSAT KHERI, or Chaunsat Kheri, an old parganah of the Saháranpur district, consisted of villages scattered amongst parganahs Tháná Bhawan, Gangoh and Núnauta, and was absorbed amongst them in 1842. It then gave a land revenue of Rs. 20,579 per annum. Fourteen of the villages were at the same time transferred to the Muzaffarnagar district, and divided amongst the parganahs of Jhanjhána, Charthával, Bidauli, Kairána and Thána Bhawan.

CHILKÁNA, a town in parganah Sultánpur of the Saháranpur district, is distant nine miles north-west from Saháranpur. The population in 1872 numbered 4,026 souls. Chilkána is situated on the road between Saháranpur and Umballa (Ambála), and possesses a second class police-station and a post-office. The principal inhabitants are some decayed families of Sayyids. The town is united with Sultánpur for the purposes of the Chaukídári Act (XX. of 1856), and together they support a force of 16 men, at an annual cost of Rs. 882. The income from all sources during 1872-73 was Rs. 3,398, giving an incidence of Re. 0-7-1 per head of the population, and Re. 1-12-3 per house. During the same year one-third of the income was expended in drainage cuts and repairs to roads. From its position on the old high road to the Panjáb, Chilkána is of some strategical importance as a military post and under the Marhattas was held by the troops of the Begam Sumru. In 1857 it was occupied by a body of plundering Gújars, who were dispersed by the arrival of a force from Jagádri.

DEOBAND, the chief town of the parganah of the same name in the Saháranpur district, is distant 21 miles south from Saháranpur in latitude 29° 41′ 50,″ and longtitude 77° 43′ 10″.

Population.

The population in 1847 was 11,634; in 1853 there were 18,638 inhabitants; and in 1865, 21,714. In 1872, out of a total population numbering 19,168 souls, 8,614 were Hindús (4,026 females); 10,554 were Musalmáns (5,059 females); and there was one Christian. Distributing the population amongst the urban and rural classes proper, there were 166 landholders, 2,047 cultivators, and 16,965 persons unconnected with agriculture. The number of enclosures in 1872 was 1,730, of which 688 were occupied by Hindús and 1,042 by Musalmáns. The number of houses in the same year was 4,079, of which 1,264 were built with skilled labour, and of these 725 were inhabited by Hindús and 539 by Musalmáns. Of the 2,815 mud huts in the town, 1,137 were possessed by Hindús and 1,678 by Musalmáns. The area of the town site is 193 acres, giving 99 inhabitants to the acre. Taking the male adult population (not less than fifteen years of age), we find the following occupations pursued by more than fifty males :—Barbers 138 ; beggars, 209 ; bricklayers, 54 ; calico-printers, 65 ; cultivators, 716 ; labourers, 1,223 ; landowners, 63 ; merchants, 311 ; money-lenders, 112 ; oil-makers, 227 ; parohits, 201 ; servants, 749 ; shop-keepers, 775 ; sweepers, 67 ; tailors, 55 ; water-carriers, 128 ; and weavers, 820.

The site lies about two and a half miles to the west of the East Káli Nadí, with which it was formerly connected by a wide natural water-way or depression known as the Jor, which runs from the south of the town eastwards. About half a mile from the town, the Jor

Site.

spreads out into a tank-like expanse, known as the Dévikund, the west and north banks of which are covered with temples, ghâts and numerous *sati* monuments, much frequented by pilgrims. There are numerous water-holes, for the flood-water of which there is no outlet and consequently there is much flooding during the rains. A scheme for draining the outskirts is now under consideration. There are four bázárs—the Chota, Bará, Sathattar and Bahra—all of which appear to be prosperous and cleanly, except the last, which contains many ruinous houses and open places used as receptacles for refuse. There are no metalled road-ways, except that leading to the railway-station, but the bázár roads are well made of earth, with side drains; the smaller ways, too, have been much improved of late years. The water in the principal well stood at 35 feet from the surface in March, the average depth being 27 feet. The people say that the average spring level has risen from 34 feet since the introduction of the canal, though there is no canal irrigation nearer than eight miles. The water in some wells has a good sweet taste, but in others is brackish. On the whole, the site is well raised, and has good drainage towards the south, and little remains to be done in the way of sanitation beyond the utilization of existing means and the enforcement of cleanliness.

The Musalmáns here are numerous and influential and are owners of the town site, in which there are now about 1,800 sharers. All these men prefer to live on the miserable pittance they receive than to follow any occupation. There are 42 masjids in the town, and a good private school, where 180 boys are taught the Koran, and Arabic and Persian. Amongst these, forty poor scholars are supported by the Muhammadan residents. Deoband is, however, essentially a Hindu town, and has an antiquity which may extend to 3,000 years. It is said that the Pandávas resided here during their first exile, and the Musalmáns assert that it was one of the first fortresses taken by the celebrated hero Sipáh Salár Masaúd Gházi. Its orignal name was Deviban or the "sacred forest," and there is still a grove near the city in which there is a temple to Devi, where a religious assembly is held yearly in the month of Chait. Deoband lies on the military route from Meerut to Landour. It is 15½ miles from the previous stage (Muzaffarnagar), and 11½ miles from the next stage (Nágal). The encamping-ground here is good. The road from Muzaffarnagar is metalled for five miles, afterwards heavy ; you leave the road to Rúrki (distant 28 miles) at four miles, and cross the Káli Nadi by a bridge at five miles. From Deoband to Nágal the road is rather heavy, and passes Saisana at 7½ miles, and Barsora at 9½ miles (see NÁGAL, MUZAFFARNAGAR). Deoband possesses a good dispensary, Anglo-vernacular school, a first class police-station, a tahsíli and a post-office. The municipality is managed by a com-

Municipality.

mittee of 15 members, of whom four hold office *ex-officio*, three are nominated by the executive authority, and eight are elected by the tax-payers. The following statements give the income and expenditure for a series of years, and at the same time indicate the character of the local trade and the incidence of taxation. In 1872-73 taxation fell at 8¼ annas per head of the population per annum :—

Statement showing Receipts and Expenditure of the Deoband Municipality for the years 1868-69 to 1872-73.

Receipts.	1868-69.	1869-70.	1870-71.	1871-72.	1872-73.	Expenditure.	1868-69.	1869-70.	1870-71.	1871-72.	1872-73.
Opening Balance ...	...	...	...	...	738	Collection ...	750	2,342	1,058	1,226	1,461
Octroi. Class I.—Food and drink ...	No details.	No details.	2,607	1,832	3,369	Head-office ...	...	...	...	...	78
„ II.—Animals for slaughter ...			10	34	46	a. Original works ...	104	...	...	155	1,189
„ III.—Fuel,&c.,			219	239	288	b. Supervision ...	...	157	...	...	...
„ IV.—Building materials ...			101	136	303	c. Repairs, &c. ...	137	601	151	306	487
„ V.—Drugs, spices ...			192	311	250	Police ...	1,515	3,036	3,044	3,138	3,174
„ VI.—Tobacco,			135	127	198	Education ...	...	...	...	...	123
„ VII.—Textile fabrics			131	1,246	954	Conservancy ...	162	...	1,122	974	1,386
„ VIII.—Metals ...			45	127	162	Charitable grants, ...	...	...	...	...	40
Total of Octroi ...	2,759	5,801	3,440	4,050	5,567	Repayment of loans ...	...	...	188	418	...
Miscellaneous ...	56	896	1,937	2,924	4,906	Road watering ... Other items ...	... 147	... 149	... 282	20 37	20 107
Total ...	2,815	6,697	5,377	6,974	11,211		2,815	6,887	5,825	6,303	8,065

The following statement shows the quantity or value of the principal imports in 1872-73, with the estimated consumption per head of the population :—

Imports.

Articles.	Weight in maunds.	Value.	Mr. Jenkinson's estimate of actual consumption per head.	Actual incidence of dutiable articles, 1871-72.	Actual incidence of dutiable articles in 1872-73.	Actual incidence of dutiable articles in maunds for 1872-73.
		Rs.	Mds. s. c.	Rs. a. p.	Rs. a. p.	Mds. s. c.
Grain and flour ...	54,790	89,102	6 0 0	4 1 3	4 9 5	2 33 0
Sugar (khand) ...	361	4,579		0 2 1	0 3 9	0 0 12
Coarse sugar ...	1,441	30,316	} 0 11 8 {	0 4 4	1 9 0	0 2 15
Gúr	216	913		0 8 0	0 0 9	0 0 7
Shíra	146	335		0 0 1	0 0 3	0 0 4
Ghí	443	10,423	0 3 0	0 9 1	0 8 7	0 0 14
Oil	53	585	0 4 0	0 0 5	0 0 5	0 0 2
Oil seeds ...	3,691	14,387	...	0 12 0	0 11 10	0 7 9
Tobacco ...	1,534	5,872	0 10 0	0 5 2	0 4 10	0 3 2
			Rs. a. p.			
Drugs and spices ...	...	10,683	0 12 0	0 11 4	0 8 10	0 1 13
European and native cloth.	...	60,890	} 5 0 0 {	4 2 5	3 4 3	...
Other cloth ...	...	2,458				
Metals	295	17,709	1 0 0	0 6 10	0 14 7	0 0 9

In compiling his estimate, Mr. Jenkinson divided the population into three classes : the first class, comprising 3,000 members, were well off; the second class had an equal number; and the third, or poor, numbered 13,000. From local inquiry he ascertained the consumption and expenditure of each class, and from the totals of the three classes struck averages per head for the whole population. Deoband is a poor town, and in framing the rates of consumption, cannot be compared with Saháranpur; accordingly the estimate is below the average of these Provinces, and the actual averages show that there must be an immense amount of smuggling. The revenue from the octroi in 1873-74 amounted to over Rs. 12,000, which will admit of the abolition of the existing house-tax. The only export of grain is to the neighbouring villages. Refined sugar and oil are exported, and a fine species of *gárá* cloth is manufactured, to the value of about Rs. 26,000.

Early in May, 1857, the villagers in the neighbourhood of Deoband attacked the town and plundered portions of it. Mr. H. D. Robertson, with a small force, proceeded to Deoband, and, after some resistance, succeeded in capturing and burning the villages of Bábupur, Fatehpur and Sampla Bakál, which had harboured and joined with a party of dakaits in plundering along the high road. Again, in August, the town was attacked by a number of dakaits, assisted by the inhabitants of certain villages in the neighbourhood of Púr in the Muzaffarnagar district, who succeeded in plundering the quarters inhabited by the Mahájans and Baniyas. The attack had been systematically conducted; certain villages confining their operations to certain quarters, but the resistance was equally determined. The quarters inhabited by the Chamárs, Gújars, and Musalmáns were untouched, though on the outskirts and undefended, and " it might be suspected that these parties had some interest in the attack." The villages of Chota Sampla, Saláhpur, Banhera, Dukhchára and Mánki were punished for their complicity in this attack. Several parties of Gújars, discovered with plunder in their possession, were seized and punished, and, this, with the exemplary defeat bestowed upon the Banjáras to the north, succeeded in freeing the town from any further alarm during the remainder of the disturbances.

The mutiny.

DEOBAND, a parganah of tahsíl Deoband in the Saháranpur district, is bounded on the west by the Rámpur parganah; on the east by Manglaur and the Muzaffarnagar district; on the north by Manglaur and Nágal; and on the south by the Muzaffarnagar district. According to the census of 1872, this parganah had then a total area of 136 square miles, of which 114 square miles were under cultivation. The area assessed to Government revenue during the same year was 129 square miles, of which 110 square miles were cultivated, 8 square miles were culturable, and 11 square miles were barren. The parganah consists of a tract west of the Hindan,

Area.

a large and high plateau between it and the Káli Nadí, the duáb between the

Natural divisions. two heads of the Káli Nadí, and a narrow strip east of that stream. The first tract comprises a portion of the old Kátia parganah, and is inhabited by the same clan of Pundír Rajpúts that is found in the remainder of the Kátha now included in Rámpur. It is drained by the depression that first gives birth to a rivulet at Umri, in the Rámpur parganah, and thence runs southwards through this group of villages. The soil is good, and yields good crops of *kusum* (safflower) and wheat. The villages lying on either side of the Hindan are also owned by Pundír Rajpúts of the Kátha. The higher lands here are poor and sandy, especially along the left bank, whilst those in the *khádir*, though better, are inferior to lands similarly situated in Nágal. No less than twenty-seven per cent. of the cultivated area is *bhúda*, or soil of the very worst description, and only eight and-a-half per cent. was irrigated at settlement. The subsoil is bad; earthen wells seldom last more than two seasons, and are nearly all situated in the *khádir*. In the uplands the water is found at a depth of twenty feet from the surface. The villages on the high central plateau between the Hindan and the Káli possess a light soil, which is fertile when irrigated, but there is little irrigation. Though the water is only twenty feet from the surface, there are few earthen wells or traces of them. On the west, just above the Káli Nadí and near the bed of the stream, there is a strip of the worst soil, *bhúda*. The population is very thin, and there is little chance of canal irrigation being extended to this tract, so that it must always remain somewhat backward. The villages about Deoband, comprising an area of about 7,600 acres, are very prosperous, with a good rich soil and a fair amount of irrigation. The last group contains the villages lying between the Káli and the Síla and a strip of land to the east of the latter. Near the banks of these streams the soil is a very low *bhúda* of the worst description, and the surface is so uneven that no moisture remains. Further inland the surface is quite level and the soil is good. Where irrigated by the canal, excellent crops of sugar-cane and wheat are produced. The water in the centre of this tract is seldom less than twenty-one feet from the surface. The principal landholders are cultivating communities of Gárás and Tagas.

The last year of the old settlement effected by Mr. E. Thornton showed a

Land revenue. land revenue amounting to Rs. 1,01,679. This was increased to Rs. 1,02,827 by Mr. VansAgnew, and Mr. Wynne, on revising the settlement, fixed the assessment at Rs. 1,03,018, on a total area of 82,012 acres, of which 73,457 acres were assessed to Government revenue; and of these, 67,222 acres were actually under cultivation at the time of settlement. The land revenue for 1872 amounted to Rs. 94,452 (or with cesses, Rs. 1,04,527), falling at a rate of Re. 1-1-4 per British acre on the total area; at Re. 1-2-4 per acre on the area assessed to Government revenue; and at Re. 1-4-9 per acre on the cultivated area. The sum paid by cultivators to the landowners as rent and cesses during the same year has been estimated at Rs. 1,49,853.

Between the years 1839-40 and 1859-60, two whole villages and 38 portions

Alienations.

of villages, having an area of 3,235 acres, and paying a revenue of Rs. 5,308, and valued at Rs. 37,850, were transferred by private arrangement in this parganah. The transfers by decree of Court comprised one entire village and 72 portions of villages, having an aggregate area of 4,595 acres, and paying a revenue of Rs. 7,007. The value recorded was Rs. 24,672. Out of the 25 whole and 89 portions of villages remaining with the original proprietors, 209 acres, bearing a revenue of Rs. 340, valued at Rs. 2,925, of the former, and 2,504 acres, bearing a revenue of Rs. 3,483, valued at Rs. 21,845, of the latter, were under mortgage. These statistics give a percentage of private transfers to the total area of four per cent., of transfers by decree of Court amounting to five per cent., and of transfers by mortgage amounting to three per cent. The average value per acre in each of these cases was Rs. 11-11-0, Rs. 5-6-0 and Rs. 9-2-0, and the land revenue assessed amounted to Re. 1-10-3, Re. 1-8-0, and Re. 1-6-0 per acre, respectively. The result from the entire parganah on twelve per cent. of the total area gives an average value of Rs. 8-4-0 per acre when the average land revenue amounted to Re. 1-8 per acre. The principal losers were Hindu Rajpúts, Tagas and Gújars.

According to the census of 1872, parganah Deoband contained 85 inhabited

Population.

villages, of which 20 had less than 200 inhabitants; 29 had between 200 and 500; 20 had between 500 and 1,000; 12 had between 1,000 and 2,000; and three had between 2,000 and 3,000. The only town containing more than 5,000 inhabitants is Deoband. The settlement records show that there are 124 estates in the parganah, of which nine are held free of revenue in perpetuity. The total population in 1872 numbered 69,430 souls (30,458 females), giving 511 to the square mile. Classified according to religion, there were 47,598 Hindús, of whom 20,183 were females; 21,831 Musalmáns, amongst whom 10,275 were females; and there was one Christian. Distributing the Hindu population amongst the four great classes, the census shows 4,212 Brahmans, of whom 1,887 were females; 8,244 Rajpúts, including 2,938 females; 3,016 Baniyas (1,360 females); whilst the great mass of the population is included in "the other castes" of the census returns, which shows a total of 32,121 souls, of whom 13,998 are females. The principal Brahman subdivisions found in this parganah are the Gaur (3,568), Acháraj, Sanádh and Dakaut. The Rajpúts belong to the Pundír (7,271), Khági (261), Gahlot, Narauliya, Gaur and Jaiswar clans. The Baniyas are chiefly Agarwáls (2,890) and Gátás. The other castes are for the most part the same as those noticed under the Rámpur parganah. The following show more than one thousand members :—Kumhárs (1,015), Kahárs (2,996), Chamárs (8,537), Khákrobs (2,202), Gújars (1,678), Barhais (1,311), and Saínís (2,213). The Musalmáns are very numerous, and have been classified under Shaikhs (2,347), converted Pundírs (479), Chauháns and other Rajpúts (589), and Patháns (1,400); the remainder have been entered without distinction. The principal landholders are Tagas, both Musalmán and Hindu; Mahájans; Gárás; Rajpúts, both Musalmán and Hindu; Musalmán Gújars, and Shaikhs.

The occupations of the people are shown in the statistics collected at the census of 1872. From these it appears that of the male adult population (not less than fifteen years of age) 726 are employed in professional avocations, such as Government servants, priests, doctors, and the like; 3,425 in domestic service, as personal servants, water-carriers, barbers, sweepers, washermen, &c.; 1,761 in commerce, in buying, selling, keeping or lending money or goods, or the conveyance of men, animals, or goods; 10,691 in agricultural operations; 3,921 in industrial occupations, arts and mechanics, and the preparation of all classes of substances, vegetable, mineral, and animal. There were 3,382 persons returned as labourers and 661 as of no specified occupation. Taking the total population, irrespective of age or sex, the same returns give 13,544 as landholders, 12,578 as cultivators, and 43,308 as engaged in occupations unconnected with agriculture. The educational statistics, which are confessedly imperfect, show 158 males as able to read and write out of a total male population numbering 38,972 souls.

Deoband is one of the old Akbari parganahs, and was the head of a *dastúr*, from which the Kátha parganah was separated in the time of Najíb Khán. The highest land revenue of the last year of the settlement previous to that made under Regulation VII. of 1822, amounted to Rs. 1,54,576. In 1841-42 it lost Rs. 28,157 by transfers, and gained Rs. 34,205, leaving the land revenue at Rs. 1,72,038. Eleven villages were transferred to the neighbouring district of Muzaffarnagar, and four villages were received in exchange. In 1855 extensive transfers again took place which are shown in the following table :—

Parganah.	Villages.	Area.	Land revenue.	Population.	Parganah.	Villages.	Area.	Land revenue.	Population.
			Rs.					Rs.	
Transferred to					Received from				
Nágal ...	113	72,365	94,069	48,713	Kátha ...	20	21,349	24,280	15,543
Rámpur ...	1	303	365	311	Rámpur ...	3	1,583	2,070	1,369
Haraura ...	21	11,334	14,500	8,107	Balance remaining.	121	87,889	1,00,199	68,683
Manglaur ...	2	765	785	226					
Bhagwánpur.	1	110	20	113					

DEOBAND, a tahsíl in the Saháranpur district, comprises the parganahs of Deoband, Rámpur, and Nágal. The total area, according to the census of 1872, is 387 square miles, of which 314 square miles are cultivated. The area assessed to Government revenue is given at 374 square miles, of which 307 square miles are cultivated, 34 square miles are culturable, and 33 square miles are barren. The land revenue during the same year stood at Rs. 3,02,057 (or with cesses, Rs. 3,33,563), falling at Re. 1-3-6 per acre on the total area, Re. 1-4-2 per acre on the area assessed to Government revenue, and Re. 1-8-1 on the cultivated area. The population numbered 198,693 souls (88,335 females), giving 513 to the square mile, distributed amongst 310 villages. The same statistics show 35 persons blind and one leper in the tahsíl. This tahsíl stretches along the border of the Muzaffarnagar district, and may be described as a series of duábs between the Kátha, the Krishni, the Hindan and the different heads of the West Káli Nadí. All other matters connected with this tahsíl will be found under the district notice, or separately under each parganah.

DHULÁPRA JHÍL is a natural reservoir of water in parganah Sarsáwa of the Saháranpur district. In connection with the drainage arrangements of the Eastern Jumna Canal, a cut was made between the Kumhárhera jhíl and the Dhulápra jhíl for the purposes of drainage. This cut starts from the right bank of the canal, within a few yards of the Jaráoli bridge. The alignment has a direction generally a few degrees north of west. After passing the Jaráoli *rájbaha* at the 80th chain, the cut enters the Kumhárhera jhíl (chain 110), and follows the jhíl for about 50 chains. It then crosses the Pilkhani (chain 210) *rájbaha*. and enters the Dhulápra jhíl (chain 290.). It runs down the jhíl for about 20 chains, and enters the khádir under the village of Agwánhera (chain 410), and tails into the Sarsáwa Nadí (chain 560) after a course of a little under 10½ miles. From its entrance into the Kumhárhera jhíl to its exit from the Dhulápra jhíl, the cut runs through low lands, the cutting seldom exceeding 2·5 feet. Beyond the latter jhíl to its descent into the low lands, the cutting is deep, averaging eight feet.

This extensive work cost Rs. 32,500, but up to the end of 1873 only about 272 bíghas of land could be put down as the net results of the reclamation attempted, whilst complaints were made of flooding in Abdullahpur and others of the neighbouring villages. The natural course of the drainage lines from both these jhíls is to the Kátha and Saindli Nadís, but instead of this course having been adopted, the cut was led across country at right angles to the natural line. Many proposals have been made to remedy this grave mistake. Until the new works are completed on the Kátha, it is impossible to use it as an escape, otherwise the swamps already existing would become so difficult to manage that greater evils than those already existing would arise. The final arrangement agreed upon seems to be the deepening of the cut. As originally designed, the cut had a

bed slope of $\frac{1}{2,400}$, and a bottom width of eighteen feet, whilst a surplus slope
of 7·5 feet was overcome by three masonry falls. By increasing the bed slope
it is proposed to do away with the falls, and thus lower the bed of the cut in
the Dhulápra jhíl by two feet, and give a flood-level so much lower. The velocity,
too, due to the increased slope, will have the effect of running off the water
more rapidly, but it has yet to be seen whether this increased power of drainage
has been so arranged as not to act injuriously to the village lands in the lower
portion of its course. Owing to the grave faults of the plan originally adopted,
the Dhulápra cut has not been of much use either as a drainage line or as a
reclamation work, and it will take much time, trouble, and money before it can
be fitted even for the ordinary purposes of a drainage work.

FAIZABAD, or Faizabad Bahat, a parganah of tahsíl Saháranpur, is
bounded on the north by the Siwáliks; on the west

Area.

by the Jumna, which separates it from the Ambála
district of the Panjáb ; on the south by parganah Sultánpur ; and on the east
by parganah Muzaffarabad. According to the census of 1872 parganah Faizabad had a total area of 182 square miles, of which 71 square miles were under
cultivation. The area assessed to Government revenue during the same year
was 118 square miles, of which 71 square miles were cultivated, 27 square
miles were culturable, and 20 square miles were barren. The area of this parganah may be divided into three tracts,—the one bordering on the hills, where,
owing to the difficulty of procuring water even for domestic purposes, and the

Natural divisions.

destruction caused by wild elephants and deer, as well
as the danger to houses by fire, as only thatched
roofs are practicable, the population is very scanty ; secondly, the highlands
lying at a distance from the hills ; and thirdly, the villages of the Jumna *khádir.*
The Búdhi Jumna and the Eastern Jumna Canal intersect the parganah from
north to south, but irrigation is only carried on from the latter, and that only
to a limited extent, owing to its being much below the level of the surrounding
country. During the rains several hill torrents (the Chupra, Gangra, and Timli)
run down the north-western portion of the parganah, and, uniting to form two
streams, flow into the Jumna. One of these (the Naugang) crosses the canal
at Shihábuddínpur, and eventually joins the Jumna in the Sultánpur parganah.
In years of unusual rain they do much damage to the area of estates lying
near their banks. *Rabi* crops predominate, and very little sugar-cane is grown.
The last year of the thirty years' settlement showed a land revenue amounting
to Rs. 48,454.   Mr. Vans Agnew increased this to Rs. 54,143, and Mr. H.
Robertson, at his revision, proposed a land revenue of Rs. 73,336 on a total area
of 75,335 acres, of which 62,236 acres were assessed to revenue, and 45,226
acres were cultivated.   The actual revenue in 1872 amounted to Rs. 65,745 (or
with cesses, Rs. 72,495), falling at a rate of Re. 0-9-0 per British acre on the

total area, at Re. 0-13-11 per acre on the area assessed to Government revenue, and at Re. 1-7-2 per acre on the cultivated area. The sum paid by cultivators to the landowners as rent and cesses during the same year has been estimated at Rs. 1,25,794.

The soil generally throughout the parganah is a soft light *rausli*, easily worked and very productive with an average rainfall, which is here from fifteen to twenty inches more than in Sahǎranpur. The characteristic soil found where-ever the parganah is not cut up by hill torrents, and in the strip of land lying between the Búdhi Jumna and the Jumna, is of a dark chocolate colour, and highly fertile when of any depth. There are also a few estates in the *khádir* of the Jumna where a clay soil is found combined with rich vegetable deposits. The northern portion is free from swamps and accumulations of water of any kind, and, owing to the great depth of the spring-level (100 to 150 feet), the construction of wells is impracticable. In the south, irrigation from wells is carried on to some extent. The cultivation generally is somewhat backward, though the people are, as a rule, prosperous and contented.

Between the years 1839-40 and 1859-60, six whole villages and 31 portions of villages, having an area of 13,107 acres, and paying a revenue of Rs. 5,804, and valued at Rs. 68,117, were

Alienations.

transferred by private arrangement in this parganah. The transfers by decree of Court comprised 34 portions of villages, having an aggregate area of 5,738 acres, and paying a revenue of Rs. 3,950. The value recorded was Rs. 39,491. Out of the 24 whole and 84 portions of villages remaining with the original proprietors, 1,023 acres, bearing a revenue of Rs. 1,058, valued at Rs. 4,760, of the former, and 10,884 acres, bearing a revenue of Rs. 6,112, valued at Rs. 58,050, of the latter, were under mortgage. These statistics give a per-centage of private transfers to the total area of 17 per cent., of transfers by decree of Court amounting to 7 per cent., and of transfers by mortgage amounting to 18 per cent. The average value per acre in each of these cases was Rs. 5-3, Rs. 6-14, and Rs. 5-2, and the land revenue assessed amounted to Re. 0-7-1 ; Re. 0-11-0 and Re. 0-9-0 per acre, respectively. The result from the entire parganah on 42 per cent. of the total area gives an average value of Rs. 5-14-0 per acre when the average land revenue amounted to Re. 0-9-3 per acre. Sayyids lost three entire villages and ten shares, and Hindu Rajpúts lost three villages and thirty-nine shares.

According to the census of 1872, parganah Faizabad contained 129 inha-bited villages, of which 61 had less than 200 inhabi-

Population.

tants; 43 had between 200 and 500 ; 21 had between 500 and 1,000; one had between 1,000 and 2,000; and three had between 2,000 and 3,000. The settlement papers showed 105 estates, of which one was held free of revenue, and another was a jungle grant. The total population in 1872

numbered 42,882 souls (19,536 females), giving 235 to the square mile. Classified according to religion, there were 25,630 Hindús, of whom 11,532 were
females; and 17,252 were Musalmáns, amongst whom 8,004 were females; and
distributing the Hindu population amongst the four great classes, the census shows
1,373 Brahmans, of whom 594 were females; 317 Rajpúts, including 124
females; 1,644 Baniyas (711 females); whilst the great mass of the population
is included amongst " the other castes" of the census returns, which show a total
of 48,796 souls, of whom 22,056 are females. The principal Brahman sub-division found in this parganah is the Gaur (1,366). Rajpúts show members of the
Khági (148) and Bais clans, and the Baniyas belong principally to the Agar-
wála (1,349), Saraugi and Dasa subdivisions. The other castes belong to the
same classes as have already been given under the notice of parganah Haraura;
Chamárs number 8,243 souls, and Málís, Kahárs, Kumhárs, &c., are proportion-
ately numerous. Of the 103 revenue-paying estates in the parganah, there are 50,
each of which forms the property of only one class, viz., Europeans, 3; Musalmáns, 3; Mahájans, 17; Rajpúts, 21; and Gújars, 3. The cultivators are chiefly
Gújars, Gárás and Saínís. The Musalmáns show Shaikhs (801), converted
Pundírs (133), Chauháns (16), other Rajpúts (794), Gújars (3,048), and Patháns
(492); the remainder are entered without distinction.

The occupations of the people are shown in the statistics collected at the
census of 1872. From these it appears that of the
Occupations.
male adult population (not less than fifteen years of
age) 212 are employed in professional avocations, such as Government servants, priests, doctors, and the like; 1,081 in domestic service, as personal servants, water-carriers, barbers, sweepers, washermen, &c.; 782 in commerce,
in buying, selling, keeping or lending money or goods, or the conveyance of
men, animals, or goods; 7,150 in agricultural operations; 1,469 in industrial
occupations, arts and mechanics, and the preparation of all classes of substances,
vegetable, mineral, and animal. There were 3,893 persons returned as labourers, and 368 as of no specified occupation. Taking the total population, irrespective of age or sex, the same returns give 659 as landholders; 17,380 as cultivators; and 24,843 as engaged in occupations unconnected with agriculture.
The educational statistics, which are confessedly imperfect, show 121 males
as able to read and write out of a total male population numbering 23,346
souls.

Faizabad is also known as Faizabad Bahat. In the time of Akbar it was
known as Raipur Tátár from the village of Raipur, which still exists on the
banks of the canal. The name was changed to Faizabad when Shahjahán
built his hunting seat at Bádsháh Mahál. It then became the centre of a
sirkár containing twenty-four maháls; whilst Saháranpur was reduced to
seventeen. In 1840-41 Faizabad had a revenue of Rs. 22,291, and in the

following year received villages assessed at Rs. 10,081, chiefly from taluka Patehar. At the same time it lost villages assessed at Rs. 6,230, leaving the land revenue at Rs. 26,142. The next great change took place in 1855, when one village was transferred to parganah Saháranpur, and 25 villages, having an area of 14,931 acres, assessed at Rs. 14,163, and with a population of 10,598 souls, were received from Bahat; and three villages, with an area of 2,236 acres, and assessed at Rs. 2,367, were received from parganah Sultánpur. These transfers left the parganah in 1855 with an area of 76,042 acres, distributed amongst 104 villages, assessed at Rs. 46,202.

FATEHPUR, a village in parganah Haraura of the Saháranpur district, is distant 15 miles from Saháranpur, 17 miles from Nágal, 15 miles from Rúrki, and 13 miles from Mohand, with a population of 579 souls in 1872. Fatehpur possesses a dák bungalow and an encamping-ground for troops half a mile from the Saháranpur road, open, large and sloping to the south, with a little shade on higher ground. Supplies are procurable, and water is plentiful. The route from Nágal lies through a well wooded and cultivated country, passing Saisana at 7½ miles, Barsara at 9½ miles, and Haraura at 10¾ miles. Up to this, the road is second-class, unmetalled and heavy, and from it the Saháranpur metalled road is travelled. Cultivation continues to 15¼ miles, when the country becomes jungly. There is a branch post-office and police-station at Fatehpur. From Rúrki the road is good, level, metalled and bridged; passes Rámpur (*q. v.*) at two miles, and junction of Haraura road at seven miles. Hence to Mohand, a small village at the foot of the pass to Dehra, the road crosses the Soláni, here called the Kandúr, by a ford which is passable except after heavy rains (2 miles); cultivation for 10½ miles; then dense jungle; no water after leaving cultivation. Road level, metalled and bridged.

GANGOH, the chief town of the parganah of the same name in the Saháranpur district, is distant 23 miles south-west from the town of Saháranpur. The population in 1847 was 6,260, and in 1865 was 10,899. In 1872 there were 10,982 inhabitants, of whom 5,049 were Hindús (2,382 females), and 5,930 were Musalmáns (2,870 females). Distributing these amongst the urban and rural classes proper, there were

Population.

258 landholders, 1,289 cultivators, and 9,435 persons pursuing occupations unconnected with agriculture. The number of enclosures in 1872 was 1,092, of which 421 were occupied by Hindús, and 670 by Musalmáns. The number of houses in the same year was 2,503, of which 1,292 were built with skilled labour, and 1,211 with unskilled labour. Of the houses built with skilled labour, 582 were occupied by Hindús, and 710 by Musalmáns, and of the 1,211 mud huts, 506 were inhabited by Hindús, and 704 by Musalmáns. The area of the town site is 99 acres, giving 111 persons to the square acre. Taking the male adult population (exceeding fifteen years of age), more than fifty pursued

each of the following occupations :—Barbers, 80 ; beggars, 152 ; butchers, 60 ; cultivators, 452 ; grain purchasers, 76 ; labourers, 431 ; landowners, 71 ; money-lenders, 52 ; painters, 66 ; potters, 64 ; purohits, 51 ; servants, 339 ; shop-keepers, 428 ; sweepers, 64 ; and weavers, 612.

The Musalmáns are chiefly Pírzádahs, and are devoted Wahábis. They are in miserable circumstances, though owning the town; but of the 1,255 sharers only a few Gújars work with their own hands, the rest are too proud to work, though not ashamed to beg.

There are five muhallas inhabited by Hindús, but the town consists really of an old and new quarter, the former said to have been founded by the legendary hero, Raja Gang, who gave his name to the place, and the latter by the famous saint Shaikh Abdul Kaddús, who has given his name to the muhalla in the western suburb known as Sarái Shaikh Abdul-kaddús. This muhalla contains three large makbaras or tombs, around which are grouped the smaller tombs of those who desired to lay their remains near the ashes of the saintly personages who repose in the larger buildings. The site of the town is fairly raised, and even becomes a mound in the centre, where the school-house now stands, and where formerly there was an old fort. Around the town there are many groves of mango, siras, jáman and sisú. To the south there is a large jhíl-like expanse known as the tálâb. The streets and bázár ways are narrow and tortuous, but most of them are now paved, and have a centre drain of brick-work. There are many good houses belonging to Mahájans, some of them double-storied, with flat roofs. The water in the wells is good, and in the higher parts of the town is found at a depth of 40 feet from the surface, and in the lower parts at 30 feet. There is no canal irrigation near, and the people enjoy tolerable health, though, in common with the upper portion of the Duáb, fever prevails here during the autumn. Act XX. of 1856 (the Chaukídári Act) is in force, and in 1873 supported a village police numbering 23 men of all ranks, at an annual cost of Rs. 1,278, which is met from a house-tax. Twelve public sweepers are also employed, and their cost is defrayed from the same source. The income from all sources in 1872-73 amounted to Rs. 5,191, giving an incidence of Re. 0-6-2 per head of the population, and Re. 1-12-11 per house. During the same year Rs. 1,580 were expended on wages, drains, culverts and paving. The town possesses a good school-house, where a tahsílí school has been for some time established, a dispensary, first class police-station, and a branch post-office. There is no trade and no evidence of prosperity, except in the houses of the money-lenders.

Gangoh during the mutiny of 1857 was frequently threatened by the Gújars led by one Fathua, who set himself up as Raja of those parts, and burned Nakúr. His head-quarters was at Bhúdakheri, which was attacked by a force under Mr. H. D. Robertson

and Lieutenant Boisragon towards the end of June. Reinforced by the Rángars of the neighbourhood, the Gújars, to the number of about 3,000 men, made
a stand near the villages of Umrpur, Shahpur and Mánpur, but were defeated
with great loss, and pursued as far as Kunda Kalán, which was captured and
burned. The object of this gathering was an intended attack upon Lakhnauti and Gangoh, which there is reason to believe was due to the instigation of
the influential Musalmán residents of Ambahta and Nakúr. These persons had
excited the Gújars generally by promises of plunder and the destruction of bonds
and records of debt, and the more influential amongst them by the hope of
regaining their traditional influence. The Rángars, who supplied large numbers
of recruits to the irregular cavalry regiments, were urged on by hopes of a
revival of purely Musalmán rule, and fought bravely against the troops, asking
and receiving no quarter.

GANGOH, a parganah of the Nakúr tahsíl in the Saháranpur district, is bounded

Area.

on the north by the Nakúr parganah; on the west by
the Jumna river, which separates it from the Karnál
district of the Panjáb; on the south by parganahs Badauli and Jhanjhána of
the Muzaffarnagar district; and on the east by parganah Rámpur. According to the census of 1872, parganah Gangoh had a total area of 131 square
miles, of which 76 square miles were under cultivation. The area assessed to
Government revenue during the same year was 119 square miles, of which 71
square miles were cultivated, 37 square miles were culturable, and 11 square
miles were barren. The same division into groups of villages for assessment
purposes was made here as in Sultánpur. The first or canal-irrigated group
is the best almost in the entire district, having at settlement more than two-

Natural divisions.

thirds of the cultivated area under irrigation either
from canals or wells. There are over two hundred
brick-built wells in this tract, and the use of earthen wells was common
until the canal, by raising the spring level, rendered their construction impracticable. The depth of water from the surface varies from six to twelve feet.
Mr. Wynne, in writing of this group, says—" The Gújars, to whom the bulk of
the group belongs, have, like those in Rámpur, been reclaimed from the
improvident habits and the tendency to cattle-lifting which characterise their
brethren in the rest of the parganah. This happy result is due to the canal.
The reward which the use of the canal water held out to industry was so great,
so immediate, and so certain, that all the traditions of caste succumbed to the
prospects of wealth, so that the Gújars throughout the region watered by the
canal are the most orderly, contented and prosperous of men." The northern
villages of this group include much of the moist land of the Kátha basin, and
those in the centre border on the Andauli jhíl and produce fine rice crops, only
inferior to the *chahora* rice of Sultánpur, and first-rate sugar-cane of the *merthi*

species. The excessive moisture has, however, resulted in the appearance of *reh* of a marked character in Fatehchandpur.

The remainder of the upland villages form the second group. Their

Second group. condition is particularly unfavourable. Five villages about Lakhnauti are held by a fast decaying colony of Turkmáns, and the remainder by an utterly improvident set of Gújars, who form a compact body, able and willing to prevent any outsider from settling amongst them. A few wealthy men have bought whole villages, but are unable to manage them from the want of cultivators, who do not settle in a place where they may see their crops carried off and their cattle lifted, whilst threats of further maltreatment are not wanting. The result is that the Gújars of these parts have no credit, and live as best they can, with their hands against every man's cattle, and with all the traditional habits of the race in full exercise. A few outsiders are now trying to establish themselves here, but, as Mr. Wynne observes " it has required, and will long require, the constant exercise of the European officer's power to make the law respected in this tract; and there must long continue cause of apprehension that, if the charge of the parganah be at any time committed to an easy going Magistrate, the lawless habits of the inhabitants will re-assert themselves, and the intending colony will be swallowed up." But here, as elsewhere, the causes of this lawlessness are not far to seek. Mr. Wynne acknowledges that the tract had been for a long time over-assessed: the soil is poor and irrigation is scanty. The Gújars of the first group, of whom he gives such a favourable account, are of the same clan and family, and were opportunities given to the men of this tract, they would, no doubt, be glad to give up the precarious livelihood, eked out by plunder, they now enjoy, for the certain results obtainable by labour under favourable conditions.

The third group of mixed upland and lowland villages is the worst of all,

Third group. containing an extremely stiff clay along the Saindli Nadí, unfitted for rice cultivation, as it is very irretentive of moisture. Irrigation is scanty; the water is only eighteen feet from the surface, but earthen wells seldom last for more than two years. The crops are bad throughout, and poor. The fourth group, comprising the *khádir* lands, is in most respects similar to the same group in Nakúr. The sandy strip covered with tamarisk jungle is succeeded by a rich alluvial soil near the Jumna. Irrigation is easy in the south, where earthen wells may, in some places, be constructed, and last for a year and-a-half Fair maize is grown here and there, and the soil is admirably adapted in some places for sugar-cane.

The last year of Mr. Thornton's settlement showed a land revenue amount-

Land revenue. ing to Rs. 86,340. This was increased by Mr. Vans Agnew to Rs. 83,981, and Mr. Wynne, at his revision, reduced the revenue to Rs. 78,859. This last assessment was made on a total area amounting to 82,546 acres, of which 72,869 acres were assessed to the land revenue, and of these 47,189 acres were actually under cultivation. According to the census the land revenue for 1872 amounted to Rs. 72,109 (or with cesses, Rs. 79,804), falling at a rate of Re. 0-13-9 per British acre on the total area, at Re. 0-15-2 per acre on the area assessed to Government revenue, and at Re. 1-7-9 per acre on the cultivated area. The sum paid by cultivators to the land-owners as rent and cesses during the same year has been estimated at Rs. 99,392.

Between the years 1839-40 and 1859-60 one whole village and 37 portions

Alienations.

of villages, having an area of 3,905 acres, and paying a revenue of Rs. 4,287, and valued at Rs. 23,739, were transferred by private arrangement in this parganah. The transfers by decree of Court comprised five entire villages and 73 portions of villages, having an aggregate area of 9,333 acres, and paying a revenue of Rs. 10,775. The value recorded was Rs. 31,761. Out of the 27 whole and 82 portions of villages remaining with the original proprietors, 925 acres, bearing a revenue of Rs. 1,242, valued at Rs. 5,529, of the former, and 1,210 acres, bearing a reve-nue of Rs. 1,657, valued at Rs. 7,463, of the latter, were under mortgage. These statistics give a percentage of private transfers to the total area of five per cent.; of transfers by decree of Court amounting to ten per cent.; and of transfers by mortgage amounting to three per cent. The average value per acre in each of these cases was Rs. 6-1-0, Rs. 3-6-5 and Rs. 6-2-0, and the land revenue assessed amounted to Re. 1-1-6, Re. 1-2-5, and Re. 1-6-0 per acre, respectively. The result from the entire pargannah on 18 per cent. of the total area gives an average value of Rs. 4-7-0 per acre when the average land revenue amounted to Re. 1-0-3 per acre. Gújars are the principal proprietors and were the principal losers.

According to the census of 1872, parganah Gangoh contained 107 inhabited

Population.

villages, of which 41 had less than 200 inhabitants; 39 had between 200 and 500; 21 had between 500 and 1,000; three had between 1,000 and 2,000; and two had between 3,000 and 5,000. The only town containing more than 5,000 inhabitants is Gangoh. The settlement records show 118 estates, of which three are held revenue-free in perpetuity. The total population in 1872 numbered 48,748 souls (24,858 females), giving 418 to the square mile. Classified according to religion, there were 30,162 Hindús, of whom 16,114 were females; 18,583 Musalmáns, amongst whom 8,742 were females; and there were three Christians. Distributing the Hindu population amongst the four great classes, the census shows 3,230 Brahmans, of whom 1,506 were females; 92 Rajpúts; 3,035 Baniyas (1,380 females); whilst the great mass of the population is included in "the other castes" of the census returns, which show a total of 29,805 souls, of whom 13,196 are females. The principal Brahman sub-division found in this parganah is the Gaur. The Baniyas belong principally to the Agarwál (2,333) and Saraugí subdivisions. The other castes belong for the most part to the same divisions as those noticed in Sultánpur. Those having more than one thousand members are as follow :—Kumhárs, 1,172; Kahárs, 3,177 ; Chamárs, 5,758 ; Khakrobs, 2,308 ; Gújars, 5,828 ; Málís, 2,079 ; and Játs, 1,152. The Musalmáns show Shaikhs (1,502), Pundírs (362), Chauháns (264), converted Rajpúts (2,366), and Patháns (1,031) ; the remainder are entered without distinction. The landholders are principally Gújars, Patháns, Brahmans and Mahájans.

The occupations of the people are shown in the statistics collected at the

Occupations.

census of 1872. From these it appears that of the male adult population (not less than fifteen years of age,) 217 are employed in professional avocations, such as Government servants, priests, doctors, and the like ; 2,054 in domestic service, as personal servants, water-carriers, barbers, sweepers, washermen, &c. ; 1,265 in commerce, in buying, selling, keeping or lending money or goods, or the conveyance of men, animals, or goods ; 7,639 in agricultural operations ; 3,295 in industrial occupations, arts and mechanics, and the preparation of all classes of substances, vegetable, mineral, and animal. There were 3,096 persons returned as labourers, and 732 as of no specified occupation. Taking the total population, irrespective of age or sex, the same returns give 501 as landholders, 20,751 as cultivators, and 27,496 as engaged in occupations unconnected with agriculture. The educational statistics, which are confessedly imperfect, show 389 males as able to read and write out of a total male population numbering 29,890 souls.

Gangoh, an old Akbari parganah, from which Jamálgarh was separated in

History.

the time of Najíb Khán, showed a land revenue of Rs. 43,540 in 1840-41. The changes that took place in the following year gave an increase of villages assessed at Rs. 66,019, and a decrease of villages assessed at Rs. 7,968. Five villages were transferred to the Muzaffarnagar district, and fifty-eight villages were received, principally from parganah Lakhnauti. The changes that took place in 1855 are shown in the following table :—

Name of parganah.	Number of villages.	Area in acres.	Land revenue.	Population.	Name of parganah.	Number of villages.	Area in acres.	Land revenue.	Population.
			Rs.					Rs.	
Nakúr ...	52	27,048	22,069	13,759	Rámpur ...	11	4,914	6,225	2,991
Rámpur ...	7	3,994	4,017	2,201	Nakúr ...	1	311	435	158
Total ...	59	31,042	26,086	15,960	Total ...	12	5,225	6,660	3,149

This left 117 villages, having an area of 83,858 acres, and assessed at Rs. 86,052 in 1855.

HARAURA, a parganah of tahsíl Sahâranpur, in the Sahâranpur district, is

Area.

bounded on the north by parganah Muzaffarabad; on the east by Sahâranpur; on the west by Bhagwânpur; and on the south by Nágal. According to the census of 1872 parganah Haraura had a total area of 105 square miles, of which 82 square miles were under cultivation. The area assessed to Government revenue during the same year was 105 square miles, of which 82 square miles were cultivated, 12 square miles were culturable, and 11 square miles were barren. There is little irrigation, as the water in the streams which intersect the parganah is at too low a level to afford facilities for irrigation. To the south, common earthen (kuchha) wells are easily constructed, but to the north the soil is more stony and wells are not so easily made. There is, however, a large proportion of the cultivated area devoted to sugar-cane and other valuable crops and altogether there is more cultivation of the *kharif* than of the *rabi* harvest. This parganah is one of the best in the district, and shows a comparatively high rental. The thirty years' settlement was made by Mr. E. Thornton, and in the year before the commencement of the present assessment amounted to Rs. 82,231. Mr. Vans-Agnew fixed the land revenue at Rs. 84,796, which at Mr. H. Robertson's revision rose to Rs. 91,611 on a total area amounting to 66,818 acres, of which 59,672 acres were assessed to revenue, and 52,387 acres were cultivated. The land revenue for 1872 amounted to Rs. 83,275 (or with cesses, Rs. 91,649), falling at a rate of Re. 1-3-10 per British acre on the total area and on the area assessed to Government revenue, and at Re. 1-9-5 per acre on the cultivated area. The sum paid by cultivators to the landowners as rent and cesses during the same year has been estimated at Rs. 1,24,488. Except in a few estates in the *khádir* of the Soláni and Hindan rivers, the soil presents considerable uniformity throughout the parganah. It is for the most part a light soft *rausli*, which becomes indurated by submersion, in which case it has been classified as *dákar*. The best soil (*misan*) forms twenty per cent. of the total cultivated area, and the worst soil only seven per cent. The soil of the northern portion of the parganah occasionally contains more sand than that of the south, and has been brought into cultivation more recently. These causes have been advanced to account for the more backward state of cultivation there.

Between the years 1839-40 and 1859-60, five whole villages and 58 portions

Alienations.

of villages, having an area of 8,855 acres, and paying a revenue of Rs. 9,212, and valued at Rs. 66,515, were transferred by private arrangement in this parganah. The transfers by decree of Court comprised three entire villages and 68 portions of villages, having an aggregate area of 11,481 acres, and paying a revenue of Rs. 12,832. The value recorded was Rs. 56,915. Out of the 27 whole and 84 portions of villages remaining with the original proprietors, 302 acres, bearing a revenue of Rs. 250, valued at Rs. 4,000, of the former, and 5,858 acres, bearing a revenue of Rs. 5,873, valued at Rs. 58,088, of the latter, were under mortgage. These statistics give a percentage of private transfers to the total area of 13 per cent., of transfers by decree of Court amounting to 17 per cent., and of transfers by mortgage amounting to 9 per cent. The average value per acre in each of these cases was Rs. 7-8-2, Rs. 4-15-3, and Rs. 9-14-7, and the land revenue assessed amounted to Re. 1-0-7, Re. 1-1-10 and Re. 0-15-10 per acre respectively. The result from the entire parganah on 39 per cent. of the total area gives an average value of Rs. 6-14 per acre, where the average land revenue amounted to Re. 1-1 per acre. Hindu Rajpúts lost five entire villages and 57 shares, or one-third of their possessions ; Shaikhs and Patháns lost one village each.

According to the census of 1872, parganah Haraura contained 118 inha-

Population.

bited villages, of which 30 had less than 200 inhabitants, 46 had between 200 and 500, 32 had between 500 and 1,000, 9 had between 1,000 and 2,000, and one had between 2,000 and 3,000. At the settlement there were 137 estates, of which one was held free of revenue. The total population in 1872 numbered 54,444 souls (24,979 females), giving 519 to the square mile. Classified according to religion, there were 37,686 Hindús of whom 17,066 were females ; and 16,758 Musalmáns, amongst whom 7,913 were females. Distributing the Hindu population amongst the four great classes, the census shows 2,889 Brahmans, of whom 1,355 were females ; 1,679 Rajpúts, including 655 females ; 1,764 Baniyas (782 females) ; whilst the great mass of the population is included in "the other castes" of the census returns, which show a total of 31,354 souls, of whom 14,274 are females. The principal Brahman sub-division found in this parganah is the Gaur (2,763). Amongst the Rajpúts, representatives of the Pundír (647), Khági (153), and Vasisht clans are found. The Baniyas chiefly belong to the Agarwál (1,106), Sangal and Saraugi sub-divisions. The other castes show Juláhas, Jogís (657), Kumhárs (951), Hajáms, Kahárs (2,870), Chamárs (12,152), Khákrobs (1,266), Gújars (1,813), Barhais (918), Lohárs (604), Garariyas, Darzís, Kolís (954), Málís (1,001). Saínís (920), Dhobís, Bháts, Játs, Orhs (284), Chhípís, Sonárs, Kulwárs, Kayaths, Kaláls, and Ahírs. Of the 136 estates paying revenue to Government there are 71 in each, of which there is but one class of proprietor, viz., Musalmáns, 19 ; Jhojas, 2 ; Rorhs, 3 ; Brahmans, 2 ; Tagas, 4 ; Mahájans, 10 ; Rajpúts, 13 ; Gújars, 11 ; Khattris 1 ; Ahírs, 5 ; and Hajjám, 1. The cultivators are chiefly Rajputs, Tagas and Saínís. The Musalmáns show Shaikhs (397), converted Pundírs (184), converted Chauháns (72), other Rajpúts (1,336), Gújars (86), and Patháns (59) ; the remainder are entered without distinction.

The occupations of the people are shown in the statistics collected at the census of 1872. From these it appears that of the

Occupations.

male adult population (not less than fifteen years of age), 489 are employed in professional avocations, such as Government servants, priests, doctors and the like ; 1,702 in domestic service, as personal servants, water-carriers, barbers, sweepers, washermen, &c. ; 915 in commerce, in buying, selling, keeping or lending money or goods, or the conveyance of men, animals or goods; 6,789 in agricultural operations ; 3,090 in industrial occupations, arts and mechanics, and the preparation of all classes of substances, vegetable, mineral and animal. There were 4,252 persons returned as labourers, and 401 as of no specified occupation. Taking the total population, irrespective of age or sex, the same returns give 511 as landholders, 18,442 as cultivators, and 35,491 as engaged in occupations unconnected with agriculture. The educational statistics, which are confessedly imperfect, show 373 males as able to read and write out of a total male population numbering 29,465 souls.

Haraura was formed by Messrs. Craigie and Ross in 1855 from the neighbouring parganahs. The following table shows the

History.

parganahs from which the villages were received, with the details of area, revenue and population, amounting in all to 137 villages, with an area of 68,507 acres, a land revenue of Rs. 80,108, and a population numbering 50,900 souls :—

Name of parganah.	Number of villages.	Area in acres.	Land revenue.	Population.	Name of parganah.	Number of villages.	Area in acres.	Land revenue.	Population.
			Rs.					Rs.	
Saháranpur ...	23	11,738	15,140	9,481	Muzaffarabad...	63	29,975	30,495	23,367
Rúrki ...	28	14,295	18,723	9,519	Deoband ...	21	11,334	14,500	8,107
Jaurási ...	1	521	500	...	Bahat ...	1	644	750	426

HARDWÁR, a celebrated town in parganah Jawálapur and tahsíl Rúrki of the Saháranpur district, is distant about 17 miles north-

Names.

east of Rúrki, and 39 miles north-east of Saháranpur. The permanent population is small, numbering only 4,919 souls in 1865, and

4,800 in 1872. Hardwár has borne several names. It was formerly called Kupila or Gupila, so named after the sage Kapila, who is said for a long time to have performed religious austerities here. The place where he lived is still shown under the name Kapilasthána, hence the pass is sometimes known as Kapila or Kupila,[1] the Kútila of Tímúr's Memoirs.[2] Another common name is Gangadwára or ' gate of the Ganges,' by which name it was known to Hwen Thsang in the middle of the seventh century,[3] and also to the Musalmán writers Abu Rihan and Rashíd-ud-dín.[4] It is now best known by the name Hardwár or Haridwár. The first name is derived from Hara, a synonym of Mahádeo or Shiva, and the second name from Hari, a synonym of Vishnu. The form Haridwára is found in the Kedarakhanda of the Skanda Purána and other Vaishnava works. In the Vishnu Purána it is called Haridwára, and the Ganges is said to flow from the " toe of Vishnu."[5] The Vaishnavas point out the *Hari ki charan* or *Hari ki pairi*, ' the print of Vishnu's foot,' in support of this belief. Amarasinha gives Vishnupadi as one of the synonyms of the Ganges. The Shaivas, on the other hand, adhere to the form Hardwár, and quote the origin of the Bhágirathi, or principal branch of the Ganges, in the Kailás of Mahádeo in support of their theory. Another name given by Wilford is Ganga-awartha, or the ' awartha of the Ganges,' which he thus explains :—" The *awartha* signifies an inclosed place of a circular form, and is more particularly applied to places of worship." This last term, and Gangadwára would seem to point out that there was originally a celebrated temple here of that name, around which the present town has sprung up.

The present town, and the ruined village of Mayapur, both lie on the right
Position.　　　bank of the Ganges, at the southern base of the Siwá-
　　　　　lik range, through which, by a gorge or natural breach,
the river enters the plains. On the left is the Chandi Pahár, on the top of which is a temple connected with those in Hardwár itself. The river occupies the whole gorge, the width of which at its narrowest point is about one mile. Owing to its proximity to the hills and the great declivity of its bed, the Ganges here divides into several channels, intercepted by large islands, many of which are placed beyond the reach of high-flood water. One of these channels commences about two and a quarter miles above Hardwár, and flows by Hardwár, Mayapur and Kankhal, rejoining the parent river a little below the last town. It is from a spot on this branch, between Mayapur and Kankhal, that the head waters of the great Ganges Canal are taken. Hardwár was visited in 1796 by Hardwicke, who calls it a small place situated at the base of the hills. Raper describes it in 1808 as very inconsiderable, " having only one street, about fifteen feet in breadth and a furlong and a half in length. Most of the houses

---

[1] Wilford, As. Res . VI., 478.　　[2] Dowson's Elliot, III., 455.　　[3] Arch. Sur. II., 231.
[4] Dowson's Elliot, I., 54.　　[5] Hall's Wilson's V. P., III., 302.

have the upper part of brick and the lower part of stone, which is of good quality." The street is now fully three-quarters of a mile long. South of the town lies the remains of the old town of Mayapura, the .Mo-yu-lo or Mayura of Hwen Thsang. The name is traditionally derived from the .temple of Máya Devi still in existence, though possibly more correctly derived from the peacocks (*mayura*) which abound in the neighbourhood.

Hwen Thsang describes the town as being 3½ miles in circumference, and very populous. General Cunningham considers that this account corresponds very closely with the site of the old city of Mayapura, as pointed out to him by the people.[1] " These traces extend from the bed of a torrent, which enters the Ganges near the modern temple of Sarovanáth, to the old fort of Raja Ben, on the bank of the canal, a distance of 7,500 feet. The breadth is irregular, but it could not have been more than 3,000 feet at the south end, and at the north end, where the Siwálik hills approach the river, it must have been contracted to 1,000 feet. These dimensions give a circuit of 19,000 feet, or rather more than 3½ miles. Within these limits there are the ruins of an old fort, 750 feet square, attributed to Raja Ben, and several lofty mounds covered with broken bricks, of which the largest and most conspicuous is immediately above the canal bridge. There are also three old temples dedicated to Naráyana-sila, to Maya Devi, and to Bhairava. The celebrated ghát, called the Pairi or 'feet ghát,' is altogether outside these limits, being upwards of 2,000 feet to the north-east of the Sarovanáth temple. The antiquity of the place is undoubted, not only from the extensive foundations of large bricks which are everywhere visible, and the numerous fragments of ancient sculpture accumulated about the temples, but from the great variety of the old coins, similar to those of Sugh, which are found here every year. The temple of Naráyana-sila, or Naráyana-bali, is made of bricks, 9½ inches square and 2½ inches thick, and is plastered on the outside. Collected around it are numerous squared stones and broken sculptures. One of the stones has belonged to the deeply carved, cusped roof of an old temple. Amongst the broken sculptures, I was able to identify only one small figure of Buddha, the ascetic, surrounded by smaller figures of ascetic attendants. The temple of Máya Devi is built entirely of stone ; and, from the remains of an inscription over the entrance door-way, I think it may be as old as the 10th or 11th century. The principal statue, which is called Máya Devi, is a three-headed and four-armed female in the act of killing a prostrate figure. In one of the hands I recognised the *chakra*, or discus ; in another there was an object like a human head ; and in a third hand the *trisúl*. This is certainly not the figure of Máya Devi, the mother of Buddha, nor is it exactly that of any goddess with which I am

Mayapur.

Temple of Máya Deví.

---

[1] Arch. Sur., II., 233.

acquainted. It corresponds best with the figures of Durga; but if the name assigned to it is correct, the figure must be that of the Pauranik Máya Devi, who, according to the Bhagavata, was the 'energy of the supreme, and by her, whose name is Máya, the Lord made the universe.' But the action of the figure is most decidedly opposed to this identification; and I am therefore inclined to assign the statue to Durga, the consort of Siva, to whom Vishnu gave his discus, and Siva his trident. This attribution is the more probable as there is, close beside it, a squatted male figure with eight arms, which can only be Siva, and on the outside of the temple there is a Lingam, and a statue of the bull Nandi. There is also a fragment of a large female statue, which may possibly have been Máya Devi, but it was too imperfect for recognition. As there was nothing about the temple to give any clue to its identification, I can only conjecture that the original figure of Máya Devi must have been destroyed by the Muhammadans, and that the vacant temple was afterwards occupied by the votaries of Siva. Outside the modern temple of Sarovanáth, I found a statue of Buddha seated in abstraction under the Bodhi tree, and accompanied by two standing and two flying figures. On the pedestal there was a wheel, with a lion on each side as supporters; and as the figure was apparently naked, I concluded that it represents Adi Buddha, the first of the twenty-four Jain Hierarchs."

The great object of attraction at the present day is the Hari ke charan, or bathing ghát, and the adjoining temple of Gangadwára.

Gangadwára.

General Cunningham notices that the original stone with the *charan*, or 'foot marks of Vishnu,' is said to have disappeared, but a second is now attached to the upper walls of the ghát. Close by, in a small temple, is a well called the Brahma-kund, which is most probably the same that was noticed by Hwen Thsang in 634 A.D., but the great temple of his days has long ago disappeared. The ghát itself is a very small one, being only 34 feet wide at the top, 89 feet at the bottom, with a flight of 39 steps to the water." Priority in ablution at the propitious moment is considered to be of great importance in a spiritual point of view, and many persons have formerly perished in the attempt to secure the advantage, being either crushed to death in the rushing crowd, or precipitated into the river and drowned. In 1819, "in consequence of a desperate rush made by the infatuated pilgrims to gain a precedency in bathing, 430 persons were squeezed to death, among whom were several British sepoys, placed as guards to prevent this very catastrophe." Owing to this accident, the Government constructed the present ghát of sixty steps and 100 feet in width, under the superintendence of Captain DeBude.[1]

---

[1] Thornton, II., 141.

The rigidly pious, and those who dread to enter the water unassisted, are

Bathing festivals.

supported by a Brahman on each side. As, however, the depth close to the ghát is not above four feet, the majority plunge in unassisted, men and women bathing together indiscriminately. The great assemblage of pilgrims is held annually on the first day of the month of Baisákh, the commencement of the Hindu solar year, which corresponds with the entry of the sun into the sign of Aries or Mesha. But this day no longer corresponds with the vernal solstice: in 1796 it fell on the 8th of April, in 1808 on the 10th, and now for many years on the 11th or 12th April.[1] Every twelfth year the planet Jupiter (Vrihaspati) is in the sign Aquarius (Kumbha) at the time of the sun's entry into Aries, and the fair is then called a *Kumbh-mela*. These are occasions of peculiar sanctity, and the fairs are attended by great multitudes. Hardwicke estimated the attendance at the Kumbh-mela of 1796 at two millions and a half, and Raper at the following Kumbh, in 1808, says—" If we estimate the number at two millions of souls, we shall probably fall short rather than exceed the reality." Bacon, writing of an ordinary year, at a much later date, puts down the attendance at from two to three hundred thousand. In these calculations, however, it must be remembered that these numbers never appeared at one time, as those who bathe come in the morning and leave in the evening or on the next day, so that there is a constant succession of pilgrims. The *Adh-kumbh* or every sixth year also attracts a great number of the devout. The ordinary attendance of late years is under 100,000, and treble that number at the Kumbh. The next Kumbh takes place in 1882. From Hardwár great numbers of pilgrims proceed to the Shaiva shrine of Kedarnáth, and the Vaishnava temple of Badrináth, both of which are situated in British Garhwal, and on their way worship at the sacred *Prayágas* (or confluences of two rivers), at Deoprayág, Rudrprayág, Karnprayág, Nandprayág and Vishnuprayág.

On the day of which the Hardwár fair is the anniversary, the Ganges is

Trade.

said to have first appeared upon earth. At the present time a very conspicuous portion of the bathers at Hardwár come from the Panjáb and distant parts of Rájputána. Religion, however, is not the sole incentive that draws these crowds together; trade and amusement are as much thought of. The Hardwár *mela* forms one of the principal horse fairs in these Provinces from which the remounts for the native cavalry are drawn, though general report shows that the class of horses now exhibited are not so good as formerly. Commodities of all kinds—Native and European—are exposed for sale, and the trade in grain and food-stuffs alone forms an important and lucrative traffic. Great attention has been paid, of late years, to the police and sanitary arrangements of these fairs, so that now there is practically

---

[1] See Thomas's Prinsep; Useful tables, 185.

very little danger to the public health or peace to be apprehended from these assemblies. The management of the funds derived from the leasing of sites for booths and flower-sellers during the fair is in the hands of the committee of the Hardwár Municipal Union, and of late years large sums have been expended on the repairs of ghâts, paving streets, metalling roads, planting trees, erecting latrines, building saráis for travellers, and other similar works of public utility. The expenditure during 1873-74 on original works amounted to over fifteen thousand rupees. The Kúmbh fair of 1867 was the largest on record since the British occupation, and a full account of the admirable sanitary, police and administrative arrangements of that year will be found in the supplement to the *Gazette of India* for August 24th, 1867.

Hardwár is mentioned in the Mahábhárata as one of the places visited by

Mythological notes.

Arjuna during his exile[1] and "many Brahmans went with Arjuna, and he made pilgrimages to all the holy places, and he went to Hardwár on the river Ganges, and bathed there ; and a damsel named Ulúpi, the daughter of Vásuki, the Raja of the Nágas, was likewise bathing there, and she saw Arjuna and besought him to espouse her, and he abode with her many days." The Ramáyana gives the Shaiva story of the descent of the Ganges from the Himálaya upon the head of Shiva. This story is told at great length in the Ramáyana, and an abstract of it occurs in the Vishnu and other Puránas, with the substitution of Vishnu for Shiva.[2] According to the Vishnu Purána, Sumati and Kesini were the wives of Ságara, and bore him, the one a son, and the other 60,000 sons. Ságara determined on performing a horse sacrifice. The horse was loosened, but was carried off. In searching for him they descended to Pátála, where they met the great sage Kapila, who reduced the 60,000 sons of Ságara to ashes on account of their ill-conduct in the world above. Ságara's remaining son, Amsúmat, was then sent to recover the horse. He succeeded in assuaging the Rishi's wrath, who not only gave him the horse but promised him that his grandson should bring down the 'river of heaven' upon earth ; and that when its waters should wash the bones and ashes of the sons of Ságara, they should be raised to heaven. " Such is the efficacy of the stream that flows from the toe of Vishnu, that it confers heaven upon all who bathe in it designedly or who even become accidentally immersed in it : those even shall obtain swarga whose bones, skin, fibres, hair, or any part shall be left, after death, upon the earth which is contiguous to the Ganges." Ságara completed his horse sacrifice, and in memory of his sons, designated the chasm that they had dug on their way to Pátala, Ságara. This myth has taken a firm hold of the people of India, and is believed in by all Hindús. Kapilasthána is still pointed out at Hardwár. Again, the ocean is now known as Ságara, and at the island of Ságar, at the mouth of the Húgli, a second Kapilasthána is

---

[1] Wheeler, I., 145.   [2] Ibid, II., 46 ; V. P. III., 297.

pointed out. There would be no incompatibility in the two sites could we imagine the tradition referred to the time when the ocean laved the slopes of the Siwálik hills, and the Ganges first forced its way through the pass at Bhím-ghora. At Hardwár is shown the place where Bhíma, one of the five Pándu brothers, was placed to guide the Ganges in its descent, and a hollow in the rock is pointed out as caused by a kick from Bhíma's horse, whence the name Bhímghora (or Bhím's horse).

On the bank of the river, two and a half miles below the Pairighát, is an

Daksha's sacrifice.

old temple sacred to Daksheswara, or lord of Daksha, a famous synonym of Shiva. It is said to mark the spot where Daksha prepared his sacrifice. The present building, says Cunning-ham, " was originally domed, but the dome was broken by a decayed banyan tree, which has now disappeared. The construction of the dome, however, shows that the temple is of later date than the Muhammadan conquest. In front of the temple there is a small square building containing a bell, which was pre-sented by the Raja of Nepal in 1848 A.D." The legend of Daksha's sacrifice is related in the Vayu[1] and other Puránas, which open with an account of Shiva's residence on one of the peaks of Meru, where, surrounded by his court, Shiva reclined upon a splended couch accompanied by the daughter of the sove-reign of the mountains. Daksha had commenced a holy sacrifice on the borders of Himávat, at the sacred spot Gangadwára, or, as the Linga Purána has it, at Kanakhala or Kankhal, at which all the gods, with the permission of Mahádeo, were present. The sage Dadhícha, enraged at the want of respect shown to the great Mahádeo, addressed Daksha and said, " Why do you not offer homage to the God who is the lord of life ?" Daksha spoke :—" I have already many Rudras present, armed with tridents, wearing braided hair, and existing in eleven forms. I recognize no other Mahádeva." The sage then prophesied that the sacrifice should never be completed. In the meanwhile Sati or Uma, the consort of Shiva, and daughter of Daksha, indignant that her lord had no share of the sacrifices, urged him to exert his power and compel the other gods to grant him a share. Mahádeo yielded to her entreaties, and created, from his mouth, a terri-ble monster, Virabhadra, who was ordered to spoil the sacrifice of Daksha. Virabhadra, accompanied by the dreadful goddess Rudrakali and her train, came to Kankhal, and destroyed the viands and beverages. In the confusion, Indra was knocked down and trampled upon, Yama had his staff broken, and Saras-wati and the Matris had their noses cut off. All fared ill,—Yajna, the lord of the sacrifice, was decapitated, and now forms the constellation Mrigasiras or Mang-sir. Daksha, too, gave up his opposition to Mahádeo, who generously granted him all the advantage that he would otherwise have reaped from the sacrifice. According to another account, Daksha was disgusted at the practices of Shiva,—

[1] Hall's edition of Willson's P. I., 120.

his going naked, smearing himself with ashes, carrying a skull, and behaving as if
he were drunk, for which Shiva was rebuked by his father-in-law, and hence his
rage. The later Puránas make Sati destroy herself through vexation at the
treatment her husband received, and the Káshikhanda makes her throw herself
direct into the sacrificial fire. Professor Wilson thinks the whole legend is
fraught with interesting historical and archæological relations. " It is intended
to intimate a struggle between the worshippers of Shiva and Vishnu, in which at
first the latter, but finally the former, acquired the ascendancy." 'It is a
favourite subject amongst the sculptures at Elephanta and Ellora. In one
cave, Bírbhadr is represented with eight arms, in one of which is suspended
Raja Daksha, a fact which would show that the legend is as old as the excavation of the caves. The Vayu and Brahma Puránas give the same story;
but as we go onwards there are additions. The Kúrma Puránа makes
Daksha say that no portion of a sacrifice is ever allotted to Shiva, and no
prayers are directed to be addressed to him or his bride. In fact, each
Puránа, according as it leans to the side of the Vaishnavas or that of the
Shaivas, distorts the story to suit its purposes. In the Linga Puránа, Vishnu
is beheaded in the fray, whilst in the Hari Vansa, Vishnu compels Shiva
to fly, after taking him by the throat and nearly strangling him. "The
blackness of Shiva's neck arose from this throttling, and not, as elsewhere
described, from his drinking the poison produced by the churning of the
ocean."

From the time of the Pándavas, bathing in the Ganges was considered a
sacred duty. Hwen Thsang calls the river *Mahábha-*
dra, or the very ' propitious,' and even in his time hundreds of thousands of pilgrims used to assemble to bathe in its waters. The
author of the Tarikh-i-Yamíni, writing in the early part of the eleventh century,
gives a similar account. Timúr, in his Memoirs,[1] relates that " the Hindu
infidels worship the Ganges, and once every year they come on a pilgrimage to
this place (Hardwár), which they consider the source of the river, to bathe and
to have their heads and beards shaved. They believe these acts to be the means
of obtaining salvation and securing future reward. They dispense large sums
in charity among those who wear the Brahmanical thread, and they throw
money into the river. When infidels die in distant parts, their bodies are
burned, and the ashes are brought to this river and are thrown into it. This
they look upon as a means of sanctification." This account of Timúr is a
curious commentary upon the promise of Kapila to the son of Ságara, given
above. Abul Fazl speaks of Haridwár as being considered holy for fourteen
kos in length. One of Akbar's mints for copper coinage was established here,
and the water of the Ganges was esteemed so much, according to Abul Fazl,

Reputation for sanctity.

_____

[1] Dowson's Elliot, III, 458.

that the Imperial Court, whilst in the Panjáb, was always supplied with drinking water from Hardwár.

The principal events connected with the modern history of Hardwár is its sack by Tímúr in 1398, noticed in the history of the Saháranpur district. The rivalry of the Bairágis and Gosháins culminated on the last day of the fair in 1760 in a pitched battle, which terminated in the defeat of the former, of whom some eighteen hundred were slain. Again, in 1796, the Gosháins, venturing to resist the better-equipped Sikh pilgrims, were defeated, with the loss of five hundred men. The accident at the ghát in 1819 is the only other fact worthy of record. The town is in the Hardwár Municipal Union, and possesses a third-class police-station and a post-office. There is a telegraph office at Mayapur in connection with the Ganges Canal works at Rúrki. Hodgson gives the elevation of Hardwár above the sea as 1,024 feet.

Hardwár forms a stage on the route from Moradabad to Landour.

Routes.

Between Asafgarh and Bhogpur (6¾ miles) the Ganges is crossed by a ferry in the rains. From Bhogpur to Hardwár (13 miles) the road is fair in dry weather, but very trying in the rains : country, jungly ; pass Ránimajra, 3½ miles; Chandpur at 6 ; Jaiputa at 7¼ ; cross the Ganges Canal at 12½, and the Rúrki road at 12¾. Hardwár also forms a stage on the alternative route from Rúrki to Dehra. From Rúrki to Bahádurabad, 9½ miles; thence to Hardwár, 7 miles; from Hardwár to Kansrao, 12 miles ; thence to Lachhiwála, 8 miles ; and from Lachhiwála to Dehra, 10¾ miles. From Baháluradad to Hardwár the country is cultivated, but the road is heavy and unmetalled; and from Hardwár to Kánsrao it is worse, and very difficult, if not impassable, in places for carts. It passes Pardúni at 4½ miles, and descends to the *ghát* at 10¼ miles ; supplies onwards through the Dún scarce and difficult, jungle exceedingly dense and water bad. Mohand is connected by a third-class forest road along the foot of the hills with Hárdwár.

The affairs of the Hardwár Municipal Union, comprising the neighbouring villages of Jawálapur, Hardwár and Kankhal, are

Municipality.

managed by a committee of 17 members, of whom five hold office *ex-officio,* and 12 are elected by the tax-payers. The following statements give the statistics connected with the levying and disposal of the municipal funds, and also show the character of the import trade. The population within municipal limits was estimated at 19,782 souls in 1873-74, and the actual income derivable from taxation during the same year amounted to Rs. 15,854, giving an incidence of 13·7 annas per head of the population, or if refunds on exports be deducted, to Rs. 14,196, showing an incidence of 11 annas 5¾ pie per head. Owing to the large moving population of pilgrims within the area of these towns, statistics as to consumption per head can hardly be accurate or complete :—

Receipts.	1871-72.	1872-73.	1873-74.	Expenditure.	1871-72.	1872-73.	1873-74.
	Rs.	Rs.	Rs.		Rs.	Rs.	Rs.
Opening Balance ...	5,064	9,317	11,284	Collection ...	1,375	1,596	1,861
Class I.—Food and drink.	...	9,928	10,142	Head Office ...	...	131	70
„ II.—Animals for slaughter.	...	77	85	a. Original works ...	4,948	7,305	15,337
„ III.—Fuel, &c. ...	...	518	749	b. Supervision ...	...	50	130
„ IV.—Building materials.	...	1,114	1,122				
„ V.—Drugs, spices.	...	280	405	c. Repairs, &c. ...	1,549	1,020	887
„ VI.—Tobacco ...	...	334	339	Police ...	3,999	4,015	4,025
„ VII.—Textile fabrics.	...	1,822	2,192	Education ...	...	100	296
„ VIII.—Metals ...	...	788	820	Conservancy ...	799	988	1,116
				Charitable grants,	55	90	220
Total of Octroi ...	9,707	14,861	15,854	Fairs ...	...	4,284	4,775
				Nurseries ...	...	225	237
Miscellaneous ...	448	7,313	12,681	Other items ...	102	404	1,825
Total ...	15,219	31,491	49,819	Total ...	12,827	20,207	30,789

The great increase under the head of miscellaneous revenue from 1872 to 1874 is due to the receipts and collections on account of the Hardwár fair being included in the accounts, and to the sale of land in 1873-74, which brought in Rs. 6,895. The local trade is almost entirely confined to supplying the wants of the pilgrims to Hardwár. A considerable through trade from the Dún passes through the town, consisting of exports of wood, string, rope and forest produce, and imports of grain, sugar, spices, cloth, and metals.

ISLÁMNAGAR, a village in parganah Nakúr of the Saháranpur district, is distant 13 miles south-west from Saháranpur. The population in 1872 numbered 2,704 souls. Islámnagar is a Pathán colony said to have been founded by Sardár Abdullah Khán, son of Jalál Khán, the founder of Jalúlabad in the Muzaffarnagar district. He quelled a Gújar insurrection in the reign of Aurangzeb, and expelling the inhabitants, changed the name from Gújarwála to Islámnagar. The site lies close to, and to the east of one of the distributary channels of the Eastern Jumna Canal, but the people do not appear to have suffered much from fever.

JABARHERA, a town in parganah Manglaur of the Saháranpur district, is distant eight or nine miles south-west of Rúrki. The population in 1872 numbered 4,601 souls, and in 1865 there were 3,591 inhabitants. It lies on the road between Deoband and Rúrki, and is also connected with Saháranpur and

Manglaur by a fair-weather road. Jabarhera was the original residence of the notorious Gújar chief, Rámdayál Singh. It possesses a pretty masjid built by Nawáb Hukím Khán, formerly governor of the district, and a village school. Act XX. of 1856 (the Chaukidári Act) is in force, and in 1873 supported a village police numbering nine men, at an annual cost of Rs. 504, which is met from a house tax. The total income in 1872-73 amounted to Rs. 1,124, giving an incidence of Re. 0-5-5 per head of the population, and Re. 1-8-3 per house. During the same year more than one-third of the income was expended on drainage works, repairs to roads, and latrines. The town of Jabarhera must be distinguished from the village of Jabarheri lying between the Síla Nadi and another branch of the West Káli Nadi.

JAHÁNGIRABAD, a small parganah of the Saháranpur district, was separated from the old parganah of Raipur Tátár in the reign of Shahjahán, and remained a separate tappa until 1842, when it was absorbed in Faizabad, Sultánpur, and Jawálapur. In 1840-41 it yielded a land revenue of Rs. 4,403 only.

JAMÁLGARH, an old tappa of the Saháranpur district, also known as Jamál Khera, was separated from parganah Gangoh in the time of Najíb Khán by one Jamál Khán, the amil of the Rohilla chief. In 1840-41 it yielded a revenue of Rs. 5,820, and was absorbed in Nakúr in the following year.

JAURÁSI, an old Akbari parganah of the Saháranpur district, from which Sakrauda was separated in the time of Zábita Khán. It remained a distinct parganah until 1855. In 1840-41 it gave a land revenue of Rs. 38,981, and in the following year lost, by transfer, villages assessed at Rs. 1,380, and gained villages assessed at Rs. 7,585. The parganah was broken up in 1855, and distributed as follows amongst the neighbouring parganahs :—

Name of parganah.			No. of villages.	Area in acres.	Land revenue.	Population.
					Rs.	
Haraura	...	...	1	521	500	...
Rúrki	...	...	91	66,189	34,254	37,612
Manglaur	...	...	26	11,265	11,168	7,304
Jawálapur	...	...	13	11,710	5,165	2,721
Bhagwánpur	...	...	22	25,624	9,461	5,362
	Total	...	153	115,309	60,549	52,999

JAWÁLÁPUR, a town in the parganah of the same name in the Sahárampur district, lies 14 miles to the north-east of Rúrki, and 36 miles east of Saháranpur. The population of Jawálápur in 1847 numbered 8,862 souls, in 1853 there were 12,162 inhabitants, and in 1865 there were 9,665. Of a total population in 1872 of 9,269 souls, there were 6,582 Hindús (3,029 females), and 2,687 Musalmáns (1,320 females). The area of the town is 120 acres, giving

77 persons to the square acre. Jawálápur lies in the north-eastern corner of the district, close to Hardwár, with which it is connected for municipal purposes (see HARDWÁR). The octroi system has been introduced here with some success. A large number of the Hindu residents consists of the Brahmans who officiate at Hardwár, and these are at feud with the zamíndárs, who are Rajpúts converted to Islám. Hence much litigation and quarrelling takes place. There is a first-class police-station, a branch post-office, a tahsíli school, and a good dispensary in the town. The present zamíndárs are said to be the descendants of the founders of the town.

JAWÁLAPUR, a parganah in tahsíl Rúrki of the Saháranpur district,

Area.

is bounded on the north by the Siwálik hills, which separate it from the Dehra Dún district; on the west by parganahs Rúrki and Manglaur; on the south by parganah Gordhanpur of the Muzaffarnagar district; and on the east by the Ganges river, which separates it from the Bijnaur district. According to the census of 1872, this parganah had then a total area of 226 square miles, of which 70 square miles were under cultivation. The area assessed to Government revenue during the same year was 129 square miles, of which 70 square miles were cultivated, 44 square miles were culturable, and 15 square miles were barren. The villages of this parganah were divided into three groups for assessment purposes. The first group comprises the villages under the Siwáliks and along the Ganges Canal.

Natural divisions.

The natural slope of the country is here excessive, and is only partly counterbalanced by the abundant rainfall. In the villages to the south of the canal, irrigation is plentiful, and the soil yields fine crops of sugar-cane, cotton, and wheat; and in the depressions, rice of a fair description. Owing to the great depth of the spring-level (30 to 70 feet), there are few earthen wells. The second group consists of a few villages which are separated from the rest by the Pathari torrent, and yield good crops of wheat and rice. The third group includes the remainder of the parganah. The villages to the north-east of the Bánganga, and on its banks in the lower portion of its course, possess a very stiff soil, producing poor crops, and the population is too scanty to work such a refractory soil. Communication between the villages is also difficult by reason of the numerous streams which intersect this tract, and which are impassable owing to the swampy nature of their beds. In the villages near the Ganges, however, the soil is lighter and more friable, though, as a rule, thinner and poorer. Close on the Ganges, cultivation is sparsely scattered amid extensive plains of tarái grass. Water is found at a depth of from six to eleven feet from the surface, and, except for tobacco and other garden produce, irrigation is not necessary. The whole of this group suffered much from the disturbances during 1857-58. Predatory bands of Gújars and Banjáras made it their home, and plundered and burned the villages. More hands to cultivate the soil, and roads to carry off its produce, are sadly needed here ; and the project of a road connecting it with Manglaur should be carried out.

The last year of Mr. Thornton's settlement showed a land revenue of
Land revenue.
Rs. 32,209, increased by Mr. Vans Agnew to Rs. 38,315. Mr. Wynne, at his revision of Mr. Vans Agnew's settlement, proposed an assessment of Rs. 41,463 on a total area of 67,933 acres, of which 58,143 acres were assessed to land revenue, and of these 30,131 acres were then under cultivation. The actual land revenue for 1872 amounted to Rs. 50,686 (or with cesses, Rs. 55,776), falling at a rate of Re. 0-5-7 per British acre on the total area, at Re. 0-9-10 per acre on the area assessed to Government revenue, and at Re. 1-2-1 per acre on the cultivated area. The sum paid by cultivators to the landowners as rent and cesses during the same year has been estimated at Rs. 94,804.

Between the years 1839-40 and 1859-60 four whole villages and twelve
Alienations.
portions of villages, having an area of 4,837 acres, and paying a revenue of Rs. 3,895, and valued at Rs. 20,902, were transferred by private arrangement in this parganah. The transfers by decree of Court comprised seven portions of villages, having an aggregate area of 1,083 acres, and paying a revenue of Rs. 521. The value recorded was Rs. 6,372. Out of the 60 whole and 11 portions of villages remaining with the original proprietors, 1,411 acres, bearing a revenue of Rs. 536, valued at Rs. 625, of the former, and 26 acres, bearing a revenue of Rs. 56, valued at Rs. 400, of the latter, were under mortgage. These statistics give a percentage of private transfers to the total area of seven per cent., of transfers by decree of Court amounting to two per cent., and of transfers by mortgage amounting to three per cent. The average value per acre in each of these cases was Rs. 4-5-1, Rs. 5-14-1, and Rs. 11-11-0, and the land revenue assessed amounted to Re. 0-12-10, Re. 0-7-8, and Re. 0-6-7 per acre, respectively. The result from the entire parganah on twelve per cent. of the total area gives an average value of Rs. 3-12-6 per acre, when the average land revenue amounted to Re. 1-10-10 per acre. The principal losers were Gújars, who still hold twelve villages.

According to the census of 1872, parganah Jawálapur contained 133
Population.
inhabited villages, of which 68 had less than 200 inhabitants, 39 had between 200 and 500, 16 had between 500 and 1,000; seven had between 1,000 and 2,000, and two had between 3,000 and 5,000. The only town containing more than 5,000 inhabitants is Jawálapur. The settlement records show that there are 146 estates in this parganah, one of which is a jungle grant. The total population in 1872 numbered 57,330 souls (25,333 females), giving 254 to the square mile. Classified according to religion, there were 45,398 Hindús, of whom 19,897 were females ; 11,923 Musalmáns, amongst whom 5,432 were females ; and there

were 9 Christians.   Distributing the Hindu population amongst the four great classes, the census shows 5,467 Brahmans, of whom 2,330 were females ; 3,735 Rajpúts, including 1,650 females ; 3,038 Baniyas (1,242 females) ; whilst the great mass of the population is included in " the other castes" of the census returns, which show a total of 33,158 souls, of whom 14,675 are females.   The principal Brahman sub-divisions found in this parganah are the Gaur (4,790), Saraswat and Acháraj.   The Rajpúts belong to the Khági (3,483) clan, and the Baniyas to the Agarwál (2,179), Choti-Saran and Sarangi divisions.   The other castes are for the most part the same as those noticed under the Rúrki parganah.   The castes having more than one thousand members in this parganah are the Kahár, 1,974 ; Chamár, 9,602 ; Khákrob, 1,038 ; Gújar, 1,311 ; Barhai, 1,134 ; Saini, 3,625 ; Lodha, 1,969, and Banjára, 1,608.   The Musalmáns are classified amongst Shaikhs (824) ; converted Pundírs, Cháuháns and Rajpúts (696); and Patháns (578) ; the remainder are entered without distinction. The principal landowners belong to the Cháuhán, Rajpút—both Hindu and Musalmán—Brahman, Gújar, Mahájan and Saini divisions.

The occupations of the people are shown in the statistics collected at the census of 1872.   From these it appears that, of the male adult population (not less than fifteen years of age) 1,578 are employed in professional avocations, such as Government servants, priests, doctors, and the like ; 2,378 in domestic service, as personal servants, water-carriers, barbers, sweepers, washermen, &c. ; 1,836 in commerce, in buying, selling, keeping or lending money or goods, or the conveyance of men, animals, or goods ; 5,617 in agricultural operations ; 2,827 in industrial occupations, arts and mechanics, and the preparation of all classes of substances, vegetable, mineral, and animal.   There were 5,280 persons returned as labourers, and 913 as of no specified occupation.   Taking the total population, irrespective of age or sex, the same returns give 128 as landholders, 15,970 as cultivators, and 41,232 as engaged in occupations unconnected with agriculture.   The educational statistics, which are confessedly imperfect, show 144 males as able to read and write out of a total male population numbering 31,997 souls.

Jawálapur was known under the name of Bhogpur in Akbar's time, and until late years the records showed the name Bhogpur *urf* Jawálapur.   It covers pretty nearly the area of the old parganah of Bhogpur, which was so called from a town of that name situated on the Ganges near Hardwár.   Tieffenthaler[1] states that Hardwár was also called Bhogpur, but Elliot[2] thinks that this statement is incorrect.   In 1840-41 Jawálapur yielded a revenue of Rs. 15,227, and in the following year received villages assessed at Rs. 1,809 from Jahángírabad.   In 1855 considerable changes took place.   Two villages, with an area of 1,409 acres, and a revenue of Rs. 750, were transferred to Rúrki, whilst 17 villages, with an

---

[1] Bernoulli, I., 147.   [2] Beames' Elliot, II., 129.

area of 15,937 acres, and a revenue of Rs. 9,023, were received from the same parganah, and 13 villages, with an area of 11,710 acres, and a revenue of Rs. 5,165, from Jaurási. This left the total number of villages at 115, with an area of 106,143 acres, and a land revenue of Rs. 45,674 in 1855.

KANKHAL, a town in parganah Jawálapur of the Saháranpur district, is distant 38 miles from Saháranpur, 16 miles from Rúrki, and about one mile from Hardwár. The population in 1865 was 4,781, and in 1872 numbered 4,904 souls, consisting principally of Brahmans attached to the Hardwár temples, who intermarry exclusively with those of Jawálapur. The temple of Daksheswara or ' Lord of Daksha,' a synonym of Shiva, lies to the south of the town, and is supposed to mark the spot where the god Mahádeo spoiled the sacrifice of Daksha, and where Sati or Uma, daughter of Daksha and spouse of Shiva, immolated herself in the fire (see HARDWÁR). Many of the houses here are very substantially built and have their walls decorated with fantastic pictures. The bank of the river is lined with shady and tastefully laid out gardens, and, notwithstanding the general want of sanitation which distinguishes it in common with other Saháranpur towns, the appearance of Kankhal is on the whole picturesque. The town is included in the Hardwár Municipal Union, and possesses an outpost of police and a village school. There are some rich mahájans resident here, and through their influence in 1857, the townsmen successfully resisted the attacks of a powerful body of dakaits. Kankhal, under the name Kanakhala, is mentioned in the Puránas and the Kátha-sárit-ságara.

KÁTHA, an old parganah of the Saháranpur district, was separated from Deoband by Najíb Khán, who established a tahsíl at Badgaon to overawe the turbulent Pundír Rajpúts. It remained a separate parganah up to 1855. In 1841-42 the land revenue amounted to Rs. 29,769, and in the following year, villages assessed at Rs. 11,480 were received from other parganahs. In 1855, the parganah was broken up, and its villages transferred to the parganahs mentioned below :—

Parganah.		No. of villages.	Area in acres.	Land revenue.	Population.
				Rs.	
Rámpur	...	8	8,313	9,229	5,232
Deoband	...	20	21,349	24,280	15,543
Nágal	...	9	7,268	7,870	4,526
Total	...	37	36,930	41,379	25,301

Mention is made of the Kátha villages in the notices of the parganahs amongst which they have been distributed. From early times this parganah has been occupied by a colony of Pundír Rajpúts, who have preserved their lands in the very midst of the tract known, from the preponderance of Gújars amongst the population, as Gújrát.

KHERI, an old tappa or subdivision of the Saháranpur district, was separated from Rúrki in the time of Zábita Khán. The proprietors are converted Rajpúts, who, on becoming Musalmáns, assumed the prefix Ráo to their names. Kheri, with the adjacent hill tracts, continued a separate tappa until the settlement in 1838, when the excessive waste was cut off to form the Kheri jungle. The cultivated portion was divided into villages and settled with the proprietors. These villages were subsequently absorbed in parganah Muzaffarabad. Some account of the tappa is given under the heads of 'waste' and 'old families' in the district notice, and a full notice of the tract and its fiscal history will be found in Mr. Thornton's report in I. Settlement Reports, 86—90. The pattís into which the estate was divided, and the arrangements made at settlement, are also detailed there. Being of purely administrative interest, and already in an available form, these details need not be repeated here.

KOTWAL, a village in parganah Manglaur of the Saháranpur district, is distant 20 miles from the civil station. The population in 1872 numbered 1,087 souls. The western half of the village is occupied by Gára Musalmáns, who possess a good masjid ; and the eastern half is inhabited by Hindu Gújars and Brahmans, who have a temple. The village belongs to the Landhaura estate. The site lies about a mile to the west of the Síla Nadi, and is fairly raised. There are about 422 mud houses separated by good open ways. The water in three brick wells stood at sixteen feet from the surface in March, and is reported good ; the village itself, too, is clean and well-kept.

LAKHNAUTI, an old Akbari parganah of the Saharanpur district, was broken up in 1842: seven villages were transferred to Rampur, one village to the Kátha parganah, and fifty-seven to Gangoh. The remainder were absorbed amongst the neighbouring parganahs of the Muzaffarnagar district.

LAKHNAUTI, a village or decayed town in parganah Gangoh of the Saháranpur district, is distant 26 miles from the town of Saháranpur. The population in 1865 was 4,157, and in 1872 was 3,998. This village lies on the road to Karnál, between Gangoh and the Jumna. It possesses a very fine specimen of an old native fort, a village school, and a branch post-office. Act XX. of 1856 is in force, and in 1872 supported a village police of nine men, at a cost of Rs. 504, which is defrayed from a house-tax. The total income from all sources in 1872-73 amounted to Rs. 1,342, giving an incidence of Re. 0-5-6 per head of the population, and Re. 1-8-5 per house assessed. Lakhnauti and the five villages in the neighbourhood are owned by a colony of Turkmáns, who are in the last stages of poverty and embarrassment. This town, however, was a place of considerable strength in the last century. In 1794 Bapu Sindhia, the Marhatta Governor of Saháranpur, was for some time engaged in reducing it to submission; and it was not until reinforcements had arrived under his lieutenant, George Thomas, and a practicable breach had been effected, that the commandant saw fit to negotiate for its surrender.

LANDHAURA, a large village in parganah Manglaur of the Saháranpur district, lies about five miles to the south-east of Rúrki, and 28 miles to the east of Sahâranpur. The population in 1853 numbered 5,197 souls, and in 1,865 there were 5,118 inhabitants. In 1872 the total population amounted to 5,023 souls, of whom 3,534 were Hindús (1,646 females), and 1,489 were Musalmáns (689 females). The town site covers 92 acres, giving 55 persons to the acre. The inhabitants are chiefly Gújars, the clansmen of the notorious Gújar chief, Raja Ramdayál Singh. Landhaura possesses a village school and a post-office. There is an old fort here surrounded by a ditch, which has been turned into a receptacle for the village sewage. The village was burned for excesses committed during the mutiny.

LIBARHERI, a village in parganah Manglaur of the Saháranpur district, is distant 25 miles from Sahâranpur, and 7½ miles due south from Rúrki. The population in 1872 numbered 3,158 souls, and in 1865 there were 3,470 inhabitants, principally Tagas and Játs. It has a village school, and forms a portion of the Manglaur Union for the purposes of the Chaukidári Act (XX. of 1856). The neighbourhood of Libarheri is celebrated for its sugar-cane, of the species known as 'merthi.' There are some trees near the town, and much rice and high-crop cultivation. Cholera and fever have been prevalent for years. The soil contains much clay used for brick-making and pottery. The drainage, however, is bad, and there are many excavations full of stagnant water around the site, which are drained towards the Ganges Canal. There are also two distributary channels close to the town, and the water-level in these and the canal is higher than the town site, hence the spring-level in the wells has risen from 30 feet from the surface to 18 feet in the cold weather, and 10 feet in the rains, and the water then becomes bad and undrinkable. The town is composed chiefly of mud huts, and the ways are unmade and full of cavities,— the receptacles of all kinds of impurities and filth. The general health, as may be supposed, is extremely bad.

MALHAIPUR, an old parganah of the Sahâranpur district, was absorbed in 1842 amongst the neighbouring parganahs. It then gave a land revenue amounting to Rs. 51,453. It was one of the old Akbari parganahs, and lay to the east of the town of Sahâranpur, having its villages very much intermixed with those of the Sahâranpur parganah. The settlement in 1838 was formed by Mr. Thornton (I., Settlement Reports, 65). The town of Malhaipur was one of the places visited by Tímúr's army in his invasion of the district in 1398 A.D.

MÁN SINGH-KE-TÁNDA, a small village on the road from Sahâranpur to the Dehra valley, is situated in parganah Muzaffarabad, 23 miles from the town of Saháranpur. There is an out-post of police stationed here for some years.

MANGLAUR, the chief town of the parganah of the same name in the Saháranpur district, is distant six miles due south of Rúrki, and 16 miles south-east of Saháranpur. The population in 1847 was 5,959, in 1853 there were 10,322 inhabitants, and in 1865 there were 9,665. In 1872, out of a total population numbering 9,202 souls, there were 3,049 Hindús (1,385 females), and 6,153 Musalmáns (2,937 females). The town site is fairly raised, and occupies 171 acres, giving 54 persons to the acre. The Musalmán inhabitants are principally Juláhas (weavers), who are now much impoverished. Some of the Hindu zamíndárs are wealthy men. There are numerous brick built

Site. houses, surrounded and divided by mud huts, and imbedded amongst groves of trees or luxuriant crops. The roadways are in fair repair. To the south is a deep depression, formerly used as a brick-field, but now irrigated from the canal and cultivated. There is a similar excavation on the west, and numerous water-holes on all sides of the town, which have of late years been drained. Many of the shops in the bázár are out of repair, and there is no trade. The water in the wells is found at a depth of eighteen feet from the surface, and is said to have risen from thirty feet since the introduction of the canal, which runs at about a quarter of a mile from the town. The Chaukidári Act (XX. of 1856) is in force, and in 1873, in conjunction with Libarheri, supported a village police numbering 21 men of all ranks, at an annual cost of Rs. 1,152, besides a staff of 16 scavengers. The total income from all sources in 1872-73 amounted to Rs. 3,276, giving an incidence of Re. 0-4-0 per head of the population, and Re. 1-7-8 per house assessed. During the same year the conservancy establishment was increased, and nearly Rs. 2,000 were expended on local improvements. Much, however, remains to be done here in the way of sanitation and drainage. The people suffer very much from ague and enlargement of the spleen, both of which are diseases due to malaria. Manglaur is said to have been founded by one Raja Mangal Sain, a Rajpút feudatory of the celebrated Vikramáditya. Traces of the foundations of the fortress of the founder are still visible near the town. Manglaur possesses a second class police-station, a post-office, and a parganah school, and was once celebrated for its carpentry, but nearly all the best workmen died during the fever epidemic of 1868-69. (See Cutcliffe's Report, Appendix A., 1.)

MANGLAUR, a parganah in tahsíl Rúrki of the Saháranpur district, is

Area. bounded on the north by parganahs Bhagwánpur and Rúrki; on the south, by the Muzaffarnagar district; on the east, by parganah Jawálapur; and on the west by parganahs Nágal and Deoband. According to the census of 1872 this parganah had then a total area of 121 square miles, of which 94 square miles were under cultivation. The area assessed to Government revenue during the same year was 120 square miles, of which 94 square miles were cultivated, 10 square miles were culturable, and 16 square miles were barren. At the time of settlement the villages in this parganah were divided into four groups. In the first group comprising those lying in the *khádir* to the east, the *rausli* soil is grey and loamy, and the *dákar* soil is stiff and brown. There are some swampy patches

Natural divisions. especially near the Hádwáha, and the spring level is found at about nine feet from the surface. The staple crop is wheat, but good rice is produced here and there. The next group consists of those villages having a mixed upland and lowland area. The low-lands in a few of these villages to the north are good, and yield fair crops of rice; but in the greater number they are swampy, the springs having risen owing to percolation from the canal. To the south the lowlands have been injured by the new cut through which the waters of the Soláni have been taken. The ridge of uplands is much cut up by ravines, and the level tract beyond, is on the whole sandy and poor. The third group consists of a few villages on either bank of the Síla Khála, containing much poor *bhúda* soil, and with little irrigation, owing to the depth of water from the surface (20 feet). The fourth group includes the upland villages irrigated from the Ganges Canal, which are well populated, irrigated and cultivated. A ridge of sand with a strip of *bhúda*, runs through this group, nearly parallel to the upland cliff. A second sandy ridge, first becoming apparent in the Rúrki parganah, runs down this par-ganah on the west, first on one side of the Síla and then on the other, and passes into the Deoband parganah, and through it into the Muzaffarnagar district. The land between these ridges is productive and easily worked, and the Ját and Gújar cultivators are both industrious and prosperous.

The last year of the old settlement effected by Mr. E. Thornton showed

Land revenue. a land revenue amounting to Rs. 96,487, which Mr. VansAgnew increased to Rs. 96,992. The late Mr. Wynne revised this assessment, and proposed Rs. 1,01,746. At that time the total area was found to be 77,070 acres, of which 66,370 acres were assessed to land revenue, and 59,311 acres were then under cultivation. The actual land revenue for 1872 amounted to Rs. 93,215 (or with cesses, Rs. 1,02,507), falling at a rate of Re. 0-8-2 per British acre on the total area, at Re. 0-13-7 per acre on the area assessed to Government revenue, and at Re. 1-5-0 per acre on the cultivated area. The sum paid by cultivators to the landowners as rent and cesses during the same year has been estimated at Rs. 1,26,659.

Between the years 1839-40 and 1859-60, fifty-two portions of villages,

Alienations. having an area of 4,509 acres, and paying a revenue of Rs. 5,759, and valued at Rs. 35,858, were transferred by private arrangement in this parganah. The transfers by decree of Court comprised one entire village and 59 portions of villages, having an aggregate area of 5,732 acres, and paying a revenue of Rs. 7,510. The value recorded was Rs. 21,111. Out of the 66 whole and 78 portions of villages remaining with the original proprietors, 620 acres, bearing a revenue of Rs. 767, valued at Rs. 3,112, of the former, and 865 acres, bearing a revenue of Rs. 1,368, valued at Rs. 10,047, of the latter, were under mortgage. These statistics give a percentage of private transfers to the total area of 6 per cent., of transfers by decree of Court amounting to 7 per cent. and of transfers by mortgage amounting to 2 per cent. The average value per acre in each of these cases was Rs. 8-12-0, Rs. 4-9-10 and Rs. 12-7-0 ; and the land revenue assessed amounted to Re. 1-3-4, Re. 1-3-8 and Re. 1-5-0 per acre respectively. The result from the entire parganah on 15 per cent. of the total area gives an average value of Rs. 6 per acre when the average land revenue amounted to Re. 1-5-0 per acre. Gújars and Játs were the principal losers, yet the former still retain 39 entire villages, and the latter 12.

According to the census of 1872, parganah Manglaur contained 115 inhabited villages, of which 36 had less than 200 inhabitants ; 36 had between 200 and 500 ; 32 had between 500 and 1,000 ; eight had between 1,000 and 2,000 ; and one had between 3,000 and 5,000. The towns containing more than 5,000 inhabitants are Manglaur and Landhaura. The records show that at settlement there were 146 estates in this parganah, of which one was a jungle grant. The total population in 1872 numbered 66,742 souls (30,152 females), giving 551 to the square mile. Classified according to religion, there were 48,272 Hindús, of whom 21,498 were females ; 18,468 Musalmáns, amongst whom 8,654 were females ; and there were two Christians. Distributing the Hindu population amongst the four great classes, the census shows 4,116 Brahmans, of whom 1,820 were females ; 135 Rajpúts, including 56 females ; 3,109 Baniyas (1,385 females) ; whilst the great mass of the population is included in " the other castes" of the census returns, which show a total of 40,912 souls, of whom 18,237 are females. The principal Brahman sub-divisions found in this parganah are the Gaur (3,786), Acháraj, Dakaut and Bharaddhwaj. The Baniyas belong to the Agarwál (1,714), Saraugi (206), Bishnoi, Goyel, Gátá, Sangal and Dasa divisions. The other castes are for the most part the same as those noticed under the Rúrki parganah. · Those castes having more than one thousand members in this parganah are the Kumhár, 1,077 ; Kahár, 2,813 ; Chamár, 13,158 ; Khákrob, 1,535 ; Gújar, 6,615 ; Barhai, 1,236 ; Garariya, 1,048 ; Saini, 1,790 ; and Ját, 4,344. The Musalmáns are returned under Shaikhs (435), converted Pundírs and Chauháns (447), and Patháns (1,436) ; the remainder are entered without distinction. The principal landholders are Gújars, Játs, Kalwárs, Shaikhzádahs, Jhojas, and Mahájans.

Population.

The occupations of the people are shown in the statistics collected at the
census of 1872. From these it appears that of the
Occupations. male adult population (not less than fifteen years of
age), 746 are employed in professional avocations, such as Government servants,
priests, doctors, and the like ; 2,894 in domestic service, as personal servants,
water-carriers, barbers, sweepers, washermen, &c. ; 1,491 in commerce, in buying, selling, keeping or lending money or goods, or the conveyance of men,
animals, or goods ; 7,762 in agricultural operations ; 4,178 in industrial occupations, arts and mechanics, and the preparation of all classes of substances,
vegetable, mineral, and animal. There were 4,935 persons returned as labourers, and 480 as of no specified occupation. Taking the total population, irrespective of age or sex, the same returns give 583 as landholders, 21,165 as cultivators, and 44,994 as engaged in occupations unconnected with agriculture.
The educational statistics, which are confessedly imperfect, show 1,128 males as
able to read and write out of a total male population numbering 36,590 souls.

Manglaur is an old Akbari parganah. It remained unchanged until 1842,
and gave a land revenue in 1840-41 of Rs. 62,607. In 1842 it received villages
assessed at Rs. 21,002, and villages assessed at Rs. 2,781 were transferred to
other parganahs. Five villages were handed over to the
History. Muzaffarnagar district, and five were received from
parganah Núrnagar (now Gordhanpur). In 1855 considerable changes took
place, which are shown in the following table :—

Parganah.	Villages.	Area in acres.	Revenue.	Popula-tion.	Parganah.	Villages.	Area in acres.	Revenue.	Popula-tion.
			Rs.					Rs.	
Transferred to Bhagwánpur.	19	4,754	9,715	4,601	Jaurási ...	26	11,265	11,168	7,304
					Deoband...	2	765	985	226
Received from Búrki.	24	13,222	17,196	16,235	Total in 1855	145	77,401	94,642	68,801

MASKHARA, a river which rises directly in the Kaluwála pass in the Siwálik
hills. Like most of the other hill streams, the bed is sandy, the fall is rapid,
and, except in the rains, it is dry. The Maskhara is fed by three other streams
rising in the same hills, viz., the Kalkar, Jaitpur, and Sansara Raos. When
the opening of the Eastern Jumna Canal was determined on, cuts were made
from the Maskhara in three places, by which its surplus waters were led into the
Chaicha, Nágadeo, and Dumaula, the head-waters of the Hindan.

MUZAFFARABAD, a parganah of the Saháranpur tahsíl, is bounded on the
north by the Siwáliks ; on the west, by the Faizabad
Area. parganah ; on the east, by Bhagwánpur ; and on the

south, by parganahs Saháranpur and Haraura. According to the census of 1872, parganah Muzaffarabad had a total area of 202 square miles, of which 78 square miles were under cultivation. The area assessed to Government revenue during the same year was 105 square miles, of which 78 square miles were cultivated, 14 square miles were culturable, and 13 square miles were barren. The northern portion of the parganah is similar to the neighbouring parganah of Faizabad, and much covered with forest. Four hill torrents intersect the parganah, two of which (the Barkala and Sahnsrao) join the Muskhara, which falls into the Jumna; a third joins the Hindan, and a fourth falls into the

Rivers.

Soláni, a feeder of the Ganges, just below Kheri. The last two contain water during the greater part of the year, and the estates on their banks have moist *khádir* lands. There is very little irrigation, and in the greater portion of the parganah earthen wells cannot be constructed, as water is found only at a great depth (100 to 150 feet) below the surface, and the soil contains a large proportion of stones and boulders. Those at present in existence are chiefly used for domestic purposes and for watering cattle. The beds of the canal distributaries, even in the south of the parganah, are too low to admit of their supplying the means of irrigation to any large extent. The *rabi* crops form 56 per cent. of the total cultivation, and but little sugar-cane cultivation is seen.

The last year of the settlement made by Mr. Thornton in 1839 showed a

Land revenue.

land revenue of Rs. 41,948, and this was raised to Rs. 43,556 by Mr. VansAgnew. Mr. H. Robertson revised the latter assessment, and proposed a revenue of Rs. 57,095 on a total area amounting to 51,621 acres, of which 42,924 acres were assessed to land revenue, and of these 33,967 acres were cultivated. The actual land revenue for 1872 amounted to Rs. 64,465 (or with cesses, Rs. 71,006), falling at a rate of Re. 0-8-0 per British acre on the total area, at Re. 0-15-4 per acre on the area assessed to Government revenue, and at Re. 1-4-8 per acre on the cultivated area. The sum paid by cultivators to the landowners as rent and cesses during the same year has been estimated at Rs. 1,14,949.

The parganah may be divided into two very distinct tracts, varying mate-

Natural divisions.

rially in the character of their soils and the facilities that they possess for irrigation. The northern portion, comprising about one-third of the total area, has the dark chocolate-coloured alluvial soil noticed under the Faizabad parganah, whilst the portion lying nearest the hills is often altogether valueless, owing to the thinness of this layer of soil. The depth of the spring-level, too, is a great hindrance to cultivation, though this is partially counterbalanced by the great rainfall, here averaging about 60 inches per annum. With the exception of a few estates in the valley of the Soláni, the remainder of the parganah is covered with a rich *rausli* soil occasionally intermixed with sand, but, as a whole, productive of luxuriant crops, and rendered still more valuable by its participation in the high rain-fall of the submontane tracts. The water here, too, is only from 10 to 18 feet from the surface, and well-irrigation is easy. In the cultivated area, first class soil (*misan*) forms fifteen per cent., and the worst soil (*bhúda*) only nine per cent. of the whole.

Between the years 1839-40 and 1859-60 six whole villages and 29 portions

Alienations.

of villages, having an area of 7,540 acres, and paying a revenue of Rs. 5,752, and valued at Rs. 46,234, were transferred by private arrangement in this parganah. The transfers by decree of Court comprised 28 portions of villages, having an aggregate area of 5,805 acres, and paying a revenue of Rs. 4,067. The value recorded was Rs. 19,625. Out of the 32 whole and 38 portions of villages remaining with the original proprietors, 4,315 acres, bearing a revenue of Rs. 2,652, valued at Rs. 18,000, of the former, and 4,923 acres, bearing a revenue of Rs. 2,913, valued at Rs. 47,265, of the latter, were under mortgage. These statistics give a percentage of private transfers to the total area of 14 per cent., of transfers by decree of Court amounting to 11 per cent., and transfers by mortgage amounting to 23 per cent. The average value in each of these cases was Rs. 6-2-1, Rs. 3-6-1 and Rs. 7-4-4, and the land revenue assessed amounted to Re. 0-12-2, Re. 0-11-2, aud Re. 0-10-0 per acre, respectively. The result from the entire parganah on 48 per cent. of the total area gives an average value of Rs. 5-13-7 per acre when the average land revenue amounted to Re. 0-11-4 per acre. Shaikhs, Gáras, Brahmans and Hindu Rajpúts were the principal losers, but still retain 3, 1, 16 and 6 entire villages, respectively, besides shares in others.

According to the census of 1872, parganah Muzaffarabad contained 136

Population.

inhabited villages, of which 62 had less than 200 inhabitants; 42 had between 200 and 500; 26 had between 500 and 1,000; 5 had between 1,000 and 2,000; and one had between 2,000 and 3,000. At the settlement there were 98 estates, of which three were held free of revenue, and fifteen were jungle grants. The total population in 1872 numbered 37,078 souls (21,020 females), giving 229 to the square mile. Classified according to religion, there were 33,809 Hindús, of whom 15,222 were females, and 12,469 Musalmáns, amongst whom 5,798 were females. Distributing the Hindu population amongst the four great classes, the census shows 1,443 Brahmans, of whom 614 were females; 1,425 Rajpúts, including 564 females; 968 Baniyas (398 females); whilst the great mass of the population is included in "the other castes" of the census returns, which show a total of 29,973 souls, of whom 13,646 are females. The principal Brahman subdivisions found in this parganah are the Gaur (1,331), and Acháraj. The Rajpúts show members of the Pundír (746), Khági, Polast and Chandrabansi clans, and the Baniyas are chiefly Agarwáls (634), Saraugís, Gargs, Goyels and Maithilas. The other castes are for the most part the same as those given under the notice of the Haraura parganah. Kahárs number 2,072 souls ; Chamárs, 11,777; Sainís, 3,469 ; Kambohs, 1,339 ; and Banjáras, 2,909. Of the 80 estates paying revenue to Government, there are 39 which belong to the same class of proprietors, *viz.*, 22 to Mabújans, 10 to Rajpúts, 5 to Gárás, and 2 to Brahmans. The cultivators are chiefly Sainís and Gárás. The Musalmáns comprise Shaikhs (295), converted Pundírs (44), Patháus (1,154), converted Rajpúts (846), and Musalmán Gújars (703) ; the remainder are entered without distinction.

The occupations of the people are shown in the statistics collected at the census of 1872. From these it appears that of the male adult population (not less than fifteen years of age) 156 are employed in professional avocations, such as Government servants, priests, doctors, and the like ; 1,211 in domestic service, as personal servants, water-carriers, barbers, sweepers, washermen, &c. ; 796 in commerce, in buying, selling, keeping or lending money or goods, or the conveyance of men, animals, or goods ; 6,552 in agricultural operations ; 1,671 in industrial occupations, arts and mechanics, and the preparation of all classes of substances, vegetable, mineral, and animal. There were 4,249 persons returned as labourers, and 309 as of no specified occupation. Taking the total population, irrespective of age or sex, the same returns give 812 as landholders, 9,419 as cultivators and 26,847 as engaged in occupations unconnected with agriculture. The educational statistics, which are confessedly imperfect, show 79 males as able to read and write out of a total male population numbering 25,258 souls.

Muzaffarabad is one of the old Akbari parganahs. In 1840-41 the land revenue stood at Rs. 37,375 ; by transfers in 1841-42 there was an increase of Rs. 19,685, and a decrease of Rs. 8,047, leaving a revenue of Rs. 49,013. The next changes took place in 1855, and are shown below :—

Transferred to				Received from				
Names of parganahs.	No. of villages.	Area in acres.	Land revenue.	Population.	Names of parganahs.	No. of villages.	Area in acres.	Land revenue.	Population.
			Rs.		Saháranpur	6	5,716	Rs. 4,660	2,310
					Bahat	57	44,254	25,557	19,545
Haraura ...	63	29,975	30,495	23,367					21,855
Saháranpur ...	4	1,767	2,088	860	Total ...	63	49,970	30,117	43,762
Bhagwáupur ...	17	18,274	7,489	6,929		96	77,674	44,925	
Sarsáwa ...	1	108	50	...	Balance ...				

NÁGAL, a village in the parganah of the same name in the Saháranpur district, is distant 10 miles from Saháranpur. The population in 1872 numbered 586 souls. Nágal is a small unimportant place on the line of march from Meerut to Landour, distant 11½ miles from the previous station (Deoband), and 17 miles from the next station (Fatehpur.) Supplies are only procurable after notice, and the encamping-ground is confined. From Deoband the country is well wooded and fairly cultivated ; the road is a second-class raised and bridged but unmetalled road ; it is rather heavy, and passes Saisara at 7½ miles, and Barsara at 9½ miles. From hence to Fatehpur you cross the Rúrki and Saháranpur road at 6¼ miles, pass Haraura at 10¾ miles, a village where water and supplies are plentiful ; road for the rest of the way is metalled. There is a third-class police-station and branch post-office here.

NÁGAL, a parganah in tahsíl Deoband of the Saháranpur district, is bounded

Area.

on the north by the Haraura parganah ; on the east by Bhagwánpur and Manglaur ; on the south by Deoband ; and on the west by Rámpur. According to the census of 1872 this parganah had then a total area of 122 square miles, of which 99 square miles were under cultivation. The area assessed to Government revenue during the same year was 121 square miles, of which 99 square miles were cultivated, 11 square miles were culturable, and 11 square miles were barren. To the west lies a small strip of the old Kátha parganah, and next to it that lying along the Hindan, and containing much bad bhúda. To the east of this, a tract of good

Natural divisions.

land runs down the centre of the parganah, and this is succeeded by a very scantily irrigated tract in the Duáb between the heads of the Káli Nadi. The villages in the first two groups resemble those similarly situated in the Deoband parganah, except that in the Kátha portion irrigation is impracticable, and in the Hindan villages the khádir is much richer and better than in Deoband. The cultivators are for the most part Gárás, Tagas and Kolís. In the central plateau there is much irrigation, and fine sugar-cane of the dhaulí species is produced. The proprietors and cultivators are chiefly Tagas and Kolís, supposed to be a branch of the Ját caste. In the villages adjoining the heads of the Káli river the soil is light, the surface undulating, and the sub-soil is not retentive of moisture. In the remainder of this group the soil is good, with a very fair sub-soil. Irrigation is scanty, and there are few wells, so that if the sub-soil were bad, there would be scarcely any crop to be found here in a season of drought. Water is to be found at 17 feet from the surface in the Western Duáb, and at 21 feet in the Eastern Duáb, which is in all respects the inferior of the two. The population over the whole area is very thin.

At the close of the last settlement the land revenue stood at Rs. 1,07,444 ;

Land revenue.

this was increased by Mr. VansAgnew to Rs. 1,04,746. Mr. Wynne then undertook the revision of Mr. Vans-

Agnew's settlement, and fixed the assessment at Rs. 1,00,860 on a total area then amounting to 77,539 acres, of which 70,240 acres were assessed to Government revenue, and of these 61,316 acres were under cultivation at the time of settlement. The actual land revenue for 1872 amounted to Rs. 91,713 (or with cesses, Rs 1,00,926), falling at a rate of Re. 1-2-10 per British acre on the total area, at Re. 1-2-11 per acre on the area assessed to Government revenue, and at Re. 1-7-2 per acre on the cultivated area. The sum paid by cultivators to the landowners as rent and cesses during the same year has been estimated at Rs. 1,44,724.

Between the years 1839-40 and 1859-60, two whole villages and 71 por-

Alienations.

tions of villages, having an area of 5,583 acres, and paying a revenue of Rs. 9,913, and valued at Rs. 36,922, were transfered by private arrangement in this parganah. The transfers by decree of Court comprised 90 portions of villages, having an aggregate area of 9,410 acres, and paying a revenue of Rs. 16,395. The value recorded was Rs. 61,624. Out of the 20 whole and 97 portions of villages remaining with the original proprietors, 391 acres, bearing a revenue of Rs. 537, valued at Rs. 3,412, of the former, and 3,736 acres, having a revenue of Rs. 6,854, valued at Rs. 28,159, of the latter, were under mortgage. These statistics give a percentage of private transfers to the total area of 7 per cent., of transfers by decree of Court amounting to 12 per cent., and of transfers by mortgage amounting to 5 per cent. The average value per acre in each of these cases was Rs. 6-9-9, Rs. 5-8-0 and Rs. 7-10-0, and the land revenue assessed amounted to Re. 1-12-4, Re. 1-12-0 and Re. 1-13-0 per acre, respectively. The result from the entire parganah on 24 per cent. of the total area gives an average value of Rs. 6-5-0 per acre when the average land revenue amounted to Re. 1-12-0 per acre. Gújars and Tagas were the principal losers, but they still retain ten entire villages amongst them.

According to the census of 1872, parganah Nágal contained 110 inhabited

Population.

villages, of which 34 had less than 200 inhabitants; 34 had between 200 and 500; 26 had between 500 and 1,000; 14 had between 1,000 and 2,000; and two had between 2,000 and 3,000. The settlement records show that there were 123 estates in this parganah, of which one was held free of revenue in perpetuity. The total population in 1872 numbered 54,537 souls (24,159 females), giving 447 to the square mile. Classified according to religion, there were 43,854 Hindús, of whom 19,304 were females; 10,680 Musalmáns, amongst whom 4,855 were females; and there were three Christians. Distributing the Hindu population amongst the four great classes, the census shows 4,171 Brahmans, of whom 1,894 were females; 1,774 Rajpúts, including 633 females; 1,358 Baniyas (587 females); whilst the great mass of the population is included in "the other castes" of the census returns, which show a total of 36,561 souls, of whom 16,190 are females. The principal Brahman sub-divisions found in this parganah are the Gaur (4,011) and Saraswat. The Rajpúts belong to the Pundír (1,631) and Solankhi clans, and the Baniyas to the Agarwál (846), Saraugi and Gálá divisions. The other castes are for the most part the same as those mentioned under the notice of the Rámpur parganah. Those having more than one thousand members in this parganah are as follow :—Kahár, 2,649 ; Chamár, 10,579 ; Khákrob, 1,655 ; Gújar, 3 917 ; Koli, 2,901 ; Saini, 2,503 ; and Taga, 3,025. The Musalmáns include Shaikhs (384), converted Pundírs (49), other Rajpúts (845), and Patháns (113) ; the remainder are entered without distinction. The principal landowners are Gárás, Rajpúts, Tagas, Kolís, Mahájans, Brahmans, Gújars, Játs, Ahírs and Rángars.

The occupations of the people are shown in the statistics collected at the census
Occupations.
of 1872. From these it appears that of the male adult population (not less than fifteen years of age) 658 are employed in professional avocations, such as Government servants, priests, doctors, and the like ; 2,065 in domestic service, as personal servants, water-carriers, barbers, sweepers, washermen, &c. ; 873 in commerce, in buying, selling, keeping or lending money or goods, or the conveyance of men, animals, or goods ; 8,588 in agricultural operations ; 2,944 in industrial occupations, arts and mechanics, and the preparation of all classes of substances, vegetable, mineral, and animal. There were 3,023 persons returned as labourers, and 421 as of no specified occupation. Taking the total population, irrespective of age or sex, the same returns give 12,921 as landholders, 10,831 as cultivators, and 31,085 as engaged in occupations unconnected with agriculture. The educational statistics, which are confessedly imperfect, show 187 males as able to read and write out of a total male population numbering 30,378 souls.

The Nágal parganah is a modern creation, having been formed from the
History.
neighbouring parganahs in 1855, when 113 villages, having an area of 72,365 acres, assessed at Rs. 94,069, and with a population of 48,713 souls, were received from Deoband, and nine villages, with an area of 7,268 acres, and assessed at Rs. 7,870, were received from Kátha, with a population of 4,526 souls. This made the area in 1855 amount to 79,633 acres, with a revenue of Rs. 1,01,939, and a population numbering 53,239 souls.

NAKÚR or Nákur, the chief town of the parganah and tahsíl of the same name in the Saháranpur district, is distant 16 miles from the town of Saháranpur, and has an area of 170 bíghas. The population in 1865 was 4,535, and in 1872 numbered 4,493 souls, chiefly Saraugís and Baniyas. Nakúr is said to have been founded by Nákula, one of the Pándavas, after whom it was called Nákul, and finally Nakúr. It has a tahsílí, a first-class police-station, a branch post-office, a Government school, and a dispensary. The site is well raised on the eastern border of a large *jhíl*, and is furnished with well-made and metalled ways, drained by saucer drains and lined by shops with ornamental fronts. The drainage runs towards the *jhíl*, which extends for a great distance as a sheet of stagnant water with muddy margins, and is much used for rice cultivation; on the north and east there are mango groves, but the other sides are bare. The water in the wells in the centre and highest parts of the town is 35 feet from the surface, in the lower outskirts it rises to 32 feet. There is a fine Jain temple here, and the school-house, tahsíldári, dispensary and sarái are all well built and cleanly kept places. Act XX. of 1856 (the Chaukídári Act) is in force, and supports a village police of eight men, at an annual cost of Rs. 432, besides a staff of eleven sweepers.[1] The total income from all sources in 1872-73 amounted to Rs. 2,005, giving an incidence of Re. 0-6-7 per head of the population, and Re. 1-12-11 per house. A portion of this was expended during the same year in paving and draining the town. Nakúr originally formed a part of the *jágír* of the Sikh Sardár, Rai Singh. There is hardly any trade, and the town has a dilapidated look, but not nearly to so great an extent as Gangoh or Lakhnauti.

Nakúr suffered severely during the mutiny. On the 20th June, 1857, it was

The mutiny.

burned by a party of Gújars before the force sent for its relief could arrive. This force, however, succeeded in recovering a portion of the plunder from the inhabitants of Fatehpur, and in punishing a body of Gújars who tried to show fight. All the town, with the exception of the Muhammadan quarter, where the police took refuge, was plundered. The police did nothing to resist the plunderers, and the Government offices were burned to the ground. Ghátampur and several other villages in the neighbourhood of Ambahta were the principals in these disturbances, and, under the leadership of Bakshi and Fathua, Gújars, continued for some time to give much trouble.

NAKÚR, a parganah in tahsíl Nakúr of the Sahâranpur district, is bounded on the north by parganah Sarsáwa; on the south by Gangoh; on the east by Sahâranpur and Rámpur; and on the west by the Jumna, which separates it

Area.

from the Karnál and Ambála districts of the Panjáb. According to the census of 1872 Nakúr had a total area of 109 square miles, of which 73 square miles were under cultivation. The area assessed to Government revenue during the same year was 96 square miles, of which 71 square miles were cultivated, 17 square miles were culturable, and 8 square miles were barren. The same division of villages into groups for assessment purposes was made here as in Sarsáwa. The villages of the first or

Natural divisions.

canal-irrigated group are better according as they lie towards the south, and worse as they lie towards the

─────────────────

[1] See Cutcliffe's Report, Appendix A., xiii.

north. The northern villages are much intersected by the drainage channels from the Kumhárhera jhíl, and many of the lands in the centre and south have a slope towards the Kátha Nála. Nearly two-thirds of the cultivated area in this group is irrigated either from canals or wells, and produces fine crops of wheat, rice and sugar-cane. Water is on an average only eight feet from the surface. In the second group, comprising the remainder of the upland villages, with the exception of six villages owned by Patháns, and a few of which the Pírzádahs of Ambahta are proprietors, the entire proprietary body are Gújars, who cultivate their own lands. They are not so industrious as their brethren in Sultánpur, and approximate more to the turbulent character of the Gújars of Gangoh. In the third group of mixed upland and lowland villages the Gújars hold all except six villages, and are here particularly indolent and improvident. In the uplands the soil is very poor, and in many places almost worthless, and in the *khádir* the soil to the north is light, but very stiff indeed to the south. Water is found at a depth of 22 feet from the surface, but the sub-soil is very irretentive of moisture, and earthen wells seldom last more than a year and-a-half. No crop grows well in any but a few detached spots in this group, and this poorness of soil may possibly account for the carelessness and improvidence shown by the Gújar inhabitants. In the fourth group or *khádir* villages, the Gújar element is not so strong. There are a number of Ját villages in the north, and several villages owned by Sayyids in the south. Water is found at a depth of eleven feet from the surface, but earthen wells hardly last six months, and brick-built wells are so expensive, that well-irrigation is scanty, and there is none from canals.

The last year's land revenue of Mr. E. Thornton's settlement amounted to

Land revenue. Rs. 60,967, which was increased to Rs. 65,262 by Mr. VansAgnew. Mr. Wynne revised this settlement, and proposed an assessment amounting to Rs. 73,143 on a total area of 68,781 acres, of which 57,791 acres were assessed to revenue, and of these 44,995 acres were cultivated. The actual land revenue for 1872 amounted to Rs. 66,119 (or with cesses, Rs. 73,550), falling at a rate of Re. 0-15-2 per British acre on the total area, at Re. 1-1-3 per acre on the area assessed to Government revenue, and at Re. 1-6-8 per acre on the cultivated area. The sum paid by cultivators to the landowners as rent and cesses during the same year has been estimated at Rs. 97,027.

Between the years 1839-40 and 1859-60, forty-three portions of villages, hav-

Alienations. ing an area of 2,857 acres, and paying a revenue of Rs. 3,468, and valued at Rs. 25,080, were transferred by private arrangement in this parganah. The transfers by decree of Court comprised one entire village and 73 portions of villages, having an aggregate area of 5,267 acres, and paying a revenue of Rs. 6,477. The value recorded was

Rs. 24,317. Out of the 38 whole and 94 portions of villages remaining with the original proprietors, 116 acres, bearing a revenue of Rs. 187, valued at Rs. 1,401, of the former, and 2,365 acres, bearing a revenue of Rs. 3,088, valued at Rs. 29,486, of the latter, were under mortgage. These statistics give a percentage of private transfers to the total area of four per cent., of transfers by decree of Court amounting to seven per cent., and of transfers by mortgage amounting to three per cent. The average value per acre in each of these cases was Rs. 8-12-0, Rs. 4-9-10 and Rs. 12-7-0, and the land revenue assessed amounted to Re. 1-3-4, Re. 1-3-8 and Re. 1-5-0 per acre, respectively. The result from the entire parganah on 14 per cent. of the total area gives an average value of Rs. 10-9-1 per acre when the average land revenue amounted to Re. 1-4-0 per acre. The principal losers were Gújars and Játs, but the former still retain 24 entire villages, and the latter hold six.

According to the census of 1872, parganah Nakúr contained 103 inhabited
Population. villages, of which 40 had less than 200 inhabitants ; 35 had between 200 and 500 ; 21 had between 500 and 1,000 ; three had between 1,000 and 2,000 ; two had between 2,000 and 3,000 ; and one had between 3,000 and 5,000. The settlement records show 136 estates in the parganah, of which three are held free of revenue in perpetuity. The total population in 1872 numbered 50,590 souls (22,636 females), giving 464 to the square mile. Classified according to religion, there were 35,912 Hindús, of whom 15,603 were females ; 14,677 Musalmáns, amongst whom 7,033 were females ; and there was one Christian. Distributing the Hindú population amongst the four great classes, the census shows 2,840 Brahmans, of whom 1,321 were females ; nine Rajpúts ; 2,973 Baniyas (1,376 females) ; whilst the great mass of the population is included in "the other castes" of the census returns, which show a total of 30,090 souls, of whom 12,903 are females. The principal Brahman sub-division found in this parganah is the Gaur (2,533). The Baniyas belong to the Agarwál (2,148) and Saraugi (413) sub-divisions. The other castes are for the most part the same as those found in the Sultánpur parganah, and there noticed. Kumhárs number 1,172 souls, Kahárs, 2,246, Chamárs, 5,778 ; Khákrobs, 2,234 ; Gújars, 7,332 ; Barhais, 1,132 ; Mális, 2,494 ; and Játs, 1,981. The Musalmáns comprise Shaikhs (1,182), converted Pundírs (996), and Patháns (2,120) ; the remainder are entered without distinction. The landholders are chiefly Gújars, Sayyids, Játs, Mahájans and Patháns.

The occupations of the people are shown in the statistics collected at the
Occupations. census of 1872. From these it appears that, of the male adult population (not less than fifteen years of age), 310 are employed in professional avocations, such as Government servants, priests, doctors, and the like ; 2,206 in domestic service, as personal servants, water-carriers, barbers, sweepers, washermen, &c. ; 1,105 in commerce, in

buying, selling, keeping or lending money or goods, or the conveyance of men, animals, or goods; 8,094 in agricultural operations; 2,707 in industrial occupations, arts and mechanics, and the preparation of all classes of substances, vegetable, mineral, and animal. There were 2,352 persons returned as labourers, and 476 as of no specified occupation. Taking the total population irrespective of age or sex, the same returns give 1,076 as landholders, 19,881 as cultivators, and 29,633 as engaged in occupations unconnected with agriculture. The educational statistics, which are confessedly imperfect, show eight males as able to read and write out of a total male population numbering 27,954 souls.

Nakúr is one of the old Akbari parganahs. In 1840-41 it yielded a land revenue of Rs. 43,385. In the following year, villages assessed at Rs. 17,142 were received from the neighbouring parganahs, and villages assessed at Rs. 4,963 were transferred. The changes that took place in 1855 are shown in the following table:—

History.

Name of Parganah.	No. of villages.	Area in acres.	Land revenue.	Population.	Name of Parganah.	No. of villages.	Area in acres.	Land revenue.	Population.
			Rs.					Rs.	
Sarsáwa ...	48	22,924	21,259	10,456	Gangoh ...	52	27,048	22,069	13,759
Gangoh ...	1	311	435	158	Sarsáwa ...	2	637	970	412
Saháranpur ...	2	1,737	2,038	1,335	Rámpur ...	2	1,522	1,592	1,054
Total ...	51	24,972	23,732	11,949	Total ...	56	29,207	24,631	15,225

This left the parganah in 1855 with 135 villages, containing 70,347 acres, and assessed at Rs. 63,193.

NAKÚR, a tahsil in the Saháranpur district, comprises the parganahs of Nakúr, Gangoh, Sarsáwa and Sultánpur. The total area according to the census of 1872 contains 423 square miles, of which 286 square miles are cultivated. The area assessed to Government revenue is given at 394 square miles, of which 278 square miles are cultivated, 77 square miles are culturable, and 39 square miles are barren. The land revenue during the same year stood at Rs. 2,62,787 (or with cesses, Rs. 2,90,498), falling at Re. 0-15-6 per on the total area, Re. 1-0-8 per acre on the area assessed to Government revenue, and Rs. 2 acre on the cultivated area. The population numbered 189,022 souls (85,569 females), giving 447 to the square mile, distributed amongst 405 villages. The same statistics show one person an idiot, five deaf and dumb, 107 blind, and 12 lepers in the tahsil. The tahsil comprises the four parganahs along the Jumna, each of which possess a portion of the *khádir*, on an average about four miles from the river bank. Then comes a high bank, often much cut up by ravines; and beyond this the uplands proper. All other matters connected with the tahsíl will be found in the district notice, or separately under each parganah.

NÁNAUTA, an old Akbari parganah of the Saháranpur district, yielded a revenue of Rs. 28,139 in 1840-41. In the following year it was broken up and distributed amongst the parganahs of Rámpur and Gangoh in the Saháranpur district, and amongst parganahs Jhanjhána and Tháná Bhawan in the Muzaffarnagar district.—

NÁNAUTA, a village in parganah Rámpur of the Saháranpur district, is distant six miles south from Rámpur and 20 miles from the civil station. The population in 1872 numbered 4,887, for the most part Musalmáns. The site is well raised, but surrounded by water-holes and irrigation channels, which assist the growth of numerous groves, in which the trees have a very dense foliage. The water in the wells stands at fifteen feet from the surface in the hot weather, and at ten feet in the rains. Out of the twelve wells in the village, the water in ten is brackish, and some of these have an oily substance floating on the top. The zamíndárs are an ill-conditioned lot of Patháns, Sayyids and Shaikhs; and the money-lenders resident here have also a bad name. The Shaikhs are descended from one Míran Bará. Their former prosperity and orthodoxy were such as to attract the Sikhs from the Panjáb, who so often visited and plundered Nánauta that it obtained the name of '*Jaláshahr*' and '*Khátashahr*' amongst the peasantry. The name Nánauta is said to have been given by the founder Nánu, a Gújar chief, who was subsequently expelled by Rája Rám of Rámpur. There is a second class police-station, a village school, and a district post-office here. Act XX. of 1856 is in force, and in 1873 supported a village police numbering eight men of all ranks, at an annual cost of Rs. 450, besides six public sweepers. The total income from all sources in 1872-73 amounted to Rs. 1,355, giving an incidence of Re. 0-4-3 per head of the population, and Re. 1-4-0 per house. A project for draining the town has been taken in hand in connection with the Krishni Nadi works. The village is clean and fairly well kept, but the people suffer much from fever (see Cutcliffe's report, Appendix A., XXII.)

NOJLI, a station of the Great Trigonometrical Survey in the Saháranpur district, in latitude 29°-53'-28", and longitude 77°-42'-52", has an elevation of 929·4 feet above the level of the sea. The upper markstone of the survey station lies 0·4 miles to the south of the village of Nojli, one mile south of Pundír, and one mile south-west of Barapur. This height is deduced trigonometrically.

PANIYALA, a village in parganah Bhagwánpur of the Saháranpur district, is distant 20 miles from the civil station. The population in 1872 numbered 2,271, souls, consisting principally of Brahmans and Baniyas. The houses, with one exception, are built of mud, and in number are about 520. There is a small bázár lined with shops, and seven brick wells, with water only eight feet from the surface. The site is well raised, but on the east is a large water-hole three-fourths of a mile long and 600 yards wide, containing water at all seasons. This was excavated to make bricks for the Ganges Canal, which flows some three miles east of Paniyála. West of the large hole are some *jhíl*-like places of smaller extent. To the west of the site are some fine mango groves, and beyond them the Síla Nadí. Fever prevailed here in 1870-71, and cattle disease was very fatal in 1871. Paniyála is a thriving little place, and now absorbs most of the grain of the neighbourhood.

PATEHAR, a taluka of the Saháranpur district, was separated from Sultánpur Bahat in the time of Najíb Khán, Rohilla, by an Afghán follower named Anwar Khán. It continued to form a separate tappa up to 1842, when it was distributed between Sultánpur and Faizabad. Patehar lay between the Eastern Jumna Canal, the Maskhara stream, and the Jumna. It formed the *mukarari* of Murtaza Khán, and comprised only 31 villages. The settlement from 1813-14 was made with village zemindárs, and before its absorption (in 1840-41) amounted to Rs. 16,227.

RÁJÚPUR, a large village in parganah Deoband of the Saháranpur district, is distant 19 miles from the civil station. The population in 1872 numbered 2,773 souls; in 1865 there were 36,028 inhabitants, chiefly Musalmán Shaikhs. Rájúpur contains 611 houses, of which 218 are brick-built, and of these, three or four fine houses belong to Baniyas. There is a good bázár containing forty shops; nine brick-built wells and a good *masjid*. The site is well raised on the eastern border of the Síla lowlands, which are cultivated as vegetable gardens by Málís, who occupy some sixty houses in the village. The water in the wells has risen to ten feet from the surface since the introduction of canal irrigation, and has changed very much in taste for the worse. During 1869-71 fever was epidemic here and very fatal: 98 persons died in 1869, 122 died in 1870, 98 died in 1871, and even in 1874 fever was very prevalent.

RÁMPUR, a town in parganah Rámpur of the Saháranpur district, is distant 14 miles from Sahárapur on the old Dehli road, and 13½ miles from Jalálabad in the Muzaffarnagar district. The population in 1853 numbered 6,566 souls, which increased to 8,464 in 1865. In 1872 there were 8,234 inhabitants, of whom 4,157 were Hindús (1,922 females), and 4,077 were Musalmáns (1,953 females), chiefly Gárás. The site is rather low and almost level, and the houses are crowded together. The lanes are narrow and uneven. Some of the houses are brick-built and have fine fronts, especially those inhabited by the Jain Baniyas known as Sarangís in the upper Duáb, who carry on a good grain trade. They have recently built a fine temple with a gilt spire. A metalled and drained road runs through the town. The bazár has been metalled and the streets have been paved, and a scheme for the drainage is under consideration in connec-

tion with the Karsuni Nadí project. The town looks well from a distance, owing
to the numerous groves which surround it and the gardens within it. The
water in the principal well is found at a depth of 20 feet from the surface, and
in many of the wells is somewhat brackish. Supplies are plentiful. Act XX.
of 1856 (the Chaukídári Act) is in force, and in 1872 supported a village
police numbering 16 men, at an annual cost of Rs. 882, besides a staff of six
public sweepers. The total income from all sources in 1872-73 amounted to
Rs. 3,715, giving an incidence of Re. 0-6-2 per head of the population, and
Re. 1-9-6 per house. During the same year, Rs. 2,609 were expended on works
of public improvement connected with the town. Rámpur is said to have been
founded by one Raja Rám, and, like Deoband, is believed to have been captured by
Sálár Masaúd. The town is noted for the manufacture of glass bangles, which
keeps six large ovens at work. There is a good parganah school, a first class
police-station, and a branch post-office. An *urs* or religious fair is held in June
at the tomb of Shaikh Ibráhím Pír, which attracts a large assemblage. (See
Cutcliffe's Report, Appendix A., XV.)

RÁMPUR, a parganah of the Deoband tahsíl in the Saháranpur district,

Area.

is bounded on the north by parganah Saháranpur;
on the west by Nakúr and Gangoh; on the east
by Nágal and Deoband; and on the south by the Muzaffarnagar district.
According to the census of 1872, parganah Rámpur had a total area of 129
square miles, of which 101 square miles were under cultivation. The
area assessed to Government revenue during the same year was 124 square
miles, of which 98 square miles were cultivated, 15 square miles were
culturable, and 11 square miles were barren. The parganah is intersected by the Jumna Canal on the west, and the Krishni Nadí on the east,

Natural divisions.

both of which have a course from north to south.
The drainage of the tract lying to the west of Rám-
pur itself is carried off along the bed of the old canal until it collects near
Anantmau, whence it is taken by the Andauli cut into the Kátha; that of the
tract to the south of this, and about Nánauta, is carried off by another cut
into the Krishni on the east, whilst in the extreme south-west a cut leads the
superfluous moisture collected in the old canal by Títron into the Kátha.
Between the Hindan and the Krishni a small drainage line carries off the
superfluous moisture from Umri southwards. The Hindan flows along the
extreme north-eastern boundary, separating this parganah from Nágal. Rampur
is still the most water-logged portion of the district, and therefore the most
unhealthy and its reclamation forms a portion of the Krishni Nadí scheme. Near
the banks of the Hindan there is some low land which grows wheat without
irrigation. On the west there is a little sandy land, but beyond, the soil is a stiff
clay, which, when irrigated, yields rice and sugar-cane, and in the *rabi*, wheat,

Portions of the parganah near Anantmau and Banhera have become so indurated by continuous submersion, that unless irrigated they would not produce any crops. In the south-east lies the tract known as the Kátha, which formerly composed a separate parganah. It is owned and cultivated by Rajpút Pundírs almost as exclusively as Rámpur proper is in the hands of Gújars. The soil here is particularly good and very retentive of moisture, but it is not adapted for earthen wells. The canal and brick-built wells fully supply all the wants of the people in this respect. In the whole parganah there were 825 brick-built and 126 earthen wells at the time of settlement. The Pundírs of the Kátha are a proud, stiff-necked generation, very clannish, and always ready to unite in open or secret opposition to the law ; but of late years there has been much improvement in these respects. They are not too proud to labour with their own hands, but make admirable horse-breeders.

The last year of Mr. Thornton's settlement of this parganah showed a

Land revenue. land revenue amounting to Rs. 1,02,249, which was increased to Rs. 1,11,467 by Mr. Vans Agnew. Mr. Wynne fixed the assessment at Rs. 1,29,108 on a total area of 80,105 acres, of which 72,247 acres were assessed to land revenue, and of these, 59,537 acres were cultivated. The actual land revenue for 1872 amounted to Rs. 1,15,892 (or with cesses, Rs. 1,28,110), falling at a rate of Re. 1-6-6 per British acre on the total area, at Re. 1-7-4 per acre on the area assessed to Government revenue, and at Re. 1-12-8 per acre on the cultivated area. The sum paid by cultivators to the landowners as rent and cesses during the same year has been estimated at Rs. 1,92,250.

Between the years 1839-40 and 1859-60 two whole villages and 57 portions

Alienations. of villages, having an area of 4,555 acres, and paying a revenue of Rs. 6,919, and valued at Rs. 39,286, were transferred by private arrangement in this parganah. The transfers by decree of Court comprised one entire village and 63 portions of villages, having an aggregate area of 4,859 acres, and paying a revenue of Rs. 6,933. The value recorded was Rs. 22,702. Out of the 43 whole and 94 portions of villages remaining with the original proprietors, 384 acres, bearing a revenue of Rs. 593, valued at Rs. 4,304, of the former, and 2,814 acres, bearing a revenue of Rs. 4,101, valued at Rs. 22,864, of the latter, were under mortgage. These statistics give a percentage of private transfers to the total area of five per cent., of transfers by decree of Court amounting to six per cent., and of transfers by mortgage amounting to four per cent. The average value per acre in each of these cases was Rs. 8-10-0, Rs. 4-10-9 and Rs. 8-0-0, and the land revenue assessed amounted to Re. 1-6-0, Re. 1-6-9 and Re. 1-1-0 per acre respectively. The result from the entire parganah on 15 per cent. of the total area gives an average value of Rs. 7-0-0 per acre when the average land revenue amounted to

Re. 1-6-0 per acre. The principal losers were Gújars, who still hold fifteen entire villages, besides shares in others.

According to the census of 1872, parganah Rámpur contained 115 villages, of which 26 had less than 200 inhabitants; 41 had between 200 and 500; 28 had between 500 and 1,000; 18 had between 1,000 and 2,000; and one had between 3,000 and 5,000. The only town containing more than 5,000 inhabitants is Rámpur. The settlement records show 140 estates, of which three are held revenue free for life, and three are free of revenue in perpetuity. The total population in 1872 numbered 74,732 souls (33,718 females), giving 579 to the square mile. Classified according to religion, there were 59,201 Hindús, of whom 26,387 were females; 15,521 Musalmáns, amongst whom 7,330 were females, and there were four Christians. Distributing the Hindú population amongst the four great classes, the census shows 3,617 Brahmans, of whom 1,644 were females; 4,436 Rajpúts, including 1,761 females; 2,556 Baniyas (1,392 females); whilst the great mass of the population is included in "the other castes" of the census returns, which show a total of 48,592 souls, of whom 21,818 are females. The principal Brahman sub-division found in this parganah is the Gaur (3,602). The Rajpúts belong to the Pundír (3,221), Khági (311), Jhotiyana, Bargoti and Rahtor clans. The Baniyas are principally of the Agarwál (1,092) and Saraugi (1,346) subdivisions. The other castes are the Jogi, Juláha (2,325), Kumhár (1,630), Hajjám, Kahár (4,166), Chamár (14,789), Khákrob (3,213), Gújar (7,905), Barhai (1,214), Lohár, Bairági, Garariya (1,116), Darzi, Máli, Saini (3,370), Dhobi, Bhát, Ját, Orh, Chhípi, Sonar, Bharbhúnja, Kalwár, Gosáin, Taga, Kayath, Miumár and Ahír divisions. The Musalmáns show amongst them Shaikhs (1,617), converted Pundírs (831), Chauháns and Rajpúts and Patháns (1,098); the remainder are entered without distinction. The principal landholders are the Gújars, who hold 20,070 acres; Rajpúts, who have 16,109 acres; Mahájans, with 6,479; Shaikhs, with 4,099; and Játs, Rorhs, Tagas, Brahmans, Musalmán Gújars, Gárás, Sayyids, and Patháns, who have each more than one thousand acres.

The occupations of the people are shown in the statistics collected at the census of 1872. From these it appears that of the male adult population (not less than fifteen years of age) 731 are employed in professional avocations, such as Government servants, priests, doctors, and the like; 3,183 in domestic service, as personal servants, water-carriers, barbers, sweepers, washermen, &c.; 1,374 in commerce, in buying, selling, keeping or lending money or goods, or the conveyance of men, animals, or goods; 9,805 in agricultural operations; 4,627 in industrial occupations, arts and mechanics, and the preparation of all classes of substances, vegetable, mineral, and animal. There were 4,779 persons returned as labourers, and 805 as of no specified occupation. Taking the total population, irrespective of age or sex, the same returns give 9,205 as landholders, 14,906 as cultivators, and 50,621 as engaged in occupations unconnected with agriculture. The educational statistics, which are confessedly imperfect, show 21 males as able to read and write out of a total male population numbering 41,008 souls.

Rámpur is one of the old Akbari parganahs, formerly included in dastúr
History.
Deoband. The land revenue in 1840-41 stood at Rs. 38,943. In the following year it lost Rs. 3,090 and gained Rs. 47,423 by transfers, leaving the revenue at Rs. 83,276. One village was transferred to Muzaffarnagar, and seven were received from that district. The changes effected in the area of this parganah in 1855 are shown below :—

Transferred to					Received from				
Name of parganah.	No. of villages.	Area in acres.	Land-revenue.	Population.	Name of parganah.	No. of villages.	Area in acres.	Land-revenue.	Population.
			Rs.					Rs.	
Nakúr ...	2	1,522	1,592	1,054	Kátha ...	8	8,313	9,229	5,232
Saháranpur ...	6	2,426	3,123	1,737	Saháranpur ...	3	1,711	2,519	1,050
Gangoh ...	11	4,914	6,225	2,991	Gangoh ...	7	3,994	4,017	2,201
Deoband ...	3	1,585	2,070	1,369	Deoband ...	1	303	365	311
Total ...	22	10,447	13,010	7,151	Total ...	19	14,321	16,130	8,794

This left 138 villages, with an area of 84,271 acres, assessed at Rs. 99,935, and inhabited by 58,066 souls.

RÚRKI (Roorkee), an important town situated on an elevated ridge overlooking the bed of the Soláni in parganah Rúrki of the Saháranpur district, is distant 22 miles east from Saháranpur in latitude 29° 52′ 25″, and longitude 77° 55′ 40″.

The population in 1853 numbered 8,592 souls, and in 1865 there were 7,588
Population.
inhabitants. Out of a total population of 10,778 in 1872, there were 6,925 Hindús (2,692 females) ; 3,551 Musalmáns (1,399 females), and 302 Christains (137 females). The town site occupies 70 acres, giving 154 souls to the acre. Distributing the population amongst the urban and rural classes proper, there were 142 landholders, 220 cultivators, and 10,416 persons pursuing avocations unconnected with agriculture in 1872. The number of enclosures in the same year was 1,469, of which 883 were occupied by Hindús, 526 by Musalmáns, and 60 by Christians. The number of houses was 3,587, and of these 2,307 were occupied by Hindús, and 1,179 by Musalmáns ; 2,188 houses were built with skilled labour, of which Hindús

possessed 1,362, and Musalmáns owned 727. Of the 1,399 mud huts in the town, 945 were inhabited by Hindús, and 452 by Musalmáns. Taking the male adult population (not less than fifteen years of age), the following occupations are found to be represented by more than fifty members each :—Blacksmiths, 64 ; cultivators, 72 ; labourers, 702 ; landowners, 62 ; servants, 2,622 ; shop-keepers, 571 ; water-carriers, 68 ; and weavers, 50.

Rúrki was, until the Ganges Çanal works were commenced, a mere mud-built village on the banks of the Soláni Nadi. It is
Site.
now a fair-sized town, with good, broad, metalled roadways meeting at right angles and lined with shops. The centre space contains an open *chauk* or market-place. The roads on each side are lined with open saucer drains leading to the lowlands beyond the town. The Ganges Canal, flowing between raised embankments, passes the town on the east. Between it and the town are several open water-holes, which during the hot weather present a large expanse of uncovered mud. On the west of the town the land is low and moist, and the Masúri (Mussooree) road passes through it by a raised embankment. On the north lies the bed of the Soláni, here fully a mile wide, always moist and green, and in the rains containing a considerable body of water. The town extends a little down into this low tract, and there the water in the wells was found to stand at six feet from the surface in March, whilst at the same time in the upper portion of the town it stood at twenty-one feet. Percolation from the canal has here, as elsewhere, raised the spring-level, and brought with it ague and other malarious diseases, but not to such an extent as is found elsewhere, owing to the greater attention to cleanliness and ordinary sanitary precautions due to the presence of an European element in the management of the town.

Rúrki possesses an excellent meteorological observatory under careful management, and the results of the observations made
Meteorology.
here are particularly worthy of record. The following table gives the mean barometer readings for five years, reduced for temperature, but not for sea level. The mean of each month
Barometer.
for the same years is also given :—

Year.	January.	February.	March.	April.	May.	June.	July.	August.	September.	October.	November.	December.
1868 ...	29·142	29·055	29·002	28·873	28·820	28·627	28·648	28·657	28·783	28·971	29·082	29·089
1869 ...	29·147	29·071	28·996	28·868	27·704	28·576	28·642	28·718	28·783	28·942	29·114	29·141
1870 ...	29·056	29·010	28·970	28·853	28·668	28·638	28·590	28·670	28·803	28·926	29·057	29·126
1871 ...	29·093	29·009	28·941	28·849	28·755	28·616	28·627	28·692	28·783	28·922	29·060	29·109
1872 ...	29·109	29·053	28·963	28·861	28·728	28·622	28·655	28·671	28·820	28·952	29·094	29·152
Mean ...	29·109	29·039	28·974	28·861	28·735	28·616	28·632	28·681	28·794	28·942	29·081	29·123

The barometric range for three years has been as follows :—

Year.	January.	February.	March.	April.	May.	June.	July.	August.	September.	October.	November.	December.
1870 ...	·086	·091	·085	·103	·069	·090	·077	·079	·079	·093	·115	·085
1871 ...	·084	·004	·880	·090	·092	·091	·100	·077	·103	·089	·093	·081
1872 ...	·084	·077	·085	·093	·105	·116	·082	·082	·058	·085	·029	·115

The thermometrical readings, as far as can can be ascertained, are shown below :—

Instrument used.	January.	February.	March.	April.	May.	June.	July.	August.	September.	October.	November.	December.
1868.												
Mean of solar radiation thermometer	106	109	117	120	126	125	128	122	122	...	134	124
Do. of terrestrial radiation do. ...	38	44	47	56	66	77	75	78	72	54	41	36
Do. of maximum in shade ...	69	70	80	96	101	101	96	98	98	94	85	74
Do. of minimum in shade... ...	44	50	55	65	72	80	78	80	75	60	49	44
Do. of standard or dry bulb ...	56	60	68	80	87	89	90	88	86	76	67	58
Do. of humidity	61	63	43	32	30	50	60	56	51	32	35	49
1869.												
Mean of solar radiation thermometer	114	119	133	152	159	154	146	150	147	140	129	114
Do. of terrestrial radiation do.	37	44	53	59	74	81	76	75	74	59	42	38
Do. of maximum in shade ...	71	74	80	97	110	107	94	94	90	87	80	76
Do. of minimum in shade ...	44	57	58	65	77	82	78	78	76	62	47	43
Do. of standard or dry bulb ...	58	62	68	82	95	95	86	85	82	75	63	58
Do. of humidity	52	61	53	24	21	35	61	67	73	55	46	52
1870.												
Mean of solar radiation thermometer	114	122	125	135	144	140	132	136	132	128	120	111
Do. of terrestrial radiation do. ...	35	42	49	52	65	74	71	66	61	47	38	34
Do. of maximum in shade ...	73	75	82	94	107	101	92	91	91	91	83	74
Do. of minimum in shade ...	41	49	55	63	74	80	78	77	73	64	48	42
Do. of standard or dry bulb ...	57	64	70	80	92	91	85	83	81	77	64	55
Do. of humidity	47	44	44	33	19	43	72	72	65	51	41	47
1871.												
Mean of solar radiation thermometer	110	118	129	138	140	137	128	132	137	132	122	111
Do. of terrestrial radiation do. ...	35	45	44	61	71	77	76	76	73	58	44	39
Do of maximum in shade ...	71	78	87	97	97	94	89	89	92	91	83	72
Do. of minimum in shade ...	43	53	53	65	73	78	78	77	74	60	49	44
Do. of standard or dry bulb ...	56	65	71	82	85	85	82	82	83	76	65	58
Do. of humidity	56	54	29	24	41	68	76	75	66	46	39	54
1872.												
Mean of solar radiation thermometer	106	114	130	134	153	160	142	135	142	141	156	126
Do. of terrestrial radiations do. ...	43	43	54	63	71	76	76	74	73	55	44	39
Do. of maximum in shade ...	66	72	88	94	103	100	90	90	90	90	83	75
Do. of minimum in shade ...	47	49	57	66	72	79	77	76	83	60	51	45
Do. of standard or dry bulb ...	57	59	73	80	86	89	83	83	81	75	66	59
Do. of humidity	70	55	35	31	33	50	74	77	69	47	42	56

The road from Rúrki to Landaur passes by Fatehpur (15 miles), by a well-
made bridged and metalled road crossing the Ganges
Routes.
Canal at ¾ mile, Rámpur *(q. v.)* at two miles, Bhagwán-
pur at 7 miles, and joining the Sahâranpur and Dehra road at Chatmalpur, one
mile south of Fatehpur. An alternative route, which should not be attempted
in the rains, is afforded by the road *viâ* Bahádurabad to Hardwár, 9¼ miles,
crossing the Soláni and Ratmau, which are fordable except after heavy rain,
the former soon after leaving Rúrki, and the latter at four miles, and arrive
at Bahádurabad ; thence to Hardwár, 7 miles, Kansrao, 12 miles, Lachhiwála,
8 miles, and Dehra, 10¾ miles. The route through the Eastern Dún is
unhealthy during and immediately after the rains. In proceeding to Sahâranpur
—the road turns off at Bhagwánpur, 9 miles, to Hindan bridge on the Sahâranpur and Dehra road,—the first stage is Umrpur (11 miles). The road is metalled
for seven miles, and after that is tolerably good. The country is well-wooded
and cultivated, supplies are procurable, water is good. In proceeding to
Meerut the first stage is Púr in the Muzaffarnagar district (15¾ miles) ; the
road passes by Manglaur, where there is a police-station and branch post-office,
and crosses the canal by a bridge at 9¾ miles.

Rúrki is said to have been founded by a Rajpút chief of some local notoriety,
who called the place after one of his wives named
Local history.
Rúri. It, however, owes its chief distinction to its
being the head-quarters of the Ganges Canal workshops and iron-foundry, established here in 1852, and the Civil Engineering College, instituted in 1847 by
the late Mr. Thomason, Lieutenant-Governor of these Provinces, both of which
have already been described in the district notice. The Sappers and Miners
of the Native Army have been cantoned here since 1853, and it has formed a
station for British troops since 1860. The garrison, European and native, now
number about one thousand men of all ranks. The Church of St. John the
Baptist was built here in 1852, and consecrated some four years afterwards. A
Cantonment Magistrate has been stationed here since 1859 (G. O. G. G., 28th
July, 1858). There is a good dispensary, under the superintendence of the
Surgeon attached to the Sappers and Miners, who is also the Civil Surgeon of
the station, besides a first class police-station, post-office and a tahsíli. The
Society for the Propagation of the Gospel has a mission school here, and there
is also another private school, called the Orman Institute, after Major Orman,
late Cantonment Magistrate of Rúrki. The Chaukídári Act (XX. of 1856) is
in force both in the cantonments and civil station and in the native town.
In the former, in 1872, a village police force, numbering 14 men, was supported
from a house-tax, at an annual cost of Rs. 1,236, in addition to a staff of sweepers. A separate collection from the native town supported during the same
year 16 men, at a cost of Rs. 792 per annum, for police purposes, besides a few

scavengers. The total income from all sources during 1872-73 amounted to Rs. 8,062, a great portion of which was expended on local improvements. At Píran Kaliyar on the Ganges Canal, about four or five miles north-east of Rúrki, a Muhammadan fair is held every year, to celebrate the death of Raja Karn. The fair takes place on the first day of the month Rabi-ul-awal, and is attended equally by Musalmáns and Hindús. There was much sickness of a malarious type prevalent here in 1867 amongst the 79th Highlanders, and some account of it is given in Dr. Cutcliffe's Sanitary Report (1868). Malarious fever is still not uncommon at Rúrki, and occasionally epidemic cholera breaks out. The last attack of cholera occurred in 1872. In a radius of eight miles around the town, containing a population of 78,619 souls, distributed amongst 60 centres of population, there were 777 cases of cholera and 323 deaths reported ; and not-withstanding a strict sanitary cordon around the cantonments, several deaths took place within both the European and native quarters.

The fiscal history of Rúrki is of some interest. From about the middle of the last century it formed part of the great estate held on a fixed revenue (*mukarari*) by the powerful Gújar family of Landhaura, and remained in their possession until the death of Raja Rámdayál in 1813. The town of Rúrki, with seventeen dependent villages, were then settled with certain of the Rajpút proprietors without any previous attempt to define the rights possessed by the individuals from whom engagements for the land revenue were taken. In fact, here as elsewhere, so long as the proprietary body, through their representatives recorded in the village papers, punctually discharged the revenue, no inquiries were ever made as to the internal consti-tution of the estate. At several of the quinquennial settlements the numbers of the proprietary body were increased without any further examination into their rights.[1] At last some members of the proprietary body became indebted to the notorious Shaikh Kalan of Rájupur, and his sons, Nijábat Ali Khán and Zámin Ali Khán. Three of their debtors were sued in the Civil Court, and a decree was obtained in an undefended suit for possession of the shares of the debtors in Rúrki which had been conveyed by a deed of conditional sale to the sons of Shaikh Kalan. Here the imperfection of the record-of-rights gave the astute Musalmáns the desired opportunity. More for form's sake than that they ever had any right to it, the names of two of the debtors were recorded in the bond as possessors of " the third portion of the sixth division of the town of Rúrki, $\frac{1}{20}$th and $\frac{1}{10}$th of Akbarpur, and one-half of Salímpur," and the third was said to own the sixth division of Rúrki, half of Rámpur, and one-fourth of Akbarpur. A decree was given in the terms of the bond, without any further inquiry, and in 1824 orders were issued for giving possession to the Shaikhs, which was effected by the Collector in the same year.

Fiscal history.

---

[1] Sel. Rev. Rec., N.-W. P., 1873, p. 272 ; 1 Set. Rep., 82.

In 1825 these proceedings came under the notice of the Board of Revenue, and from inquiries made, it was found that in the portion of Rúrki and its dependencies transferred to the Shaikhs, there were actually seventy-two individuals in possession by virtue of proprietary right, and not three, as had been stated in the decree; and such was the lax procedure in vogue in those days, that these three individuals were able not only to convey the title in their own lands, but practically the title of sixty-nine of their fellow sharers. After putting their heads together, the great legal authorities declared that, as the Shaikhs had been once in possession they could not be ousted again save by a regular appeal to the proper court. This court lay then in Bareilly, more than 130 miles off, and in that day the roads were not so easy as they are now; and if the Rúrki Rajpúts desired to save their property, which became imperilled through no fault of their own, they had to undergo the trouble, expense and danger of a journey to Bareilly in the hope of getting justice done to them. At the settlement in 1838 thirteen out of the fifteen dependent villages were settled with the zamíndárs of Rúrki, and for the remaining two they were allowed a charge of five per cent. on the land revenue, whilst the settlement was made with the actual resident proprietors.

RÚRKI, a parganah in the Rúrki tahsíl of the Saháranpur district, is bounded on the north by the Siwálik hills; on the east by parganah Jawálapur; on the west by parganah Bhagwánpur; and on the south by parganah Manglaur. According to the census of 1872, parganah

Area.

Rúrki had then a total area of 198 square miles, of which 71 square miles were under cultivation. The area assessed to Government revenue during the same year was 107 square miles, of which 69 square miles were cultivated, 18 square miles were culturable, and 20 square miles were barren. The villages of this parganah were divided into four groups for the purposes of assessment. The first of these comprises a few villages on the high plateau south of Rúrki, and bordering on parganah Manglaur. With

Natural divisions.

few exceptions, the surface here is perfectly level, the soil is good, and the sub-soil is retentive of moisture. The spring level is 32 to 34 feet from the surface, so that irrigation from wells is impracticable, and the level of the country is too high for canal irrigation. Still good sugar-cane and wheat crops are grown in ordinary years without watering. The second group includes the villages with mixed uplands and lowlands. The lowlands are subject to the denudating action of the Solání, but when removed from its influence, produce excellent sugar-cane, cotton and wheat. Near Jaurási the highlands are much broken up into ravines, which, owing to the indolence and apathy of the people, are year by year cutting more and more into the cultivable area. With the exception of one narrow strip on the west, the remainder of the highlands possess a soil similar to that described under the first group, and with similar capabilities if irrigated, but owing to the depth at which water is found (20 to 32 feet), irrigation is practically unknown, and only *bájrá* and *joár* are grown.

The third group contains the villages on the northern plateau of the uplands. In those lying between the Haljaura and Ratmau torrents, there are several strips of good *khádir* along both those streams, which produce good wheat and sugar-cane, and in places good rice. The uplands of these villages are very undulating, with a light soil, and a spring level varying from 23 to 42 feet from the surface, so that there is no irrigation, and the only fair crops are *bájrá* and *joár*. The villages in the tract lying between the Ratmau torrent and the Siwáliks are intersected by the Pathari, a mountain torrent, causing much diversity of surface. The water in this portion of the third group is found at a depth of from 16 to 40 feet from the surface, the population is thin, and the cultivation of the more valuable crops is very restricted. The fourth or lowland group of villages possesses a fairly level surface, with a gradual slope from west to east, and also to the south-east. In the latter direction there is much swampy land near the banks of the Pathari, and in the *dákar* tracts where the Hadwáha takes its rise. A rich *rausli* soil prevails in the west, and *dákar* is the characteristic soil on the east. In the marshy tract, rice, and in the rest, wheat, sugar-cane and cotton grow well where the cleaning of the crops from weeds is attended to. Water is found at a depth of from eight to twelve feet from the surface.

The last year of Mr. Thornton's settlement of this parganah showed a

Land revenue.

land revenue of Rs. 42,023, increased on revision to Rs. 45,835. Mr. Wynne was then appointed to examine the assessments made on revision by Mr. VansAgnew, and proposed a land revenue amounting to Rs. 50,661 on a total area of 60,046 acres, of which 47,741 acres were assessed to land revenue, and of these 35,648 acres were then under cultivation. The actual land revenue in 1872 amounted to Rs. 53,034 (or with cesses, Rs. 58,464), falling at a rate of. Re. 0-6-8 per British acre on the total area, at Re. 0-12-5 per acre on the area assessed to Government revenue, and at Re. 1-2-8 per acre on the cultivated area. The sum paid by cultivators to the landowners as rent and cesses during the same year has been estimated at Rs. 88,566. Between the years 1839-40 and 1859-60, four whole villages and 19 portions of villages, having an area of 2,676 acres, and paying a revenue of Rs. 4,127, and valued at Rs. 16,189, were transferred by private arrangement in this parganah. The transfers by decree of Court comprised one entire village and 18 portions of villages, having an aggregate area of 1,780 acres, and paying a revenue of Rs. 2,710. The value recorded was Rs. 10,418. Out of the 52 whole and 34 portions of villages remaining with the original proprietors, 208 acres, bearing a revenue of Rs. 193, valued at Rs. 1,201, of the former, and 134 acres, bearing a revenue of Rs. 108, valued at Rs. 390, of the latter, were under mortgage. These statistics give a percentage of private transfers to the total area of four per cent., and of transfers by decree of Court amounting to three per cent. The transfers by mortgage are merely nominal. The average value per acre in the case of transfers by private and public sale was Rs. 6-0-4 and Rs. 5-13-7, and the land revenue assessed amounted to Re. 1-9-0 and Re. 1-8-4 per acre respectively. The result from the entire parganah on seven per cent. of the total area gives an average value of Rs. 4-14-0 per acre when the average land revenue amounted to Re. 1-7-10 per acre. Patháns, Brahmans and Rajpúts lost one entire village each, and Gújars lost four ; Hindú Rajpúts still hold 27 entire villages.

According to the census of 1872, parganah Rúrki contained 107 inhabited villages, of which 37 had less than 200 inhabitants; 37 had between 200 and 500 ; 18 had between 500 and 1,000 ; 12 had between 1,000 and 2,000 ; two had between 2,000 and 3,000. The only town containing more than 5,000 inhabitants is Rúrki. The settlement records show that there are 118 estates in this parganah, of which two are held free of revenue in perpetuity, and twenty-two are jungle grants. The total population in 1872 numbered 54,881 souls (24,747 females), giving 277 to the square mile. Classified according to religion, there were 34,657 Hindús, of whom 15,606 were females ; 19,895 Musalmáns, amongst whom 9,004· were females ; and there were 302 Christians. Distributing the Hindú population amongst the four great classes, the census shows 1,786 Brahmans, of whom 737 were females; 749 Rajpúts, including 277 females ; 1,940 Baniyas (774 females); whilst the great mass of the population is included in "the other castes" of the census returns, which show a total of 30,182 souls, of whom 13,818 are females. The principal Brahman subdivisions found in this parganah are the Gaur (1,611) and Kanaujiya. The Rajpúts belong to the Pundír (560), Chauhán and Panwar clans, and the Baniyas to the Agarwál (1,235), Saraugi, Bishnoi and Garg divisions. The other castes comprise the Juláha, Jogi, Kumhár, Hajjám, Kahár (1,678), Chamár (11,270), Khákrob (1,068), Gújar, Barhai, Lohár, Bairági, Garariya, Darzi, Koli, Máli, Saini (4,357), Dhobi, Bhát, Ját, Orh (997), Chhípí, Sunár, Bharbhúnja, Kalwár, Gosháin, Tagas, Kamboh, Kayath, Ahir, Khatík, Lodha, Banjára (932), Khatri, Lohera, Chauhán, Káchhi, Aheriya, Nuniya and Pási castes. The Musalmáns comprise Shaikhs (607), converted Pundírs (107), converted Chauhán (24), other Rajpúts (300), and Patháns (810) ; the remainder are entered without distinction. The principal landholders belong to the Gújar, Rajpút, both Hindu and Musalmán, Gosháin, Mahájan, Saini and Jhoja divisions.

The occupations of the people are shown in the statistics collected at the census of 1872. From these it, appears that, of the male adult population (not less than fifteen years of age), 433 are employed in professional avocations, such as Government servants, priests, doctors, and the like ; 4,120 in domestic service, as personal servants, water-carriers, barbers, sweepers, washermen, &c. ; 1,141 in commerce, in buying, selling, keeping or lending money or goods, or the conveyance of men, animals, or goods; 6,016 in agricultural operations ; 2,368 in industrial occupations, arts and mechanics, and the preparation of all classes of substances, vegetable, mineral, and animal. There were 4,460 persons returned as labourers, and 413 as of no specified occupation. Taking the total population, irrespective of age or sex, the same returns give 465 as landholders, 17,196 as cultivators, and 37,220 as engaged in occupations unconnected with agriculture. The educational statistics, which are confessedly imperfect, show 952 males as able to read and write out of a total male population numbering 30,107 souls.

Occupations.

Rúrki is one of the old Akbari parganahs, formerly included in Dastúr Deoband. It remained unchanged until 1842. The land revenue in 1840-41 amounted to Rs. 74,793, and in the following year it received by transfer villages assessed at Rs. 44,241, and lost villages assessed at Rs. 4,461. In 1855 considerable changes took place in its area, which are shown by the following table :—

History.

Transferred to					Received from				
Name of parganah.	Number of villages.	Area in acres.	Land revenue.	Population.	Name of parganah.	Number of villages.	Area in acres.	Land revenue.	Population.
			Rs.					Rs.	
Haraura ...	28	14,295	18,723	9,519	Jaurási ...	91	66,189	34,254	37,612
Bhagwánpur ...	69	40,208	56,803	35,066	Jawálápur ...	2	1,409	750	1,289
Jawálápur ...	17	15,937	9,023	6,731					
Manglaur ...	24	13,222	17,196	16,233					
					Total ...	93	67,598	35,004	38,901
					Balance ...	119	82,208	52,251	55,849

RÚRKI, a tahsíl in the Sahāranpur district, comprises the parganahs of
Rúrki, Jawálápur Manglaur and Bhagwánpur. The total area according to
the census of 1872 contains 789 square miles, of which 330 square miles are
cultivated. The area assessed to Government revenue is given at 503 square
miles, of which 328 square miles are cultivated 108 square miles are culturable,
and 67 square miles are barren. The land revenue during the same year stood
at Rs. 2,76,588 (or with cesses, Rs. 3,04,345), falling at Re. 0-8-9 per acre on
the total area, Re. 0-13-9 per acre on the area assessed to Government revenue,
and Re. 1-4-11 on the cultivated area. The population numbered 242,696 souls
(109,010 females), giving 307 to the square mile, distributed amongst 498
villages. The same statistics show 20 persons insane, 5 idiots, 46 deaf and
dumb, 604 blind, and 52 lepers in the tahsíl. This tahsíl occupies the whole of
the east of the district from the Siwáliks to the Muzaffarnagar district, and
fully two-thirds of it is covered with forest, or lies in the lowlands drained by
the Soláni, Ratmau, Pathari and Ránipur torrents. Other matters connected
with the tahsíl are given under the district notice, or separately under each
parganah.

SAHÁRANPUR, the chief town of the Sahāranpur district, is situated in the
parganah of the same name in latitude 29°-28'-15", and longitude 77°-35'-15".
The population in 1847 numbered 34,294 souls; in 1853 there were 31,968
inhabitants; and in 1865 there were 44,119. In 1872 the population was
returned at 43,844, of whom 19,528 were Hindús (8,665
females); 24,296 were Musalmáns (11,898 females), and
20 were Christians and others not included in the above two classes. Distributing the population amongst the rural and urban classes proper the same
returns show 613 landholders, 2,124 cultivators, and 41,107 persons engaged
in occupations unconnected with agriculture. In 1872 there were 4,992 enclosures in the city, of which 1,705 were occupied by Hindús, 3,283 by Musalmáns, and four by Christians. During the same year there were 9,364 houses,
of which 4,621 were built by skilled labour, and of these 2,257 were inhabited
by Hindús and 2,361 by Musalmáns. Of the 4,743 mud huts in the town,
2,824 were occupied by Hindús and 3,916 by Musalmáns. The area occupied by the town is 550 acres, giving 80 inhabitants to the acre. Taking the
male adult population (not less than fifteen years of age) we find the following
occupations represented by more than fifty males :—Barbers, 240 ; beggars,
286 ; blacksmiths, 82 ; bricklayers, 55 ; butchers, 140 ; carpenters, 82 ; cultivators, 775 ; dyers, 51 ; goldsmiths, 140 ; grain-parchers, 55 ; green-grocers, 54 ;
herdsmen, 127 ; labourers, 3,090 ; landowners, 199 ; letters of carriages, 109 ;
merchants, 385 ; money-lenders, 108 ; oil-makers, 115 ; polishers, 61 ; potters,
221 ; purohits, 114 ; servants, 4,166 ; shopkeepers, 2,304 ; shoemakers, 334 ;
singers, 131 ; stone-masons, 60 ; sweepers, 234 ; washermen, 90 ; water-carriers,

Population.

129; and weavers, 995. Out of the whole population only 327 males are shown as able to read and write. The Musalmáns are a very influential body here, and have recently commenced to build a new masjid on the plan of the Dehli Jamai Masjid.

Saháranpur is the head-quarters of the district, and the residence of the Collector-Magistrate and his assistants. The mission, the stud, and the botanical-gardens have already been noticed in the account of the district. In addition to these institutions, there is a very good dispensary, schools, a distributing post-office, a telegraph office, a first-class police-station, the head-quarters of the Jumna Canal establishment, the tahsílí, an old Rohilla (Ruhela) fort now used as an office, a district jail, a fine new mosque, and St. Thomas's Church, built in 1854, and consecrated in 1858. The railway was opened here in 1869, and there is one hotel and a travellers' bungalow in the European quarter near the railway station. This being the point of departure from the rail for travellers to Masúri (Mussooree), the station presents a busy appearance during the commencement and close of the hot season, and the hotel and dák bungalow are usually crowded with Europeans passing to and fro during those months. Saháranpur was the principal station in the Great Trigonometrical Survey of the Himálayas, where all the most valuable observations, whether of latitude, longitude or azimuth, were taken. According to the spirit-levelling records of the survey, the surface of the stone slab on the west side of the south porch of the Church is 902·73 feet above the level of the sea. The top of the first milestone on the Meerut road, or thirty-sixth from Muzaffarnagar, is 906·55 feet, and the top of the fourth milestone in the Dehra road is 912·07 feet above the level of the sea.

The civil station lies on both sides of the Damaula Nadi, which is crossed by a low bridge. The railway station is close to the city side of the nadi, which flows through the centre of the civil station past the north-west suburb of the city. The site of the city itself is low and moist, the water is near the surface,—at a depth of seven to ten feet in March, and close enough in the rains to reach it from above. All the surrounding land is, as a rule, irrigated from the canal. On the west was a large excavation known as the Raiwála Jor, which has recently been filled up, and is now cultivated. The drainage which used to fall into it has been taken right through the town by a large masonry drain, which in two places passes through cuttings. Within the north-eastern suburb of the city is the Pandhoi Nadi, which joins the Damaula near the civil station. This was, until the recent improvements were carried out, a mere sluggish swamp, used as a receptacle for all manner of filth, overgrown with jungle, and choked with mud. In 1870, a project embracing the effectual surface drainage of the city, the thorough reclamation to purity of the Pandhoi Nadi, and the straightening

Public institutions.

Site.

and depening of the Damaula to its junction with the Hindan, a distance of quite eight miles was carried out under the superintendence of Mr. G. H. Howe, C.E. This has resulted in a marked decrease in the malarious diseases for which the city of Saháranpur had been some time notorious. The gháts on the Pandhoi were repaired, and better arrangements made for the removal of refuse.

About one-half the houses are built of brick, and these are being added to daily. The ganj or principal market place is an important busy spot. The bázár way is narrow but long, and lined on each side by good shops, the floors of which are raised about three feet above the road level, whilst on each side an open saucer drain renders the permanent accumulation of impurities impossible. The smaller roadways however contain open, deep, narrow brick drains, which are too often neglected. This evil however is in process of removal. The principal streets are metalled with kunkur. Only one muhalla lies to the east of the Pandhoi, the remainder all lying to the west. Cultivation formerly extended close to the houses on the western side, but the growing of high rain crops close to the site has recently been put a stop to, as has been done with marked advantage in other large centres of population. Rheumatism, ague, influenza, fever, and occasionally small-pox as an epidemic, are common in Saháranpur. Dr. Planck thinks that there is reason to suppose that fever has been prevalent here since the foundation of the city, and cites its abandonment as a military station many years ago in proof of his surmise. At the same time the introduction of the canal has had much to do with the ague from which the people now universally suffer. The water level has been raised, and drainage has not been attended to, whilst the flow of the natural existing lines of drainage has been impeded by the same causes. At the same time the character of the well-water has been changed for the worse. There are now few good wells, and the surface impurities held in solution have a smaller depth through which to percolate before mingling with the well-water. In many places where the well-water used to be clear and sparkling, it is now of a dull colour, with a brackish or unpleasant taste. The new drainage and other works have already effected an improvement in these matters, but it will take some time and much close supervision before the sanitary arrangements of the city can be considered to be in a satisfactory state.[1]

Saháranpur possesses a municipality supported by an octroi tax, which in
1872-73 gave a revenue of Rs. 38,324. The affairs of
Municipality.
the municipality are managed by a committee of fifteen members, of whom five are appointed *ex-officio*, two are nominated by the house-proprietors and inhabitants of the civil station, and the remainder are elected by the tax-payers. The following statements give the statistics of the octroi

---

[1] For an elaborate description of the drainage system, see Dr. Cutcliffe's Report, App. A., q. v.

collections for a series of years, and at the same time indicate the nature and relative importance of the local trade. The population within the limits of the municipality numbered 45,019 souls in 1872-73, and the incidence of taxation fell at 13⅜ annas per head of the population:—

Receipts.	1868-69.	1869-70.	1870-71.	1871-72.	1872-73.	1873-74.
	Rs.	Rs.	Rs.	Rs.	Rs.	Rs.
Opening balance	...	6,878	14,421	10,843	21,240	12,642
Octroi { Class I.—Food and drink	No details.	No details.	No details.	13,878	21,450	28,614
,, II.—Animals for slaughter				395	686	605
,, III.—Fuel, &c. ...				1,5.9	2,387	2,490
,, IV.—Building materials				1,507	3,308	3,649
,, V.—Drugs, spices				3,090	3,109	2,856
,, VI.—Tobacco				359	583	489
,, VII.—Textile fabrics				5,588	5,189	5,922
,, VIII.—Metals ...				2,063	1,602	2,638
Total of octroi ...	25,246	29,087	22,235	28,458	38,324	47,264
Rents ...	134	...	...	...	298	1,002
Ordinary income other than taxation,	...	...	...	3,829	1,990	1,313
Extraordinary ...	545	4,150	827	4,350	20,661	27,169
Total ...	25,924	40,115	37,463	36,637	82,513	89,390

Expenditure.	1868-69	1869-70.	1870-71.	1871-72.	1872-73.	1873-74.
I.—Collections	2,101	2,598	2,252	2,230	2,728	2,546
II.—Head-office	...	...	297	500	412	217
III.—Public Works—						
a. Original works,...	...	4,109	6,114	5,115	32,034	41,057
b. Supervision	...	250	1,353	120	620	171
c. Repairs	8,749	3,996	1,428	2,234	1,300	8,838
d. Compensation	...	...	...	1,512	18,406	6,369
IV.—Police ...	4,880	8,328	6,525	6,500	6,691	6,794
V.—Education	...	...	120	90	399	344
VI.—Charitable grants	253	639	1,118	919	1,033	1,213
VII.—Conservancy	2,253	4,025	5,589	5,589	5,904	6,225
VIII.—Road watering	...	...	...	16	107	71
IX.—Lighting	...	845	96	648	375	544
X.—Public gardens, &c.	...	...	...	233	...	10
Other items	811	897	1,749	336	622	4,834
Total ...	19,047	25,687	26,641	26,042	69,871	79,871

Statement showing the estimated Imports and Exports in 1872-73, and the actual Imports and Exports in 1873-74.

Article.	Imports.		Exports.		Balance.		Collector's estimate of consumption per head in 1872-73.	Actuals of 1873-74.
	1872-73.	1873-74.	1872-73.	1873-74.	1872-73.	1873-74.		
	Mds.	Mds.	Mds.	Mds.	Mds.	Mds.	M. s. c.	M. s. c.
Grain and flour,	320,431	503,305	42,215	90,677	278,216	412,428	7 4 11	9 6 14
Refined sugar ...	16,960	23,798	7,157	14,054	9,803	11,744	0 15 1	0 10 6
Gúr and shakr ...	15,221	17,691	2,555	2,446	12,666	15,245	0 15 5	0 13 8
Ráb ...	15,500	16,098	71	...	15,429	16,098	0 13 12	0 14 5
Shira ...	3,535	3,236	385	...	3,150	3,236	0 3 2	0 2 14
Ghí ...	3,627	4,172	872	1,952	2,755	2,220	0 3 2¼	0 1 15½
Oil ...	4,593	2,388	473	2,233	4,120	155	0 4 1¼	0 0 2
Oil-seeds ...	8,845	16,358	433	1,042	8,410	15,316	0 7 15½	0 13 9
Tobacco ...	7,957	6,452	966	739	6,985	5,713	0 7 1	0 5 2
Metals ...	5,342	10,520	250	1,280	5,092	9,240	0 4 11	0 8 3
	Rs.	Rs.	Rs.	Rs.	Rs.	Rs.	Rs. a. p.	Rs. a. p.
Drugs and spices,	1,32,512	88,794	33,700	42,060	98,812	46,734	2 15 3¼	1 0 7¼
Cloth, ...	3,50,177	3,75,950	52,080	90,280	2,98,097	2,85,670	7 13 5	6 5 6

The export table is based on nine months' actual registration, with the addition of one-fourth for the first quarter not registered. It is therefore not absolutely accurate, as it will not correctly record the annual export in the case of any article which is principally on the move during the first three months of the year. The returns for 1873-74 are based on the actual registration of exports and imports for the whole year. In 1872-73 the export of grain amounted to about one-eighth the imports; 7,821 maunds of rice, 4,252 of wheat, and 1,269 of barley were exported to the Panjáb, and 6,839 maunds of rice, 3,850 of wheat, and 1,034 of barley went to districts in these provinces. The rice was chiefly taken by Muzaffarnagar, Meerut and Háthras, and the wheat by Cawnpore and Dehra. Of refined sugar 3,941 maunds were consigned to the Panjáb, and 598 to these provinces; of *gúr*, half the exports went to the Panjáb; *shira* was chiefly consumed by the neighbouring parts of the district. The cloth exported was taken for the most part by the north-western districts. The consumption per head in regard to saccharine substances, oil, tobacco, spices and metals seems too high when compared with the average for these provinces, which shows 15 sers, 4½ sers, 3 sers, Re. 1-2-4 and Rs. 2-8-4 respectively. The rate of taxation for the last nine months of the year 1872-73 for the principal articles paying duty was as follows:—

	Per maund. As.		Per maund. As.		Per maund. As.		Each. As.
				Country tobacco...	2	Sheep and goats	0½
Cleaned rice	1	Other sugars	1½	Chewing tobacco...	2¾	Cattle ...	1
Other sorts of rice	0½	Ráb	0¼				Per cent.
Superior grains	0½	Shíra	0¼	Copper ...	0¾		As.
Inferior grains	0¼	Ghí	6½	Manufactured iron	1¼	Cloth ...	24
Fine wheaten flour	1	Fish	1	Vessels of brass ...	10	Essences ...	40
Coarse ditto	0¾	Potatoes	1	Ditto of copper,	13½	Drugs and spices	32
Other flours	0½	Oil-seeds	1	Charcoal ...	0½	Timber ...	32
Refined sugar	4	Oil	4	Country string ...	1¼	Bricks, stone...	24

Sahâranpur is passed on the route from Meerut to Ambála (Umballa), and

Routes. is distant 9⅜ miles from Nágal, and 10¼ miles from Sarsáwa. The road from the border of the district is unmetalled as far as the Hindan (5 miles); thence on it is metalled. The railway is crossed by a level-crossing just beyond Sahâranpur. The encamping ground is near the city. Hence to Sarsáwa the road passes the Karnál road and railway at two miles, and crosses the Eastern Jumna Canal by a bridge at 3¼ miles. From Sahâranpur to Dehli the first stage is Rámpur (14 miles); the road is sandy and heavy in places, and crosses numerous canal channels and the Krishni river on the way. From Sahâranpur to Rúrki (23¾ miles) the first stage is Umarpur (11½ miles); the road crosses the Nágadeo by a bridge at 3 miles, the Hindan by a bridge at 6¼ miles, and the West Káli Nadi close to Sikandarpur. Both these latter rivers are always fordable, except after heavy rains. The road is rather a good one.

SAHÁRANPUR, a parganah of the Sahâranpur district, is bounded on the north by parganah Faizabad Bahat; on the south by Rámpur; on the east by

Area. Haraura; and on the west by Sarsáwa and Sultánpur. According to the census of 1872 it comprised a total area of 129 square miles, of which 97 square miles were under cultivation. The area assessed to Government revenue during the same year was 113 square miles, of which 92 square miles were cultivated, six square miles were culturable, and fifteen square miles were barren. The Jumna Canal passes through the western portion of the parganah, and irrigates a very large proportion (four-fifths) of the irrigated area, which amounts to about 57 per cent. of the cultivation. There is also some irrigation from wells and tanks. To the east of the

Natural divisions. canal runs the Krishni river, and east of this the Pandhoi and Dumaula, which unite at the city of Sahâranpur. On the extreme east the Hindan intersects the parganah. The course of all these streams is from north to south. The soil is generally good, showing eighteen per cent. of the first class, and only seven per cent. of the worst class in the whole cultivated area. The soil of the parganah may be divided into three belts or zones. In the northern zone it is light, and of the class called *rausli*, similar to that found in the parganahs to the north. In the southern belt it is generally a hard clayey *rausli*, resembling that found in the parganahs to the south; whilst the central zone combines the character-istics of both descriptions, and according to its elevation presents clay or sand in larger porportion. The produce of each season is about equal.

The thirty years' settlement of this parganah was made by Mr. E. Thornton,

Land revenue. and in the year before the commencement of the existing settlement, amounted to Rs. 95,070. Mr. VansAgnew's new assessment rose to Rs. 95,561, and Mr. H. Robertson's revision gave a land revenue of Rs. 1,28,332, based on a total area amounting to 76,945 acres, of which 65,886 were charged with Government revenue, and of these 58,691 acres were cultivated. The land revenue for 1872 amounted to Rs. 1,18,033 (or with cesses, Rs. 1,30,506), falling at a rate of Re. 1 6-10 per British acre on the total area, at Re. 1-10-1 per acre on the area assessed to Government revenue, and at Re. 1-14-5 per acre on the cultivated area. The sum paid by cultivators to the landowners as rent and cesses during the same year has been estimated at Rs. 1,74,011.

Between the years 1839-40 and 1859-60, five whole villages and 105 por-

Alienations. tions of villages, having an area of 16,288 acres, and paying a revenue of Rs. 14,433, and valued at Rs. 74,543, were transferred by private arrangement in this parganah. The transfers by decree of Court comprised one entire village and 108 portion of villages, having an aggregate area of 16,831 acres, and paying a revenue of Rs. 12,569. The value recorded was Rs. 70,537. Out of the 33 whole and 141 portions of villages remaining with the original proprietors, 942 acres, assessed at Rs. 1,155, and valued at Rs. 8,461, of the former, and 13,227 acres, assessed at Rs. 11,014, and valued at Rs. 1,02,600, of the latter, were mortgaged. These statistics give a percentage of private transfers to the total area of 20 per cent., of transfers by decree of Court amounting to 21 per cent., and of transfers by mortgage amounting to 7 per cent. The average value per acre in each of these cases was Rs. 4-9-1, Rs. 4-6-1, and Rs. 7-15-0; and the land revenue assessed amounted to Re. 0-14-2, Re. 0-11-11, and Re. 0-13-0 per acre respectively. The result from the entire parganah on 48 per cent. of the total area gives an average value of Rs. 5-7-0 per acre where the average land revenue amounted to Re. 0-13-3 per acre. Patháns, Brahmans and Gújars lost one entire village each, and Hindú Rajpúts lost two entire villages and 63 shares, but still retain nine villages.

According to the census of 1872, parganah Sahásranpur contained 140 inhabited villages, of which 39 had less than 200 inhabitants, 47 had between

Population. 200 and 500, 41 had between 500 and 1,000, nine had between 1,000 and 2,000, two had between 2,000 and

3,000, and one had between 3,000 and 5,000. The only town containing more than 5,000 inhabitants is the city of Saháranpur itself. At the time of settlement there were 179 estates, of which nine were held free of revenue. The total population numbered 109,767 souls (50,825 females) in 1872, giving 851 to the square mile. Classified according to religion, there were 60,220 Hindús, of whom 27,084 were females ; 49,627 Musalmáns, amongst whom 23,732 were females ; and there were 20 Christians. Distributing the Hindu population amongst the four great classes, the census shows 3,614 Brahmans, of whom 1,600 were females ; 2,095 Rajpúts, including 789 females ; 5,715 Baniyas (2,639 females) ; whilst the great mass of the population is included in " the other castes" of the census returns, which show a total of 48,796 souls, of whom 22,056 are females. The principal Brahman sub-divisions found in this parganah are the Gaur, numbering 3,199 souls, and the Saraswat and Acháraj, numbering 75 and 92 members respectively. They own two entire estates. Amongst the Rajpúts are the Pundír (386), Khagí (176), Polast, Bais and Banáphar clans. They own three entire estates. Agarwál Baniyas number 4,355 souls, and Saraugis, 388 ; other Baniya divisions represented here are the Bishnoi, Garg, Goyel, and Dasa. They possess nine entire estates. The other castes show Juláhas (1,155), Jogís (543), Kumhárs (1,586), Hajjáms (617), Kahárs (4,339), Chamárs (17,355,), Khákrobs (2,705), Gújars (3,829), Barhais (1,379), Lohárs (560), Garariyas (444), Málís (4,223) ; Sainís (2,933), Játs (462) ; Chhípís (358), Sonárs (660), Tagas (711), Kayaths (492), Khatíks (536), Khattrís (465), and Ahírs (440). Kaláls possess two entire estates, Sainís have one, Khattrís three, Kayaths one, Gújars nine, Játs one, and Tagas hold five. Musalmáns possess 24 entire estates in the parganah. The cultivators are chiefly Gáras, Gújars and Sainís. The Musalmáns comprise Shaikhs (5,614), converted Pundírs (1,144), Khagís (298), other Rajpúts (671), and Patháns (2,675) ; the remainder are entered without distinction.

The occupations of the people are shown in the statistics collected at the census of 1872. From these it appears that, of the *Occupations.* male adult population (not less than fifteen years of age) 886 are employed in professional avocations, such as Government servants, priests, doctors, and the like; 6,980 in domestic service, as personal servants, water-carriers, barbers, sweepers, washermen, &c. ; 3,666 in commerce, in buying, selling, keeping or lending money or goods, or the conveyance of men, animals, or goods ; 9,346 in agricultural operations ; 6,920 in industrial occupations, arts and mechanics, and the preparation of all classes of substances, vegetable, mineral, and animal. There were 8,360 persons returned as labourers, and 894 as of no specified occupation. Taking the total population, irrespective of age or sex, the same returns give 1,890 as landholders, 24,684 as cultivators, and 83,193 as engaged in occupations unconnected with agriculture. The educational statistics, which are confessedly imperfect, show 1,886 males as able to read and write out of a total male population numbering 58,942 souls.

This parganah received by transfer, in 1842, portions of taluka Patehar and parganahs Jahángírabad and Malhaipur, giving a land revenue of Rs. 16,537, and lost lands yielding a revenue of Rs. 50,939. The more important changes that took place in 1855 may be shown by the following table :—

History.

	Transferred to					Received from				
Names of par- ganahs.	Number of vil- lages.	Area in acres.	Land revenue.	Population.	Names of par- ganahs.	Number of vil- lages.	Area in acres.	Land revenue.	Population.
Haraura ...	23	11,738	15,140	9,481	Muzaffarabad ...	4	1,767	2,088	860
Muzaffarabad ...	6	5,716	4,560	2,310	Bahat ...	7	1,732	5,466	3,318
Sarsáwa ...	14	4,919	4,001	3,013	Sultánpur ...	1	146	200	83
Sultánpur ...	2	915	1,230	1,123	Faizabad ...	1	578	902	1,255
Rámpur ...	3	1,711	2,519	1,05	Rámpur ...	6	2,428	3,123	1,737
				16,977	Nakúr ...	2	1,737	2,038	1,333
Total ...	48	24,999	27,450						

This left 180 villages in the parganah, with a land revenue amounting to Rs. 93,226, an area of 81,279 acres, and a population numbering 95,201 souls.

SAHÁRANPUR, a tahsíl in the district of the same name, comprises the parganahs of Saháranpur, Faizabad, Muzaffarabad, and Haraura. The total area, according to the census of 1872, contains 618 square miles, of which 328 square miles are cultivated. The area assessed to Government revenue is given at 441 square miles, of which 323 square miles are cultivated, 59 square miles are culturable, and 59 square miles are barren. The land revenue during the same year stood at Rs. 3,31,518 (or with cesses, Rs. 3,65,656), falling at Re. 0-13-5 per acre on the total area, Re. 1-2-10 per acre on the area assessed to Government revenue, and Rs. 1-9-3 on the cultivated acre. The population numbered 253,371 souls (116,360 females), giving 410 to the square mile, distributed amongst 523 villages. The same statistics show 11 persons insane, 2 idiots, 32 deaf and dumb, 267 blind, and 30 lepers in the tahsíl. This tahsíl lies in the centre of the district, running up on the north to the Siwálik hills. Formerly there was an extensive forest on this side, but this has long been divided into grants and let out on clearing leases, most of which have now fallen into the hands of the Saháranpur money-lenders. The other matters pertaining to the history of this tahsíl will be found in the district notice, or separately under each parganah.

SAKRAUDA, an old tappa of the Sahāranpur district, which was separated from parganah Jaurásí and formed into a separate tappa by Rao Kutb-ud-dín in the time of Zábita Khán. Sakrauda, with the adjacent hill tracts, remained in the possession of the descendants of Rao Kutb-ud-dín until the settlement in 1838, when Mr. Thornton separated the waste from the cultivated lands, and broke up the tappa, distributing the villages between parganahs Jaurási and Muzaffarabad. The Raos of Sakrauda are Rajpúts converted to Islám, and some account of them is given under the heads of 'waste lands' and 'old families' in the district notice. A full account of the arrangements made at the settlement under Regulation VII. of 1822 will be found in Mr. Thornton's report in I. Set. Rep., 90. These being of purely administrative interest, and already in an available form, need not be repeated here.

SARSÁWA or Sirsáwa, the chief town of the parganah of the same name in the Sahāranpur district, is situated on the road from Ambála to Sahāranpur, 10¼ miles from Sahāranpur and 14¾ miles from Jagádri. The population in 1865 was 3,706, and in 1872 numbered 3,433 souls. Sarsáwa has a second-class police-station, a post-office, and a village school. Supplies are plentiful and water is abundant. Act XX. of 1856 (the Chaukídári Act) is in force, and in 1873 defrayed, from a house-tax, the cost (Rs. 504) of a village police numbering nine men. The total income from all sources in 1872-73 amounted to Rs. 1,250, giving an incidence of Re. 0-4-1 per head of the population, and Re. 1-6-4 per house. The site lies on the high land above the basin of the Jumna, and the houses, though for the most part built of mud, are kept in better repair than is usual in this district. A small trade to and from the Panjáb passes through the town. Sarsáwa has been identified with Sharwa, the city of Raja Chand in the eleventh century, and is noticed in the local history of the district (p. 245). Sarsáwa forms a stage on the route viá Sahāranpur to Ambála (Umballa). From Sahāranpur the road is metalled, and crosses the Karnál road and railway at two miles, and the Eastern Jumna Canal at 3¼ miles by a bridge. Hence to Jagádri the road is very heavy, and descends into the Jumna khádir, crossing that river by boats in the rains and by a bridge-of-boats in the dry season at 5½ miles. The stone bench-mark of the Trigonometrical Survey, imbedded in front of the sarái doorway, is 896·45 feet above the level of the sea.

SARSÁWA, a parganah of tahsíl Nakúr in the Sahāranpur district, is bounded on the north by parganah Sultánpur, on the south by parganah Nakúr, on the east by parganah Sahāranpur, and on the west by the Jumna river. According to the census of 1872, parganah Sarsáwa had a total area of 95 square miles, of which 70 square miles were under cultivation. The area assessed to Government revenue during the same year was 92 square miles, of which 69 square miles were cultivated, 14 square miles were culturable, and nine square miles were barren. The character and appearance of this parganah is in many respects similar to those to the north and south, and, like Sultánpur, it was divided into

Natural divisions.
four groups for settlement purposes. In the first or canal-irrigated group the proprietors and cultivators are for the most part Gújars, but they are decidedly less industrious and less prosperous than their clansmen in the similarly situated group in Sultánpur. In the second group of upland villages the soil is, as a rule, light, but capable, with manure and water, of producing excellent rice. Patches of stiff *dákar* soil afford good crops without irrigation. Irrigation is easy, and earthen wells last from three to four years, with a depth of water from the surface of from nine to fifteen feet. Gújars, Játs and Mahájans own between them about two-thirds of this tract. The third group comprises the mixed upland and lowland villages, but possesses little *khádir*, and this, too, is devoid of wells. In the *bangar* portion the water is found at a depth from the surface varying from ten to sixteen feet. Here irrigation is deficient, earthen wells seldom last more than two years, and the subsoil is not retentive of moisture. The bulk of the villages in the north of the fourth or *khádir* group belong to Rajpúts, and in the south to Mahájans of Nakúr. This group resembles the corresponding one in Sultánpur, except that there is much poor land in the villages bordering on the Jumna. Irrigation is very scanty, and the subsoil is not retentive of moisture. Water is found at a depth of from ten to fourteen feet from the surface, but earthen wells seldom last more than one year. The only want is a denser population and a greater expenditure of capital to bring this group up to the standard found in Sultánpur. There the population shows 516 souls to the square mile, here there are only 403. Wheat and rice are the principal crops throughout the whole parganah, though cotton and sugar-cane are also cultivated to some extent.

The last year of Mr. Thornton's settlement showed a land revenue of

Land revenue.
Rs. 60,883, increased to Rs. 62,687 by Mr. VansAgnew. Mr. Wynne proposed an assesment of Rs. 69,804 on 59,683 acres, of which 53,947 acres were assessed to revenue, and of these 43,257 acres were cultivated. The actual land revenue for 1872 amounted to Rs. 63,462 (or with cesses, Rs. 69,935), falling at a rate of Re. 1-0-8 per British acre on the total area, at Re. 1-1-3 per acre on the area assessed to Government revenue, and at Re. 1-6-8 per acre on the cultivated area. The sum paid by cultivators to the landowners as rent and cesses during the same year has been estimated at Rs. 88,930.

Between the years 1839-40 and 1859-60 eight whole villages and 56 por-

Alienations.
tions of villages, having an area of 5,840 acres, and paying a revenue of Rs. 7,486, and valued at Rs. 37,288, were transferred by private arrangement in this parganah. The transfers by decree of Court comprised 63 portions of villages, having an aggregate area of 4,163 acres, and paying a revenue of Rs. 5,800. The value recorded was Rs. 24,248. Out of the 32 whole and 85 portions of villages remaining with

the original proprietors, 278 acres, bearing a revenue of Rs. 265, valued at Rs. 1,600, of the former, and 1,542 acres, bearing a revenue of Rs. 1,526, valued at Rs. 15,753, of the latter, were under mortgage. These statistics give a percentage of private transfers to the total area of nine per cent., of transfers by decree of Court amounting to seven per cent., and of transfers by mortgage amounting to 18 per cent. The average value per acre in each of these cases was Rs. 6-6-0, Rs. 5-13-2, and Rs. 9-9-5, and the land revenue assessed amounted to Re. 1-5-0, Re. 1-6-3, and Re. 1-3-3 per acre respectively. The result from the entire parganah on 34 per cent. of the total area gives an average value of Rs. 4-7-6 per acre when the average land revenue amounted to Re. 0-14-0 per acre. Tagas lost eight villages, nearly all their possessions in this parganah.

According to the census of 1872, parganah Sarsáwa contained 93 inhabited villages, of which 32 had less than 200 inhabitants, 37 had between 200 and 500, 17 had between 500 and 1,000, six had between 1,000 and 2,000, and one had between 3,000 and 5,000. The settlement records show 129 estates, of which five are held revenue-free in perpetuity. The total population in 1872 numbered 38,306 souls (17,157 females), giving 403 to the square mile. Classified according to religion, there were 28,705 Hindús, of whom 12,644 were females ; and 9,601 Musalmáns, amongst whom 4,513 were females. Distributing the Hindu population amongst the four great classes, the census shows 2,196 Brahmans, of whom 1,018 were females ; 1,779 Rajpúts, including 692 females ; 1,694 Baniyas (803 females) ; whilst the great mass of the population is included in "the other castes" of the census returns, which show a total of 23,036 souls, of whom 10,131 are females. The principal Brahman sub-division found in this parganah is Gaur (1,978). The Rajpúts belong to the Khagí (1,583) and Pundír clans, and the Baniyas are chiefly Agarwáls (919). The other castes belong for the most part to the same classes mentioned under the notice of the Sultánpur parganah. Juláhas number 1,046 souls ; Kahárs, 1,715 ; Chamárs, 6,214 ; Khákrobs, 1,312 ; Gújars, 4,936 ; and Málís, 1,692. Musalmáns show 7,278 Shaikhs, 454 converted Pundírs, 1,026 converted Rajpúts, and 787 Patháns. The landholders are principally Gújars, Mahájans, Sayyids, Játs, Gárás, and Rajpúts, both Hindu and Musalmán.

The occupations of the people are shown in the statistics collected at the census of 1872. From these it appears that, of the male adult population (not less than fifteen years of age), 463 are employed in professional avocations, such as Government servants, priests, doctors, and the like ; 1,270 in domestic service, as personal servants, water-carriers, barbers, sweepers, washermen, &c. ; 667 in commerce, in buying, selling, keeping or lending money or goods, or the conveyance of men, animals, or goods ; 6,110 in agricultural operations ; 1,749 in industrial occupations, arts and mechanics, and the preparation of all classes of substances,

Population.

Occupations.

vegetable, mineral, and animal. There were 2,428 persons returned as labourers, and 312 as of no specified occupation. Taking the total population, irrespective of age or sex, the same returns give 273 as landholders, 16,525 as cultivators, and 21,508 as engaged in occupations unconnected with agriculture. The educational statistics, which are confessedly imperfect, show 6 males as able to read and write out of a total male population numbering 21,149 souls.

Sarsáwa is one of the old Akbari parganahs. In 1840-41 it yielded a revenue of Rs. 56,440, and in the following year received lands assessed at Rs. 1,152, and lost others assessed at Rs. 8,072. In 1855 further changes took place, which are shown in the following table :—

	Transferred to					Received from				
Names of parganahs.	Number of villages.	Area in acres.	Land revenue.	Population.	Names of parganahs.	Number of villages.	Area in acres.	Land revenue.	Population.
Nakúr ...	2	637	970	413	Nakúr ...	48	22,924	21,259	10,456
Sahâranpur ...	44	20,421	18,330	11,653	Sahâranpur ..	14	4,919	6,001	3,013
					Muzaffarabad ...	1	108	50	...
Total ...	46	21,058	19,300	12,065	Sultánpur ...	1	631	750	256

This left in the parganah in 1855 an area of 60,536 acres, assessed at Rs. 59,570, and distributed amongst 127 villages.

SHAIKHPURA, a village in parganah Sahâranpur of the Sahâranpur district, lies four miles south-east of Sahâranpur town on the road to Deoband. The population in 1872 numbered 2,767 souls.

SHIUPURI, a station of the Great Trigonometrical Survey in parganah Rúrkí of the Sahâranpur district, lies in latitude 29°-19,′ and longitude 78°-1′-59,″ at an elevation of 870·7 feet above the level of the sea. The upper markstone is on an elevated earthen mound on the high bank which bounds the bed of the Ganges to the western side, apparently the site of a ruined fort. The village of Shiupuri lies to the west, about half a mile from the station of Gangadáspur close by, and Mírapur south-east, three miles. This height was deduced trigonometrically.

SIKANDARPUR, a village in parganah Bhagwánpur of the Sahâranpur district, on the road from Sahâranpur to Rúrkí, is distant 14 miles from the former, and 9¾ miles from the latter town. The population in 1872 numbered 1,160 souls. Supplies and water are procurable, and the encamping-ground is good. Road from Rúrkí metalled for seven miles, remainder good : it crosses the canal close to Rúrkí by a bridge, passes Rámpur at 1¼ miles, and Bhagwánpur at 6½ miles. From Sikandarpur to Sahâranpur the road is rather good, and crosses the Káli close to the village, the Hindan at 7¾ miles, and the Nágadeo at 11 miles. The two latter are bridged, and are also fordable except after heavy rain; the Káli is unbridged. The district officers say that the better encamping-ground is at Umarpur Begampur, a small village of 324 inhabitants, 12 miles from Saháranpur and 11¾ miles from Rúrkí.

SULTÁNPUR, the chief town of the parganah of the same name in the Saháranpur district, is distant about nine miles north-west from Saháranpur. The population in 1872 numbered 3,022 souls. Sultánpur and Chilkána have between them one village school, and are also united for the purposes of the Chaukídári Act (XX. of 1856). From this source a village police, numbering 16 men of all grades, was entertained in both villages in 1872, the cost of whom, amounting to Rs 882, was defrayed from a house-tax. Sultánpur is noted for the number and wealth of its Jain or Saraugi residents, who carry on a considerable trade in sugar and salt with the Panjáb. It is said to have been founded by Sultán Bahlol Lodí in 1450-1488 A. D.

SULTÁNPUR, a parganah of tahsíl Nakúr in the Saháranpur district, is
Area. bounded on the north by parganah Faizabad, on the west by the Jumna which separates it from the Ambála district of the Panjáb, on the south by parganah Sarsáwa, and on the east by parganah Saháranpur. According to the census of 1872, parganah Sultánpur had a total area of 88 square miles, of which 67 square miles were under cultivation. The area assessed to Government revenue during the same year was 87 square miles, of which 67 square miles were cultivated, 9 square miles were culturable, and 11 square miles were barren. This parganah may be broadly divided into two tracts,—the one lying in the *khádir* of the Jumna, and the other on the *bangar* or upland. For settlement purposes the villages were distributed into four groups. The first comprised the villages watered by the
Natural divisions. Jumna Canal. Mahesri and Badgaon, the two most northern of these, are intersected by the bank separating the upland from the basin of the Maskhara river, and grow some of the best rice in the district. Hence, too, a ridge of red sand runs southward, to the east of which is a fine strip of *dákar* soil. To the west and on the *bangar* bank the soil is poor and light. To the south the land abruptly sinks to the Síkri swamp, a great rice-growing tract. Water along the ridge is found at 17 to 18 feet from the surface, and elsewhere at from 6 to 10 feet. Earthen temporary wells can easily be dug, but have been seldom used since the introduction of canal irrigation. The sugar-cane and rice grown here are some of the best of their kind; the cotton and wheat, though a little inferior to that found elsewhere, are still excellent.

The second group comprises those villages having portions of both *bangar* and *khádir* lands. In them the *khádir* produces the best rice in the district. Much land on the bank of the Búdhi Nálá is kept as a reed and grass preserve, which at certain seasons are cut down and sold in Saháranpur. The soil of the *bangar* portion is very light and poor. The subsoil, too, unlike the upland

group, is not retentive of moisture, and earthen wells can only be dug with
difficulty. This, added to the fact that the proprietors are either money-
lenders or non-resident Sayyids, will account for the backwardness of these
villages when compared with those in the neighbourhood. The third group,
or those villages lying in the basin of the Síkrí swamp, formerly belonged to
Sayyid Zámin Ali of Chilkána, but they have long gone out of the possession
of his family. The irrigation here is wholly from wells, which are easily dug
and last two or three seasons. The fourth group comprises the *khádir* villages,
where the Gújars predominate both as cultivators and proprietors, and are fairly
prosperous and industrious. Except in the high, sandy tract near Gordhanpur, irrigation even from wells is hardly necessary or resorted to in this group.
The subsoil consists of a friable blue soil, which would in any case prevent the
construction of other than brick-built wells here.

The last year of Mr. Thornton's settlement showed a land revenue of

Land revenue.

Rs. 51,205, which was increased by Mr. VansAgnew to
Rs. 57,021, and revised by Mr. Wynne, who proposed
a revenue of Rs. 67,052, on a total area amounting to 56,717 acres, of which
49,632 acres were assessed to Government revenue, and of these 40,329 acres
were cultivated. The actual land revenue for 1872 amounted to Rs. 61,097
(or with cesses, Rs. 67,205), falling at a rate of Re. 1-1-4 per British acre on
the area assessed to Government revenue, and at Re. 1-15-9 per acre on the
cultivated area. The sum paid by cultivators to the landowners as rent and
cesses during the same year has been estimated at Rs. 88,608.

Between the years 1839-40 and 1859-60 two whole villages and 56

Alienations.

portions of villages, having an area of 4,564 acres,
and paying a revenue of Rs. 4,606, and valued at
Rs. 37,620, were transferred by private arrangement in this parganah. The
transfers by decree of Court comprised three entire villages and 76 portions
of villages, having an aggregate area of 10,592 acres, and paying a revenue of
Rs. 9,527. The value recorded was Rs. 42,131. Out of the 30 whole and 86
portions of villages remaining with the original proprietors, 266 acres, bearing
a revenue of Rs. 309, valued at Rs. 2,515, of the former, and 5,813 acres,
bearing a revenue of Rs. 5,538, valued at Rs. 45,743, of the latter, were under
mortgage. These statistics give a percentage of private transfers to the total
area of eight per cent., of transfers by decree of Court amounting to 18 per cent.,
and of transfers by mortgage amounting to 11 per cent. The average value
per acre in each of these cases was Rs. 8-3-11, Rs. 3-15-7, and Rs. 7-14-9, and
the land revenue assessed amounted to Re. 1-0-1, Re. 0-14-6, and Re. 0-15-5
per acre respectively. The result from the entire parganah on 37 per cent. of
the total area gives an average value of Rs. 6-0-5 per acre when the average
land revenue amounted to Re. 0-15-0 per acre. Patháns and Gárás were the
principal losers. Gújars hold twelve entire villages; Tagas, one; Patháns, one;
and Hindu Rajpúts, two.

According to the census of 1872, parganah Sultánpur contained 102
inhabited villages, of which 39 had less than 200

Population.

inhabitants, 37 had between 200 and 500, 18 had
between 500 and 1,000, six had between 1,000 and 2,000, one had between
2,000 and 3,000, and one had between 3,000 and 5,000. There were 121 estates
at the time of settlement, all of which paid land revenue to Government. The
total population in 1872 numbered 45,378 souls (20,918 females), giving 516
to the square mile. Classified according to religion, there were 24,244
Hindús, of whom 11,498 were females; and 20,134 Musalmáns, amongst whom
9,420 were females. Distributing the Hindu population amongst the four
great classes, the census shows 1,527 Brahmans, of whom 706 were females;
51 Rajpúts, including 13 females; 2,045 Baniyas (980 females); whilst the
great mass of the population is included in "the other castes" of the census
returns, which show a total of 21,621 souls, of whom 9,799 are females. The
only Brahman sub-division found in this parganah is the Gaur, and the Baniyas
belong to the Agarwál (1,667) and Jaini divisions. Amongst the other castes the
following sub-divisions are found :—Juláha (561), Jogi, Kumhár (799), Hajjám,
Kahár (2,324), Chamár (7,381), Khákrob (1,039), Gújar (2,337), Barhai (803),
Lohár, Bairági, Garariya, Darzi, Koli, M**á**lí (1,672), Dhobi, Bhat, Ját (549),
Chhípí, Sonár, Bharbhunja, Kulwár, Gosáin, Taga, Kamboh, Kayath, Bohra,
Ahír, Khatík, Lodha, and Banjára. The Musalmáns show 'Shaikhs (495),
Pundirs, Chauháns, and Patháns (794); the remainder are entered without
distinction. The principal landholders are Mahájans, Gújars, Gárás, Patháns,
Tagas, and Sayyids.

The occupations of the people are shown in the statistics collected at the
census of 1872. From these it appears that, of the

Occupations.

male adult population (not less than fifteen years of
age), 527 are employed in professional avocations, such as Government servants, priests, doctors, and the like; 1,294 in domestic service, as personal
servants, water-carriers, barbers, sweepers, washermen, &c.; 840 in commerce,
in buying, selling, keeping or lending money or goods, or the conveyance of
men, animals, or goods; 6,258 in agricultural operations; 2,394 in industrial
occupations, arts and mechanics, and the preparation of all classes of substances, vegetable, mineral, and animal. There were 3,521 persons returned
as labourers, and 358 as of no specified occupation. Taking the total population, irrespective of age or sex, the same returns give 1,232 as landholders,
16,685 as cultivators, and 27,461 as engaged in occupations unconnected with
agriculture. The educational statistics, which are confessedly imperfect, show
489 males as able to read and write out of a total male population numbering
24,460 souls.

Sultánpur, or Sultánpur Bahat of Shahjahán's reign, represents the Bahat
Kanjáwar of the Aín-i-Akbari. Bahat and Sultánpur

History.

were made separate parganahs in the time of Najíb

Khán, and remained separate thereafter. In 1840-41, Sultánpur yielded a land revenue, amounting to Rs. 39,674. This was increased by the transfer from other parganahs of villages assessed at Rs. 23,007 in 1842, and it also then lost villages assessed at Rs. 24,804. Further changes took place in 1855, which are shown in the following table:—

Name of parganah.		Number of villages.	Area in acres.	Land revenue.	Population.	Name of parganah.		Number of villages.	Area in acres.	Land revenue.	Population.
Faizabad	..	3	2,231	2,366	1,366	Bahat	...	1	357	265	93
Saháranpur	...	1	146	200	83	Sarsáwa	...	44	20,421	18,330	11,653
Sarsawa	...	1	631	750	256	Saháranpur	...	2	915	1,230	1,123
Total	...	5	3,013	3,316	1,705	Total	...	47	21,693	19,845	12,869

This left in 1855 an area of 57,048 acres, assessed at Rs. 54,717, and distributed amongst 120 villages.

THÁNÁ BHAWAN, or Tháná Bhím, was an old Akbari parganah formerly belonging to the Saháranpur district. It received portions of Nánauta, and in 1840-41 yielded a revenue of Rs. 72,030. In the following year eighty villages were transferred to the Muzaffarnagar district, and the remainder was distributed amongst other parganahs.

TÍTRON, a village in parganah Gangoh of the Saháranpur district, is distant 26 miles south-east from Saháranpur. The population in 1872 numbered 3,825 souls, chiefly Gújars and Patháns. Títron lies on the road between Saháranpur and Pánipat, and possesses a post-office and a village school. Act XX. of 1856 (the Chaukidári Act) is in force, and in 1873 supported a village police numbering eleven men, at an annual cost of Rs. 612, which is defrayed from a house-tax. The total income from all sources in 1872-73 amounted to Rs. 1,956, giving an incidence of Re. 0-6-4 per head of the population, and Re. 1-10-2 per house. During the same year one-fifth of the collections was expended upon works of public utility, such as drains, culverts, and roads. The neighbourhood of Títron is celebrated for its excellent sugar-cane of the species known as merthi. The town is situated to the west of the Kátha Nadi about 1½ miles, but close by there is a canal distributary. The site is raised and the streets slope down to the outskirt, so the surface drainage is good and the soil in general is clayey and retentive. To the north-east is a large extent of swamp covering one hundred acres and lying between the canal and the Kátha. The water level in wells in low ground is about six feet, and in high ground about twenty feet from the surface. Many of the wells and houses are built of brick, and some of the streets are paved with brick and sloped towards a narrow central drain. The town has improved very much of late years, and the reputation that it once possessed for unhealthiness is no longer justly due to it.

ALIGARH DISTRICT.

CONTENTS.

ALIGARH, the most southern district of the Meerut division, is bounded on the

Boundaries and area. north by the Bulandshahr district and a portion of Budaon; on the south by the Muttra and Agra districts; on the east by Eta; and on the west by the Gúrgaon district of the Panjáb and by the Muttra district. The parganahs of Bulandshahr adjoining Aligarh on the north are Jewar, Khúrja, Pahásu, and Dibái ; and the Sahiswán parganah of Budaon, also on the north, is separated from this district by the Ganges. The Eta parganahs on the east are Faizpur Badariya, Pachlána, Bilrám, and Márahra. The Jumna separates the Tappal parganah of this district from the Palwal parganah of Gurgaon on the west; and the Noh Jhíl and Mát parganahs of Muttra also lie on the western boundary. Parganahs Mahában and Sadabad of Muttra and Jalesar of Agra form the southern boundary. The district lies between north latitude 27°-29′ to 28°-10′-30″, and east longitude 77°-32′-30″ to 78°-42′-30″, with an area of 1,957·41 square miles, or 1,252,747 statute acres, of which 897,172 acres are cultivated, 121,168 acres are culturable, 20,165 acres are held free of land revenue, and 214,242 acres are barren. The population in 1865 numbered 926,538 souls, and in 1872 there were 1,073,108 inhabitants, giving 546 to the square mile. The extreme length from north to south is 45 miles, with an average length of 40 miles ; the greatest breadth from east to west is about 70 miles, with an average breadth of 50 miles. The shape of the district is somewhat that of an irregular hexagon, the rivers Jumna and Ganges, opposite each other, forming the two shortest sides.

The following table gives the existing administrative sub-divisions of the district, with statistics of their area, revenue, and population[1]:—

Administrative divisions.

Present Tahsíl.	INCLUDES						In the Police jurisdiction of station.
	Parganah.	Entered in the Ain-i-Akbari in	Number of estates in 1874.	Land revenue in 1874.	Area in acres in 1874.	Population in 1872.	
				Rs.			
I.—Koll {	1. Koll ...	Koll ...	321	2,91,600	175,274	194,160	Koll.
	2. Murthal ...	„	66	58,379	36,000	26,857	Harduaganj.
	3. Barauli ...	„	25	20,590	16,623	9,652	Jawá.
			412	3,60,569	227,897	230,669	
II.—Atrauli {	4. Atrauli ...	Atrauli ...	203	1,47,275	108,022	80,647	Atrauli.
	5. Gangiri ...	Gangiri ...	160	1,44,909	118,349	76,727	Gangiri.
			363	2,92,184	226,371	157,374	
III.—Sikandra Rao, {	6. Sikandra ...	Sikandra ...	205	2,56,340	141,586	128,864	Sikandra Rao.
	7. Akrabad ...	Akbarabad ...	113	1,30,980	74,226	64,747	Akrabad.
			318	3,87,320	215,812	193,611	

[1] The principal authorities for this notice are, for the period preceding the mutiny, the Aligarh Statistics by Mr. J. R. Hutchinson, C.S.: Rúrkí, 1856 ; and the Settlement Reports of Mr. J. Thornton and Messrs. Rose and Wright. For the period since the mutiny, the Settlement Report of Mr. W. H. Smith, C.S, and a few notes by Mr. E. S. Robertson, C.S., are my chief sources of information. All statistics as to area, assessments, and the like are based on Mr. Smith's final figures.

Present Tahsil.		Parganah.	Entered in the Ain-i-Akbari in	Number of estates in 1874.	Land revenue in 1874.	Area in acres in 1874.	Population in 1872.	In the Police jurisdiction of station.
					Rs.			
IV.—Khair	{	8. Khair ...	Koil ...	144	1,74,070	98,305	71,951	Khair.
	{	9. Tappal ...	Tappal ...	100	1,36,090	95,499	59,809	Tappal.
	{	10. Chandaus...	Chandaus ...	75	90,890	66,343	38,699	Chandaus.
				319	4,01,050	260,147	160,459	
V.—Iglás	{	11. Hasangarh,	Koil ...	117	1,65,584	79,771	66,838	Gonda.
	{	12. Gorai ...	„ ...	116	1,22,110	56,797	47,827	Iglás.
				233	1,87,694	136,568	114,665	
VI.—Háthras	{	13. Háthras ...	Jalesar ...	257	3,11,635	139,345	159,834	Háthras.
	{	14. Mursán ...	„ ...	143	1,06,891	46,607	47,496	Mursán.
				400	4,18,526	185,952	207,330	
			GRAND TOTAL,	2,045	20,47,343	1,252,747	1,073,108	

In the time of Akbar the Sirkár of Koil contained twenty-one maháls or parganahs, divided among the four dastúrs of Koil, Márahra, Akbarabad, and Thána Farída. The following ing table gives the names of the maháls and their land revenue in dáms :—

Administrative changes.

Maháls.			Land revenue in dáms.	Maháls.			Land revenue in dáms.
Atrauli	...	...	54,34,459	Dibái	...	...	21,69,933
Akbarabad	...	...	30,03,409	Sikandra Rao	...	...	44,12,631
Ahár	...	...	21,06,554	Soron	...	...	8,05,016
Pahásu	...	...	25,02,562	Sirhpura	...	...	9,89,458
Bilrám	...	...	21,31,765	Shikárpur	...	...	19,84,824
Pachlána	...	...	6,24,825	Koil	...	...	1,04,12,305
Tappal	...	...	18,02,571	Gangíri	...	...	3,72,050
Thána Farída	...	...	2,12,759	Márahra	...	...	36,79,582
Jaláli	...	...	29,57,910	Malakpur	...	...	14,46,132
Chandaus	...	...	17,49,238	Noh	...	...	13,11,955
Khúrja	...	...	37,03,090				
				Total	...		5,38,12,949

Taking the rupee at twenty double dáms,[1] the land revenue of this Sirkár was about Rs. 2,69,06,474, or 2,690,647 pound sterling. It was also bound to furnish a contingent of 4,035 cavalry and 78,950 infantry. Mursán and Háthras, formed out of Jalesar, belonged to Sirkár Agra, and all the remaining parganahs

---

[1] See Thomas's *Pathan Kings*, 431.

of this district to Sirkár Koil. Saidhupur is the same as Sirhpura, and Malakpur or Malikpur has been converted into Anúpshahr since the time of Shahjahán. The changes that have occurred since the Musalmán occupation may be briefly noticed here. In 1802, by the treaty of Faizabad, the British frontier came within fifteen miles of Koil, and included parganahs Sikandra Rao, Márahra, Akbarabad, Jaláli, Pachlána, and Gangíri. On the fall of Aligarh, on the 4th September, 1803, the territories to the north as far as the Siwáliks, and to the east as far as the Sárda, fell into the hands of the British. On the 2nd of October of the same year, Mr. R. Cunynghame, Collector of Etáwa ; Mr. Leycester, Collector of Moradabad ; and Mr. Claude Russell, Governor-General's Agent at Farukhabad, were directed to distribute the conquered territory into three divisions, and attach one division to each of their respective districts, in order to commence the settlement.[1] The Collectors met at Koil on the 28th of October, and, modifying the instructions received by them, submitted to Lord Lake, as Commander-in-Chief, statements of a proposed division into four portions of the conquered districts. The first portion comprised the present districts of Saháranpur, Muzaffarnagar, and the parganahs in the neighbourhood of Meerut and Hápur, containing altogether fifty-three maháls or parganahs. The second portion included Khúrja, Sikandarabad, Baran, Shikárpur, Dádri, Dásna, Kásna, Dankaur, Gházi-ud-dínnagar (Ghaziabad), Begamabad, Malikpur, Garhmuk-tesar, and some other neighbouring parganahs, amounting altogether to thirty maháls. The third portion, to be attached to Fatehgarh, contained Koil, including Kanka, Atrauli, Dibái, Chharra, Bhamauri, Pindráwal, Khair, Noh, Chandaus, Barauli, Murthal, and Pítampur, altogether twelve maháls. The fourth portion, to be attached to Etáwa, included Fíruzabad, Sadabad, Sahpu, Khandauli, Ráya, Joár, Mursán, Mát, Mahában, Hasangarh, Gorai, Husain, Tuksán, Háthras, Jalesar, Khalílganj, Daryapur, Moheriya, and Sonri, or fifteen maháls. The third and fourth divisions were sanctioned at once ; the second was placed under charge of Colonel Ochterlony, the Resident at Dehli; and the first was sub-divided into the northern and southern divisions, the latter of which was annexed to the Moradabad district.[2]

In 1804 the Aligarh district was formed by the union of the second, third, and fourth divisions, with the addition of parganah Anúpshahr from Moradabad[3] and parganah Sikandra Rao from Etáwa ; and on the 1st of August, 1804, Mr. C. Russell was appointed Collector of the new district. In 1816 the Kásganj tahsíl, comprising parganahs[4] Bilrám, Faizpur Badariya, Soron, and half Márahra, were annexed to Aligarh from Etáwa, and Fíruzabad, Khandauli, and

---

[1] For a more detailed account of the several parganahs see the alphabetical arrangement following the district notice. [2] November 4, 1803. [3] Board's Records, 18th February, 1805, No. 19, Etáwa transfers ; Ibid, 28th July, 1809, No. 33 ; and 8th August, 1809, No. 15. [4] Ibid, 31st December, 1816, No. 16.

Sahpu were transferred to Agra. In 1818 A.D., Ahár Tilbegampur, Sikandar-abad, Dankaur, Kásna, Baran, Málágarh (Agauta), and Malikpur were transferred to Meerut.[1] The next great change occurred in 1824, when parganahs Bilrám, Faizpur Badariya, Soron, and half of Márahra were annexed to the newly created district of Sahiswán, now known as Budaon. Parganahs Sadabad, Sikandra Rao, Mahában, Mát, Sonai, Ráya, Jalesar, Awa Mísa, and Noh Jhíl were transferred to the newly-created district of Sadabad, now known as Muttra ; and parganahs Dibái, Shikárpur, Anúpshahr, Jahángírabad, Khúrja, half Pítampur, and Ahmadgarh were transferred to the newly created district of Bulandshahr.[2]

In 1828-29 parganahs Somna and Chandaus were transferred to Buland-shahr,[3] but were re-annexed to Aligarh two years afterwards. Parganah Sikandra Rao was also re-annexed from Sadabad in 1832-33, and half of Márahra from Fatehgarh in 1837. The Budaon parganahs were shortly afterwards transferred to Fatehgarh, but were re-annexed to Budaon in 1837, and again separated in 1845 and attached to the Patiáli sub-division (now Eta), to which Márahra and Pach-lána were transferred in 1856. In 1854, 17 villages from Barauli and one from Atrauli were transferred to Bulandshahr. Of the parganahs appearing in the present list, Koil, Atrauli, Gangíri, Sikandra, Tappal, and Chandaus were in existence in the time of Akbar. The origin of Mursán and Háthras has been explained. Khair, Hasangarh, Gorai, Murthal, and Barauli are talukas detached from Koil, and Akrabad is the modern rendering of Akbarabad.

There were originally two Sadr Amíns, besides the covenanted Judge and Registers (Registrars), for the trial of civil suits. The latter were salaried officers, and the former received each Rs. 50 a month besides the institution fees until 1815, when, by section 49 of Regulation XXIII., 1814, the remuneration for themselves and their establishments was confined to the value of the stamps on the plaints in cases decided on the merits or by compromise. In 1816 the Judge reported these as amounting to Rs. 927 only, of which Rs. 600 were disbursed for establishment, leaving only Rs. 27 a month to the Sadr Amíns. In 1815 munsifs were appointed under Regulation XXIII., 1814, instead of kázis or native commissioners, and were remunerated by institution fees. They were appointed to eleven stations,—Sikandarabad, Bulandshahr, Khúrja, Anúpshahr, and Dibái, now in the Buland-shahr district ; Atrauli, Khair, Kauriyaganj, and Sikandra Rao, now in Aligarh ; Jalesar, now in Agra ; and Mahában, now in Muttra. The number of munsifis was shortly afterwards reduced to eight. In 1833 there were seven munsifis,—Koil, Khair, Atrauli, Háthras, Kásganj, Ráya, and Jalesar. In 1846 the two last were removed to Agra. In 1856 the munsifis in Aligarh were

Civil administration.

---

[1] Board's Records, 4th August, 1818. [2] *Ibid,* 15th September, 1823, No. 21 ; 27th February, 1824, No. 1 ; 23rd June, 1828, No. 1. [3] *Ibid,* 4th August, 1826, No. 2.

Koil, Atrauli, Khair, Háthras, and Kásganj; the last was transferred to Eta in the same year. At present there are four of these courts of original civil jurisdiction, *viz.*, Akrabad, Koil, Khair, and Háthras. The munsif of Akrabad has jurisdiction over tahsíl Atrauli, parganah Akrabad, and part of Sikandra Rao; the munsif of Koil over tahsíl Koil; the munsif of Khair over tahsíls Khair and Iglás; and the munsif of Háthras over tahsíl Háthras and portions of Sikandra Rao. The Judge of Aligarh has appellate civil and criminal jurisdiction, and original criminal jurisdiction in sessions cases throughout the district.

The number and distribution of the magisterial and other courts and officers from 1803 to 1855 have been given in detail in Mr. Hutchinson's Memoir. In 1860-61 there were 21 magisterial courts, 12 civil and revenue courts, and five covenanted officers serving in the district; in 1870-71 the numbers were 25, 13, and 6 respectively. The revenue and magisterial staff in 1874 consisted of a Magistrate-Collector and his Assistant, five Deputy Collectors, six tahsíldárs, three of whom have revenue powers and magisterial powers of the second class, and six Honorary Magistrates. There is also a Deputy Inspector of Customs and of Schools, an Inspector of Post-offices, District Superintendent of Police, and a Civil Surgeon, besides the railway staff and the officers of the Canal and Public Works Departments.

The district consists of one vast plain drained by six streams, and possesses
General appearance. no natural inequality of surface nor any artificial one of any importance. The height of the Duáb at Somna is 622·31 feet above the level of the sea, at Háthras it is 586·01 feet, and at Aligarh 605·85 feet. Where the Ganges and Jumna bound the district there are tracts of low-lying land, rich and well cultivated, and for the most part dry, except in the rains. The old bed of the Ganges is known as the Búrh Ganga, besides the term *khádir* commonly applied to such lands. To the south of the district there is no *khádir*, and altogether the *khádir* of the great rivers comprises no more than nine entire villages and portions of eleven others on the Jumna side, and eighteen entire villages with portions of twelve others on the Ganges side; with a river frontage on the west of about twelve miles, and on the east of about ten miles. On the Jumna the *khádir* is well raised and but little subject to inundation, whilst on the Ganges it is lower, and its appearance changes with the floods of almost every year. From the Ganges and the Jumna the land rises, at first abruptly, and afterwards gradually, to the watershed along which passes the Ganges Canal. Taking a section of the country from east to west the change in elevation is well marked by the high bank of the Ganges, to the west of which the heights are only varied by the depressions through which the smaller streams flow southward.

The following table of ascertained heights above the level of the sea

Heights. in this district is compiled from the records of the Great Trigonometrical Survey. See further under ALIGARH, SOMNA, CHANDAUS, and HÁTHRAS, in the alphabetical arrangement:—

On the Dehli and Agra road by Aligarh—

						Feet.
Masonry pillar on railway at Somna	...	...	...	...		628·98
Somna bench-mark ...	...	...	...	...	...	622·31
Top of post on 65th mile from Dehli	...	...	...	...		632·19
Ditto 66th ditto	...	...	...	...		626·31
Kanhaiya Deota crossing, pillar on bank, ...	...	...	...			624·76
Top of pillar on embankment ...	...	...	...	...		622·75
Top of stone on 68th mile from Dehli	...	...	...	...		624·18
Surface of plinth of 69th milestone from Dehli	...	...	...			624·17
Top of post on 70th mile from Dehli	...	...	...	...		622·79
Top of stone on 71st ditto	...	...	...	...		621·34
Ditto 72nd ditto	...	...	...	...		622·45
Ditto 73rd ditto	...	...	...	...		622·26
Top of post on 74th ditto	...	...	...	...		621·97
Top of stone on 75th ditto	...	...	...	...		617·58
Top of post on 76th ditto	...	...	...	...		612·58
Top of stone on 77th ditto	...	...	...	...		610·99
Ditto 78th ditto	...	...	...	...		613·50
Well in encamping-ground, Aligarh	...	...	...	...		609·89
Ditto on surface of largest block of stone	...	...	...			610·49
Bench-mark opposite rest-house in ditto	...	...	...	...		605·85
Platform of railway engine-house	...	...	...	...		608·75
Surface of plinth of 2nd milestone on Agra road	...	...	...			602·45
Ditto 4th ditto	...	...	...	...		602·41
Bench-mark, 1¾ miles north of bungalow	...	...	...			602·57
Surface of plinth of 9th milestone from Aligarh	...	...	...			596·52
Ditto 10th ditto	...	...	...	...		592·39
Ditto 11th ditto	...	...	...	...		593·87
Ditto 12th ditto	...	...	...	...		589·93
Sásni bench-mark ...	...	...	...	...		589·20
Surface of plinth of 13th milestone from Aligarh	...	...	...			587·08
Ditto 14th ditto	...	...	...	...		591·39
Ditto 15th ditto	...	...	...	...		587·99
Ditto 17th ditto	...	...	...	...		588·04
Surface of plinth of Sidh Gopál's temple	...	...	...	...		581·40
Ditto 19th milestone from Aligarh	...	...	...			584·04
Háthras bench-mark ...	...	...	...	...		586·01
Surface of plinth of 23rd milestone from Aligarh	...	...	...			578·97
Ditto 24th ditto	...	...	...	...		576·88
Ditto 25th ditto	...	...	...	...		580·02
Ditto 26th ditto	...	...	...	...		575·40
Kewalgiri bench-mark	...	...	...	...		575·17
Surface of plinth of 28th milestone	...	...	...	...		574·41

The soil throughout may be said to consist of a rich fertile loam which
becomes much indurated wherever it comes into con-
Soils.
stant contact with water, whilst here and there are large
tracts of sandy soil. To the north-east, in parganah Atrauli, the land bordering
the Ganges possesses a more or less sandy soil. To the west, along the high bank
of the Jumna, the soil is sandy for a few miles, but then comes pure loam, and
wherever sand occurs it appears in the form of high ridges or hillocks, running
from north to south in irregular lines, sometimes interrupted for a space, but
traceable throughout. Thus three ridges run through the Khair tahsíl: the
western ridge forms the natural boundary between Tappal and Chandaus; the
middle ridge follows the line of the Karwan; and the eastern ridge is less
defined and most interrupted. All three ridges are continued through the upper
portion of Iglás, and two of them extend into Mursán. Occasional spurs are
thrown off from these lines of sand, and gradually intermingle with the plain.
In the other tahsíls there are tracts of land of varying extent, but none in any
way remarkable and with irrigation the soil is always fertile. To the north
the eastern tracts are inferior to the western, and neither are so fertile as the
tracts to the south. The substratum is entirely kunkur,—a formation composed
of nodules of impure carbonate of lime, which is found everywhere at a few
feet below the surface, and in several places crops out even at the surface. In
many cases it takes the form of blocks, and is used for building purposes, and
in the form of coarse gravel for metalling roads.

The conventional distribution of soils in this district comprises (1) *bára*, or the
lands immediately adjoining the village site, and highly cultivated and manured; (2) those more distant, known as *manjha* (middle); and (3) the outlying
lands called *barhá*. The natural classification of soils is into *dumat, mattiyár,
bhúr*, and *píliya* or sand. At the recent settlement, the soil was divided into seven
classes for settlement purposes, *viz., bára*—irrigated (*cháhí*), and unirrigated
(*kháki*)—comprising the manured land around the village site; *manjha*, irrigated
and unirrigated, the manured fields between the *bára* and the unmanured outlying lands; *barha*, the outlying lands which are always unmanured, divided
into irrigated and unirrigated. The unirrigated *barha* is sub-divided, according
to quality and consistency of land, into four classes :—*chiknot* (clay), *mattiyár*
(loam), *píliya* (light sandy loam), and *bhúr* (sand). Though almost all irrigated
barha is of equal value as to productive power, unirrigated *barha* presents
marked differences in quality. So little, however, exists between unirrigated
chiknot and *mattiyár* and between *bhúr* and *píliya*, that the two former constitute
the first class, and the latter form the second class unirrigated *barha* of
the settlement records. These artificial distinctions are well understood by
the people, and form the foundation of their own system of assessment of
rents. The following statement gives the soil areas of the cultivated area

in acres by parganahs for the whole district, as ascertained at the recent settlement :—

Parganahs.	Irrigated.				Unirrigated.					Total cultivated area.
	Bára.	Manjha.	Barhá.	Total.	Bára.	Manjha.	Barhá (I).	Barhá (II).	Total.	
Atrauli ...	3,032	3,639	33,9'9	40,590	350	373	a11,419	b17,992	30,137	70,727
Gangíri ...	3,176	3,690	25,950	32,816	495	819	c12,390	d33,058	46,762	79,578
Hasangarh	4,600	5,1?0	40,904	50.634	41	75	5.979	12,1u8	18.203	68,837
Gorai ...	3,182	4,047	31,659	38,888	34	74	4,604	5,060	9,772	48,660
Akrabad...	2,746	3,425	39,464	45,635	31	28	1,503	2,655	4,217	49,852
Sikandra...	7,237	8,471	69,648	85,356	86	94	5,175	3,346	8,701	94,057
Barauli ...	335	434	5,328	6,397	18	18	2,288	1,787	4,106	10,203
Koil ...	6.345	7,778	77,826	91,949	77	146	12,693	11,187	24,103	116,062
Morthal ...	1,098	1,177	18,749	21,024	30	48	1,820	2,679	4,577	25,601
Tappal ...	2,399	2,703	26,275	31,377	129	196	22,372	14,092	36,789	68,166
Chandaus,	1,754	2.020	20,009	23,783	47	57	9,333	9,807	19,244	43,027
Khair ...	8,657	4,799	36,298	44,754	76	206	15,431	15,323	31,036	75,790
Mursán ...	4,336	5,026	26,389	35,751	40	35	743	2,336	3,154	38,905
Háthras ...	9,505	11,126	79,530	100,161	40	56	4,677	2,783	7,556	107,717
Total ...	53,402	63,465	531,948	649,115	1,489	2,225	110,427	134,213	248,357	897,172

Extensive plains or tracts of barren land, impregnated with noxious salts,

Usar plains. and known as *usar* or *reh* lands, occur on or near the watersheds of the district, and always close to good loam or clay soil. One irregular line of *usar* soil follows the line of the main canal, and is continued between the two branches of the canal, which bifurcate at Nánu, on into the adjacent district. Another line of *usar* runs north and south along the watershed between the Ním and the Káli; and a third line takes a course between the sandy tract near the Jumna in Khair and the Karwan Nadí. To the north of the Háthras tahsíl there are a few detached *usar* plains, but to the south and in Iglás they are practically absent. These plains are now, and have always been, unculturable. Regarding the spread of *usar* in this district Mr. W. H. Smith writes :—

" The results of an observation of some years lead me to the opinion that in the dry tracts, where well irrigation alone is possible, and where the soil is subject only to the natural action of the seasons, it has never manifested any signs of a liability to spread. Both the old maps and the statements of the people agree in showing that to this day there are the same patches, within exactly the same limits, as were observable at last settlement, nearly 40 years

a includes 374 acres 1st class *khádir.*   *b* includes 437 acres 2nd class *khádir.*   *c* includes 1,003 acres 1st class *khádir.*   *d* includes 1,812 acres 2nd class *khádir.*

ago. No change is known to have taken place in this long period. It is in tracts near the Ganges Canal that a very different state of things appears to have arisen since the canal has been opened. What has happened to a small extent near the Káli Nadí has occurred to a considerable extent in some parts adjacent to the canal, and from apparently similar causes. There is and must be a considerable amount of percolation from so large a body of water, flowing at so high a level, and the line of *usar* plain runs almost parallel with the parent canal in the Koil tahsíl, and in Sikandra Rao actually between the two branches. At present, however, the total income of the proprietors has been so much increased by the means of additional irrigation supplied by the canal, insomuch that the whole area perhaps is now watered when formerly not half was irrigated, that the damage is scarcely, if at all, felt. But if the present state of things continues, it seems to me to follow that a great part of the tract must become waste, and with a reduced culturable area, there will be considerable loss both to the State and the proprietor. In the Koil tahsíl, where there is only one canal channel, the increase of *usar* is comparatively insignificant, and is confined almost wholly to low lands near jhíls. The appearance presented by the 'reh' on the tracts where it is increasing is very singular. It forms a white crust on the ground, and the plains on which it lies stand out from the landscape glistening white in the sun, like snow on a bright winter's day in England. After rain it renders the ground so slippery as to be almost impassable. In the drier tracts the 'reh' rarely exudes, and there is no white incrustation. But even grass refuses to grow on the soil it frequents, and an almost complete absence of vegetation marks its presence."

The district is partly bounded on the east by the Ganges, and on the west by the Jumna. The character of these rivers present no

Rivers.

peculiar features in this district. The former touches parganah Atrauli, and the latter borders on parganah Tappal. The Jumna *khádir* has here a breadth of about six miles, which is largely used for grazing purposes. There are thousands of acres of cultivation, but the land, as a rule, is inferior in quality to the uplands of the interior. The Ganges bed, especially that portion known as the Búrh Ganga, is little better, containing for the most part an excessive proportion of sandy and unirrigated land. There are ferries across the Ganges at Sánkra or Sánkura and Dinapur in the Atrauli tahsíl; across the Jumna at Lálpur in parganah Tappal, leading to Biloipur in parganah Palwal in the Gurgaon district; and at Antasani, leading to Mahiwála. The Jumna *khádir* is so raised as to be almost above the level of the highest floods, except such an exceptional one as that of 1871, which continued during the whole of August. The Ganges *khádir* is low, and the deep stream continually changes from one side to the other;—one year it lies under the Budaon side, and the next year, perhaps two miles away, close under the high land at Sánkura on the Aligarh side. Old land is constantly cut away, and new land is formed every year. The fresh soil is not at once fit for cultivation, and the alluvial deposits of several years are required to render it available for the plough: it is then, however, singularly fertile. The permanency of the Jumna khádir always ensures a crop, and therefore, though the culturable land is of inferior quality, rents are higher than along the Ganges. The Búrh Ganga or old bed of the Ganges is dry in this district, except during the rains.

The head-waters of the Rind are closely connected with those of the Sengar,

Rind.

and collect between the Cawnpore and Etáwa terminal branches of the Ganges Canal, close to their bifurcation from the main branch at Nánu. The principal sources of the Rind are a series of hollows containing water, which lie near the fourth, sixth, and ninth miles of the Cawnpore branch of the canal. The hollow at the fourth mile, near the village of Ladhawa, is the most distinct, and is traceable to a set of shallow depressions which lie to the north of Nánu. From these jhíls or hollows the drainage appears to pass around by Akrabad to the west of Ladhawa. It then crosses the line of the canal, and sweeping around the village of Kanakpur in a defined line of water-course, assumes under that shape the name of Rind. The maximum depth of the main hollows lying to the north of Nánu, and which form the true Rind, is only three feet below the surface of the neighbouring country, whilst in its course around Akrabad and Ladhawa it does not exceed twelve inches in depth. At the sixth mile of the canal, near Gopi and Rudain, the hollow is of the same character in its immediate junction with the canal, and the drainage passes off towards the Rind without any perceptible depression. The hollow at the ninth mile, near Ginauli, is less extensive, and drains into the Rind. To the west of the Nánu branch of the Rind, and close to the village of Saháoli, lies a depression which is so intimately connected with the head-waters of both the Rind and Sengar, that not even the most careful examination could discover the difference, or lead to any other conclusion than that the drainage was common to both rivers. The alignment of the Etáwa branch of the canal has, however, entirely turned its waters towards the Rind. The Rind flows onwards into the Eta district, and drains the depressions on each side of its course. The Rind is also known by the name of Ratwa in this district, and further south it is called Arind. Reh is common along the course of this stream, and has increased very much of late years, so that hardly a village close to the river is now free from this destructive salt.

The Sengar rises in this district near the great Adháwan jhíl, and, taking a

Sengar.

southerly course at first, continues onward inclining to the east. It has a total length of 190 miles through this district, Etáwa, Mainpuri, and Cawnpore, and joins the Jumna near the town of Musanagar in the Cawnpore district, at a point centrically situated between the two stations of Kálpi and Hamírpur. The increasing width and depth of the channel characteristic of the Duáb rivers renders the Sengar a formidable stream in the lower part of its course, where it runs through deep and raviny ground on its approach to the Jumna. This line of drainage receives the rain-fall from the south of Koil, almost due south. For two or three years the Sengar, in its course through Háthras, has been used as a canal distributary, but in the hot and cold weathers this stream is dry.   In the rains it has a breadth of about 42 feet and a depth of about four feet. The banks are sloping, and the bed is soft and clayey.

The Isan rises in a tract to the east of Sikandra Rao, amidst a series of jhíls
Isan.
or extensive flats near the villages of Ikbálpur, Kheriya, and Bargawán ; to the east of the Rind and between the two, the Cawnpore terminal branch of the Ganges Canal runs along the water-shed southwards. These depressions, like those forming the sources of most of the Duáb rivers, are so very shallow, that their irregularities in depth can only be traced by the levelling instrument. They continue onwards parallel to and almost fringing the line upon which the Cawnpore branch runs, as far as its twenty-fourth mile, where the Jinwar jhíl in the Etá district is met with. The Isan is dry except during the rains, when it has a breadth of about 100 feet and a depth of about six feet. The banks are sloping, and the bed is soft and muddy.

The Karon or Karwan Nadi rises in the Bulandshahr district, and runs through
Karon Nadí.
the west of this district through parganahs Chandaus, Khair, Hasangarh, Gorai, and Mursán.   The fields lying close to this stream are often benefited by the percolation of moisture during the rains, but, as a rule, in the hot and cold weathers it is dry. The Karon has a breadth of about 29 feet, and a depth of about five feet in the rains. The banks are generally sloping, and the bed is soft and muddy. The Chohiya rises in the Bulandshahr district, and after entering this district joins the Ním near Shaikhupur in parganah Atrauli. The breadth in the rains is about 170 feet, with a depth of eight feet. At other times it is dry.

The Ním is a considerable stream, which enters this district from parganah
Ním Nadí.
Dibái of the Bulandshahr district, near the village of Dhuro in parganah Atrauli. It flows slightly south-west, approaching closer and closer to the Káli, which it eventually joins to the south in the Etá district. It is seldom dry, and is used for irrigation purposes. There is a certain amount of *tarái*, or low-lying land liable to inundation during the rains, along the Ním towards its confluence with the Káli. The Ním is bridged at Malsái and Bhíkampur. It has a breadth of 200 feet, and a depth of eight feet in the rains, with a sandy bed and sloping banks.

The Káli or Kalindri Nadí flows from north-west to south-east through
East Káli Nadí. parganahs Atrauli, Jaláli, and Akrabad, and, forming
the boundary between Gangíri and Sikandra Rao,
enters the Etá district. It is not navigable in this district, but is used for irrigation, and for some years has formed an escape for the excess water from the
canals. Inundation from this cause has occasionally been a source of loss to
the villages lying along its banks in this district. Another evil, due to the
increased volume of water in the Káli, is the exudation of *reh*, which renders
patches of land quite unculturable. The facilities afforded for irrigation would,
however, appear to more than counterbalance the losses from floods and *reh*.
The canal escapes are situated at Kásimpur on the main line, and at Ginauli on
the Cawnpore terminal line. There is a fair amount of *tarái* or low-lying land
along the banks of this river. The Káli is bridged on the eleventh mile of the
road from Aligarh to Moradabad, and here the width of the stream in high
flood is 187 feet, and depth 14 feet ; width in ordinary flood 95 feet, and
depth $7\frac{1}{2}$ feet ; and width in hot season 30 feet, and depth 3 feet. It is also
bridged at mile 22 on the Aligarh and Kásganj road, and here the width
of the stream in flood is 250 feet, with a depth of $14\frac{1}{2}$ feet ; width in ordinary
flood 237 feet, with a depth of 8 feet ; width in hot season 60 feet, with a depth
of $5\frac{1}{2}$ feet. The bed is generally sandy, and the banks are sloping in this
district.

The Ganges Canal enters the district at the village of Dánpur in parganah
The Ganges Canal. Barauli, bordering on the village of Khera Khás of
parganah Pahásu of the Bulandshahr district. The
canal continues on a straight south-easterly course, whilst the East Káli Nadí
maintains its relative position with regard to the canal as far as Dabthala,
opposite the 160th mile, where it takes a bend to the eastward, regaining its
former position a few miles southward, opposite Sálgarhi. The distance between
the Karon and Káli at Khúrja on the 140th mile is only 11 miles, whilst at the
160th mile this has been increased to 24 miles. The slope of the country in
this section is 27·73 feet, or 1·38 feet per mile, from north to south. The canal
passes along the watershed, and on its 160th mile the surface of the country is
15·62 feet above the bed of the Karon, and 25·33 feet above that of the Káli.
In advance of the 160th mile the alignment continues direct to Sumera, at which
village there is a curve on a radius of 20,000 feet, which brings the canal on
the direct bearing of the head-works of the Etáwa and Cawnpore terminal lines,
and of the villages of Nánu and Rájupur, between which these head-works are
situated. This point is 180·8 miles from the regulator of the canal head at
Mayapur, and the main line of canal terminates here. The slope from north to
south of the surface of the country from the 160th to the 180th mile is 26·86 feet,
giving an average per mile of 1·34 feet. Its transverse slope tends towards the

westward from the Káli to the Karon, and further south to the heads of the
Sengar river. The canal alignment has been kept as near as possible to the
Káli, in order to avoid the low tracts in which the Sengar collects, and in the
neighbourhood of Harduaganj the canal is only 1·75 miles from the Káli. The
width between the Karon and Káli at the 160th mile is, as above mentioned,
24 miles, and this continues nearly to the 180th mile. Here, however, the
intervention of the heads of the Sengar, which now have a well-defined section,
reduces the width to ten miles, through which, about midway and along the
highest ground, runs the canal. The country throughout this section is well
cultivated, except near the heads of the Sengar, and the depth of the water in
wells from the surface varies from 16 to 49 feet.

Taking up the Cawnpore terminal line from Nánu, its total length is 169
miles 3,700 feet. It is thus described by Colonel
P. Cautley[1] :—" After leaving Nánu, and after having
overcome the difficulties of the flats and hollows between that place and Sikandra
Rao, the channel proceeds in an easterly direction, keeping to the line of main
canal of my original survey, and maintaining an almost direct course centrically between the Isan and Rind rivers, as far as the 98th mile at the village
of Dingari ; south of this point the Rind river discontinues its parallelism with
the Isan, and proceeds onwards on a more southerly course, whilst the Pándu
river, the heads of which lie on the left of the Rind and in the neighbourhood
of Sabhad and Bándmau (villages situated to the south-east of Dingari), takes
up the bearing which the Rind has deserted and continues on a course
parallel to the Isan river. At the 98th mile, therefore, the line of canal turns
the heads of the Pándu and proceeds onwards, keeping to the left of that
river and between it and the Isan, until it reaches the 139th mile ; at this
point, and on the left, the Nún, a line of drainage connected with the Ganges
and the lowland lying between Cawnpore and Bithúr, rises ; keeping this low
land connected with the Nún on the left, and still maintaining its parallelism with
the Pándu river, the canal proceeds onward to the village of Bára, or to the
160th mile, from thence it takes a long sweep to the north-east, and passing
between the town and military bazárs of Cawnpore, enters the Ganges river by
a series of lock and falls."

The total length of the Etáwa terminal branch, from the Nánu regulator to the
Jumna, is 175 miles. It leaves the regulator at an angle
of 21·5,° corresponding with that of the departure of
the Cawnpore branch. After passing the fort of Bijaigarh, where it takes a curve
bringing it directly parallel to the Cawnpore branch and the course of the Rind,
it proceeds onwards in the same direction on a length of 65 miles. At this point,
near the village of Gangsi, "it makes a turn to the right, and leaving the Rind,

Cawnpore terminal line.

Etáwa terminal branch.

_____

[1] Ganges Canal, I., 250.

it keeps clear of the heads of the Ahniya and Phúra, two rivers which join the Rind in one connected channel under the village of Bhímwamau. Avoiding the drainage connected with the above two rivers, the line regains its parallel direction to the Rind, which it maintains from the 116th to the 145th mile. At this point a comparatively sharp turn to the right, near the village of Gajamau, not far from the town of Akbarpur, clears the heads of the Nún, a river that, rising near Akbarpur, takes a course almost parallel to the Rind. From thence the canal, passing to the right of the Ním, reaches the Jumna river at the village of Fatehabad, eight miles east of the town of Musanagar. From the above general description it will be understood that the Etáwa terminal line, throughout its whole course, runs to the right of the Rind river, keeping as much as possible out of the influence of the tributaries and drainage which are connected with it. The Sengar river, the heads of which lie in the neighbourhood of Koil and the town of Bijaigarh, throughout its whole course maintains a parallel direction to the canal flowing on its right, so that, in fact, the Etáwa branch, from its head at the Nánu regulator to its terminus in the Jumna, passes between the Rind and the Sengar rivers on a course as equidistantly marked out as the position of the ridge or watershed would admit of."

Having described the course of the canal, I now turn to the works on the main line and its branches. At Dánpur there is a

Works on the canal.

bridge with a water-way of three bays of 40 feet each, rájbaha and inlet heads; ghâts and a second-class chauki are attached, and similar bridges exist at Barauli and Dabthala. Near Sumera, on the 163rd mile of the course of the canal, falls have been constructed with a drop of five feet in perpendicular height, to meet the lower level found near the heads of the Sengar and Rind on the right, and the Isan on the left. This work consists of five bays of 20 feet each, giving a clear water-way of 100 feet, with a navigable channel, locks, mills, rájbaha heads, &c. Three miles below Simra, near the village of Kásimpur, an escape leads into the Káli, with a water-way of 60 feet divided into ten sluices of six feet each, attached to the up-stream side of the bridge, with its head well protected by masonry revetments constructed in the step form. The distance from the Káli is 20,577 feet, and the total fall between the escape flooring and the bed of the river is 21·35 feet. The other works between Káimpur and Nánu are the bridges at Barautha, Machúa, Changeri, and Shaikha, each with a water-way of three bays of 40 feet each, rájbaha and inlet heads, ghâts and a second-class chauki. From Rúrki to the 50th mile, where the Fatehgarh or Anúpshahr branch is given off, the height of the top of the bank from the canal bed has a minimum of 15 feet, and that of the berm or towing path from the canal bed is 12 feet. The latter is a constant quantity, and although it is exceeded in many places where the depth of excavation is great, the depth of 12 feet for the trapezoidal portion which is intended for the retention of the canal water is always maintained. The height and width of embankments vary with the amount of earth excavated from the channel, but the earth is always spread out so as to form an even esplanade.

Southwards from the Anúpshahr branch head the width of the canal falls from 140 feet to 130 feet, and the depth from the top of the bank from 15 feet to 14 feet, and from the berm to the bed of the canal from 12 feet to 11 feet. These are continued as the minimum measurements as far as Khátauli or the 62nd mile, and from this point to the 105th mile the width is reduced to 120 feet ; from the 105th to the 144th mile it is 110 feet, and the berm is reduced from 11 feet to 10 feet from the bed of the canal, leaving an average depth of 8 feet of water in the canal. From the 144th mile to Nánu the width is gradually reduced to 80 feet by decrements averaging 10 inches per mile. The depth of trapezoidal channel, or from the surface of the towing path to the canal bed, is maintained at ten feet, to allow of a clear two feet above the high-water level in the canal. The width of the water-way of the bridges from the 110th to the 180th mile has been maintained on two uniform dimensions, viz., of 135 and 120 feet, the former having three bays of 45 feet each, and the latter three bays of 40 feet each. Every bridge, except Damkaura and Acheja, from the Bulandshahr head downwards, has two rájbaha heads attached to it, one on each side of the canal, with channels ten feet in width. The sill or flooring of the rájbahas is laid two feet above the bed of the canal and of the flooring of the bridge to which it is attached.

The following diagram [1] gives a section and plan of the general arrange-
Plan of the canal.
ment of the canal, and shows the lining out of the road at a point where it comes in contact with a milestone. These stones are numbered from the Mayapur regulating bridge in a continued series to Nánu. They are situated away from the road on a platform kept clear for their especial purpose. " They consist of a square prism of stone imbedded in a cylindrical mass of masonry, the top of which acts as a bench-mark, and the figures engraved on the stone, independently of the mileage, give the exact depression of that particular point from the flooring of the regulating bridge at Mayapur. On the following diagram the width of the bank is supposed to be much greater than that laid down as a minimum dimension ; in fact, as it really is on the greater part of this section of the canal, the road is here 20 feet wide, with an additional 10 feet between it and the plantations, so as to prevent the passage being interrupted by boughs of trees. The road by these means actually maintains a width of 30 feet ; it has a slight slope internally, so that all drainage may flow away from instead of towards the canal channel, and there is a low edging of earth carried along the crest of the interior slope,

---

[1] From Cautley's Ganges Canal, I., 244.

for the purpose of preventing the action of the water from destroying its uniformity."

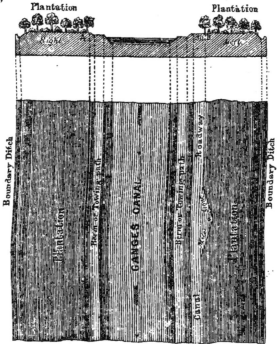

At the Sumera falls near Jawá, a small portion of the water-power in the navigation channel is utilised for driving mills ; one containing six pairs of stones has been erected there, and each pair turns out about one maund (82℔.) of flour per hour.

The position of the drainage areas of the Sengar and Rind influenced in a great measure the direction of the line of main canal from the 152nd mile, in the neighbourhood of Somna, downwards, and the intervention of the Isan determined the site for the bifurcation of the Etáwa and Cawnpore terminal lines, so as to reach the high land stretching between the Isan and the Rind along which the Cawnpore line is taken. The slope of 15 inches has been continued along both lines as far as the natural profile of the country would admit of it, and when this ceases to be the case, the slopes are reduced to 12 inches per mile, the superfluous fall being overcome by masonry descents and lockage. The regulating bridges at Nánu have each a water-way of 100 feet divided into five bays of 20 feet each, and are connected with each other by a line of curved revetment, resting upon a redan-shaped platform, which projects its acute angle towards the point of

The Nánu works.

bifurcation. The main line as it approaches this point bears on a line which bisects the angle of departure of the two branches. This angle is equal to 43,° and the main line meets it on an angle of 158·5°. The object of this lining out of the works is, that ordinarily each branch may have an equal supply, which can be increased or decreased by the regulators over each branch as occasion may require, and, if necessary, either branch can be left entirely dry without interfering with the other, the excess water being passed off by the Kásimpur and Munda Khera escapes. The staple material for building throughout this and the Bulandshahr district has been block kunkur, the use of bricks being confined to arches and to those works where block kunkur was not procurable.

With the exception of a slight curve, which gives the Cawnpore branch of the canal a direction to the south of the town of Sikandra Rao, the bearing for thirty miles is almost due south-east; at points near the fourth, sixth and ninth miles, and before its arrival at Sikandra Rao, the line of canal crosses low country which is connected with the heads of the Rind (see "Rivers" ante). Here there are three bridges, at Kailanpur, Rudáin and Ginauli, each of which is provided with masonry inlets. These inlets have been constructed more with a view of preventing the accumulation of water by the interference of the bridge approaches with the drainage of the country than to relieve the drainage itself. To obviate the difficulties attendant upon these obstructions to the natural drainage, an escape cut was made from the Ginauli bridge to the Káli, and cross cuts were made connecting the escape with the hollows in the fourth, sixth and ninth miles above mentioned. The distance of the canal from the Káli is eleven miles, and the difference in level between the sill of the escape and the bed of the Káli is 28·67 feet, or 2·42 feet per mile. The breadth of the cut is ten feet, and it is further connected with an escape head from the canal channel itself, which may be used should necessity arise for relieving the canal of its surplus waters. From Ginauli the canal passes onwards on the same bearing into the Eta district.[1] The only other works besides those already mentioned that exist along this branch in this district are the bridges at Baramai, Purdilnagar, Jarauli and Jansoi, with rájbaha and inlet heads.

The Etáwa terminal branch passes to the west of the head-waters of the Rind river, and "proceeds onwards, touching the heads of some drainage connected with the Sengar, in the neighbourhood of the fort of Bijaigarh; the contact is very slight, occurring at the fourth mile near Bajrangpur, and at the 5½ mile near the village of Dupur; the country is exceedingly flat throughout, so much so, that on the right of the canal as it passes by the fort of Bijaigarh, which lies at a distance of half a mile, the eye wanders over sheets of waste and uncultivated plain, the whole of which throws its drainage into the Sengar river. As far as the fort of Bijaigarh, the line of canal is carried on a bearing almost

---

[1] Its description will be carried on under the notice of the Eta district in Gazetteer, III.

due south; from thence, however, it takes a turn to the left, proceeding onwards in a south-easterly direction, running parallel to the Rind as well as to the Cawnpore terminal line; at the tenth mile the canal comes in contact with a hollow in the neighbourhood of the village of Jáo, over which it passes under the inconvenience of heavy embankments, but with little interference with drainage; at the twelfth mile, another hollow, but small as compared with that at Jáo, is crossed under similar circumstances; the canal, in fact, at the above two points, is fringing a line of drainage that passes into the Sengar under the town of Jalesar. On its onward course, and between the 17th and 23rd miles, or between the villages of Janera and Rudarpur the canal crosses the heads of a third line of hollows, which is also connected with the Jalesar Nála." Bridges are built at Chitrauli, Bajrangpur, Bijaigarh, Jáo, Lodipur, Katai, and Sítapur with three arches each, an eighteen feet roadway, rájbahas, inlet heads, gháts, and a second-class chauki attached.

There has been some little extension of canal distributaries of late years. Feeders from Bulandshahr now enter Khair, and give water where it was much needed. The Koil rájbaha, too, when in full work, will irrigate all the country between the railway and the Karon; and the Sikandra Rao distributary will supply water to the tract between the Cawnpore branch canal and the Isan river.

Though not yet completed, the Lower Ganges Canal is so far advanced that a short account of what it is intended to perform, and the present state of the works, must be given here. It is designed to be taken from the right bank of the Ganges at Narora, on the border of the Aligarh district, about four miles below the Rájghát station of the Oudh and Rohilkhand Railway. It will thence cross the Káli, and running down the Duáb between the Isan and the Káli, will cross the former river and the Cawnpore branch of the Ganges Canal. It will then turn the head of the Pándu Nadi, and keep between that river and the Rind to a little below Cawnpore, and afterwards follow a course south of the railway to Allahabad.

The Lower Ganges Canal.

The committee appointed in 1866 to examine into the various projects for strengthening the irrigating power of the Ganges Canal, and the means to be adopted for providing water for the tract lying between the canal and the Ganges, recommended Rájghát in the Bulandshahr district as the point from which water should be drawn, either for a separate canal, or to supplement the Ganges Canal. It was proposed to construct a weir, 4,500 feet in length, to raise the low-water level eight feet, of which 5½ feet should be raised by a masonry weir, and 2½ feet by a movable board, thus raising the flood level estimated at 300,000 cubic feet per second about 1½ feet, and giving a velocity of 12 feet per second over the weir in high floods. The project provided for wells and the use of block kunkur in the works, and for a channel capable of carrying 5,000 cubic feet per second. The discharge

History of the project.

at Rájghát on the 10th April, 1866, was only 5,630 cubic feet per second, and at Cawnpore, on the 5th of April, it was 5,438 cubic feet per second, so that with the Ganges Canal at Hardwár drawing its full supply, it was thought that this canal could not always be relied upon to receive more than about 3,000 cubic feet per second. The cost was estimated at 192 lakhs of rupees, and the return at eight per cent. on the outlay, or, with a reduced volume of water, at five per cent.

In November, 1869, the Government of India forwarded a proposal by Colonel Strachey, C.S.I., to the Government of the North-Western Provinces for the construction of this canal. The inquiry into the merits of the work was entrusted to Mr. R. Forrest, who submitted to Government, in 1870, four alternative projects for lines to be constructed from alternative heads. His work was never completed, but to him is due the credit of having selected from amongst many alternatives the best position for the weir and head of the canals, of effecting a large saving of expense by projecting a passage across the *khádir* of the Ganges, and of designing an arrangement of the various lines, which has been substantially adhered to in the ultimate project. The design was completed by Major Jeffreys, R.E., and Colonel Brownlow, R.E., arranged for the distribution of the water from a discharge fixed at 3,500 cubic feet in the cold weather and 6,500 cubic feet in the rains,—the same quantities that are allotted to the Ganges Canal.[1] The water will be raised to fill the canal by a weir 6½ feet above the cold-weather level of the river, which is also the level of the sill of the canal entrance. Shutters will be used on the weir to increase the depth of water to ten feet when required. The main canal commences with a bottom width of 216 feet, a slope of six inches per mile, and a full supply depth of ten feet. A branch, intended as a distributary, will be thrown off at the 26th mile, to water the Káli-Ganges Duáb in the Fatehgarh District; and at mile 39, a supply channel will be thrown off to feed the Cawnpore and Etáwa branches of the Ganges Canal, which are intersected by the new canal on the 39th and 37th miles respectively of their course below Nánu. Henceforth the demands on the stream entering the Ganges Canal at Hardwár will cease at these points, and the upper canal will be relieved of irrigation from 128 miles from Cawnpore on the Cawnpore branch and on 130 miles of the Etáwa branch. The Lower Ganges Canal will then pass on through the Etá and Mainpuri districts, and will cross the valleys of the Isan and Káli rivers by aqueducts at miles 34 and 112, and the Cawnpore branch of the Ganges Canal at mile 115 in its own mile 94. Then heading the Pandu Nadi, the line will pass through a corner of the Etáwa district, and will intersect the Cawnpore district, running on a narrow watershed between the Pándu and the Rind to the Fatehpur district, which it will traverse in close proximity to the railway. Through this

---

[1] Project of the Lower Ganges Canal : Allahabad, 1874.

portion of its course it interferes little with the natural drainage of the country, and on approaching the Sasúr Khaderi Nála, skirts the right bank to the Jumna, to which the surplus waters will find their way by a dry ravine. From the Etáwa branch will be taken the Bhognipur line, to water the tract between the Sengar and the Jumna, and lower down the Ghátampur rájbaha, and to supply these two important channels with water it is intended to lead a second feeder, to be called the Jhínjhak branch, into the Etáwa branch. A still-water channel will go on to Allahabad itself, and the main line will be navigable to this point. The supply branch to the Cawnpore and Etáwa branches will be made navigable, while the Cawnpore branch is already navigable, and the Etáwa branch will be made so. A still-water channel will connect the town of Fatehgarh main with the main line, and the tail of the Cawnpore branch will be linked on to the line by a channel crossing the Pándu river. The details of the works in each district are given in the district notices, and need not be further noticed here.

The scheme embraces in all 555 miles of new main canals and 942 miles of distributaries. The cost of these is estimated at Rs. 1,82,58,451, and if we add to this the original cost of the Cawnpore and Etáwa branch channels, which this project now, absorbs, the capital account will stand at Rs. 2,22,65,232. The gross income is taken at Rs. 25,80,000, and the net income at Rs. 19,50,000, which would give a direct profit of 8·8 per cent. From these estimates and the actual cost of the Upper Ganges Canal, it would appear that the ultimate cost of the whole of this great system of works for the Duáb will not exceed five millions sterling. The only great work in the upper portion of the Lower Ganges Canal is the weir and head-works at Narora. These were estimated to cost Rs. 19,61,828, besides Rs. 2,40,600 for temporary accommodation, such as workshops, bungalows, &c.

Three divisions (Narora, Kásganj, and Bhongaon), comprising 107 miles

Progress of the work.

of main canal and 24 miles of supply channel, were started during 1873-74. The workshops form a separate charge. The outlay during the year on works, including the workshops, was Rs. 14,92,735; tools and plant, Rs. 105,979; manufacture of materials, Rs. 6,27,250; and establishment Rs. 2,10,687; or a total of Rs. 24,36,651. The work taken in hand on the weir comprised the under-sunk foundations for the left wing wall, those of 800 feet run of the weir proper adjoining it, and those of the weir sluices. The left wing wall will stand on twenty-seven circular wells, 12 feet in diameter, and all these were sunk to within five feet of their proper depth in 1873-74. The weir proper contains in its foundations a line of blocks ten feet square and sunk to 18 feet, and a line of wells eight feet in diameter; nearly all of these were sunk before the rains of 1874, and concretion was commenced. The foundations of the weir sluices contain 152 blocks under the superstructure, 80 blocks under the partitioning floor, 32 wells 12 feet in diameter, and 54 wells eight feet in diameter; of these all were in hand except 31 of the first set of blocks, and eight of the second. The sinking of the blocks varies from 12 to 20 feet, and that of the wells is about 33 feet. A branch railway connected with the Oudh and Rohilkhand line has been made for the carriage of block kunkur and other materials. Brick and mortar are brought from the brick-fields near Narora, where six steam mortar mills are at work near the lime-kilns adjoining the weir. The foundations sunk to the close of the year aggregated 1,227 feet in length, and, in addition, the right and left revetment foundations were completed. In a few years the entire works will be finished, and the great scheme of irrigation for the whole Duáb, from the Siwáliks to Allahabad, after forty years of thought and work, will be brought to a conclusion. Twenty years hence it will be time to review the effect of these recent extensions upon the prosperity of the Lower Duáb. As I have already shown, canals have not been an unmixed benefit to the people; but it is promised that the experience gained by the department shall not be lost sight of, and that the "error committed in the Upper Duáb of diverting drainage from its natural course into other natural channels which were not created for its reception, without duly enlarging their capacity, shall be avoided."

There are now no public ferries in this district. By Regulation VI. of

Ferries.

1819, seven ferries and fourteen dependent gháts were made public ferries, and yielded in 1820 a net revenue of Rs. 7,673; in 1821, Rs. 6,658; and in 1822, Rs. 7,260. In 1823 the ferries were leased to Mr. James Gardner of Kásganj for Rs. 22,000. In 1832 the ferries were again placed under the Magistrate; and in 1837, the last remaining ferry, that of Jasupur on the Ganges, was transferred to the Budaon Magistrate, who still controls the Ganges ferries, while those on the Jumna are under the Deputy Commissioner of Gurgaon.

The general surface of the country is, as a rule, dry, and the few jhíls or

Jhíls.

natural reservoirs of water are confined to the depressions in the higher level of the country through which the Ganges Canal and its branches pass. Some of these have been drained by the canal authorities, and measures are being taken to drain the rest. Occasionally in the rains strips of land, several miles in extent, are slightly flooded in parganah Akrabad, and the Adháwan jhíl, near the sources of the Sengar, is of considerable size in the rains. There are also fair sized jhíls at Gopi, Bhawan Garhi, Shaikha, Ikri and Gursikaran in Koil. The Shaikha jhíl on the borders of parganah Husain and that near Husain itself are of fair size. The Sikandra Rao parganah contains a large number of jhíls, and the one near the town of that name is said to affect particularly the health of the inhabitants. To the north of the district, the Aligarh and Barauli parganahs contain a fair number of jhíls, but there are none in the other parganahs of the district that deserve the name.

The railway stations on the East Indian Railway within this district are

Communications. Somna, 14 miles north-west of Aligarh; the Aligarh civil station, which forms the junction with the Oudh and Rohilkhand line to Moradabad; Páli, seven miles south-east, and Háthras road, 19 miles south-east. The stations of the Oudh and Rohilkhand line are Aligarh, Rámpur for Harduaganj, and Raipur for Atrauli. The statistics of the traffic of the district by rail show a maximum from October to April, and thence a gradual falling off, until the minimum is reached during the rains. The returns of the East Indian Railway for 1871 were—

HÁTHRAS.			PÁLI.			ALIGARH.			SOMNA.		
Goods.			*Goods.*			*Goods.*			*Goods.*		
Inwards.	Outwards.	Passengers.	Inwards.	Outwards.	Passengers.	Inwards.	Outwards.	Passengers.	Inwards.	Outwards.	Passengers.
315,938	306,415	37,820	3,718	6,820	1,415	173,386	143,652	84,221	194	1,474	5,233

The following table shows the detail of traffic on the Rohilkhand line :—

	ATRAULI ROAD.						ALIGARH.							
	GOODS.		PASSENGERS AND PARCELS, &c.				GOODS.		PASSENGERS AND PARCELS, &c.					
			Inwards.		Outwards.				Inwards.		Outwards.			
Period.	Inwards.	Outwards.	Number of passengers.	Earnings.	Number of passengers.	Earnings.	Inwards.	Outwards.	Number of passengers.	Earnings.	Number of passengers.	Earnings.	Total earnings.	Cost of establishment.
	£. s.	£. s.		£. s.		£. s.	£. s.	£. s.		£. s.		£. s.	£. s.	£. s.
1st half of 1872,	4 3	4 17	4,024	65 9	4,253	70 6	170 9	1,948 17	15,151	410 18	17,557	514 4	3,189 7	31 2
2nd ditto ...	9 0	4 17	5,488	98 16	5,959	108 3	352 4	442 6	2,558	1,185 19	24,849	1,007 4	3,157 12	28 0
1st ditto 1873 ...	29 15	5 5	6,818	156 12	6,922	158 11	3,651 4	2,567 18	38,398	2,195 11	38,382	2,391 8	11,359 7	286 5
2nd ditto ...	24 17	132 6	6,533	152 9	7,417	173 12	3,794 10	4,361 5	13,013	3,053 16	38,103	2,549 8	14,242 6	31 15
1st ditto 1874 ...	42 11	1,954 16	7,689	199 2	8,331	221 7	9,462 19	8,943 7	44,027	3,358 4	42,614	3,367 4	27,548 12	44 10

The Háthras road station of the East Indian Railway is about six miles from Háthras town, and the Atrauli road station of the Rohilkhand line is about the same distance from Atrauli. A new line of light railway on the narrow guage system, now in process of construction between Háthras and Muttra, is intended to accommodate the Háthras traffic towards the west, and the pilgrim traffic to and from Muttra. It will run nearly parallel to the metalled road from Háthras to Muttra, on a nearly level line, and will cost a comparatively small sum when compared with other lines : about 15 miles of this line lie within the Aligarh district. To avoid the great expense and delay experienced in the transhipment of goods from broad gauge wagons to narrow gauge wagons, two lines of rail, constituting a narrow and broad guage, will run between Háthras city and the East Indian Railway station. The Ganges Canal also constitutes a means of communication, chiefly for through traffic,[1] and for timber and bambús as far as Barautha and Nánu.

The principal metalled and bridged first class roads in the district are the —(1)

Roads.

Grand Trunk Road, which enters the district at the 276th mile from Allahabad, at the south-east corner, and proceeds by Sikandra Rao, Koil and Somna to the Bulandshahr district, where one branch leads to Dehli and another, viá Bulandshahr, to Meerut. The total length of this road in this district is 49 miles 5·3 furlongs. It crosses the Ganges Canal at Nánu and the East Indian Railway near Chúhanpur ; (2) Koil to Moradabad by Atrauli and Ramghát, 24¼ miles in this district, passes by the important marts of Harduaganj and Atrauli, and crosses the Káli by a handsome bridge, built in 1851 on the eleventh mile ; (3) Koil to Anúpshahr by Jawá, 12·3 miles, crosses the canal by a bridge ; (4) Koil to Tappal 31 miles 7·5 furlongs, of which 20 miles are metalled and the remainder is raised and bridged ; (4) Háthras to Kásganj by Sikandra Rao and the railway station, nearly 30 miles from the town and 23 miles 7·7 furlongs from the railway station ; (5) Koil to Agra through Sásni and Háthras, 29 miles 5 furlongs ; (6) Koil to Muttra through Iglás, 24·68 miles ; (7) Aligarh to Kásganj by Panehtí, has a total length of 20·08 miles in this district, of which 9¾ miles are metalled, and it is intended to macadamize the whole road in connection with the Eta authorities. At present the road is raised and bridged, and, when metalled, will complete all the principal lines of communication in this district : this road crosses the Káli by a bridge in the 22nd mile from Aligarh ; (8) Háthras by Mursán to Muttra, 15¼ miles. Besides these metalled roads, a network of cross country roads connect each great branch with the other, and with all the principal marts, towns, police-stations and bridges on the canals. There are good bridges over the Ním at Malsái, built in 1841 at Bhíkampur, built by subscription in 1856 ; and over the Káli at Haidaramai, built by Government in 1830 ; and over the same river at Datauli.

The following table gives a list of the second-class roads which, though unmetalled, are raised and bridged, and the third-class roads which are not raised with the distances of each within this district :—

Second class roads.

						M.	F.	Ft.
1.	Khair to Iglás	...	...	...	...	16	4	160
2.	Iglás to Sadabad	...	..	...	...	16	0	220
3.	Nánu to Dúdu	...	...	...	...	17	0	500
4.	Koil to Barauli	...	...	...	...	13	0	0
5.	Sásni to Nánu	...	...	...	...	12	7	380
6.	Harduaganj to railway-station	...	...	...	...	3	4	0
7.	Dádu to Sánkura	...	...	...	...	7	1	390
8.	Khair to Brindaban	...	...	...	...	6	4	460

Third class roads.

						M.	F.	Ft.
1.	Akrabad to Bijaigarh	...	...	...	...	6	5	300
2.	Ditto to Pilkhana	...	...	...	...	3	1	560
3.	Sásni to Gopi	...	...	...	...	16	2	470
4.	Háthras to Jalesar	...	...	...	...	16	0	0
5.	Atrauli to railway-station	...	...	...	...	4	0	0
6.	Gangíri to Atrauli	...	...	...	...	16	0	0
7.	Iglás to Sásni	...	...	...	...	8	2	180
8.	Sásni to Jalesar	...	...	...	...	15	2	380
9.	Barauli to Somna	...	...	...	...	6	3	170
10.	Somna to Khair	...	...	...	...	10	0	500
11.	Somna to Chandaus	...	...	...	...	6	6	60
12.	Chandaus to Tappal	...	...	...	...	16	7	580
13.	Rohina to Jawá	...	...	...	...	15	5	400
14.	Ládpur to Katái	...	...	...	...	5	2	30
15.	Hasanpur to Ináyatpur	...	...	...	...	3	6	593
16.	Purdilnagar to Pilkhana	...	...	...	...	6	2	170
17.	Husain to Sikandra Rao	...	...	...	...	7	5	0
18.	Kachora to Bhánkri	...	...	...	...	11	6	0
19.	Chharra to Máchhua	...	...	...	...	12	0	200

The principal encamping-grounds from Koil to Cawnpore by the Grand Trunk Road are at Akrabad, 14 miles ; Sikandra Rao, 10 miles ; and Bhadwás, 10 miles (Eta) : Koil to Agra by the Grand Trunk Road, there is Sásni, 13 miles; Háthras, 9 miles; Sadabad, 10 miles: on Koil to Muttra by Iglás there is Iglás, 15 miles; and Ráya, 14 miles (Muttra). All these roads are metalled and bridged, and there are *bardáshtkhánas* or supply-houses at the halting stages in all except the last, but at Iglás there is a sarái, and provisions are procurable on indent. Troops could march in cases of emergency along the following roads :—Koil towards Anúpshahr (Jawá, 9 ; Dánpur, 12), the halting places are mere villages ; Koil to Rámghat (Atrauli, 16 ; Rámghat, 13), bridged and metalled ; Koil to Kúsganj (Jaláli, 13 ; Gangíri, 13.), Ním and Káli Nadís bridged ; Koil to Tappal (Khair 14 ; Tappal, 18); Koil to Jalesar (Sásni, 13 ; Mahu, 11; Jalesar, 9); roads from Háthras to Ráya (13½), Jalesar (18), Sikandra Rao (20). See further the alphabetical arrangement.

Table of distances of the principal towns and villages from the head-quarters of the district in Aligrah.

Akrabad	...	...	12	Iglás	...	15
Aksoli	...	...	28	Jaláli	...	12
Atrauli	...	...	16	Jao Ináyatpur	...	19
Barauli	...	...	13	Jattári Salímpur	...	27
Barla	...	...	20	Kachora	...	30
Beswán	...	...	22	Kauriaganj	...	15
Bhánkri Khás	...	...	6	Kailora	...	18
Chandaus	...	...	16	Khair	...	14
Chharra Fatehpur	...	...	23	Madrák	...	7
Chherat Surhál	...	...	6	Mendu	...	20
Dádon	...	...	28	Mítái	...	23
Daryapur	...	...	16	Mursán	...	22
Datáoli	...	...	21	Naráyanpur	...	21
Ehan	...	...	23	Panehti	...	6
Gambhira or Bijagarh	...	14	Pilkhana	...	12
Gangíri	...	...	22	Purdilnagar	...	26
Gopi	...	...	16	Sabal or Gonro	...	11
Harduaganj	...	...	7	Salímpur	...	20
Hastpur Chandphari	...	10	Sásni	...	14
Hatísa Bhagwantpur	...	22	Sikandra Rao	...	22
Háthras	...	...	21	Somna	...	14
Husain	...	...	22	Tappal	...	82

The climate of Aligarh does not differ from that of the other Duáb districts.

Climate. The year is divided into the rainy season, the middle of June to the middle of October; the cold season follows, and lasts until the beginning of April, when the hot season comes on and continues until the rains. There is generally a little rain in December and February. The following table, compiled by Dr. Stewart Clark, gives the temperature during 1853:—

Mean temperature.	January.	February.	March.	April.	May.	June.	July.	August.	September.	October.	November.	December.
Sunrise ...	44·0	48·5	61·0	64·5	79·0	84·0	73·0	78·5	76·5	64·0	52·5	44·0
At 10 A. M.	56·5	69·0	80·5	87·5	94·0	96·5	86·0	90·0	92·0	80·6	70·0	62·5
At 2-30 P. M.	60·0	78·0	88·5	89··	98·0	99·5	87·0	92·5	94·0	83·5	77·0	70·0

The rain-fall at several places in the district for the years 1862-63 to 1871-72:—

Registering station.	1862-63.	1863-64.	1864-65.	1865-66.	1866-67.	1867-68.	1868-69.	1869-70.	1870-71.	1871-72.	Average of ten years.
Koil ...	66·8	34·2	14·8	19·5	29·7	30·2	8·8	26·0	28·7	30·0	29·0
Háthras ...	22·2	26·2	21·1	18·9	26·7	34·4	16·3	30·6	32·9	34·5	26·5
Sikandra ...	23·0	27·4	24·1	19·4	17·2	38·5	21·0	29·6	26·1	28·3	25·4
Atrauli ...	21·2	40·4	26·0	30·5	19·8	32·3	18·8	32·6	31·6	34·4	28·7
Khair ...	27·4	22·9	15·9	17·3	25·8	23·8	10·5	21·3	29·1	25·2	21·9
Iglás ...	24·7	35·1	21·1	16·5	27·1	30·6	12·1	23·3	29·8	21·7	24·2
Average ...	30·8	31·0	20·5	20·3	14·3	31·6	14·9	27·5	29·7	29·0	25·9

The following table gives the same statistics, distributed according to seasons, for the whole district:—

Period.	1860-61.	1861-62.	1862-63.	1863-64.	1864-65.	1865-66.	1866-67.	1867-68.	1868-69.	1869-70.	1870-71.
1st June to 30th September ...	11·3	42·2	28·4	29·6	16·9	18·6	22·0	26·4	11·8	17·1	25·9
1st October to 31st January ...	0·7	0·3	1·5	0·3	0·3	1·3	0·6	2·4	1·3	6·4	1·4
1st February to 31st May ...	0·4	1·2	0·9	1·1	3·3	0·4	1·8	2·8	1·8	2·0	2·4
Total ...	12·4	43·7	30·8	31·0	20·5	20·3	24·4	31·6	14·9	27·5	29·7

The following table gives the total rain-fall at the principal stations of the district for the years 1844-45 to 1849-50, from returns existing among the records of the Board of Revenue.

Names of Stations.	1844-45	1845-46.	1846 47.	1847-48.	1848-49.	1849-50.	Average.
Aligarh ...	22·78	25 37	18·58	31·32	24·65	24·67	24·56
Akrabad ...	26·45	14·03	23 40	24·83	26 40	21·67	22 81
Atrauli ...	22 90	34·12	11·50	26 67	24 84	26 00	27·67
Háthras ...	32·50	32·76	16 48	28·23	26·65	24·71	30 22
Khair ...	37·42	26·19	20·03	30·92	13·45	21 67	25 01
Iglás ...	15·30	21·10	14·58	17 26	16·97	27 64	18·86
Sikandra Rao ...	22·79	30 77	20·12	27·06	19·95	20·40	23·51
Tappal ...	...	...	20·42	18·84	18·23	29·23	22 13

	1847-48.	1848-49.	1849-50.		1847-48.	1848-49.	1849-50.
Harduaganj ...	28·50	17·48	29 53	Hasangarh ...	33·31	15·53	22·43
Chharra ...	32·79	31·70	21 22	Bhadwás ...	36·62	20·57	29·92
Sásni ...	30·64	20·17	23 97	Husain ...	23·89	18·75	20·09
Mursán ...	26·45	22·29	25·69	Somna ...	28·83	2 ·42	19·40

The average rain-fall is about 26 inches. The western tahsíls of Iglás and
Khair have a smaller rain-fall than the remainder of the district, and the winter
crops in Khair and Atrauli are dependent upon the winter rains. On the whole,
the rain-fall is adequate, and there is so much irrigation that even in seasons of
drought there can now be little distress in this district.

PART II.

PRODUCTIONS OF THE DISTRICT.

There are no species of animals, either wild or domesticated, peculiar to this
district as distinguished from the other districts of
Animals. the Meerut division. Cows sell at from ten to thirty
rupees each, and plough cattle can be obtained at from ten to fifty rupees each.
Ponies fetch from ten rupees upwards, but a serviceable country-bred horse
costs two hundred rupees. Riding camels are not bred in the district, but
camels for burden can be bought for about Rs. 75. Sheep sell at from half a
rupee to one rupee each, and when prepared for sale to Europeans, they fetch
two rupees each. Government stallions from the stud stand at Bhilpur
Mítái, Daryapur, Somna and Kauriyaganj, and a few stud bulls are distributed
throughout the district with good results. The black buck or antelope is very
common, and there are a few nílgái (*Portax pictus*). Game birds are generally
scarce, but peacock and, in the cold-weather, all kinds of wild duck and geese
are plentiful. Rewards are given for the destruction of wolves : one rupee for
every full-grown male, two rupees for full-grown females, and eight annas for
cubs. The following table shows the deaths recorded as due to the attacks of
wild beasts and snake-bites for the years 1869 to 1873 :—

	1869.	1871.	1872.	1873.	Total of four years.	Average of four years.
Males ...	27	16	47	28	118	29
Females ...	21	18	33	32	104	26
Total ...	48	34	80	60	222	55

Fish is not a common article of consumption. The kinds usually sold are for the most part scaleless and are caught in tanks. The more common are the *saur, potra, jhinga, singi, láchi, rohu, karol, rotiya, chilka, dor, soteliya, bhúr,* and *mughara.* There are no regular fisheries in this district, and no colonies of persons living by river industries. The census returns show only forty men who have no other trade than fishing.

The mode of husbandry in this district differs so little in any important

Agriculture. respect from that practised in the other districts of the division, that it would be useless repetition to describe it here. The facts relating to the practice of agriculture given under the Meerut district will hold equally good for Aligarh. I will therefore confine myself to a general view of the present state of the district, its cultivation, amount and value of produce, irrigation, and the few peculiar agricultural products worthy of notice. The great extent to which, at last settlement, cultivation had already been carried, left comparatively little room for the increase which steadily advancing prices and the introduction of canal irrigation would have led us to expect.

Cultivated and culturable area. Still the change, such as it is, has everywhere been on the side of increase. The total cultivated area, which at the last settlement amounted to 839,127 acres, has now increased to 897,172 acres, or by seven per cent. The settlement statistics of cultivation for Atrauli and Iglás respectively represent the maximum and minimum of increase. From the same records it appears that the proportion of the cultivated area to the culturable area has risen from 82 per cent. at the past settlement to 88 per cent., so that now only 12 per cent. of the culturable area, or 121,168 acres, remains untilled, and of this 5,676 acres are under groves. The greater portion of this culturable waste consists of wide tracts of poor sand or alluvial *khádir* lying in tahsíls Atrauli and Khair (75,769 acres, or 62½ per cent.), and there cultivation reaches only 81 per cent. of the culturable area, whilst in the remainder of the district it covers 92 per cent., and the culturable waste comprises only small patches devoted to grazing purposes. The area under grass for pasturage is very restricted, so much so, that in several parganahs, as Mursán, where cultivation is 96 per cent., and Háthras, where it is 95 per cent. of the culturable area, the *kharíf*, which is specially useful for growing crops for fodder, has had to be increased at the expense of superior produce in the *rabi*. As a general rule, the more extensive the *rabi* the richer and more productive the crop, and here only in exceptional cases does the *kharíf* in any way exceed the *rabi*. The few wide uncultivated pasture lands in Atrauli and Khair must sooner or later come under the plough, and in a very short time cultivation must reach its maximum in this district. The pressure of the population on the land is even now severely felt; and when extension of cultivation can no longer be resorted to, emigration must be attempted; and it would be wise to commence this in time, so as to gain the experience which will ultimately be found necessary.

Great fertility is the characteristic of the district, and in the cold-weather it presents an almost unbroken sea of green, with the village sites appearing at intervals. Though only a portion of the total area is sown with *rabi* crops, a considerable portion of the *kharíf* is also resown, so that the intervals of unoccupied ground are scarcely seen. Mr. Smith thinks that, of all the parganahs, Háthras has best retained its old pre-eminence of being the most fertile. As early as the beginning of the present century, the Commissioners who visited Háthras compared its appearance favourably with that of other portions of the district, and now, though there is more equality in the various sub-divisions of the district, Háthras is still supreme. "Next to Háthras in natural advantages comes Iglás, then Sikandra Rao and Koil, and then the two tahsíls of Khair and Atrauli. There are tracts, indeed, in these two last tahsíls which equal or surpass anything in other parts of the district, but on the whole the sub-divisions stand pretty much in the order named so far as soil and natural capability of irrigation are concerned." *Bára* and *manjha* lands are always manured, but *manjha* to a less extent than *bára*. The cost of manuring is not great, and the benefit is enormous. These lands yield both the rain and cold-weather crops, and sometimes an intermediate crop. Nearly all the other lands yield but one crop in the year, the *kharíf* or *rabí* crop being taken according to circumstances.

The principal crops are wheat, barley, *joár*, *bájra*, gram, cotton and indigo.

Principal crops.

Within the last twenty years the quality of both cotton and indigo has improved, whilst that of the other kinds of agricultural produce has remained much as it was. The statement given below shows the acreage of the various crops on the ground during the year in which each sub-division of the district was surveyed at the recent settlement. The estimate of average produce is formed "chiefly on the results of constant and unremitting inquiry from cultivators and landholders in every portion of the district for every quality of soil, and as the knowledge of the cultivator or landowner is based on the experience of many lives available over the whole area of the district, and is itself, in fact, the outcome of innumerable and trustworthy trials," Mr. Smith has depended almost wholly on this source of information, having found the actual cutting and weighing of specified areas, in practice, both not to be relied upon and misleading. The estimate of chaff or *bhúsa* is very difficult to frame correctly. By far the larger portion is privately consumed by the cultivators for their own cattle, and but very little is sold. Some kinds of chaff, such as that of gram, *múng*, *urd*, *masúr*, and peas are especially prized, and fetch a high price. The price is the harvest price, or that actually received by the cultivator, and is necessarily much below the price ruling in the market at the time. These prices were obtained from the patwáris or village accountants of the various sub-divisions. I give Mr. Smith's statement here. The value of cotton includes that of seed, of *moth, arhar,* &c., and the cereals includes the value of the chaff:—

Statement showing the area under each crop, the produce and value.

Name of crop.	Area in acres at settlement.	Average produce per statute acre in maunds and sers.	Amount of produce in maunds.	Harvest rate.	Value in rupees.	Average produce of straw per acre.	Produce in maunds.	Value per rupee in maunds.	Value. Rs.	Total value. Rs.
		M. S.		KHA-RIF. Per md. Rs. a.		M. S.				
Cotton ...	119,715	2 0	239,430	11 0	26,33,730	4 15	523,753	1	5,23,753	31,57,483
Red pepper ...	24	3 0	72	6 0	432	...	...	...	...	432
Indigo ...	29,013	42 0	1,218,546	0 4¾	3,65,564	...	...	...	...	3,65,564
				Per acre.						
Chari (fodder)...	1,416	...	...	10 8	14,868	...	...	...	...	14,868
Water-nuts ...	114	...	...	35 0	3,990	...	...	...	...	3,990
Sweet potatoes...	5	...	...	10 0	50	...	...	...	...	50
Sugar-cane ...	1,548	...	...	61 0	94,428	...	...	...	...	94,428
Vegetables ...	357	...	...	35 0	12,495	...	...	...	...	12,495
Rawas ...	78	...	...	5 0	390	...	...	...	...	390
				Per rupee M. S.						
Joár ...	159,106	10 20	1,670,163	0 35	19,09,272	30 0	4,773,180	4	11,93,295	31,02,567
Bájra ...	70,405	8 30	616,044	0 30	8,21,392	...	...	...	...	8,21,39..
Moth ...	33,615	7 0	235,315	0 30	3,13,740	14 0	470,610	3	1,56,870	4,70,610
Maize ...	3,581	10 20	37,600	0 30	50,133	...	...	...	...	50,133
Gawár ...	3,066	7 0	21,462	1 10	17,169	...	...	...	...	17,169
Arhar ...	1,245	7 0	8,715	...	17,430	...	3,735	...	1,245	18,675
Múng ...	4,328	5 10	22,722	0 21	43,280	10 0	43,280	3	14,427	57,707
Paddy ...	1,324	12 0	15,888	1 0	15,888	...	...	...	...	15,888
Urd ...	2,504	7 35	19,719	0 21	37,560	15 0	37,560	3	12,520	50,080
San ...	118	5 0	590	0 20	1,180	...	...	...	...	1,180
Masína ...	3	7 0	21	0 30	28	14 0	42	3	14	42
Til ...	161	1 0	161	0 15	429	...	...	...	...	429
Kangni ...	70	10 20	735	0 20	1,470	...	...	...	...	1,470
Kurti ...	1,720	5 0	8,600	1 0	8,600	...	...	...	...	8,600
Total Kharif ...	433,516	...	...	...	63,63,518	...	...	...	19,02,124	82,65,642

Name of crop.	Area in acres at settlement.	Average produce per statute acre in maunds and sers.	Amount of produce in maunds.	Harvest rate.	Value in rupees.	Average produce of straw per acre.	Produce in maunds.	Value per rupee in maunds.	Value.	Total value.
									Rs.	Rs.
				RABI.						
				Per acre. Rs. a						
Carrots ...		...	...	30 0	82,110	...	....	...	...	82,110
Vegetables ...	2,737	...	...	35 0	56, 60	...	...	...	...	56,560
Melons ...	1,616	...	...	35 0	2,275	...	...	...	..	2,275
Fenugreek ...	65	...	...	10 0	210	...	...	...	...	210
Arwi ...	21 12	...	...	35 0	420	...	...	...	...	420
				Per md.						
Onions ...	13 18 0		234	1 8	351	..	...	.	...	351
				Per rupee M. S.						
Wheat ...	182,045 17 20	3,185,787	0 25	50,97,256	26 0	4,733,170	4	11,83,292	62,80,548
Barley ...	93,463 16 0	1,495,408	0 35	17,09,037	24 0	2,243,112	4	5,60,778	22,69,815
Bejar ...	91,963 14 0	1,287,482	0 30	17,16,642	21 0	1,931,223	4	4,82,805	21,99,447
Gram ...	56,274 8 20	478,329	25 0	7,65,326	8 20	478,329	2	1,91,331	9,56 657
Goá ...	14,035 17 20	245,612	0 30	3,27,482	25 0	350,875	4	87,719	4,15,211
Dúa ...	1,253 4 0	5,012	25 0	8,019	...	...	...	...	8,019
Oats ...	54 20 0	1,080	0 25	1,728	...	...	...	...	1,728
Masúr ...	1,469 10 0	14,690	0 30	19,587	8 20	12,486	3	4,096	23,683
Peas ...	291 14 0	4,074	0 35	4,656	8 20	2,473	3	824	5,480
Chaina ...	1,398 21 0	29,358	0 30	39,144	...	...	...	...	39,144
Tobacco ...	2,921 14 0	40,894	0 16	1,02,235	...	...	...	...	1,02,235
Tára ...	39 4 0	156	0 25	250	...	...	...	...	250
Dhaniya ...	51 4 0	204	0 10	816	...	...	...	...	816
Kar ...	993 1 0	993	0 5	7,944	...	...	...	...	7,944
Rál ...	19 4 0	76	0 12	253	...	...	...	...	253
Sarson ...	183 4 0	732	0 20	1,464	...	...	...	...	1,464
Haldi ...	20 3 20	70	0 8	350	...	...	...	...	350
Sonf ...	11 4 0	44	0 12	147	...	...	...	...	147
Total Rabi...	450,946	...	...	...	99,44,262	...	...	...	25,10,845	1,24,55,117
Fallow (báhan),	12,710	...	...		...	...	...	...	...	...
GRAND TOTAL,	897,172	...	...	...	1,63,07,780	...	...	...	44,12,969	2,07,20,759

It will be seen that out of the total cultivated area, 433,516 acres, or 48·3

Results of this inquiry. per cent., are under *kharíf* or rain crops, and 450,946 acres, or 50·3 per cent., are under *rabi* or cold-weather crops, whilst 12,710 acres are fallow (*báhan*), ploughed and ready for sowing. The area under wheat, cotton and *joár* is 460,866 acres, or 51 per cent. of the whole cultivated area, of which wheat occupies 20, and *joár* 17 per cent. ; next come barley and *bejar*, the latter a mixture of gram and barley, or peas and barley, which occupy 185,426 acres, or 20 per cent. of the cultivated area. *Bájra* and gram cover 126,679 acres, or 14 per cent. of the cultivated area ; the pulses *moth*, *múng*, and *urd* and *gojái*, a mixture of wheat and barley, occupy 54,482 acres ; and indigo appears on 29,013 acres. The valuable crops of tobacco and vegetables only show 4,894 acres, and Mr. W. H. Smith considers this to be the chief defect of the returns. A much larger area is cultivated under these crops—such as maize, tobacco, vegetables, *chaina*, onions, fenugreek, spices, &c.—than is shown above. These crops are chiefly ' *dofasli*,' that is, one of a double crop in the same year, and only the crop on the ground was recorded. In the case of indigo, only that which was sown as one crop for the year of measurement was recorded, whilst it is notorious that always in *bára* and *manjha* lands, and often in *barhá* lands, indigo ground is re-sown with cold-weather crops. It is estimated that at least ten per cent. of the cultivated area is *dofasli*, or bears two crops in the year. The estimate is also defective under the miscellaneous crops. Where *sarson* is sown with wheat, *dúa* with barley, *arhar* with cotton, *múng* and *urd* with *joár*, and *moth* with *bájra*, the chief crop only is stated. The estimate of their value is about two per cent. of the total value of all produce. For these reasons the total value of the produce given above must be increased from Rs. 2,06,40,749 to Rs. 2,31,17,637, or Rs. 25-12-3 per statute acre. The Government demand according to this estimate would amount to 9·4 per cent. only of the value of the total produce during a fair average year.

It will be seen from the table above given that there is no poppy and

Staple crops. very little sugar-cane cultivation, and that, besides grain, the staple crops are indigo and cotton. Grain naturally takes up by far the greater part of the cultivated area,—in fact wheat, barley, *joár*, *bájra*, gram, *bejar* and *gojái* occupy 73·2 per cent. of the cultivated area ; and if *báhan*, or land ploughed and prepared for sowing, be excluded, then these grain crops comprise 74·3 per cent. of the entire cultivation. Similarly, cotton occupies 119,715 acres, or 13·6 per cent. of the actual cultivation, and the indigo cultivation covers 29,013 acres, or 3·4 per cent.; so that the principal grains, indigo and cotton taken together, form 91·3 per cent. of the total produce. The area under both cotton and indigo has increased very much of late years, but there has been no such great or sudden displacement of the area under food-grains to make way for cotton and indigo as to afford any reasonable ground for alarm. In fact, the increase in cultivation more than counterbalances the increase in the area devoted to other than food grains.

Indigo being a crop of special importance to the district, some account of its cultivation and the manufacture of the dye appears to be necessary here.[1] The peculiarity in the cultivation of indigo in this district is that the plant occupies the ground only for six months (April to September), and there is not a *khunti* or second crop as in the Benares Division. The monsoon breaks so very late in the Upper Duáb that recourse must be had to irrigation either from wells or the canal before sowing the seed. Towards the end of the spring, as soon as the approaching hot-weather tempers the coldness of the nights, the seed is sown. If the seed were sown earlier, there would be danger of its germination being checked, or perhaps killed altogether, by the excessive cold. It is therefore not considered advisable to sow earlier than the end of March or beginning of April. The seed is sown broad-cast and roughly harrowed in by the *henga*, or even a bundle of branches of trees, and in five or six days the young plants spring above the ground. Weeding operations commence within about a month from the appearance of the plant above ground, and have to be repeated at least twice, and sometimes oftener. In August the plant has generally attained to its full growth, and the cutting commences. When cut it is tied into bundles and taken on carts to the place of manufacture, where it is weighed in presence of the cultivator. The manager of the factory loses no time in having the plant packed into the vats, and the pressure requisite for fermentation being effected by means of several strong beams tightly fastened down between posts fixed into the opposite walls of the vats, and water being applied, the process of steeping commences.

The first process, or the steeping of the plant, continues from eleven to fifteen hours, according to the temperature prevailing at the time. Thus one day and one night have been occupied in cutting, leading and steeping the plant. The second process consists in beating the fermented water and separating the fecula. The plant having been sufficiently steeped, the water therefrom is drawn into a lower vat, and by the aid of coolies (who beat the water with sticks) the separation of the particles of colour is brought about. This process in fine weather occupies two to three hours. The third process is boiling the fecula. In the course of this process, during the second day, the water is drawn off from the

Marginal notes: Cultivation of indigo. Sowing. Steeping. Separation of the fecula.

---

[1] Agra Exhibition Catalogue, 1867.

lower vat, leaving the dye deposited at the bottom, from which it is conducted

Boiling.

in a drain to the boiler. Here no time should be lost in lighting the boiler furnace, care being taken that the colour be well stirred in the boiler until the boiling is considered sufficient. These operations generally occupy five to six hours from the time of lighting

Collecting the dye.

the fire. The fourth process consists in cooling and collecting the dye. Below the boiler (and roofed over) is a large shallow vat, in which (a few inches from the bottom) rests a framework of bambu, over which is stretched a stout sheet. When the boiling has been concluded, the contents of the boiler are drawn off into this cooling vat, the water being drained off under the bambus, and the now thickened dye

Filling the frames.

remaining on the sheet. The fifth process consists in filling the frame with the dye, and pressing the same by means of screws. As soon as it has become quite cool, the sheet is unfastened at the far end and sides, and the whole of the colour drawn together to facilitate its removal. This is then taken in buckets and put into perforated boxes or frames, inside of which strong cloth has been previously placed to prevent any of the dye escaping from the holes by which the water trickles out when pressure is applied.

Pressing the dye.

The sixth process is pressing the dye. The mass of colour now filled into the frames (12 inches) in a liquid state is compressed down to about $3\frac{1}{2}$ inches by means of screws. After remaining pressed down for some hours, until all the water has escaped, the screws are all unloosed, and the dye, now comparatively firm, and forming a slab of $3\frac{1}{2}$ inches in thickness is cut into cakes of $3\frac{1}{2}$ inches square. The cakes having been thus cut are placed upon an open bambu framework, fitted in stages, in a house from which the wind is carefully excluded. This precaution is rendered necessary from the tendency which indigo has to crack and fall to pieces if allowed to dry rapidly. Indigo when presenting a sound and uncracked appearance in the chests, when exposed for sale in Calcutta, will find a much readier market than it would have met with had the cakes been allowed to crack and crumble. When the cakes have dried sufficiently, the assortment of the colours may then be made. The indigo cakes are then packed into chests according to the assortment, and a specimen cake is kept from each chest and placed in the box of samples, with the number of the chest attached, and the whole is then sent to the Calcutta market. The facilities for irrigation being intimately connected with the production of the more valuable crops have next to be considered.

Irrigation is extensively practised from wells (*cháhi*), tanks and rivers (*ábi*),

Irrigation.

and canals (*nahari*.) The following statement shows the irrigated area of each parganah divided into the three classes abovementioned, and the relative importance of each mode of irrigation in each parganah :—

Parganah.	Cháhí (wells).	Abí (tanks).	Naharí (canals).	Total.	Total unirrigated cultivated area.	Total cultivated area.	Total culturable area.	Barren.	Revenue-free.	Total.	Grand total area.
	IRRIGATED CULTIVATED AREA.							UNASSESSED.			
Atrauli ...	39,288	349	954	40,590	30,137	70,727	87,396	20,464	162	20,626	108,022
Gangíri ...	30,421	2,080	315	32,816	46,762	79,578	103,211	14,822	316	15,138	118,349
Hasangarh...	50,531	103	...	50,634	18,203	68,837	73,564	5,802	.412	6,207	79,771
Gorai ...	38,855	33	...	38,888	9,772	48,660	51,014	4,020	1,763	5,783	56,797
Akrabad ...	20,292	1,068	24,275	45,635	4,217	49,852	94,904	19,169	153	19,322	74,226
Sikandra ...	41,423	2,015	41,918	85,350	8,701	94,057	102,029	38,473	1,084	39,557	141,586
Barauli ...	2,087	290	3,120	6,097	4,106	10,203	11,502	5,121	...	5,121	16,623
Koil ...	71,011	2,068	18,840	91,949	24,103	116,052	128,330	41,377	5,567	46,944	175,274
Murthal ...	5,817	242	14,965	21,024	4,577	25,601	28,402	6,590	8	6,598	36,000
Tappal ...	28,119	263	2,997	31,379	36,789	68,168	87,422	8,077	...	8,077	95,499
Chandaus ...	20,515	352	2,916	23,783	19,244	43,027	51,933	13,382	1,028	14,410	66,343
Khair ...	41,026	636	3,092	44,754	31,036	75,790	43,095	14,645	365	15,210	98,305
Mursán ...	35,709	42	...	35,751	3,154	38,905	40,557	2,514	3,536	6,050	46,607
Háthras ...	98,683	465	1,013	100,161	7,556	107,717	113,981	19,563	5,791	25,364	139,345
Total ...	524,400	10,005	114,406	648,817	246,357	897,174	1,013,340	214,212	20,165	234,407	1,252,747

Water-level.

Towards the Jumna and Ganges, and along their high bank, the depth of water from the surface is from 50 to 60 feet, whilst in portions of the interior of the district it is only from 16 to 18 feet. Except in the *khádirs* of the rivers, and close to the canals, water is nowhere very near the surface, whilst at the same time it is not so far below as to prevent the formation and use of temporary earthen wells. The driest portions of the district are the parganahs of Khair and Atrauli, on the Jumna and the Ganges, and of these the portions nearest to the high bank of those rivers are particularly dry. The same rule holds good generally—"that on or near the watershed, and consequently the highest part of the Duáb, water is comparatively near the surface and the sub-soil is generally firm, while as the two rivers are approached the water-level sinks, the sub-soil becomes loose and sandy, and wells are made with difficulty and expense." Mr. W. H. Smith notices that in Iglás, which lies nearer the Jumna than Háthras, the water is generally farther from the surface than in the latter tahsíl, though the average irrigation capability is very good. For these reasons it is difficult to give the average depth of the level of the water from the surface of the ground in this district, but from 20 to 30 feet may be considered a fair approximation to the fact.

From the imperfection of the records, it is not easy to give the areas irrigated during the last settlement, but Mr. Smith, from the existing data for Háthras and Mursán, estimates a total irrigated area at last settlement amounting to 506,485 acres, and an unirrigated one of 332,642 acres, in the proportions of 60 and 40 per cent. of the cultivated area respectively. The irrigated area, according to the records of the recent settlement, amounts to 648,815 acres, with an unirrigated area of 248,357 acres, as shown above, or 72·3 and 27·7 per cent. on the cultivated area respectively. From these figures it would appear that irrigation has increased by 142,330 acres, or 28 per cent. The cost per acre of irrigation under each class is a much debated point. Some officers think that canal irrigation is cheaper than well irrigation, whilst others hold the opposite view. General experience goes to show that home-circle lands (*bára* and *manjha*) are usually irrigated from wells, even though canal water be available. The coldness of the canal water is supposed to be injurious to the tender plants. In the outlying lands (*barha*) canal water usually supersedes wells, and always does so in the case of indigo. Most of the wells in the district have been constructed by the cultivators themselves. There are over 51,000 wells, which roughly give an average area watered by each well of 10·5 acres. Generally speaking, the wells may be divided into two classes, —percolation wells and spring wells. Little dependence can be placed on the former, as half a day's labour will often suffice to exhaust the supply. The water in spring wells, where the *sot* or spring is reached, is practically unlimited. The popular classification of wells is, however, into *pukka* and *kuchcha*. Percolation wells are usually *pukka* or brickbuilt. Spring wells are of three kinds—(1) *pukka*, where the sub-soil to the spring is sandy, and masonry is necessary throughout; (2) *garáwari*, where the sub-soil is clay, but a layer of sand intervenes, and wooden frames are necessary to prevent the walls from falling in; or *ajár*; where wicker-work is used for the same purpose; (3) *kuchcha* wells, made of clay throughout. The *pukka* wells number 11,000, and irrigate some 42 per cent. of the wet area irrigated from wells; *kuchcha* wells number 40,000, and irrigate the remainder. Comparing percentages with areas, the figures do not appear to tally; but it must be remembered that whereas *pukka* wells have always two láos (buckets) or runs, and sometimes three or four, *kuchcha* wells have rarely more than one. The average area irrigated per run of a *pukka* well is nine to eleven acres, and per *kuchcha* well is six to eight acres. As a rule, wells can easily be constructed, except in the tracts close to the canal. Irrigation

Increase in irrigation.

Wells.

from ponds and tanks only amounts to 10,005 acres, and is confined to a few parganahs.[1]

The length of the main Ganges Canal running through the district is 48·62 miles, and from it 260·12 miles of rájbahas or principal
Canals.
distributaries, 49·5 miles of minor rájbahas, and 487·62 miles of small channels (*gúls*) are fed. In a few places, where the surface drainage has been impeded, and where percolation has taken place, the efflorescence of *reh* along the line of canal has increased. As a rule, it disappears with efficient drainage, and where it does exist, up to the present, the increased facilities for irrigation afforded by the canal more than reimburse the loss caused by *reh*. The following statement, taken from the annual irrigation reports, shows the area, according to season, irrigated by the Ganges Canal from 1866-67 to 1872-73 in each parganah :—

Year.	Chandaus.	Khair.	Baraul.	Morthal.	Atrauli.	Koil.	Sikandra Rao.	Háthras.	Tappal.	Total.
1866-67.	Acres.	Acres	Acres.	Acres.	Acres.	Acres.	Acres.	Acres	Acres.	Acres.
Kharíf ...	470	390	400	4,520	1	6,654	17,340	1,027	...	30,802
Rabi	396	764	1,876	9,724	1,014	13,286	38,214	2,188	...	67,462
Total ...	866	1,154	2,276	14,244	1,015	19,940	55,554	3,215	...	98,264
1867-68.										
Kharíf ...	249	806	670	5,383	...	6,582	19,348	921	...	33,459
Rabi ...	198	831	1,794	8,086	1,039	10,848	30,324	1,783	...	54,903
Total ...	447	1,137	2,464	13,469	1,039	17,430	49,672	2,704	...	88,362

[1] The following table shows the number of masonry and earthen wells and the percentage of the cultivated area watered from each class of well in five tahsíls :—

	Masonry.	Percentage of area.	Earthen.	Percentage of area.
Sikandra Rao	1,987	52·7	3,574	47·3
Khair	2,232	54·0	4,240	46·0
Háthras	814	9·0	17,342	91·0
Iglás	1,084	28·0	8,563	72·0
Koil	3,043	68·0	2,832	32·0

Year.	Chandaus.	Khair.	Baraul.	Morthal.	Atrauli.	Koli.	Sikandra Rao	Hâthras.	Tappal.	Total.
1868-69.										
Kharíf ...	573	1,214	950	6,542	...	8,398	26,534	1.191	633	46 240
Rabi ...	2,611	2,611	3,132	11,591	8	16,573	40,693	1,993	3,640	82,857
Total ...	3,184	3,825	4,082	18,133	8	25,171	67,232	3,184	4,278	129,097
1869-70.										
Kharíf ...	1,512	1,799	1,374	8,369	...	12,859	27,633	1,093	1,261	55,900
Rabi ...	2,415	2,363	1,272	7,618	2	11,362	32,065	1,500	1,330	59,947
Total ...	3,927	4,162	2,646	15,987	2	24,241	59,698	2,593	2,591	115,847
1870-71.										
Kharíf ...	1,812	1,748	843	6,359	...	8,884	22,763	1,235	1,227	44,871
Rabi ...	1,759	3,276	1,790	9,170	59	12,864	35,761	1,606	1,725	68,010
Total ...	3,571	5,024	2,633	15,529	59	21,748	58,524	2,841	2,952	112,881
1871-72.										
Kharíf ...	1,185	1,184	936	6,908	...	8,760	25,093	1,343	793	46,202
Rabi ..	893	1,054	1,417	7,702	2	9,586	25,750	1,204	249	47,767
Total ...	1,988	2,238	2,353	14,610	2	18,346	50,843	2,547	1,042	93,969
1872-73.										
Kharíf ...	1,273	978	864	6,566	...	7,489	21,215	1,072	612	40,069
Rabi ...	1,548	1,409	1,142	8,503	...	9,026	26,494	2,346	595	51,063
Total ...	2,821	2,387	2,006	15,069	...	16,515	47,709	3,418	1,207	91,132

The following statement shows the character and extent of the cultivation for which water is taken from the canal. Cereals in the *rabi*, and indigo and cotton in the *kharíf*, are the principal crops watered from the canal. In a good year for indigo the cultivation nearly doubles, falling again with reduced prices. A similar rule seems to hold good in regard to cotton ; and owing to the presence of the canal, prices, when

Influence of the canal on particular crops.

remunerative enough, can always obtain a full proportional supply of the raw material from this district:—

Crops.	1869-70.	1870-71.	1871-72.	1872-73.	Crops.	1869-70.	1870-71.	1871-72.	1872-73.
Gardens ...	1,435	1,257	1,478	1,890	Gram ...	4,259	1,613	1,489	2,243
Sugar-cane ...	147	206	245	401	Other pulses ...	318	585	177	170
Wheat ...	32,887	30,425	28,336	28,998	Cotton ...	9,147	6,307	2,960	1,961
Barley ...	21,130	24,942	17,144	17,833	Other fibres ...	17	3	113	3
Rice ...	2	619	576	595	Indigo ...	38,783	35,631	40,776	35,689
Other cereals ...	7,520	2,157	565	751	Drugs ...	93	74	53	159
Fodder ...	199	15	45	39	Oil-seeds ...	...	9	4	...

The district has suffered, in common with the rest of the Upper Duáb, from

Droughts.

hailstorms and droughts. The first great drought that is still remembered is that of 1783-84. It was felt very severely in the district, and the sites of many villages are pointed out that were devastated during the *chalísa* (1840 Sambat). Many died from starvation and others emigrated. For the previous two years the rains had been unfavourable and the produce very scanty. The famine year itself opened with an entire absence of rain in Asárh and Sáwan (June to August). Then Bhádon came and clouds appeared, but no rain. The land remained unploughed, and the full force of the calamity fell at once upon those portions of the Duáb that were most distant from the rivers. About the middle of September the rains began and fell with such regularity that seed which had lain in the ground for two years, is said to have germinated. In 1803-04 and 1805-06 there were scarcities from a want of rain, the prevalence of hailstorms, and the disturbed state of the country, as no one knew whether he should be able to reap the crop that he had sown or should be obliged to leave it to another. In 1806-07 no rain fell until the 15th August, and no steady rain set in until the 4th of September.[1] The distress continued to be felt to such a degree that in February, 1808, Government granted remissions to all except the great zamíndárs, at the rate of three annas in the rupee.[2] In September, 1808, there was still want of rain, and serious consequences were apprehended, as only one good shower had fallen during the previous month. The district participated in the droughts between 1813 and 1837.

[1] Board's Records, 26th July, 1806, No. 8. [2] *Ibid*, 26th February, 1808, No. 1 ; 25th August, 1808, No. 48.

Writing in 1826, the Collector represented that the preceding rain crop was very poor in Aligarh, and had been the source of great loss. The district had not had a good shower for six months, and many of the cultivators had emigrated. The Collector estimated that the cultivation of the cold-weather crops had fallen off by 8,000 bíghas. " Though the crops on the irrigated lands looked flourishing, yet the fields not under the influence of wells gave no room for hope of a tolerable harvest."

In 1837 the *chauránawe* famine occurred, so called from 1894 *Sambat*, the corresponding year of the Hindú calendar. It is the year from which, until the mutiny, most of the poorer classes used to reckon their time, and to which they referred all their misfortunes. The mutiny has since taken the place of the *chauránawe kál.* In June, 1837, there was a shower of rain, but none fell in this district in July or August, and very little in September. The price of food-grains rapidly rose, crime increased and immense numbers of people flocked into the district from Rajputána. Relief works were opened, but still the distress lasted for nearly a whole year ; and to add to the sufferings of the people cholera broke out amongst the low Musalmán population who lived on inferior meat. It is a curious fact that both in 1837 and 1856 easterly winds prevailed, and meat became bad in an abnormally short space of time. The suffering was intense, and far greater than that felt in 1860-61, when the introduction of the canal to a certain extent removed the ever-impending dread of starvation in seasons of drought. The influence of the canal was more clearly seen in 1868-69, when the returns showed 59 per cent. of the cultivated area as irrigated, and of this 129,088 acres got their water from the canal, and three-fourths of this area were under food-grains. Still the drought was very injurious to tracts like Khair and Atrauli which were unprotected by canals

1868-69. or wells. " Owing to the late and scanty rains of July, 1868, a less breadth than usual of food-crops was sown, and the produce on dry lands was stunted and withered. The rain in September was of the utmost benefit in securing the spring sowings in quarters where irrigation was defective ; but the autumn crop was too far gone for recovery, and the farmers showed their sense of the imminent danger of famine by planting carrots in every available spot round the wells. Towards the close of the year 1868 great fears were entertained for the spring crops. The long drought which intervened between the September storms and the middle of January, 1869, rendered it generally impossible to sow on any lands that were without means of irrigation ; still, so beneficial were the effects of the cold-weather showers when they did arrive that not less than seven-eighths of an average crop was expected. The want of fodder was very pressing and farmers were obliged to supplement the usual food for cattle with the leaves of the bábul tree. This was of course mitigated by the cold-weather rain."

" In respect of the grain traffic, the official reports from this district give no figures, but observations, here and there, indicate that the course of trade was much the same as elsewhere in the Northern Duáb, and the market no less sensitive. On the 18th September, the Collector informed Government that the heavy rain down country had checked exports. But on the 25th idem it was said that the prices of grain were kept up by the exports to the Panjáb, thus showing that the current had immediately turned westwards. In the middle of October, the exports slackened and prices fell, only to rise again in November, when the prospects of the *rabi* looked extremly bad. Generally it may be said regarding the grain trade that large supplies were attracted to the important mart of Háthras. Thence, to September, 1868, the export was eastwards. In September, October, and November grain was sent westwards and southwards, but chiefly to native states. With the beginning of 1869 the great drain for the Panjáb commenced, though the Collector says that he saw at the close of 1868 dispatches lying on the Háthras railway station, and destined both for Jalandhar and Jabalpur. Prices were considerably lowered by the spring harvest in April. They soon, however, rose again, and the Collector did not expect a decline until favourable rain should fall. But it seems more probable that the demand elsewhere ruled the market than that the out-look of the local agriculture was thought precarious. The rains of 1869 were in due time and abundant; a slight break occurred in August, 1869, but it was followed by magnificent showers all over the district. Still there was no decline in prices, on the contrary wheat was as dear in the autumn of 1869 as it had been in the winter of 1868."

Prices during the season of scarcity.

Month.		Wheat.		Barley.		Bájra.		Joár.		Common rice.		Gram.	
		M.	s.	M.	s.	M.	s.	M.	s.	M.	s.	M.	s.
February, 1869	...	14	6	18	0	14	8	15	0	10	0	15	8
March	,,	...	15	0	19	0	12	0	14	0	11	0	14	0
April	,,	...	13	8	18	12	12	0	13	0	11	0	13	8
May	,,	...	14	8	19	0	...		...		11	0	13	8
June	,,	...	14	8	18	0	10	0	10	0	11	0	14	0
July	,,	...	13	0	16	8	10	0	9	0	11	0	13	0
August	,,	...	12	8	16	0	11	0	12	0	11	0	11	8
September	,,	...	12	8	16	8	14	0	16	8	11	0	11	8
October	,,	...	11	8	17	0	19	0	16	0	9	8	11	8
November	,,	...	10	8	18	0	18	0	25	0	11	0	10	8
December	,,	...	8	4	16	0	16	0	19	8	11	0	8	0
January, 1870	...	9	8	16	8	21	0	23	0	12	0	1	0
February	,,	...	10	0	20	0	20	0	21	0	13	0	12	0
March	,,	...	12	8	25	0	21	0	25	0	13	0	14	8
Average		...	13	2	16	0	15	2	16	3	10	9	13	9

The prices given are those ruling during the last week of the month, as given in Mr. Henvey's report.

Tahsíl Háthras is infested with the weed called *baisurái*. The roots of this

The weed *baisurái*.

plant are said to penetrate the soil to a depth of twenty feet or more, so that where it once takes possession of the soil it is in effect ineradicable. " The rains seem to keep it down, and in the case of the kharíf crop it entails little inconvenience ; but immediately after the conclusion of the rainy season, wherever it has taken root, it completely covers the ground, and from a distance looks like a dense green cultivated crop. Constant cutting is the only remedy, and this must be done three or four times during the growth of a *rabi* crop. The weed generally grows so thickly that the operation of cutting requires much more labour and time than ordinary weeding, and cultivation therefore, where the weed abounds, is expensive. Opinions as to its ultimate effect on the crop are various. Some assert that it materially diminishes produce, some deny this ; my own view is that it is a matter of industry only.[1] When it is cut as often as it emerges from the soil, and is never allowed to grow high enough to incommode the rising crop, it has very little (if any) deleterious effect on the produce. When the cultivation has been careful, I have seen the very finest and richest crops on *baisurái*-infested land ; on the other hand, where husbandry is lax and the weed is allowed to make head, the crop naturally grows up thin and poor. Its worst characteristic is its tendency to spread. It is now common in numbers of villages, which, at the time of last settlement, were not affected." *Baisurái* and, to the south-west, *káns* are the greatest enemies to good cultivation that are to be met with in these Provinces.

At the commencement of British rule the surface of the country was covered

Jungle.

with large tracts of jungle, principally of *dhák (Butea frondosa).* These have generally given way before increasing cultivation, and what remains is fast disappearing. In fact, with the exception of a preserved tract in Chandaus belonging to the Piśáwa zamíndárs, there is now little *dhák* jungle, and there are few trees of any size or value in any part of the district. The total area under groves, such as mango and other fruit trees, &c., is 5,676 acres, of which nearly one-half is in Gangíri and Sikandra Rao. There are few districts which have such a bare appearance, and none where more efforts should be made to induce the people to plant trees. This has been partially attained by the Government allowing a remission of revenue for lands under groves as long as they are maintained ; and no doubt in a few years we may expect some improvement in this direction. The principal plantation trees are *nim, mango, jáman, pípal, bábul, mahúa, farás,* and *ber. Sál* and the better sorts of timber for building purposes are imported.

---

[1] Mr. W. H. Smith.

The building materials of the district are brick and block kunkur ; there is no
Building materials, &c. stone. Block kunkur costs about a rupee per hundred
cubic feet to quarry, and eight annas per hundred cubic
feet per mile to transport. Bricks, the smaller size, Rs. 150 to 200 per lakh.
The larger size (*gumban*), Rs. 500 to 800 per hundred thousand. Kunkur
lime is worth about ten rupees per hundred maunds ; kunkur for roads, 24 to 32
annas for digging 100 maunds, and the transport per mile is about the same as
for block kunkur. Kunkur quarries exist in considerable numbers all over the
district. Road kunkur can be laid down on the side of the road at a cost of about
Rs. 225 per mile of twelve feet wide and six inches deep. *Nim karts* or joists
sell at a rupee each ; mango, *jáman*, and the like at Rs. 18 a score ; and *farás*
and *ber* at Rs. 8 a score.

PART III.

INHABITANTS OF THE DISTRICT.

The first census took place in 1847, and gives a total population of 739,356
Census of 1847. souls, or 455 to the square mile. There were 651,792
Hindús, of whom 336,150 were engaged in occupations
unconnected with agriculture. The Musalmáns numbered 87,564 souls, of whom
21,880 were engaged in cultivation. The villages numbered 1,964, of which 1,895
were inhabited ; and of these 1,782 had less than 1,000 inhabitants, 106 had
between 1,000 and 5,000, and there were seven towns containing more than 5,000
inhabitants, *viz.*, Harduaganj, 5,942 ; Sásni, 5,524 ; Patti Umda Begam (Sikandra Rao), 7,195 ; Ahmadnagar, 6,740 ; Atrauli, 12,722 ; Háthras, 22,903 ; and Koil,
36,181. The town population therefore numbered 97,207 souls, or 11·7 per cent.
of the total population, whilst in the whole district the agricultural population
amounted to less than one half the total number of inhabitants.

This enumeration was followed by the regular census taken in 1852 and
Census of 1853. reported in 1853, which showed a total population of
1,134,565, or 527 souls to the square mile. There were
1,013,374 Hindús, of whom 502,513 were cultivators ; and 121,191 were Musalmáns, of whom 29,522 were agriculturists. There were only fourteen villages
added to the district in the interval between 1847 and 1852, and this will not
account for the great difference in the results. Mr. J. Hutchinson, who conducted the census of 1852, declares the enumeration of 1847 "to be totally incorrect,
and no dependence can be placed upon it." Subsequent enumerations would
lead one to suppose that he was right in his estimate, for though Márahra and
Pachlána were transferred to Eta between 1852 and 1865, and deducting their
population the figures for Aligarh should be 1,026,690, or 516 to the square
mile, the census taken in 1865 more nearly approaches the total given in 1852

than that given in 1847. The relative population of the villages remain nearly the same, but the number of towns having more than 5,000 inhabitants has increased from eight in 1847, to twelve in 1852, by the inclusion of Jaláli, Tappal, Khair, Shahgarh, Mursán, and Márahra, whilst Harduaganj and Ahmadnagar were excluded. The urban population in 1852 was 153,463 souls, or 13·5 per cent. of the total number of inhabitants, whilst the proportion of agriculturists remained about the same.

The census of 1865 shows the total population at 926,588, giving 498 souls to the square mile. The distribution according to sex, age, religion, and occupation of the Hindú and Musalmán population may be briefly shown as follows :—

Census of 1865.

| | AGRICULTURAL. | | | | | NON-AGRICULTURAL. | | | | | |
| | Males. | | Females. | | | Males. | | Females. | | | |
	Adults.	Boys.	Adults.	Girls.	Total.	Adults.	Boys.	Adults.	Girls.	Total.	Grand Total.
Hindús	133,179	73,099	109,361	60,504	376,143	148,210	90,805	139,805	67,510	446,330	822,473
Musalmáns & others.	7,427	4,766	6,669	3,903	22,765	26,069	16,094	25,458	12,679	80,300	103,065
Total	140,606	77,865	116,030	64,407	398,908	174,279	106,899	165,263	80,189	526,630	925,538

In addition to the above, there were 484 persons employed in the railway, 566 in military occupations, and 166 Europeans and Eurasians. The number of villages is given at 1,799, of which 1,625 had less than 1,000 inhabitants, 166 had between 1,000 and 5,000, and only eight towns existed with more than 5,000 inhabitants, viz., Mursán, Tappal, Jaláli, Harduaganj, Sikandra Rao, Atrauli, Háthras, and Koil. The decrease between 1853 and 1865 amounts to ten per cent., and is wholly inexplicable.

The census of 1872 gives the total population at 1,073,333, or 547 persons to the square mile. Of these, 955,121 were Hindús, 117,911 were Musalmáns, 239 were non-Asiatics, and 62 were Native Christians. There were 1,750 villages, giving an average of 0·9 villages to each square mile, and 613 inhabitants to each village. The actual classification of villages showed 422 with less than 200 inhabitants, 693 with between 200 and 500, 411 with between 500 and 1,000, 168 having from 1,000 to 2,000, 47 having from 2,000 to 5,000, and nine above 5,000. These last include the towns mentioned in 1865, with the addition of Bijaigarh or Gambhíra. The

Census of 1872.

settlement records give the average area in acres of the villages in each tahsíl as follows :—Koil, 639 ; Iglás, 604 ; Atrauli, 737 ; Háthras, 481 ; Sikandra Rao, 853 ; and Khair, 922. The next table gives the population, divided into agriculturists and those following other occupations ; and the succeeding table shows the details of population for each parganah according to sex, age, and religion, from the census returns of 1872.

Religion.	Land-owners.		Agriculturists.		Non-agriculturists.		Total.	
	Male.	Female.	Male.	Female.	Male.	Female.	Male.	Female.
Hindús	12,350	10,522	225,189	184,840	278,022	244,198	515,561	439,560
Musalmáns ...	1,745	1,903	10,796	9,245	49,115	45,105	61,656	56,255
Christians ..	14	15	...	...	32	15	46	30
Total, ...	14,109	12,442	235,985	194,085	327,169	289,318	577,263	495,845

Parganah.	Hindús.				Muhammadan, and others not Hindu.				Total.	
	Up to 15 years.		Adults.		Up to 15 years.		Adults.			
	Male.	Female.	Male.	Female.	Male.	Female.	Male.	Female.	Male.	Female.
Koil ...	34,458	28,462	52,594	45,547	6,382	5,883	10,781	10,053	104,215	89,945
Baraulí ..	1,967	1,575	2,591	2,458	249	217	310	285	5,11	4,535
Murthál	5,8·6	4,578	7,765	7,004	349	314	595	446	14,515	12,342
Sikandra Rao	25,957	20,907	37,133	31,476	2,910	2,518	4,035	3,928	70,035	58,629
Akrabad ...	12,987	10,362	17,921	15,628	1,675	1,499	2,433	2,242	35,016	29,731
Gorai ...	9,929	8,068	14,598	12,561	609	484	843	735	25,979	21,848
Hasangarh ...	13,724	10,777	20 877	17,910	740	658	1,119	1,033	36,460	30,378
Gangíri ..	14,709	11,861	19,269	17,485	2,998	2,635	3,920	3,850	40,896	35,831
Atrauli ..	16,088	13,059	21,460	19,521	2,201	2,012	3,134	3,172	42,883	37,764
Háthras ..	30,755	25,551	47,411	41,970	2,998	2,543	4,635	3,971	85,799	74,035
Mursán ...	9,336	7,844	14,444	12,425	727	606	1,113	1,001	26,620	21,876
Tappal ...	12,352	9,698	16,769	15,432	1,006	885	1,304	1,363	31,431	27,378
Chandaus ...	7,9·4	6 502	10,800	9,886	784	689	1,098	956	2·,666	18,033
Khair ..	14,586	11,974	21,297	19,039	1,092	948	1,662	1,859	38,631	33,320
Total ..	210,632	171,218	304,929	265,342	24,720	21,891	36,982	34,394	577,263	495,845

The number of Hindú males was 515,561, or 54·0 per cent. of the entire Hindú population ; Hindú females number 439,560, or 46·0 per cent.; Musalmán males, 61,656, or 52·3 per cent. of the entire Musalmán population ; and Musalmán females, 56,255, or 47·7 per cent. The percentage of Hindús on the total population is 89·0, and of Musalmáns is 11·0, or one Musalmán to every nine Hindús. The percentage of males in the total population is 53·8, and of females is 46·2, whilst the divisional percentages are 54·0 and 46·0 respectively.

The statistics relating to infirmities show that in 1872 amongst the total

Infirmities.

population of the district there were 83 insane persons (35 females), or 0·7 per 10,000 of the population; 62 idiots (13 females), or 0·6 per 10,000 inhabitants; 167 deaf and dumb (53 females), or 1·6 per 10,000; 3,222 blind (1,634 females), or 30·0 per 10,000; and 240 lepers (23 females), or 2·2 per 10,000. The statistics of age were first

Ages.

collected in 1872, and exhibit the following results for the Aligarh district. The table gives the number of Hindús and Musalmáns according to sex at different ages, with the percentage on the total population of the same religion. The columns referring to the total population include the inhabitants of all creeds, but preserve the sex distinction :—

Ages.	HINDÚS.				MUSALMÁNS				TOTAL POPULATION.			
	Males.	Percentage on total Hindús.	Females.	Percentage on total Hindús.	Males.	Percentage on total Musalmáns.	Females.	Percentage on total Musalmáns.	Males.	Percentage on total population.	Females.	Percentage on total population.
Up to 1 year ...	28,393	5·5	26,371	6·0	3,381	5·4	3,825	5·9	31,777	5·5	29,696	5·9
Between 1 and 6...	78,432	15·4	70,786	16·1	9,224	14·9	8,851	15·7	88,664	15·3	79,642	16·0
„ 6 and 12...	74,531	14·4	55,029	12·5	8,758	14·2	7,125	12·6	83,355	14·4	62,156	12·5
„ 12 and 20...	87,866	17·0	70,660	16·1	10,109	16·8	9,643	17·1	98,280	17·0	80,305	16·1
„ 20 and 30...	93,842	18·2	84,113	19·1	11,666	18·9	10,768	19·1	105,519	18·2	94,894	19·1
„ 30 and 40...	70,014	13·5	58,931	13·4	8,162	13·2	7,290	12·9	78,185	13·5	66,226	13·3
„ 40 and 50...	44,165	8·5	37,864	8·6	5,088	8·2	4,668	8·2	49,257	8·5	42,534	8·5
„ 50 and 60...	24,855	4·8	23,74	5·2	3,080	4·9	2,834	5·0	27,935	4·8	25,908	5·2
Above 60...	12,403	2·4	12,732	2·9	1,888	3·0	1,751	3·1	14,291	2·4	14,484	2·9

The proportion of Hindú males under 12 to the total Hindú population is 35·4 per cent., and of Hindú females is 34·6; amongst Musalmáns the percentages are 34·6 and 34·3 respectively. Taking the quinquennial periods up to 15 years of age, or 0 to 5, 5 to 10, and 10 to 15 years, the percentage of both sexes to the total population is 18·9, 11·8, and 9·1 respectively; or taking females only, the numbers are 19·6, 11·4, and 7·9 per cent. Here, as all throughout the division, females are slightly in excess of males in the first period, and considerably below them in the other two. In the third period males show 10·1 to 7·9 females. This is no doubt due to the systematic concealment of the females of a marriageable age. Again, taking the total population of the same sex and religion, only the proportion of Hindú males of the ages of 10 to 13 to all the

Hindú males is 5·7, and of Hindú females to all Hindú females is only 4·5; whilst Musalmáns show 5·4 and 4·4 respectively. From the ages of 13 to 20 the proportion of Hindú males to the total of the same sex and religion is 16 per cent., and of Hindú females is 15·2 per cent., whilst Musalmáns show 16 and 16·3 per cent. These results support the conclusion that the enumeration of females from ten to fifteen years of age is defective.

Distributing the Hindú population, numbering 955,121 souls, amongst the four great classes, we have 148,249 Brahmans (67,556 females), 88,414 Rajpúts (38,900 females), 53,544 Baniyas (24,999 females), and the great mass of the inhabitants included in 'the other castes' of the census returns, which number 664,914 souls, of whom 308,095 are females. Amongst the Brahmans, 24,393 belong to the great Gaur ·subdivision, 8,299 are Sanádhs, 7,488 are Saraswats, 1,226 Kanaujiyas, and the remainder are unspecified in the census returns, or belong to minor subdivisions. The Gaurs connect their name with the ancient kingdom of Gaur in Bengal, and say that they came to the Upper Duáb to assist Raja Janamejáya in his great snake-sacrifice, and, like the Tagas, received a grant of lands in return for their services. The Máhábhárata opens with an account of the snake-sacrifice performed by Janamejáya in revenge for the death of his father, Parikshit, who had been bitten by a snake. Janamejáya subsequently killed a Brahman, and in expiation of this crime, amongst other austerities, he listened to the recital of the Mahábhárata by Vaisámpáyana, a pupil of Vyása. Some time afterwards a dispute as to the ritual to be observed in certain cases arose between the Raja and the Brahman, and the former perished in consequence of the curse pronounced upon him by the enraged priest.[1] The story of the immigration from Bengal is too improbable to be accepted. The Gaurs would have to pass through the country of the Jajhotiya and Kanaujiya Brahmans, where now hardly a trace of them is to be found, and they are almost confined to the Meerut Division and the adjacent districts of Rohilkhand. Gaur, too, was only made the capital of Bengal a short time before the Musalmán invasion, and the present tribes of Gaur Brahmans, Tagas, and Rajpúts were settled here long before Mahmúd ever left Ghazni. There can be little doubt but that the name is connected with Gauda or Gaura (now called Gonda), a subdivision of the district of Uttara Kosala in Oudh, lying to the south of the Rapti (Ráwati). The ancient city of Srávasti is said in the Puránas to be in Gauda, and modern research identifies Srávasti with Sahet-mahet, 12 miles from Balrámpur in the Gonda district.[2] Srávasti was the seat of a powerful dynasty of the solar race who ruled until the fourth century, when they appear to have fallen amid the general dissolution of the eastern kingdoms. About the beginning of the Christian era

Castes.

Brahmans.

---

[1] Vish. Pur., IV, 162.   [2] Arch. Sur., I., 380; Beames' Elliot, I., 102.

religious differences may have led to the emigration of the Brahmans and others from the Gaurian kingdom, for we know that fierce disputes raged between the Buddhists and the followers of the old law about that time, and that at the same time the Gaurians settled in the Upper Duáb. There are a few Gautam Brahmans who say that they belong to the Maithila division. The Sanádhs are a branch of the Kanaujiyas, and intermarry with both Kananjiyas and Gaurs. As landholders they form cultivating communities, and are good agriculturists, and, as a rule, do not claim or expect favour in rent. The Saraswats are those who come from the sacred river Saraswati or Sarsuti in the Panjáb. Brahmans altogether form an important portion of the proprietary body in this district, and they own 244 villages, with an area of 113,576 acres.

Amongst the Rajputs the following clans are the most important:—Jádon (36,423), Chauhán (15,408), Kirár (9,352), Pundír (6,125), Janghára (3,490), Bargújar (3,429), Gahlot (3,085), Surajbansi (1,160), Bhál (1,009), Bais (948), Panwár (952), Gaharwár (905), Rahtor (801), Tómar (749), Sikharwár (354), Gaur (459), Jaiswár (490), Bachhal, Bangar, Barkhar, Bharadwáj, Chandel, Chhonkar, Dhákra, Gautam, Joliya, Kachhwáha, Porach, Parwal, Mandwal, Khajuniya, Raghubansi, Raikwár, Solankhi, Sengar, and Tanak. The remainder are unspecified. The Jádons belong to the Bágri or inferior division of the tribe, and are not on an equality with the Jádons of Jewar in Bulandshahr and those of the native state of Karauli. The principal landed proprietors of this tribe are the talukadárs of Somna in this district, and Awa Mísa in the Muttra district, noticed hereafter under the principal families of the district. The Jádons claim descent from Sri Krishna, and through him from Yádu of the Lunar race. Those living in this district trace their origin to Muttra and Batesar, whence they spread over all the neighbouring country. They are now most numerous in tahsíl Koil and in parganahs Akrabad, Sikandra, Atrauli, Gorai, Hasangarh, and Khair. Many, however, belong to the pure Yádava race, and an account of them will be found under Muttra. The Chhonkars or Chonkars claim descent from the Karauli Jádons, but common report makes them a spurious branch derived from the marriage of a Jádon and a *chokri* or female servant. The Chauháns are scattered all over the district, but are the prevailing clan in Khair, Chandaus, and Morthal. Bhupál Singh of Khair, the head of the clan in this district, was hanged for rebellion in the mutiny. They claim descent from Raja Sangat, the great-grandson of Cháhara Deva, the brother of Prithiráj, one of whose numerous progeny settled in Khair. The Chauhán clan will be noticed at length under the Mainpuri district. Kirárs are a numerous clan, and, though numbered amongst Rajputs, are held to be of very inferior rank. They are good cultivators, but as proprietors they have lost more than half their villages during the last settlement. They claim to be a branch of the Júdons, and say that they came from the west, and are descendants of one Kunwar or Karauli Pál. They have occupied villages in this and the Mainpuri district since the middle of the fifteenth century.

The Pundírs, also called Purírs, form an important clan, and in this district are more prosperous than any other of the old Rajpút clans. The Jangháras give the derivation of their name as *jang* (war) and *áhára* (hungry), or those who hunger after war ; but their enemies say that they might as well derive the name from '*jang*' and '*hára*' (worsted), those who were overcome in war. The Bargújars have been noticed under the Bulandshahr district. Gahlots are one of the thirty-six royal tribes, and formerly held large possessions in this district. This clan

Gahlots.

is divided into two great branches, the Sisodhiya and Ahária. The branch in this district is the Sisodhiya, which is the same as that to which the Rána of Udépur or Mewár, the premier Raja of Rajputána and the "sun of the Hindús," belongs. Tod[1] devotes a large portion of his first volume to the annals of the Gahlots of Mewár. The Gahlots are of the Solar race, and trace their descent from Lava, the eldest son of the deified hero Ráma. They emigrated from Oudh and settled at Dwárka in Gujrát, and on their expulsion from thence settled in Mewár and changed their name to Gahlot. One branch made the town of Ar or Ahár, in the valley of the present capital of Udepur, their chief seat, and were hence called Aháriyas, whilst another branch settled in Sisodha on their expulsion from Chítor, and founded the present house of Mewár. The origin of the name Gahlot is said to be in this wise: on the expulsion of the clan from Gujrát, the queen Pushpávati alone escaped the sack of the capital (Balabhi), where her husband, the celebrated Siláditya, was slain. This event[2] happened in 523 A.D. The queen fled to a cave in the hills and was there delivered of a son, whom she named Guha or the cave-born. His descendant Bappa seized on Chítor in 727 A.D., and founded the Gahlot dynasty of Mewár, who subsequently removed to Udepur. The Persian historians make Naushizád, son of Naushírwán, or Maha Banu, daughter of Yezdijird, the source of the present Sisodhiya line.[3] The Gahlot prince of Chítor married the sister of Prithiráj, and it is to this connection is due the presence of Gahlots in the Upper Duáb. They all say that they came to assist the Chauhán prince of Dehli in his numerous wars, and that in reward he gave them over the lands of the Meos and the Dors. Chand Bardai mentions Gobind Rao, Gahlot, as one of Prithiráj's auxiliaries. The Bulandshahr Gahlots say that they settled near Dásna under Raja Khumán at an early period. A long inscription in a *math* behind the temple of Achalesvara on mount Abu, bearing date 1286 A.D., speaks in high praise of the liberal race of Guhila, so early had the name been fixed. But here Guhila is made the son of Vappaka, and

---

[1] Madras Edition, I., 175-561. [2] Thomas's Prinsep, U. T., 252. Their enemies say that the correct derivation is from *gahla*, a slave girl. [3] Tod, I., 198.

it is said that the name Guhila " is attached to the princes who have been born in his race." Some say that the Guhila Rajpúts are distinct from the Gahlots, and this may be due to a branch formed by this Guhila, son of Bappu, the conqueror of Chítor.

The Bháls are noticed under the Bulandshahr district. The Bhattis or Jaiswárs also call themselves a branch of the Jádon stock. They came from Jaisalmír, and many of them have become Musalmáns in this and the neighbouring districts. They say, as usual, that they came here in the time of Prithiráj; in fact this era is quite as common in the district as ' the Norman Conquest' is in England. The Porach clan formerly possessed Daryápur, Háthras, Mendu, and Husain, but all have now passed out of their hands. They are old settlers in the district, and were contemporaries of the Dors and Meos before the Musalmán conquest. The returns of 1872 show only 82 Dors in this district, which once ' almost entirely' belonged to them. None of the other Rajpút clans require any particular notice here. Altogether Rajpúts still possess 544 villages, with an area of 346,648 acres in this district, in full proprietary right.

Baniyas belong to the following subdivisions:—Bárahsaini (14,049),

Baniyas.

Agarwál (15,027), Dasa (4,512), Jaiswár (2,684), Mahesri (3,472), Gaharwál (2,890), Chausaini (2,521), Khandelwál (1,172), Sarangi (1,222), Lohiya, Máhar, Bádbpeta, Bishnoi, Baranwál, Ghoi, Rastaugi, &c., They are an important and wealthy class, and have now 210 villages, comprising 115,450 acres in this district. They are chiefly absentees, following their trades of money-lending and brokerage in the principal towns. Before the last settlement they held only 41 villages, and have occupied their present position entirely of late years. The Ágarwáls claim descent from Raja Ugrasen of Agroha in the Sarsa district of the Panjáb. They are divided into two great branches,—the Bísa and Dasa. Ugrasen is said to have married the daughter of Vásuki, the Rasa of the Nágas, and by her he had eighteen sons, of whom seventeen founded the *gots* of the Agarwáls, and the eighteenth became the *guru* of the rest. Agroha was destroyed by Shiháb-uddin Ghori. The Dasas of the original stock are descendants of the concubines of Ugrasen, and are called Kadími Dasas, to distinguish them from the new families of impure origin who adopt the name. They are also called Raja-ke-barádari, from one of their members having obtained the title of Raja in the reign of Farrukhsiyár. The Chausaini or Chausení is considered rather a low caste even amongst Baniyas. They say that they came from Muttra and are descendants of one of the wrestlers of Raja Kans, to whom the Chamárs also look up as their progenitor. The Dhusars are said to have come from Riwári. They are a spurious clan, who assume to themselves the name of Brahman, and often that of Bhárgava or descendants of the Muni Bhrigu.

As in other districts, the great mass of the population comes under the head

Other castes.

of other castes. The following table gives the names and numbers of each of the principal other castes found in Aligarh in 1872 :—

Ahár	...	1,308	Habúra	...	909	Mathuriya	...	18
Aheríya	...	7,461	Hajjám	...	22,076	Meo	...	30⁵
Ahír	...	26,578	Ját	...	89,292	Mochi	...	50₃₅
Baheliya	...	9	Jotishi	...	834	Nat	...	3?5
Banjára	...	2,352	Juláha	...	321	Nunera	...	492
Barha	...	23,183	Káchhi	...	19,211	Orh	...	3,886
Bári	...	357	Kahár	...	26,949	Patwa	...	93
Beda	...	66	Kalál	...	12,296	Ramaiya	...	46
Bharbhunja	...	1,834	Kanjar	...	1,139	Riwári	...	554
Bhát	...	4,125	Kayath	...	8,842	Sangtarásh	...	23
Bhísti	...	13	Khákrob	...	24,832	Sunár	...	5,918
Borah	...	173	Khetík	...	19,994	Taga	...	7
Chamár	...	178,126	Khattri	...	1,516	Tamoli	...	328
Chhípi	...	2,709	Koll	...	35,081	Tawáif	...	21
Chobdar	...	216	Kumhár	...	10,520	Teli	...	3,680
Darzi	...	6,347	Kunjara	...	218	Thathera	...	144
Dhanak	...	467	Kármi	...	460	Aghori	...	552
Dhobi	...	13,338	Lodha	...	38,526	Bairági	...	5,089
Dhuna	...	7,285	Lohár	...	2,068	Fakír	...	14
Dom	...	17	Miumár	...	1,110	Gosháin	...	2,752
Gararíya	...	32,883	Máli	...	5,786	Jogi	...	5,097
Ghosi	...	602	Malláh	...	2,159	Marwári	...	29
Gújar	...	640	Manihár	...	81	Mína	...	496

The Chamárs are the most numerous, and form the bulk of the labouring population, and even 16·5 per cent. of the total population. Some few of them have attained to considerable prosperity, but as a rule they are mere serfs of the proprietor, tied to the soil, and going with it on occasions of transfer. In fact no sharer will think a partition complete until an adequate number of Chamárs has been allotted to his share in proportion to his interests in the estate. Játs are the most industrious and painstaking of all the cultivating classes. There is a great spirit of rivalry between them and the Rajpúts, so that these two castes seldom reside in the same village, and if let alone would at once fly at each others' throats. In the mutiny " the old Ját and Rajpút feud raged strongly in the western portions of the district, and was only stopped by news arriving of the fall of Dehli."

The Játs are decidedly the most powerful amongst these 'other castes.' They

Játs.

hold amongst them 452 villages as proprietors, and belong chiefly to the Tenwa, Thákurel, Khandiya, and Chábuk subdivisions. They occupy nearly the whole of the western portion of the district. A notice of the clan is given under the Meerut district, and a short sketch of their local history is only necessary here. The Khandiya *got* prevails in Tappal, the Thákurel in Hasangarh, and the Tenwa in Gorai, Mursán, and Háthras. The history of the Tenwa *got* will be found hereafter under the history of the Mursán and Háthras talukas. The Thákurels of the Hasangarh or Lagaswán parganah, say that they came here in 1046 A.D. under Vikrama Thákur, and expelled the Jangháras and Kalárs, whose lands they formed into 54 villages, and held possession of these until the British occupation, when very many of the villages fell into the hands of the money-lenders. The Khandiya Játs take their name from the village of Khandiya in parganah Tappal, where they settled at a very early date, and spread all over the parganah. The Pisáwa talukádárs are of the Chábuk *got*, and are noticed hereafter. The Játs in the eastern parganahs are chiefly those who settled in the district during its usurpation by the Bhartpur Raja, towards the close of the last century. They do not seem to have settled and multiplied in the way that the western Játs have done, and are altogether not so prosperous.

Ahars and Aheriyas are chiefly found in the Atrauli parganah, in the sandy tracts towards the Ganges, where they eke out their professional livelihood of robbery and cattle-breeding by tilling the land for enough food to support themselves throughout the year. Mr. Smith writes of the Aheriyas :—" Their profession is theft, robbery, or dakaiti, and the Aheriyas of Aligarh are notorious in the adjoining districts to which their crimes are mostly confined. They form a sort of powerful secret society, and under the name of cultivators are mere robbers and murderers ; and there can be little doubt, whether from fear or sympathy, they receive ample support and assistance from many of the proprietors of their villages." Ahírs own some ten villages, and are pretty numerous in Sikandra Rao and Atrauli. In the former tahsíl they have the character of being fair cultivators, but in Atrauli they are said to be idle, lazy and careless. The soil may have something to do with this state of things, as in Atrauli it is sandy, and the Ganges khádir affords good pasturage for cattle, the breeding of which is the Ahírs' hereditary occupation. In Sikandra Rao there is no waste land, and the peasantry must depend upon the cultivation of the soil for their maintenance. Lodhas hold 25 villages in Koil, Atrauli, and Akrabad, and seem to have acquired the management of their villages during the troubled times of the Marhatta supremacy in the last century. Khattris hold 18 villages. Káchhis are chiefly found in Háthras, Sikandra Rao, and Atrauli, and here, as elsewhere, are market gardeners. They are few in number in each village, and cultivate the small holdings that they possess very highly. The more they work the more is exacted from them, whilst with the lazy Gújar and the Aheriya dakait, the less they do and the more they make their neighbours afraid of them, the better off they are.

Garariyas are chiefly found in Sikandra, Koil, and Atrauli. As a rule they
are sheep breeders, but many villages in this district are altogether cultivated
by them, and they own one : they make fair agriculturists. Kayaths hold 77
villages, most of which are hereditary amongst the descendants of former parganah officials. They held 61 of these villages in 1838. The Lodhas are among
the best agriculturists in the district, and hold 25 villages as proprietors. They
are chiefly to be found in Koil, Atrauli, and Akrabad, and assumed the management of their villages during the struggle for life at the close of the last century.
The Meos, who once owned so much of the land, the Ishmaelites of the twelfth to
the fifteenth centuries, now have but one village. Bohras, a money-making class,
vie with their trade-fellows, Baniyas and the usurer Brahmans, in their careful
money-getting habits. But it would appear that the Brahman money-lender
is more grasping than either. " To the power derived from the possession of
money they add the influence of caste, and some of them have been among the
largest accumulators of property in the district. As a class they are accused
of every sort of fraud and chicanery ; and if half the tales told are founded on
truth, in times not so long past, when there was less careful supervision than
now over the subordinate civil courts, their predecessors must have been a
curse to the country. They have had most success among the formerly heavily-
assessed proprietary communities ; and within the last 50 years two wealthy
families have grown up in the south of the district,—one, that of Ganga Ram
of Kanchirauli among the Játs of Iglás; and another, that of Gaj Singh of
Lakhnau, among the Játs and Porach Thákurs of Háthras."

The Musalmáns in the census returns of 1872 are divided into Shaikhs

Musalmáns.

(16,459), Sayyids (4,180), Mughals (1,192), Patháns
(15,226), Miwátis (2,040), and unspecified, 78,774.
Amongst the latter class must be included the great mass of converted Hindús or
Nau Muslims, who hold 78 villages in the district. Many of them are absentees
and residents of Bulandshahr, but many also live in the district. The Jaláli
Sayyids are the most noteworthy of their class in the district. Though a small
community, they are distinguished by the number of servants that they have
given to the State. The Sayyids hold 55 villages. Mughals hold only 7 villages,
and are of little importance. Shaikhs hold 35 villages, and Patháns are owners
of 222 villages, many of which are included in the Datauli and Bhíkampur
talukas. A fakír has one village. The Musalmáns as a rule are exacting,
though not absolutely severe landlords, like the money-lenders and the Jádons of
Awa Misa. They get as much as they can out of their tenants, but help them
largely in times of scarcity and need. Europeans, or rather Eurasians, hold 21
villages ; they make good landlords when they look after their villages themselves, but as a rule they are more in the hands of their agents than others.
The district returns of 1872 showed 123 English, 12 Scotch, 16 Irish, 10 French,

and 17 Europeans whose nationality was not specified. There were also two Australians, 61 Eurasians, and 62 Native Christians. Few of these are permanent residents ; the railway brings an ever-changing population from all countries amongst its servants, and the European census above given may not hold good for a single year.

The census of 1872 for the first time has attempted to collect statistics regarding the occupations of the people. The distribution of the population into the two great divisions of agriculturists and those following occupations unconnected with the cultivation of the soil has been sufficiently noticed in the preceding pages. The agriculturists as a body will be described hereafter, and here we have chiefly to speak of the subdivision of the non-agricultural classes. The whole population was divided for the purposes of the census of 1872 into six great classes, each of which had several subdivisions, and included all the male adults engaged in the occupations it represents. The first or professional class embraces all Government servants, soldiers, and persons following the learned professions, literature, the arts and sciences, and numbered 4,319 male adults (not less than fifteen years of age), amongst whom are included 1,296 uprohits or family priests, 1,686 pandits, 160 *baids* or physicians, 376 singers, &c. The second class numbered 45,965 members, and comprised all males engaged in domestic service, as cooks, washermen, sweepers, water-carriers, and the like. The third class represents commerce, and numbered 22,849, amongst whom are all persons who buy or sell, keep or lend money and goods of various kinds, as money-lenders (1,527), shopkeepers (11,934), bankers (375), and all persons engaged in the conveyance of men, animals, or goods, as pack-carriers, ekka-drivers, porters, &c. (4,923). The fourth class includes persons possessing or working the land as proprietors (8,988), cultivators (146,040), ploughmen, gardeners and nut-growers, and every one engaged about animals, as shepherds, graziers, &c., they number 1,974 male adults. The fifth class, containing 50,955 members, included all persons engaged in industrial occupations, the arts and mechanics, in the manufacture of textile fabrics and dress, or articles of food and drink, as well as dealers in animal, vegetable, and mineral substances. The sixth class contained 76,193 males, including labourers and others (67,752), persons of independent means (18), and persons supported by the community and of no specified occupation (8,423); altogether there are 357,354 males classified by occupation in this district, nearly one-half of whom belonged to the agricultural population.

The five municipal towns of the district contain an aggregate population of 121,168 souls, and besides these there are only four other towns having a population exceeding 5,000, *viz.,* Jaláli, Tappal, Mursán, and Bijaigarh, aggregating 251,53 souls, giving a total town population of 146,321. But in all these towns there is a proportion of inhabitants who live by cultivation, and, roughly speaking, the five municipal towns may be said to contain all the non-agricultural population of the district, and the cultivators who live in the municipal town smay be set off against the few artisans and other non-agriculturists of the rural towns. Thus the bulk of the population is agricultural ; the only manufacture (indigo) is the mere working up of an extensively grown plant, and the only other trade (cotton) is nothing more than a carrying trade of agricultural raw materials.

The census of 1872 gives the number of enclosures inhabited by Hindús at 99,322, whilst Musalmáns occupy 14,856, and Christians 18, or a total of 114,196. This shows 58 enclosures to the square mile, and nine persons to each enclosure. The separate houses, their character and distribution, are shown as follows :—

Houses.

Class of house.	INHABITED BY				Number of inhabitants.
	Hindús.	Musalmáns.	Christians.	Total.	
Built with skilled labour ...	21,528	2,876	16	24,420	121,963
Ditto unskilled labour ...	165,770	21,249	7	187,026	951,145
Total ...	187,298	24,125	23	211,446	1,073,108

This return gives 107 houses to the square mile, and five inhabitants to each house. The proportion of persons inhabiting the better class of houses in the total population is only 11·3 per cent., whilst the divisional average is 10·2 per cent., showing a low standard of comfort in this division, which, however, ranks second in the province in this respect.

The district, and especially the northern half, abounds in the remains of old forts ; few of them, however, have any claims to any antiquity, and the greater number owe their origin to the necessity that was felt for a means of defence against the lawless bands who overran the Duáb towards the end of last century. Many of the old Rajpút forts were improved and strengthened by their successive owners. Háthras was built of brick by the Ját Raja, and nearly every respectable landholder constructed a mud fort into which he could retire at the approach of danger. Even for some years after the British occupation fort-building was the daily occupation of all the more powerful talukadárs ; and that they succeeded in their own unscientific way in turning out something formidable is shown by the story of Sásni, Kachaura, and Bijaigarh, which were not taken until after great loss in 1802. Mau, Mursán, and Lutsán in tahsíl Háthras, Morthal in Koil, Tappal, Chandaus, Pisáwa, Beswán, Gorai, Deori, Chharra, Barla, and Atrauli must all have been

Forts.

places of considerable strength, sufficient to withstand any attacks of native troops, and only to be attempted by Europeans when well led and skilfully handled.

Passing from the people and their houses to the customs that prevail

Customs.

amongst them we find that "panchâyats are chiefly resorted to by the lower castes, with whom these meetings appear to be a kind of promiscuous assembly of as many of the caste brotherhood as can be got together, to discuss the business in hand, whatever it may be.[1] Breaches of caste rules and matrimonial affairs are the most usual subjects of discussion. In nearly all low castes, widows are re-married to the deceased husband's brother, and this observation applies to Játs and Ahírs, though they can hardly be called low castes. Panchâyats also arrange divorces and re-marriages of divorced women. Their procedure is untrammelled by any system of rules, and, so far as can be ascertained, even the decision of a majority is not binding. Indeed it is not easy to say how they arrive at their conclusions. Nearly all trades and bodies of artisans have chaudhris. Here, again, it is not easy to say how these men come to enjoy the office. In some cases it is admittedly hereditary. In others it seems to depend on a kind of scramble ; the man with most vigour and audacity being recognized as chaudhri, to the exclusion perhaps of the last chaudhri's heir. In no case does it appear that election is in use by the trades-people themselves, and in a case where election was suggested by the authorities as the best means of settling an inveterate dispute, although a formal majority was obtained, the dispute raged with as much vigour as ever."

Aligarh was one of the districts selected and placed by Mr. Thomason under

Education.

Mr. H. S. Reid for experimental schools. Schools were opened at each of the eight tahsílis in 1850-51. In 1845 the number of Persian and Arabic schools was 159, attended by 1,432 pupils, and the number of Hindi schools amounted to 137, attended by 1,473 pupils—total, 2,905, of whom 682 were Musalmáns and 2,223 were Hindús. The percentage of male children at school to the number fit for school in 1845 was 4·7 per cent. In 1851 the number of schools had increased to 548, and the pupils to 4,948, of whom 3,882 were Hindús. At the same time there were eight tahsíli schools with 366 pupils, and three Anglo-vernacular schools with 21 pupils. The halkahbandi or village schools were opened in 1853. The zila school was opened in 1858 ; the new school-house was built, partly by subscription, in 1870, and has a master's residence and boarding-house attached, to the support of which grants-in-aid are made by the Koil and Háthras Municipalities. The Anglo-vernacular schools are placed at Háthras, Sikandra Rao, and Atrauli, and are kept up by local contributions and municipal grants.

The female normal school was opened in 1867, and is under the charge of the Inspectress of Girls' Schools, whose salary is charged to the establishment. Aligarh

---

[1] Note on Customs, by Mr. E. S. Robertson, C.S.

is the residence of the Assistant Inspector of the First Circle, subordinate to the Inspector of the First or Meerut Circle. The local educational arrangements are made in concert with the local educational committee, of which the Collector is president. The following statement gives the educational statistics of the district for the years 1860-61 and 1871-72, from the records of the Education Department.

Class of School.	1860-61.			1871-72.						
	No. of schools.	No. of pupils.	Cost.	No. of schools.	No. of pupils.		Average daily attendance.	Cost per head.	Proportion borne by State.	Total charges.
					Hindús.	Musalmáns.				
			Rs.					Rs. a.	Rs. a.	Rs.
GOVERNMENT. { Zila (superior),	1	83	1,721	1	146	17	137	78 15	45 5	12,633
Tahsíli ...	8	589	2,467	6	580	105	524	4 4	3 8	2,620
Halkahbandi ...	160	1,258	4,104	95	3,440	308	2,745	3 8	...	11,773
Female ...	...	...	...	42	622	36	440	4 2	4 1	2,604
AIDED ... A.-vernacular ..	...	...	...	3	119	39	134	40 0	16 0	5,242
UNAIDED, Indigenous ...	255	3,034	14,857	232	1,799	670	2,469	6 0	...	14,858
GOVERNMENT. } Normal (female),	...	...	...	1	20	...	13	302 5	302 5	4,534
Total ...	427	4,964	23,149	370	6,766	1,175	6,462	...	...	54,264

The census statistics of education.
An attempt was made during the census of 1872 to collect statistics in regard to the state of education amongst the people. The following statement shows the results,—the number of Hindús and Musalmáns who can read and write (literate), and the percentages of the same to the total population of the same religion, sex and age. The Christian population is so small that the statistics referring to them have been omitted :—

Ages.	HINDÚS.					MUSALMÁNS.				
	Males.			Females.		Males.			Females.	
	Number.	Literate.	Percentage.	Number.	Literate.	Number.	Literate.	Percentage.	Number.	Literate.
1 to 12 ...	182,416	2,888	1·5	152,186	4	21,363	369	1·7	19,201	Nil.
12 to 20 ...	87,866	4,169	4·7	70,660	Nil.	10,409	414	3·9	9,643	1
Above 20 ...	245,279	14,646	5·9	216,714	...	29,684	1,331	4·4	27,311	Nil.
Total ...	515,561	21,703	4·2	439,560	4	61,656	2,114	3·4	56,255	1

These statistics must be very imperfect, for the girls' schools mentioned above must have turned out more than five pupils able to read and write. The educational statistics also show a total of 7,941 boys attending school in the district, without counting those privately educated, whilst the census shows only 7,840 males up to 20 years of age as able to read and write. Few remain at school after they have passed 18 years of age, so that these returns palpably under-estimate the number of literate persons in the district. The census shows 102,807 males between 6 and 15; and taking two-thirds of those between 15 and 20, we have 138,597 males of a school-going age. Comparing these figures with the school returns, we find only about one boy in every seventeen attending school, whilst there is but one school for every 374 boys. This much may at least be gathered, that there is much room for the extension of the lower class or village schools.

The Aligarh Institute and Scientific Society, founded in 1864 by Sayyid Ahmad Khán, C.S.I., at present Judge of the Small Court at Benares, is thus described by Mr. Smith :—" The main design of the society was an ambitious one,—it was an endeavour to bring to the knowledge of the general native public the more important results of modern science and historical investigation by means of translations into the vernacular from works in English or other European languages. This design has been steadily kept in view, and during the last nine years various translations have issued from the Society's Press. Some histories, treatises on farming, on electricity and on political economy, and many of Todhunter's elementary as well as more advanced mathematical works, have opened out a new course of possible study to the native who knows no language but his own. A captious critic might find objections in some cases to the books selected for translation; but when the end aimed at is so good, and the obvious difficulties in the way are so numerous, it is scarcely fair to criticize with severity. Defects in execution there must be, and these are chiefly due to the want of a European supervisor, who should not only be possessed of considerable scientific attainments, but should have a perfect knowledge of both English and Urdu. Such a man is not easy to obtain, nor could the Society afford the price of his services. The Institute boasts of a library of more than 2,000 volumes, and in the building is a public reading room furnished with the leading English and vernacular papers. In connection with the society, a newspaper called the *Aligarh Institute Gazette* is published. Part of its contents are printed in Urdu alone, part in English, and a portion also in both languages. It consists largely of extracts from the English papers, but general subjects of social or political interest are frequently discussed in its columns, and the moderation of its tone is attested by the fact that Government is a large subscriber for copies of the paper for use in its various schools." The ' *Tahzib-ul-Akhlak*,' or ' Muhammadan Social Reformer,' is also printed here, but is published at Benares. Thákur Giri Parshád of Benares publishes a paper called the *Mangal Samáchar*.

The language of the peasantry is very pure Hindi, which, in the southern parganahs, is strongly tinged with the Braj dialect of Muttra; but the language used by the better classes is the Urdu of Dehli. There is only a very small congregation of Native Christians, and there is no Brahmo Samáj. The religion of Islám is not believed to be making much progress amongst the people, nor is the Wahábi movement popular. It must, however, be admitted that the teaching of the more zealous amongst the Aligarh Musalmáns has had the effect of inducing all classes of Muhammadans to adopt stricter views of their religion, and to be disposed to abandon many of the customs and observances which Indian Muhammadans have borrowed from their Hindú neighbours, or which remained untouched with their conversion to Islám. On the one hand, the zealous and bigoted, who form the mass of the population, hold that the Kurán claims political supremacy for the religion of Islám. On the other hand, the most eminent, most learned, and most intelligent of the Musalmáns deny that this claim of political supremacy is of the essence of Islám, and strongly assert the duty of loyalty to the sovereign, of whatever faith, who permits the free exercise of their religious rites to Muhammadans. As might be expected from its proximity to Dehli, there has been much Muslim colonization and conversion in this district. Converted Badgújars and Chauháns hold large estates near the Bulandshahr border ; and in connection with the Puritan movement amongst the Musalmáns, it may be mentioned that these talukadárs have dropped the Hindú title of Thákur which they formerly used, though the word has no necessary connection with Hindú superstition of any kind. Some few Játs have embraced Islám in the southern portion of the district, but no family of any note. Indeed there are few Hindu castes that have not given some of its members as converts to the Muhammadan religion.

Previous to 1846 there was no district dák ; the letters from police-stations were brought to the Court, by the post when practicable, and in other cases by policemen. In 1846 a district post was organized, and defrayed by a cess from the landholders known as *dakána*. The statistics [1] for the years 1846-47 to 1851-52 were as follow :—

Post-office.

Year.		Amount of cess realised from samindárs.	Cost of establishment.	Number of private letters.		Amount of postage.		
				Posted at police-stations.	Posted at Sadr office.	Received at police-stations.	Received at the sadr-station.	Total.
		Rs.	Rs.			Rs.	Rs.	Rs.
1846-47,	...	1,599	1,599	2,258	3,457	61	78	139
1847-48,	...	1,560	1,557	3,542	4,383	102	94	196
1848-49,	...	1,596	1,592	3,163	5,225	127	114	241
1849-50,	...	1,516	1,564	7,250	6,017	196	162	358
1850-51,	...	1,543	1,635	8,596	7,041	239	169	428
1851-52,	...	1,686	1,642	9,605	8,898	237	227	465
1852-53,	...	1,593	1,710	10,149	9,306	252	220	471
Total,	...	11,093	11,098	34,563	44,327	1,214	1,084	2,298

The postal charge on private letters was six pie, or half an anna, per tola.

The great increase in the number of letters posted and postage received will be seen from the following tables, which comprise the returns of both the district and imperial post-offices. There are fifteen imperial post-offices in the district, viz.,—Aligarh, Akrabad, Atrauli, Beswán, Dádon, Háthras, Harduaganj, Iglás, Jaláli, Khair, Mursán, Sásni, Sikandra Rao, Tappal, and Somna. There are fourteen district post-offices, viz.,—Ahan, Bijaigarh, Barla, Chandaus, Daryapur Gonda, Gangíri, Husain, Jarauli, Jawá, Jatári, Salímpur, and Aksoli.

Year.	RECEIPTS.						CHARGES.					
	Miscellaneous savings, fines.	Passengers and parcels.	Deposits, guarantee funds, family funds.	Remittances.	Postage.	Total receipts.	Charges fixed and contingent, salaries, &c.	Mail service.	Remittances.	Other charges, refunds, advances, printing.	Cash balance.	Total charges.
	Rs.	Rs.	Rs.	Rs.	Rs	Rs.	Rs.	Rs.	Rs.	Rs.	Rs	Rs.
1861-62,	9,61k	21,489	797	2,84,991	14,014	3,70,849	18,545	2,64,576	50,044	649	283	3,34.097
1865-66,	403	164	...	82,448	16,171	99,191	19,050	56,613	23,243	2	283	99,190
1870-71,	865	...	292	61,513	13,665	76,33‹	30,812	19,714	14,822	10,840	150	76,338

In addition to the above, the receipts in 1860-61 from staging bungalows amounted to Rs. 4,670, and the expenditure to Rs. 1,422 ; the receipts for service postage to Rs. 14,301, and the expenditure to the same amount, making a total receipt of Rs. 3,49,820. The following table gives the number of letters, newspapers, parcels, and books received and despatched during 1861-62, 1865-66, and 1870-71 :—

	1861-62.				1865-66.				1870-71.			
	Letters.	Newspapers	Parcels.	Books.	Letters.	Newspapers.	Parcels.	Books.	Letters.	Newspapers.	Parcels.	Books.
Received,	148,667	9,424	2,097	729	201,810	14,425	2,803	1,444	268,383	20,355	2,406	3,740
Despatched,	141,799	882	1,589	121	170,293	4,511	3,563	1,657	213,341	20,064	5,325	1,236

On the formation of the district in 1804, two small houses were hired as a jail.

Jails.   There were only forty prisoners in 1805, but yet this temporary jail was insufficient for their accommodation. In 1810 the criminal jail was built, and in 1816 the first civil jail and hospital. In 1806 the duty of guarding the prisoners at work was given to a corps of peons, and from 1817 to 1831 the jail guards were supplied from the Agra Provincial Battalion. In the latter year special guards were entertained. The jail administration is now conducted under Act XXVI. of 1870. The jail statistics for five years previous to the mutiny were as follow :—

Year.	Aggregate number of prisoners during the year.	Daily average number of prisoners.	Cost of permanent jail establishments.	Cost of permanent jail guard.	Cost of contingent jail guard.	Miscellaneous charges.	Cost of native medicine.	Cost of rations.	Cost of clothing and bedding.	Cost of additions and repairs.	Grand total of expenditure.
			Rs.	Rs	Rs.	Rs.	Rs.	Rs.	Rs.	Rs.	Rs.
1844 ...	255,113	6:9	1 394	5,976	6,781	1,714	231	11,097	1,374	318	28,885
1845 ...	234,18^	641	1,254	5,976	5,28	1,963	209	9,556	1,117	346	25,701
1846 ...	238,230	652	1,176	5 976	4,833	1 277	190	8,932	1,391	4,609	28,384
1847 ...	253,651	695	1,808	4,717	4,779	778	84	8,069	393	86	20,714
1848 ...	225,522	609	2,124	5,871	4,138	831	76	7,660	345	597 / 191	} 21,642

The following table gives the average cost per head per annum of the main items of expenditure, except rations, which gives the daily cost per head :—

Year.	Average cost of permanent guard.	Contingent guard.	Rations per diem.	Rations per annum.	Clothing.	Total cost.	Total cost, exclusive of additions and repairs.	Total cost, exclusive of permanent establishment and repairs.
	Rs. a. p	Rs. a. p.	Pie.	Rs. a. p.	Rs. a. p 1 15 5½	Rs. a. p.	Rs a. p	Rs. a. p.
1844 ...	8 6 9½	9 11 2	8½	15 13 11	1 11 10½	41 5 2	40 2 5½	30 5 2½
1845 ...	9 5 2	8 3 9	7¾	14 14 3	2 2 1½	40 1 6	39 8 10¾	28 4 5
1846 ...	9 2 7¾	7 6 7	7½	13 10 11	0 9 0½	43 8 6	36 4 11¾	25 7 11
1847 ...	6 12 7	6 14 0	6	11 9 6		29 12 10	29 10 10½	20 4 8
1848 ...	9 10 3	6 12 8½	6½	12 9 1	0 9 3½	35 8 7½	34 8 11½	21 6 10½

1850, 1860, 1870. The later statistics of the Aligarh Jail are as follow :—The average number of prisoners in jail in 1850 was 562, in 1860 was 481, and in 1870 was 470; the ratio per cent. of this average number to the population, as shown in the census of 1865 (925,538), was in 1850, ·067; in 1860, ·056; in 1870, ·051. The number of prisoners admitted in 1860 was 1,660, and in 1870 was 1,260, of whom 26 were females. The number of persons discharged in 1870 was 733. In 1870, there were 314 admissions into hospital, giving a ratio of admissions to average strength of 66·98; 4 patients died, or ·85 of the average strength. The cost per prisoner per annum in 1870 was for rations Rs. 18-2-1; clothing, Rs. 2-14-3 ; fixed establishment, Rs. 6-11-3; contingent guards, Rs. 3-7-10; police guards, Rs. 2-4-9; and additions and repairs, Rs. 12-6-0, or a total of Rs. 45-14-2. The total manufactures during the same year amounted to Rs. 2,437, and the average earnings of each prisoner to Rs. 5-3. In 1870 the Muhammadan prisoners numbered 165, and the Hindú 499 ; there were 17 prisoners under 16 years of age, 879 between 16 and 40, 123 between 40 and 60, and 22 above 60. The occupations of the majority of the male prisoners were—agriculturists, 402, labourers, 319, and domestic servants, 153.

In the year 1804 Government undertook the police duties in all large towns,

Police and crime.

and intrusted the interior police to the tahsíldárs, who were remunerated by a fee of one-half per cent. on the collections. Regulation XIV. of 1807 relieved the tahsíldárs of all police duties, and ordered the establishment of regular thánás or police-stations, which was carried out in 1809, when thirty-eight stations were formed in what then constituted the Aligarh district, employing 1,187 officers and men, at a yearly cost of Rs. 78,696.[1]

The attention of the Magistrate was early directed towards the suppression

Highway robbery.

of the crime of kazáki, or robbery by mounted highwaymen, which in those days assumed such proportions that, as a matter of fact and not a figure of speech, the highways were unoccupied, and the travellers walked through bye-ways. The facility of escape into the Begam Sumrú's territories, the protection afforded by the heavy jungles and numerous forts which then studded the country, and the ready sale for plundered property, contributed to foster this crime, which probably had its origin in the recent disbandment of the Marhatta forces, by which hundreds of mercenary adventurers were left to their own resources. In 1806, the Magistrate reported to Government that the kazáks had become so daring as to rob and plunder travellers in the extensive plains near the town of Koil, and that he had as a matter of necessity entertained fifty horsemen for the protection of the roads. Government immediately sanctioned this establishment, and when, in 1809, it was found that still more vigorous measures were required for the suppression of kazáki, and also of thagi and dakaiti which had begun to prevail

---

[1] The cost of police under the first system amounted to Rs. 91,020, viz., tahsíldár's commission, Rs. 21,756 ; sadr kotwáli establishment, Rs. 16,560; and police of towns under Regulation XXXV., 1803, and XXI., 1806, Rs. 52,704. These figures and facts are taken chiefly from Hutchinson's Aligarh Statistics.

in these provinces, orders were issued to Colonel Gardner to raise a corps of irregular cavalry for the support of the police and for other local purposes. Next year Regulation II. of 1810 was passed, containing very stringent enactments against *kazáks*, and in the same year the office of superintendent of police was instituted. One of the first steps this officer (Mr. Guthrie) took, was to establish a horse patrol of one hundred and forty-five sawárs from Colonel Gardner's corps, for the protection of the roads in this district. In 1812, he placed subordinate stations of footmen to co-operate with the horse patrols in the suppression of crime along the high roads, but, even after the adoption of these measures, the roads were so insecure that it was the practice of passengers to travel in company, and to be conveyed from station to station by parties of the patrols. Colonel Gardner's exertions for the suppression of *kazáki* were completely successful for in a short time, many of the *kazáks* surrendered to him and were pardoned at his recommendation, on giving security for future good conduct. Not content with arresting the offenders themselves, he struck at those who sheltered them, and denounced Thákur Híra Singh, talukadár of Awa Mísa in the Muttra district, as a notorious harbourer of these criminals and participant in their spoils.

The Magistrate was ordered by Government to inquire into the conduct of Híra Singh; but as no positive proof was elicited against him, the matter was allowed to drop. In 1815 Colonel Gardner's corps was removed for military service, and was replaced in its police duties by a small party of irregular cavalry, and by a detachment of 50 men from Major Lumsdaine's dromedary corps. The dromedaries were found to be of little use for patrolling, and in 1817 the Magistrate was authorised to entertain a local force, numbering 78 men, at a monthly cost of Rs. 1,615. In the meantime, whilst *kazáki* was being put down with a strong hand, every other description of crime was committed almost with impunity. On the 23rd February, 1809, the Magistrate (Mr. Ross) reported to Government that since the 12th of the preceding month, three dáks had been robbed not far from Koil; since the commencement of the year, 40 cases had occurred of robbery, 24 of house-breaking, and 81 of thefts of magnitude; in all which crimes 684 persons were concerned, of whom only 70 were apprehended. The old system of police had been abolished, and no other had been introduced in its stead. The tahsíldárs, in name at least, still continued in charge of the police, but relieved of all responsibility, and knowing that even the work of supervision would remain but a short time in their hands, they cared little for the suppression of crime, and their efforts to preserve the public peace were guided and directed by the influence which such proceedings would have on the collection of the public revenue. The punctual discharge of the duty of the office of collector of the revenue was found more profitable than any other, and consequently more

Raja of Awa Mísa, chief harbourer of thieves.

attention was paid to it than to the less show duties of the magistrate. Two years later the Magistrate reported that there was an increasing spirit of disobedience amongst.the zamíndárs, who all possessed strongholds which enabled them to defy the officers of police ; and that scarcely a process was issued which was not either evaded or openly resisted. In 1814 Ajít Singh, zamíndár of Sumera, in Khandauli, plundered a treasure party, wounding two of the chaprásis on guard. The Magistrate applied for the assistance of the military, and in the meantime sent the darogahs of Sadabad, Itmádpur, and Khandauli, with 55 footmen, to act against Ajít Singh. The latter attacked them, killed the darogah and jamadár of Khandauli, wounded three footmen, and took the darogah of Itmádpur prisoner. After this he remained unmolested in his fort until a detachment of two companies of the 13th Regiment, with two 6-pounders, was sent against him under Major Maxwell, when he made his escape, and his fort was destroyed.

For many years this district was the head-quarters of gangs of thugs and dakaits, the extent of whose depredations may be inferred from the following extracts from a report by the Superintendent of Police, dated 30th April, 1816 :—"The most heinous robberies committed in these provinces are perpetrated by gangs of Budhiks and Shughal Khors. These gangs are almost exclusively settled in the district of Aligarh and in that part of the territory of the Nawáb Vazír bordering the district of Gorakhpur. After much enquiry I am disposed to believe that the Budhiks of Aligarh and the Shughal Khors of Bharáich are connected with each other, and are one and the same people, the name constituting the sole difference. Exclusive of the Shughal Khors established in the country of the Nawáb Vazír, the following tribes are notorious in the western provinces:—Budhiks, Kanjars, Bhauriyas, Gidhiyas, and Habúras. All of these subsist by robbery, and are more or less attached to a vagrant life, eating the flesh of jackals, lizards, &c. The Budhiks of Aligarh and the Shughal Khors of Gorakhpur are outcasts of Musalmán as well as Hindú tribes ; the majority, however, are Rajpúts. Formerly numbers of Budhiks infested different parts of the districts of Aligarh, Etáwa, Farukhabad, and Agra. At present those residing in the North-West Provinces are settled on the estates of the chieftains of Mursán, Háthras, &c, in Aligarh, and some few in the district of Agra. The gangs generally make excursions once a year, in the prosecution of which they journey several hundred miles. Those in Aligarh have been known to visit Saháranpur, Hardwár, Lucknow, Allahabad, Benares, and Jaipur for the purpose of plunder, and those in Bharáich have visited Chupra in the district of Sáran, Hazáribágh in Ramgarh, and Allahabad. The high roads leading through Etáwa, Aligarh, and Farukhabad are for the most part the scenes of the atrocities committed by a class of thugs who rob and murder on the highways.

Thagi and dakaiti.

To so great an extent did this crime prevail in former years, that during 1808 and 1809 not less then sixty-seven bodies were taken out of wells in the single district of Etáwa. The gangs composing this class were established and fostered in the estates of Híra Singh of Awa Mísa, Bhagwant Singh of Mursán, Daya Rám of Háthras, and Himmat Singh of Eta. In 1811 a list of sixty-eight persons and several sirdárs called jamadárs, composing these gangs, was given into this office by persons who were induced to deliver themselves up to Colonel Gardner under hopes of pardon. They were all Musalmáns, and chiefly of the Mewati tribe." The chief gangs of Budhiks quitted these provinces on the fall of Háthras. The fall of Háthras and the subsequent establishment of police-stations and outposts in the parganahs of Háthras, Mursán, Awa and Beswán effected immediately a reformation in police matters which the Magistrates had hitherto vainly attempted to obtain. The rebellious and disaffected were deprived of their last rallying point, outlaws lost a refuge inaccessible to our police, and the robber gangs no longer had a safe home where they could divide and dispose of their spoils, and from whence they could issue unchecked on their plundering expeditions.

At present the chief crimes of this district are petty burglaries, thefts,

Habúras.

and cattle-stealing. The worst cases of burglary and highway robbery are generally committed by Habúras, a kind of gipsy tribe, notorious as vagrants and ruffians, and whose sole profession is thieving. These Habúras infest those parts of the district which border on Muttra and Bulandshahr, and when disturbed in their avocations by a zealous police-officer, they usually cross the boundary into the neighbouring jurisdiction, to return again at a favourable opportunity. In the police circles to the south and east of Koil the tribe of Aheriyas (also called Baheliyas) are the perpetrators of most of the cases of burglary and theft. They are well known as a thieving caste, but they generally conceal their real occupation under the nominal profession of agriculture. Suicides are numerous, especially amongst females; the impelling motive appears generally to be a sudden impulse of passion, or jealousy or revenge, and in some few cases self-destruction is effected from fear of shame or dread of exposure. In 1806 it was found that several instances had occurred of persons killing their children from an impulse of passion, with the intention of revenging themselves for an insult or injury offered to them, under the idea that the guilt of the innocent victim's death would be on the head of the person offering such insult or injury. To put a stop to this practice, a proclamation was issued by the Court of Circuit that persons convicted of so flagrant and cruel an offence would be invariably punished with death. Judging from the records, sati was seldom practised: only twelve cases were recorded from 1815 to its abolition by law in 1829. From 1817 to 1831 the duty of jail, treasury, court and personal guards was performed by sepoys of the Agra Provincial Battalion, which was disbanded in 1831, and from that time to the mutiny the guards were furnished from the native regiments cantoned at Aligarh. The chaukidárs or village watchmen are now organised under Act XVI. of 1873, and in 1873 numbered 2,000 men, maintained at a cost of Rs. 72,000, and giving one chaukidár to every 485 of the inhabitants. The **Existing police.** regular police are enrolled under Act V. of 1861, and during the same year numbered 1,057 men of all ranks, entertained at a cost of Rs. 1,14,210 per annum, of which Rs. 30,184 were chargeable to the provincial revenues. The proportion of police to area is one to 1·75 square miles, and to total population is one to every 1,015 inhabitants. The average number of offences for seventeen years before the mutiny (1836 to 1852), distributed under the heads then adopted, was as follows :—Murder, 7·5 ; homicide, 7·4 ; dakaiti, 1·1 ; highway robbery, 8·2 ; burglary, 541·4 ; cattle-theft, 88 ; theft with poisoning from 1843 to 1852, 3 ; other thefts, 1,012·4 ; affrays, 7·2 ; assault with wounding, 40 ; arson, 2 ; rape, 1 ; receiving stolen property, 13 ; attempts and other offences, 1,081. The average value of property stolen from 1843 to 1852 was Rs. 25,905, and of property recovered was Rs. 5,028, showing only 19·5 per cent. of recoveries. The average number of cases during the same ten years was 512, concerning 925 persons, of which 43 cases and 109 persons were committed, and 334 cases and 917 persons were acquitted. The percentage of convictions for the ten years is 60·09. The following statement shows the crime statistics and the results of police action for seven years after the mutiny :—

Year.	Cases cognizable by the Police.					Value of property		Cases.			Persons.			Proportion of convictions to persons tried.
	Murder.	Dakaiti.	Robbery.	Burglary.	Theft.	Stolen.	Recovered.	Total cognizable.	Under inquiry.	Prosecuted to conviction.	Brought to trial.	Convicted and committed.	Acquitted.	
						Rs.	Rs.							
1865 ...	6	...	15	766	1,231	30,053	4,981	2,404	619	312	795	457	300	57·6
1867 ...	5	1	9	752	952	23,395	5,905	2,392	1,201	598	1,583	1,325	159	83·7
1868 ...	5	...	10	589	879	28,661	6,821	2,164	1,280	662	1,595	1,301	208	81·5
1870 ...	10	...	10	528	651	22,865	7,551	2,114	1,176	508	1,146	953	193	83·1
1871 ...	3	...	13	899	724	23,756	8,596	1,996	1,082	507	1,149	915	204	82·24
1872 ...	12	1	15	1,047	721	30,177	11,685	2,241	2,035	544	1,427	1,151	249	80·66
1878 ...	11	2	17	924	713	27,908	22,524	2,112	1,998	629	1,541	1,143	142	74·17

The administration comes out well of late years in serious cases against the person ; but in heinous cases against person and property, or property alone,

the police here, as in the greater part of the Meerut division, have comparatively failed to render that security to the persons and property of travellers
which one should expect in a well-governed British district. The junction of
the Oudh and Rohilkhand Railway with the East Indian line at Aligarh has
led to an influx of travellers, who are the prey of regularly organized bands
of plunderers.

The first-class police-stations in the district are Khair, Iglás, Háthras, Sásni,
Sikandra Ráo, Akrabad, Atrauli, Dadon, Jawá, Aligarh, and Harduaganj. The second-class police-stations are Tappal, Gonda, Naráyanpur, Mursán, Husain, Agsoli, Sánkora, Barla, Gangíri, Somna, and Chandaus. The
third-class stations are Hastpur, Mitái, Hatísa, Alam, Gopi, Jáo, Chherat,
Panehti, Madrák, Bhánkri, junction of roads from Sásni to Jalesar and from
Háthras to Kásganj.

Orders were issued under the Infanticide Act (VIII. of 1870) at an
early period in Aligarh, and the result at first was
much difference of opinion. The Magistrate reported
that he did not think that the crime prevailed to any extent in this district;
but he sent up a list of 127 villages, and another of certain clans in which the
percentage of female minors on the total minor population fell below 40 per
cent., the standard then in force. The statistics, however, were incomplete, and
further information was called for. A special census was taken in the cold
weather of 1871-72, and on this basis, as all Rajpúts in the district had already
been proclaimed, the Pundír, Jádon, and Chauhán tribes were brought under the
rules from the beginning of 1872 in 85 villages where the minor population
exceeded 25 souls with less than 40 per cent. of girls. The total population of
the proclaimed villages was then 9,657, with 2,253 boys and 1,146 girls. On
receipt of the census statistics of 1872, and orders lowering the standard of
exemption to 35 per cent., 54 villages were removed from supervision by the
police, whilst inquiries were directed to be held in regard to the Rajpút, Ját,
Ahír and Banjára villages in which, from the census statistics, it appeared that
there was reason to believe that the practice still continued. The result of these
inquiries was that 37 villages were exempted. There are now 85 villages on the
proclaimed list —12 Jádon villages, 14 Chauhán, 8 Pundír, 1 Gahlot, 1 Solankhi, 1 Badgújar, 25 Ját, 22 Ahír, and 1 Gújar village.

After the conquest in 1803, the first settlement of the Fíruzabad division
of the conquered provinces was made by Mr. R.
Cunynghame of Etáwa for 1211 *fasli* (1803-04) almost
entirely with farmers. Parganahs Mahában, Mát, Sonai, Ráya, Sahpu, Hasangarh, and talukas Káras and Joár were farmed by Raja Daya Rám of Háthras
and Raja Bhagwant Singh of Mursán, besides their ancestral lands of Háthras
and Mursán. Sadabad and Khandauli were given in farm to one Puran Chand,

Infanticide.

Fiscal history.

and Báh Panáhat to Brijbási Lál. Fíruzabad and Jalesar were held *amdní*, the *amíns* appointed to settle and collect the revenue receiving ten per cent. on the collections. The Koil parganahs also under Mr. C. Russell were chiefly settled on the *amáni* system. Owing to the disturbed condition of the district, assessments could only be made on an estimate of the crops, as they stood, or those of the preceding years were accepted. The parganahs of Khair, Noh Jhíl, and Malikpur were farmed to obtain the farmer's assistance in restoring them to order, and parganahs Shikárpur, Pitampur, and Barauli were then held in open rebellion by Dúndi Khan.

In October, 1804, instructions were issued for the new settlement. Lands

Settlement of 1212 *fasli*, 1804-05 A. D.

were to be leased at a fair assessment by a comparison of the rent-roll of each village for some years back, and in all cases possible, the village proprietors were to be admitted to engagements and encouraged by easy assessments. *Nankár* allowances not exceeding ten per cent. were to be deducted from the land-revenue, and engagements were to be taken for the remainder under Regulation VIII. of 1793. If subordinate proprietors existed in a taluka, the settlement was to be made with them, and in any case with the parties in possession. The troubled state of the district, however, rendered it advisable to continue the practice of giving most of the parganahs in farm to the more powerful talukadárs. The Rajas of Háthras, and Mursán were confirmed in their farms with the addition of Sadabad and Khandauli, and Báh Panáhat was given in farm to Sheonandan Dichit, the agent of the Bhadauriya Raja. Mr. J. R. Hutchinson gives the assessment of 1803-04 at Rs. 18,19,250, and that of 1804-05 at Rs. 19,86,483.[1] Although these assessments were fixed on a comparatively moderate estimate of the rental assets, not much more than three-fourths of the demand were realized; and remissions to the extent of Rs. 9,78,440 were granted for both years. This was necessary from losses caused by drought, hailstorms, and war. Dúndi Khán was in rebellion and plundered the parganahs now forming the Bulandshahr district; Holkar and Amír Khán made irruptions into the Duáb, and the Banjáras carrying supplies to the English army at Bhartpur and Muttra devastated the country through which they passed. The drought of 1803-04 is still remembered as having been very severely felt in the Upper Duáb.

The Government attempted to relieve the cultivators by a system of advances,

Triennial settlement, 1213-1215 *fasli*.

but this soon became a source of emolument to the native officials instead of a privilege to the landholders, so that on inquiry being made much of it had to be remitted. Regulation IX. of 1805 gave instructions for a triennial settlement, 1213 to 1215 *fasli* (1805-06 to 1807-08), at the expiration of which another settlement for a similar term was to be concluded with all those willing to engage. After 1218 *fasli* a new

---

[1] The charges for collection amounted to Rs. 1,66,279 and Rs. 1,95,445 respectively.

settlement was to be concluded with the same persons for a further term of four years (1811-12 to 1814-15), the assessment being formed by adding to the annual revenue of the second three years, three-fourths of the net increase of revenue during one year of that period. At the same time the following instructions[1] were issued to the Collectors:—"In those instances in which the land-revenue assessed on the lands in the Ceded Provinces under the late settlement has been proved to be too heavy, adequate deductions must necessarily be granted in fixing the land-revenue of 1213 *fasli*, but it will be the duty of the Collectors, in all practicable cases, to restore the land-revenue of 1212 by a progressive assessment previously to the expiration of the approaching settlement. The Governor-General in Council does not however consider it to be proper to rescind his orders of the 22nd of April, for the conclusion of a settlement on the land-revenue of 1212 *fasli* with those landholders and farmers who have fulfilled their engagements, although some loss may be sustained by Government in the adjustment of the land-revenue of those lands which have been too highly assessed. It is of the utmost importance, with reference to the improvement of the resources of the country, that the assessment should in all cases be moderate, and the temporary diminution of the public revenue which may result from the principles on which the approaching settlement is to be made will be amply compensated by the confidence they will inspire in the moderation of the British Government, and by the encouragement which will be afforded to the improvement of the lands, and by the increasing prosperity of our subjects of every description in the Ceded Provinces." Though orders had repeatedly issued for the settlement with the village proprietors, Mr. C. Russell in the Koil parganahs continued the great farms. The Rajas of Háthras and Mursán, and Harkishan Singh of Beswán, were confirmed as farmers; Dibái was given to Thákur Mardán Ali Khán; Malakpur to Akbar Ali Khán; Noh Jhíl, Khair, Pítampur, and Shikárpur were settled with Ranmast Khán, the son of the rebel leader Dúndi Khán; while Chandaus was leased to Puran Chand, a banker of Mahában. Mr. Russell considered that it was necessary to conciliate the principal land-owners at any cost, without bestowing any attention on the rights of the village proprietors, who were left to their mercies.

That the difficulties connected with the settlement of the land-revenue with the actual proprietors of the land were real is shown by the following letter[2] from the Collector :—" In the column specifying the names of the farmers, the Board will observe that Raja Daya Rám holds the principal farms in this district. The parganahs which compose them,

Mr. Russell's difficulties.

---

[1] Extract from Board's Proceedings, No. 25, of June 14th, 1805.   [2] *Ibid*, No. 17, dated July 29th, 1806, containing a letter from Collector of Aligarh; see also Board's Records, 22nd October, 1805, No. 1 ; and 21st January, 1806, Nos. 5-6.

with the exception of Khandauli, were placed under his superintendence by Lord Lake immediately after the conquest of these provinces, and they were continued to him by the late Acting Collector of the Firuzabad division in that year, with the approbation of His Lordship. In the last year the same arrangement was directed by His Lordship, and the parganah of Khandauli was added to his farm by the Acting Collector, with the concurrence of His Lordship, as he had in vain attempted to realize the collections or to preserve tranquillity and good order by the appointment of a tahsíldár. From the same causes, and under similar circumstances, the parganah of Sadabad was also given in farm to Raja Bhagwant Singh in that year, as the refractory and violent spirit of the zamíndárs set the authority of the tahsíldár at defiance. The farm of Noh Jhíl and Khair the Board are already informed to have been granted to Ranmast Khán, the son of Dúndi Khán, according to the conditional offer of pardon to the latter by the Right Hon'ble Lord Lake, and any observations upon this point are unnecessary.

"Independent of these places, there are only three small farms, of Chandaus, a part of Dibái, and of Ahár Malikpur. The former has been farmed, as I could not procure any adequate security for the collections upon the tahsíldári system upon the percentage of Government, owing to the mutinous habits and character of the zamíndárs, and their not being able to produce any securities. Dibái was originally under a tahsíldár, but in consequence of the separation of the taluka Gangapur, the remainder was given in farm to Mardán Ali Khán, in consideration of the attachment and fidelity he had manifested to the British interests. The zamíndár of Gangapur had been in rebellion against the Government. He was pardoned by the Right Hon'ble Lord Lake, and his lands being restored to him, his revenues are paid into the head treasury. The same circumstances apply with respect to Ahár Malikpur, from which parganah the three talukas of Jadaul, of Payama, and of Sonai, have been separated in the present settlement, and the collections of them are payable at the head treasury. The remaining villages are farmed by Akbar Ali Khán, the person who held them in farm in the past year. Under the head of *amáni* are included the *istimrári* tenures of Yahiya Khán of Karáoli and of Maloi, and Muhammad Kádir Baksh of Jhajhar, upon which subjects I have already had the honour to address the Board. The towns of Koil and of Khurja, which have always been held *khás*, are also included in it, as likewise one or two small disputed *mukarari* tenures, and two or three different talukas (some villages of which have been separated and granted in *jágír* by the Right Hon'ble Lord Lake to individuals, and no engagements yet entered into for the remainder), as well as a few other villages which are at present held *khás*. The zamíndári lands of Ranmast Khán are also included, until he may think proper to conclude a final settlement."

Another of Mr. Russell's letters shows his opinions on the tenure question.[1]

His opinions on tenures. In replying to objections raised by certain village proprietors against the grant of their lands in *jágír* to one Gopál Kishan, he writes in the following terms :—" Any objections of the zamíndárs upon occasions of *jágírs* are erroneously founded ; their rights are preserved and secured to them, and any oppressive grievances can be redressed by law. The right of soil, indeed, rested formerly solely and exclusively with the king, and not with the immediate landholders. I am not aware, therefore, of any obstacle to Government granting in *jágír* any lands which they may think proper in this country, nor can the objections of the zamíndárs be considered valid." The Board in reply stated that they did not concur in the Collector's opinion regarding the rights of zamíndárs, and declared that the grant of *jágírs*, except in cases where Government is the actual proprietor of the soil, is objectionable, inasmuch as it tends to affect the rights of individuals.

Although the Collector was so unmindful of the interests of the inferior proprietors, he was quite aware of the defective title by

On talukas. which the talukadárs held their large possessions. In April, 1808, he writes thus to the Board of Commissioners :—"It is notorious that in the majority of the talukas and the nominal zamíndári estates of our principal landholders, the proprietary right in the soil is not vested in the possessors. A vast proportion of the lands have been successively annexed to their estates from time to time through intrigues and by means of that power and influence which they have possessed. They have taken advantage of the distractions and revolutions which have prevailed, and have in many instances founded their own consequence and authority upon the weakness of the ruling power. The talukadárs possess pattahs granted under former Governments, in which they are styled zamíndárs and talukadárs, and they attach the validity of regular sanads to them." More than forty years after the date of this letter, the claims of the talukadárs in this district to the absolute proprietary right of the whole of their talukas were finally negatived by the civil courts, as will be seen further on. This settlement was based on a progressive revenue rising from Rs. 23,56,464 in 1218 *fasli* to Rs. 24,21,575 in 1219, and Rs. 24,57,253 in 1220. The average number of persons engaging for the land-revenue was only 827, and the average charges for collection amounted to Rs. 2,03,362.

As Government relinquished all extra cesses, and had forbidden the zamíndárs

Cesses abolished. to collect them, deductions were made on this account in the assessment. The sums remitted to some of the chief talukadárs as compensation for the abolition of transit *(rahdári)*, salt and

[1] Board's Records, 28th June, 1806 ; *Ibid.*, 22nd October, 1805, No. 1 ; and 21st January, 1806, Nos. 5, 6.

bázár *(ganj)* duties were considerable, amounting in the case of Daya Rám of Húthras[1] to Rs. 20,000 a year, and in the case of Bhagwant Singh of Mursán to Rs. 10,000. Not content with this, Daya Rám claimed an additional remission of Rs. 10,000 a year, on the ground of custom, for 1211 and 1212 *fasli.* He was then as farmer paying Rs. 3,30,000 per annum as land revenue, and as proprietor Rs. 1,35,000, and put in a letter of the Marhatta General DuBoigne allowing Rs. 10,000 as ' *muáfi bamújib mamúl*' or 'customary deduction,' and one of Perron's allowing Rs. 16,062 for 1802, and Rs. 10,000 for 1803.[2] This claim was disallowed, but neither he nor the Mursán Raja refrained from collecting the illegal cesses until the fall of Háthras and Mursán. In 1806, the want of rain was much felt. None fell up to the 15th of August, and it was not until the 4th of September that the regular monsoon commenced. Similar complaints were received in 1808, when the rains did not set in until

Droughts and remissions. August. The consequence of this was, that remissions amounting to three annas in the rupee were granted to all except the most powerful zamíndárs. These remissions amounted in 1806 to Rs. 1,88,278 for loss caused by the marching of troops ; Rs. 60,980 for damages alleged to have been committed by field mice *(muskhori),* besides the three annas in the rupee.[3] Mr. Grant, writing in 1806, says, with regard to these remissions[4]:—" I am convinced that the intention of Government has been nearly rendered abortive, and that of the considerable remissions which have been authorised in this district, a very small proportion has been granted to the inferior classes of zamíndárs and ryots, for whose relief I conceive the indulgence of Government to have been intended." Besides the remissions of land revenue, large remissions of advances *(takkávi)* were granted, so that it is not surprising that during the first five years of our rule no sales for arrears of land revenue were necessary.

The Board of Commissioners, appointed under Regulation X. of 1807, met at Aligarh in December of that year, and issued instructions for a permanent settlement. The Collector stated that, owing to wars and bad seasons, only three-fifths of the culturable land were then under cultivation ; that with improved management he expected an increase of eight lakhs of rupees to the revenue in six years ; and deprecated the introduction of a permanent settlement. The

---

[1] Board's Records, 20th June, 1806, No. 17; *Ibid* 27th June, 1806, Nos. 16—20; 26th August, 1806, Nos. 7— 8 ; 23rd January, 1807, No. 28. Daya Rám also received compensation for the abolition of the Háthras mint. [2] Board's Records, 22nd April, 1806, No. 5; 23rd January, 1808, No. 28; 25th May, 1808, No. 5; 25th April, 1809, Nos. 46-53. [3] As to drought, see Board's Records 26th August, 1806 Nos 7, 8; 26th February, 1808, No. 1 ; 25th September, 1808, No. 48 ; and Remissions, 26th February, 1808, No. 1; 23rd September, 1808, No. 34. [4] Again, in Board's Records, 16th January, 1809, 40, Collector reports that " but few of the people have received the benevolent indulgence of Government," whereon he was directed in forming the settlement to make *further inquiries.*

Board then directed a settlement with farmers for three years, and with pro-
prietors for a similar term, with a stipulation that the revenue assessed for the last year should remain fixed for ever, in case the zamíndárs were willing to engage for its payment in perpetuity, subject to the sanction of the Court of Directors. This sanction was, fortunately for the State, never obtained. The Court of Directors were informed of this intention in a despatch dated 31st July, 1807, and again in 1808, and in their reply, dated 27th February, 1810, they express their determination not to proceed immediately to the settlement of the ceded and conquered provinces in perpetuity until all the proceedings regarding the current settlement were before them.[1] In 1811 they disallowed the permanency of the existing settlement, and the conditions laid down in Regulation X., 1807, were rescinded by Regulations IX. and X. of 1812, which again reverted to the declarations contained in the Regulations of 1803 and 1805.

With this settlement [2] was introduced the system of tahsílís, by which tahsíldárs received fixed salaries instead of the commission of ten per cent. on the collections formerly given. Mr. Russell was succeeded by Mr. Trant, who carried out the new settlement with the village proprietors of the Muttra and
eastern parganahs which had been held in farm by Daya Rám, Bhagwant Singh and Harkishan. Mr. E. Elliott joined in December, 1808, and carried out the settlement of the remainder of the district, with the exception of two parganahs. The land revenue of Aligarh in the year 1218, exclusive of the lands formerly held in farm or at a fixed revenue, stood at Rs. 20,74,010, or Rs. 4,00,906 above the land revenue of 1215. The revenue of the resumed farms was fixed at Rs. 8,12,835, and exceeded the revenue paid by the farmers by over three lakhs of rupees, yet the people did not complain, and only rejoiced at being delivered from the oppression of the late farmers. The total revenue of 1216 *fasli* (1808-9 A. D.) is given by Mr. Hutchinson at Rs. 26,03,825, of 1217 at Rs. 28,60,661, and of 1218 at Rs. 31,03,793, and the number of persons allowed to engage at 3,324.

The settlement was too hurried to admit of that scrutiny into the rights of the proprietors which Government desired ; and in 1810 Mr. Fortescue, whilst regretting the frequency of sales for arrears, suggested that the separate possession and responsibility of sharers might be attempted, when he believed that fewer sales would occur. The Board, accordingly, instructed Collectors to
allow all persons to claim admission to the proprietary right, whether they had previously been admitted to engage for the Government revenue or not. Another cause of distress was

---

[1] A full account of the arguments and proceedings in relation to this attempt at a permanent settlement is given in Selections from Revenue Records, N. W. P., 1818-20 : Calcutta, 1866; see page 29.   [2] 1st January, 1808.

the system of taking security for one-fourth of the revenues from the zamíndárs, which Mr. H. Newnham thus describes.[1] " In this district many estates are confessedly in the actual possession of the securities,—in some cases on the strength of the security bond, in others by *katkina*. Possession of the securities, on whatever grounds, is equally injurious to the landholders and to Government. A process is issued to the landholder, who attends and says he is not in possession ; the security is then called upon, who frequently confesses possession, but complains of loss, claims a settlement of accounts, and advances a variety of private engagements and pecuniary concerns. Legally, if the security has paid a fourth of the revenue for which he is responsible, he is released from every public demand. Supposing him to have paid the fourth, but to have realized the whole demand from the estate, in which way is the revenue recoverable ? The ruin of the estate is too often the object of the security, and possession gives him full means to effect that purpose. As many talukas have arisen through this cause, the landholders of large estates become security to ruin the smaller zamíndárs, and thereby increase their estates by the purchase of the former zamíndárs' lands. The sufferings of the former class from this one cause are numberless, and I have reason to believe that nearly one-eighth of the whole landed property in this district is in this predicament." The Board replied that they were aware of the inconveniences to which landholders were exposed by the requisition of security, and contemplated proposing to Government, from the expiration of the present leases, the exemption of actual proprietors of land from the necessity of furnishing it. But it was not till November, 1817, that the Board authorized the Collector to dispense with the requisition of security in cases where it appeared unnecessary for the safety of the revenue.

The settlement in the parganahs lately farmed was in every instance a progressive one, and was adopted with a view of affording temporary relief to the newly admitted village proprietors, and, at the same time, of retaining ultimately the

Settlement of 1816-18 worked badly in resumed farms.

assessment which these talukadárs were understood to have realized from them. It was also adopted in Fíruzabad and Jalesar for the sake of securing the highest obtainable assessment for the last year of the lease, as such final assessment was, under the provisions of Regulation 7, 1807, to become permanent. This object failed in most of these parganahs. Mr. Newnham, writing[2] in 1811, says :—"The change in the management of the lands (from farmers to zamíndárs) appears to have failed in continuing the same state of high cultivation ; in the place of a floating capital, of the command of labour, and all the ready powers of agriculture, men who had no wealth but their industry and proprietary rights were introduced, and who could not be expected to be able to entice

[1] To Board, 1st January, 1811.   [2] To Board 30th July, 1811.

into their villages, ryots to cultivate the lands which had been tilled by the personal servants of the talukadár as labourers, or as assignments in lieu of money wages, which compensation was not omitted in the account of the assets. The newly acknowledged zamíndárs could only look to their ryots, on whom they increased the demand in proportion that the Government demand increased towards themselves. A ryot, insolvent through misfortune, or resisting a claim he could scarcely discharge, soon gave rise to difficulties, and the ruinous vacancy which the flight or death of ryots or labourers occasioned was in no way to be remedied."

The next settlement was for four years. Since the revocation by the autho-rities in Europe of the promised permanency of the second triennial settlement

Quartennial settlement, 1219-1222 *fasli* (1811-12 to 1814-15 A.D.)

might have been understood to authorize a recurrence to the original provisions of Regulation IX. of 1805, which had prescribed that, on the expiration of such second triennial settlement, a third settlement for four years, from 1219 to 1222 *fasli* was to be formed on specified principles, it would probably have been advisable to have adopted this measure to equalize the assessments on particular estates; but as Regulation X. of 1812, which rescinded Regulation X. of 1807, was silent in regard to such intermediate re-settlement, the only modifications attempted during the four years preceding the expiration of the decennial period from the conquest (1223 *fasli*), for which provision was made, consisted of annual expedients for the management of the deteriorated estates, while those who continued to pay the assessments of 1218 *fasli* were left undisturbed.

Mr. C. F. Ferguson in 1812-13 slightly increased the revenue, and the number of persons admitted to engagements rose from 3,324 to 4,612, show-ing that the Board's directions in 1810 were not overlooked. Though the charges of collection were decreased, and there was more supervision, heavy balances accrued, with remissions, reductions, and partial re-settlements, in con-

Distribution of fiscal ad-ministration.

sequence of landholders absconding and sales of land not meeting purchasers. The accounts of the re-settlement of farmed villages show a decrease in the revenue of Rs. 90,443 in 1219, Rs. 23,474 in 1220, and Rs. 1,03,600 in 1221. Attempts at the demarcation of village boundaries were now for the first time made. In 1814-15, the Western Board sent Messrs. Calvert and Boulderson to take charge of a portion of the district. Parganahs Anúpshahr, Akrabad, Gangíri, Jahángírabad, Jalálí, Pachlána, and Sikandra Rao were made over to Mr. Calvert, together with some parganahs of Etáwa and Fatehgarh. Parganahs Sadabad, Khandauli, Mahában, Mát, Firuzabad, Jalesar, Ráya, Sonai, and Sahpu were intrusted to Mr. Boulderson, and Mr. Ferguson retained charge of Koil and the remaining parganahs. In 1816, Mr. Ferguson resumed charge of the eastern division on Mr. Calvert's departure. In the same year, three parganahs, Fíruzabad, Sahpu and Khandauli, were transferred to Agra, and at that time paid a revenue of Rs. 3,77,711.[1] At the same time Noh Jhíl and Sikandra were given over to Mr. Boulderson, and the Kásganj tahsíl was received from Etáwa.[2]

The fourth settlement for five years was made by Messrs. Ferguson, Calvert and Boulderson for the parganahs under their respective charges, giving an aggregate land revenue of Rs. 30,29,833, being an increase on the former settlement

Fourth settlement, 1223 to 1227 *fasli*, or 18.5-.6 to 1819-20 A.D.

of Rs. 2,74,638. In the old farmed parganahs the rates established by Mr. Boulderson reached the highest assessment of 1218. In submitting an account of the portions of the district settled by Messrs. Ferguson and Calvert, the Board of Commissioners, after noticing the considerations which led to the exten- sion of the settlement of 1218 for four years, and the principles on which that measure was founded, remark :—" A progressive settlement, which should rest on a speculation of prospective improvement, will generally defeat itself. The landholders seldom look beyond the immediate operations of the current year, and will thoughtlessly bind themselves to a future incumbrance of any extent for the sake of a present relief. A moderate enhancement would perhaps stimulate their exertions, and industry to meet it, particularly if it be limited to a portion of the lease, so as to leave to them in the remainder of the term the benefits of such industry. But, generally speaking, when the actual pressure of a load (the weight of which they did not estimate) falls upon them, they recede in despair from the struggle, and the result not only disappoints the anticipated increase from expected improvement, but will frequently produce a retrograde falling off in the former cultivation. This remark is fully exemplified in several of the accounts now submitted to your Lordship, where the deficiency on the ultimate demand of the former settlement far exceeds the difference between that demand and what had been punctually realized in the early part of the lease. The remark might also be deemed as affording an argument against the new arrangements which are proposed for your Lordship's sanction, as a large proportion of them are at a progressive assessment. But in the present instance the measure is principally confined to the re-establishment of temporary abatements. Those cases in which the progres- sive assessment is at an increase upon the former settlement are comparatively few, and of inconsiderable amount, and the further additions to the assessment of the current year, which has been realized with sufficient punctuality, are trifling. In taking a view of these settlements, and of the accounts of the other portion of the district, we cannot hesitate in offering to your Lordship our deliberate opinion that no increase of revenue can be expected from any future

[1] Sahpu, Rs. 40,028: Khandauli, Rs. 68,255; Firuzabad, Rs. 2u9,428 ; see Board's Records, 5th November, 1816, No. 1. [2] *Ibid*, 31st December, 1816, No. 16.

re-settlement of this district. These arrangements have certainly remedied many errors and inaccuracies which have occurred in the former settlement ; but, exclusive of errors, which are perhaps unavoidable in a general settlement, and of probable embarrassments from unfavourable seasons, much counteraction to any future re-settlement is to be apprehended from the landholders themselves, who have learnt the mode of anticipating the requisition of an increase by a reduction of the assets towards the expiration of the lease, either by throwing the land altogether out of cultivation, or by discontinuing the culture of the more valuable produce, such as sugar-cane, cotton, &c. This latter measure affects also the revenue of the customs. Section 7, Regulation IX., 1805, held out to the landholders of the conquered provinces the hope of a permanent settlement from the year 1223. The promise may, indeed, be said to be partial, and to be not very clearly defined, as it is restricted to those lands which may be in a state of cultivation to warrant the measure. But the land-holders looked only to the promise, and did not calculate on the reservation attached to it. The disappointment is accordingly general. Even under this reservation, a majority of the parganahs in this district would, on a comparison of the improvable land with that in actual cultivation, be found not to possess more of the former than what the landholders might be deemed entitled to as the future reward of their industry. Considerable abatements were granted (in some cases apparently on insufficient grounds) in the first years of this settlement ; but the Board deemed it expedient to waive a retrospective revision of them, an indulgence which has probably contributed to the punctuality with which the revenue has, generally speaking, hitherto been paid. The land fit for cultivation is stated at more than two-thirds of the land under tillage, so that of the arable land little more than seven-twelfths are in cultivation. The waste also appears very extensive,[1] —the twenty-five parganahs, regarding which this information is furnished, exhibit 281 farms out of an aggregate of 1,692 estates.''

This quinquennial settlement was extended in the ceded parganahs for five

lettlement extended. years by Regulation XVI. of 1816, and again for five years by order of Government in 1822, and for a further term of five years, from 1235 to 1239 *fasli* (1827-8 to 1831-2 A. D.), by Government orders of the 13th April 1826. In the conquered parganahs it was extended for five years, from 1228 to 1232 *fasli*, by orders of Government in 1818. Soon after the formation of this settlement it was found advisable to restrain tahsíldárs from exacting interest on balances and from taking villages under direct management without the express sanction of the Collector. These settlements were again extended from 1233 to 1237 *fasli* (1815-16 to 1829-30, A. D.), to allow time for the inquiries directed by Regulation VII. of 1822,

---

[1] Settlement Records, N.-W. P., 32.

while certain parganahs in which the errors were most glaring were exempted from the rule of extension and were immediately settled.

For the settlement under Regulation VII. of 1822 scarcely any extra establishment was allowed in this district, and the Collector's time was too much occupied by the other duties of his office to admit of his careful attention being given to the detailed and laborious enquiry prescribed by Regulation VII. of 1822. It was found at the next settlement of this district, that villages settled under this Regulation were generally over-assessed. Mr. H. Rose, in reporting the settlements of parganahs Jaláli, Akrabad, Sikandra Rao and Márahra in 1839, writes that " out of 37 villages settled under Regulation VII. of 1822, 35 required reduction of revenue to the extent of Rs. 6,440, on a jama of Rs. 47,533. The system of settlement under that Regulation undoubtedly tended to cause over-assessment; but that system, faulty as it was, had not fair play in this district, where the Settlement Officer, when he was not satisfied with the revenue which his papers warranted him to demand, was in the habit of appointing native assessors for the express purpose of raising the estimate of assets. That under such a method of settlement some estates should have broken down and others should now exhibit marks of over-assessment is not to be wondered at. The matter for surprise is that the whole have not been ruined long ago."

Inadequate provision for revision of settlement.

Mr. Stirling gives the following lamentable description of the state of the district in his time :—" The consequence of the inadequacy of the tahsili establisments, and their inefficiency, has been that almost all the villages in this district have been mortgaged, farmed, sold or given over to creditors. A few intriguing, dishonest and avaricious men, have by indirect means possessed themselves of the greater portion of the most flourishing estates in this district. These changes of property have upset all kinds of village rights, and the individual claims of cultivators, amongst whom tenfold more distress has been occasioned than has been experienced in any district of which I have had charge." In a subsequent letter to the Commissioner of Agra, dated 19th May, 1832, Mr. Stirling attributes much of the prevailing distress in the country to the abolition of the Benares mint, the bankrupty of indigo factories, and the reduced purchases of Government. He stated the effects of the abolition of the mint to be, first, a considerable enhancement of the price of coin as compared with silver bullion ; second, an unavoidable continued debasement of the currency ; third, a growing scarcity of the circulating medium ; and he considered the commerce and agriculture of the country to have suffered from these causes at the rate of eleven per cent., and that the prices of commodities and of grain and labour had fallen to that extent. The bankruptcy of all the indigo manufactories not only occasioned the failure of many respectable native houses, but swept away a large amount of currency from those channels of circulation in which it had been long employed, and had afforded occupation to the industry of a great number of commercial men and agriculturists. Such a convulsion caused no inconsiderable distress ; but happily the immediate loss did not fall with too great a weight on the country. Owing to the practice of making large advances, the people had received perhaps more than the full price of their labour and commodities, and when the treasure usually expended on indigo works ceased to flow, they had only to turn their attention to the production of grain. Mr. Stirling calculated the diminution of the Company's purchases to be about ten lakhs of rupees annually. At the same time Mr. Smith thinks[1] that, during this period, though at first much land was left out of cultivation and many of the old proprietors lost their villages, still there had been much general progress. In 1815, the total cultivated area of the district as it then stood, exclusive of the large talukas, was only 934,078 acres ; and if 100,000 acres be taken as the area under cultivation in the talukas, the total cultivated area will have been 1,034,078 acres. " But the cultivated area of the district, reduced to its present size at the time of last settlement, was 839,127 acres, or 81 per cent. of the total cultivation of about three districts in 1815. I am rather under the mark in concluding that by the time the last settlement was finished, cultivation in Aligarh, even since 1815, had at least doubled, and that since 1803 it must have more than doubled. In 1815 the revenue fell at Rs. 3-6-5 per cultivated acre, and at last settlement (1838) though the revenue was increased, it fell at only Rs. 2-3-1 per cultivated acre."

In 1833, Mr. John Thornton was appointed to officiate as Deputy Collector of Aligarh, and was intrusted with the revision of the settlement under Regulation IX. of 1833. He joined his appointment in December of that year, and remained in charge of the settlement office five years, during which time he finished the settlement of parganahs Háthras, Mursán, Gorai, Hasangarh, Khair, Chandaus, Somna, Koil, Atrauli, Murthal and the talukas of Bhamauri Náh and Dátauli. He also made a summary settlement for six years of parganah Tappal, part of the jágir of the Begam Sumru, which had lapsed by her death in 1837. Mr. Thornton was succeeded by Mr. H. Rose, who took charge in December, 1838, and finished the settlement of the remaining parganahs, viz., Sikandra Rao, Márahra, Akrabad, Jaláli and Barauli in July, 1839. Both Mr. Thornton and Mr. Rose were ably assisted by Mr. W. B. Wright, formerly Superintendent of the Customs line at Hansi, who was appointed, at Mr. Thornton's recommendation, in 1837, as Assistant in the settlement. In 1840, parganah Tappal was resettled by Mr. Wright, at a revenue of Rs. 1,18,206.

Mr. John Thornton's revision.

_____

[1] Settlement Report, p. 63 : the opinion of Mr. Smith as Settlement Officer is particularly valuable on this point.

By this revision of the settlement a total increase in the assessment was

Principles of assessment in 1838. gained of Rs. 75,785, but this increase was mainly effected on the estates of some of the talukadárs, who, during the past settlements, had contrived to conceal their real resources. Under the new system of settlement, such an evasion of the just demand of Government was almost impossible. The Settlement Officer no longer trusted to arbitrary valuations of assets and estimates of area formed by the kanúngoes and patwáris. Each village was accurately surveyed, measured and mapped, field by field, and the lands divided into four classes with reference to their proximity to the village, as at present. These four classes were comprehended in the two great divisions of irrigated and unirrigated lands, and for each class average parganah rent-rates were framed from the results of a careful enquiry into the actual rents paid by cultivators for such lands, and by a comparison with the rates in neighbouring parganahs. These rates, applied to the areas of each class of land, gave the village rent-roll or gross assets of each village, and the jama or Government demand was then obtained by a deduction in favour of the zamíndárs of not less than 30 per cent. on the gross assets. This demand was further tested by an examination of the recorded assets of the estate for the past ten years, and by the *daul* or estimate of the tahsíldárs. Nothing could be more fair than such an assessment, provided that the lands were rightly classified. Mr. Thornton and Mr. Rose were careful to satisfy themselves on these important points ; one or two of the talukadárs tried to obtain easy terms by throwing a great proportion of their lands out of cultivation at the time of settlement, and by stopping up their earthen wells; but Mr. Thornton readily detected the fraud. The revenue survey was made between the years 1833 and 1837, when parganah Tappal was surveyed by Captain Brown, and the remaining parganahs by Captain Wroughton. In most instances the *khasrahs* or indices, and *shajrahs* or field maps were furnished by the survey establishment, but it is to be regretted that these important documents were in general drawn up very incorrectly, especially the field maps.

Mr. W. H. Smith made the existing settlement of the district between 1866

Mr. W. H. Smith on past settlements. and 1873. In reviewing the past fiscal history of the district, he writes :—" From all the authorities and facts which I have considered, my deductions are as follow:—That at the time of the conquest the entire district was in a terrible state of disorganization ; that population was defective and much land out of cultivation ; that the zamíndárs generally were in a depressed and unsettled state ; and that they were called upon to pay a very heavy revenue before they had recovered from the injurious results of former misrule, but that the good effect of our rule very soon became manifest. With the aid of remissions and reductions, which were largely resorted to, in other words, by lenient treatment, they tided over times of difficulty.

Meanwhile population and cultivation alike increased, and within 30 years there was double as much land under the plough as before, while the assessments having been, with few exceptions, left untouched after 1819, the incidence of the revenue rate on the cultivated acre fell lower and lower, and at the end the people were paying half the rate for double the amount of land. No doubt the revenue was even then heavy, and from time to time bad seasons may have caused much individual and partial distress, but on the whole the landholders of the district maintained their original position, and the general results of the 30 years was a constantly improved revenue administration, and in the mass an enormous amelioration in general progress and prosperity."

The principles of assessment adopted at the present settlement were substantially the same as those described above, but in working out the average rates, the particular rates which each class of soil actually paid were first discovered, and then these rates were applied to the soils as classified, and the general total of these rates was taken as the estimate for the tract of country for which they had been selected. The classification of soils adopted has already been noticed (p. 352); and here it may be said that this classification is the one acknowledged by the people in their own transactions; and the rates found to prevail, and on which the assessment is based, represent actual facts. The general rates, modified by the peculiar local characteristics of each estate, form the basis of the individual assessment of these estates. The following statement shows the initial and expiring revenue of the past settlement, and the new revenue for each tahsíl in the district :—

Principles of assessment in 1866-74.

Tahsíl.	Initial revenue of past settlement.	Expiring revenue of past settlement.	Initial revenue of present settlement.	INCIDENCE OF THE LAND REVENUE ON						
				Cultivated area in 1868.	Total area in 1868.	Culturable area in 1868.	Cultivated area in 1868.	Present total area.	Present culturable area.	Present cultivated area.
	Rs.	Rs.	Rs.	Rs. a. p.	Rs. a. p.	Rs. a. p.	Rs. a. p.	Rs. a. p.	Rs. a. p.	Rs. a. p.
Atrauli	2,47,136	2,46,407	2,92,124	1 13 3	1 1 5	1 4 9	1 10 3	1 4 7	1 8 6	1 15 1
Koil	3,01,600	3,01,959	3,60,569	2 1 6	1 5 2	1 12 6	1 15 9	1 9 4	2 2 1	2 5 11
Iglás	2,64,991	2,67,976	2,87,694	2 5 4	1 15 4	2 2 5	2 4 5	2 1 8	2 4 11	2 7 2
Khair	3,55,177	3,54,496	4,01,050	2 1 3	1 5 9	1 9 6	1 14 4	1 8 8	1 12 10	2 3 4
Háthras	3,91,751	3,98,074	4,16,526	2 12 9	2 2 3	2 9 2	3 11 5	2 4 0	2 11 4	2 13 8
Sikandra Rao	2,80,587	2,78,857	3,87,320	2 1 0	1 4 8	1 12 5	1 15 0	1 12 8	2 7 6	2 11 0
Total	18,41,242	18,47,769	21,47,343	2 3 1	1 7 7	1 13 0	2 0 11	1 11 5	2 1 6	2 6 3

The new assessment has resulted in an increase of Rs. 3,06,100, or 16·6 per cent. over the initial revenue of the old assessment, and of Rs. 2,90,573, or 16·2 per cent. over the current revenue, and this, too, though the proportion taken by the State has fallen from 68·9 per cent. to 50 per cent. of the rental assets. The causes of this increase are the increase in cultivation, population and irrigation, and the rise in the value of land, rents and prices. Besides the land revenue,

Rs. 2,14,551-7-6 are collected for the ten per cent. cess under Act XVIII. of 1871, and Rs. 1,08,117 for patwáris' fees, bringing up the total demand from the district to Rs. 24,70,011, and giving an increase of 23·8 per cent. on the old demand. In tahsíls Koil and Atrauli, the new demand was collected in 1871-72; in Iglás and Khair in 1872-73; and in Háthras and Sikandra Rao in 1873-74. The settlement will probably be confirmed from 1871 to 1901.

The following statement gives the official account of the revenue demand, collections, and balances from 1860-61 to 1872-73.

Year.	Demands.	Collection.	Balances.	PARTICULARS OF BALANCE.				Percentage of balance and demand.
				Real.				
				In train of liquidation.	Doubtful.	Irrecoverable.	Nominal.	
	Rs.	Rs.	Rs.	Rs.	Rs.	Rs.	Rs.	
1860-61 ...	18,32,750	17,12,038	1,20,712	1,20,712	...	...	...	6·58
1861-62 ...	18,42 705	17,86,684	56,111	51,311	3,823	977	...	3·04
1862-63 ...	18,48,697	17,98,823	49,874	43,114	...	...	6,760	2·69
1863-64 ...	18,41,874	18,33,883	7,991	6 065	...	...	1,926	·43
1864-65 ...	18,41,592	18,22,736	18,856	17,313	...	...	1,543	1·02
1865-66 ...	18,41, 25	18,24,228	16,897	15,398	...	...	1,499	·92
1866-67 ...	18,40,905	18,37,180	3,725	1,776	...	...	1,949	·20
1867-68 ...	18,40,601	18,39,45 ·	1,149	...	...	...	1,149	·06
1868-69 ...	18,40,060	18,38,249	1,811	...	...	·	1,811	·10
1869-70 ...	18,40,423	18,37,843	2,580	...	...	...	2,580	·14
1870-71 ...	18,40,659	18,93,163	1,496	...	...	...	1,496	·08
1871-72 ...	19,52,605	19,51,775	830	416	98	277	39	·04
1872-73 ...	20,05,468	20,05,050	418	237	20	142	19	·02

Turning from the land to the proprietary body, I shall now take up the great talukas for which the district is noted. For the history of the Ját talukás of

Ját talukas.

Háthras, Mursán and Iglás, we have the valuable report of Mr. John Thornton, from which the following account is mainly taken.[1] All these families trace their origin to a man named Makan, who about the end of the sixteenth or the beginning of the seventeenth century came from Rajputána to the neighbourhood of Mursán. He was a Ját of the Tenwa tribe, and on his arrival found the country occupied by Rajpúts and Játs of the Khokhen tribe. Makan married a woman of the Khokhen tribe, and partly through the influence of her clansmen, and partly, probably, on account of the surrounding country being imperfectly cultivated, he and his descendants, during the next three generations, were enabled to obtain possession of a considerable tract of country, which they divided amongst themselves. Each sub-division became the parent of a number of hamlets (dákhili mauza), the occupants of which are all of the same caste, and trace their origin to the common ancestor who founded the parent village (asli

[1] Settlement Reports, N.-W. P., I., 247.

mauza). These clusters of villages in the course of time became known as talukas. The tract occupied by the Tenwa Játs was known as tappa Joár, because the town of Joár or Jawár was the principal place therein, or the residence of the head of the family. Tappa Joár belonged to parganah Jalesar, but in the reign of Shahjahán (in 1652 A. D.), Sadullah Khán took 200 villages from Jalesar, including the Ját tappa, 80 villages from Mahában, and 7 from Khandauli, and formed them into a new parganah, which he called after his own name, Sadabad. The Ját confederation had become firmly established at the death of Shahjahán in 1658 A. D.; and during the wars that ensued for the possession of the throne, Nandrám, a great-grandson of Makan, found means to establish himself as head of his tribe. Possessed of great abilities, and supported by the Porach Raja of Daryápur, Nandrám not only refused to pay the land-tax, but succeeded in incorporating several villages not owned by Játs into the Ját tappa of Joár. When Aurangzeb became firmly established on the throne, Nandrám submitted to the emperor, and was rewarded with the *khidmat zamíndárí* or revenue management of Joár and Tochigarh. He subsequently received a grant, conferring the police management also upon him, with the title of faujdár.

Nandrám's influence remained unimpaired until his death in 1695 A. D. He left fourteen sons, of whom three only need be mentioned here :—Zulkaran, the eldest ; Jai Singh, the second son ; and Bhoj Singh, the seventh son. The Háthras family is descended from Jai Singh, and that of Mursán from Zulkaran Singh. Zulkaran died before his father, and for some years Bhoj Singh took the lead amongst the brethren. It is probable that the authority of Bhoj Singh varied just as he was able to secure the favour of the local Government officers. At last, in 1716 A. D., Bhoj Singh obtained from Sayyid Abdullah, the famous minister of Farrukhsiyár, a grant in terms similar to that conferred upon Nandrám by Aurangzeb, and in the following year a remission of revenue as *jágír*. The two brothers, Jai Singh and Bhoj Singh, divided the tappa equally between them, and transmitted their possessions to their sons. Bhoj Singh died in 1750 A. D. and left three sons. Of these, Mohan Singh obtained taluka Simardhari ; Jagat Singh, the eldest son, received talukas Barha and Tuksán, and left Barha to his eldest son, Partáb; whilst his second son, Muktáwal Singh, received Tuksán, and transferred it to Phup Singh of Mursán. Kanjal Singh, the third son of Bhoj Singh, received Chotwa and Kotha Patta, but he was ousted in 1768 on account of arrears, and the talukas were divided between the Háthras and Mursán Rajas.

We have now to trace the history of the family of Jai Singh. He died in 1749 A.D., and left two sons : Sáwant Singh, the younger son, received a number of villages as his share, which he formed into a taluka named Gubrári ; but the greater portion of the estate came into the hands of the eldest son, Baran Singh, a man of great activity and determination of character. In 1752 Baran Singh induced the amil of the Oudh Vazír to transfer to him Háthras and the surrounding villages, held until then by a clan of Porach Rajpúts, and when Surajmal, in 1760, expelled Ratan Singh, the Porach talukadár of Mendu, Baran Singh had influence enough to secure the revenue management for himself. Baran Singh died in 1668 and left two sons. The younger of these, by name Sakat Singh, succeeded to most of those villages included in his father's estate which had formed a portion of the old tappa Joár. These were divided after his death into two smaller talukas, Káras and Karíl,—the former fell to the share of his son Durga Singh, and the second son, Udai Singh, obtained Karíl. But all the individual acquisitions of Baran Singh descended to his eldest son, Bhúri Singh, who did not survive many years, and during whose time the estate appears neither to have increased nor diminished. Bhúri Singh died in 1775 A. D., and Daya Rám, his youngest son, found means to supplant his elder brother, Nawal Singh, in by far the larger part of his father's possessions. The latter retired to Beswán and founded the Beswán taluka.

Before commencing the history of Daya Rám, I will give the genealogical

Daya Rám.

tree of the family, from Makan the founder, which will show the ancestors from whom the several talukadárs in Háthras are descended. It is taken from Mr. Thornton's report, and purposely omits mention of those sons of Nandrám whose descendants are extinct, or who obtained portions of territory which never came at a subsequent period into the possession of Daya Rám, and which have therefore never been included in parganah Háthras :—

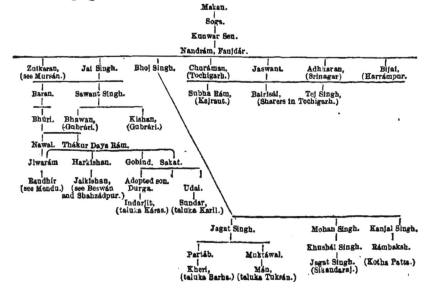

The descendants of Churáman and Jaswant held possession of Tochigarh and Bahrámgarhi at Mr. Thornton's settlement. They had possession of other villages also at different times; but as all but these two had been in possession of Daya Rám for 38 years, the possession of the descendants of these two sons of Nandrám was confirmed in these two villages only. The descendants also of Bijai Singh were confirmed in the possession of Harrámpur as a subtenure of talukas Barha and Gujrát. Muktáwal Singh, son of Jagat Singh, was dispossessed of his estate by Phup Singh of Mursán, who also acquired Kanjal Singh's share in Kotha Patha, and his share in Chotwa fell to Daya Rám.

" A few separate villages were added to the estate by Thákur Daya Rám,

Daya Rám. through arrangements made with the amils of the neighbouring parganahs ; but his chief efforts appear te have been directed towards the expulsion of the other descendants of Nand Rám from their several estates, and the annexation of the latter to his own extensive possessions. In 1776 A. D., taluka Simardhari fell into his hands. In 1779, taluka Tochigarh met the same fate. Taluka Gubrári followed in 1794, and taluka Barha in 1799 A. D. The last named taluka had been taken out of the talukadár's hands by the Marhattas 22 years before, during which interval the revenue was collected by amils from the village communities. These transactions are said by Thákur Daya Rám to have taken place in the way of sale, mortgage or the like, but it is probable that little option was allowed to the weaker party. The subsequent possession of the Thákur was not uninterrupted, as the Government of the time in some years preferred to collect its dues from each village by means of its own officers. Talukas Káras and Karíl were allowed to remain in the hands of their former occupants, who were more nearly related to Daya Rám, as the foregoing account will show ; but they were considered as included in the main estate, and the revenue required from them by the Government was paid by Thákur Daya Rám himself. Such was the state of things at the commencement of our rule in 1803 A. D."

After the conquest of Aligarh, the Commander-in-Chief used every means

1803-14. in his power to conciliate Daya Rám. He was confirmed in the possession of his ancestral lands in Háthras on the same terms on which he had held them under the Marhatta Government. The revenue was fixed at Rs. 1,62,828, and remained at that sum until 1807-8. In the following year talukas Gubrári and Simardhari were assigned to him in *jágír*, and he was allowed to engage for the remainder of the parganah at a revenue, fixed for his life at Rs. 93,620. No kind of interference was made with his interior management, and indeed he was allowed to remain so independent that the people count the introduction of British rule in the parganah from the date of Daya Rám's expulsion. It was probably the injudicious relaxation of our due authority and superintendence which led to his eventual ruin.[1] During the commotions caused by the war with Holkar and the rebellion of Dundi Khán, Daya Rám certainly did good service : he kept his part of the district free from the rebels, and he also raised a force of cavalry, for which however he was paid liberally by the Commander-in-Chief. But he soon displayed a spirit of insubordination and disaffection, and as early as September, 1806, the Resident of Dehli wrote to the Magistrate of Aligarh to the effect that letters had been received by Holkar from Daya Rám expressive of discontent, and recommending the Magistrate to keep a watchful eye on him. Daya Rám and the other chiefs of his tribe, viz., Bhagwant Singh of Mursán, and Harkishan Singh of Beswán, appear to have made it a point of honour never to pay the Government demand till the last moment to which they could safely put it off; and the Collector, conscious of his inability to enforce the demand, was obliged to content himself with repeated remonstrances, and an occasional vigorous representation to the Board of Commissioners of the state of affairs in those talukas. On one occasion, 8th August, 1810, the Collector stated that " the principle on which these talukadárs withhold their revenue is, that in the event of hostilities they may have a supply of cash, or that Government, with a view to the debt, may be prevented from proceeding to extremities." Not less frequent were the complaints of the Magistrates against these talukadárs for affording a secure asylum to offenders of all descriptions, for levying arbitrary duties, for omitting to report the occurrence of heinous crimes, and for disregarding the authority of the courts of judicature. At length, in July, 1816, the Magistrate (Mr. Majoribanks) reported the gross misconduct of Thákur Daya Rám in refusing, after repeated injunctions, to deliver up four offenders in a case of murder; and he strongly recommended that both Daya Rám and Bhagwant Singh should be deprived of their privilege of exemption from the police system introduced in the other parts of the district. This report reached the Supreme Government at a time when it was particularly politic not to pass over such misconduct, as a rising of the Pathán population of Rohilkhand a few months before had shown that the minds of the people in this part of our dominions were very unsettled. " It was therefore important to strike a blow that should impress all ranks with a proper estimate of our vigour and military means. At the close of 1816 it was resolved to reduce both Daya Rám and

---

[1] In 1806 Daya Rám held a farm of Rs. 3,31,000 revenue, and was proprietor of an estate assessed at Rs. 1,35,000. For matters connected with his history see Board's Records, 22nd April, 1806, No. 6; 20th June, 1806, No. 17; 27th June, 1806, Nos. 17 to 20 August 1806, No. 1; 26th August, 1806, Nos. 7-8; 5th, September, 1806, No. 17-23; 23rd September, 1806; 18th January. 1807, Nos. 6-7; 6th February, 1807, No. 7; 23rd January, 1808, No. 28; 28th May, 1808, No. 5; 29th August, 1808, No. 22; 21st February, 1809, No. 25; 26th February, 1809, No. 48; 25th March, 1809, Nos. 46-53; 8th June, 1809, No. 27; 21st November, 1809, No. 31A; 21st November 1809, No. 29.

Bhagwant Singh to the level of subjects, and to employ an overwhelming force for that purpose, as well to beat down all opposition as to give *eclat* to the measure. The divisions from Cawnpore, Meerut and Muttra were accordingly ordered to concentrate upon Háthras, and place themselves under the immediate command of Major-General Marshall, the officer commanding in the field. Háthras was reckoned one of the strongest forts in India. It was kept in the completest state of repair, and every improvement that was introduced into the neighbouring fortress of Aligarh, such as preparing a covered way, raising a glacis, and levelling the height of the ramparts, was carefully copied by Daya Rám. On the 21st of February the place was invested on all sides; and Daya Rám was then summoned to surrender a gate of his fort, and allow of its being dismantled. After some evasion on his part, and a negotiation which lasted till the 16th, he finally refused, when the siege immediately commenced. The *katra* or fortified town was breached and evacuated on the 23rd; approaches were then made to the fort, and batteries erected under a smart though ineffectual fire from the ramparts. By the 1st of March the works of the besiegers were completed, and on the following morning forty-two mortars and three breaching batteries of heavy guns began to play on the fort. Such powerful means had never yet been employed against any fortified place in India, and the effect was beyond measure destructive and astonishing to the garrison. The batteries continued to play till evening, when at 5 o'clock a large magazine blew up within the place, destroying half the garrison and nearly all the buildings. The effect is described to have been awful. Daya Rám with a few horse made his escape in the dark that same night, and, though challenged and pursued by a piquet of the 8th dragoons, got off with little damage. The rest of the garrison, in attempting to follow, were driven in and obliged to surrender at discretion. Bhagwant Singh agreed to dismantle his fort on the first summons; and thus was this important object gained, with the loss of only one European and five natives killed on our side, while the impression of the utter[1] futility of resistance spread far and wide through Hindustan."

On the expulsion of Daya Rám his property was confiscated, and an opportunity arose for restoring the condition of the village occupants, and for admitting them to the same liberal terms and the same direct intercourse with Government that were allowed to men of a similar class in other places. Notwithstanding the oppressive and arbitrary rule of Daya Rám, the original proprietors, in the greater number of villages, " still adhered to the soil, which they claimed as their own, and even where this was not the case, there frequently existed individuals or families who, though originally located by the talukadár himself, and therefore not strictly entitled to protection, might have been considered worthy of it from

Measures consequent on the expulsion of Daya Rám.

_____

[1] Prinsep's Transactions in India, I., 419.

long possession, improvement of the cultivation, or other causes. If this liberal and just course had been then pursued after due and careful enquiry, all the distress and confusion which subsequently existed might have been avoided, and there would still have remained a considerable number of estates, to the occupancy of which no one could with reason lay claim, and which might therefore have been made over by Government to any one whom they wished to favour. But though all correspondence which took place at the time shows clearly that the intentions of Government coincided with the above views, yet those intentions were defeated by the superficial way in which the question was taken up by the local officers, and the too ready acquiescence of the Board of Revenue in their representations. Misled by the title of zamíndár, which Daya Rám had enjoyed in the greater part of the parganah, and considering, as was then too often done, that the unrestricted power which the Thákur had exercised was the true index to his just and rightful interest, the Collector thought that no individuals or communities throughout the parganah could be entitled to protection, for the sole reason that none had hitherto been protected. It followed as a necessary corollary to this proposition, that the Government were authorized, after Daya Rá'n's forfeiture, to make over any portion of the estate, to whomever they chose, in absolute proprietary tenure, and to derive a larger revenue from such part as they might keep in their own hands than would have been demanded from a tract of equal size and fertility elsewhere.

"In consequence of these unfortunate and erroneous conclusions, the five talukas of Joár, viz., Simardhari, Barha, Gubrári, Karíl and Káras, were restored to the descendants of the former talukadárs, who, in the three first cases, had been wholly dispossessd for the respective periods of forty-one, forty, and twenty-three years, while the real owners or occupants of the soil in every separate village, who still retained and cultivated it, were admitted to no engagements, and were left in the condition of tenants-at-will. The rest of the parganah was composed of single and independent villages, of which 31 were made over to Thákur Jíwa Rám as a mark of the favour of Government under the name of taluka Mendu, and 20 were committed in the same manner to Thákur Jaikishan, under the appellation of taluka Shahzádpur. These two individuals, of whom the former was a son, and the latter a grandson, of Nawal Singh, elder brother of Daya Rám, were supposed to have shown good will to our authority during the operations against Háthras. This indeed was a politic, and in their case, owing to the supersession of Nawal Singh before narrated, a natural course to adopt. After the success of those operations they applied to be admitted as farmers of part of the forfeited estate ; but the Governor-General thought fit to direct, as a fuller means of evincing his approbation of their services, that they should be installed

Establishment of the talukas.

as proprietors of some of those villages which might have been held by Thákur Daya Rám, ' in undisputed proprietary tenure.' No injustice could have been caused by this order if it had been properly executed ; but as it was left to the Collector to decide what villages had really been thus held by Daya Rám, the objections which were urged by the people, whose estates were selected by the new talukadárs, against this transfer of them to other masters were disregarded in every instance.

When these arrangements had been decided upon, the new settlement,

Formation of the settlement of 1226 *fasli.* which was to commence with 1226 *fasli* (1818-19 A. D.), came under consideration. This settlement was intended to last for only five years, but unfortunately, with the exception of 13 villages and certain modifications of the land revenue in others, it remained in force till Mr. Thornton's revision. Though the higher authorities were still anxious that all under-rights should be protected as well in the different talukas as in that part of the parganah which remained under the immediate management of the Government officers, this object was most imperfectly attained, either as regarded the real and effectual preservation of the under-tenures themselves, or the selection of the parties who were entitled to hold them. A very hasty and incomplete inquiry took place into the names of those who were termed *mukadams* in every village. Under this unmeaning title were included individuals of all classes, from the original zamíndár to the *ínámi* of Thákur Daya Rám, who had obtained possession of a village on condition of furnishing a certain number of horses. And while it was clearly considered indispensable that some persons should be recorded in every case under the appellation in question, even when no one claimed it, it seems to have been thought of little moment, when claimants did appear, to select those who could show the best title. The gross assets of every village being then assumed, in most cases at a very full, and in many at an excessive amount, the revenue payable by these *mukadams* to the talukadárs in talukas Mendu and Shahzádpur, and to Government in the miscellaneous villages, was determined by a deduction of only 10 per cent. to cover all risks and expenses, including the patwári's fees. From the amount thus payable by the *mukadams* in Mendu and Shahzádpur, 15 per cent. was deducted for the profit of the talukadárs, and the remainder formed the Government revenue. In the five Joár talukas no deduction whatever was made in favour of the *mukadams* ; and though it would seem to have been vaguely intended that no more than the assumed gross rental, under the name of the *raibandi*, should be demanded from them, yet this intention, if it really existed, had never been enforced. In these talukas the revenue demandable by Government from the talukadárs was determined by a reduction of somewhat more than 20 per cent. from the above mentioned rental or *raibandi*."

The settlement, above described from Mr. Thornton's report, remained in
force until 1822-23, and was then extended as regarded
the *mukadami* villages for five years, and subsequently,
owing to the misleading advice given by the Collector of the time, up to Mr.
Thornton's revision. The Collector's object seems to have been to extract from
the already overburthened estates a further allowance for the sons of Daya Rám.
Daya Rám himself was pardoned, and a residence was provided for him near
Koil, with a pension of Rs. 1,000 for himself and Rs. 750 for his family.[1] He
died in 1823.[2] The condition of the Háthras estates in 1835 was most deplora-
ble. Deeds of mortgage existed for parts of almost every estate, and the general debt could not be less than two lakhs of rupees. In talukas Mendu and
Shahzádpur the people were in still greater difficulties. In the five talukas of
Joár, the condition of the cultivating communities was perhaps least miserable
where they appeared at first sight to have been most hardly treated. For
when they had been excluded from the management of their estates, though still
poor and destitute, they escaped being involved in debt, except such as they might
have incurred in cultivating their own separate fields. Mr. Thornton adopted
the same principles that were followed by him in the settlement of Mursán.
Where there were no village proprietors in existence, he conferred proprietary
rights on the talukadár; but where the original proprietors existed, and no transfer of their rights had taken place, he admitted them to engagements. These
persons, formerly known as *mukadams*, were styled *biswadárs*, and the rates of
deduction from the rental by which he determined the Government revenue were
the same as those which he adopted in Mursán, and which are noticed hereafter.
Gobind Singh, son of Daya Rám, continued to live at Koil on a pension of
Rs. 750 a month, and during the mutiny did such good service that he was
rewarded with the gift of several villages, including the zamíndári of Koil itself.
He died too soon to enjoy his well earned honours, and his estates are now
managed by his widow and adopted son.

As already mentioned, the Mursán family is descended from Zulkaran, the
eldest son of Nandrám. Zulkaran predeceased his
father who himself died in 1695, A. D. He left a
son, Khushál Singh, who resided with his mother at Rahatpur and Mánkraul,
—two villages made over to him by his uncle, for his support. When he grew
up to manhood he attracted the favour of the Oudh Vazír, Saadat Khán,
who gave him the farm of the following talukas, some of which had probably been in a greater or less degree subject to his grandfather's authority,
and had afterwards recovered their independence, but most of them appear not

Marginal notes: Mr. Thornton's revision. / Mursán family.

---

[1] Board's Records, 11th August, 1818, No. 35; 11th September, 1818, No. 6; 20th January, 1818,
No. 31; 30th June, 1818, No. 32; 3rd April, 1818, No. 21; 14th August, 1818, No. 34; 6th
October, 1818, No 34; 2nd November, 1819. [2] *Ibid*, 17th October, 1823, No. 2.

to have been so subject :—Talukas Dayálpur, Mursán khás, Gopi, Puteni, Ahri, Dáramái, and six other villages. Phup Singh succeeded his father about the year 1749 A. D., and increased his estates very largely by obtaining, from the amils of the neighbourhood, the lease of all such villages as had fallen out of cultivation, or in which the revenue was from any cause collected with difficulty. He also acquired a great portion of the estates held by the heirs of Bhoj Singh. Phup Singh was expelled from the Mursán estate by Surajmal, the Ját Raja of Bhartpur, in 1757, and retired to Sásni, over which he acquired complete authority. He recovered possession of Mursán in 1761, but was again expelled by Najf Khán in 1776. He did not again occupy Mursán until 1785, and it was some years before he recovered all the talukas that he formerly held. Shortly before his death he relinquished the management of the estate to his son ·Bhagwant Singh. Phup Singh was the first of his family to assume the title of Raja. His acquisitions were the greater part of taluka Moheriya, talukas Rohi, Bisana or Lashkarpur, Kotha Patta, Chotwa and Tuksán, and about seventeen single villages.

Bhagwant Singh obtained entire control of the estate on the death of his
Bhagwant Singh father in 1798 A D. He added talukas Sonk and Madan to it in 1795, and taluka Dunaitiya in 1796. In 1803 he was allowed to engage for the whole of the estates held by him, and in the engagement papers is styled zamíndár in some places, talukadár in others, and farmer in others. On this point the Collector seems to have been guided by the leases which the Raja had received from the former Government. At the close of the year 1215 *fasli* (1807-8 A.D.) a lease was granted to him for his own life, at a fixed revenue of Rs. 80,000, for the whole estate, exclusive of talukas Sonk and Madan, which were granted to him in *jágír* for good service performed in Lord Lake's campaign. The following table shows the descent of the Mursán family from Makan to Raja Tíkam Singh, C. S. I., the present representative. The *ráj* has always descended to the eldest son, but the collateral branches are entitled to be maintained by the Raja of the time being.[1]

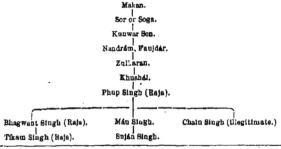

```
                        Makan.
                          |
                     Sor or Soga.
                          |
                     Kunwar Sen.
                          |
                   Nandrám, Faujdár.
                          |
                       Zulkaran.
                          |
                       Khushál.
                          |
                   Phup Singh (Raja).
     _____|_____
     |                    |                     |
Bhagwant Singh (Raja).  Mán Singh.   Chain Singh (Illegitimate.)
     |                    |
Tíkam Singh (Raja).   Suján Singh.
```

[1] Mr. Thornton gives a full table of the collateral branches of the family in Set. Rep. I., 245.

No investigation was made in 1803 with regard to the internal circumstances of the taluka, nor was the Raja's management in any way controlled or interfered with until the death of Bhagwant Singh. During this interval several indivi-duals petitioned for the recovery or the maintenance of their rights in particular villages, but they appear to have been all referred to a future opportunity for the investigation of their claims. Bhagwant Singh could not resist the example of his brother Ját, Daya Rám, and joined with the latter in setting at nought the orders of the civil courts ; but on the fall of Háthras he surrendered and con-sented to dismantle his own fort of Mursán. Raja Bhagwant Singh died in 1823, leaving a son, Tikam Singh,[1] and the whole of his estates were held under direct management by the Collector for the year 1823-24. All persons who con-sidered themselves to possess rights as being the descendants of those who were the original zamíndárs previous to the annexation of their respective villages to the parganah, as well as those who only rested their claims on long residence and management, came forward and prayed for the protection of Government. In the settlement for 1232-36 *fasli* (1824-25 to 1828-29 A.D.), all these claimants were permitted to engage for their respective villages with the title of *mukadams*, and those villages in which no claimant came forward were left with the far-mers. Tikam Singh was declared the *sudder malguzar* or principal engager for the revenue, and was given a *malikána* allowance of fifteen per cent. on the land revenue paid by those who engaged for each village, besides a sum of Rs. 644 per mensem on account of expenses of collection. Between 1232 and 1237 *fasli*, Tikam Singh lost nearly a lakh of rupees by this arrangement, and this led to a summary settlement in 1238, conducted on the former system of allowing Tikam Singh to collect only a fixed sum from each village, on which he received *malikána*. Farmers were again selected for those villages to the management of which there existed no rightful claimant, and security was demanded from each one admitted to engage ; but bad seasons and insufficient security were again said to be a cause of loss to the Raja.

In 1832-34, when Mr. John Thornton was appointed to revise the settlement

Mr. John Thornton.

of the district, the Mursán estate comprised some 300¼ villages, of which 231 were hamlets dependent on parent villages. These had all been drawn from time to time from parga-nahs Jalesar, Sadabad, Mahában, Ráya and Koil, and were then distributed amongst eighteen talukas, each consisting for the most part of a parent village with its surrounding hamlets. Taluka Moheriya contained several minor talukas which had become obsolete through the extinction of the original settlers, and one other comprised all the villages not in the other talukas. Mr. Thornton's first care was to " discover in what villages there existed individuals or com-munities who were entitled to retain the management under the Raja, and to

---

[1] Board's Records, 7th April, 1815.

determine the relation in which the two parties should stand towards each
other." Mr. Thornton's remarks on the formation of the taluka so well apply
to the other talukas of this district, that I shall give his conclusions in his own
words. He writes :—" I have found that in about two-thirds of parganah
Mursán, the descendants of the original zamíndárs who held the villages
before they came under the Raja's authority are still forthcoming, and that
neither by their own act, nor by the will of the former Government, have they
forfeited their right of managing their respective estates as long as they shall
pay the revenue demanded from them. With the exception of the three talukas
of Sonk, Madan, and Dunaitiya, it was not even alleged by the Raja that the
rights of the original zamíndárs had been transferred to his ancestors in any
legal manner, ; but he relied upon the assertion that the descendants of those
zamíndárs were extinct, and that the ancestors of the present claimants had
been located by his predecessors as common cultivators. This assertion, however,
was in itself vague and improbable ; it was supported by no proof, and opposed
to all evidence, oral or documentary. The holders of the several villages give
a clear and credible account of their descent and past history, which is attested
by all those who could be supposed to have any knowledge on the subject.
Their rights were acknowledged by the former Government when opportunity
offered, as is proved by some original papers from the office of the parganah
registrar (kanúngo) of the latter part of the last century. By these papers,
it appears that during the time that Raja Phup Singh was expelled from his
estate, the ancestors of the present village occupants were recorded by the
Government of the time as zamíndárs or *mukadams* (for the terms appear to
have been used indiscriminately) of their respective villages. Even during
the life of the late Raja Bhagwant Singh the management of the land was left
to these men, except when some reason presented itself to the contrary. All
others were called farmers *(mustájirs)* ; and even when any village was leased
out to an individual of the latter class, the hereditary village occupants frequently continued to hold as *kitkinadárs* under him, and if totally deprived of
the management, they still retained their seer land, which they repeatedly
mortgaged as necessity occurred. These points, taken together and combined
with the total absence of proof on the other side, form as strong evidence as
can generally be looked for in inquiries of this nature. But in Mursán the
assertion of the Raja is still more powerfully refuted by the circumstances of
the cases themselves, and particularly by the formation of the talukas mentioned
above. No race of mere tenants-at-will could have obtained the sole occupancy
of a large tract ; caused by such occupancy the villages which arose therein
to be so connected as to be termed a taluka ; divided that taluka from a remote
period into separate portions, each known by the name of one of the early
members of the family ; held each of those portions distinct to the present day ;

settled their several shares without dispute as soon as they were allowed to engage in 1825-26 ; and finally procured the sanction and the testimony of the neighbouring inhabitants to their claim of being the parties to whom, under whatever superior, the right of cultivating and managing the soil belongs. In the three talukas above mentioned, the Raja allowed the descent of the present *mukadams* from the original zamíndárs, but rested his claim for their expulsion from the management on the plea that their ancestors had sold them to his father, Bhagwant Singh, in return for his discharging some arrears of revenue due to the Government of the time. But it appeared, upon examination, that these transactions were rather between the amils and Bhagwant Singh than between the Raja and the zamíndárs, or at all events, that the inconsiderable number of the latter who were present at the time, contemplated nothing more than the annexation of their villages to the parganah and the consequent transfer of their future payments from the amil to the Raja. I have, therefore, admitted to engagements all those who have established their descent from the original zamíndárs, and who consequently inherit rights which existed at a period anterior to the Raja's authority. Those who have derived their tenures from the Raja himself, or his ancestors, have been directed to apply to the same quarter for their renewal. In about one-third of the parganah the stock of the old zamíndárs was extinct, and these villages have, in consequence, been made over to the exclusive management of the Raja, with the title of zamíndár. A similar course has been pursued with regard to a few villages, in which the rightful occupants have been prevailed upon, by certain equivalents, to withdraw their claims of every kind in favour of the *sudder malguzár.*"

Those villages which were settled with the Raja, under the title of zamíndár, in consequence of the absence of other claimants, were classed as *zamíndári*. Those which were settled solely with the Raja, on account of the refusal of the village occupants, were termed *talukadári*, and the remaining villages settled with the village communities were classed under *mukadami* (see parganah MURSÁN). The Raja made every effort in the civil courts to obtain a reversal of Mr. Thornton's proceedings but without effect.[1] During the currency of Mr. Thornton's settlement, Raja Tikam Singh held his own amid the fall of all around him. Notwithstanding his dissatisfaction with the changes made by Mr. Thornton, the Raja proved a staunch friend to the British during the troubles of 1857, and was rewarded with the decoration of ' Companion of the Star of India,' the proprietorship of several large villages, such as Gonda in Iglás and others, and the remission of the revenue of five villages, assessed at Rs. 6,550 per annum, for two generations. Though in debt, he is not embarrassed, and will leave to his

---

[1] In 1846, the Raja instituted 57 civil suits in the local courts to contest Mr. Thornton's proceedings, all of which, except five, which were compromised, were dismissed in appeal to the superior courts.—Hutchinson, 140.

son and grandson one of the finest estates in all the surrounding country. He is of fearless and independent character, and commands the respect of all who know him. Raja Tikam Singh is an honorary magistrate of the district.

Mr. Thornton, with his final proceedings, drew up a set of rules for prevent-

Rules for settlement of disputes between the talukadárs and biswadárs. ing any doubt or uncertainty in future as to the relations between the two parties that he found in the parganah. First, as regards the village occupants, the following principles were formulated : —

" 1. I consider them entitled to retain the management of their respective villages as long as they shall pay the land revenue which may be settled by the Collector at any revision of the settlement as that which the Raja is to obtain from them. This land revenue shall at least be so moderate as to be paid easily in an average year, in order that even in case of an unfavourable season, the *malguzárs* may be able to make arrangements for its liquidation.

2. If they shall at any time be deprived of the management on account of refusing to engage at the time of settlement, or on account of balances afterwards due from them, they shall retain the lands which are in their own seer cultivation, and shall not be called upon to pay more for the same than the rates fixed at the time of settlement.

3. In all such cases of dispossession, they shall be allowed the option of recovering the management at any ensuing settlement, provided they then discharge the arrears due from them, in cases where failure in paying the revenue may have been the cause of their deprivation.

4. They shall be termed ' *biswadárs,* ' and their representatives ' *mukadam biswadárs.*'

5. Whenever the holders of any *thok* or *patti,* the revenue of which is separate from that of the remainder of the village, shall fall into balancea, the holders of the other *thoks* shall have the option of taking it into their own hands upon discharging the balance, and of holding it as mortgagees till they shall have been repaid the amount.

6. The abovementioned rights shall be considered to be hereditary and transferable, that is to say, while in possession of management they may transfer their share or interest, and, when dispossessed, their seer land, subject to the payment of the settlement rates.

Secondly, as regards the Raja—

1. The Raja being established by length of possession as *sudder malguzár* of the parganah, is entitled to the difference between the revenue required by the State from each village and the sum which it may fix that he shall receive from the village communities. It follows that if the Government demand should at any time be pressed to the utmost extent that each village can regularly pay, his

interest will cease in the villages settled with the *mukadams*, or remain in abeyance, though the revenue may still be paid through his hands.

2. When the malguzars of any village may fail to pay their revenue in any year, the Raja shall sue them before the Collector, and after establishing his claim, if neither they nor their securities shall discharge the balance, he shall be entitled to make his own arrangements for the future management. He shall also assume the management in cases when the mukadams may decline engaging on the terms proposed at the time of settlement.

3. Whenever the descendants of the old zamíndárs, who have now been recorded as biswadárs, shall become extinct in any village, the Raja shall succeed to their rights and title in the same manner as he has now been allowed to succeed to the original occupants in those estates which have been settled with him as zamíndár.

4. As long as the abovementioned descendants continue to exist, and are forthcoming on the spot to assert their claims to the occupancy of the soil, the Raja shall, in such villages, retain the appellation of talukadár.

5. The talukadárí rights which the Raja has been above described to possess shall be considered to be hereditary and transferable. His successor will be of course in exactly the same position with respect to the village malguzárs as has now been assigned to himself. "

As has been seen, taluka Beswán owes its origin to Nawal Singh, eldest

Taluka Beswán and Shah-zádpur.

brother of Daya Rám, who, when worsted in the contest with his energetic younger brother, retired to Beswán, which with 26 other villages had been set apart for his maintenance during the life of Bhúri Singh, his father. Nawal Singh does not appear to have ever taken any measures to press his claims to the Háthras estate by right of seniority. He was succeeded by his two sons, Jíwa Rám and Harkishan. The former received Beswán and the estate connected with it, partly in jágír and partly on a fixed revenue for life, and the latter shared with him.[1] Harkishan was succeeded by his son Jaikishan or Jaikishor, who, on the downfall of Háthras, obtained the grant of taluka Shahzádpur, formed partly from Háthras and partly from Mendu. Jaikishan was succeeded by Girdhar Singh and Gír Parshéd ; the latter still holds Beswán and Shahzádpur. Jíwa Rám having previously squandered, through extravagance and folly, much not only of his paternal possessions but also of taluka Mendu, granted to him in 1817, died in 1835. He left five sons, and was succeeded by the eldest, Randhir Singh, who has succeeded in retaining but

Talukas Kanka and Kaj-raut.

little of the family property. From the genealogical table given on a preceding page it will be seen that

---

[1] Board's Records, 29th September, 1809, No. 30 : 18th November, 1809, No. 8 : 30th December, 1809, No. 15: 24th March, 1818, No. 4: 5th May, 1818, No. 7: 3rd July, 1818, No, 9: 11th August, 1831, No. 8.

Jaswant Singh, one of the sons of Nand Rám, had three sons—Subha Rám, Bairisál, and Tej Singh. The two latter received Tochigarh, whilst Subha Rám obtained a few villages in Tappa Joár. In the troublous times of Muhammad Sháh, Subha Rám increased his possessions, and his son Umed Singh, during the Ját usurpation (1757 to 1775), succeeded in obtaining the lease of a considerable tract of country. On the accession of Najaf Khán to power, Umed Singh was dispossessed (1775) and his farm was given in *jágír* to one Rustam Beg Khán, who held it until the arrival of the Marhattas in 1785. Umed Singh then recovered possession and divided the taluka with his nephews, Shiu Singh and Sáhib Singh, sons of Sumer Singh. One share was called Kanka and the other Kajraut. Both have since been more than once subdivided. In 1792 the talukas were given in *jágír* to a Marhatta named Gulábji Kadam, who remained in possession until a short time before the conquest. The Játs were then again admitted to engage and settlements were made with Nihál Singh, son of Umed Singh, Shiu Singh and Kishan Singh, son of Sumer Singh, in 1805-06, and continued with them until 1836. Mr. Thornton at the revision found that the talukadárs had so thoroughly exterminated the old proprietors that he could only restore four villages to the real owners, the Janghára Rajputs. The following table shows all that is necessary concerning this family up to the last settlement.:—

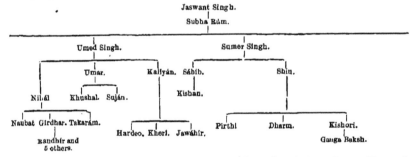

The shares of Pirthi and Dharm, sons of Shiu Singh, have been alienated, those of several others have been mortgaged, and the talukas, for all purposes, have now been broken up and separate interests have been created.

The Játs of the Chábak *got* hold taluka Pisáwa. They first obtained a footing in the district by Mukhrám, their leader, undertaking the lease of Pisáwa and the neighbouring villages from Perron. At Mr. Elliot's assessment Mukhrám was dispossessed of all the villages except taluka Pisáwa, and the real proprietors were allowed to engage. Taluka Pisáwa itself was settled by Mr. Sterling in 1833 for twenty years. Mukhrám Singh was succeeded by Bharat Singh, and he by his three sons, Tej Singh, Shib Singh, and Gobind Singh. Like most others of

Taluka Pisáwa in Chandaus.

the influential Játs, the proprietors of Pisáwa sided with the British during the mutiny of 1857 and received a few villages as reward. They have increased their paternal possessions by purchase, but of late years have shown a grasping, quarrelsome disposition, and their " constant disputes with their own tenants and the neighbouring zamíndárs have, to a certain extent, impaired the general good estimation in which they were formerly held."

The Pundírs or Purírs of Nái, represented by Thákur Kundan Singh,

Pundírs of Nái.

received two villages in reward for their service during the mutiny. Mr. Bramly writes :—" Kundan Singh's estates are small, but his influence in his clan is great. His presence in the neighbourhood of Sikandra Rao continually served as a check to the Muhammadan population of that town, who never dared to do any overt act of rebellion without the help and screen of rebel troops, on whom they could afterwards throw the blame. During the month of June and a portion of July, the Tahsíldár, though his functions were entirely in abeyance, still was allowed to live in the town without molestation. During this time the only two men who visited him, or showed him any countenance, were Kundan Singh and Debi Parshád, Baniya. After the departure of Mr. Watson for Agra, the Tahsíldár, being no longer safe in the town, took shelter with Kundan Singh. In the end of August, after the defeat of Ghaus Khán's followers near Koil, Kundan Singh having been made Názim of the Parganah, entered the town of Sikandra Rao with a body of some 1,500 of his own followers, reinstated the Tahsíldár, and maintained him in that position till our authority was thoroughly established. I have always heard Kundan Singh well spoken of as an upright man. He is one of the best specimens of the home-bred, untravelled Rajpút I have ever met."

Raja Pirthi Singh, the adopted son of the late Pitambar Singh of Awa Mísa,

Pirthi Singh of Awa Mísa.

in the Muttrá District, in common with many other members of the spurious offshoots of the great Jádon stock, claims kinship with the Jádons of the Karauli State, but his claim is not allowed by any of the pure Jádava families. His history will be given under the Muttra District. The family is noticed here as having acquired of late years talukas Daryápur and Husain, which belonged to the Porach Rajpúts, and the greater portion of the Bijaigarh taluka, which belonged to the Pundír Rajpúts. The Awa family are more money-lenders than landholders, and have always proved severe and grasping landlords. They are now the largest single owners in the Sikandra Tahsíl.

Talukas Dátauli and Bhamauri Náh are held by a clan of Sarwáni Afgháns

Afgháns of Dátauli.

who settled here some two hundred years ago. One of their leaders, Muhammad Mír Khán, obtained possession of Dátauli in the reign of Akbar. Abdul Rahman Khán increased the ancestral possessions considerably by the purchase of estates at sales for arrears of revenue during the early years of British rule, and was succeeded by his son, Muhammad Husain Khán. The latter died soon after signing the engagement papers at the settlement in 1838, and was succeeded by his brother, Faiz Ahmad Khán, then only twelve years of age. The estate was placed under the management of Muhammad Daúd Khán, one of the talukadárs of Bhamauri Náh, whose sister had married Abdul Rahman Khán, and whose daughter had married Muhammad Husain Khán, and so well was it managed that specie enough was accumulated to complete the purchase money of the valuable Malikpur estate in the Bulandshahr district from the assignees of Mercer and Co., indigo-planters. Dátauli now consists of 25 villages, paying a revenue of Rs. 30,246, and situated in the most fertile portion of the parganah. Malikpur contains 32 villages, all of which will descend to the eldest son according to the custom of the family.

Taluka Bhamauri was acquired by Afgháns of the same stock, named Yúsaf and Sulaimán, during the reign of Shahjahán. They resided at Bhíkampur, which now frequently gives its name to the family. They added considerably to their possessions, but were twice ejected, once by the Bhartpur Játs in 1757 A.D., and again by Indurgír Gosháin, who during the government of Najaf Khán established a temporary supremacy in these parganahs. Náh was originally held by Megdwár Rajpúts who were dispossessed by the Játs, and their lands were given to Báz Khán by De Boigne in 1793-94 A.D. The grant was confirmed by the British Government in 1803, and the two talukas were joined together under the name of Bhamauri Náh. In 1856 they comprised 61 villages, paying a revenue of Rs. 42,313. Báz Khán had three sons—Muhammad Khán, Khanzamán Khán, and Daúd Khán, who divided the estates between them. Hádi Yár Khán, the son of Muhammad Khán, now owns one-third, and has taken up his residence at Dádon. Khanzamán's share has been divided into three smaller talukás,—two held by his sons, Abdul Shakúr Khán and Muhammad Takí Khán, and one by his grandson. Daúd Khán's share again has been equally divided between his two sons, Ináyatullah Khán and Ghulám Ahmad Khán. In spite of these subdivisions each member of the family still retains a considerable property. Hádi Yár Khán holds 32 villages in Aligarh and the large estate of Mohanpur in Eta. Abdul Shakúr Khán and his brother and nephew hold 48 villages in Aligarh and several estates in Eta, and the sons of Daúd Khán hold 15 villages each, besides estates in the adjoining district. During the mutiny Daúd Khán's conduct was very suspicious. Mr. Sapte writes that he refused to furnish supplies to the Bulandshahr force on their way to Eta, and "for two days we were put to great inconvenience, and his personal bearing towards us was disrespectful in the extreme. Of the movements and intentions of the rebels at Kásganj he feigned complete ignorance, though his house was but a few miles from that town. If he had been, as he professed, a well-wisher of the British, he must have felt anxiety for himself if the rebels had advanced, but his conduct plainly showed that he was under no apprehension from them."

A branch of the Badgújar family converted to Islám by Sábit Khán, the well-known Governor of Koil in the beginning of the last century, owns taluka Chakáthal. They claim descent from Dán Saháì, a lineal descendant of Partáp Singh, and in the last century, Rúp Singh the son, and Tára Singh the. grandson, of Dán Saháì became converts to Islám. Tára Singh died in 1811, and his widow, Maha Kunwar, succeeded to the property. Maha Kunwar died in 1859. During her life, Nitanand, the father of Jawála Baksh, Brahman, a servant of the estate, induced her to transfer it to him. On the death of Mahá Kunwar, her sister Ratta Kunwar succeeded and contested the transfer to the Brahmans. The case was recently decided in the Privy Council adversely to her. One-fourth of the remainder was decreed to be the property of Arám Singh, the grandson of a cousin of Tára Singh. Ratta Kunwar has made over all her rights to. Mashúk Ali Khán, the son of her daughter. The death of Ratta Kunwar will be the signal for another appeal to the Courts, and there are grave doubts whether the estate can stand the expense. The converted Badgújars of Taluka Pilkhana also belonged to the Sábitkháni family, but their importance ended with the sale of the taluka by auction in 1815, when it was purchased by Mardán Ali Khán.

Taluka Barauli is held by a family of Badgújar Rajpúts who claim to be the eldest branch of the clan settled in this and the Bulandshahr Districts (see BULANDSHAHR DISTRICT). Even at the last settlement five villages were mortgaged and the estate was sadly neglected. The zamíndárs were idle and extravagant and deeply involved in debt, and by 1856 one-half of the villages had passed into the hands of the Musalmán Badgújars of Pahásu, Pindráwal, and Chatári in the Bulandshahr District. The present owner, Rao Karan Singh, has increased the debt by a protracted litigation concerning his right to one-half the estate. The suit has been decided by the Privy Council in his favour, and if he only pays attention to his estate, there can be no doubt that he will eventually be able to clear off the present incumbrances, as Barauli has been much improved of late years by the canal. The families of Muhammad Ali Khán of Chatári, Bákir Ali Khán of Pindráwal, and Faiz Ali Khán of Pahásu, are noticed in the account of the Bulandshahr District. They are Musalmán Badgújars, and have acquired by purchase considerable estates in this district.

The Somna taluka belongs to Jádon Rajpúts[1] of the Bágri *got*. The taluka belonged to Chauhán Rajpúts,[2] but in the troubled times of Marhatta rule, during the last decade of the eighteenth

Taluka Chakáthal.

Badgújars of Barauli.

Taluka Somna.

---

[1] Board's Records, 31st August, 1822, No. 7.   [2] Settlement Report, 345 : Board's Records.

century, Jairám Singh, of the Jádon clan, obtained the farm of the taluka from General Perron. Though he appears to have had no sufficient title to the proprietary right in most of the villages of the taluka, the settlement of 1803 and successive settlements were made with him as zamíndár until his death in 1826. Before his death, two of his collateral relatives, Khushál Singh and Rámparshád, sued for and obtained a share in the estate, and the remainder was divided amongst his three sons, Híra Singh, Chandan Singh, and Balwant Singh. At the revision of settlement Mr. Thornton found that he could not restore the original zamíndárs, as they had been so long out of the management of their estates, and he found that their exclusion was mainly due to the policy adopted by Jairám, who used his utmost endeavours to keep the old zamíndárs satisfied with his management of the estate. To the few Ját communities he granted indulgences which left them the entire management of their villages, and so stopped them from engaging in a doubtful contest to prove their undoubted rights, whilst the Chauháns were allowed certain privileges which sufficed for their support. His sons, however, pursued a different course. They not only deprived the original proprietors of every privilege granted to them by Jairám, but those men who were weak enough to trust to Rajpút honour were not even allowed to reside within the limits of the taluka: and so the injustice done by the nature of the early summary settlements was allowed to continue by the arbitrary, though salutary, influence of our limitation laws. All these brothers are now dead. Balwant Singh alienated his portion of the estate through extravagance. The widow of Híra Singh is still alive and in possession of her husband's share. Chandan Singh died childless, leaving an estate largely increased by judicious purchases to his two widows and his adopted son. One of the widows now manages the estate.

Jaláli is noticeable for a family of Sayyids who have settled here from the time of Ala-ud-dín, when Sayyid Kamál-ud-dín married the daughter of the Kázi. In the time of Shahjahán they expelled the original Pathán proprietors. They have supplied a large number of men who have attained to considerable distinction in the civil and military service of the State. (See JALÁLI.)

Sayyids of Jaláli.

Taluka Husain was acquired by Raja Ratan Singh of the Porach tribe of Rajpúts, about 1760, shortly after his expulsion from Mendu and Háthras by the Játs. Ratan Singh retired to Farukhabad and subsequently acquired the favour of Nawal Singh of Bhartpur, who, in 1770, gave him a *jágír* and allowed him to engage for taluka Husain. The taluka had, originally, been farmed by one Muhammad Shákir, who had been allowed to withdraw certain villages from Pargœnah Jalesar and to hold them as farmer, but about seven years before Ratan Singh obtained the taluka, the Musalmán had been expelled and the village proprietors had again paid direct to the Jalesar amil. Neither Ratan Singh nor his predecessors had

Taluka Husain.

ever before had any portion of the taluka beyond a few houses in Husain Khás. The arrangement in favour of Ratan Singh continued in force only until 1786, when the dominion of the Marhattas commenced. Ratan Singh died in 1787 and was succeeded by his son Mitrsen, who was deprived of the taluka. Husain was then made over to an Afghán named Kotal Khán, and afterwards in *jáedád* to Bápúji Sindhia. It subsequently formed a portion of Perron and DeBoigne's possessions, who collected the revenue separately from each village. So that from 1786 to 1803 the Raja retained no portion of the estate except three revenue-free villages. During the confusion of the earlier years of our government Mitrsen found means to have himself admitted to engage for the taluka, and from 1803-04 to 1807-08 he was entered as the chief engager for the revenue. In the latter year, in consequence of the indebtedness of Mitrsen,[1] the old proprietors were recorded, and it was directed that engagements should be taken from them, but the settlement was again made with the Raja as farmer on his giving security, and was continued to his son Jaswant Singh and grandson Naráyan Singh. Mr. Thornton revised the settlement in 1836, and found that the taluka consisted of forty revenue-paying and three revenue-free estates, held by the Raja on a conditional and temporary lease, without prejudice to the rightful owners ; but in only 17 villages could these owners be found, and the remainder of the taluka was settled with the Raja as proprietor. Naráyan Singh mortgaged his rights to Pirthi Singh of Awa Mísa, in the Muttra District, and on his death in 1846 was succeeded by his two widows as heirs. His *malikána* allowance, in accordance with rule, was reduced to ten per cent. on the land assessment, and a pension of Rs. 600 per annum was allowed to each of his widows. They brought a suit for redemption against the mortgagees, and obtained a decree in the lower Courts, which was reversed on appeal. The Jádon talukadár of Awa Mísa is now in possession, and the only member of the old family now living is the childless widow of Naráyan Singh. Taluka Daryápur, another old possession of the Porach Rajpúts, was the head-quarters

Taluka Daryápur.

of the Raja who first assisted Nandrám, the ancestor of the Háthras and Mursán families ; his descendants retained possession until the last settlement, when they borrowed money from the Raja of Awa Mísa, who is now in possession of their estates.

Taluka Iglás was held under the Marhatta Government by one Gangadhar

Taluka Iglás.

Pandit as a grant for religious and charitable purposes, and it was confirmed to him by the British Government. On his death the grant was resumed, and in 1816[2] one-fourth of the

---

[1] Board's Records, 23rd May, 1809; No. 11 : 16th June, 1809, No. 14: 4th July, 1809, No. 35 : 11th July, 1809, No. 39 : 29th September, 1809, No. 33 : 17th November, 1802, No. 19. [2] G. O., 5th January, 1816 : Board's Records, 12th April, 1814, No. 8 ; 13th October, 1815, No. 1 ; 16th February, 1816, No. 2 ; 23rd February, 1816, No. 1 ; 21st December, 1821, No. 35.

produce was appropriated for his heirs, and three-fourths to public and charitable purposes. The entire revenue from the eleven villages of the taluka is paid into the treasury, and the public three-fourths now go to make up part of the endowment of the Agra College. The revenue assessed at the present settlement is Rs. 7,740 per annum, of which the Agra College gets Rs. 5,805 and the heirs of Gangadhar the remainder.

Taluka Gambhíra, more commonly known as Bijaigarh, in the old Parganah Jaláli, and Tahsíl Sikandra Rao, belongs to an old family of Pundír Rajpúts, who formerly held the greater portion of Parganahs Akrabad and Sikandra Rao. Rao Mánik Singh was expelled by the Ját-Marhatta Government, and his taluka was given to Raja Bhagwant Singh of Mursán. The fort of Bijaigarh was taken, after great loss, by the Commander-in-Chief in 1802. The graves of those who fell in the attack are in the low *duhur* lands below the fort. In 1805-06 Rao Mánik Singh was admitted to engage for the revenue, and was succeeded by his son Khawan Singh, with whom the settlement under Regulation IX. of 1833 was made and whose extravagance and weakness ruined the estate.[1] In 1838 Khawan Singh mortgaged the taluka to Mán Singh, a banker of Koil, who in 1840 sub-mortgaged it to Mr. J. O'B. Saunders, at that time an indigo-planter in this district. In 1852 Khawan Singh obtained a decree in the local Courts for redemption of the mortgage, but this was reversed by the Sadr Diwáni in 1853. Khawan Singh died the same year, leaving as his heirs his widow, Baldeo Kunwar, a son, Balwant Singh, only four years of age, and his mother, Jai Kunwar. He left the estate encumbered with debt to the amount of Rs. 75,000. The taluka originally contained 32 villages, of which eight were sold prior to the revision of settlement in 1838, and thirteen were sold subsequently. Balwant Singh now holds only eleven villages, most of which are small. "He would appear to have accepted the warning taught by the ruinous excesses of his father, and limits his expenditure by the reduced amount of his income." The new settlement has enhanced the demand on his villages, but with ordinary prudence he ought to be able to pay the increased land-revenue without difficulty.

Parganah Sikandra Rao was originally composed of talukas Agsoli, Deori, Pora, and Naukhail. After the cession, taluka Agsoli was farmed to Hurmat Ali Khán, and the other talukas to Muhammad Núr Khán, both residents of Sikandra Rao.[2] In 1809 the farm of Agsoli was discontinued, and the villages of the taluka were settled with the several zamíndárs; but at the special request of the real proprietors of the remaining talukas, Núr Khán was allowed to continue as farmer. In 1810 the tahsíldár absconded, and Núr Khán became bankrupt. The Government took Núr

---

[1] See Board's Records, 15th July, 1814, No. 4: 2nd August, 1814, No. 7: 29th September, 1813, No. 6. [2] Board's Records, 24th June, 1809, No. 23: 19th July, 1809, No. 13.

Khán's fort of Deori in part payment of his arrears, and the three talukas were broken up and the villages were separately settled with the old proprietors.

Major Louis Derridon was an officer in the Marhatta service, whose sister

Major Derridon. married M. Perron. Perron held the village of Bhamola in *jágír* by sanad from Sindhia and by a farmán of Shah Alam. After leaving the Marhatta service he made over his *jágír* to his brother-in-law by deed of gift, dated Chinsurah, June 11th, 1804. Major Derridon refused to give up this village to the British, and was ejected by force, but was afterwards reinstated. Part of the village being subsequently required for cantonments, the village of Dodhpur and half of Alampur were given in exchange for Bhamola on a revenue-free tenure to Major Derridon and his heirs for ever (October 13th, 1821).[1] Major Derridon died in 1845, and his estate was divided amongst his heirs, most of whom are now in comparatively poor circumstances. Alampur has been sold and is now in the hands of Mahmúd Ali Khán of Chatári, and the greater portion of the interests in Bhamola and Dodhpur has been lost to the family. Those left of the family reside in Agra.

Amongst the minor estates in this district may be mentioned taluka Raipur

Minor estates. in Parganah Atrauli, which formerly belonged to a family of Musalmán Rajpúts, but before the mutiny it passed into the hands of a Baniya of Atrauli, the Afghans of Bhamauri Náh, and other creditors. Similarly, taluka Lohgarh was purchased by a servant of the Barla indigo factory, and taluka Sahnaul came into the hands of one Khushwakt Ali, son of one Wazír Irshád Ali of Cawnpore. Taluka Badesra fell into the hands of the Játs of Kuchchesar in the Bulandshahr district. In Parganah Koil, talukas Aísa and Manchaura, belonging to Mír Mahar Ali, and taluka Sikháran, belonging to Hakím Zulfakár Ali, have been broken up: the former in 1810 and the latter in 1816. Taluka Sukrawáli, in the same parganah, has been divided amongst the heirs of Nandrám Ját, who acquired the estate at the first settlement. Taluka Sáhibabad belonged to a Kayath family who held the hereditary kanúngoship of the parganah. They founded Keshopur, Gadrána, and Gambhírpur, but the latter village subsequently passed into the hands of the adopted sons of Mán Singh, a well-known banker of Koil. The Chauháns of Bámauti, in Parganah Khair, formerly held the whole of the parganah. Rao Pirthi Singh was dispossessed by Perron, and on the British occupation, Rao Lachhman Singh, son of Pirthi Singh, obtained certain allowances which terminated with his death. Lachhman Singh was succeeded by Híra

---

[1] Board's Records, 24th January, 1806, Nos. 3-5; 18th February, 1806; 24th June, 1806, No. 2; 28th October, 1806; 26th June, 1807, No. 1; 8th November, 1808, No. 32; 8th June 1821, No. 7.

Singh, and he by Bhúpál Singh, who attacked and plundered Khair in 1857. He was subsequently captured and hanged. The bankers of Duchíta, in Khair, have also large possessions in the parganah.

All proprietary tenures fall under one or other[1] of the three great classes already explained, *viz., zamindári, pattidári,* and *bháya-*
Proprietary rights.
chára. Of the 2,046 estates or mahals, including those held free of revenue, 1,064, or 52 per cent., are *zamindári* ; 854, or 42 per cent., are *bháyachára;* and 128, or 6 per cent., are *pattidári.* Both these latter tenures indicate the existence of numerous co-sharers and mostly of cultivating communities, and, on the other hand, *zamindári* tenures are often confined to a single owner, though in the majority of cases there are here also several co-sharers. Counting the two latter classes as one, it will be found that the whole district is pretty equally divided between small village communities and those who are, in some cases, the possessors of considerable property. Cases of perfect *pattidári* with complete division of the land and joint responsibility are few and exceptional ; for once separation is complete the holders prefer to remain unfettered and to erect their shares into distinct estates. But a very considerable number exhibit a combination, or rather a commixture, of the two former systems, partial separation and partial union in one and the same village, the division being founded on hereditary right, or (specially when the proprietary body is numerous and the lands tilled by the sharers) depending on ability to cultivate and to pay the recognized *báchh.* In Iglás and Khair villages of this kind constitute more than half the entire number ; in Háthras they are 168 out of a total of 400, and in Koil they number 202 out of 412 estates. Zamindári estates are most numerous in Atrauli and Sikandra Rao.

No description of tenures would be complete without a reference to that condition of landed property known as the talukadári,
Talukadári.
which prevails to a considerable extent in Iglás and Háthras, and in which there are two distinct classes of proprietors—the superior and inferior. This was the subject that engaged the attention of Mr. J. Thornton in 1838, and he was the first to grasp the real nature of these holdings and lay down the principles on which they should be dealt with by the State. The Mughal conquerors,[2] and, in imitation of them, their Marhatta successors, seem to have applied the term zamindár to all those from whom they received the revenue, whether of a large tract or a single village, provided the tenure of such persons was of a permanent nature. Thus, when Phup Singh was expelled from Mursán, the ancestors of the present village proprietors enjoyed the same title as the ousted Raja. It is clear, therefore, that the term 'zamindár' was never intended, at that time, to convey or express a right to the occupancy in the soil itself. In the district held by the larger zamindárs, the land was

---

[1] See page 222.   [2] Thornton's Mursán Repeot : I., Settlement Report, 147.

still retained by those to whom it belonged before the appointment of any permanent officer between them and the State, and who were emphatically termed ' bhumiyas, ' as being indissolubly connected with the soil ; and although these large zamíndárs were frequently enabled, by the apathy of the native governments, and especially of an usurping power like the Marhattas, to encroach upon the rights of those whom they were bound, by the terms of all their leases, to protect, the condemnation of such tyranny by the general voice of the country was sufficient to prove that in so doing they exceeded the power entrusted to them. If, then, the title of zamíndár had still retained its original meaning, Mr. Thornton considered that there could be no objection to apply it still, in the sense of ' sudder malguzár ' or principal engager for the revenue, to all individuals of that class in the country.[1] " But from the first period of our sway we seem to have been misled, partly by the etymology of the word, and partly by the absence of any class in our own country corresponding with these large farmers of revenue, and the term zamíndár has thus been brought to signify the possession of a proprietary right in the land itself. In compliance with this new signification of the word, those who have it in the lower provinces have been constituted absolute masters of the tract of which they were found to pay the revenue, whether that tract were large or small, and whether the occupancy of the soil really belonged to them or not. And it appears that the people of the country have entirely adopted the term in its new sense, and they have learned to prize it as the official title which conveys the same idea as the more familiar ones of ' bhumiyas, ' ' biswadárs, ' &c., which are in use among themselves. In the case of Mursán, for example, they would have considered the recognition of the Raja as zamíndár of the whole parganah to be fatal to the security of their tenures. Since then the native governments, whose usage in this respect was the only foundation of the Raja's claim, have passed away, and different views have since been adopted, as well by the mass of the people as by the Government itself," Mr. Thornton thought that it would be neither just nor expedient to admit the claim alluded to; nor was there anything in the documents conveying the grants to Nandrám and Bhoj Singh which could affect this question. The argument will equally apply against the concession of the title to the Raja, whether his ancestors obtained that title by a formal grant, or merely from custom and courtesy, and, moreover, it is evident that no formal grant was intended in either of those cases. Such a grant would have required an imperial farmán and the Emperor's seal, and would have clearly conveyed an hereditary title. But the simple order of the minister of the day was sufficient to commit the fiscal and faujdári charge of a district to any individual, and to assign him a jágir therein as the reward of his services, both arrangements

---

[1] Settlement Report, 257. The biswadárs are chiefly cultivating proprietors, tilling the land without the intervention of any non-proprietary cultivating class.

being equally liable to cease on the death of the individual in question or at the minister's own pleasure. The real grounds for upholding the tenure were its long continuance and the principle laid down by Government of maintaining any arrangement which was found to be in force at the time of the cession or conquest. Mr. Thornton found that in quite two-thirds of the great talukas the original proprietary body still survived. In these he acknowledged the rights of the village communities, but owing to the long continued connection with the taluka-dárs, he allowed to the latter a certain right, called the " superior " or taluka-dári right, by which the talukadár received a certain percentage (*malikána*) of the revenue paid by the "inferior" proprietors. These words " superior" and "inferior" are not used as indicative of the quality of the respective rights, but refer to the position of the holders with regard to the State. The inferior proprie-tors or biswadárs pay their revenue through the superior proprietors to Government.

The proportion of the assets allowed as *malikána*, or the dues of the superior proprietors, varied with each taluka. In all cases the biswadárs were allowed 20 per cent. of the gross rental assets, and of the remainder 30 per cent. was allowed to the talukadárs of Kanka and Kajraut, and 18 per cent. to the other Ját talukadárs. Mr. Thomason[1] ruled that of the 22½ per cent. of the revenue (or 18 per cent. of the assets) thus alienated, only ten per cent. should remain as a heritable and trans-ferable right to the heirs of the talukadárs on the demise of the existing incum-bents. This rule has not been always observed, and in the case of Raja Tíkam Singh of Mursán, Government has conferred on him and his heirs for ever the same amount of *malikána* as that fixed at last settlement. This is very hard on the village proprietors, for, as noticed by Mr. Smith, whilst they would have only had to pay 55 per cent. of the assets as land-revenue under the existing rules on the death of Tíkam Singh, or, in other words, 50 per cent. of the assets *plus* 10 per cent. on the revenue, they will have now to pay 65·4 per cent. of the assets for ever, and thus pay the reward which Government certainly intended should be paid out of its own resources. Mr. Thornton hoped that his new arrangements would place the rights of both parties on a firm basis, which should be equally advantageous to the superior and inferior proprietor, but Mr. Smith shows that these hopes have scarcely been realized. "On the whole, indeed, the policy has been favourable to the pros-perity and maintenance of the high position of the talukadárs, and where it has appeared to fail, its failure is not due to the nature of the policy itself, but to the minute subdivision of property consequent on the laws of Hindú inheritance, or to the extravagance of the original talukadár. But it has been fatal to the great majority of the inferior proprietors or biswadárs."

Malikána.

---

[1] Thomason's Desp., I., 24; II., 199.

The following tables show the changes in the talukadári rights during the last settlement :—

No. of villages.	Where malikána is paid to original incumbent or heirs.				Where talukadári villages have been absorbed by talukadár.				Where talukadári allowances have been partly transferred.				Where talukadári allowances have been wholly transferred.			
	No. of villages.	Land-revenue.	Malikána.	Total.	No. of villages.	Land-revenue.	Malikána.	Total.	No. of villages.	Land-revenue.	Malikána.	Total.	No. of villages.	Land-revenue.	Malikána	Total.
219	119	Rs. 1,02,694	Rs. 29,868	Rs. 1,32,562	15	Rs. 12,033	Rs. 3,175	Rs. 15,208	14	Rs. 13,028	Rs. 4,038	Rs. 17,066	70	Rs. 85,243	Rs. 25,246	Rs. 1,10,489

Of the villages where the talukadári rights have been preserved intact, the Raja of Mursán holds 84, Gír Parshád Singh of Shahzádpur holds 19, and the remaining 16 belong to various small talukas of the Háthras and Mursán families. Of the 70 estates where the superior rights have gone to strangers, 30 belonged to the Mendu estate, 14 to Husain, and the remainder to various small talukadárs whose rights were sold as they became more minutely subdivided by the increase in the number of co-sharers. On the whole, 53 per cent. of the talukadári rights remains with the original owners, 40 per cent. has been permanently alienated, and seven per cent. has been temporarily alienated between 1838 and 1868.

The biswadári rights have suffered still greater vicissitudes. Of the 218 villages, 79 have entirely passed out of the hands of the original proprietors; in 71 villages half and more than half the area of the village has been alienated ; in 49 less than one-half the area has been transferred, and in only 19 villages is the stock of the old proprietors in possession. In other words, in nine per cent. of the malikána villages paying six per cent. of the original demand the original stock remains ; in 22·5 per cent. of the villages paying 24 per cent. of the demand they have lost nearly half their estates; in 32·5 per cent. of the villages paying 34 per cent. of the entire revenue assessed they have lost more than half their possessions, and have lost all in 36 per cent. of the villages paying the same percentage of the land-revenue. This state of things is much to be regretted. The purchasers of both the

Fate of the inferior or biswadári rights.

superior and inferior interests belong to the Baniya and Maháján money-lending classes. Mr. Smith writes :—" There can be little doubt that the cause of their (biswadárs) decay has been the large percentage of assets which was deducted as their joint dues to Government and the talukadár. Eighty per cent. was too large a proportion to be paid at a time when prices were low and the effects of the former heavy assessments were still being felt. Those who have held on until now are mostly in a very different position ; their revenue has long been paid with ease, and the present settlement has added practically nothing to the demand." * * * " The Háthras Baniyas and the village money-lenders, who have taken the place of the Játs and Rajpúts of thirty years ago, bought their estates well knowing their liabilities, and at a time when the profits of zamíndárs were much lower than they are now ; and now land has so greatly increased in value, and so much greater importance is attached to its possession, they are not likely to turn defaulters. Those of the old proprietors still remaining are in a more prosperous condition than they were, and their prosperity is still increasing with high prices and rising rents. The enhancement in their total payments, result-ing from the retention of the old malikána allowances, is probably not sufficient to ruin them."

Mr. Smith notices a peculiar tenure to be found amongst certain village

Certain tenures in bháya-chára estates.

communities, especially in Khair and Iglás. " The village, as a whole, is held in imperfect pattidári tenure ; each proprietor holds a certain portion of the area in severalty, and, besides, enjoys his share of common rights of whatever value or kind they may be. But apart from the general body of proprietors, who all share on the same principles, will be found one or two individuals who are admitted to be proprietors, but are allowed no share whatever in the interests held in common. They own so many acres of land, which they cultivate or lease out as they please, and for which they pay Government revenue, but have no further concern with the general management of the estate, and no voice in the settle-ment of village accounts. The origin of these tenures is various. Sometimes the holdings have been granted to returned absentees or their descendants, who claim relationship with the coparcenary body, but whose ancient rights have been forfeited by lapse of time and non-possession. Sometimes they are held by Brahmans, whose ancestors obtained them from former proprietors. In some cases they are the result of the settlement of a disputed claim to a share in the common property. The holdings are mostly of small extent and value."

Dividing the proprietary body into three classes,—1st, petty proprietors, or

Distribution and value of proprietary rights.

those possessing one-fourth or less of a single villáge ; 2ndly, those possessing more than one-fourth, and not more than an entire village ; and 3rdly, those who are proprietors of more than one village, the following statement shows the distribution of the land amongst the proprietors in this district at the recent settlement : —

Class of proprietor.	Number of shares.	Total area in acres.	Average area per share in acres.	Revenue in rupees.	Rate per acre in rupees.	Average revenue per share in rupees.	Total area cultivated by tenants in acres.	Average area per share cultivated by tenants.	Total area cultivated by sharers.	Average area per share cultivated by sharers.
1.	2.	3.	4.	5.	6.	7.	8.	9.	10.	11.
1st or petty,	26,209	426,082	16·2	10,49,408	2 7 5	40 0 8	282,852	10·8	143,230	5·
2nd or middling.	770	166,520	216	3,94,961	2 5 1	5!5 12 0	132,515	172	34,005	44·
3rd or large,	196	304,570	1,554	7,02,974	2 4 11	3,587 0 0	276,867	1,412	27,703	142·
Total ...	27,175	897,172	33	21,47,343	2 6 3	79 0 3	692,234	25·4	204,938	7·6

These statistics show that the district is held either by very large or very small proprietors. The first class in the above table holds 47·5 per cent. of the entire cultivated area, the second class holds 18·5 per cent., and the third class has 34 per cent. Each proprietor cultivates a portion of his share as his seer or home-farm, and leases out the remainder to tenants. The average amount retained by each class of proprietor will be the difference between columns 9 and 4, and the profits will be represented by the difference between the rental and the revenue of the plots leased *plus* the net profits of the home-farm. Taking with Mr. Smith the first class or petty proprietors, the area of the portions leased to tenants amounts to 10·8 acres, of which the land-revenue is Rs. 26-11-2, and the rental therefore paid by tenants will be Rs. 53-6·4. As shown elsewhere (page 377), Mr. Smith estimates the produce of the land as worth, on an average, Rs. 25-12-3 per acre, and therefore the produce of the 5·4 acres retained as his home-farm by the petty proprietor will amount to Rs. 139-2-1. From this must be deducted the cost of production apart from rent or revenue, which may fairly be set down at two-fifths of the produce. The results are as follows :—

Expenditure.	Rs.	a.	p.		*Receipts.*	Rs.	a.	p.
Land-revenue of entire holding ...	40	0	8		Rent of tenant's land, ...	53	6	4
Cesses and patwaris' fees ...	6	0	6		Value of produce of home-farm,	139	2	1
Cost of cultivation of home-farm,	55	10	7					
Total Rs. ...	101	11	3		Total ...	192	8	5
					Balance left to proprietor, Rs. ...	90	13	2

This gives a monthly income of Rs. 7-9-1 per month to the petty proprietor, and, as far as one can see, Mr. Smith's figures are incontrovertible. "No doubt the income of the zamíndár is supplemented in various ways. There is the common pasture land of the village on which he can graze his cattle; his wood for fuel or for agricultural implements is grown on his own estate; his hired labour is obtained at a cheap rate, some kinds of labour are given gratis, and custom assigns to him certain dues from his tenants at marriages and other ceremonies. If, too, he is out of the money-lender's hands, he can store his grain and sell it at a higher rate than the harvest price. But, after all, the great majority of the members of the proprietary communities are poor men, who make a rudely comfortable subsistence perhaps, but nothing more." Calculated in the same way, the average income of proprietors of the second class will amount to Rs. 65-3-0 per mensem, or Rs. 782-4-3 per annum; and similarly the income of the third class amounts to Rs. 4,580 per annum, or Rs. 381 per mensem. Mr. Smith explains the difference in the incidence of the revenue on the first and third classes of proprietors as due to the fact that, in Atrauli, the poorest subdivision in the district, "petty proprietors hold a much smaller, and great proprietors a much larger area than in any other portion of the district." Deduct the area and revenue belonging to the two classes in this tahsil, and the rate paid by each for the remainder of the district comes out exactly the same, or Rs. 2-7-11. The villages held by the laborious proprietary communities have not been, "as was often the case in former times, assessed at a higher rate than those of other landholders." On the whole, the portion of the proprietary body included in the second and third classes is fairly well off. Many of the third class possess estates in other districts, or are engaged in trade or service, and their actual profits from the land here is but a small item of their income. Again the increase of population and the subdivision of estates continually tends to drive the proprietor to the money-lender, and to the accumulation of land in the hands of the wealthy capitalists.[1]

The revenue-free (*mudfi*) tenures may be divided into—(1) those which are
Revenue-free tenures.
granted for ever; (2) life grants and groves, the revenue of the latter of which will be assessed on the removal or decay of the trees; and (3) certain lands part of the revenue of which is paid to Government, but is devoted to special purposes and does not form a portion of the general revenue of the State. The permanent alienations may be further subdivided into—(a) whole estates, (b) small plots, and (c) patches of less than ten bighas. The returns of the revenue-free plots and patches of land for the Háthras and Sikandra Rao tahsíls are incomplete, and give only an estimate.

---

[1] The settlement accounts of 1805-06 show that the number of persons admitted to engagements as proprietors was then only 827; these increased to 3,324 in 1808-09, and to 4,612 in 1812-13.

The following statement gives the returns for the whole district under each class :—

Class of grant.	Area in acres.	Estimated land-revenue remitted.	Cesses.	Remarks.
1. In *perpetuity*—		Rs.	Rs.	
(a.)—Entire villages (12),	4,337	6,720	672	
(b.)—Permanent plots ...	2,335	4,500	450	Estimated.
(c.)— Less than ten bíghas,	4,030	10,360	1,036	Ditto.
2a.—Revenue-free for two generations—				
Five villages ...	...	6,000	600	Rs. 550 excess are paid into the treasury.
2b.—Revenue-free for life—				
Entire villages (11) ...	2,668	6,030	603	
Plots and groves ...	4,683	12,274	1,227	
3. Special grants—				
Eleven villages ...	...	7,740	774	Taluka Iglás (see page 447).

Taking these figures, the estimated amount of revenue permanently alienated will be about Rs. 23,000 ; the temporary alienations are about Rs. 24,300, and the Iglás grant, which is really perpetual, amounts to Rs. 7,740, or a total of Rs. 55,040. This gives 2·5 per cent. on the total demand, and only one per cent. of this will eventually revert to the State.

Of the twelve villages held revenue-free in perpetuity, two belong to the

History of these grants.

dargáh of Sháh Jamál (see ALIGARH town) ; Lál Garhi to a Hindú temple near Háthras ; Mominabad and Háshimpur to a temple at Brindaban in Muttra ; three villages to the Derridon family or their representatives (page 449). Bádhesi was given to one Naubat Rái in Akbar's time, and still belongs to his descendants ; and Kheriya Khwajah Budha, Husainpur, and Salímpur were Musalmán grants for religious purposes. The remaining grants in perpetuity are small plots and patches given by the village proprietors either for the support of small shrines and temples, or for the subsistence of Brahmans and fakírs. Few of these have ever been confirmed by the State. At Mr. Thornton's settlement those patches not exceeding ten bighas, found in the possession of members of the priestly clan, were granted to them as such, and those to which the occupants seemed to have no claim were resumed at once, or only granted free of revenue until the next settlement. Of the latter class, Mr. Smith has resumed land assessed now at Rs. 1,823, but the account is incomplete. The five villages granted revenue-free for two generations comprise a portion of the reward given to Raja Tíkam Singh of Mursán for his services in the mutiny. The villages are assessed at Rs. 6,550, and the Raja pays the excess above Rs. 6,000 into the treasury. He also holds nine villages as a life grant, assessed at Rs. 4,190 per annum, which will be paid by his heirs. Two other life villages, Oghipur and Imlahra, were with

Timukhiya, in the Meerut District, granted by the Marhattas to the man who captured Ghulám Kádir on his escape from Meerut. They were originally granted in perpetuity, but owing to the loss of the *sanad*, the Aligarh estates will be resumed on the death of the present grantee, whilst the Meerut village still remains with his representative. The Iglás villages are those of which the revenue is granted partly (one-fourth) to the heirs and assignees of Ganga-dhar Pandit, and partly for the support of the Agra College. At the recent settlement of the district, the holders of resumed revenue-free grants have been recorded as absolute proprietors of their lands.

The following statement shows the distribution of the cultivated area amongst proprietary and non-proprietary cultivators.

Non-proprietary tenures.

Of the entire cultivated area, 29 per cent. is held by cultivators with a right of occupancy, 48 per cent. by tenants-at-will, and 23 per cent. as seer by the proprietors. Of the area cultivated by tenants only, those having a right of occupancy hold 37 per cent., whilst tenants-at-will hold 63 per cent. of the tenant area :—

Statement showing classes of cultivators and areas[1] held by them.

Parganas.	Cultivated by proprietors.			Cultivated by tenants with rights of occupancy.			Cultivated by tenants without a right of occupancy.		
	Number of holdings.	Area.	Average area per holding.	Number of holdings.	Area.	Average area per holding.	Number of holdings.	Area.	Average area per holding.
Atrauli	668	10,847	16·23	2,195	22,511	10·25	4,715	37,369	7·92
Gangiri	348	9,198	26·43	2,730	2,148	7·86	5,150	48,912	9·49
Hasangarh	2,924	24,569	8 4	1,228	8,734	7·11	3,842	35,534	9·24
Goral ...	926	9,184	9 91	913	8,986	9·84	2,354	30,490	12 95
Akrabad ...	706	8,33	11 8	3,175	25,425	8·	1,598	16,096	10.0
Sikandra Ráo	1,255	19,016	15·15	5,144	50,104	9·74	4,008	24,937	6·22
Barauli	28	757	27·	194	2,850	14 69	454	6,596	14·52
Koil	2,098	29,851	14·22	4,166	33,694	8·	5,081	52,507	10·33
Morthal	216	4,680	21·43	·07	6,483	9 85	1,718	12,488	7·29
Tappal ...	2,052	31,605	15·4	1,256	9,587	7·63	3,120	26,974	8·64
Chandaus ...	793	15,039	18·96	560	6 286	11·24	1,351	21,702	16 0
Khair	1,367	20,356	14·89	1,219	12,567	10 3	2,609	42,867	16·43
Mursán	861	7,973	9·26	1,500	12,296	8·19	2,452	18,636	7·6
Háthras	951	13,582	14·28	3,193	35,753	11·1	5,305	58,377	11·0
Total ...	15,193	204,938	13·42	28,380	258,749	9·12	43752	4,33,485	9·9

Mr. Smith writes that " on the whole there seems to be good reason for believing that the area held by tenants with a right of occupancy has not decreased during the last settlement." In the first place those only were recorded then as having a right of

The occupancy-tenant.

[1] The total number of holdings is 87,325, occupying 897,172 acres, and giving an average area of holdings of all classes of 10 27 acres.

occupancy, who had really cultivated for generations in the village, and were of the better castes and classes. Those of menial and inferior castes, though they always held land in a village, never seem to have attained the privilege of a right of occupancy. Act X. of 1859 changed all this ; it recognized no distinctions of caste or class, and put altogether aside the custom of a village if the custom was ruled by any other standard than the mere occupancy of twelve years' duration. It was only probable, therefore, that when that law was passed many tenants would find themselves in possession of occupancy rights which they had never thought of claiming before. The effect of every succeeding year was to increase the number of these tenants. At first neither tenants nor zamíndárs perfectly understood their position ; as years went on and the law became gradually better known, a struggle arose between the two classes, and this struggle has been continuously going on. Where the zamíndár is very powerful and at the same time inclined to be exacting, the tenant goes to the wall, and very few *maurúsi* cultivators are now found on the large estates held by the Nau-Muslim talukadárs of Koil and Morthal, by the Pathán zamíndárs of Atrauli, or by the wealthier Rajpút proprietors of Sikandra and Akrabad. But on the other hand, where the zamíndár is easy going, like the Raja of Mursán, or comparatively weak, like the general run of smaller proprietors, the cultivator will fight for his rights, and has little difficulty in establishing them. The cases instituted in the Settlement Courts with the object of obtaining a record of *maurúsi* rights have been very numerous. On the whole I am inclined to think that the cultivator has got the best of the battle ; and that if the records of last settlement survived, it would be found that the *maurúsi* area had increased. But it is doubtful if it will increase much further. The zamíndárs are now fully alive to the disadvantages of the position, as far as they themselves are concerned, and few tenants will henceforth ever be allowed to hold beyond the limit of eleven years, within which term the power of dispossession remains with the proprietor." Many artifices were resorted to in order to induce the old cultivators to resign their rights at the time of settlement, but fortunately the recording officer thought it necessary to note only facts, and so disappointed many who then wished to get rid, once and for ever of " the 12 years' man." The new revenue laws, if judiciously worked, will smooth over much of the present difficulty, for the Settlement Officer will now have power to increase the rents of the cultivators *pari passu* with the increase of the land-revenue, and the doubtful litigation which up to the present time inevitably ensued after each revision of settlement will be avoided. The custom of subdividing the land under the operation of the laws of inheritance has lessened the average extent per holding, and will continue to work in this direction. Occupancy rights are frequently the subject of temporary transfer, but permanent transfers seem to be unknown in this district.

The bulk of the agricultural classes in this district are drawn from the
Brahman, Ját, Chamár, Rajpút, Ahír, and Lodha castes,
more especially from the three first mentioned. Of
these the Játs and Chamárs are the best cultivators. The Játs unite with untiring diligence an intelligent‧discrimination as to rotation of crops, and the
treatment and selection of soils, and are almost alone in the practice of regularly and constantly employing their women in field labour. The Chamárs
are laborious and painstaking, but are less enterprising cultivators. The mass
of the agricultural classes are fairly well-to-do, but while some are substantial
farmers with a good stock of cattle and a reserve for a bad season, many still
discount the harvest at the door of the village money-lender, and rely upon his
advances for food and seed alike. The average extent per holding is 9·12
acres for cultivators with a right of occupancy and 9·9 acres for tenants-at-will.
Perhaps 10, 30, and 50 acres, respectively, would fairly represent the local
idea of a small, a middle-sized, and a large holding. Many holdings, however, sink
below ten acres, and many rise above fifty acres. With regard to the question
as to whether a five-acre holding is as good as eight rupees cash wages a month
the Assistant Settlement Officer writes:—" The answer to the question depends
upon the quality of the soil and the character of the cultivator. As a rule five
acres in this district do not represent a value equal to eight rupees cash wages.
Usually a holding consists of a small portion of the best and a large portion of
inferior land. Now eight rupees a month would represent a clear profit of eleven
rupees per standard bígha, which is an exceptionally high figure here. I should
say that the produce of an ordinary five-acre holding is equivalent‧to an income of five rupees a month." Curiously enough the average area per holding
(10·27 acres) nearly coincides with the average area under tillage per plough
(11 acres), and accords pretty closely with the popular estimate of fifty village
bíghas per plough. The total number of ploughs is over 70,000, and each
requires two bullocks. Ploughs with only one bullock are exceedingly rare,
and if a cultivator cannot afford two bullocks, he falls back on the chance of a
loan, or works the land with his own hand. The following statement shows
the number of ploughs in each tahsíl and the average cultivated area in acres
to each plough :—

Tahsíl.		Ploughs.	Area.	Tahsíl.		Ploughs.	Area.
Sikandra Rao	...	14,202	10·0	Iglás	...	9,454	12·4
Khair	...	14,183	13·0	Koil	...	13,105	11·0
Háthras	...	13,155	11·4	Atrauli	...	13,325	11·0

Throughout the district cash rents are the rule. In a few estates *batái*
or division of the produce, and *zabti* or fixed cash rates
according to the crop, still prevail. In the latter case,
should the crop fail, a proportional deduction is allowed in the rent demanded.
As a rule, the tenant holds on a written lease for a long or a short term, as the
case may be: often the agreement is a verbal one, generally made at the commencement of the agricultural year, or a particular rent is sanctioned by the
usage of years, and in some cases of generations. *Batái* is dying out, as with
the advance of cultivation the tenant finds it more his interest to have a fixed
sum to pay, and the practice now only obtains where, from the character of the
soil and the absence of irrigation, the outturn is uncertain and the cultivation
is a mere matter of speculation. It is now wholly confined to the khádir
lands and the high sandy soil above the two great rivers in the Khair and
Atrauli tahsíls. In Atrauli the system chiefly prevails in the sandy estates of
the Dátauli and Bhamauri Náh talukas, which are cultivated by Ahars and
Aheriyas, and there is good reason to believe that the system suits these tracts.
In Khair the system is dying out. As a rule, the standard of division is half to
the landowner and half to the tenant; and only in a few cases, chiefly
the headmen of the Atrauli villages, does the landowner restrict himself to two-
fifths of the produce. Altogether there were 252 cases of commutation of
produce rents to cash rents from 1866 to 1873, of which 132 cases and 7,824
acres belong to Atrauli, 96 cases and 930 acres to Khair, and 24 cases and
511 acres to Koil. The rent-rate fixed averages Rs. 2-15-7 per acre, "whilst
the general rent-rate of the whole district is Rs. 4-12-6, or a rate sixty per
cent. higher than that found possible to apply to *batái* lands." Rates of rent
vary to same extent throughout the district, but the following details give the
average rates found at settlement:—

Tahsíl.	Bára.		Manjha.		Outlying lands.		
	Irrigated.	Dry.	Irrigated.	Dry.	Irrigated.	1st class dry.	2nd class dry.
	Rs. a. p.	Rs. a. p.	Rs. a. p.	Rs. a. p.	Rs. a. p.	Rs. a. p.	Rs. a. p.
Sikandra Rao ...	12 0 0	5 4 0	8 12 0	3 8 0	4 12 0	2 12 0	1 12 0
Atrauli ...	12 4 8	5 4 3	8 12 6	3 8 2	4 6 3	2 10 2	1 10 4
Koil ...	11 8 0	5 4 0	8 4 0	3 8 0	4 9 0	2 12 0	1 12 0
Iglás ...	11 6 0	5 4 0	8 4 0	3 8 0	4 12 0	2 12 0	1 12 0
Parganah.							
Khair ...	12 0 0	5 4 0	8 12 0	3 8 0	4 12 0	3 0 0	2 0 0
Chandaus ...	12 0 0	5 4 0	8 12 0	3 8 0	4 12 0	3 0 0	2 0 0
Tappal. ...	11 8 0	5 4 0	8 4 0	3 8 0	4 9 0	3 0 0	2 0 0
Háthras ...	11 8 0	5 4 0	8 8 0	3 8 0	5 0 0	3 0 0	2 0 0
Mursán ...	11 0 0	5 4 0	8 0 0	3 8 0	4 9 0	2 12 0	1 12 0
						2 12 0	1 12 0

Increased prices, competition for land, and increased population have all

Enhancement.

tended to raise the rent-rates beyond those prevalent at the last settlement. The settlement records show that the percentage of rise during the settlement operations varies from 17 to 38, the average for the whole district being about 31 per cent. From 1866 to the middle of 1873, 2,359 enhancement cases were decided by the settlement courts, involving an extent of 52,769 acres, or one-sixteenth of the entire cultivated area. The former rent-rate of this tract was Rs. 1,91,303, and the rental now fixed is Rs. 2,50,699 ; the old rate was Rs. 3-10-0 per acre, and the new rate is Rs. 4-12-0, giving a rise of 31 per cent. The greatest number of enhancement cases has been decided in tahsíl Sikandra Rao, which has so largely benefited of late years by canal irrigation ; next in order come the Koil, Iglás, Háthras, Atrauli, and Khair tahsíls.

Tahsíl.	No. of cases.	Area in acres.	Former rental.	Former rent-rate.	Amount enhanced.	New rental.	New rent-rate.	Per-centage of rise.
			Rs.	Rs. a. p.	Rs.	Rs.	Rs. a. p.	
Atrauli ...	177	5,803	20,685	3 9 0	7,930	28,615	4 12 8	38
Iglás ...	193	9,214	35,124	3 12 11	10,024	45,148	4 3 9	28
Sikandra Rao ...	889	16,692	56,760	3 12 9	18,522	75,282	4 7 11	32
Koil ...	517	10,476	36,853	3 8 3	13,449	50,303	4 12 6	36
Khair ...	168	4,566	15,154	3 5 1	4,816	19,970	4 6 8½	31
Háthras ...	415	6,018	26,726	4 7 0	4,656	31,382	5 3 1½	17
Total ...	2,359	52,769	1,91,303	3 10 0	59,396	2,50,700	4 12 0	31

Regarding these enhancement suits, it would at first sight appear that they

There were really few enhancement suits.

have been very few when the area and the increase of revenue at assessment is considered: " But," writes Mr. Smith, " it must be remembered, in the first place, that these suits are only instituted against tenants with a right of occupancy, and that the total area held by this class of tenants in this district is only 258,749 acres, so that the amount of land hitherto affected by suits is rather more than one-fifth of the full amount to which suits are applicable, and meanwhile more cases are being instituted. In the next place the characteristics of the Aligarh tenures are on the whole unfavourable to the institution of an excessive number of cases. Talukadárs and zamíndárs owning large collections of villages abound on the one hand, and, on the other, proprietary brotherhoods, cultivating their own land, are very numerous. With neither class are rent suits in favour. The tenants of the more powerful proprietors, whether tenants with a right of occupancy or tenants-at-will, find it to their interest to meet the views of their zamíndárs, and when an enhancement of revenue has taken place are generally willing to pay an enhanced rent. In the village communities, the cultivators are either of the same brotherhood, or are, at all events, on terms of amity and almost equality with the proprietary body. The new revenue is provided for by an increased rate on the holdings of the members of the community ; while each cultivator, not a proprietor, readily acknowledges the justice of a similarly increased rent on his own patch of land. In neither cases are the courts needed or sought. It is in villages held by what may be called the middle class of proprietors, those who own one or two villages only, or even less, and have little wealth or hereditary influence, or in estates where new purchasers have crept in, that enhancement cases chiefly arise. Proprietors of these classes are compelled to have recourse to the courts for assistance in raising rents. But nevertheless, at the time of settlement, the cultivators as a body admit their liability to an enhanced demand, when they see that a corresponding increase is exacted by the State from the zamíndárs, and all proprietors alike, if they use tact and show a wish to conciliate, can at such a time get their tenants to agree to rents which on other occasions they would in vain demand ; and hence it is that in Aligarh a very large number of rents have been settled by mutual agreement."

As shown elsewhere the increase in cultivation during the past settlement General increase of rental throughout. has been 7 per cent., and the increase in irrigation has been 28 per cent. Taking Rs. 4-4-0 per acre as the irrigated rent-rate of the past settlement, and Re. 1-9-0 as the unirrigated rent-rate, and applying these rates to the former areas, there results a rental for the whole district of Rs. 26,72,014. The rental actually assumed in 1838 was Rs. 26,71,273. Applying the same rates to the increased cultivated and irrigated areas of the present settlement, the result is a rental of Rs. 31,54,947, or an increase of 18 per cent. on the application of the old rates. The rate of this rental will be Rs. 3-8-1 per acre, and the former rent-rate was Rs. 3-2-11 per acre. " If the above assumption," writes Mr. Smith, " approximate to correctness, a rise of 10 per cent. in the general rent-rate will represent the combined effects of an increase of 7 per cent. in cultivation and 28 per cent. in irrigation. This is as much as could be expected, when it is considered that the proportion of irrigation to cultivation has only altered by 12·3 per cent., and that the increase in cultivation itself, though small, has a tendency at least to lower the general rate. If not exactly the truth, this calculation is near enough for all practical purposes."

Taking the figures given above and the rentals recorded in the village papers, it will be seen that rents have actually risen. The village papers give the rents which purport to be actually paid by cultivators, both hereditary and tenants-at-will, as well as the nominal rents entered for the land held as seer by proprietors. Taking the seer land at non-occupancy rates, being those at which it would be leased if not cultivated by the proprietors, the total recorded rental

of the district is found to be Rs. 36,53,016, or 36·7 per cent. above the rental
of 1838. The old rent-rate of 1838 was Rs. 3-2-11 per acre, and the new
rental according to the village papers amounts to Rs. 4-0-11 per acre, giving a
rise of 27 per cent. in the rent-rate. But these records are imperfect if taken
as they stand. In many cases the rents are purposely under-stated, and in others,
though correctly given, they are much below the rents paid elsewhere for similar
land. Still materials are forthcoming for the ascertainment of the true rental ;
rent suits, the examination of the accounts of farmed villages, and personal
enquiry were all brought in as aids to the correction of the rental as recorded
in the village papers, and the result was a rental of Rs. 42,94,685 and a rent-
rate of Rs. 4-12-6 per acre, which allows for purposely under-stated rent-rolls,
under-rented villages, and for future enhancement where needed. Thus ascertained facts show that the effect of the rise in prices and the increase in population, cultivation, irrigation, means of communication, &c., has been an increase
in the rental of about 50 per cent., and the tendency is still towards a rise.
" On the whole there can be very little doubt that any approximation to the
true idea of rent is only beginning to be grasped by the zamíndár, and that until
of late years, rents have meant little more than a slight arbitrary increase on the
revenue-rates."

As might be expected, one of the results of peace was the enhanced value

Transfers before 1838.

of land, and with it the possibility of making the land
a security for the advancement of money. The first
sale for arrears of revenue took place in June, 1810, for the balances of 1216
and 1217 *fasli*, and was quickly followed by others, so that during 1810-11,
45 estates, paying an aggregate revenue of Rs. 27,868, were put up for auction
for arrears amounting to Rs. 11,253, and were sold for Rs. 2,359. Thirty-
four of these were bought in by Government for nominal prices.[1] This went
on from bad to worse, so that hundreds of estates were put up for sale, but found
few purchasers. Not so much harm as might have been expected was done by
this multiplicity of sales. Few estates were actually sold, and the remainder
were re-settled, in many cases with the original zamíndárs, at reduced assessments. In other cases, when they were temporarily re-settled with farmers,
they were subsequently restored to the real proprietors on their paying up the
balances for which they had been sold. In fact the zamíndárs seem to have
regarded the sale regulation as a kind of Insolvent Act, which released them
from their embarrassments, and gave them a fresh lease of their villages on
more favourable terms. Another device which they occasionally resorted to
was the throwing up of their engagements, in hopes of thereby compelling the
revenue authorities to lower the demand. This practice became so general
that the Board of Commissioners found it advisable to issue a circular[2] in

---

[1] Hutchinson, p. 39.   [2] 17th February, 1817.

1817, directing that in cases where zamíndárs gave in their resignation in hopes of the assessment being lowered, the Collectors should make it a rule to settle with the farmer, and not to re-admit the zamíndárs on a lower assessment.

Year.				Number of estates.	Land-revenue.	Arrears.	Sale proceeds.	Number purchased by Government.
					Rs.			
1810-11	...	...	...	45	27,868	11,253	2,359	34
1812-13	...	...	...	59	53,639	18,097	3,558	24
1813-14	...	...	...	122	1,41,891	1,35,301	7,310	82

Mr. Stirling, writing in 1831, says that "almost all the villages in this district have been mortgaged, farmed, sold, or given over to creditors." Mr. Smith, writing in 1874, qualifies this statement and says that the alienations which took place previous to last settlement cannot be compared in extent with those which occurred subsequent to 1833. The changes were mostly in individual villages, and nothing approaching a general transfer of ownership took place. It was only when rights were established and consolidated by the elaborate proceedings of the last settlement that radical changes began. As has been seen, land formerly had no marketable value and purchasers could not be found. The system of requiring security for advances, the handing over the village communities to the tender mercies of the talukadár, the system of rewarding the sub-collectors of revenue by a commission, the sudden changes made by the conferment of a proprietary right on persons little accustomed to understand its responsibilities, and the withdrawal of the capital invested in indigo and the company's trade all prepared the way for the accrual of indebtedness which led to the introduction of capitalists and other speculators that is characteristic of the period between 1838 and 1868.

Leaving out the transfers by confiscation on account of rebellion, the alien-
Transfers of landed property from 1839 to 1868. ations by revenue process[1] from 1839 to 1868 have amounted to 144,452 acres, or 11·9 per cent. of the total area (1,213,779 acres), and 870,717 acres, have been alienated by private or forced sale, or 71·7 per cent. of the total area. If sales of all kinds are reckoned as permanent transfers, while revenue farms and private mortgages are considered as temporary alienations only, then 608,650 acres, or 50 per cent., have been permanently, and 406,519 acres, or 33 per cent. of the total area, have been temporarily transferred during the short period of thirty years. Though

[1] From Mr. W. H. Smith's Report, 1875.

these figures represent the total area alienated, and where, as it often happened, a village was transferred more than once, the area has been calculated as many times, the transfers are abnormal and exceed those recorded in any other district in this division. Mr. Smith divides the period of thirty years into three decades and gives the following table of transfers :—

Decade.	Transfers by revenue process.[1]	Transfer by other processes.	Total.
1st (1839 to 1848)	95,285	316,809	412,091
2nd (1849 to 1858)	19,779	248,823	268,602
3rd (1859 to 1868)	19,488	305,085	324,573
Total ...	134,552	870,717	1,005,269

In explanation of this table he writes :—" From this table it will be seen that nearly eight per cent. of the total area was transferred by revenue process during the first decade, and of the whole area transferred nearly 41 per cent. changed hands during the first ten years. In the second ten years transfers of all kinds were fewer than in either the previous or succeeding decades ; land was increasing in value, rents were beginning to rise, and new owners had to a large extent taken the place of the former defaulters. But this period was one of low prices, and the effects seem to have been felt in the succeeding decade, when transfers again became more numerous. The reign of high prices did not set in until those proprietors who were embarrassed had lost the opportunity of recovering themselves. From the excess of mortgages over other modes of transfer in the second decade, and that of private sales in the third, it would seem that they first had recourse to a temporary alienation which probably only too often ended in a permanent loss of property. Mortgage in this country mostly involves the surrender of possession to the mortgagees, and generally ends in an absolute sale, when the mortgagor finds himself unable to meet his engagements. With all these transfers, therefore, it follows that the proprietors who were holding land at last settlement have to a large extent been displaced by strangers. In Atrauli, Játs and Rajpúts together have lost more than half their former possessions ; in Murthal the Chauháns have yielded to the Nau-Muslim Badgújars, who with their old religion seem to have given up the thriftless tendencies of their caste ; in Khair, Játs, Nau-Muslims and Chauháns have all suffered in various degrees; in Tappal the Chauháns have been almost obliterated from the list of zamíndárs ; in Háthras and Mursán few of the old clans of Rajpúts survive, and even in Sikandra Rao and Akrabad there have been great changes of ownership. In Iglás the Játs have offered a tough resistance, but with moderate success.

---

[1] Except Koil and Atrauli.

In more exact terms the kanungo's returns show that in Atrauli and Gangiri together about 50 per cent. of the old proprietors have been replaced by others , in Iglás 52½ per cent. of the area has changed hands; in Khair 47 per cent. of the land is no longer held by the old zamíndárs, 38 per cent. having been permanently, and 9 per cent. temporarily alienated ; in Sikandra 30 per cent. has gone for ever, while 25 per cent. is in mortgage and farm, and in Háthras 54¼ per cent. of the proprietary interests have suffered the former, 11½ per cent. the latter fate "

The following statement shows the relative gains and losses of the various

Relative gains and losses of the various castes.

castes in land paying revenue to Government, giving the areas held by each caste at the commencement of the past settlement and at the beginning of the present settlement :—

Caste.	Area held at former settlement.	Present area.	Caste.	Area held at former settlement.	Present area.
	Acres.	Acres.		Acres.	Acres.
Rajpút	466,921	346,648	Lodha	16,180	14,918
Ját	303,055	284,328	Ahír	8,728	4,743
Brahman	111,047	113,576	European ...	13,585	23,335
Kayath	30,927	38,381	Nau-Muslim ...	47,822	72,218
Baniya	21,699	115,450	Mughal	7,873	4,368
Khatri	6,603	11,095	Pathán	125,261	116,148
Gosháin	9,581	1,821	Shaikh	11,970	19,972
Gararíya	2,294	322	Fakír	382	396
Bohra	...	4,019	Mewati	2,604	456
Bhát	...	405	Sayyid	25,879	29,857
Sonár	...	63	Other castes ...	1,373	...
Saraugi	...	215			
			Total ...	1,213,799	1,242,749

This statement does not include 29 estates held free of revenue and comprising 9,998 acres, nor does it give the fate of individual proprietors. Játs have bought from Játs, Brahmans from Brahmans, and the Jádon Rajpút of Awa Mísa has laid hold of the patrimony of the Porach Rajpúts of Daryapur and Husain, but these changes are not shown. Játs, Rajpúts, and Brahmans still hold more than one-half the whole district, and though there have been many changes amongst individuals, the relative position of the castes in the proprietary body remains pretty much as it was. At the last settlement Khatris, Baniyas, Bohras, and Europeans, who may fairly be said to represent the speculators in land, held 41,887 acres, or only 3·4 per cent.; they now hold 153,899 acres, or 12·3 per cent. The increase is most marked in the case of the Baniyas. Besides the purely speculative classes, the Nau-Muslim Badgújars, Patháns, Kayaths, and notably the Awa Mísa family, have largely increased their possessions by purchase. Altogether the old Ját and Rajpút proprietary body has been to a large extent displaced, and Mr. Smith attributes much of this to the severity of the past settlement. Though Mr. Thornton did not over-estimate the assets, yet the proportion of the assets taken by him was too high, and averaged 69 per cent. of the assets of the district. Then, in addition to this, the various cesses for roads, post-office, schools, patwáris and watchmen were put on, so that the proprietor seldom had more than 26 per cent. of the assets. In the talukadári estates the proprietor had, in addition, to pay the *malikána* allowance of the talukadár. "Had there been a large margin of culturable waste, the zamíndárs would probably have been able to hold out; but this was not the case. The increase in cultivation, during the 30 years, has been only 7 per cent., and there is now in most tahsíls little enough left even for the pasturage of cattle. The cultivated area at the present time is 88 per cent. of the culturable; while, therefore, prices and rents were low, as they remained for many years after last revision, it was difficult for all and impossible for some proprietors to keep out of debt. Many were ruined at once, others held on for years by means of mortgages and loans, which only increased their liabilities, until at last they were obliged to succumb. Those who have survived the struggle are prosperous enough, and the new proprietors are to a large extent men of wealth and position; but the history of this settlement supplies strong grounds for a conviction that the demand of 69 or 70 per cent. of the assets as the share of the State, if assessed with care and rigidly collected, is far too high to be imposed with safety." The following table gives the official return of transfers from 1868-69 to 1872-73 :—

Year.	UNDER ORDERS OF COURT.				BY PRIVATE TRANSFER.				
	Sale.		Number of other cases.	Total number of cases.	Sale.		Succession, number of cases.	Mortgage, &c., number of cases.	Total number of cases.
	Number of cases.	Aggregate revenue of property transferred.			Number of cases.	Aggregate revenue of property transferred.			
1868-69	90	4,243	77	167	159	4,672	534	255	948
1869-70	87	10,428	47	134	160	8,350	606	253	1,019
1870-71	57	740	39	96	105	3,491	601	189	895
1871-72	119	6,095	4	123	164	18,431	684	474	1,322
1872-73	78	9,907	49	127	131	15,772	622	401	1,154

The following table shows the results of each mode of transfer of each class

Increase in the value of land.
during each decade of the last settlement (1838 to 1868) derived from the settlement records :—

Mode of transfer.		Area transferred in acres.	Land-revenue in rupees.	Price in rupees.	Price per acre in rupees.			Year's purchase.
1839 48.								
Private sale	...	50,997	71,946	3,79,100	7	6	11	52
Mortgage	...	104,531	1,52,764	4,24,887	4	1	0	27
Public sale	...	76,047	1,14,861	4,79,296	6	4	10	41
Total	...	231,575	3,39,571	12,83,233	5	8	8	37
1849-58.								
Private sale	...	68,597	1,04,057	6,51,998	9	8	0	62
Mortgage	...	75,347	1,10,807	5,84,842	7	12	2	52
Public sale	...	48,467	76,186	3,40,385	7	0	4	44
Total	...	192,411	2,91,050	15,77,225	8	3	1	54
1859-68.								
Private sale	...	103,194	1,57,815	12,59,661	12	3	3	79
Mortgage	...	88,367	1,43,924	9,81,177	11	1	7	68
Public sale	...	59,514	98,893	4,54,938	7	10	3	46
Total	...	251,075	4,00,632	26,95,776	10	11	9	67

During the second decade the average price shows an increase of 47 per cent. over the prices ruling from 1839 to 1848, whilst the price obtained in the third decade is 93 per cent. above that obtained in the first ten years. It may be noted that the increase obtained at auction sales is very small, and that if this item be eliminated from the account, we find that land changed hands during the first decade at Rs. 5-2-8 per acre, and at 3½ years' purchase of the land-revenue. During the last decade the averages were Rs. 11-11-1 per acre and 7·4 years' purchase—that is, these last ten years exhibit an average increase of 126 per cent. in price and 111 per cent. in the number of years' purchase. The cause of the lower price at auction sales is undoubtedly the dread of future litigation as to the rights or interests purchased, or the fear lest some claimant with a prior lien should spring up. For this reason Mr. Smith considers that private sales and mortgages more correctly show the actual increase in the value of land. "By common consent six or seven per cent. is considered a fair return for investment in land. Suppose, then, a man buys a village assessed now with a revenue of Rs. 1,000. Under existing arrangements the rental in full should be Rs. 2,000. From this must be deducted the land-revenue of Rs. 1,000 ; cesses at ten per cent. of the land-revenue, Rs. 100 ; patwáris' fees at five per cent.

Rs. 50 ; and, as the purchaser is generally a non-resident, Rs. 50 for expenses
of collection. His full profits will therefore be Rs. 800. Assuming this sum
to represent six or seven per cent. on the outlay, the buyer will have had to pay
from Rs. 11,400 to Rs. 13,300 for the estate ; in other words, from about 11½ to
13 years' purchase of the land-revenue. Special reasons will, of course, at times
greatly enhance the value of any particular village, but in average cases the
above estimate is not far from the truth. Even during the last decade of the
settlement, in certain parganas where the revenue was not heavy and the assessment pretty evenly distributed, as much as this was paid ; as, for instance, in
Atrauli, where private sales were effected at an average of 11·7 years' purchase,
in Akrabad all kinds of sales at 11 years, in Sikandra private sales again at
11·2. It is quite certain that the value of land has not decreased since 1868."
In the early days of British rule, as shown in the history of the fiscal arrangements, the land had no value and found no purchasers, but as soon as Mr. Thornton's settlement established the various rights in land and placed a limit on the
Government demand, land began to have a marketable value, and as the character and importance of our fiscal laws became better known, this value increased
until now, as shown above, land which sold for Rs. 7-6-11 per acre in the first
decade of the last settlement brought over Rs. 12 in the last decade. And this
increase in the value is progressing, as land is becoming more and more, every
day, a favourite investment of capitalists.

　　　Grain, cotton, indigo, indigo-seed, and to a small extent oil-seeds, form the
principal articles of export. Though much of the grain
is consumed in the district itself, still there usually exists
a considerable surplus which is collected in the larger marts and disposed of by
the grain-dealers. Much of the surplus grain goes down-country and to Rajputána by the Makanpur ghát on the Jumna. A great
proportion of the grain actually consumed in the district
also is first collected in the hands of the grain-dealers, and is then distributed
according to the demand. The principal marts are Háthras, Koil, Atrauli,
Sikandra Rao, and Harduaganj, and the imports of grain into those towns will
be found under the notices of them in the alphabetical arrangement hereafter.
The exports of food-grains by rail from March, 1871, to April, 1872, amounted
to 18,955 maunds. In 1872-73 Aligarh alone exported 92,899 maunds, and
Háthras exported 17,150 maunds. During the same year the canal carried off
6,838 maunds. The trade to Rajputána is entirely by cart and has not been
registered. The imports into Rewari in the Gurgaon District through Palwal
and Dehli from these provinces amounted to Rs. 4,47,962 in 1870-71. Most
of this traffic passes through the Aligarh and Muttra Districts. Allowing three-
quarters of a ser, or one and a half pounds, of grain per diem as the food
allowance per head of the population, we find that 7,344,083 maunds represent

Exports and imports.

Food-grains.

the annual consumption of food-grains. In a former page the estimate of the annual production of food grains is set down at 9,367,652 maunds, and thus a margin amounting to 2,023,569 maunds is left to meet seed, fodder, and export requirements. Mr. Smith estimates one-fourteenth of the total produce, or 669,118 maunds, as the seed requirements, which would leave 1,354,451 maunds of food-grains for cattle, reserves, and exportation. Nearly all the rain-crops, except the pulses, are consumed locally, and the exports are confined to wheat, barley, *bejar*, gram, and the pulses.[1] Cotton cultivation has increased of late years to such an extent as to make it one of the characteristic products of the district. Mr. Smith estimates the yield from the acreage under cotton

Cotton.

at the settlement as 239,430 maunds of 82℔s., or 19,154,000℔s. The population, according to the census of 1872, is 1,073,108 souls, and allowing a local consumption of two pounds per head, there would still be left for exportation 212,603 maunds. In the neighbouring district of Bulandshahr, Kunwar Lachhman Singh estimated three pounds of cleaned cotton as the average consumption per head, of which two pounds consist of country cloth and one pound of foreign cloth. Mr. Smith remarks :—" Nearly every one of the great mass of the Hindús, who constitute 89 per cent. of the total population, buys at least one new *dhoti* of country cloth every year, and a *dhoti* weighs from about 2½ to 3½℔s. The poorer classes, too, wear jackets of the same cloth, and in this part of the country there are few without a large cloth or *dopatta* to cover themselves with, besides. With women's *langas* and *dopattas* taken into consideration, the estimate seems low, even though imported cloth is largely used." From April, 1872, to the end of March, 1873, the export of cotton by rail from Aligarh (63,649 maunds) and Háthras (50,518 maunds) amounted to 114,167 maunds, whilst 45,930 maunds passed down by the canal to Cawnpore. This gives a total of 160,097 maunds without counting the considerable traffic by road and river. The exports by rail during the previous year amounted to 146,441 maunds, and estimating the canal export at the amount registered in 1872-73, the total exports during 1871-72 by canal and rail reach the high figure of 192,000 maunds. The register of traffic passing down the Grand Trunk Road by Bhongaon in the Mainpuri district, from October, 1870, to July, 1871, shows that 253,180 maunds of cotton passed down by cart alone from Aligarh and the north. During the year from 1st April, 1870, to the end of March, 1871, 32,914 maunds of cotton were sent by river from places above Cawnpore on the Ganges to places below Cawnpore, and 1,77,500 maunds of cotton passed through the Jhusi bridge-of-boats at Allahabad. These facts show that the road and river traffic must be consider-

---

[1] The following statement of the canal traffic (in maunds) downwards to Cawnpore during 1272-73, will show its character ; there was no upward traffic :—Wheat, 2,292 ; Arhar, 2,462 ; Múng, 434 ; Oilseeds, 2391 ; Bejar, 1,650 ; Cotton, 45,930 : Salt, 6858 ; Miscellaneous, 2,333.

able, and support Mr. Smith's high estimate of the local produce, which nearly equals the outturn from the whole of Rohilkhand. Cotton presses are to be found in many of the large townships, and several in Koil itself and Háthras.

The following table shows the average price of cleaned cotton per maund in rupees annas and pies for different periods from 1828 to 1873 in this district :—

Rise in price of cotton.

1828-36.	1837-40.	1844-53.	1854-63.	1864-73.	1841-57.	1858-73.
Rs. a. p.	Rs a. p.	Rs. a. p.	Rs. a. p.	Rs. a. p.	Rs. a. p.	Rs. a. p.
6 0 0	6 8 0	7 12 4	11 9 4	14 0 0	7 9 5	14 5 0

The increase in 1854-63 over 1844-53 amounts to 49 per cent., and the last decade (1846-73) shows an increase of 20 per cent. over the previous decade, and 80 per cent. over the first decade (1844-53). The increase in price since the mutiny has been 88 per cent., or very nearly double what it was for seventeen years before, and if we take the Koil rates since 1828, the price has more than doubled. During the last four years the prices have been Rs. 14½, 15, 12¼, and 13½ per maund, and even allowing for the difference between market and harvest rates, this rate is high enough to pay the cultivators well, and to ensure the cultivation of much above the present area devoted to the plant.

The first indigo-planters settled in this district under DeBoigne, the Mar-

History of indigo-plant-ing.

hatta Governor.[1] They were M. Jourdan, who settled at Khair; Mr. Orr at Mendu; Mr. John Thornton at Koil and Máchhua; Mr. Longcroft at Koil and Jaláli, and Messrs. Robertson and Stewart at Maloi and Allahdádpur. The other factories have been established since the British occupation in 1803. M. Jourdan died at Aligarh, and one of the monuments in the grounds of the late Judge's house is believed to mark his grave. Mr. Thornton also died there in 1848. His house was the same as that lately purchased by Mr. Bramly and presented to the Aligarh Dispensary. Mr. Longcroft lived where the garden of Badari Parshád is now situated. Mr. Stewart removed to Calcutta; and was succeeded at Allahdádpur by Mr. Hashman, whilst Mr. Orr went to Lakhwa in Oudh. The Sásni factories were built after the conquest by Mr. R. Carruthers from the ruins of the fort of Sásni; Chotwa was built in 1806 by Mr. George Mercer; Barla and Anúpshahr at the same time, and Mr. George Blunt formed the Háthras factory in 1817. During this time indigo-planting flourished. Mr. W. Morton, formerly a captain in the Bengal Engineers, introduced a system by which the tahsíldárs or sub-collectors of the land-revenue contracted with the European planters

[1] From notes by Mr. W. Connor, Honorary Magistrate, and an anonymous letter in the *Dehli Gazette,* 1874.

for supplying the green indigo plant. Under this system the tahsíldárs received the advances made by the planters and applied them to meet the land-revenue due from the estate. They, moreover, managed the cultivation, and were rewarded by presents both from the factory and from Government. Notwithstanding the general prosperity of indigo speculators, there were many serious obstacles to successful trade during the Marhatta administration; chief amongst these was the number and excessive nature of the tolls on exports. Indigo and cotton, then, as now, the chief exports, used to be shipped at Farukhabad for Calcutta, but had to pay the following duties on their way to the river :—to the Koil authorities from Koil to Jaláli ; to the Sásni Raja from Jaláli to Sikandra Rao ; to the Kachaura Thákur from Sikandra Rao to Eta; to the Eta Raja from Eta to Karáoli, and to the Mainpuri Raja from Karáoli to Bhongaon. These dues were all abolished by the British, and remissions of revenue were allowed in lieu of them to the several petty Rajas. The indigo trade prospered until 1830, when the failure of the Calcutta houses involved the Aligarh factories in their ruin. Many valuable estates and enormous outstanding debts were sold by auction for very inadequate prices in 1834. The purchasers were chiefly hangers-on about the Courts, pleaders and money-lenders who bided their time, and when things began to look better, pressed for the debts that they had purchased, and in this manner acquired, at auction sale, under their own decrees many villages from the people indebted to the factories. Hence the numerous shares and fractions of shares in villages in the hands of the money-lending classes in this district. The indigo trade revived a little in 1862, but soon fell again, and though the area under indigo has increased very much of late years, it has never equalled the area previous to 1830. The withdrawal of the Europeans from the indigo trade was a great loss to the district, and gave its prosperity a shock from which it has hardly yet recovered. Though the native manufacture has increased so much, yet natives look more to quantity than quality, and even now their indigo averages only Rs. 120 per maund, where indigo from a neighbouring factory grown on similar soil, but manufactured under European superintendence, brings Rs. 180 per maund.

The district is now literally studded with factories. The following state-

Area under indigo and outturn.

ment shows that there were 171 factories, producing 3,625 maunds of marketable indigo, in 1873 :—

Tahsíl.		Number of factories.	Produce in maunds.	Tahsíl.		Number of factories.	Produce in maunds.
Koil	...	33	885	Khair	...	18	274
Sikandra	...	91	1,799	Iglás	...	5	157
Atrauli	...	18	162	Háthras	...	6	348

The quantity of indigo annually produced in the Upper Provinces was reckoned by Mr. Stirling in 1830 at an average crop of 20,000 maunds, and this at Rs. 200 per maund made the value of the annual supply of indigo about 40 lakhs of rupees. The effect of the abstraction of this sum from the general commerce of the country must have been immense, for it did not find investment in other channels; it was a sort of foreign capital which nourished so long as it lasted, but did not take root in the country. We have some means of testing the local estimate of produce. The imports of indigo into Riwári in 1869-70 was 106 maunds, and in 1870-71 was 273 maunds; more than one-half of this may be credited to Aligarh, or, say, about 150 maunds per annum. Then we have the returns of the Calcutta brokers (W. Moran & Co.), which for the European factories give the following results for eleven years; the out-turn is shown in chests which average about $3\frac{1}{8}$ factory maunds of 74 lbs. 10 oz. 10·666 dr. avoirdupois each. The price is per factory maund, and the minimum and maximum rate of exchange is also given:—

Factory.	1863-64. Exchange, 2*s.* $1\frac{3}{4}$*d.* to 2*s.* $3\frac{1}{4}$*d.*		1864-65, Exchange, 2*s.* 1*d.* to 2*s.* $1\frac{1}{8}$*d.*		1865-66. Exchange, 2*s.* 1*d.* to 2*s.* $1\frac{7}{8}$*d.*		1866-67. Exchange, 1*s.* $11\frac{3}{4}$*d.* to 2*s.* 1*d.*		1867-68. Exchange, 1*s.* $10\frac{1}{2}$*d.* to 1*s.* $11\frac{3}{4}$*d.*		1868-69. Exchange, 1*s.* $11\frac{5}{8}$*d.* to 2*s.* $0\frac{1}{4}$*d.*	
	Chests.	Price per maund.	Chests.	Price per maund.	Chests.	Price per maund.	Chests.	Price per maund.	Chests.	Price per maund.	Chests.	Price per maund.
		Rs. a.		Rs. a.		Rs. a.		Rs. a.		Rs. a.		Rs. a.
Bela ...	143	144 12	209	158 12	276	168 12	262	161 6	192	210 3	125	225 10
Háthras ...	33	136 0	24	164 8	26	173 0	19	156 0	33	208 14	27	226 8
N.-W. Indigo Association,	36	118 8	136	125 6	110	163 0	105	150 2	59	20c 8	28	226 8
Total Chests	212	...	369	...	411	...	386	...	184	...	160	...

Factory.	1869-70. Exchange, 1*s.* $11\frac{1}{8}$*d.* to 2*s.* $0\frac{1}{16}$*d.*		1870-71. Exchange, 1*s.* $10\frac{7}{8}$*d.* to 1*s.* $11\frac{1}{8}$*d.*		1871-72. Exchange, 1*s.* $11\frac{5}{8}$*d.* to 2*s.* $0\frac{1}{16}$*d.*		1872-73. Exchange, 1*s.* $11\frac{3}{8}$*d.* to 1*s.* $11\frac{5}{8}$*d.*		Decennial average.	1873-74.	
	Chests.	Price per maund.	Chests.	Price per maund.	Chests.	Price per maund.	Chests.	Price per maund.		Chests.	Price per maund.
		Rs. a.		Rs. a.		Rs. a.		Rs. a.	Rs. a.		Rs. a.
Bela ...	149	226 1	199	192 14	163	258 8	146	172 12	192 0	186	184 14
Háthras ...	43	210 12	43	184 4	43	238 6	44	122 6	178 7	33	191 6
N.-W. Indigo Association,	70	218 5	44	180 12	25	229 12	29	140 10	175 1	25	141 4
Total Chests,	262	...	286	...	251	...	219	...	...	244	...

It is not so easy to give the outturn from the native factories. The accounts of the brokers show the native manufacture of the Duáb and Rohilkhand under one head as follows (in factory maunds) :—

Year.	1863.	1864.	1865.	1866.	1867.	1868	1869.	1870.	1871.	1872.
Outturn ...	1,781	3,983	4,574	4,716	10,142	9,995	23,376	15,026	13,317	11,000

It will be seen from this that there has been an extraordinary advance in cultivation by natives during the last ten years, and examining all the data before us, there is much reason to believe that the local estimate is far under the real outturn. Taking the area under indigo, and allowing 42 maunds of green plant per acre and 325 maunds of the green plant to one maund of manufactured indigo, the outturn should show 3,749 maunds of indigo. This too, though it has been proved that the area under indigo has been considerably understated in the settlement returns. Tahsil Atrauli shows only 162 maunds, whilst the Barla concern alone, for the same year, turned out 351 maunds, or more than double the estimate given for the whole tahsíl.

The local prices for the green plant at the Barla concern for a series of years, both for *badni* (or advance terms) and *khush kharíd* (or

Prices of indigo plant.

ready market prices) in rupees per 100 maunds has been as follows :—

From	Advance.	Cash price.	From	Advance.	Cash price.	For	Advance.	Cash price.	For	Advance.	Cash price.
1837-56,	16—19	21—24	1859-65,	19—23	23	1870...	20—24	26—30	1872...	20—28	30
1857-56,	20	23	1866-69,	20—24	26—28	1871...	20—26	26—30	1873...	20—28	30

" *Badni* is an arrangement for the supply of plant to be furnished at a fixed price at the time of manufacture, on consideration of an advance of money at the time of the arrangement; *khush kharíd* is plant sold at the time of manufacture by the cultivator who has planted it on speculation. Taking the highest prices paid, we find that the price has risen for *badni* plant from Rs. 19 per 100 maunds in 1837 to Rs. 28 in 1873, or 47 per cent., and for *khush kharíd* from Rs. 24 to 30, or 25 per cent. This rise in the price of indigo plant especially illustrates the rise in the rentable value of land, for though the price of plant has considerably increased and the increased price in *badni* operations has been maintained this year, yet last year was conspicuous for an enormous fall in the price of manufactured indigo, and it was not expected that it would be much higher when the sales took place this cold weather (1873). Whether the manufacturer, erroneously called the planter in this district, gains or loses, the cultivator gets a price for plant, which enables him to pay a higher rent than was exacted from him in past years." The Calcutta prices for the manufactured dye have been given on a previous page. As a rule, the Duáb indigo is inferior to that of the Benares Division, whilst the latter is inferior to the Bengal and Tirhút plant. Prices during 1872-73 for *gand* and low native indigo ruled from Rs. 75 to Rs. 105 per maund: for ordinary and middling plant quality (European and native) Rs. 115 to Rs. 150, and for good quality Rs. 180 to Rs. 200. A few European factories turn out indigo of very superior quality, and some few lots of these particular marks sold as high as Rs. 220 to Rs. 230, and one lot as high as Rs. 247-8-0. Prices during 1872-73 ruled from Rs. 85 to Rs. 100 per maund below those of the previous year. A considerable amount of indigo seed is sent to Bengal, but as most of this traffic passes by boat down the Ganges, there are no accurate returns in existence for judging of its real importance.

Oil-seeds were exported in 1871-72 by rail to the amount of Rs. 61,145

Oil-seeds.

maunds, and in 1872-73 there were 54,480 maunds sent out of the district by rail and 2,391 maunds by the canal. This trade centres in Háthras and Koil.

In 1856 there were 37 saltpetre manufactories in the district, producing

Saltpetre.

about 50,000 maunds per annum. In 1872-73 the outturn was only 25,000 maunds, but the number of refineries has increased from two in 1856 to sixteen in 1873, with an outturn of 10,190 maunds of refined saltpetre, valued at Rs. 6 per maund, or Rs. 61,140. Crude saltpetre is valued at Rs. 3-6-0 per maund, so that the entire value of this manufacture, all of which is exported, is nearly a lakh and a half of rupees. The returns of the five municipalities in the district show the imports very fairly. They consist of sugar, rice, European cloth goods, spices, metals, tobacco, rice, timber, bambus, and pedlar's wares generally. The details there given show the extent of the external trade of the district and the importance of Háthras as a distributing centre of commerce for this and the surrounding districts. The line of railway under construction from Háthras to Muttra and from the East Indian Railway to the town of Háthras will still further raise its position as one of the most flourishing marts of the upper Duáb; and if to these-lines be added the projected line from Háthras by Kásganj to the Ganges, Aligarh will be better off in the way of communication by road, rail, canal and river than many counties in England.

The following table shows the goods and passenger traffic on the East Indian Railway for one year, and is sufficient to exhibit the relative importance of each station :—

1871.	HATHRAS.			PALI.			ALIGARH.			SOMNA.		
	Goods.		Passengers.	Goods.		Passengers.	Goods.		Passengers.	Goods.		Passengers.
	Inwards.	Outwards.	Outwards.	Inwards.	Outwards.	Outwards.	Inwards.	Outwards.	Outwards.	Inwards.	Outwards.	Outwards.
	Rs.	Rs.	Rs.	Rs.	Rs.	Rs.	Rs.	Rs.	Rs.	Rs.	Rs.	Rs.
January 1871 ...	38,099	20,557	2,589	705	150	100	13,543	10,144	7,283	42	280	667
February ,, ...	33,923	22,568	3,535	719	561	126	10,466	11,930	7,202	75	...	463
March ,, ...	33,141	21,519	3,701	452	330	192	7,249	7,387	8,406	5	...	551
April ,, ...	41,380	25,935	3,336	147	944	130	33,780	5,710	7,330	2	...	342
May ,, ...	29,306	22,085	3,251	372	1,094	146	8,424	3,366	6,823	3	...	443
June ,, ...	19,468	30,728	2,973	340	579	89	29,924	3,349	7,733	15	...	530
July ,, ...	11,817	25,096	2,249	363	690	76	5,525	8,314	5,944	4	39	337
August ,, ...	9,481	11,267	2,617	262	657	101	7,935	4,971	5,641	...	22	434
September ,, ...	17,529	10,122	2,854	164	351	124	5,799	3,084	5,275	5	...	329
October ,, ...	24,055	20,120	2,103	39	245	76	3,870	9,773	5,900	16	845	323
November ,, ...	25,509	40,570	3,227	3	819	124	14,207	31,911	8,711	9	282	354
December ,, ...	29,408	55,848	5,385	152	400	131	32,064	43,714	7,973	24	6	460
Total, ...	3,15,938	3,06,415	37,820	3,718	6,820	1,415	1,73,386	1,43,652	84,221	194	1,474	5,233

Fairs.

From the 17th to the 23rd October the Ramlíla religious fair is held in most of the large towns in the district, and about 12,000 persons come into Koil for its celebration during this period. Similarly at the Musalmán festival of the Muharram large crowds assemble at the principal shrines. In September the Hindús hold a fair at Barhad, near Sikandra Rao, in honour of Raghunáthji, where some 8,000 people assemble, and a small trade in mules, asses, leathern buckets for water and wooden utensils is carried on. The *baráha* fair during the last week in October attracts some small assemblages of people in the large Hindú towns. Sweetmeats, toys, European and country cloths are the staple articles of trade at these fairs, and none of them are large enough to assist, in any way, in the spread of contagious diseases. The only places where special police and sanitary arrangements are necessary are the Koil and Háthras Muharram fairs, the Koil Ramlíla fair, and the Sikandra fair. Of the mere market towns the most important are Sásni, Akrabad, Bijaigarh, Gangíri, Tappal and Khair; but small market towns exist everywhere. Excluding the municipal towns there are 180 markets in the district: 26 in tahsíl Síkandra Rao, 43 in Háthras, 34 in Koil, 31 in Iglás, 23 in Atrauli, and 23 in Khair, or one to every ten villages and to every 5,961 persons. Cattle, grain, country cloth, vegetables, sweetmeats, toys, brass utensils, and the numerous articles of domestic consumption are the chief commodities of trade.

For corals and pearls the weights used are : 12 grains of rice make one

Weights and measures. *rati*, and 24 *ratis* make one *tank*, which is equivalent to 2 dwts. 19 grains Troy. For weighing gold and silver, 8 grains of rice go to the *rati*, 8 *ratis* to the *másha*, and 12 *máshas* to the *tola*, equivalent to 7 dwts. 12 grains Troy. The common bazar weight for goods is 5 *tolas* make one *chhaták*, and 16 *chhatáks* one *ser*, weighing 2 ℔s. 6 oz. Troy ; 40 sers make one maund ; a smaller *ser* starting with three *tolas* to the *chhaták*, and 9 *chhatáks* to the *ser* makes the latter only 1℔. 6ozs. Troy, and the maund of 24 *sers* known as a *kuchcha* maund. In selling unrefined saltpetre a *ser* of 16 *chhatáks*, with 7½ tolas to each, or weighing 3 ℔s. 9 ozs. Troy is used. Indigo and refined saltpetre are weighed with a *ser*, of which the *chhatáks* weigh 6¾ *tolas* each ; the *ser* therefore weighs 3 ℔s. 2 ozs. 5 dwts. The *ser* of 80 *tolas* is now generally used, but in Háthras and Koil metals and spices are sold at the *ser* of 85 *tolas*, called the *ser* of 28 *taka* of Jaipur or Bharatpur pice.[1] The linear measures for cloth gives a yard of 36 inches divided into two *háths* or cubits, each of which contains three *giras*, which are again subdivided into three *angasht* or digits. Masons and carpenters use the miumári yard of 2 feet 9 inches, in which 12 thread breadths make one *tasú* and 24 *tasús* make one yard. The Iláhi *gaz* or yard is generally used for all purposes, including stone-cutter's work, land-measuring, cloth-measuring, &c. It contains 33 British inches, and a bígha of land-measured with this yard is exactly five-eighths of an acre. Two Iláhi yards make one *dand*, and 2,500 *dand* make one *kos*. In the official measurement of land, at the settlement of 1838 the *jaríbi gaz* amounted to 2 feet 7½ inches ; one span or eight digits made one *kuri*, and three links made one *jaríbi gaz* or yard, and eight yards made one *gatta*, and twenty *gatta* made one *jaríb*.

The subdivisions of a bígha are as follows :—20 nanwánsi = 1 kuchwánsi : 20 kachwánsi = 1 biswánsi : 20 biswánsi = 1 biswa : and 20 biswa = 1 bígha. Here the local bígha of the greater part of the district is equivalent to 2,756·25 square yards or 0·5694 of an acre : 1·7560 bíghas make one acre. The standard or Shahjaháni bígha used in a few villages annexed from Bulandshahr is equivalent to 3,025 square yards, or 0·625 of an acre. The Government have adopted the British acre for all purposes. Three kuchcha bíghas are equivalent to one pukka bígha. In the early days of our rule rupees coined at different places were current in the district. The following are the rates established in 1805 for their conversion into Lucknow rupees, then considered the standard rupee :—Farukhabad, Re. 1-8-1 per cent. ; Háthras, Rs. 2-9-4 ; Muttra, Rs. 8-3-7 ; Dig, Rs. 12-1-0, and Brindaban, Rs. 16-7-2.

[1] The *taka* is equal to two Jaipur pice.

Prices.

The following statement shows the prices of the chief agricultural products in this district for the years 1861 to 1870 in *sers* of 80 *tolas* each (one *ser* is equal to 2·057 ℔ avoidupois):—

	1861.	1862.	1863.	1864.	1865.	1866.	1867.	1868.	1869.	1870.	Average of the ten years.
Paddy	28	27⅓	29¾	30	28	22⅓	25	25	16	15¼	24¾
Common rice (husked)	12¾	15½	14⅓	14¼	12	10⅓	13¾	13¾	12¼	11¾	13¼
Best rice (husked)	9	10	9⅓	9½	8	7¾	9	8¾	8	7¾	8⅓
Wheat	16⅓	85¼	26	24¾	18½	19	24	25⅓	16¼	18⅓	22⅓
Barley	20	48	33¾	31	26	26¼	33½	33⅓	22½	28⅓	30¼
Bájra	21¾	36⅓	28¼	27¼	27⅓	25¼	28	27¾	42⅓	22¾	27
Joár	21⅓	35	26½	26	28⅓	27¾	30½	28¼	25¼	26¾	27½
Indian-corn	32	37	35	36	33	31	32	25	23	26	31
Urd	21¼	24	33	18⅓	15⅓	20	26½	22	9	19	21
Mung	19	30⅓	30	15⅓	18	24	23⅓	20	15⅓	24	22¼
Arhar	27⅙	27	32	35	33	32	40	32	35	40	33¼
Moth	30	29	28	26	25	25	25	25	25	25	26⅓
Gram	18¾	32⅓	29⅓	25	23⅓	24¼	26½	26	16	19⅓	24
Lentils	16¾	29¾	36	24⅓	23¼	23	26	25¼	16	20¼	24
Clean cotton	3¼	3¼	1¾	1¾	2⅓	3	3	3	2	2	2¼
Sugar (raw)	8¼	8⅓	10	10¾	11	9¾	8	7	8⅓	9	9
Sugar (refined)...	3¼	3¼	3⅓	4	3¾	3¼	3¼	3¼	3¼	3¼	3⅓
Salt	7	7	6¾	6⅓	6½	6¾	6⅓	6¾	6¾	6¾	6¾
Ghi	1¾	2	2¼	2	2	1¾	1¾	1¾	1¾	1½	1¾
Til seed	12	11	10⅓	15	18	14	14	11	10	12	12⅓
Mustard seed	15⅓	14½	13	18	22¼	24	17⅓	19⅓	15⅓	15⅓	17⅓

In connection with his inquiries into the effects of the rise in prices on the rental of the district, Mr. W. H. Smith gives some valuable notes on the rise of prices in general throughout the district. He shows that there has been a considerable and steady rise in the price of the four standard grains—wheat, barley, *joár*, and *bájra*. The following table is arranged in periods from 1828 to 1870-71, and the percentages of the rise or fall of price in each period as compared with the other are calculated. The *ser* of 80 *tolas* is used throughout:—

Grain.	Averages per rupee during									Percentage of rice or fall of column						
	1828-37.	1838-39 to 1847-48.	1848-49 to 1857-58.	1858-59 to 1867-68.	1838-39 to 1856-57.	1857-58 to 1867-68.	1868-69.	1869-70.	1870-71.	3 on 2.	4 on 2.	4 on 3.	5 on 2.	5 on 3.	5 on 4.	7 on 6.
1.	2.	3.	4.	5.	6.	7.	8.	9.	10.	11.	12.	13.	14.	15.	16.	17.
	S. C.	S. C.	S. C.	S. C.	S. C.	S. C.	S. C.	S. C.	S. C.	Fall.	Fall.	Fall.	Rise.	Rise.	Rise.	Rise.
Wheat ...	33 8	33 15	38 5	24 1	36 2	25 9	14 13	11 15	24 15	1	13	11	39	41	59	41
Barley ...	44 3	47 4	55 8	33 2	49 4	34 2	18 7	18 11	35 4	6	20	15	33	42	67	44
										Rise.						
Joár ...	48 7	41 5	49 8	27 8	46 10	29 15	12 8	18 0	29 3	16	2	17	76	50	80	55
Bájra ...	40 1	33 14	48 7	26 5	43 5	28 4	...	16 0	25 12	18	17	30	52	29	84	53
Total ...	41 9	39 1	47 15	27 12	43 14	29 7	...	...	..	6	13	18	50	40	72	49

From the above it will be seen that from 1827 to 1858 prices ruled very low, and that since the mutiny there has been a great and permanent rise. The first decade of all includes the famine of 1837, and the famine of 1868-69 is left out of the calculation of percentages. The prices of 1870-71, though lower than those of the two preceding years, are higher than the average of the decade preceding the mutiny, and the tendency is still on the side of rise. With the present improved communications this must continue, and can only change in an unusually good season. The prices of cotton and indigo are given under the head of 'trade,' and need not be further noticed here.

The present rates of daily wages of artizans are :—For blacksmiths, carpenters and masons five annas ; labourers as beldárs, 2½ to

Wages.

3 annas ; coolies 2, women 1½, and boys 1¼ annas. The wages of agricultural day labourers are about 2 annas, and in addition half a *ser* of chapátís or unleavened bread, or the same quantity of grain. Weeders receive 3 annas a day and the grass they pick out, which is often worth 2 annas more. The following statement shows the official returns as to wages for six years after the mutiny :—

	1858.		1860.		1862.		1864.		1866.		1874.	
	Near Koil.	In the District.	Near Koil.	In the District.	Near Koil.	In the District.	Near Koil.	In the District.	Near Koil.	In the District.	Near Koil.	In the District.
	a. p.	a. p.	a. p.	a. p.	a. p.	a. p.	a. p.	a. p.	a. p.	a. p.	a. p.	a. p.
Beldárs	2 0	1 6	2 0	1 6	2 0	1 6	2 0	1 6	2 6	1 6	3 0	2 0
Bhistis	2 6	1 0	2 6	1 6	2 6	1 6	2 6	1 6	2 6	1 6	3 0	1 6
Kahárs	4 0	4 0	4 0	4 0	4 0	4 0	4 0	4 0	4 0	4 0	4 0	4 0
Tailors	4 0	3 0	4 0	3 0	4 0	3 0	4 0	3 0	4 0	3 0	4 6	3 0
Washermen	4 0	2 0	4 0	2 0	4 0	2 0	4 0	2 0	4 0	2 0	4 0	2 0
Blacksmiths	3 0	2 6	3 0	2 6	4 0	4 0	3 0	4 0	3 0	4 0	5 0	3 6
Barbers	4 0	2 6	4 0	2 6	4 0	3 6	4 0	2 6	4 0	2 6	4 0	2 6
Carders	2 0	2 0	2 0	2 0	2 0	2 0	2 0	2 0	2 0	2 0	3 0	2 0
Carpenters	3 0	2 0	3 0	2 0	4 0	3 0	4 0	3 0	4 0	3 0	5 0	3 6
Dyers	3 0	2 0	3 0	2 0	4 0	3 0	4 0	3 0	4 0	3 0	4 0	3 0
Goldsmiths	5 0	2 0	5 0	2 6	5 0	2 6	5 0	2 6	5 0	2 6	5 0	3 0
Shoe-makers	4 0	3 0	4 0	3 0	4 0	3 0	4 0	3 0	4 0	3 0	5 0	3 0
Grooms	1 6	1 0	1 6	1 0	2 6	1 6	2 6	1 6	2 6	1 6	3 0	2 0
Masons	4 0	3 0	4 0	3 0	4 0	3 0	4 0	3 0	4 0	3 0	5 0	3 0
Tile-makers	4 0	2 6	4 0	2 6	4 0	2 6	4 0	2 6	4 0	2 6	4 6	3 0
Brick-layers	2 0	1 6	2 0	1 6	3 0	2 0	3 0	2 0	3 0	2 0	4 6	3 0
Bracelet-makers	3 0	1 6	4 0	2 0	4 0	2 0	4 0	2 0	4 0	2 0	4 0	2 0
Painters	4 0	3 0	4 0	3 0	4 0	3 0	4 0	3 0	4 0	3 0	5 0	3 0

The following statement sufficiently explains the revenue and civil expenditure of this district for the years 1860-61 and
1870-71 :—

Revenue and expenditure.

Receipts.	1860-61.	1870-71.	Expenditure.	1860-61.	1870-71.
	Rs.	Rs.		Rs.	Rs.
Land-revenue ...	17,82,993	19,66,550	Revenue charges ...	1,21,286	1,67,560
Profit and loss, Revenue Department.	51,611	...	Judicial charges ...	1,17,765	1,09,220
Stamps ...	79,230	38,594	Police charges ...	1,31,369	78,108
Revenue charges ...	10,625	...	General charges ...	12,857	...
Judicial charges ...	37,168	1,75,320	Stamp charges ...	4,624	7,045
Police ...	1,197	...	Mutiny profit and loss,	72,824	...
Mutiny profit and loss,	12,796	...	Pensions ...	36,550	20,154
Public works ...	2,752	...	Public works ...	13,634	...
Income-tax ...	...	99,319	Profit and loss, Revenue Department.	10,556	...
Miscellaneous ...	...	266	Interest and refund ...	...	13,588
Abkari ...	...	57,043	Excise and cess ...	...	4,935
			Medical and education,	...	33,130
			Miscellaneous ...	...	988
Total ...	19,78 372	23,37,092	Total ...	5,21,465	4,34,728

The revenue from December, 1857, to April, 1858, was Rs. 11,46,715,
and the expenditure during the same period was Rs. 2,39,551.

The actual assessment of the income of the district at six pies in the rupee,
calculated upon profits exceeding Rs. 500, for the pur-
poses of the income-tax of 1870, during 1870-71, was

Income-tax.

Rs. 1,25,467. There were 1,410 incomes between Rs. 500 and Rs. 750 per an-
unm; 354 between Rs. 750 and Rs. 1,000; 316 between Rs. 1,000 and Rs. 1,500;
136 between Rs. 1,500 and Rs. 2,000; 356 between Rs. 2,000 and Rs. 10,000;
44 between Rs. 10,000 and Rs. 100,000, and one above Rs. 1,00,000; total persons assessed were 2,617.

Canal revenue.

The following statement shows the receipts and
charges on account of the canal for a series of years:—

Year.	Collections.	Patwáris' fees.	Establishments.	Contingencies.	Total.	Percentage of payments to collections.
	Rs.	Rs.	Rs.	Rs.	Rs.	Rs.
1866-67	1,82,691	3,481	485	...	3,966	2·11
1867-68	2,04,563	4,166	478	26	4,670	2·288
1868-69	1,98,045	3,797	458	27	4,282	2·162
1869-70	2,72,293	6,489	1,133	...	7,622	2·79
1870-71	2,11,080	7,273	1,183	...	8,456	4·00
1871-72	2,26,388	8,302	563	...	8,865	3·91
1872-73	1,81,272	6,822	...	567	7,388	4·07

Stamps were imposed on petitions and documents from an early period of our
rule. The following table shows the receipts and charges
for eight years previous to the mutiny :—

Stamps.

Year.	Value of stamps sold.	Charges and refunds.	Net receipts	Year.	Value of stamps sold.	Charges and refunds.	Net receipts.
	Rs.	Rs.	Rs.		Rs.	Rs.	Rs.
1845-46 ...	59,867	5,362	54,204	1849-50	64,361	5,161	59,200
1846-47 ...	75,636	5,059	70,577	1850-51	69,980	3,865	·66,095
1847-48 ...	74,770	5,959	68,810	1851-52	69,037	3,543	65,495
1848-49 ...	66,195	5,176	61,019	1852-53	75,106	2,893	72,213

Stamp duties are now collected under the General Stamp Act (XVIII. of
1869) and under the Court Fees Act. The following statement shows the
revenue and charges under this head for eleven years since the mutiny :—

Year.	Adhesive stamps and bundis.	Blue-and-black document stamps.	Court fees.	Duties and penalties realised	Total receipts.	Gross charges.	Net receipts.
	Rs.	Rs.	Rs.	Rs.	Rs.	Rs.	Rs.
1862-63 ...	5,981	79,306	...	670	85,957	4,581	81,376
1863-64 ...	7,693	80,403	...	474	88,570	5,461	83,109
1864-65 ...	6,451	84,818	...	776	92,045	5,478	86,567
1865-66 ...	5,314	94,079	...	2,135	1,01,529	6,970	94,560
1866-67 ...	6,031	84,955	...	1,719	92,705	5,670	87,035
1867-68 ...	6,271	1,32,444	...	550	13,265	8,506	1,30,759
1868-69 ...	5,356	1,54,683	...	922	1,60,962	8,847	1,52,115
1869-70 ...	5,939	1,71,472	...	1,170	1,78,580	10,136	1.68,445
1870-71 ...	4,936	37,810	1,30,294	3,903	1,72,943	11,645	1,61,298
1871-72 ...	5,917	33,762	1,30,248	1,180	1,71,106	5,474	1,65,632
1872-73 ...	5,116	38,096	1,33,426	495	1,77,133	7,158	1,69,975

In 1873-74 there were 8,982 documents registered under the provisions of
the Registration Act (VIII. of 1871) on which fees to
the amount of Rs. 17,352 were collected. The expenses
of establishment, &c., during the same period amounted to Rs. 5,843. There
were 3,823 registrations affecting immoveable property in which the registration was compulsory under Section 17 of Act VIII. of 1871, and 2,192 in which
the registration was optional ; the aggregate value of the property transferred
by these instruments being Rs. 31,92,377. These figures include immoveable
and moveable property, wills, &c., and give the total aggregate values of all the
documents registered.

Registration.

For the collection of inland customs a post was established at Aligarh under
the charge of the Collector of the land-revenue. This
was withdrawn under Regulation IX. of 1810, and
for the five years of its continuance the total receipts amounted to Rs. 6,25,757,

Customs.

and the charges to Rs. 95,246. For the same years the receipts from town duties were Rs. 30,085, and the charges were Rs. 6,344. Subsequently the town duties were farmed, and rose gradually from Rs. 6,200 in 1810 to Rs. 12,500 in 1836, in which year they were abolished, together with inland customs duties. During the ten years 1826-1836 upwards of Rs. 30,345 were expended from these funds in local improvements in Koil alone.

The excise in this district consists of a tax on the sale of spirituous liquors and intoxicating drugs, which for many years was real- ised by the system of farming out the taxes by parganahs.

Excise.

The following table shows the collections for ten years before the mutiny:—

Year.	Amount of lease of liquor vend	Amount farm of drugs.	Amount farm of opium.	Total revenue.	Collected during the year.	Subsequently realised.	Remitted by Go- vernment.
	Rs.	Rs.	Rs.	Rs.	Rs.	Rs.	Rs.
1843-44 ...	11,250	3,700	2,200	17,150	15,936	1,103	111
1844-45 ...	11,700	3,900	2,400	18,000	16,136	1,303	561
1845-46 ...	13,050	4,225	2,725	20,000	16,863	3,045	53
1846-47 ...	12,500	4,000	2,500	19,000	17,201	1,679	120
1847-48 ...	14,000	4,350	3,800	22,100	19,091	3,009	...
1848-49 ...	14,850	4,099	3,701	22,650	20,440	2,210	...
1849-50 ...	15,200	4,575	...	19,775	18,731	1,044	...
1850-51 ...	17,807	4,700	3,300	25,807	23,542	2,121	154
1851-52 ...	21,550	5,200	3,300	30,050	27,469	2,577	...
1852-53 ...	21,550	6,050	4,000	31,600	22,416	...	...

The consumption of opium rose from nearly six mounds in 1843-44 to $8\frac{1}{4}$ mounds in 1846-47; then falling again, it suddenly rose in 1849-50 to 22 mounds $22\frac{1}{2}$ sers, and in 1852-53 was 22 mounds 27 sers.

The following table gives the statistics connected with the excise for ten years after the mutiny :—

Year.	License fees for vend of spirits.	Duty on spirits.	Opium.	Madak.	Tári.	Intoxicating drugs.	Fines, &c.	Gross charges.	Net receipts.
	Rs.	Rs	Rs.	Rs.	Rs.	Rs.	Rs.	Rs.	Rs.
1862-63 ...	945	10,362	13,500	16	35	4,745	...	667	27,969
1863-64 ...	3,202	9,586	14,700	84	45	4,813	87	1,153	31,364
1864-65 ...	5,239	10,685	20,160	275	33	5,532	233	11,774	30,050
1865-66 ...	6,184	11,411	21,760	251	18	4,768	196	13,847	30,739
1866-67 ...	6,947	12,512	27,200	408	7	4,205	412	16,559	35,152
1867-68 ...	8,383	14,951	33,920	476	32	7,421	107	20,343	44,848
1868-69 ...	8,595	11,064	24,880	442	69	8,103	124	20,487	42,789
1869-70 ...	1,119	11,372	35,542	402	31	6,964	8	21,088	34,350
1870-71 ...	5,382	10,058	36,272	478	45	7,394	4	21,242	38,392
1871-72 ...	6,404	10,025	37,648	373	60	10,629	99	21,425	43,812

Tee town of Kol or Koil[1] is of undoubtedly great antiquity. Local

History.

tradition identifies it with the Kosam or Kosambhi to which Nichakru removed his capital after Hastinápur had been swept away by the Ganges. · But Kosambhi has been identified with Kosam on the Jumna near Allahabad, so that this suggestion cannot be accepted.[2] Indeed Ahár in the Bulandshahr District and other towns in other districts make similar pretensions. To carry out the story, the founder is said to be a Kshatriya of the lunar race, named Koshárab. The present name was given to the city by Bálaráma, who slew here the great Asura (demon) Kol, and with the assistance of the Ahírs subdued this part of the Duáb. Bálaráma is said to have gone from Koil to Rámghát on the Ganges, where he founded a town, and Hardeva (Harduaganj) is said to have been founded by the Ahírs of Rámá's army, and named after another of the many names of their chief (Hardeo). Another legend connects the foundation of Koil with the Dor tribe of Rajpúts, of whom so much has been said in the Bulandshahr District.[3] The story runs that in 429 *Sambat* (or 372 A.D.) Raja Vikrama Sen, of the Dor tribe, ruled at Baran (Bulandshahr), and his brother Káli held Jaláli, and both were tributary to Raja Anangpál of Dehli. Vikrama Sen had two sons, Indur and Mokindur; the former succeeded his father in Baran, and the latter his uncle at Jaláli. Mokindur was succeeded by Gobind Sen, and he by Náhar Singh, the founder of Sambhal. After him came his grandson Dasrath Singh, the founder of Jalesar, who, dying childless, was succeeded by his brother Bijai Rám, and he was followed by Budh Sen. "One day as Budh Sen was riding from Jaláli to Dehli, considerably ahead of his followers, he came to a *jhíl* (called in old Hindi ' *kol*') and dismounted. Whilst waiting for his retinue a fox came up and barked at him, which so irritated the Raja that he drew his sword and struck the fox. The fox retreated to a hole and continued to bark at the Raja and attack him until his suite arrived. After consoling their master, they suggested that there must be some excellent inherent quality in the soil which had imparted to a contemptible creature like the fox, vigour and audacity enough to enable him to set at nought a royal Rajpút; and that therefore it would be a desirable site for the foundation of a city and fort. Raja Budh Sen, after consulting his astrologer, found that it was an auspicious moment for the purpose, so at once he dug up a little clay from the jhíl with his own dagger, and laid the foundation of a city which he named Kol after the jhíl. In a few ·years the fortress and city were finished, and the seat of government was removed from Jaláli to Koil, which became the capital of a large kingdom, comprising Patiáli, Jalesar, Budaon, Sambhal, Kampil, and Baran. After a reign of 55 years the Raja was succeeded by his son Mangal Sen. The

¹ Spelled Kol and pronounced Koil.   ² Bhilsa Topes, Chaps. 2, 3. Arch. Sur., I., 301.
³ Vol. III. of the Gazetteer.

latter made an alliance with the Raja Bena of Atranji and Etáwa, and gave his daughter Padmávati in marriage to the heir of the Etáwa Raja. On Raja Bena's death his sons deposed and murdered their eldest brother, and Padmávati returned a widow to her father's house at Koil. She became a devotee of Ganga, and her father built for her a lofty column in the centre of his fortress, from whence she might be able to view daily the sacred river. Another version of the legend is that the unfortunate Padmávati was built up alive in this column.[1]" It has been shown in the introduction that Anang Pál cannot have ruled in Dehli earlier than A.D. 736, and the inscription on the column in the fort shows that it was erected in 1253 A.D. by Balban, so both the main facts of the story want corroboration.

This much, however, may be said, that some time before the Musalmán invasion the district was held by the Dor Rajpúts, and that in the time of Mahmúd of Ghazni the chief of the Dors was Hardatta of Baran. Koil continued an outpost of the Raja of Baran until the close of the twelfth century, when, weakened by the attacks of the Meos, the Dors fell an easy prey to the Badgujars. Prithiráj has left an inscription boasting of his victory over the Dors, and the Badgujar traditions all agree in stating their settlement here as due to the grant of 150 villages as dowry with his daughter by the last Dor Raja to Partáb Singh, the Badgujar leader. The Badgujars were the principal tribe at the time of the Musalmán invasion. There is some reason to believe that Koil was once the seat of a Buddhist community. Statues of Buddha and other Buddhist remains have been found in excavations made in the eminence on which the citadel of Koil stood. So also have Hindú remains indicating that in all probability the citadel contained in succession a Buddhist and a Hindú temple. As will be seen, these were superseded in their turn by a Muhammadan building (see KOIL). For Koil, as for most places in Upper India, authentic history commences with the Muhammadan invasion, and I shall now turn to the Musalmán historians, and mention the few events, connected with the district, recorded by them.

In the year 1194 A.D. Kutb-ud-dín marched from Dehli to Koil, "which,"

Kutb-ud-dín.

writes Hasan Nizámi,[2] "is one of the most celebrated fortresses of Hind. Those who were wise and acute were converted to Islám, but those who stood by their ancient faith were slain with the sword. The nobles and chiefs of the State entered the fort and carried off much treasure and countless plunder, including one thousand horses." From Koil the conqueror proceeded to Benares, and on his return occupied himself in chasing a certain tribe in the neighbourhood of the fort, which, "after the manner of foxes playing with lions, had occasioned much trouble by

[1] Ledlie's Miscellany in Aligarh Statistics, 340.   [2] Tajul Maásir in Dowson's Elliot, II, 222-224, 242, 358, 380.

their deceits and stratagems ; therefore by the edge of the sword they were despatched to the fire of hell. Three bastions were raised as high as heaven with their heads, and their carcases became the food of beasts of prey. That tract was freed from idols and idol worship, and the foundations of infidelity were destroyed." Kutb-ud-dín appointed Hisám-ud-dín Ulbak as the first Musalmán governor of Koil. The conversions boasted of by the Muhammadan writers must have been partial, as few (if any) converted Hindú families trace back the change in their religion to so early a period.

Nizám-ul-Mulk Mahzab-ud-dín was governor of Koil in 1242 A.D., dur-

Balban.

ing the reign of Sultán Ala-ud-dín Masaúd Shah *bin* Firuz Shah, but so disgusted the Turki nobles by his insolence and avarice that they caused him to be assassinated. Ten years later there would seem to be some attempt to throw off the Musalmán yoke, for we find the great Vazír Ghaiás-ud-dín Balban sent as governor to Koil to quell a rebellion of the Native Rajas. He was son-in-law of the great Altamsh (Iltitmish), and was powerful enough to succeed his brother-in-law, the Sultan Násir-ud-dín, on his death in 1265. To him we owe the great *minár* that until lately stood in Koil, and an inscription on it, bearing date in the eighth year of the reign of Násir-ud-dín, runs as follows :—

" This building was built during the reign of the great Sultán, the owner of the neck of nations, Násir-ud-dunya wá-ud-dín, king of kings, the protector of the people of the faith, the heir of the kingdom of Sulaimán, the lord of the seal in the kingdom of the world, Abul Muzaffar Mahmúd, son of the king. May God perpetuate his kingdom and his rule ! By order of the learned great Malik Azam Kutlugh Khán, Bahá-ul-hak wá-ud-dín, the Malik of the Maliks of the east and of China, Balban, the Shamsi, during the days of his governorship—May his high office continue—on the 10th Rajab A. A. 652[1] (17th August, 1253 A.D.)".

The pillar was pulled down in 1862. Balban seems to have been relieved of his government by Malik Sher Khán, who, in 1259 A.D., received the districts of Bayána, Koil, Bálárám, and Gwaliar. He was nephew of the great Ulugh Khán, and owed his appointment to the good offices of his uncle. On his accession to the throne, Balban gave the fief of Koil to Muhammad Sherandáz, who, with his brother Malik Mukaddir, took part in the Bengal campaign against the rebel Tughril.[2] Under Firúz Shah, Kikí Malik was governor of Koil (1291 A.D.) During the reign of Alá-ud-dín, in 1300 A.D., the Mughals under Targhi

---

[1] The inscription is in the Toghra character, and I am indebted for the translation to Mr. Blochmann of Calcutta, from a rubbing procured at Koil. Mr. Thomas gives a facsimile of the inscription in his ' Pathan Kings of Dehli,' p. 129, Lond., 1871. He also gives a faulty reading, but no translation. Mr. Blochmann notes that " Thomas imagines that the inscription was traced by Násir himself, but of this there is no proof, and in page 130 he mistakes ' *Malik-ul-Alim* (' the learned malik') for ' *Malik-ul-Alam*' (king of the world). Balban, whose real name was Bahá-ud-dín, is here called Shamsi, which means related to Shams-ud-dín Altamsh. His title, Kutlugh Khán, (not Kutlagh Khán), is Turkish, (1), the word ' Kutlugh' meaning ' a standard-bearer' in Turki."　　[2] Tarikh-i-Firúz Shahi, Elliot, III., 117, 190, 538.

invaded Hindustán and encamped on the banks of the Jumna between Dehli and the imperial forces, which were shut up in Baran and Koil, and were unable to advance towards Dehli. Ibn Batuta gives us a glimpse of the state of Koil in the reign of Muhammad *bin* Tughlik. He mentions the town in his account of his embassy from Dehli to China (1342 A.D.) From him[1] it would appear that the district was then in a very disturbed state, since the escort of the Emperor's embassy had to assist in relieving Jaláli from an attacking body of Hindús, and lost one of their officers in the fight. Ibn Batuta calls Koil " a fine town surrounded by mango groves." From these same groves the environs of Koil would appear to have acquired the name of Sabzabad, or ' the green country.' In 1376-77, during the reign of Fíruz Shah Tughlik, the fiefs of Oudh and Sandíla (Shadída) and the Shikk of Koil were placed under Malik Hisám-ul-Mulk and Hisám-ud-dín Nawá. " These nobles showed such zeal in establishing order in their respective commands that the Sultán had no anxiety about the safety of these parts of his dominions." The next great event of local importance was the invasion of Tímur, detachments of whose cavalry are said to have swept through the north of the district. On his departure this portion of the Duáb fell into the hands of Ikbál Khán, who made several expeditions against the refractory Hindú tribes throughout the Duáb. In one of these petty raids Ikbál Khán was joined by Sultán Mahmúd, who had taken refuge in Dhár during the late troubles. Ikbál Khán took the Sultán with him to Kanauj and left him there, whilst he himself proceeded towards Jaunpur. From 1400 until his death in 1405 A.D. Ikbál Khán was master of Upper India, whilst Sultán Mahmúd resided, with the mere semblance of power, at Kanauj. The nominal king was little better off by the death of his keeper, for when, towards the end of 1405 he went to Dehli and sent the family of Ikbál Khán to the *khitta* of Koil, Daulat Khán was made Faujdár of the Duáb, and Koil became the scene of many a battle between the Jaunpur and Dehli forces.

One result of this absence of control was that the successors of Mahmúd found the whole of the Duáb in utter confusion. The imperial authority was only recognized in Koil as long as the army remained, and in 1419 A.D. Khizr Khán, the first of the Sayyid Sultáns, found it necessary to march against Koil in person. In the following year Táj-ul-Mulk was sent again to chastise the rebels in the neighbourhood of Koil. In 1426 A.D. the imperial forces encamped at Atrauli for a season, under Sultán Mubárik Sháh II., in order to oppose the advance of the Jaunpur forces under Ibráhím Sháh Sharki, and pursued the latter prince through the Etáwa district and across the Jumna. In 1445 A.D. Isa Khán Tarkbacha held Koil along with Jaláli, and was confirmed in his office by Sultán Bahlol Lodi on the defeat of Sultán Husain of Jaunpur, who had hitherto retained possession of the Duáb as far as Jalesar and Jaláli.

---

[1] Cathay and the way thither, II., 412.

During the reign of Ibráhím Lodi, the zamíndúrs of Jartoli, a place dependent on Koil, were chastised by the governor of Sambhal, and the district
was completely brought under subjection by Bahlol Lodi in 1478. We next
hear of Koil in connection with the Mughals. After the capture of Dehli
Bábar appointed his dependant Kachak Ali governor of Koil (1526 A.D.), but
as soon as the reverses of the Mughals threatened the stability of their government, Kachak Ali was attacked by a body of Duáb bowmen under one Ilyás
Khán and was taken prisoner. The success of the insurgents was very short-
lived, for in the following year Ilyás Khán was taken prisoner and was flayed
alive.

An inscription in the fort of Koil records its construction during the reign of
Ibráhím Lodi by the Shikkdár Muhammad, son of Ummar, in 1524-25 A.D.
The text runs as follows :—

" In the name of God, the Merciful and the Clement !

1. At first I said:—' Praise be to God, who has created Mustafa.'

2 I then wrote several verses on account of the fort. I shall not remain, a monument (of
me) shall remain.

3. A strong fort, a firm foundation, completed in the reign of my king,

4. Whose name is Ibráhím Sikandar, who bestows silver and gold on beggars.

5 During the shikkdári of Muhammad, son of Ummar, when Shiháb, son of Munawar, was
councillor.

6. He has suffered much hardship on account of the building, and raised the structure, in
a short time.

7. It was in 931 H. when the fort was completed.

8. May I, a helpless man, whose name is Ahmad, find on the day of resurrection the shadow
of Ahmad (the prophet)."

In the reign of Akbar, Koil was made a Sirkár, and included the dastúrs
of Márahra, Kol ba Haveli, Tháná Farída, and Akbar-

Akbar.

abad. The greater portion of dastúr Thána Farída
is now in the Meerut district, and of dastúr Márahra is now in Eta. The names
and revenue of the parganahs forming this district are given elsewhere. In
the beginning of Shahjahán's reign Nijábat Khán was faujdár of the district,
and in 662 A.D. Hasan Ali Khán, tuyuldár, was sent to suppress a local rebellion by Aurangzeb. An inscription on the Idgah in Koil dates from the reign of
Akbar and runs as follows :—

" In the name of God, the Clement and the Merciful !

In the reign of the victorious ruler, in the time of the faith cherishing Shah Jalá-ud-
dín Muhammad Sháh, over all Sháhs greater (Akbar), Muhammad Gesu, the benevolent, erected
this building as fruit of life (devoted) to the prophet, and as a radiant eye to Ali. This building
was well erected in the month of Ramazan, in the year of the Hijra 900 and 70 over (i. e., 970,
or June, 1563 A.D)."

Muhammad Gesu was clearly a Shiah, and may be the same as the Mír
Muhammad Gesu, a servant of Akbar's faujdár of Meerut in 1582 A.D., and
eventually murdered there. The next inscription is one on the dargah of Sháh
Iláhbaksh, bearing date in the reign of Farrukhsiyár :—

"This tomb was built for the rest and peace of Shah Ilâhbaksh (the saint), acquainted with hidden truths and revelations, by the slave, the servant of the fakírs, Sábit Khán, *alias* Jafur Beg, son of Muhammad Beg, in the year 1129 H. (1717 A.D.), the sixth year of the reign of Muhammad Farrukhsiyar, Padisháh-i-Ghâzí, with the assistance of Bhau Singh, the architect."

The mention of Sábit Khán brings us to the best known and best remembered of all the governors of Koil in modern times.

Sábit Khán.

He repaired the old Lodi fort and called it, after his own name, Sábitgarh, and the great mosque in the centre of the town, also built by him, bears the following inscription[1] :—

"The praise belongs to God ; let us praise him without ceasing: and the thanks belong to God ; let us thank him without end, that with sums for benevolent purposes, for the sake of Muhammad, may God bless him. The servant of the throne of him with whom all creatures take refuge, Sábit Khán Bahádur, Sábit Jang, son of Muhammad Beg, a Turkmán Mughal, living in Koil, built the Jámah Masjid and the well ; commenced in 1137 H. and finished in 1141 H , or the eleventh year of Muhammad Shah, Padisháh-i-Ghazi (A. D. 1728.) Who can sufficiently perform the duty of thanking God."

He was a pious, careful ruler, and induced many of the Hindús to become Musalmáns. One important branch of the Badgújars of Bulandshahr was converted by his influence, and to this day bears the name 'Sábit Kháni.' The descendants of Sábit Khán reside to the present day in Koil, and assume the name of Nawáb as a title of honour,·though most of them are common labourers. Soon after the death of this governor the district fell into the state of confusion common to the whole empire, and which has been slightly sketched in the introduction to the present volume. The Marhattas commenced their incursions, and the Játs soon followed. These latter were invited by Safdar Jang to assist him in his campaign against the Afgháns of Farukhabad, and having once obtained a footing in the Duáb, knew well how to increase the advantages of their position. About the year 1757, Surajmal, the Ját leader, took the fort of Sábitgarh, and changed the name to Rámgarh, still the name of a village close to the fort. The Játs soon became masters of the entire country, and no doubt their new capital must have materially aided them in their conquests. The fort lies about two miles to the north of the city of Koil, and must always have been a place of strength and importance. The roads leading from Muttra and Agra towards Dehli and Rohilkhand all centre here.

The Játs, however, did not remain long in ·possession for, in 1759, the Afgháns, under Ahmad Sháh Abdáli, expelled[2] them from Koil, which was made a portion of the Afghán head-quarters, and appears to have been the encampment of the Rohilla detachments also. As soon as the Dauráni retired

---

[1] For this translation also I am indebted to Mr. Blochmann. Sábit Khán and his family are buried in the garden, now known as Kinlochganj, in the city of Koil. [2] Life of Háfiz Rahmat Khán, 59.

to Kandahár, Súrajmal, with his Játs, again crossed the Jumna, and taking possession of Agra proceeded up the Duáb. He was opposed by Najíb-ud-daula between Tappal and Jewar on the banks of the Jumna. The Rohilla had intrenched himself in a strong position, and Súrajmal erected batteries to make the attack at leisure, whilst with his horse he intercepted his adversary's supplies.[1] One day, whilst in a battery, a sally was made by the royal troops, and Surajmal was shot, and his troops retired to Bhartpur. Six months later Jawáhir Singh, the son and successor of Surajmal, re-entered the Duab accompanied by a large Marhatta force (1765 A.D.), but retired the following year. Aligarh was frequently, for a time, in the possession of the Játs until 1773 A.D., when Nawal Singh, the Ját leader, was completely defeated by Najf Khán, who followed up his successes so well that in 1776 A.D. Díg alone remained to them, and Najf Khán himself undertook the government of the Duáb.[2] He repaired the fort of Rámgarh and changed its name to Aligarh.

Najf Khán died in 1782 without issue, and there was at once a contest for his offices. Afrasyáb Khán succeeded him as amír-ul-umara, but he met with powerful rivals in Shafi Khán, who commanded in the Panjab, and Muhammad Beg Hamadáni, who held Agra. The latter did all he could to plunder and lay waste the country towards Koil, now held by Afrasyáb Khán. All these subsequently united their forces, and Afrasyáb Khán was left in possession of the Duáb and the tracts to the south-west of the Jumna jointly with Muhammad Beg. In 1784 Afrasyáb Khán was assassinated with the connivance of Madhoji Sindhia, who became amír-ul-umara. All the accumulations of Afrasyáb were at this time in Aligarh, which was held by his brother Jahángír Khán. "He had a strong garrison, and the siege was expected to be long and bloody. Early in the month of July of the current year Sindhia appeared before the place. Contrary, however, to all expectations, it held out but a short time. It has been imagined that the fears of the women for the preservation of their honour and effects had inclined the commandant of the fort to pacific measures. Certain it is that Jahángír Khan, signifying his readiness to negotiate, a treaty was accordingly drawn up and agreed to by the respective parties. To Khádim Husain, eldest son of the deceased Nawáb, a *jágír* was allotted amounting to a yearly revenue of a lakh and a half of rupees. To the Begams were promised an honourable asylum, and to Jahángír Khan personal safety. It appears, however, that this treaty was very ill adhered to by the Marhatta Chief; for, on the place being surrendered, the Begams and Jahángír Khán were sent under a strong guard to the fort of Gwalior and there detained in confinement. The young Nawáb, indeed, was received by Sindhia with great

---

[1] Life of Háfiz Rahmat Khán, 84. Other accounts say that Surajmal was shot whilst on a hunting party near Síkandarabad in the Bulandshahr district, a little to the north of Jewar.
[2] Francklin's Shah Aulum, 99.

attention, and directed to remain in the royal camp, but Sindhia took possession of the fort, and with it the whole of the treasures of Afrasyáb Khán, amounting, as it has been affirmed, in specie, jewels, and valuable articles to a krore[1] of rupees." Khádim Husain assisted Lord Lake at the conquest, and received taluka Teothi free of revenue for his life. He died in 1837, and was succeeded by his son Ghulám Husain Khán, who received a pension of Rs. 130 per mensem from Lord Auckland. He had nearly persuaded Lord Ellenborough to restore the taluka to him revenue-free, when it was found that his *sanad* had been tampered with in order to introduce the words '*naslan bad naslan*,' signifying a grant in perpetuity. The consequence was that he lost the pension as well as the estate.

Aligarh remained in possession of the Marhattas until 1788, when Ghulám Kádir Khán, abandoning his associate Ismaíl Beg at Agra, made a rapid march on Aligarh and took the fortress by storm. He obtained a considerable booty, and leaving a Rohilla garrison behind him proceeded to Dehli. Sindhia recovered Aligarh the same year, and it remained in the hands of the Marhattas until 1803. Aligarh, under the Marhattas, is chiefly remarkable as the place

Marhattas.

where Sindhia, with the aid of De Boigne, organised those regular battalions drilled and armed after the European fashion, which subsequently did such good service on many a hard-fought field. It was here that De Boigne completed the arrangements of his corps, and received nearly the whole of the Meerut Division in *jaedád* for their support. Two battalions were raised in 1784 and placed under the control of Apa Khandi Rao, and did such good service at Chaksána and Agra in 1785 and 1786, and at Lálsont in 1788, that on his restoration to power Sindhia ordered De Boigne to raise fourteen more battalions in 1789, and form them into two brigades, with one hundred pieces of cannon. This was completed in 1790, and shortly after their formation they were drawn into action in the famous battle of Mairta in 1790, where they defeated the Rathors, and again the combined forces of the Jaipur Raja and Ismaíl Beg. In the quarrel between Holkar and Sindhia regarding the division of the spoil of Hindustan, De Boigne's battalions won for Sindhia the battle of Lakhairi, though opposed to Dudrenec's battalions fighting on behalf of Holkar. They also won the battle of Kanond against the forces of Ismaíl Beg and the widow of Najf Kúli Khán. In fact all the Marhatta successes from the Chambal to the Himálayas since 1784 A.D. were due to these troops alone.[2] In 1796 De Boigne was succeeded by Perron. At this time there were three brigades: one commanded by Major Perron at Poona, one under Major Sutherland at Muttra, and one under Captain Pedron at Aligarh.

---

[1] Francklin's Shah Aulum 136: London, 1798.   [2] L. F. Smith's Regular Corps in the service of Native States : Calcutta, 1804.

Perron came to Aligarh in 1797 and assumed the supreme command.

Perron.

He at once arranged and pursued a systematic plan to aggrandise his authority and riches. From Lahore to Kota and from Aligarh to Jodhpur the country obeyed his authority and dreaded his frown : his only rivals, Tantia Pagnavís and Lakhwa Dáda, perished in 1801, and in the following year George Thomas' fell. Another brigade was added in 1802, which increased the disciplined forces to four brigades, or thirty-two battalions. A storm, however, broke out at Ujjain, and Perron, at the risk of his life and place, was obliged to proceed to court and appease his enemies, which having accomplished by the liberal use of money, he returned in safety to Aligarh. At this time (November, 1802) the Peshwa demanded assistance from Sindhia against Holkar, and Sindhia ordered Perron to send him some of his brigades but Perron hesitated, and so long, that when he did despatch them they arrived too late, and the Peshwa had already joined the British. The result of this step was the triple alliance between Holkar, Sindhia, and the Raja of Nágpur against the British, the Nizám, and the Peshwa. Perron drew up the plan of the campaign and advised Sindhia to attack the Nizám's country whilst he held the northern Duáb, and Holkar attacked Surat and Ambaji Inglia, and Shamsher Bahádur from Bundelkhand ravaged the lower Duáb, then held by the British.

By the treaty of 1802 the British frontier had been advanced to within fifteen miles of Koil. " Such was the weakness of the former administration that the zamíndárs tyrannized over the people with impunity, levying imposts at their pleasure, and applying the revenues solely to their own use. These petty despots, whose treachery could only be exceeded by their rapacity, were, at the time of the cession, becoming every day more dangerous to the neighbouring states, in erecting fortresses and training soldiers on their domains, thereby opposing the legitimate authority, opening new sources of contention, and forming numerous banditti, who acknowledged no law but the commands of their respective chiefs. To such a degree of power and confidence had these refractory zamíndárs arrived through the debility of the Government of Oudh, that even some trouble was experienced in reducing their strongholds, after the change had taken place by the transfer of the country to the British authority. This was particularly instanced at Sásni and Bijaigarh (then in Parganah Jaláli), two forts belonging to Raja Bhagwant Singh of Mursán, which, though attacked by the Commander-in-Chief in person, were not carried without the loss of many lives. It was the introduction of our system of customs and transit duties which prompted the Raja and other zamíndárs to rebel. Hitherto in every large village they had their toll-house, at which they levied arbitrary duties on goods passing through their estates, and they resisted by force of arms the transfer to the British Government of a source of revenue which they greatly valued as adding to their power and dignity no less than to their wealth. Raja Bhagwant Singh was expelled from his forts in March, 1803, and his possessions in Parganah Jaláli were confiscated." Petty expeditions against the neighbouring chiefs were of daily occurrence, and all prepared for the grand struggle which they knew must sooner or later come. The Marhatta chiefs formally adopted Perron's plan of campaign, but with little intention of adhering to its spirit, should that be opposed to what they considered their own interests.

The first result of this condition of affairs was a declaration of war in 1803.

Capture of Aligarh. On the 29th August the British force under Lord Lake advanced towards the frontier and were met by Perron with about 8,000 good horse, but nothing was done, and the cavalry dispersed at the first round of grape from the British horse artillery. Perron himself fled to Háthras, and thence to Muttra. On the 5th September he wrote to General Lake from Muttra and proposed to surrender himself on assurance of protection to his person and property. This was readily granted, and Perron having sent for his family from Agra, contrived to elude the vigilance of his troops by giving them liberal largesses, and joined the British force at Sásni. In the meantime every preparation was made for the assault of the fort then commanded by Colonel Pedron and garrisoned by about two thousand men. The 4th of September was fixed for the assault, and Colonel Monson was appointed to lead the attack with four companies of Her Majesty's 76th Regiment under Major McLeod, two battalions of the 4th Native Infantry under Colonel Browne, and four companies of the 17th Native Infantry under Captain Bagshaw. During the night immediately preceding the attack, two covering batteries of four 18-pounders each were erected,—one at a village near the fort, and the other near Perron's house, to protect the storming party.

" About 3 A. M. the whole of the attacking party left the camp, marching in a circular direction towards the gateway, which was the only entrance into the fort across the ditch, on their arrival within four hundred yards of which they halted till daybreak. While thus waiting in breathless expectation, an officer who had been reconnoitring reported his having seen about sixty or seventy of the enemy seated round a fire and smoking under a tree in front of the gateway. On receiving this intelligence, a small party from Her Majesty's 76th Regiment was sent with the view of taking these men by surprise, and to endeavour, amidst the confusion, to enter the fort with them, when the gate might be secured till the arrival of the main body. This design, however, unluckily failed through the ardour of those employed; but though the surprised party gave an alarm on discovering our soldiers, not one of them escaped to relate the particulars, so that the assailants had an opportunity of retiring as quietly as they came ; and the sentries on the ramparts, while they opened a brisk fire in that direction, took the affair for nothing more than a near approach of our videttes. On the firing of the morning gun, which was the appointed signal for the assault, the storming party, covered by a heavy fire from the two batteries already mentioned, moved on till they came within one hundred yards of the gate, in front of which was a traverse, recently thrown up, and mounted with three 6-pounders, from which, however, the enemy were dislodged before they had time to discharge them. Colonel Monson then pushed forward with the two flank companies of the 76th Regiment, and attempted to enter the fort along with the guard stationed behind this breast-work; but on reaching the place it was found abandoned and the first gate shut, while the entrance or sortie was raked by two or three guns, and flanked by the bastions, particularly the lower one of the renny opposite to it, and which kept up a most destructive fire of grape shot. Two ladders were then instantly applied to the walls, and Major McLeod, of the 76th, with the grenadiers, attempted to mount, but being opposed by a formidable row of pikemen, threatening death to all assailants, they were obliged to desist. A 6-pounder was then planted before the gate to force it open, but without effect; on which a 12-pounder was brought up, though some time elapsed before it could be properly placed, on account of the peculiar situation of the gate, which was near the flank of a bastion. Four or five rounds were fired before any impression was made upon the gate; and during the whole of the interval, which lasted full twenty minutes, the storming party was exposed to a most severe and raking fire, not only of musketry but grape, from the great guns and wall-pieces. The scaling ladders placed against the walls were crowded with the enemy, who left the ramparts and came down by them to contend with us while engaged in the effort to force an entrance. This was the arduous crisis; and here we sustained our principal loss. Colonel Monson was wounded by a pike on this spot; and here four grenadier officers were killed, together with the adjutant of the 76th Regiment and Lieutenant Turton of the 4th Native Infantry. Dreadful, however, as the struggle was, with death flying and grappling in every direction, nothing could appal the determined spirit of the British troops, who by their perseverance amidst these fearful odds and perilous circumstances succeeded in overcoming all obstacles. As soon as the first gate was thrown open, the whole party advanced in a circular direction along a narrow road, defended by a strong round tower built of masonry. This tower was pierced with loop-holes from which a constant and most deadly fire was kept up by a number of matchlock-men, while showers of grape poured from the neighbouring bastion and the narrow passage. After forcing the second gate, which was easily accomplished, the troops proceeded along a narrow-causeway to another gate, of which they gained possession by taking advantage of the confused state of the enemy, who, in crowding to get through, gave our party an opportunity of passing, before it could be shut against them. During this time the troops were severely annoyed by a heavy cross fire in every direction, but nothing could repress their ardour in the pursuit, which was continued till they arrived at a fourth gate leading into the body of the place."

" Here new delay and mortification occurred, for Captain Shipton, of the artillery, who had charge of the guns, and who, though wounded, still remained actively at his post, experienced some difficulty in bringing up the 12-pounder; and when it actually came, the gate was found too strongly secured to be forced. Major McLeod, however, having succeeded in passing through the wicket and ascending the ramparts, resistance gradually lessened, till this fortress, hitherto considered impregnable, fell, a hard-earned conquest to the intrepid band of assailants, after a most vigorous defence which lasted nearly an hour. Though our loss was necessarily considerable, it was far exceeded by that of the enemy, who had at least two thousand killed, the surrounding ditch being almost filled with dead bodies, owing to the attempts made by many of the garrison to effect their escape that way after the entrance of our troops into the interior of the fort. Many who could swim were enabled to gain the plain on the outside, but numbers were drowned; and even the former, through their obstinacy in refusing to surrender, were cut up by a picquet of the 27th Dragoons. They who yielded were permitted to quit the fort and be at large by the Commander-in-Chief, who was close to the place all the time, observing with the utmost anxiety the result of his energetic and ably arranged plan of attack. The fort being carried, M. Pedron, who had commanded it, was conducted as a prisoner to General Lake. He was an elderly man, clad in a green jacket, with gold lace and epaulettes; the second in command, a Marhatta chief, was killed; and two other chiefs were taken prisoners. It should here be observed that the achievement was materially facilitated by the loyal and gallant conduct of Mr. Lucan, a British officer, who had lately quitted the service of Sindhia to avoid fighting against his countrymen. On joining our army he undertook to lead Colonel Monson to the gate and point out the road through the fort, which he effected in such a manner as to gain the particular[1] thanks of the Commander-in-Chief and the public acknowledgments of the Government." The British lost in the attack 26 Europeans and 21 natives killed, and 76 Europeans and 105 natives wounded.[2] Guns of various descriptions to the number of 281 were captured in the fort, besides large supplies of powder and shot, accoutrements, and some tumbrils containing Spanish dollars.

[1] Thorn. Mem., War in India, 447.   [2] Major Smith gives the names of the officers killed, viz., Cameron, Browne, Fleming, Campbell, and St. Aubin of the 76th Regiment, and Turton of the 4th Native Infantry. The officers of the 76th were interred in front of their standard guard, in presence of General Lake and his staff. Eleven officers were wounded. It was not until 1851 that a medal was given for the storming of Aligarh (see further under ALIGARH in the alphabetical notices).

From the importance attached to Aligarh by M. Perron, and his retaining it as his place of residence, it may be naturally supposed that nothing was omitted which the skill and experience of French engineers could devise, for the purpose of adding to its natural strength. The elevated plain in the midst of which it stands, being interspersed with large swamps and deep morasses, becomes so completely inundated during the rainy months as to render the fort perfectly inaccessible, nor can any military operations be then carried on against it. The ditch is from one to two hundred feet in breadth, and thirty-two in depth, of which there are always ten feet of water. The several bastions and faussebraies lined with guns, bearing upon the only entrance into the fort, are, from their peculiar situation, extremely formidable ; and had the garrison cut the narrow passage in front of the gate, so as to unite the two ditches, it would have been impossible to have carried the place by assault. They had, indeed, the day before the attack commenced, a mine on the outside of the gate, under the traverse recently erected, and, no doubt, the junction of the ditches would soon have followed, if we had allowed time for it, by adopting the slow operations of a siege, or deferred the attack a few days longer. This neglect of an obvious advantage on the part of the enemy could not escape observation, and therefore our first care after the capture was to render the fort completely insular, by uniting the ditches, substituting a drawbridge for the causeway, and thus making the place impregnable, at least to a native army.

The formation of the district and its fiscal history is told elsewhere, and here I will merely give the general history of the pacification of the district. Scarcely had the district been formed, when the war with Holkar broke out, and his emissaries poured into the Duáb, exciting the hopes and fears of all those who had managed to assume some semblance of right over the collection of villages known as talukas. These talukas were undoubtedly due to the disorders of the previous half century, when revenue had to be collected by some means, and there was no regular assessment. Amils were appointed as farmers who were obliged to pay a certain sum within a fixed time into the treasury, and in order to meet their engagements they sublet their farms to others who had full power to collect all that they could lay hold on. Some energetic individuals engaged for a cluster of bad villages, and by force or persuasion managed the cultivators, provided for the cultivation, and paid the revenue as it became due. No inquiry was ever made into proprietary rights ; success in collecting the revenue was the sole standard of fitness, and the amil supported the title, though the persons engaging for the revenue never possessed an acre of land in the tracts for which they engaged. Gradually the most unscrupulous and most energetic survived and assumed the title of talukadárs, and, owing to their local knowledge and experience, could not be passed over by the successive Imperial, Ját and Marhatta governors of the district. In this manner the Badgújar,

The British.

Ját, Rajpút, and Musalmán talukas arose and increased, and flourished more and more with anarchy and disorder. Sindhia himself with all his power failed, in many cases, to recover the just demands of the State from those to whom lands had been granted in *jágír* for services rendered to the contending factions, who were almost year by year compelled in this way to purchase the support of the military communities. Even De Boigne and Perron thought themselves fortunate if they could collect a nominal revenue from the more powerful talukadárs and grantees. Perron's administration was undoubtedly a strong one. His subjects enjoyed peace from the hands of marauders, who used occasionally to visit the towns for plunder ; but still there was no real safety for person or property. Cash and valuables were buried, no money-lending could be carried on, trade was crushed by vexatious imposts, there was no export of grain and cultivation languished, no one wore good clothes in order to avoid contributions, mud houses, for the same reason, were alone built, and altogether insecurity and ' the right of might' showed their natural results in the total disorganisation of society. Such was the state of things at the British occupation, and our early rulers at once set themselves to the task of reducing chaos to order. Inquiries were made into the rights of the talukadárs, the levying of transit dues was prohibited, and those whose own will had hitherto been their sole law began to feel that a really strong power had, at last, sprang up and would make itself respected.

Holkar's emissaries had, therefore, good material to work upon in 1804. Amongst the first to join the Marhattas were Náhar Ali Khán and Dundi Khán, converted Badgújars[1] of Pítampur, now in the Bulandshahr district, who held the whole of the northern and north-eastern parganas. Holkar's amils held the country to the west and north-west, whilst Abhai Singh, a leader of banditti, occupied Chandaus, and in Koil itself an insurrection broke out in September which lasted for nine days. Mr. Claude Russell joined his appointment as Magistrate and Collector in December, 1804, and with the assistance of the talukadár of Beswán expelled the Marhattas from Noh Jhíl and Khair.[2] Colonel Grueber expelled Abhai Singh from Chandaus, and Captain Cruttenden recovered Parganahs Atrauli and Dibái. When Colonel Grueber retired, Atrauli and Dibái were again occupied by the Badgújars and Chandaus was menaced. The commandant at Aligarh could not spare sufficient troops for the Collector's support, and at length Colonel Richardson was sent against the Badgújars, and their rebellion was put an end to by the capture of Túrkipura in July, 1805. Dúndi Khán was pardoned and his estates were given to his son Ranmast Khán, who at once set about repairing the losses suffered during the recent campaign, and, unchecked and unwarned, restored his numerous forts to order. The estates of Náhar Ali Khán also were confiscated, but on his death, a

---

[1] The history of this family is given in full under the Bulandshahr district.   [2] Board's Records, 18th February, 1805, No. 19.

short time afterwards, they were restored to his son. In February, 1805 the Amír Khán, with his Pindaris, crossed the Jumna at Mahában and marched upwards celebrated through the Duáb to Kamona, the fort of Dúndi Khán. Colonel Grueber with two battalions and two companies of regular troops and 1,500 of Skinner's horse was at that time investing Kamona, and retired on the approach of the Pindaris, but Amír Khán stayed only one day, and passed northwards to the Meerut district closely pursued by General Smith. A fortnight after, on their way back, the Pindaris defeated a body of the Háthras Raja's troops at the fords of the Jumna, but made no further disturbance in this district. Notwithstanding the lenity with which he had been treated, or perhaps in consequence of that mistaken lenity, Ranmast Khán soon showed fresh signs of disaffection and refused to engage for his share of Pítampur and the farm of Shikárpur on any reasonable terms.[1] He was expelled in 1806. In October, 1806, the Magistrate (Mr. Cunyngham) reported to Government that Dúndi Khán had marched with an armed force against the zamíndárs of Masmana in Noh Jhíl, had expelled them, and fired a salute of eleven guns. In August, 1807, the Magistrate (Mr. Spedding) reported that Dúndi Khán and Ranmast Khán were prepared to resist any force sent against them, and that they had mounted cannon on their forts of Kamona and Gannaura. In the following month the Collector (Mr. Russell) reported Ranmast Khán's general and systematic disregard of authority, his uniform disaffection to the Government, and his positive violation of the conditions of his pardon, and in consequence of these reports the Governor-General, on the 25th September, ordered a military force against Dúndi Khán, to apprehend him and reduce his forts, unless he should pay his revenue, dismantle his forts, and surrender his person. But the troops were directed not to commence operations till the legal forms required by Regulation III. of 1804 had been fulfilled. Accordingly the Magistrate summoned[2] Dúndi Khán and Ranmast Khán to attend, but instead of answering the summons they commenced laying in provisions and making preparations for defence, and Ranmast Khán increased the list of his offences by plundering the town of Shikárpur. On the 12th of October Major-General Dickens invested the fort of Kamona ; on the 19th November a breach was effected, and an attempt made to carry the place by storm, but the assailants were driven back with great slaughter, the loss of men and officers exceeding that sustained in many of the pitched battles of the time.[3] The impression however made on the garrison was such that Dúndi Khán evacuated the fort on the 24th and threw himself into Gannaura, from which place he made his escape on the 13th of December. A reward of Rs. 10,000 was offered for his apprehension, and Rs. 5,000 for the arrest of

1806-07.

---

[1] Board's Records, 3rd July, 1807, No. 12 ; 25th September, 1807, No. 15.   [3] *Ibid,* 29th September, 1807, No. 1.   [2] *Ibid,* 31st October, 1807, No. 72.

each of his sons. His ancestral estate of half Pítampur was given by Government to Mardán Ali Khán, who, though a near relation of Dúndi Khán, was a zealous partizan of our Government during Dúndi Khán's rebellion. It is now known as Chatári. (See BULANDSHAHR District).

After this the peace of the district was not disturbed for several years until the
The Háthras and Mur- rebellion of Daya Rám of Háthras and Bhagwant Singh
sán Rajas. of Mursán rendered military operations on a somewhat
extensive scale necessary. An account of the subjugation of these talukadárs has already been given (pages), 430,436 and from this time until the mutiny of 1857 there is little worth recording beyond what has been given in the fiscal history of the district.

News of the outbreak at Meerut arrived at Aligarh on the 12th May,
The mutiny. 1857.[1] Messrs. Watson, Lane, and F. B. Outram represented the civil administration of the district, and the military garrison comprised 300 men of the 9th Native Infantry under Major Eld. A period of the usual uncertainty and dismay ensued, but the troops appeared quiet and orderly, and beyond the burning of an empty bungalow no overt act of disaffection occurred until the 20th of May. On the 19th the infantry were reinforced by a detachment, and on the 20th the right wing of the 1st Gwaliar Cavalry marched in under Captain Alexander. On the same day a Brahman named Naráyan, a resident of a village close to Aligarh, was found tampering with the sepoys and was sentenced to death the same evening. The execution had hardly terminated when the 9th broke out into open mutiny. The officers, civilians and ladies escaped to Háthras, and the station was occupied by rebel troops and the rabble from Koil and the neighbouring villages. The Courts were plundered and burned, and seven lakhs of rupees in specie were divided amongst the insurgents. The prisoners were released from the jail, and the large bullock train at the post-office was plundered chiefly through Rasúl Khán, khánsámah of the dák bangalow, and Mír Khán, mail-guard. Messrs. Connor, Cline, and Nichterlein, who had been left behind on the 20th, made their way to Sawámái, close to Sásni, on the 22nd, where they were attacked and plundered by the Mewatis, and Mr. Nichterlein, junior, was killed. The party was, however, released the same night by Panna Lál, a resident of Sásni, and was conducted in safety to Háthras. On the 24th 100 men of the Gwaliar Cavalry mutinied and left for Dehli, and the Europeans retreated to Khandauli in the Agra district. On the 29th the planters of the Maloi factory were released by the Agra volunteers, who remained with Mr. Watson until the arrival of the Nímach rebels, and the mutiny of the remainder of the Gwaliar Cavalry obliged that officer to retire to Agra (July 2nd).

---

[1] The following account is taken from Mr. W. J. Bramly's official narrative and the other mutiny memoirs.

Mr. Watson communicated with the Meerut and Bulandshahr authorities throughout, but they were unable to afford him any assistance.

The volunteers comprised forty men commanded by Lieutenant W. H. Greathed. On the 28th May they advanced to Aligarh and occupied the station. Whilst at Aligarh intelligence was received from Khair that Ráo Bhúpál Singh, Chauhán, had deposed the tahsíldár and proclaimed a Rajpút government. Mr. Watson and Dr. S. Clarke, with the volunteers, made a night march to Khair, about fourteen miles west of Aligarh, and whilst the town was surrounded by videttes to prevent the rebel chief's escape, Mr. Watson, with a few volunteers, gallantly rode straight through the town to the tahsíli, where Bhúpál Singh was surprised and captured with sixteen followers. Rao Bhúpál Singh was hanged on the spot, and the party returned to Aligarh. Mr. Paterson Saunders then took command of the volunteers. About the middle of the month the Chauháns, joined by the Játs, re-occupied Khair and plundered and destroyed nearly all the Government buildings, as well as the houses of the Baniyas and Mahájans. Until about the middle of June the volunteer force remained intact. Mr. Cocks writes:—" It was sufficiently strong to overawe the Muhammadan population of the town of Koil, as well as the refractory villages, which were ever ready to take advantage of the state of anarchy. On several occasions we were obliged to saddle at a moment's warning and descend on these villagers, who met us with matchlocks, swords, and bludgeons, but were on every occasion well punished. Our greatest danger, however, arose from the frequent arrival at Koil of large bands of mutineers from Oudh and the districts which had been abandoned. When we felt unable to face those in the open field, we occasionally harassed their movements, by firing at their advanced guards, and then made an orderly retreat to some position capable in a certain measure of defence. We were never attacked by those parties, owing to their anxiety to reach Dehli. Our military duties were very heavy; not a night passed but we were told off for either sentry or patrol; and during the day, when not employed on some expedition, we were without the convenience or even necessaries of life; and it was considered a luxury to get a thatch or tree to sleep under. I consider myself bound to remark here that, so long as the volunteers remained in the district, their conduct was soldier-like and creditable, and many displayed a dashing courage which was afterwards memorably proved at Agra on the 5th of July, and at Aligarh on the 24th of August."

About the 21st June the Lieutenant-Governor recalled most of the volunteers to Agra, and there remained with Mr. Watson but eleven men.[1] With this reduced force Aligarh was again abandoned, and the deserted factory of Mandrák, situated about seven

Defence of Mandrák.

---

[1] Messrs Cocks and Outram of the Civil Service; Ensigns Marsh and Olivant; Dr. Stewart Clark and Messrs. P. Saunders, J. Tandy, H. B. Harington, Hind, Castle, and Burkinyoung.

miles from Aligarh on the Agra road, was occupied. At the same time Captain Burlton held Sásni between Mandrák and Háthras, and Captain Alexander remained at Háthras. From Mandrák various expeditions were undertaken to the different towns, and the month of June passed by without anything more stirring than the news brought by camel-riders of fresh mutinies and whispers of a projected rising amongst the Gwaliar troopers at Sásni and Háthras. A *jahád* was preached in the town of Koil, and the *jahádis* boasted that they would fix the heads of the Europeans on the gates of the city before night. On the 2nd July news came of the mutiny of the Gwaliar troopers, and on the same day some one thousand of the Musalmán rabble of Koil appeared before Mandrák. Mr. Cocks writes :—" On that date (2nd July), at 3 p. m., we sat down to our mess dinner. In the midst of it we heard the buzz of an enraged populace; soon tom-toms were beating, flags flying, and the country swarming with white clothes, each Government chauki in a blaze added to the excitement of the scene. Scarcely a word was spoken, but each seemed to understand his neighbour's thoughts, saddled his horse, and drew his sword. We rode forth, the gallant Watson at our head. On reaching the road we were met by a salute from a hundred matchlocks ; a hundred more were aimed, but missed fire, owing to the damp state of the atmosphere. " Charge" was the order, and well was it obeyed. Stirrup to stirrup, and man to man, we dashed through the mass of cowards, scattering them like so many sheep, and not stopping till nearly 15 corpses remained as trophies of our victory. Watson was wounded, as was his horse, and two or three got contusions. When we charged, I believe not one expected to have come back alive ; and when darkness compelled our return, it was with feelings of intense satisfaction and thankfulness that we finished our repast and talked over our escapes and adventures." It is such gallant acts as this that have won us India, and that will keep India, and I have no doubt that when occasion arises, Englishmen will always be found ready to emulate the heroes of 1857. The same day the traitorous Gwaliar Cavalry broke out into open mutiny, and their officers were obliged to fly to Agra. This necessitated the retreat of the gallant volunteers, and, sad to relate, the noble Watson died of cholera at Agra. Naturally of a weak constitution, the exposure and anxiety rendered him an easy prey to Asiatic cholera, and no less a victim to the mutiny than those who died on the field. One who knew him well writes:—" I fully believe he had, from the commencement of the outbreak, made up his mind to be killed or die in the defence of the district in which he took so much interest." So long as he remained in Aligarh communication with Meerut was maintained, and the establishment of a rebel government in Koil was delayed.

From the 2nd July, 1857, until the 24th August, 1857, the district was in the hands of the rebels. A committee (panchágat) was formed to preserve order and save the city of Koil

Rebel government.

from plunder by the Mewatis, butchers, and other low Musalmáns. One Nasím-ullah, a vakíl of the Judge's Court, took umbrage at his exclusion from the pancháyat and invited Muhammad Ghaus Khán, of Sikandra Rao, to Koil. Nayáz Ahmad, Inspector of Schools, assisted Nasímullah, and both procured for Muhammad Ghaus Khán the appointment of deputy from Walidád Khán of Málágarh in the Bulandshahr district. They ousted the committee of safety, and Nasímullah became sub deputy governor of Koíl, Máhbúb Khán was created tahsíldár, and Hasan Khán was placed in charge of the police (kotwál). Forces were levied and the police and jail guards took service with the usurpers, but Ghaus Khán never extended his power beyond the city and never collected any revenue. On the 20th August, Mr. Cocks, with a force under Major Montgo-mery, was despatched from Agra to succour Háthras, which was supposed to be threatened by the Koil rebels. On the 24th the British force moved upon Koil and attacked the rebels under Ghaus Khán and Maulvi Abdul Jalíl near the garden of Mán Singh close to the city. The rebels were defeated, the Maulvi himself was killed, and the Musalmáns abandoned the city. Mr. Cocks was accompanied in his advance by the troops of the Mursán Raja and Thákur 'after-wards Raja) Gobind Singh. To the latter was assigned the charge of the city, with the aid of a council composed of Aftáb Rái, an experienced old tahsíldár, Sundar Lál, a Subordinate Judge, and Rái Durga Parshád, a Deputy Collector. All the tahsílis were reoccupied, though the authority of the officers was neces-sarily, but weakly, established. On the 25th September Gobind Singh was surprised by a rebel force under Nasímullah and expelled from the city, and on the same day the tahsíldár of Atrauli was murdered at his post. The follow-ing day Major Montgomery's force was obliged to leave Háthras to avoid the large force of rebels in retreat from Dehli. This body of rebels arrived at Háthras, on the 3rd October and Sikandra Rao on the 4th, where they halted on the 5th, and marched again southward on the 6th.

On the 5th Colonel Greathed's column occupied Koil without resistance. The rebels fled to Akrabad pursued by Major Ouvry's Lancers, when many of the Gújar raiders were punished. Akrabad was occupied on the 6th, and the rebel leaders Mangal Singh and Mahtáb Rai were slain, and a considerable number of guns and much ammunition was captured. Colonel Greathed's column arrived at Agra on the 10th October, and shortly after the action of the Karwan Nadi, Mr. Cocks with Major Eld, 150 Europeans, two guns, 100 Sikhs, and Mr. Bramly as Magistrate, were sent to re-occupy the district. They took possession of the fort and easily held their own. The police and revenue estab-lishments were strengthened, Gobind Singh was reinstated in Koil, and the collec-tion of the land-revenue proceeded steadily with the returning confidence in the stability of our Government. Payment, except in a few cases, was withheld only where there was real inability to pay. During the month of November the district was continually harassed by flying parties of rebels proceeding from across the Jumna eastwards : but these did little or no harm in their passage, though they caused a great feeling of insecurity at our police and revenue posts, where the mere cry of ' rebels' was sufficient to put to flight the raw levies.

In December a body of the Fatehgarh rebels threatened the district from the south. Colonel Farqubar, commanding in Bulandshahr, deemed it advisable to march in their direction with a view to holding them in check, if possible, until the arrival of the column which was being formed at Dehli and Meerut under Colonel Seaton, C.B., to convey a quantity of stores and ammunition for the use of the troops at Cawnpore. The Bulandshahr force occupied Pindrá-wal, and marched thence by Atrauli to Chharra, a small village close to the residence of Daúd Khan, talukadár of Bhíkampur. On the 11th December Colonel Seaton's column arrived at Aligarh, and on the 14th joined the Bulandshahr force, and the same day completely routed the enemy at the Ním Nadi. After this the Dúab was completely cleared of the rebels, and the only danger lay on the Rohilkhand side, for even after the occupation of Fatehgarh the whole river face between it and Aligarh was at the mercy of the rebels. In March, 1858, General Penny's force marched down and took up a position at Patiáli, and afforded some show of protection.

The old Rajpút and Ját feuds broke out with their accustomed fury during the mutiny. In the western portions of the district, and especially towards Sadabad of Muttra, internal struggles raged until the fall of Dehli. The feeling of animosity between the Musalmáns and Hindús was also generally very bitter, especially after the excesses of Nasímullah and the elevation of Thá-kur Gobind Singh. No officer of Government above the rank of jamadár of police joined the rebels except the Inspector of Schools and the Jailor. Only one Christian was murdered, and Mr. Hoggan and his family, (five persons) were kept concealed in a sweeper's house in Koil for six days after the departure of the Europeans, whilst Mr. Ryan of Nánu was rescued by a zamíndár, and sent into Háthras. One large indigo factory was plundered and burned by the villagers, and three others by the mutineer troops. The remainder were saved by the village zamíndárs. The records of the head-quarters offices and those of four out of eight tahsíls were destroyed and the towns of Khair and Harduaganj were plundered. Mr. Bramly thus sums up his experiences of the mutiny :—" Little trust can be placed in the humanity of the lower classes, whether Hindú or Musalmán. They have proved themselves little better than savages, and all that can be said is that they treat us not worse, but perhaps better than they treated each other. Though aid in the struggle has been rendered us in many instances by the natives, especially by the Hindús after they had a foretaste of a Musalmán government, still their general attitude

must be characterized as apathetic. The large number of persons who had so
much to gain from the overthrow of our Government was content to annex
their lost estates and await the result of the struggle. That the people plundered when they suddenly found authority overthrown by the mutinous troops
and anarchy ready made for them was natural. What people would have
done otherwise, but to take an active part and assist the mutineers, the small
Muhammadan section excepted, they showed in this district little desire. Much
as they love plunder, they love life and security more ; and the same with the
sepoys. A hard contest, even though successful, formed no part of their pro-
gramme. The treacherous and easy slaughter of their officers and other
Europeans, accompanied with the certain plunder of treasuries, the wiping
out of debts, and the prospect of a new régime in which they must necessarily play a leading part, was the pleasing picture they had before them,
when they shouted ' dín! dín!' The storming of forts and entrenchments,
though held by a few Europeans, and they worn and exhausted, was a service
of danger to meet which there was no sense of duty of spirit or patriotism, no
sense of injuries to be avenged, to spur them on. In such a cause they
could not meet death."

The confiscations for rebellion amounted to 21,912 acres, paying a land-

Confiscations.
revenue of Rs. 34,708. These punishments were imposed
more for isolated acts of plunder amongst the people
themselves than for overt acts of rebellion against the Government.

Tahsíl.			Areas con-fiscated in acres.	Land reve-nue in rupees.	Tahsíl.	Area confis-cated in acres.	Land reve-nue in rupees.
Atrauli	...	...	1,252	2,195	Khair ...	5,810	8,550
Koíl	...	...	4,969	6,959	Háthras ...	1,115	2,616
Iglás	...	...	8,650	8,798	Sikandra...	5,566	5,589

With the exception of malarious fevers, there are no endemic diseases pre-

Medical aspects of the district.
valent in the district. The country is flat, and level, and
in many cases it has been found very difficult to carry
off the extra moisture caused by the canal. The natural drainage lines are
shallow, sluggish streams incapable of further extension as receptacles for
the excessive rain-fall : hence swamps arise, and with them appear the malarious fevers. Some improvement has taken place near Koil and in other parts
of the district by judicious draining, and with the increase in cultivation and
the planting of trees the general health seems to have improved throughout the
district. Cholera first broke out in 1817 and committed great ravages. In
1821 again cholera visited the district, and the people say that "firewood

became scarce in consequence of the quantity used for burning the dead." The next cholera year was 1827, following on the famine of 1825-26, and again after the *chauránawe* famine of 1837-38 cholera raged. From June to August, 1856, and after the famine of 1860-61, cholera was again very destructive in this district. In 1837 a malignant typhoid fever broke out in the Sásni subdivision. Some say that it was conveyed into the district by travellers from Bombay ; others that it was due to the fact that some Chamárs had eaten the decayed flesh of a cow that had died of the murrain which raged at the same time. The fever held possession of the patient for four or five days, and ended in delirium, during which the crisis took place. This epidemic lasted for six months. In 1856 fever followed the cholera epidemic of that year, and extended its ravages well on into the cold-weather. This outbreak was characterised by its rapid course in individual cases, and death generally resulted on the fourth day after seizure, while those who survived this period ultimately recovered. It was calculated that 34,000 persons died during its prevalence, or three per cent. of the total population. Fever also followed the famine of 1860-61, especially in Koil and Harduaganj. It broke out in April and May, when the fresh grain was brought into the market, and, the old stocks having been exhausted, was, at once, used for food. In February, 1850, there was an outbreak of small-pox, which was much intensified by the imperfect disposal of the bodies of those who had died of the disease. The following statement, compiled from the sanitary reports, gives the mortuary statistics of the district for the years 1867 to 1873 :—

Year.	Fever.	Small-pox.	Bowel complaints.	Cholera.	Other causes.	Total.	Percentage of deaths to 1,000 of the population.
1867	6,086	426	1,023	1,104	1,965	10,604	11·4
1868	5,662	1,938	967	106	1,768	10,441	11·2
1869	6,668	6,449	1,601	429	1,819	16,966	18·3
1870	8,603	518	...	68	3,419	12,608	13·60
1871	12,954	701	2,093	61	1,524	17,338	18·69
1872	15,307	593	3,036	799	1,232	21,027	19·85
1873	14,063	4,678	4,152	350	1,605	24,848	23·13

In 1873-74 there were 14,743 vaccine operations, of which 12,229 were successful, 1,637 were unsuccessful, and the results in 877 cases were unknown.

Amongst the deaths from other causes the following are recorded as due to injuries :—

Year.	Suicide.			Wounds.			Accidents.			Snake-bites.			Total.
	Male.	Female.	Total.	Male.	Female.	Total.	Male.	Female.	Total.	Male.	Female.	Total.	
1871 ...	23	9	32	6	10	16	75	83	158	16	18	34	240
1872 ...	27	16	43	29	27	56	64	72	136	47	33	80	315
1873 ...	8	27	35	7	4	11	30	30	60	11	12	23	129

Cattle disease is very common, and assumes a virulent form in the rainy season. The poor half-starved cattle gorge themselves with the rank grass which flourishes as soon as the rain falls. Foot-and-mouth disease seems to be produced by the cattle standing in and cropping the wet herbage in the rains. The local treatment of this disease consists in placing the hoof of the animal on a heated brick and washing the diseased part with wine *(sharáb)* and water. A mash of *dál* (split pulse), flour and oil is also given. In *bádan* or dysentery, black-pepper, ghi, aniseed, sugar, and rice-water are the remedies employed. . In *aphara* or windy colic, ammonia, salt, borax, and *gúr* are given. Cattle disease is also attributed to the existence of a noxious insect on certain grasses during the rains. In 1871 it was estimated that about one thousand head of cattle died of these diseases during the year.

Cattle disease.

Amongst the indigenous drugs used by the native physicians in this district the following may be mentioned :—Opium as a sedative ; capsules of the poppy plant as a stimulant and expectorant ; *ispaghul (Plantago ispaghula)* useful in diarrhœa ; *bel (Ægle marmelos)* as a tonic and febrifuge ; pomegranate fruit in dysentery ; flowers of the *madár (Calatropis Hamiltonii)* used in cholera and dyspepsia ; tobacco used as a sternatatory ; *tulsi (Ocymum sanctum)* a demulcent ; *imli* or tamarind used as a laxative ; *amaltás (Cassia fistula)* used as a purgative ; castor-oil ; *dhatúra (Datura alba)* in cough and leprosy ; gum arabic, muriate of ammonia, and ginger are also used. Dr. Jackson thus describes the local practice of medicine in this district :—" The treatment adopted by both Hindú and Musalmán physicians is based on a system of physiology which divides the active principles in the system into air, blood, and bile, and the remedies are divided into hot and cold, as also the temperament. The system has been handed down for ages, and is the very essence of empiricism. The Muhammadan *hakím* is certainly ahead of the Hindú, having less faith in *mantras*

Indigenous drugs.

and charms, and it is not uncommon to find him well versed in European remedies. He looks on derangement of the stomach and digestion as the source of all disease. The stomach is likened to a retort, gases from which during the process of digestion proceed to the brain, where they are distilled in the form of fluid which may exercise a most pernicious effect. Filtering downwards this fluid causes catarrh, and attacking the lungs is the source of hemoptysis and consumption, and, if it finds its way to the intestinal canal, dysenteries, cholera, and other bowel complaints are the result. In the treatment of disease the *hakim* has travelled in the same groove as his forefathers, and his patient is perfectly satisfied with hot and cold remedies, while the result, successful or the reverse, is attributed with stoical resignation to all-powerful *kismat*."

There were dispensaries at Koil, Háthras, Sikandra Rao, and Khair in 1872, which treated 12,915 out-door patients and 742 in-door patients. The Koil dispensary was established by private subscriptions through Mr. Blunt in 1849, and was placed under Government in 1851, when branch dispensaries were also opened at Sikandra Rao and Háthras. In 1853 the average attendance at these three dispensaries was 3,328 per annum, it is now 3,414. In 1872, Mr. Bramley, C.S., gave a good house to the Koil dispensary, which now affords ample accommodation to the whole city.

GAZETTEER

OF THE

ALIGARH DISTRICT.

CONTENTS.

AHAN or Ehan, a town parganah Háthras of the Aligarh district, is distant 10 miles from Háthras and 25 miles from Aligarh. In 1865 there were 1,296 inhabitants, and in 1872 there were 1,380. It has a police-station.

AKRABAD, a village in parganah Akrabad and tahsíli Sikandra of the Aligarh district, is situated on the Grand Trunk Road, 12 miles from Aligarh and 11 miles from Sikandra. The population in 1861 was 2,008 ; in 1865, 2,199 ; and in 1872, 2,197. There is a police-station, encamping-ground, and munsifi here. The Chaukidári Act (XX. of 1856) is in force in Akrabad, and in 1873 supported a village police numbering six men of all grades, at an annual cost of

Rs. 324. The number of the houses in the town in 1872-3 was 477, and of these, 460 were assessed with a house-tax averaging Re. 0-13-3 per house and Re. 0-2-1 per head of the population per annum. The income for the same year was Rs. 532, including a balance of Rs. 149 from the previous year, and the expenditure was Rs. 520. In 1857 Mangal Singh and Mahtab Rai of Akrabad not only allowed their followers to plunder the tahsíl after the mutineers had looted the treasure, but refused all aid to the tahsíldár, and lived a life of open rebellion. On the 6th October, 1857, Akrabad was captured by Colonel Greathed's column, and the two rebel leaders were captured, tried, and executed. Their brethren, Tej Singh and Jawáhir Singh, proved loyal. Akrabad or Akbarabad is said to have been founded by the Emperor Akbar during one of his hunting excursions.

AKRABAD or Akbarabad, a parganah of the Aligarh district, is bounded on the north by parganah Gangíri; on the south by parganahs Háthras and Sikandra; on the east by Gangíri and Sikandra; and on the west by Koil and Háthras. According to the settlement records, Akrabad in 1873 comprised an area of 74,226 acres, of which 19,322 acres were unassessable, 5,052 acres were culturable, and 49,852 acres were cultivated. The physical features of the parganah present no peculiarities, being a level plain bounded by the Káli or Kalindri Nadi on the north-east, and the Isan for a short distance on the south-west. There are a few small jhíls at Gopi, Akrabad, and Golahra Saháwali. At the last place the fourth division of the Ganges Canal branches off for Etáwa. The Grand Trunk Road to Meerut runs through Akrabad, which is also connected by cross roads with Jaláli, Barla, and Bijaigarh, and externally with Sásni, and through Kauriyaganj with Kásganj. The principal towns are Akrabad, Pilkhana, Bijaigarh, and Kauriyaganj.

The parganah is made up of portions of parganah Jaláli on the north and
Fiscal history.
parganah Akrabad or Akbarabad on the south. These were originally separate tahsíls, the head-quarters of Jaláli being at Pilkhana; but they were united in 1840, and the head-quarters were fixed at Akrabad on the Grand Trunk Road. Both parganahs belong to the Ceded Provinces. At the revision of settlement under Regulation IX. of 1833, parganahs Pachlána[1] and Gangíri belonged to the Akrabad tahsíl, and were subsequently transferred to Atrauli in exchange for taluka Datauli. Similarly, parganah Jaláli contained taluka Sásni, transferred in 1840 to Háthras. Akrabad and Jaláli were settled by Messrs. H. Rose and W. B. Wright in 1839, and Datauli by Mr. J. Thornton in 1836. The proportion of irrigation in Akrabad at the settlement was 59 per cent., and in numbers of the estates *kuchcha* wells were impracticable. In Jaláli the percentage of irrigation was 76. The increase in the former was Rs. 1,674, falling at Re. 1-14-6 on the

[1] Pachlána is now in the Eta district.

cultivated, and at Re. 1-12-6 on the assessed area per acre ; in the latter the increase was Rs. 932.

The new settlement has been made by Mr. W. H. Smith, and shows the following statistics :—

Total area.	Revenue-free.	Barren.	Culturable area.	Cultivated area			Total culturable.
				Irrigated.	Unirrigated.	Total.	
Acres.	Acres.	Acres.	Acres.	Acres.	Acres.	Acres.	Acres.
74,226	153	19,169	5,052	45,635	4,217	49,852	54,904

The percentage of unassessable land to the total area is 26, and of the culturable area to the total area is 74, but 92 per cent. of the culturable area is cultivated, and 91 per cent. of the cultivated area is irrigated. There has been an immense increase in the proportion of irrigation to cultivation since the last settlement, entirely due to the opening of the canal. The new assessment amounts to Rs. 1,30,980 for land revenue, and Rs. 13,098 for cesses. The initial revenue of the past settlement stood at Rs. 92,817, and the expiring revenue at Rs. 90,627, thus giving an actual increase of Rs. 40,353, or 44 per cent. The incidence of the new revenue on cultivation is Rs. 2-10-0 per acre, against a former incidence of Re. 1-14-11. The results of the last settlement, as regards the transfer of property, show that 8,202 acres were farmed on account of arrears of revenue, whilst the changes due to voluntary transfers, such as private sale, mortgage, &c., and to transfers by auction under orders of the Civil Courts, were as follow :—

		Area in acres.	Land revenue.	Price per area.	Years' purchase.
			Rs.	Rs. a. p.	
Private sale	...	17,070	21,770	13 0 7	10·0
Mortgage ...	...	16,415	22,471	10 0 1	7·8
Auction ...	...	11,914	14,740	4 7 1	3·5
Total	...	45,399	58,984	9 11 0	7·4

The selling price of land in this parganah is shown to have risen soon after the expiry of the first decade of Mr. Thornton's settlement. From 1839 to 1848 the price fetched by land at private sales was 8·5 years' purchase of the land-revenue ; in the next ten years this had risen to ten years, and in the last decade to eleven years. The permanent transfers from the old proprietors have amounted to 41·3 per cent. of the total area, whilst mortgages are only 11·4 per cent.

Out of 24 villages owned by the Pundír Thákur of Bijaigarh, only 17 now remain to him. Rajpúts, Brahmans, Kirárs, and Musalmáns have been the principal losers. In this parganah, out of 40,990 acres transferred, 25,922 acres belonged to persons who owned three-fourths or more of an estate. The following statement shows more clearly the nature of the changes amongst the proprietary body from 1838 to 1868 :—

Caste.	Area held in 1838 in acres.	Lost between 1838 and 1868 by			Remaining.	Caste.	Area held in 1838 in acres.	Lost between 1838 and 1868 by			Remaining.
		Sale.	Mortgage, &c.	Total.				Sale.	Mortgage, &c.	Total.	
Brahman,	3,649	480	411	891	2,758	Ahír, ...	299	246	...	246	53
Khatri, ...	1,327	1,327	...	1,327	...	Baniya,...	45r	...	...	...	458
Kayath,...	6,216	2,507	1,0r5	3,512	2,7o4	Lodha, ...	1,529	717	483	1,200	329
Rajpút, ...	51,561	21,01i	9,235	:0, 69	2!,315	Ját, ...	3u9	...	...	...	369
Gosháin, .	339	259	...	245	80	Garariya,	358	...	358	358	...
Dhusar,...	3,114	...	..	...	...	Musalmán,	6,735	772	2,179	2,951	3,764

Of the 110 estates found in the parganah during the year of measurement, 77 were held in zamíndári and 33 in imperfect pattidári tenure. Thirty-four per cent. of the total area was held by proprietors possessing more than one village ; 36 per cent. by proprietors who were less than six in number, and possessed one village or less than one village ; and the remainder by proprietors who numbered over six sharers. The percentage of the land-revenue paid by each of these classes was 32·5, 40, and 27·5 per cent. respectively. Kharíf crops during the season of measurement occupied 22,144 acres of the cultivated area, and the rabi crops covered 27,698 acres. Amongst the kharíf crops, cotton occupied 7,470 acres, jodr 8,126 acres, indigo 3,039 acres, and bájra 2,226 acres. The principal rabi crops were wheat, 22,144 acres ; barley, 12,425 acres ; bejar, 5,656 acres ; and goji, 4,747 acres. 497 holdings were held by proprietors as seer, 2,541 by hereditary tenants, and 1,724 by tenants-at-will. Only 6 acres out of 49,842 acres leased to tenants paid rent in kind, and the average rental per acre was Rs. 4-6-4, viz., Rs. 4-1-8 for hereditary tenants and Rs. 4-12-0 for tenants-at-will. Seventeen per cent. of the total area is held as seer by proprietors, 46 per cent. is cultivated by hereditary tenants, and 37 per cent. by tenants-at-will. The average area of the holdings of each class is 17 acres, .8·9 acres, and 10·6 acres respectively. In 1855 hereditary tenants possessed 996 holdings, averaging 12·4 acres, and paying an average rental of Rs. 3-10-6 per acre ,whilst tenants-at-will cultivated 2,466 holdings, averaging 12·6 acres each, and paying an average rental of Rs. 4-3-11 per acre. Altogether here, as in Sikandra Rao, the rental has increased, whilst the average area of the holdings has decreased.[1]

According to the census of 1872 pargana Akrabad contained 87 inhabited villages, of which 13 had less than 200 inhabitants, 33 had between 200 and 500, 25 had between 500 and 1,000, 10 had between 1,000 and 2,000, 2 had between 2,000 and 3,000, and 3 had between 3,000 and 5,000. The only town containing more than 5,000 inhabitants is Bijaigarh, with 5,652. The settlement records show that there are 113 maháls or estates in the parganah, containing 89 villages, which have an average area of 834 acres each. The total population in 1872 numbered 64,747 souls (29,731 females), giving 566 to the square mile. Classified according to religion, there were 56,898 Hindús, of whom 25,990 were females ; 7,845 Musalmáns, amongst whom 3,739 were females ; and 4 Christians. Distributing the Hindú population amongst the four great classes, the census shows 7,585 Brahmans, of whom 3,417 were females ; 7,448 Rajpúts, including 3,261 females ; 3,232 Baniyas (1,519 females) ; whilst the great mass of the population is included in " the other castes" of the census returns, which show a total of 38,633 souls, of whom 17,793 are females. The principal Brahman subdivisions found in this parganah are the Gaur (412), Saraswat (214), and Sanádh (162). The Rajpúts belong to the Gahlot (199), Chauhán (433), Badgújar (115), Jádon (489), Janghára, Tomar, Pundír, and Panwár clans. The Baniyas are chiefly Agarwáls (369), Chausainis (143), Dasas, Mathuriyas, and Jaiswárs. The principal divisions of the other castes are the Ját, Sonár, Barhai (1,300), Hajjám (1,287), Ráj, Máli, Bhát, Kalál (1,904), Gosháin, Ahír (2,901), Káchhi (1,455), Joshi, Darzi, Kahár (1,910), Jogi, Bairági, Dhobi, Lohár, Koli (1,276), Chamár (9,843), Khatík, Khákrob (1,547), Kumhár, Garariya (3,741), Aheriya (726), Orh, Banjára, Kayath, Lodha (2,068), Dhúna, Bharbhúnja, Teli, Kanjar, Ghosi, Chhípi, Bári, and Nuniya. The Musalmáns are distributed amongst Shaikhs (1,545), Sayyids (258), Mughals (116), and Patháns (508) ; the remainder are unspecified.

The occupations of the people are shown in the statistics collected at the census of 1872. From these it appears that of the male adult population (not less than fifteen years of age), 256 are employed in professional avocations, such as Government servants, priests, doctors, and the like ; 2,782 in domestic service, as personal servants, water-carriers, barbers, sweepers, washermen, &c. ; 2,106 in commerce, in buying, selling, keeping or lending money or goods, or the conveyance of

Population.

Occupations.

---

[1] See Rev. Rep., N. S., II., 105.

men, animals, or goods ; 9,388 in agricultural operations ; 2,830 in industrial occupations, arts and mechanics, and the preparation of all classes of substances, vegetable, mineral and animal. There were 4,234 persons returned as labourers, and 367 as of no specified occupation. Taking the total population, irrespective of age or sex, the same returns give 1,475 as landholders, 25,251 as cultivators, and 38,021 as engaged in occupations unconnected with agriculture. The educational statistics, which are confessedly imperfect, show 1,328 males as able to read and write out of a total male population numbering 36,016 souls. In 1863, 22 villages of Akrabad were transferred to Atrauli, aggregating 43,624 acres and giving a land-revenue of Rs. 50,707, and in 1862, 23 villages were transferred to parganah Koil, and 4 to Háthras.

ALIGARH, the head-quarters of the district, with the town of Koil, may, for all practical purposes, be regarded as one and the same place. Aligarh is so called from the neighbouring fort of that name, known at different times as Muhammadgarh, Sábitgarh, Rámgarh, and, since the time of Najf Khán as Aligarh. It lies in latitude 27°-55'-41" and longitude 78°-6'-45."

In 1847 the city of Koil had 36,181 inhabitants ; in 1853 the population numbered 55,001. and in 1865 there were 48,403 inhabitants. The site has an area of 400 square acres, giving 146 souls to the acre. According to the census of 1872 there were 58,539 inhabitants, of whom 39,012 were Hindús (17,343 females), 19,489 were Musalmáns (9,422 females), and 38 were Christians (12 females.) Distributing the population amongst the rural and urban classes, the returns show 417 landholders, 1,982 cultivators, and 54,128 persons pursuing occupations unconnected with agriculture. The number of enclosures in 1872 was 7,142, of which 2,571 were occupied by Musalmáns. The number of houses during the same year was 11,276, of which 3,963 were built with skilled labour, and of these 995 were occupied by Musalmáns. Of the 7,313 mud huts in the town, 3,153 were owned by persons of the same religion. Taking the male adult population, 19,718 souls (not less than fifteen years of age), we find the following occupations pursued by more than fifty adult males :—Attornies, 61 ; barbers, 322 ; beggars, 473 ; blacksmiths, 189 ; bricklayers, 179 ; butchers, 271 ; carpenters, 202 ; carpet-makers, 104 ; cartmen, 406 ; cotton-cleaners, 82 ; dancing boys, 144 ; druggists, 86 ; dyers, 416 ; flour-dealers, 82 ; goldsmiths, 219 ; grain-dealers, 134 ; grain-parchers, 127 ; green-grocers, 167 ; inn-keepers, 129 ; labourers, 3,300 ; leather-dyers, 330 ; lime-burners, 82 ; merchants, 506 ; money-lenders, 215 ; oil-makers, 93 ; painters, 71 ; porters, 498 ; potters, 160 ; purohits, 121 ; servants, 6,368 ; shopkeepers, 1,557 ; sieve-makers, 67 ; sweepers, 289 ; tailors, 161 ; tobacconists, 79 ; washermen, 214 ; water-carriers, 423 ; weavers, 1,719 ; and wine-sellers, 214. From these figures it would appear that the population has increased by 22,358 souls since 1847.

Koil is rather a handsome town in its general appearance, and is particularly well situated. The centre of the town is occupied by the high site of an old Dor fort, now crowned by Sábit Khán's mosque, which forms a conspicuous object in the landscape from whichever side the town is approached. The

The site. precincts of the mosque have been much improved of late years by clearing and levelling the space around and paving it with kunkur. The new tahsíli, also, is placed here, and, close to it, a number of fine shops have been built by the municipality. From this central space one wide road runs to the north-east, to the railway station, and another runs westward to the Khair road, whilst it is contemplated to make a third road to the southward, to eventually wind to the westward and open up a portion of the city that most needs improvement. The really business part of the city lies to the eastward, between the high central site and the railway. The principal bazarway runs from north to south, and is crossed by the road to the railway station, and a branch connecting it with the Grand Trunk Road, which serves as the main line of communication for the east of the town. The road from Muttra to Rámghat, on the Ganges, also furnishes an important commercial way. All these roads are well made, drained and paved with kunkur, and even many of the small connecting ways are paved, and all are drained to a certain extent. The smaller lanes have room for improvement, but vigorous efforts are being made by the municipality, and it is hoped that within a few years the whole town will be effectually paved and drained. The situation is decidedly healthy, and the facilities for drainage, on the whole, are fairly good. The heavy rains of 1871 and 1874, however, caused considerable lodgements of surface water in some places, but the remedy for this is practicable. In the principal streets the houses are chiefly built of bricks, but the greater number are made of earth. The outskirts, especially to the east and south, are low, so that the drainage there passes off very slowly, and, as a rule, they are not so well kept as the interior of the town.

The town contains 101 muhallas or wards, many of which go by the name of Sarái, as Hakím-ke-Sarái, Babu-ke-Sarái, and the

Subdivisions of the town. like. A good part of the town probably originated in clusters of saráis, this being a central halting-place for travellers to Dehli, Agra, Muttra, Rohilkhand, &c. The northern part of the principal bazarway is called Miyánganj, and from it branch off the large market-place of the same name and Perronganj. Russellganj was founded by Mr. Claude Russell in 1805, and in rivalry with it, one Hakím Asad Ali built the sarái known by his name. The descendants of the Hakím still reside in the city in very poor, circumstances. Neither De Boigne nor Perron did anything for the city. De Boigne's residence lay outside the city towards the fort, and is the same as that occupied by Perron before the siege in 1803. It is called the Sáhib Bagh.

It consists of a large two-storeyed building situated in the midst of a garden and surrounded by a high wall and bastions. It was here that Perron held his court and kept a garrison consisting of his body-guard and a few artillery with light field-pieces. Of late years it has been used as a settlement office, but is now in a very dilapidated condition. Portions of the premises still belong to the Messieurs Derridon, great-grandsons of M. Perron's sister, and there are still some remains of the bastion and the garden. Perron had another large garden opposite Thornton's factory, now occupied by one Nasr-ullah. Both Perron and De Boigne were fond of gardening, and formed plantations of fruit trees obtained from all parts of India, and even from Europe and Persia. M. Pedron, who commanded in Aligarh at the conquest in 1803, had his house in the midst of an extensive garden, where the Judge's Court now stands. Dudrenec lived in a house in the outskirts now occupied by one Khushwakt Ali. The city in De Boigne's time extended only as far as the large masonry building on the edge of Perronganj, and that quarter is still known as Aligarh darwáza. Beyond this house to the north-west there was only a bare open plain ; close to it, on the road, were the cotton screws and indigo factories of Mr. John Thornton, one of the first planters in the district. Mr. Longcroft's factories lay on the Meerut road, where the remains of old vats are yet to be seen, and his garden is now in the possession of one Badari Parshád. Messrs. Robertson and Stewart had also residences near the city. Mr. John Thornton's house was recently purchased by Mr. Bramly, C.S., and presented to the city for a dispensary. Kinlochganj, named after the Collector of that name, stands on the site of Sábit Khán's garden, and contains Sábit Khán's tomb and those of his family. Sábit Khán purchased many estates for his family, but through extravagance and carelessness his descendants are now in penury, and the only sign now remaining of their former position is the self-assumed title of Nawáb.

Nawáb Sábit Khán's mosque stands on an eminence in the centre of the city known as the Bála Kila. From the inscription given in the history of the district (page 498) it appears to have been commenced in 1724 A.D., and it was finished in 1728 A.D. The architecture is the debased style of the last century. The building has five cupolas,—three in the middle and one on each side. The side cupolas are of the peculiar shape which Mr. Ferguson declares to be borrowed from the bambu roof of a hut in the Lower Provinces ; yet the mosque, as seen from a distance, is by no means without beauty and even dignity. The materials are block kunkur, brick in the domes, and here and there red sandstone. The last must have been brought from some place beyond the Jumna. The mosque at present, notwithstanding the glitter of its gilded pinnacles, is not in a good state of repair, and reflects little credit upon the Musalmán population.

The mosque.

Buddhist and Hindú remains have been discovered in making excavations in the Bála Kila, and there must be still many more there. Several of the fragments found have been placed in the compound of the Institute, and contrast in their elegance with the ugly fountain erected there. Near the fort of the Bála Kila, and south-east of the Jámah Masjid or great mosque, is a smaller and somewhat more ornate mosque, attributed also to Sábit Khán, and known as the Moti Masjid. Another memorial of the Nawáb is the tank near the mosque.

Although the tomb of Shaikh Jamál is held in most reverence by the pious,
Gesu Khán. the tomb of Gesu Khán is undoubtedly the most beautiful of the mortuary buildings around the town. It is an open pillared *chhatri*, such as the early Musalmáns imitated and modified from the Hindús. Close behind it is an Idgáh bearing an inscription showing that it was built by Gesu Khán in 1563 A.D. (page 448). Local tradition makes this personage governor of the town during the reign of Akbar. Altogether there are nearly one hundred imámbarahs in the town. The Hindús have many temples, but none of them are of any antiquity or deserving of notice. The temple of Achaleswar, in the southern portion of the city, borders the Achal tank; it is built of kunkur blocks. The tank is of considerable size, and is supplied with tolerably pure water from the Ganges Canal. The temple was a common building until the Játs came, who presented several valuable gifts to the priests and enlarged the temple. There is a large masonry tank on the Dehli road, built about 200 years ago by Jálu Rai, a Kayath, which is now in ruins and used as a melon garden.

The site of the present fort was originally known as Rámgarh, from the
Fort. village of that name close to it. The oldest inscription as yet discovered connects it with one Muhammad, who was holder of the *shikk* of Koil under the Lodis in 1524 A.D., and who called it Muhammadgarh after his own name.[1] This name was changed to Sábitgarh at the beginning of the last century (about 1717 A.D.), and to Rámgarh by the Játs about 1757. Najf Khán took the fort and changed the name to Aligarh, which it has since retained. Its successive holders, and notably Afrásyáb Khán, repaired and strengthened the works in every possible way, and the Marhattas only obtained possession by stratagem. De Boigne and Perron both employed all the military skill available in those days to render the fortress impregnable. Nature itself assisted them. The vicinity of the fort for some distance is interspersed with marshes and shallow pieces of water, which become so much swollen during the rains as to render the place inaccessible, and consequently secure from attack at that season. The outline of the works at the time of the capture by the British was a polygon of probably ten sides, having at each

---

[1] Page 488.

angle a bastion, with a renny or fausse-braie, well provided with cannon. Outside this line of defence was a ditch, above 100 feet wide, thirty feet deep from the top of the excavation, and having ten feet of water. Across this ditch was no passage, but by a narrow causeway, defended by a traverse, mounted with three 6-pounders. The result of the attack by the British has already been related.[1] After the capture the fort was insulated by cutting away the causeway and replacing it by a drawbridge; the entrance was strengthened by a ravelin, the ramparts were lowered, a glacis and covered way were added, and the interior was cleared of numerous buildings, which it was thought might interfere with the defence. It was occupied by a few of the rebels for a short time in 1857. The walls and bastions were again repaired in 1858, and barracks for Europeans were built inside, and the trench outside deepened so as to contain seven feet of water in the rains. The fort is now, however, quite unoccupied and garrisoned only by a single watchman under the Public Works Department. There can be no doubt that it could easily be refitted for military purposes, but it is unhealthy. Besides, a force of British soldiers sufficient to garrison the fort should be able to hold their own in the field against any odds, and it is, of course, highly undesirable that it should be occupied by a hostile or insurrectionary army.

The Koil Minár, as we have seen, was erected in 1253 A.D. to commemo-

The Koil Minár.

rate the victories of Sultán Násir-ud-dín.[2] A writer in Ledlie's Miscellany gives an account of the pillar, and winds up with " a hope that the local authorities or the Government may be induced to interpose on behalf of this relic of antiquity. Though vastly inferior to the Kutb Minár at Dehli in size and beauty, it is almost equal in historical interest, and deserves to be rescued from the grasp of decay's effacing fingers." Alas for his hopes, for in August, 1862, it was pulled down with the sanction of Mr. G. Edmonstone, Lieutenant-Governnor, to make room for improvements around the mosque, and for a row of shops which have never yet been let. The Minár stood on the high ground of the Bála Kila. It consisted of a round tower on a square base, apparently divided by external cornices into stages, or it may be that balconies were at one time thrown out as in the Dehli pillar. At the time of demolition, the first stage and a part of the second still remained. The base was of block kunkur, with a few pieces of red sandstone ; the first stage was entirely of block kunkur, and the second of burned bricks. To the north, a doorway opened on a spiral staircase made of block kunkur which originally led to the top of the column. The staircase was lighted by several apertures, and opened on the balcony at the top of the first stage. The lower stage was 54 feet high, and what remained of the second stage was 20 feet. The external circumference at the base was

---

[1] Page 502.　　[2] Page 486. The inscription is preserved in the Aligarh Institute.

80 feet, and the walls here were six feet, diminishing at the top of the first stage to four and a half feet. Immediately where the kunkur staircase terminated, there was an ornamental Hindú pillar laid across the stairway, and above this several beams of wood, which would appear to show that the second stage was built by other hands, and was of comparatively recent origin. It is a little remarkable that the Hindús of Koil appear to have invented a mythical origin for their pillar, just as those of Dehli did for the Kutb; and as in the Dehli tradition so in that of Koil, the tower was erected at the desire of the pious daughter of the king, who wished to look daily upon the sacred stream of the Jumna or Ganges. The coincidence can hardly be accidental, and we may well admire the ingenuity which thus disguises a badge of defeat and slavery.

The tomb of Iláh Baksh stands close to the Moti Masjid. It is small, but handsome and cupola shaped. From the inscription

Tomb of Iláh Baksh. given on a previous (page 489), it would appear to have been built by Sábit Khán for the fakír Iláh Baksh in 1717 A.D. Local tradition says that the tomb was originally built by the Nawáb for his own remains, but that warned by the fakír Sháh Iláh Baksh that he should never lie in the tomb that he had built, the Nawáb defiantly or jestingly replied that either he or the fakír should lie in it, whichever died first. It so happened that the fakír did die first, and his heirs claimed the fulfilment of the promise. So his remains were laid in the Nawáb's sepulchre, whilst Sábit Khán himself was buried in his own garden now occupied by Kinlochganj.

About a quarter of a mile to the west of the Jámah Masjid, there is a curious group of tombs to the south of the Khair road. The

Sháh Jamál. central one, and that which is most venerated by natives, is called the dargáh of Sháh Jamál, Shams-ul-Arifin. The building itself is insignificant, but the surrounding graveyard contains a number of slab tombs and head stones, many of them evidently of considerable antiquity. The inscriptions on a good many are in Arabic. Sháh Jamál is supposed to have been one of the original invaders of Koil, and the tombs in the neighbourhood probably contain the remains of some of the besiegers. Local tradition makes Jamál to be a Tátar darvesh who took up his abode near Koil previous to the siege and capture by Ala-ud-dín Ghori. The darvesh predicted the capture, when the assailants were reduced to despair by the long resistance of the town and the sickness that prevailed amongst themselves. Two of Jamál's disciples perished in the attack which took place the next day, and in which the town was taken. It is possible that Sháh Jamál and his disciples were spies of the Ghorian invader, as fakírs have been both before and since his time. One of his disciples is buried in the Mámu Bhanja Muhalla in the city, and the other at the tomb called Aulia Ambia; others are buried in the nameless tombs about the city, near which are some fine tamarind trees.   Many of these tombs had endowments, but owing to mismanagement and extravagance and the subdivision of property, the khádims have fallen into poverty and the tombs are now in very bad repair.

Pír Bahádur was a cavalry commander of some note in Ala-ud-dín's army,

Pír Bahádur.

who was killed in the assault on Koil.   His remains lie near the (late) Military Hospital, and there used to be a superstition that it was dangerous to gallop a horse in the vicinity of the tomb. In corroboration of this belief, a story is told of the son of a former tahsíldár of Koil who was thrown from his horse, and, becoming entangled in the stirrup, was dragged along the road till he died, because he galloped close to the tomb.   However of late days the station race-course has been established not far from it, without any manifestation of resentment on the part of the Pír.

Sháh Jamál was another chief in the Muslim army whose tomb is not far

Sháh Jamál.

from the railway station.   The villages of Jamálpur and Dhorera are still held as a revenue-free grant for the support of the dargáh of Sháh Jamál.   The estimated land-revenue of these villages amounts to Rs. 1,440 per annum.   An *urs* (or religious gathering) is held at the tomb of Sháh Jamál in June, at which about 2,000 persons assemble for worship.   In former times the city had several gates, of which the names of the Madár, Dehli, Túrkmán, Sásni, and Aligarh darwázas still survive. Of these, only the vestige of one pillar of the Aligarh gate now remains near the dargáh of Kalan Shahíd.

I now pass from the city to the precincts occupied by the civil station or

Public institutions.

Aligarh proper.   The station is admirably kept, and consists of a series of private residences and the post-office on one side of a large central space, and on the other the public offices, courts, zila school, the institute building, and the cemetery.   The telegraph office is on the south-side of the East Indian Railway, on the outskirts of the city.   The old cemetery of 1802 lies towards the fort.   There was a military cantonment here until 1870, when the cantonment was abandoned and the lands were handed over to the Koil municipality.   Besides the Judge's and the Magistrate's Courts, the principal buildings are as follow :—The Anglo-vernacular school, with an average attendance of 125 boys, of whom 25 are boarders : the latter live in a separate house specially built for them and adjoining the school.   The Aligarh Institute and Scientific Society has already been described in the district notice (page 403).   The post-office workshops were first started about 32 years ago by Dr. Paton, Postmaster-General, when the custom of carrying mails by the agency of runners was superseded by the innovation of wheeled carriages, mail-carts, and bullock wagons.   The experiment was found to be so successful that almost every part of India was supplied from these workshops, not only with carts and wagons, but also with bags, stamps, and other postal apparatus. Soon there arose a colony of workmen, and skilled labour was never wanting in times of emergency. Thus, after the mutiny, as many as 2,000 workmen were employed, and to the workshops is the credit due of the rapidity with which postal communication was re-established at that critical period. Since the opening of the railway the operations of the workshop have been considerably curtailed: at present only between 300 and 400 workmen are employed, consisting of carpenters, iron-smiths, leather-workers, stamp-cutters, &c. The net cost of articles manufactured, exclusive of all profit, is upwards of Rs. 70,000 per annum. The district jail stands to the west of the station : it is built for over 500 prisoners and is usually full.

The East Indian Railway Station, a well constructed and commodious building, lies between the city and the civil station. The line of the railway here runs in a north-westerly direction, and the traffic between the city and the country lying beyond the civil station passes the railway by level crossings north-west and south-east of the railway station. A junction station for the Oudh and Rohilkhand Railway is under construction. There is a small church in the centre of the station, built by Mr. T. P. Woodcock in 1838. Just where the railway passes the jail, at the south-west corner of the jail enclosure, stands a small, plain and indeed ugly, domed monument commemorating the officers who fell in the assault on the Aligarh fort in 1803. Near the premises of the dispensary and the Government Telegraph Office, and also in the grounds of a house in the civil station belonging to Mr. Bramley, C.S., are some old brick tombs, the inscriptions on which have perished. They are certainly not Muhammadan, and most probably mark the burial-place of some of the French residents of M. Perron's time. Mr John Péche, the last survivor of Perron's companions, died in February, 1872. In Koil there is a dispensary in Russellganj and an important vernacular school known as the " *Madrassah-i-mafíd-i-khaláik.*"

Dr. Whitwell analysed the waters of the civil and military stations, as well as those of the jail and railway station, in August, 1869. He remarked[1] that the station had been abandoned as a military post owing to the prevalence of fever, and that all the drinking water with one exception was unusually foul, being greatly contaminated by sewage matter, and the water in the well on the railway platform, from its proximity to the latrine and urinal, was particularly unwholesome. The exception was the Ganges Canal water, which appeared to be so free from impurities of any kind that it would be desirable to supply the whole population from it. The physical properties of all the waters examined when passed through filter

Drinking water.

---

[1] Sixth Report on Analyses of Potable Waters, 1870.

paper were found to be good, with an alkaline reaction. The results of some of the analyses were as follows :—

Date of analysis.	Position of water source, and by whom used.	Degrees of total hardness.	Degrees of permanent hardness.	Degrees of removable hardness.	Grains of oxygen required for oxidation of roadily oxidisable organic matter of 1,000 grains of water.	Total solids in 70,000 grains of filtered water.	Volatile matters.	Mineral matters.	Earthly salts, silica, oxide of iron insoluble in water.	Lime calculated as carbonate.	Silica.	Soluble salts.	Chloride of sodium.	Sulphate of soda.	Carbonate of soda.
16th Aug., 1869.	Well No.1, Infantry Lines.	5·4	3·0	2·4	·00025	30·59	2·2	41·5	29·0	10·5	11·5	12·5	3·0	5·5902	5·7078
18th do.,	Well No. 5, in the School compound.	9·95	3·2	6·75	·000375	33·25	1·75	31·5	18·55	10·955	3·57	12·95	5·25	8·4155	2·5681
20th do.,	Well No. 3, in the Jail Garden.	12·21	1·81	10·4	·0002	21·525	1·75	19·775	12·775	6·3	4·025	7·0	1·89	4·5	5·898
21st do.,	Tank, south-west part of city.	2·318	2·18	·138	·00075	12·6	1·4	11·2	7·0	3·465	3·5	4·2	2·1	5·1924	·47565
23rd do.,	Branch of Ganges, Canal, 3 miles above the native city.	3·2	3·2	None.	·00045	8·925	·975	8·05	5·775	3·71	2·43	2·275	·535	3·979	·66591
25th do.,	Well No. 6, on the Railway platform.	10·91	10·4	·54	·0009	69·3	5·25	64·05	25·735	14·35	4·723	8·325	20·478	15·09	·8539

The local rainfall for a series of years as recorded by the canal authorities has been as follows :—

Year.	April.	May.	June.	July.	August.	September.	October.	November.	December.	January.	February.	March.	Total.
1866-67 ...	...	...	·5	10·8	14·2	1·2	·3	...	...	·4	...	1·0	28·4
1867-68 ...	·5	·8	1·1	12·8	7·9	1·4	1·0	...	·9	·6	2·1	·4	29·5
1868-69 ...	·2	1·8	·7	4·6	·3	·5	...	...	...	1·2	·2	1·3	10·8
1869-70 ...	...	...	...	4·7	6·2	5·9	5·8	...	·9	·3	...	4·2	28·0
1870-71 ...	...	...	...	7·4	7·6	6·8	2·1	...	·9	·7	2·8	...	28·3
1871-72 ...	...	...	·6	4·7	15·1	7·3	·8	...	1·0	·8	...	...	30·3
1872-73 ...	...	...	...	2·9	11·8	13·5	1·5	...	...	·2	·70	...	30·6

There is reason to believe that from the middle of the twelfth century up to the middle of the eighteenth century the land comprised in the town of Koil was held free of revenue by various grantees. Sábit Khán, during the reign of Muhammad Sháh, resumed many of the grants, but these were again released by Najf Khán. Anand Rao, Desmukh of the Marhattas, in 1785, again resumed all the old holdings, allowing in some cases to the ex-grantees six annas of the produce, and in other

Settlement of the town.

cases ten annas. Hence the terms *shashani* and *dasani* applied to these tenures. Those who appealed to Sindhia were restored to their original holdings, whilst very many accepted the new state of things. Previously to the revision of settlement by Mr. Rose, grants to the yearly value of Rs. 4,500 were resumed by Mr. Harvey, but many of his proceedings were reversed, and Mr. G. Blunt assessed the town at only Rs. 5,272. Hitherto the sums due to the grantees were paid from the Government Treasury; but Mr. Blunt placed farmers in possession, confirming Government as landholder. The town was then divided into four maháls or estates, — the Dehli Darwáza, Budaun Darwáza, Míthi Kirki, and Khari Kirki, and the revenue was distributed in the following manner :—

Area in acres.	Assumed rental.	Grantees' allowance.	Residue for the State.	Collection fees to farmer.	Net result.
	Rs.	Rs.	Rs.	Rs.	Rs.
1,736	7,217	1,945	5,272	529	4,743

This state of things lasted until after the mutiny. A complete change was then effected. " The city was conspicuous for its disloyalty, and many of the residents and ex-muáfidárs were found deserving of punishment. Of the ten farmers, eight were Muhammadans and two Hindús. No charge was made against the latter; of the former, one was an absconded rebel, and a son of another had been killed in action with our troops. The Muhammadans indeed had been notoriously refractory, and Mr. Bramley, the Collector, wrote:— ' Against the others, if no overt act can be proved, still the fact of their disaffection has been sufficiently obvious.' He then went on to recommend the immediate transfer of the farm held by the Muhammadans to Raja Gobind Singh of Háthras, who had specially distinguished himself by his good services in behalf of order, leaving the share of the Hindús in their possession for the time, but proposing that it also should be conferred on the Raja on the expiry of the term of settlement in 1868. Not only was this proposal, as far as it went, sanctioned by the Governor-General, but, in addition, the zamíndári rights of Government in the city were conferred on the Raja and his heirs for ever by a sanad dated 5th June, 1866."

The gift was not a valuable one, as it merely placed Gobind Singh in the position of the farmers, whilst the same allowances were paid to Government. At the recent settlement the names and arrangements of the maháls were altered. There are now five pattis or subdivisions forming one mahál, *viz.*, (1) Rání Sáhib Kunwar, including the former revenue-paying land and the revenue-free land which has come into the possession of Gobind Singh and his heirs ; (2)

Patti Muáfi Muzabta, comprising all the resumed revenue-free lands in the possession of the original grantees and assessed at half assets; (3) Patti Muáfiat comprises all revenue-free land a portion or all of which is cultivated ; and (4) Patti Abádi includes sites of houses, bungalows, and land taken up for public purposes.[1] The statistics of each patti are as follows :—

Name of patti.	Total area.	Barren.	Waste.	Cultivated.	Land-revenue.	Cesses.	Fees of lamberdárs.	Total.
	Acres.	Acres	Acres.	Acres.	Rs.	Rs.	Rs.	Rs.
1. Ráni Sahib Kunwar,	758	259	184	315	1,123	112	...	1,235
2. Muáfi Muzabta ...	1,540	57	66	1,417	5,577	558	558	6,693
3. Muáfiat ...	1,345	109	163	1,073	...	480	...	480
4. Abádi	1,058	721	323	14	...	...	...	...
Total ...	4,701	1,146	736	2,819	6,700	1,150	558	8,408

Koil was plundered during the mutiny by the Mewatis of the neighbouring villages, by the passing rebel troops, by Nasím-ullah during his eleven days' rule, and by the British troops.

, There are no manufactures in Koil except a very trifling trade in pottery introduced by Dr. J. Henderson in 1823. The same gentleman made considerable improvements in the manufacture of cotton, indigo, and fine gunpowder. He also founded the Agra United Service Bank and established the *Agra Ukhbar*, under the editorship of Mr. Harry Tandy, who died in Aligarh in 1842. The chief trade is in cotton, for which there are screws near the railway station, and about 8,434 bales of cotton, weighing 31,154 maunds, were exported by the East Indian Railway alone in 1872. The indigo manufacture is altogether in the district ; there are no factories allowed in the town. The affairs

Municipality. of the town are managed by a municipality, numbering fifteen members, of whom five are official and ten are elected by the tax-payers. The income is raised by an octroi tax on imports, which in 1872-73 fell at a rate of Re. 0-11-6 per head of the population. The following table shows the income and expenditure for a series of years, and

---

[1] See further regarding this settlement in Smith's report, 114.

the succeeding table shows the net imports in quautity or value for the year 1872-73 :—

Receipts.	1871-72.	1872-73.	1873-74.	Expenditure.	1871-72.	1672-73.	1873-74.
	Rs.	Rs.	Rs.		Rs.	Rs.	Rs,
Opening balance ...	4,303	5,961	368	Collections ...	5,003	5,114	5,021
Class I.—Food and drink.	29,319	26,699	27,818	Head office ...	273	419	402
				a. Supervision ...	600	515	666
„ II.—Animals for slaughter.	1,012	750	1,740	b. Original works,	12,660	8,784	9,611
				c. Purchase of land	...	2,376	53
„ III.—Fuel, &c.	4,318	2,314	2,282				
„ IV.—Building materials.	2,540	2,263	2,576	d. Compensation,	1,285	...	...
				e. Repairs ...	4 624	2,859	2,791
„ V.—Drugs & spices.	1,493	950	992	Police ...	14,890	14,569	14,415
„ VI.—Tobacco	1 210	948	1,232	Education ...	2,245	2,355	2,392
„ VII.—Textile fabrics.	5,837	5,312	6,830	Charitable grants,	1,093	710	835
				Conservancy ...	2,870	4,024	4,252
„ VIII.—Metals ...	1,293	386	473	Road-watering ...	331	470	473
				Lighting ...	1,795	1,954	1,869
Total Octroi ...	47,022	39,622	43,443	Gardens ...	806	262	449
				Extraordinary ...	600	600	600
Rents ...	408	232	335	Miscellaneous ...	635	2,140	2,044
Gardens ...	41	18	384				
Fines ...	230	48	59				
Pounds ...	934	313	154				
Extraordinary ...	371	432	1,962				
Miscellaneous ...	1,362	895	1,236				
Total ...	54,671	47,521	47,941	Total ...	48,710	47,151	45,273

Articles.				Net imports in quantity.	Net imports in value.	Consumption per head.		
				Mds.	Rs.	Mds.	s.	c.
Grain of sorts ...	...	...		387,478	7,74,530	7	0	13
Rice and kbil ...	...	...		12,560	37,677	0	9	2
Sugar, refined ...	...	...		16,745	2,00,928	0	12	2
Ditto, coarse ...	...	...		70,112	2,79,736	1	10	12
Ghi	...	...		7,085	1,41,703	...		
Fruits and sugar-cane	...	...		7,722	1,49,734	...		
Fodder	...	...		66,169	21,295	...		
Vegetables and milk	...	...		19,540	40,576	...		
Oil	...	...		6,489	51,907	0	4	11
Wax ...	...	...		79	1,579	..		
Oil-seeds ...	...	...		30,318	60,635	0	21	15½
Fuel ...	...	...		176,565	48,298	...		
Soap-nuts, soap, &c.,	...	...		24,337	1,646	...		
Building materials	...	...		73,615	46 096	...		
Iron ...	...	...		1,470	14,641	...		
String, bambús, &c.	...	...		22,950	30,595	...		
Drugs, spices, &c. ...	...	...		14,828	58,934	...		
Tobacco ...	...	...		2,974	9,215	...		
Cloth ...	...	...		...	6,27,259	11	5	9¾
Metals ...	...	...		1,635	49,132	0	14	2¼

From Aligarh military routes branch off by Sásni and Háthras to Agra
(distant 53¼ miles, or five marches); by Jalúli and Kás-

Routes.

ganj to Budaun (distant 73 miles, or 7 marches); by
Jawa and Anúpshahr to Budaon (distant 96¾ miles, or 8 marches); by Somna
and Khúrja to Dehli (distant 80½ miles, or 7 marches); by Jawa and Anúpshahr to Moradabad (distant 80⅝ miles, or 8 marches); by Somna and Bulandshahr to Moradabad (distant 110 miles, or 10 marches), and by Iglás to Muttra
(distant 38⅞ miles, or 3 marches). Each of the stages will be found noticed
in the district alphabetical arrangement under the names of the towns or
halting-places where they occur.

ATRAULI, the chief town of the parganah and tahsíli of the same name in
the Aligarh district, is distant 16 miles from Koil on the Rámghat road.

In 1847 Atrauli had 12,722 inhabitants; in 1853 the population numbered
15,410; in 1858, 14,329; and in 1865 there were

Population.

15,052 inhabitants. The site has an area of 163
square acres, giving 98 souls to the acre. According to the census of 1872
there were 15,941 inhabitants, of whom 9,829 were Hindús (4,643 females), and
6,112 were Musalmáns (3,059 females). Distributing the population amongst
the rural and urban classes, the returns show 483 landholders, 2,070 cultivators,
and 13,388 persons pursuing occupations unconnected with agriculture. The
number of enclosures in 1872 was 2,020, of which 761 were occupied by Musalmáns. The number of houses during the same year was 3,419, of which 960
were built with skilled labour, and of these 283 were occupied by Musalmáns.
Of the 2,459 mud huts in the town, 1,021 were owned by the same religionists.
Taking the male adult population, 4,985 (not less than fifteen years of age), we
find the following occupations pursued by more than fifty males :—Barbers,
90; beggars, 142; bullock-dealers, 73; butchers, 60; calico-printers, 90;
confectioners, 64; flower-sellers, 212; goldsmiths, 81; labourers, 853; merchants, 134; money-lenders, 69; pandits, 59; petty dealers, 75; potters, 55;
servants, 530; shepherds, 99; sweepers, 66; water-carriers, 113; and weavers,
502.

The town is well built, clean and healthy, and the principal ways are fairly
wide, well-drained, and metalled. A good road runs

Site.

under Atrauli to Rámghat on the Ganges. The Káli
is crossed by a fine well-built masonry bridge at the extremity of the Ukhlána
boundary on this road. The three ways of entrance to the town from the
Aligarh road converge on the market-place in the centre of the town, and from
it two bazarways branch off to the east, and then to the south known as the
Mandi and Bara bazárs. In the southern border of the town, these two bazarways join by a curving road, so that the business portion of the town forms an
oval, well-metalled and drained throughout. The Bara bazar is the more

important of the two, and has a fair trade in cotton, iron, brass utensils, and country produce. The Mandi bazar-houses are poor, and many are in a ruinous state. The southern portion of the town is chiefly inhabited by agriculturists and Chamárs, who cultivate the rich lands in the vicinity. The water in wells is found at a depth of 20 feet from the surface, and is good as a rule, though occasionally brackish. There is no canal irrigation near, and drainage could easily be effected to the Káli, distant 2½ miles to the west. There is a tahsíli, police-station, post-office, and a school here. The tahsíli is on a high-raised site in the centre of the town formerly occupied by a fort. It consists of a group of buildings surrounded by a high wall, and communicates by a metalled road, planted with trees, with the market-place below. The sarái lies in the centre of the town between the two bazárs. The school is a church-like building, with many windows ; it is of faulty construction and but badly attended, as the Musalmáns have many private schools at which Persian and the reading of the Korán is taught.

Atrauli has had municipal government since 1865. The committee now

Municipality.

consists of nine members, of whom three are official, three are elected by the tax-payers, and three are nominated by the Collector. There is very little trade, and no manufacture of any importance. The following statement shows the income and expenditure for three years :—

Receipts.	1870-71.	1871-72.	1872-73.	Expenditure.	1870-71.	1871-72.	1872-73.
	Rs	Rs.	Rs.		Rs.	Rs.	Rs.
Opening balance ..	2,295	1	5˚3	Collection ...	1,166	1,366	1,359
Class I. – Food and drink.	3,200	3,170	3,500	Head-office ...	79	67	103
„ II.—Animals for slaughter	597	515	280	a. Original works	3,561	817	1,700
„ III.—Fuel, &c,	132	134	1·65				
„ IV.—Building materials	100	221	202	b. Repairs, &c.,...	160	1,248	377
„ V.—Drugs, spices.	620	416	243	Police ...	937	1,041	1,068
„ VI.—Tobacco,	508	532	418	Education ...	263	300	288
„ VII.—Textile fabrics.	...	414	393	Conservancy ...	792	792	909
„ VIII.—Metals ...	...	225	144	Charitable grants,	139	220	260
Total of octroi, ...	5,15˚	5,626	5,345	Road watering ...	35	24	32
Rents ...	95	95	160				
Extraordinary ..	181	146	645	Repayment of loans.	...	100	...
Fines ...	53	99	37	Miscellaneous ...	18	10	192
Miscellaneous ...	16	1,123	14	Lighting ...	646	562	560
Total ...	7,797	7,090	6,734	Total ...	7,796	6,557	6,847

The following statement gives the imports for the year 1871-72 and 1872-73, in quantity or value, and the average consumption per head of the population.. The incidence of the octroi per head during 1872-73 was only 5½ annas :—

Articles.			Value in 1871-72.	Value in 1872-73.	Quantity in 1872-73.	Consumption per head.					
						1871-72.			1872-73.		
			Rs.	Rs.	Mds.	Rs.	a.	p.	Rs.	a.	p.
Grain	...	...	88,781	88,746	59,164	5	9	4	3	28	7
Sugars	...	...	33,081	49,057	9 041	2	8	3	0	22	8
Ghi	...	...	8,305	8,663	433	0	8	4	0	1	1
Vegetables	...	.	2,534	3,849	3,208	...			...		
Fruits	...	...	2,459	15,898	1,046 bundles	...			...		
Pán	...	...	636	1,304	5,216 Mds.	...			...		
Fodder	...	..	2,294	3,250	13,660	...			...		
Building materials	...	...	4,844	7,694	...	0	4	5	0	7	8
Spices, &c.,	...	...	6,648	15,320	...	0	6	8	0	14	2
Cloth	...	...	41,384	50,325	...	2	9	7	3	2	1
Metals	...	...	22,504	18,452	...	1	6	2	1	2	6
Oil	...	...	...	1,512	217	...			0	0	9
Oil-seeds	...	...	...	7,510	2,504	...			0	6	4
						M.	s.	c.	M.	s.	c.
Tobacco	...	...	1,720	2,751	...	0	4	5	0	6	8

History.

Atrauli is said to have been founded in the twelfth century by one Uttara Kumár, son of some Raja whose name is lost in oblivion, and little is known about its local history. I have only found it mentioned once in the Persian stories as the halting-place of Mubárak Sháh's forces in 1426 A.D, in his contest with the Jaunpur Sultan.[1] The Musalmán inhabitants have always had a bad reputation. From June until the early part of September, 1857, they remained in possession of the town. They are converted Hindús, and from the first showed disaffection to the British rule. Early in September, Mr. Cocks, the Special Commissioner, sent Muhammad Ali, a devoted servant of Government, as Joint Magistrate to Atrauli, with Daúd Khán as his deputy. But the Musalmáns refused to acknowledge his authority, and on the 25th September they broke out into open rebellion and murdered Muhammad Ali on his leaving the tahsíl. On the restoration of order several of the more prominent leaders of rebellion suffered punishment.

ATRAULI, a parganah in the tahsíl of the same name in the Aligarh district, is bounded on the north by the Bulandshahr district; on the east by pargana Gangíri ; on the south by parganahs Koil and Gangíri ; and on the west by parganahs Morthal and Koil. In 1874 the area comprised 108,022 acres, of which 70,727 acres were cultivated (40,590 irrigated),

[1] Dowson's Elliot, IV., 63.

16,669 acres were culturable, 20,464 acres were barren, and 162 acres were held free of revenue.

The eastern portions of parganah Atrauli as it stood before 1870, viz., those estates which immediately adjoin the low ground in the old bed of the Ganges (or Burhganga) are of the worst description, containing for the most part a large portion of sandy and unirrigated land. The lowlands themselves are not of large extent, but their produce, especially where the soil is suited to sugar-cane, or to the double crop of wheat and rice, is exceedingly sure and abundant. The villages on the extreme western boundary are chiefly of inferior quality, while the remainder of the parganah is on the whole comparatively good. This parganah is traversed by three streams, of which the Káli Nadi skirts the western boundary, whilst the Chohiya and Ním Nadis enter the parganah at different points, and, after uniting at the village of Ramamái, flow out in a southerly direction. These two last streams do not add much to the fertility of the parganah, for their overflow in the rainy season seems rather to deteriorate than to improve the soil, while they dry up so soon as to be of little use, except below the junction, for the purpose of irrigation. The Káli Nadi, on the other hand, retains its water through the year, and wheat is consequently raised in most places on its banks. But the lands through which it flows are not commonly of a superior kind, and they have moreover suffered much of late years by the exudation of reh, which has caused much of them to remain out of cultivation.

The changes in area since the last settlement have been considerable, and are noted hereafter. The former settlement in taluka Bhamauri Náh took 62 per cent. of the assets; in Datauli 65 per cent. was taken; in Faizpur Badariya, 66 per cent.; and in Atrauli Khás, Morthal, Akrabad, and Jaláli, 70 per cent. was taken. The new assessment is at half assets.[1] The following statement gives the statistics of the present settlement of the assessable area :—

Fiscal history.

Culturable.				Cultivated.			Total.
New fallow.	Old waste.	Groves.	Total.	Irrigated.	Dry.	Total.	
Acres.	Acres.	Acres.	Acres.	Acres.	Acres.	Acres.	Acres.
2,053	14,019	597	16,669	40,590	30,137	70,727	87,396

The proportion of culturable land to the total area is 81 per cent., and the proportion of cultivation to the culturable area is the same. The proportion of irrigated area to cultivated area is 57. The character of the culturable waste

---

[1] See detailed observations on new assessment in Revenue Reporter, IV., 87.

is of three kinds—dhák jungle, bhúr or sand, and the lowlying lands in the river bed. The first does not abound; as to the second, which lies chiefly about the Ním and above the Ganges, much of it is covered with *káns* grass, and can only be cultivated at intervals of from two to four years. The settlement of five villages lying within the river-bed has been made for only five years, as the land within their area is seldom used except for grazing purposes, and is subject to injury from *reh*, and even if cultivation would pay, the habits of the Ahars and Aheriyas who inhabit these tracts are little favourable to a settled life. The land-revenue assessed at the recent settlement amounts to Rs. 1,47,275, and the cesses to Rs. 14,625, falling at a rate of Re. 1-5-10 per British acre on the total area, at Re. 1-11-0 per acre on the area assessed to Government revenue, and at Rs. 2-1-3 per acre on the cultivated area. The sum paid by cultivators to the landowners as rent and cesses during the year 1871 has been estimated at Rs. 2,64,023.

Talukas Bhamauri Náh, Datauli, Chakáthal, Raipur, Lohgarh, Sanaul, and Badesara are mentioned in the district notice. Taking this parganah and Gangíri together, though two-thirds belong to the talukadárs of Bhamauri Náh and Datauli, the transfers during the currency of the expired settlement have been considerable. Out of a total of 6,120 shares into which the estates in both parganahs had been divided, 3,928 shares changed hands between 1838 and 1868. Many of these shares were transferred several times, and the net result is that 2,970 shares, comprising one-half of the old parganah of Atrauli and one-third of the old parganah of Gangíri, have been permanently lost to the old proprietors. Much of these changes must be attributed to the severity of the assessment. The following table shows the mode of transfer, the area, revenue and average price per acre of transfers made during each decade of the expired settlement :—

Mode of transfer.	1839-1848.			1848-1858			1859-1867.		
	Area.	Price.	Average per acre.	Area.	Price.	Average per acre.	Area.	Price.	Average per acre.
	Acres.	Rs.	Rs. a p.	Acres.	Rs.	Rs. a. p.	Acres.	Rs.	Rs. a. p.
Private sale ..	13,112	95,964	7 3 7	12,720	1,41,800	11 2 4	10,706	1,51,008	14 1 8
Mortgage ...	15,081	88,292	5 13 0	7,050	37,985	5 6 2	7,051	75,570	10 11 5
Auction sale ...	26,508	1,80,644	6 13 0	4,614	56,988	12 2 0	6,657	54,057	8 1 11
Total ...	55,001	3,64,900	...	24,384	2,36,773	...	24,414	2,80,635	...

The average value for the whole 20 years in both parganahs is roughly seven years' purchase of the land-revenue. In the old parganah of Atrauli the price has risen from 5·9 years' purchase in the first decade to 9·2 years' purchase in the last nine years, and in the old parganah of Gangírif rom 2·8 years' purchase in the first decade to 6·8 years'purchase in the last nine years. The soil in the latter tract is inferior to that in the former, and consists of a continuation or part of the Atrauli sandy tract. Hereditary tenants held, in the whole tahsil in 1868, 4,134 holdings, comprising 34,448 acres, or 23 per cent. of the cultivated area ; tenants-at-will held 9,900 holdings, comprising 93,823 acres, or 62 per cent. of the same area ; and the seer of proprietors comprised 978 holdings, equal to 22,222 acres, or 15 per cent. of the cultivation. Their holdings averaged respectively 8 acres, 9·5 acres, and 23 acres. In 1867-68 hereditary cultivators paid an average rental of Rs. 3-7-2 per acre, whilst tenants-at-will paid Rs. 3-14-8 per acre, a rate Rs. 13-5-0 per cent. higher than that paid by tenants with a right of occupancy. Comparing the statistics of 165 villages for which records from the last settlement exist, the statistics of the holdings of hereditary tenants in 1838 and 1868 are as follows :—

Year.	Area.	Number of holdings.	Average area.	Year.	Area.	Number of holdings.	Average area.
1838 ...	Acres. 22,306	2,591	8·6	1868 ...	Acres. 18,755	2,249	8·3

This shows a diminution of 14 per cent in the number of holdings and of 16 per cent. in the area held by hereditary cultivators—a result seldom met with elsewhere, and only to be accounted for by the disinclination of the Bhíkampur talukadárs and the new Baniya landowners to permit the growth of occupancy rights. One-third of the area in both parganahs is leased on rents in kind. This system is, however, almost entirely confined to the sandy tracts along the Ganges and Káli, cultivated by the notoriously unthrifty Ahárs and Aheriyas—the first devoted to breeding and grazing cattle, and not seldom stealing them, and the latter lazy and worthless as cultivators.

According to the census of 1872 parganah Atrauli contained 161 inhabited villages, of which 50 had less than 200 inhabitants ; Population, 71 had between 200 and 500 ; 28 had between 500 and 1,000 ; 10 had between 1,000 and 2,000 ; and one had between 2,000 and 3,000. The only town containing more than 5,000 inhabitants is Atrauli, with 15,941. The settlement records show that there are 203 maháls or estates in the parganah.

The total population in 1872 numbered 80,647 souls (37,764 females), giving 477 to the square mile. Classified according to religion, there were 70,128 Hindús, of whom 32,580 were females ; 10,519 Musalmáns, amongst whom 5,184 were females. Distributing the Hindú population amongst the four great classes, the census shows 9,040 Brahmans, of whom 4,088 were females ; 2,393 Rajpúts, including 1,041 females ; 3,011 Baniyas (1,422 females) ; whilst the great mass of the population is included in " the other castes" of the census returns, which show a total of 26,029 souls, of whom 20,655 are females.

The principal Brahman subdivisions found in this parganah are the Gaur (608), Saraswat (426), and Sanádh (243). The Rajpúts chiefly belong to the Chauhán (686), Badgújar (1,157), Gahlot, Jádon, Janghára, Tomar, Pundír, Panwár, Mandwár, and Bais clans. The Baniyas are of the Agarwál (394), Chausaina, Dasa, Ghoi, Jaiswár, Rastaugi, Saraugi, and Badpeta subdivisions. Amongst the other castes the following have more than 1,000 members :—Barhai (1,568), Hajjám (1,471), Ahír (1,847), Kahár (2640), Koli (2,895), Chamár (11,069), Khatík (1,640), Khákrob (1,614), Garariya (3,017), and Lodha (12,538). The following have less than 1,000 and more than 100 members :—Ját, Sonár, Máli, Bhát, Kalál, Gosháin, Káchhi, Darzi, Jogi, Bairági, Dhobi, Lohár, Kumhár, Aheriya, Banjára, Káyath, Dhúna, Malláh, Teli, and Chhípi. The Musalmáns are distributed amongst Shaikhs (1,717), Sayyids (391), Patháns (1,471), and Mughals (142). The remainder are unspecified.

The occupations of the people are shown in the statistics collected at the census of 1872. From these it appears that of the male adult population (not less than fifteen years of age), 285 are employed in professional avocations, such as Government servants, priests, doctors, and the like ; 2,378 in domestic service, as personal servants, water-carriers, barbers, sweepers, washermen, &c. ; 1,069 in commerce, in buying, selling, keeping or lending money or goods, or the conveyance of men, animals, or goods ; 12,767 in agricultural operations ; 4,303 in industrial occupations, arts, and mechanics, and the preparation of all classes of substances vegetable, mineral, and animal. There were 4,468 persons returned as labourers, and 560 as of no specified occupation. Taking the total population, irrespective of age or sex, the same returns give 2,013 as landholders, 36,770 as cultivators, and 41,834 as engaged in occupations unconnected with agriculture. The educational statistics, which are confessedly imperfect, show 1,623 males as able to read and write out of a total male population numbering 42,883 souls.

Since 1838 constant changes have taken place in the area of this parganah : thus from 1848 the following alterations may be noted :—

Year.	Number of villages.	Transferred to	Area in acres.	Land-revenue.	Year.	Number of villages.	Received from	Area.	Land-revenue.
				Rs.					Rs.
1848	1	Bulandshahr	576	951	1851	2	Morthal	1,512	1,456
,,	1	Morthal	249	797	1854	14	Faizpur	5,617	5,573
1854	3	Gangíri	2,927	1,732	1863	29	Jalálí	23,677	27,554
					1863	22	Akrabad	19,947	23,153
Total	5		3,752	3,480	Total	67		50,758	57,736
Increase	62		47,001	54,256					

In 1873 [1] further changes were sanctioned which resulted in the addition of 91,252 acres to Gangíri; at the same time four villages were transferred from Gangíri to Morthal and two were received from Morthal.

ATRAULI, a tahsíl of the Aligarh district, comprises the parganahs of Atrauli and Gangíri. The total area according to the settlement records of 1874 contains 226,371 acres, of which 478 acres are held free of revenue and 35,286 acres are barren. Of the remaining assessable area (190,607 acres) 150,305 acres are cultivated, and of these 73,406 acres are irrigated. Of the culturable area (40,302 acres) 1,663 acres are under groves, 33,547 acres are old culturable waste, and 5,092 acres are now fallow. The new land-revenue assessed on the parganah amounts to Rs. 2,92,184, and the cesses to Rs. 29,218. The revenue falls at a rate of Re. 1-15-1 on the cultivated acre. In 1872 the population numbered 157,374 souls (73,595 females), giving 445 souls to the square mile, distributed amongst 294 inhabited villages. The agricultural·population numbers 80,371 souls, and possess 1·8 acre per head and 9 acres per family. There are altogether 306 villages, with an average area of 739 acres, and ranging from 3,907 acres to 47 acres. The same statistics show 447 persons as blind, 34 lepers, 28 deaf and dumb, 8 idiots, and 15 insane persons in the tahsíl in 1872.

The Ním Nadí runs through the centre of Atrauli and the southern portion of Gangíri, and the Chhoiya joins the Ním in the centre of Atrauli. These streams are dry except during the rains. The Kálí affords some irrigation throughout the year, but owing to the efflorescence of *reh*, that which is cultivated one year may be barren the next, and here *reh* was known before the introduction of the canal and cannot be attributed to its action. The physical conformation of the tahsíl is similar to that of other tracts throughout the Duáb. First are the lowlands of the Ganges comprising the old bed of the river to the extreme east. Next come the uplands known as the *bángar* or *pahára*, which rise sharply from the lowlands and for some distance contain light and sandy soil. This soil is gradually exchanged for a clay and loam as one proceeds westward, and these soils are characteristic of the central portions of the tahsíl. Here and there extensive *úsar* plains occur. Further west and near the Kálí comes a second long strip of sand, but of much less extent than the similar tract near the Ganges, and then we have the *tarái* or lowlands of the Kálí itself. Though so much of the old area has been permanently alienated between 1839 and 1868, the increased value of land and improvement in prices must conduce to put a stop to these transfers, and one ought not to hear much of them in future. The culturable area of the whole tahsíl is 84 per cent. of the total area; cultivation covers 79 per cent. of the culturable area, but irrigation only reaches 49 per cent. of the cultivation, and of the culturable waste one per cent. is under groves.

---

[1] G. O. No. 182, dated February 7, 1870.

There is a less proportion of irrigation and a greater of unirrigated sandy soil here than in any other subdivision of the district.

Unirrigated *bhúr* and *píliya* occupy 32 per cent., or one-third, and irrigated and unirrigated *bhúr* and *píliya* together 46 per cent., or nearly one-half the entire cultivated area. *Bárah* and *manjha* comprise only nine per cent. of the cultivated area. The crops too are inferior. There is more barley (18 per cent.) and less wheat (18 per cent.), more bájra (16 per cent.) and other inferior rain-crops than elsewhere. The cold-weather crops are 48·5 per cent. of the whole crops. The old rate on cultivation amounted to Re. 1-13-3 per acre, and is now Re. 1-15-1 per acre. The increase in revenue on the two parganahs amounts to 18 per cent. on the old revenue of Rs. 2,47,136. The general result of the new revision is that enhancement of the Government demand has taken place in 79 per cent. of the villages and 83 per cent. of the former revenue : in 4 per cent. of the villages and 2 per cent. of the revenue the assessment remains as it was before, and in the remainder reductions have taken place. These last comprise the sandy villages (8) east of the Ním, and on the high lands above the Ganges and the villages (19) lying in the khádir of the Ganges. The khádir villages are generally thickly studded with patches of *reh*, and if cultivated will only give the poorest crops. In twelve of them the settlement has been made for five years only, and will then be revised, as, owing to the scanty cultivation at present existing, it was found impossible to assess them for a longer term. The soils here were divided into three classes—(1) khádir *bárah* and *manjha*, with an average rental of Rs. 5-4-3 per acre ; (2) first-class outlying khádir or sugar-cane land, with an average rental of Rs. 7-14-5 per acre; and (3) second-class outlying khádir, with an average rental of Rs. 2-10-2 per acre.

BARAULI, a village in parganah Barauli and tahsíl Koil of the Aligarh district, is distant 13 miles from Aligarh. The population in 1865 numbered 2,274 souls, and in 1872 there were 2,523 inhabitants, chiefly Badgújars. The Chaukidári Act (XX. of 1856) is in force in Barauli, and in 1873 supported a village police numbering four men of all grades at an annual cost of Rs. 234. The number of the houses in the town in 1872-3 was 469, and of those 348 were assessed with a house-tax averaging Re. 1-0-5 per house and Re. 0-2-3 per head of the population per annum. The income for the same year was Rs. 458, including a balance of Rs. 99 from the previous year, and the expenditure was Rs. 385.

BARAULI is a small taluka, now called a parganah, lying to the extreme north of the Aligarh district. It is bounded on the north-east and north-west by the Bulandshahr district, and on the south by parganahs Koil and Khair of the Aligarh district. The census of 1872 shows that it had then a total area of 25 square miles and 617 acres, of which 15 square miles and 603 acres were under cultivation. The area assessed to Government revenue during the same year was 17 square miles and 622 acres, of which 2 square miles and 19 acres were culturable, and the remainder was cultivated.

There is nothing peculiar in the physical appearance of this tract, and the history of the Badgújar family who own it is given in the district notice (page 445). Mr. Rose made the assessment in 1838. There was then 52 per cent. of irrigation, and the rate on cultivation fell at Re. 1-10-5 per acre. The present settlement was made by Mr. W. H. Smith, and the statistics of area are as follows : —

Settlement.	Unassessable.		Culturable.		Cultivated.		Total assessable.	Total area.
	Barren.	Free of revenue.	Fallow.	Groves.	Irrigated.	Dry.		
	Acres.	Acres.	Acres.	Acres.	Acres.	Acres.	Acres.	Acres.
Former ...	4,680	346	In correct.		5,050	4,712	11,247	16,273
Present ...	5,121	...	1,283	16	6,097	4,106	11,502	16,623

The proportion of the culturable to the total area is only 69 per cent., but the proportion of cultivation to the culturable area is 89, and of irrigation to cultivated area is 60, showing an increase of 22 per cent. The new assessment amounts to Rs. 20,590, and the cesses to Rs. 2,059. The increase in the revenue has therefore been 27 per cent. There have been very few changes in the proprietary possession of the soil since 1833. The alienations have chiefly been temporary through mortgage, and these incumbrances are now being paid off. The returns show that in 12 out of the 25 villages in the parganah 9,153 acres, out of a total of 16,074 acres, have been transferred, but the greater portion of these transfers are only temporary by mortgage. The following statement shows the particulars of the transfers made between 1838 and 1868 ; 24 out of the 25 villages in the parganah still belong to one owner :—

Mode of transfer.	1839-1848.			1849-1858.			1859-1868.		
	Area.	Average price per acre.	Years' purchase.	Area.	Average price per acre.	Years' purchase.	Area.	Average price per acre.	Year's purchase.
	Acres.	Rs. a. p.		Acres.	Rs. a. p.		Acres.	Rs. a. p.	Rs.
Private sale ...	815	12 14 1	11·0	...	...	...	65	21 3 6	16·6
Mortgage ...	3,640	5 12 9	2·0	320	9 8 10	8·7	104	8 13 2	9 3
Auction sale ...	...	...	...	...	...	...	3	21 9 2	26·2
Total ...	4,455	7 1 5	3·7	320	9 8 10	8·7	172	12 4 11	11·9

Mortgages form the great bulk of the transfers in this parganah. Mr. Rose, in his report on the assessment in 1838, remarks that " the present managers are deeply in debt, and it is not probable that the property will in a few years pass out of their possession ; and, so far as the prosperity of the cultivating community and the interest of the State are concerned, the sooner such a change takes place the better." These expectations have not been realised ; the proprietor of the day; though still in debt, is in possession. Few sales have taken place and the mortgages are being gradually reduced, whilst the general rise in the value of land will probably enable him to clear off all his present incumbrances. There have been no farms or sales on account of arrears of the land-revenue between 1833 and 1868 in this parganah, and the present easy assessment can without difficulty be paid from the assets. In Barauli, in 1857, hereditary tenants paid an average rental of Rs. 1-12-5; this had increased in 1868 to Rs. 2-14-5 ; tenants-at-will, in 1857, paid on an average Rs. 2-13-8 per acre, and this has been increased by 37·2 per cent., or to Rs 3-14-8 per acre. The land-revenue for 1872 amounted to Rs. 20,590 (or with cesses Rs. 22,649), falling at a rate of Re. 1-3-10 per British acre on the total area, at Re. 1-2-6 per acre on the area assessed to Government revenue, and at Rs. 2-0-2 per acre on the cultivated area.

According to the census of 1872 parganah Barauli contained 24 inhabited villages, of which 6 had less than 200 inhabitants; 15 had between 200 and 500 ; 2 had between 500 and 1,000 ; and one had between 2,000 and 3,000. The settlement records show altogether 25 villages distributed amongst mahals or estates. The total population in 1872 numbered 9,652 souls (4,535 females), giving 445 to the square mile. Classified according to religion, there were 8,591 Hindús, of whom 4,033 were females, and 1,061 Musalmáns, amongst whom 502 were females. Distributing the Hindú population amongst the four great classes, the census shows 1,631 Brahmans, of whom 749 were females ; 1,433 Rajpúts, including 617 females ; 406 Baniyas (200 females); whilst the great mass of the population is included in " the other castes" of the census returns, which show a total of 5,121 souls, of whom 2,467 are females. The principal Brahman subdivisions found in this parganah are the Gaur (249) and Saraswat (43). The Rajpúts belong chiefly to the Chauhán (113), Jádon (1,223), Gahlot, Badgújar, and Janghára clans. The Baniyas comprise Agarwáls (263), Dasas, Chausainis, and Mahesris. Amongst the other castes the only one that has more than one thousand members is the Chamár (1,442). The following have more than one hundred and less than one thousand members each :—Ját, Barhai, Hajjám, Kahár, Jogi, Koli, Khatik, Khákrob, Kumhár, and Garariya. The Musalmáns comprise Shaikhs (577) and Mewátis (456).

Population.

The occupations of the people are shown in the statistics collected at the census
of 1872. From these it appears that of the male adult
population (not less than fifteen years of age) 25 are
employed in professional avocations, such as Government servants, priests,
doctors, and the like ; 385 in domestic service, as personal servants, water-
carriers, barbers, sweepers, washermen, &c. ; 61 in commerce, in buying, selling, keeping or lending money or goods, or the conveyance of men, animals,
or goods ; 1,490 in agricultural operations ; 456 in industrial occupations, arts
and mechanics, and the preparation of all classes of substances, vegetable,
mineral, and animal. There were 519 persons returned as labourers and 94
as of no specified occupation. Taking the total population, irrespective of age
or sex, the same returns give 104 as landholders, 4,342 as cultivators, and
5,206 as engaged in occupations unconnected with agriculture. The educational statistics, which are confessedly imperfect, show 210 males as able to
read and write out of a total male population numbering 5,117 souls.

Occupations.

Barauli is in reality a taluka still held almost intact by Badgújars. It belonged to the old parganah of Koil, and was not detached from it until the
last century ; for all practical purposes it is now regarded as one with taluka
Morthal under the name of parganah Morthal (see MORTHAL). In 1854, 17
villages were transferred from Barauli to parganah Pahásu in the Bulandshahr
district.[1])

BESWAN, a village in parganah Gorai and tahsíl Iglás of the Aligarh district,
is distant 26 miles from Aligarh and 4 miles from Jewar. The population in
1865 was 3,253, and in 1872 there were 3,541 inhabitants, chiefly Játs. Beswán gives its name to a taluka, an account of which has been given in the
district notice under the head of " old families." The Chaukidári Act (XX. of
1856) is in force in the village, and in 1873 supported a village police numbering
seven men of all grades, at an annual cost of Rs. 396. The number of the houses
in the town in 1872-73 was 826, and of those 695 were assessed with a house-
tax averaging Re. 0-13-10 per house and Re. 0-2-9 per head of the population
per annum. The income for the same year was Rs. 666, including a balance
of Rs. 64 from the previous year, and the expenditure was Rs. 629.

BIJAIGARH, or Gambhíra as it is often called, a town in parganah Akrabad
and tahsíli Sikandra Rao of the Aligarh district, is 12 miles from Aligarh and
10 miles from Sikandra. The population in 1853 numbered 4,449 souls, and
in 1865 there were 4,798 inhabitants. In 1872 there were 5,652 inhabitants,
of whom 5,228 were Hindús (2,359 females) and 424 were Musalmáns (197
females). The town site occupies 41 square acres, giving 138 souls to the acre.
A fair kuchcha road runs from Iglás by Sásni, and passing the fort of Bijaigarh joins the Grand Trunk Road above Akrabad. The neighbourhood is

[1] G. O. No. 1159, dated March 8, 1854.

irrigated from a rájbaha of the Ganges Canal. There is a watchman's post, a school, and a post-office here. The town is purely an agricultural one, but rapidly advancing in prosperity. The Chaukidári Act (XX. of 1856) is in force in Bijaigarh, and in 1873 supported a village police numbering nine men of all grades at an annual cost of Rs. 516. The number of the houses in the town in 1872-73 was 963, and of these 795 were assessed with a house-tax averaging Re. 1-1-2 per house and Re. 0-2-5 per head of the population per annum. The income for the same year was Rs. 856, including a balance of Re. 0-8-11 from the previous year, and the expenditure was Rs. 729.

Bijaigarh was held by Bhagwant Singh in 1803, and was not taken without some trouble. There is a monument here to Colonel Gordon, who was killed by the accidental explosion of a tumbril after the fort had been taken. The neighbouring fort of Kachaura was held by Thákur Harkishan Singh of Beswán, and in the attack Major Nairn, of the 2nd Cavalry, lost his life. The slab erected to his memory was in 1853 removed to Bhadwás, on the Grand Trunk Road between Eta and Aligarh. The graves of those who fell at Bijaigarh are in the low *duhar* lands below the fort, and those who fell at Kachaura are buried in Lohár-ke-Nagla.

CHANDAUS, a town in parganah Chandaus and tahsíli Khair of the Aligarh district, lies in latitude 28°-5'-2" and longitude 77°-54'-7", at an elevation of 699·3 feet above the level of the sea. The upper markstone of the Great Trigonometrical Survey station is on a high bank of accumulated sand about 400 yards from the village of that name. The village of Umri lies to the south-west of the station 5·9 miles, and Elampur north-west 2·4 miles. This height was deduced trigonometrically. Chandaus is distant 20 miles from Aligarh and 6 miles from Somna. The population in 1865 was 2,512, and in 1872 was 2,931. There is a police-station and a post-office here. The Chaukidári Act (XX. of 1856) is in force in Chandaus, and in 1873 supported a village police numbering seven men of all grades at an annual cost of Rs. 396. The number of the houses in the town in 1872-73 was 620, and of these 570 were assessed with a house-tax averaging Re. 1-3-7 per house and Re. 0-3-9 per head of the population per annum. The income for the same year was Rs. 724, including a balance of Rs. 28 from the previous year, and the expenditure was Rs. 627.

CHANDAUS, a parganah of tahsíl Khair in the Aligarh district, is bounded on the north by parganah Khúrja of the Bulandshahr district, on the south by Khair, on the east by Khúrja and Koil, and on the west by parganah Jewar of the Bulandshahr district and Tappal of this district. According to the census of 1872 this parganah had then a total area of 103 square miles and 137 acres, of which 68 square miles were under cultivation. The area assessed to Government revenue during the same year was 102 square miles, of which

67 square miles were cultivated, 14 square miles were culturable, and 21 square miles were barren. Chandaus is drained by the Karon Nadi, which is dry except during the rains. Three separate lines of *bhúr* or sandhills run through this parganah and Khair, and of these the western ridge, which may be said to form the natural boundary between Chandaus and Tappal, is almost unbroken. The middle ridge follows the course of the Karon Nadi, crossing the stream from the left to the right bank near Doohíta, whilst the eastern ridge, rising here and there among lowlying villages, is less easily traced as a continuous line ; occasional short spurs jut out from each range. Water is found at a depth of 18 to 30 feet from the surface, and wicker-lined wells, which last from two to three years, are easily made. Of the 79 estates at settlement, 39 were zamíndári, 37 were imperfect pattidári, one was imperfect pattidári, and two were held free of revenue, and in all these estates only 10·57 per cent. of the land-revenue was paid by landholders possessing one or more villages.

The following statement shows the changes that have occurred in this parganah since 1838 :—

Caste.				Area held in 1838.	Area transferred.	Area held in 1868.	
						Area.	Revenue.
				Acres.	Acres.	Acres.	Rs,
Chaubán	...	...	...	28,091	13,676	14,415	15,854
Ját	...	...	...	15,756	4,098	11,658	15,281
Jádon	...	...	...	3,881	1,624	12,257	3,068
Brahman	...	...	...	4,421	2,683	1,738	1,01
Gosháin	...	...	...	605	101	504	738
Nau-Muslim	...	...	...	12,613	5,846	6,767	5,962
Sikh	...	...	...	309	154	155	223
Total			...	65,676	28,182	37,494	43,207

Chandaus includes taluka Pisáwa, which is separately mentioned in the district notice. The present settlement was made by Mr. W. H. Smith. The statistics of area show a total area of 66,343 acres, of which 13,382 acres are entered as barren and 1,028 as held free of revenue. The assessable area is distributed as follows:

Culturable.				Cultivated.			
New fallow.	Old waste.	Groves.	Total.	Irrigated.	Dry.	Grand Total.	Total.
648	8,101	157	8,906	23,783	19,244	43,027	51,933

These figures show that the proportion of culturable land to the total area amounts to 78 per cent., and the proportion of cultivation to the culturable area is 83 per cent. Irrigation reaches only 55 per cent. of the cultivated area, and only 17 per cent. of the culturable waste is available for the extension of cultivation. Much of this culturable waste is under dhák jungle which sooner or later must come under the plough, but much of it also is of such a character as will prevent any attempt at its cultivation, so that on the whole the actual margin of available land fit for cultivation is hardly more than ten per cent. of the cultivated area in this parganah.

By the recent settlement the land-revenue has been fixed at Rs. 90,890 and the cesses at Rs. 9,089. The new land-revenue falls at Rs. 2-1-9 on the cultivated acre, and gives a rise of 14 per cent. on the old assesment (Rs. 79,308). Irrigation has increased by 32·5 per cent., and cultivation by 3·6 per cent., since last settlement.

The statistics of the successive revisions of settlement in this parganah may be shown as follows :—

Year.	No. of villages.	Land-revenue.	Year.	No. of villages.	Land-revenue.
		Rs.			Rs.
1809-11 ...	...	48,232	1821-37 ...	61	60,661
1812-15 ...	60	53,929	1838-68 ...	64	79,577
1816-20 ...	61	60,661	1868 ...	...	79,141

During the first settlement several villages now separated were then included in others, but, on the whole, the parganah was much as it is now, and two villages were then and are still held free of revenue. The revenue of four villages of the second settlement and of three villages of the third settlement cannot now be traced. 4,441 acres were farmed for arrears of land-revenue during the currency of the past settlement, and 2,926 acres were sold, aggregating 11 per cent. of the total area and 14 per cent. of the revenue. Much of this was due to the difficulty found in borrowing money, owing to the smallness of the security that could be offered by the petty proprietary body and the absence of any wealthy body of traders. Rs. 4,728 were remitted from the revenue demand in Chandaus during 1860-61, but, as a rule, the revenue has been punctually paid in this parganah. The following statement shows the mode of transfer, the average price per acre, and the average number of years' purchase of the land-revenue brought by the areas transferred between 1838 and 1868. It is to be noted that if a single plot or estate has changed hands ten times, ten entries have been made in this account :—

Mode of transfer.	1838-1848.			1849-1858.			1859-1868.			Total.		
	Area.	Price per acre.	Years' purchase	Area.	Price per acre.	Years' purchase.	Area.	Price per acre.	Years' purchase.	Area.	Price per acre.	Years' purchase.
	Acres.	Rs. a. p.		Acres	Rs. a. p.		Acres.	Rs. a. p.		Acres.	Rs. a. p.	
Private sale,	1,108	3 15 6	4·26	2,774	8 8 9	6·	11,737	9 2 1	7·	15,619	8 10 7	6·74
Mortgage ...	5,573	2 5 11	2·7	4,866	6 1 10	4·96	8,393	4 11 8	4·27	18,832	4 6 3	4·
Auction sale,	5,204	4 5 8	3·43	2,577	4 6 9	3·35	4,373	4 13 5	3·66	12,254	4 8 8	3·54
Total ...	11,885	3 6 2	3·21	10,317	6 5 3	4·86	24,503	6 13 9	5·56	46,705	5 13 9	4·87

The transfers by revenue process have also been considerable, amounting to 2,866 acres during the first ten years of the expired settlement, and showing for the whole term 4,441 acres farmed for arrears of revenue and 2,926 sold on the same account. The average price brought at these sales was only Rs. 2-4-10 per acre, or 1·48 year's purchase on the revenue. Private sales are the true standard of the value of land, and in this parganah the price at private sales during the last twelve years of the expired settlement was 102·6 per cent. higher than during the first eleven years. On the whole, 32 per cent. of the area bearing 34 per cent. of the land-revenue had been permanently alienated in 1868, and 11 per cent. of the area bearing 12 per cent. of the revenue was mortgaged or in farm. Out of 28,182 acres transferred, 11,728 acres belonged to proprietors owning three-fourths of a village or more. The kharíf crop occupies 44 per cent. of the entire cultivated area, and in it joár covers 16 per cent. of the total area, bájra 12 per cent., cotton 9 per cent., and moth 6 per cent. Amongst the rabí crops, wheat occupies 17 per cent. of the total cultivation, bejar 20 per cent., and gram 8 per cent. 4,092 acres, or 9 per cent. of the cultivation, are leased on payments in kind. There were 9,245 bulls and bullocks, 5,192 buffaloes, 6,244 cows, 522 horses, and 6,375 goats and sheep in the parganah in 1868. 640 holdings are held as seer by proprietors, 623 by hereditary tenants, and 1,505 by tenants-at-will, including revenue-free estates, with an average area of 22·2 acres, 11·1 acres, and 15 acres respectively. The average rental is Rs. 3-7-2 per acre, and hereditary tenants pay on an average Rs. 3-1-8 per acre, whilst tenants-at-will pay Rs. 3-8-10 per acre. Altogether 30 per cent. of the cultivated area is held by cultivating proprietors. At the commencement of the expired settlement only 70 holdings were entered as possessed by hereditary tenants, with an average area of 15·2 acres and an average rental of Rs. 2-7-0 per acre, whilst tenants-at-will held 1,493 holdings, with an average area of 17 acres and an average rental of Rs. 2-12-5 per acre. The comparative areas held by each class are as-follows :—

	1868.		1869.	
	Area.	Rent.	Area.	Rent.
Hereditary tenants	1,064	2,596	6,925	21,510
Tenants-at-will	25,479	70,819	22,672	80,570

According to the census of 1872 parganah Chandaus contained 64 inhabited
Population.
villages, of which 12 had less than 200 inhabitants; 20 had between 200 and 500 ; 21 had between 500 and 1,000; 9 had between 1,000 and 2,000; and 2 had between 2,000 and 3,000. The settlement records show that in 1874 there were 76 maháls or estates in the parganah, and 66 villages, with an average area of 1,005 acres; the largest having 3,835 acres, and the smallest having 105 acres. The total population in 1872 numbered 38,699 souls (18,033 females), giving 376 to the square mile. Classified according to religion, there were 35,172 Hindús, of whom 16,818 were females ; 3,527 Musalmáns, amongst whom 1,645 were females. Distributing the Hindú population amongst the four great classes, the census shows 6,456 Brahmans, of whom 2,999 were females; 4,828 Rajpúts, including 2,164 females ; 1,603 Baniyas (760 females); whilst the great mass of the population is included in " the other castes" of the census returns, which show a total of 22,285 souls, of whom 10,465 are females. The principal Brahman subdivisions found in this parganah are the Gaur (4,080), Saraswat (291), and Kanaujiya. The Rajpúts belong to the Chauhán (2,538), Badgujar (140), Gahlot (61), Jádon (1,221), Janghára (179), and Bhál clans, and the Baniyas to the Agarwál (454), Dasa (538), Chausaini, Mahesri, Bárahsaini, and Gurákú subdivisions. Amongst the other castes, the following have more than one thousand members each :—Ját (4,381), Chamár (5,700), Khatík (1,787), and Orh (1,055) ; the following having between one hundred and one thousand members :— Sonár, Barhai, Hajjám, Máli, Bhát, Kalál, Gosháin, Ahír, Darzi, Kahár, Jogi, Bairági, Dhobi, Lohár, Koli, Sweeper, Kumhár, Garariya, Aheriya (376), Banjára, Dhúna, Teli, and Riwári. The Musalmáns comprise Shaikhs (232), Patháns (98), Musalmán Rajpúts (89), and those entered without distinction.

The occupations of the people are shown in the statistics collected at the
Occupations.
census of 1872. From these it appears that of the male adult population (not less than fifteen years of age) 114

are employed in professional avocations, such as Government servants, priests, doctors, and the like ; 1,308 in domestic service, as personal servants, water-carriers, barbers, sweepers, washermen, &c. ; 558 in commerce, in buying, selling, keeping or lending money or goods, or the conveyance of men, animals, or goods ; 6,750 in agricultural operations ; 1,444 in industrial occupations, arts and mechanics, and the preparation of all classes of substances, vegetable, mineral, and animal.   There were 1,928 persons returned as labourers and 365 as of no specified occupation.   Taking the total population, irrespective of age or sex, the same returns give 723 as landholders, 18,909 as cultivators, and 19,667 as engaged in occupations unconnected with agriculture.   The educational statistics, which are confessedly imperfect, show 810 males as able to read and write out of a total male population numbering 20,666 souls. In 1838 Chandaus comprised 62 villages, with an area of 60,441 acres and a revenue of Rs. 72,266, and in 1840-41 one village was received from parganah Koil, two villages from Khúrja in the Bulandshahr district, and one village from Khair, leaving Chandaus possessed of 66 villages.   Chandaus was ori-ginally occupied and owned by Chauháns ; but even at last settlement the Játs of the Tappal family held nearly half the parganah.   The Chauháns, however, still retain 17 out of 21 villages held by them in 1838.

CHHABRA RAFATPUR, a town in parganah Gangíri of the Aligarh district, is distant 23 miles from Aligarh and 11 miles from Atrauli.   The population in 1865 numbered 2,130 souls, and in 1872 there were 2,072 inhabitants. The Chaukidári Act (XX. of 1856) is in force in Chharra, and in 1873 supported a village police numbering three men of all grades, at an annual cost of Rs. 162. The number of the houses in the town in 1872-73 was 454, and of these 402 were assessed with a house-tax averaging Re. 1-2-9 per head and Re. 0-3-8 per head of the population per annum.   The income for the same year was Rs. 627, including a balance of Rs. 155 from the previous year, and the expen-diture was Rs. 470.

DÁDON, a town in parganah Gangíri of the Aligarh district, is distant 28 miles from Aligarh and 14 miles from Atrauli.   The population in 1865 numbered 1,797 souls, and in 1872 there were 2,092 inhabitants.   There is a police-station here since 1851, now a first-class station.   The Chaukidári Act (XX. of 1856) is in force in Dádon, and in 1873 supported a village police numbering five men of all grades at an annual cost of Rs. 288.   The number of the houses in the town in 1872-73 was 427, and of these 359 were assessed with a house-tax averaging Re. 0-9-2 per head and Re. 0-1-7 per head of the population per annum.   The income for the same year was Rs. 240, includ-ing a balance of Rs. 34 from the previous year, and the expenditure was Rs. 235.   Dádon is the residence of a branch of the Bhíkampur talukadári family.

DARYAPUR, a town in parganah Háthras of the Aligarh district, is distant six miles from Háthras and 14 miles from Aligarh. The population in 1865 numbered 2,729 souls, and in 1872 there were 2,763 inhabitants. Daryapur was the seat of an old *ráj* held by the Porach Rajpúts. It was taken from them by the Játs, and the Porachs retired to Husain, which they have also recently lost. The Chaukidári Act (XX. of 1856) is in force in Daryapur, and in 1873 supported a village police numbering seven men of all grades, at an annual cost of Rs. 396. The number of the houses in the town in 1872-73 was 594, and of these 549 were assessed with a house-tax averaging Re. 1-0-10 per house and Re. 0-3-4 per head of the population per annum. The income for the same year was Rs. 689, including a balance of Rs. 110 from the previous year, and the expenditure was Rs. 632.

DATAULI, a town in parganah Atrauli of the Aligarh district, is distant 21 miles from Aligarh and 10 miles from Atrauli. The population in 1865 was 2,934, and in 1872 there were 3,437 inhabitants. Datauli gives its name to a taluka held by Patháns, some account of whom is given under the district notice. The Chaukidári Act (XX. of 1856) is in force in Datauli, and in 1873 supported a village police numbering seven men of all grades at an annual cost of Rs. 396. The number of the houses in the town in 1872-73 was 722, and of these 588 were assessed with a house-tax averaging Re. 0-15-2 per house and Re. 0-2-7 per head of the population per annum. The income for the same year was Rs. 558, including a balance of Re. 0-1-0 from the previous year, and the expenditure was Rs. 558.

GANGÍRI, a parganah in the Atrauli tahsíl of the Aligarh district, is bounded on the north by parganah Atrauli and the Ganges, on the east by the Eta district, on the west by Atrauli and Koil, and on the south by Akrabad and Sikandra Rao. According to the census of 1872 this parganah had then a total area of 185 square miles and 30 acres, of which 125 square miles were under cultivation. The area assessed to Government revenue during the same year was 184 square miles, of which 124 square miles were cultivated, 37 square miles were culturable, and 23 square miles were barren. Until 1870 Gangíri was confined to a narrow strip of land running along the eastern side of parganah Atrauli from north to south, and containing only 26 villages, with an area of 27,097 acres, or 42·3 square miles. More than three-fourths of its present area has been received from parganah Atrauli since then. As these changes were made subsequent to the preparation of the rent-rate reports, it is very difficult to make any comparison with past statistics.[1] It will be merely necessary here to refer to the results of the present settlement as affecting the present area. The area in 1874 amounted to 118,349 acres, or 184 square miles and 589 acres, of which 14,822 acres were barren,

---

[1] For an account of Gangíri as it was, see Rev. Rep., IV., 87.

and 316 acres were held free of revenue. The assessable area was distributed as follows :—

	Culturable.				Cultivated.			
New fallow.	Old waste.	Groves.	Total.	Irrigated.	Dry.	Total.	Total.	
Acres.	Acres.	Acres.	Acres.	Acres.	Acres.	Acres.	Acres.	
3,039	19,528	1,066	23,633	32,816	46,762	79,578	103,211	

Here the culturable area is 87 per cent. of the total area, the cultivated area is 77 per cent. of the culturable area, and the irrigated area is 41 per cent. of the cultivated area. The actual margin left for increased cultivation is 22 per cent. of the culturable area. Seven villages in the Ganges khádir are assessed for terms of five years only. The total land-revenue of the parganah at present is Rs. 1,44,909, and the cesses are Rs. 14,413.

According to the census of 1872 parganah Gangíri contained 133 inhabited

Population.

villages, of which 33 had less than 200 inhabitants ; 51 had between 200 and 500 ; 33 had between 500 and 1,000 ; 8 had between 1,000 and 2,000 ; 6 had between 2,000 and 3,000, and two had between 3,000 and 5,000. The towns containing more than 5,000 inhabitants were the total population in 1872 numbered 76,727 souls (35,831 females), giving 415 to the square mile. Classified according to religion, there were 63,324 Hindús, of whom 29,346 were females ; 13,396 Musalmáns, amongst whom 6,483 were females ; and 7 Christians. Distributing the Hindú population amongst the four great classes, the census shows 4,783 Brahmans, of whom 1,283 were females ; 2,124 Rajpúts, including 905 females ; 2,399 Baniyas (1,131 females) ; whilst the great mass of the population is included in "the other castes" of the census returns, which show a total of 54,018 souls, of whom 25,127 are females. The principal Brahman subdivisions found in this parganah are the Gaur (217), Saraswat, aud Kanaujiya. The Rajpúts chiefly belong to the Chauhán (306), Badgújár, Gahlot, Jádon (652), Pundír, Solankhi, Gaharwár, Bais, Gaur, and Aghaya clans ; and the Baniyas to the Dása Chausaini (269), Agarwál, Bárahsaini and Mahesri subdivisions. Amongst the other castes the following show more than one thousand members :—Ját (3,293), Barhai, Hajjam, Kalál (1,753), Ahír (8,633), Káchhi (2,666), Kahár, Koli (2,271), Chamár (12,969), Khatík, Khákrob, Garariya (2,396), and Lodha (5,932). The following castes have less than one thousand, but more than one hundred members each:—Sonár, Máli, Gosháin, Darzi, Jogi, Bairági, Dhobi, Kumhár, Aheriya, Banjára, Káyath, Malláh, and Teli. The Musalmáns comprise Shaikhs (1,640), Sayyids (646), Mughals (71), and Patháns (4,222); the remaining Muhammadans are unspecified.

The land-revenue for 1872 amounted to Rs. 1,44,909 (or with cesses Rs. 1,66,541), falling at a rate of Re. 1-3-7 per British acre on the total area, at Re. 1-3-8 per acre on the area assessed to Government revenue, and at Re. 1-13-1 per acre on the cultivated area. The sum paid by cultivators to the landowners as rent and cesses during the same year has been estimated at Rs. 2,73,939.

The occupations of the people are shown in the statistics collected at the

Occupations.

census of 1872. From these it appears that of the male adult population (not less than fifteen years of age) 108 are employed in professional avocations, such as Government servants, priests, doctors, and the like; 2,777 in dom:stic service, as personal servants, water-carriers, barbers, sweepers, washermen, &c.; 1,171 in commerce, in buying, selling, keeping or lending money or goods, or the conveyance of men, animals, or goods; 13,434 in agricultural operations; 2,891 in industrial occupations, arts and mechanics, and the preparation of all classes of substances, vegetable, mineral, and animal. There were 3,792 persons returned as labourers and 395 as of no specified occupation. Taking the total population, irrespective of age or sex, the same returns give 1,169 as landholders, 40,379 as cultivators, and 35,179 as engaged in occupations unconnected with agriculture. The educational statistics, which are confessedly imperfect, show 1,172 males as able to read and write out of a total male population numbering 40,896 souls. In 1854 parganah Gangíri received three villages from Atrauli, making in all 26 villages. Its present boundaries were fixed[1] in 1370, and increased the area from 27,097 acres to 118,319 acres, by the addition of villages from parganah Atrauli (see ATRAULI parganah). One-third of the proprietary rights in the old parganah has changed hands and been permanently alienated from the original owners between 1839 and 1868, or 170 shares out of 520.

GANGÍRI, a village in parganah Atrauli of the Aligarh district, is distant 24 miles from Aligarh and 16 miles from Atrauli. The population in 1865 numbered 1,284 souls, and in 1872 there were 2,253 inhabitants. Gangíri lies on the route from Koil by Jaláli and Kásganj to Budaon, distant 11¼ miles from Jaláli and 12¾ miles from Kásganj. For the road from Jaláli see JALÁLI. To Kásganj the road is unmetalled throughout, and crosses the Ním Nadi by a bridge at Malsái, and passes Dholna at five miles. The Chaukidári Act (XX. of 1856) is in force in Gangíri, and in 1873 supported a village police

---

[1] G. O., N. W. P., No. 182, dated 7th February, 1870.

numbering 4 men of all grades at an annual cost of Rs. 216. The number of the houses in the town in 1872-73 was 469, and of these 387 were assessed with a house-tax averaging Re. 0-15-3 per house and Re. 0-2-7 per head of the population per annum. The income for the same year was Rs. 417, including a balance of Rs. 49 from the previous year, and the expenditure was Rs. 365. There is a police-station here and a post-office.

GAUNDA, a town in parganah Gorai of the Aligarh district, is distant 16 miles from Beswan and 12 miles from Aligarh. In 1865 there were 2,052 inhabitants, and in 1872 there were 2,312. There is an outpost of police here.

GHARBARA, a town in parganah Khair of the Aligarh district, is distant 37 miles from Aligarh and 6 miles from Tappal. The population in 1865 numbered 2,578 souls, and in 1872 there were 2,351 inhabitants.

GORAI, a parganah in tahsíl Iglás of the Aligarh district, is bounded on the north by Hasangarh, on the south by part of Hasangarh and the Mahában parganah of Muttra, on the east by parganah Háthras, and on the west by the Muttra district. According to the census of 1872 this parganah had then a total area of 88 square miles and 462 acres, of which 79 square miles were under cultivation. The area assessed to Government revenue during the same year was 80 square miles, of which 71 square miles were cultivated, 3 square miles were culturable, and 6 square miles were barren. The general features of the parganah resemble those of Hasangarh, and both are described under Iglás. The changes that took place during the currency of the past settlement have been so great as to render any comparison of the state of the parganah as it now exists with the statistics of previous settlements difficult without details which are out of place here. The existing settlement was made by Mr. A. B. Patterson. The total area was then found to comprise 56,797 acres, of which 4,020 acres were barren and 1,763 acres were held free of revenue. The statistics of the assessable area are as follows:—

CULTURABLE.				CULTIVATED.			TOTAL.
New. Fallow.	*Old.* Waste.	Groves.	Total.	Irrigated.	Dry.	Total.	
325	1,982	47	2,354	38,888	9,772	48,660	51,014

These figures show that the percentage of the culturable to the total area is 90, of cultivation to the culturable area is 95, and of irrigation to cultivation is 80. Only five per cent. of the culturable area remains to come under the plough. Cultivation has increased by 0·8 per cent. since last settlement, and irrigation by 19·2 per cent. The land-revenue assessed amounts to Rs. 1,22,110, and the cesses to Rs. 12,211. During the currency of the past settlement, 18 whole villages and 54 parts of villages, comprising 20,816 acres, were transferred in Iglás, and of these 16,394 acres passed for ever from the hands of the old proprietary body. In addition, 7,613 acres were temporarily farmed on account of arrears of land-revenue. As the settlement went on the rise in prices told on the value of the land, and by the close of the settlement the average price per acre increased by 65 per cent. Talúkás Kauka, Iglás, Beswán, and Kajraut are separately mentioned in the district notice.

The following table shows the mode of transfer, the area transferred, the price per acre, and the number of years' purchase on the land-revenue of the areas transferred during the three decades of the expired settlement. The average price from all sources was Rs. 9-2-11 per acre, and the average years' purchase was 4·05 years.

Mode of transfer.	1839-1848.			1849-1858.			1859-1868.		
	Area.	Average price per acre.	Years' purchase.	Area.	Average price per acre.	Years' purchase.	Area.	Average price per acre.	Years' purchase.
	Acres.	Rs. a. p.		Acres.	Rs. a. p.		Acres.	Rs. a. p.	
Private sale ...	1,385	6 14 7	$3\frac{1}{10}$	3,171	6 3 2	$4\frac{1}{16}$	4,584	11 9 2	5
Mortgage ...	4,544	6 3 3	$2\frac{1}{10}$	2,569	8 2 6	$3\frac{1}{2}$	4,008	12 7 8	$5\frac{7}{10}$
Auction by Court	5,479	7 7 5	$3\frac{1}{2}$	2,937	10 1 7	$4\frac{3}{4}$	2,966	10 10 10	$4\frac{1}{16}$
Sale for arrears of revenue.	236	5 2 1	$\frac{1}{2}$	...	...	...	1,038	7 3 9	$4\frac{1}{2}$
Total ...	11,643	6 13 6	$2\frac{3}{4}$	8,677	9 3 10	$4\frac{1}{16}$	12,596	11 4 9	$5\frac{1}{10}$

In Gorai, out of 48,787 acres under cultivation at measurement, 38,355 acres, or 78·6 per cent., were held by tenants; and of these, 10,959 acres, or 28·5 per cent., were held by tenants with a right of occupancy, each of whose holdings on an average covered 11·9 acres, whilst the average holding of tenants-at-will was 14·1 acres, and of all tenants was 13·2 acres. Tenants with a right of occupancy paid an average rental of Rs. 3-13-3 per acre, and tenants-at-will paid Rs 4-1-8 per acre, the average for all being Rs. 4-0-5 per acre. Sixty villages are held on a zamíudári tenure, four villages in perfect pattidári, and 59 villages in bháyachára tenure. Fifty-two villages, paying a revenue of Rs. 45,587, belong to proprietors who own more than one village; 15 villages, paying a revenue of Rs. 11,713, belong to one owner or to less than six sharers; and 46 villages, paying Rs. 52,208, to more than six sharers. Rs. 7,030 were remitted in 1838 on account of the famine of 1837, and Rs. 2,516 were remitted in 1862 on account of the famine of 1860-61.

According to the census of 1872 parganah Gorai contained 105 inhabited villages, of which 39 had less than 200 inhabitants; 35 had between 200 and 500; 19 had between 500 and 1,000; 11 had between 1,000 and 2,000, and one had between 3,000 and 5,000.

Population.

The settlement records show 113 villages distributed amongst 116 maháls or estates in 1874. The average area of each village is 503 acres. The total population in 1872 numbered 47,827 souls (21,848 females), giving 537 to the square mile. Classified according to religion, there were 45,156 Hindús, of whom 20,629 were females ; 2,671 Musalmáns, amongst whom 1,219 were females. Distributing the Hindú population amongst the four great classes, the census shows 10,845 Brahmans, of whom 4,925 were females ; 752 Rajpúts, including 341 females ; 2,229 Baniyas (1,030 females) ; whilst the great mass of the population is included in " the other castes" of the census returns, which show a total of 31,330 souls, of whom 14,333 are females. The principal Brahman subdivisions found in this parganah are the Saraswat (1,229) and Gaur (370); the Rajpúts chiefly belong to the Jádon (230), Janghára, (188), Chauhán, Badgújar, Gahlot and Jaiswár clans, and the Baniyas belong to the Agarwál (1,254), Dása, Chausaini, Mahesri, and Bárahsaini subdivisions. Amongst the other castes the following show more than one thousand members :— Ját (9,958), Barhai, Hajjám, Káchhi (1,118), Koli (1,283), Chamár (7,514), Khatík, Khákrob, and Garariya (1,131). The following have between one hundred and one thousand members each :—Sonár, Bhát, Kalál, Darzi, Kahár, Jogi, Bairági, Dhobi, Kumhár, Aheriya, Káyath, Dhúna, Malláh, and Teli. Musalmáns comprise Shaikhs (111) and Patháns (177) ; the remainder are unspecified.

The occupations of the people are shown in the statistics collected at the census of 1872. From these it appears that of the male adult population (not less than fifteen years of age) 174 are employed in professional avocations, such as Government servants, priests, doctors, and the like ; 1,814 in domestic service, as personal servants, water-carriers, barbers, sweepers, washermen, &c. ; 902 in commerce, in buying, selling, keeping or lending money or goods, or the conveyance of men, animals, or goods ; 7,893 in agricultural operations ; 2,014 in industrial occupations, arts and mechanics, and the preparation of all classes of substances, vegetable, mineral, and animal. There were 2,862 persons returned as labourers and 407 as of no specified occupation. Taking the total population, irrespective of age or sex, the same returns give 1,433 as landholders, 21,340 as cultivators, and 25,054 as engaged in occupations unconnected with agriculture. The educational statistics, which are confessedly imperfect, show 1,249 males as able to read and write out of a total male population numbering 25,979 souls. At the last settlement Gorai contained 38 villages, with an area of 28,426

Occupations.

acres. Since then 65 villages have been added from Koil and 10 from Muttra ; in all 75 villages, with an area of 27,171 acres and a revenue of Rs. 45,901.

HASANGARH, a parganah in tahsíl Iglás of the Aligarh district, is bounded on the north by parganahs Khair and Koil, on the south by Gorai, on the west, by Muttra, and on the east by Koil. A portion of the parganah lies to the south of Gorai and between it and Mursan. According to the statistics of the census of 1872 the parganah had then a total area of 125 square miles, of which 109 square miles were under cultivation. The area assessed to Government revenue during the same year was 124 square miles, of which 108 square miles were cultivated, seven square miles were culturable, and nine square miles were barren.

As the general features of both parganah Hasangarh and parganah Gorai are the same, they are noticed as one under tahsíl Iglás (see IGLÁS). The changes that have taken place in the area of the parganah during the currency of the last settlement render any comparison of its fiscal returns difficult without going into a detail which appears to be unnecessary. The existing settlement was made by Mr. A. B. Patterson. The total area was then found to be 79,771 acres, of which 5,805 acres were barren and 402 acres were held free of revenue. The statistics of the assessable area are as follows :—

Culturable.				Cultivated.			Total.
New fallow.	Old waste.	Groves.	Total.	Irrigated.	Dry.	Total.	
Acres.	Acres.	Acres.	Acres.	Acres.	Acres.	Acres.	Acres.
779	3,673	75	4,727	50,634	18,203	68,837	73,564

From the above it will be seen that the proportion of culturable land to the total area is 92 per cent., of cultivation to the culturable area is 94 per cent., and of irrigated to cultivated area is 73 per cent. Only six per cent. of the total culturable area is available for the extension of cultivation. Cultivation has increased by 5·6 per cent. since last settlement, and irrigation by 28 per cent. The new assessment amounts to Rs. 1,65,584, and the cesses to Rs. 16,558. During the currency of the past settlement, 18 whole villages and 82 parts of villages, comprising 38,960 acres, changed hands, or more than one-half the total area, and of this 28,394 acres were permanently transferred from the industrious Játs ; and besides these, 10,492 acres were farmed for arrears of revenue. At first land in this parganah fetched only 2·5 years' purchase of the land-revenue; but by the close of the settlement in 1868 the value of land had increased by ninety per cent., and this enhancement has fallen into the hands of the land speculators who bought up the land during the earlier years, when the pressure of the assessment was most felt. On the whole the parganah is one of the most fertile and the most flourishing in the district. Cultivation and irrigation have nearly reached their maximum, and the recent arrangements have left a sufficient margin to the cultivators, from which they can easily keep out of fresh debts and meet those already in existence. One should not hear of excessive transfers again in this parganah. The following table shows the mode of transfer, area transferred, average price per acre, and average number of years' purchase of the land-revenue in each decade of the expired settlement. The average price per acre from all sources was Rs. 8-9-1, and the average years' purchase was 3·12 :—

Mode of transfer.	1839-1848.			1849-1858.			1859-1868.		
	Area.	Average price per acre.	Years' purchase.	Area.	Average price per acre.	Years' purchase.	Area.	Average price per acre.	Years' purchase.
	Acres.	Rs. a. p.		Acres.	Rs. a. p.		Acres.	Rs. a. p.	
Private sale ...	3,631	3 14 8	1 ¾	5,112	5 3 1	2₁%₀	8,322	8 .0 9	3¾
Mortgage ...	2,881	4 9 1	1₁%₀	5,279	9 6 6	3₁%₀	6,946	12 11 9	5¾
Auction by Courts.	7,381	7 11 7	3 ⅜	5,500	12 10 6	5¾	6,931	10 9 11	4¼
Sale for arrears of revenue.	1,638	1 14 6	1	138	2 8 11	1⅞₀	395	2 2 5	⅞₀
Total ...	15,531	5 10 4	2 ⅓	16,029	9 2 1	3₁%₀	22,094	11 3 3	4½

In Hasangarh tenants cultivate 44,972 acres, or 63·7 per cent. of the total cultivated area. Of this, 9,082 acres, or 21·2 per cent., are held by tenants with a right of occupancy, whose average holding is 8·6 acres. Tenants-at-will cultivate holdings averaging 9·6 acres each. The latter pay an average rental of Rs. 4-3-8 per acre, whilst the former pay Rs. 3-14-6 per acre, the average for all tenants being Rs. 4-2-7 per acre. Though Hasangarh is inferior in its soil to the neighbouring parganah of Gorai, the average rent-rate is higher, which is partly attributable to the greater influx of new landholders into Hasangarh, and an effort on their part to raise the general rate. In Hasangarh only 13 villages, paying a revenue of Rs. 10,775, belong to proprietors who own more than one village; 12, paying Rs. 12,385, belong to less than six sharers; and the remainder, paying a revenue of Rs. 1,35,307, belong to cultivating communities. In these property is generally much subdivided. In 1838 Rs. 10,117 were remitted on account of the famine of 1837, and Rs. 9,602 were remitted in 1862 on account of the famine of 1860-61. From the statistics of 97 villages in the whole tahsíl, the following facts in regard to the growth of tenant-rights during the currency of the past settlement are gathered :—

Year.	Hereditary tenants.			Tenants-at will.			Total.		
	Holdings.	Area.	Rent.	Holdings.	Area.	Rent.	Holdings.	Area.	Rent.
			Rs.			Rs.			Rs.
18:8 ...	150	3,013	10,692	2,641	26,210	95,462	2,791	29,223	1,06,154
1868 ...	1,179	9,869	34,143	3,871	37,741	1,61,362	5,050	47,610	1,95,505

These hereditary tenants in 1838 paid Rs. 3-8-9 per acre ; they now pay Rs. 3-7-4, showing a decrease of 2·5 per cent : the tenants-at-will then paid Rs. 3-10-3 per acre ; they now pay Rs. 4-4-4 per acre, showing an increase of 17·3 per cent. The general rise in rents amounts to 13 per cent. The assumed average rental per acre at assessment was Rs. 5-10-11 for irrigated land in the tahsíl and Rs. 2-2-4 for dry land, or a cultivation rate of Rs. 4-13-5.

According to the census of 1872 -parganah Hasangarh contained 107

Population. inhabited villages, of which 27 had less than 200 inhabitants ; 36 had between 200 and 500 ; 28 had between 500 and 1,000 ; 10 had between 1,000 and 2,000 ; 4 had between 2,000 and 3,000, and two had between 3,000 and 5,000. The towns containing more than 5,000 inhabitants were

The settlement records show 113 villages, distributed amongst 117 maháls or estates in 1874. The average area of each village is 705 acres. The total population in 1872 numbered 66,838 souls (30,378 females), giving 535 to the square mile. Classified according to religion, there were 63,288 Hindús, of whom 28,687 were females ; 3,550 Musalmáns, amongst whom 1,691 were females. Distributing the Hindú population amongst the four great classes, the census shows 10,653 Brahmans, of whom 4,886 were females ; 206 Rajpúts, including 89 females ; 3,124 Baniyas (1,436 females) ; whilst the great mass of the population is included in "the other castes" of the census returns, which show a total of 49,305 souls, of whom 22,276 are females. The principal Brahman subdivisions found in this parganah are the Saraswat (879) and Gaur (346). The Rajpúts are chiefly members of the Janghára (148), Chauhán and Jádon clans, and the Baniyas belong to the Agarwál (905), Dása (484), Chausaini, Mahesri, and Bárahsaini (1,194) subdivisions. Amongst the other castes the following have more than one thousand members each :—Ját (20,552), Barhai, Hajjám, Kahár, Bairági, Koli (3,246), Chamár (9,345), Khatík, Khákrob, and Garariya. The following castes have less than one thousand and more than one hundred members each :—Sonár, Bhat, Kalál, Kúchhi, Jogi, Darzi, Dhobi, Kumhár, Orh, Káyath, Dhúna, and Teli. The Musalmáns comprise Shaikhs (135) and Patháns (151) ; the remainder are unspecified. The old parganah comprised 50 villages of Thákurel Játs´and four villages of Brahmans, known as the " *Chauwan* (54) *gaon*" but the Játs have lost a good portion of their property owing to the severity of the last assessment, and have been replaced by Baniyas and land speculators.

The occupations of the people are shown in the statistics collected at the census of 1872. From these it appears that of the

Occupations.

male adult population (not less than fifteen years of age) 305 are employed in professional avocations, such as Government servants, priests, doctors, and the like ; 2,090 in domestic service, as personal servants, water-carriers, barbers, sweepers, washermen, &c. ; 1,671 in commerce, in buying, selling, keeping or lending money or goods, or the conveyance of men, animals, or goods ; 10,596 in agricultural operations ; 3,540 in industrial occupations, arts, and mechanics, and the preparation of all classes of substances, vegetable, mineral, and animal. There were 3,935 persons returned as labourers and 750 as of no specified occupation. Taking the total population, irrespective of age or sex, the same returns give 1,255 as landholders, 27,748 as cultivators, and 37,835 as engaged in occupations unconnected with agriculture. The educational statistics, which are confessedly imperfect, show 1,495 males as able to read and write out of a total male population numbering 36,460 souls. Hasangarh, at the past settlement, comprised 54 villages, with an area of 51,951 acres and paying a revenue of Rs. 1,05,315. Since then 43 villages have been added to it from Hathras, 6 from Mursán, 5 from Koil, and 1 from Khair ; in all 55 villages, with an area of 26,941 acres and a land revenue amounting to Rs. 53,127.

HATHÍSA BHAGWÁNTPUR, a town in parganah Háthras of the Aligarh district, is distant 3 miles from Háthras and 24 miles from Aligarh. In 1865 there were 1,654 inhabitants, and in 1872 there were 1,336. There is a police-station here.

HÁTHRAS, or Háthras Khás as it is sometimes called, is a town in the parganah of the same name in the Aligarh district, situated in lat.. 27°-35′-31," and long. 78°-6′-9″, distant from Aligarh 21 miles, 29 miles from Agra, and 24 miles from Kásganj in Eta.

In 1847 Háthras had 22,903 inhabitants, in 1853 the population numbered 20,504, and in 1865 there were 23,722 inhabitants.

Population.

The site has an area of 256 square acres, giving 92 souls to the acre. According to the census of 1872 there were 23,589 inhabitants, of whom 21,121 were Hindús (9,795 females) and 2,468 were Musalmáns (1,076 females). Distributing the population amongst the rural and urban classes, the returns show 30 landholders, 624 cultivators, and 22,935 persons pursuing occupations unconnected with agriculture. The number of enclosures in 1872 was 2,897, of which 332 were occupied by Musalmáns. The number of houses during the same year was 5,057, of which 2,610 were built with skilled labour, and of these 149 were occupied by Musalmáns. Of the 2,447 mud huts in the town 338 were owned by the same religionists. Taking the male adult population, 8,296 souls (not less than 15 years of age), we find the following occupations pursued by more than fifty males :—Attorneys, 56 ; barbers, 177 ; beggars, 186 ; brokers, 232 ; cart-drivers, 245 ; confectioners, 238 ; cotton-cleaners, 147 ; flower-sellers, 142 ; goldsmiths, 98 ; grain-dealers, 56 ; grain-parchers, 118 ; greengrocers, 190 ; labourers, 973 ; merchants, 147 ; milk-sellers, 56 ; money-lenders, 95 ; painters, 166 ; pandits, 201 ; porters, 62 ; potters, 210 ; purohits, 99 ; servants, 1,971 ; shop-keepers, 1,009 ; sweepers, 99 ; tailors, 217 ; water-carriers, 137 ; weavers, 124 ; and weighmen, 72. The town is essentially a great centre of commerce, and most of the merchants belong to the Baniya class. The Bárahsaini and Agarwáls (here of the Chúruwála *gotra*) are the leading subdivisions. The Musalmán portion of the population is insignificant, both in number and influence.

The general plan of the town is compact and the houses stand close together. A broad metalled road skirts the entire city where the walls once stood. One wide way passes through the centre from east to west, and two good roads pass from north to south dividing the town into six principal divisions known as the Nayaganj, Puránaganj, the Anáj (grain), Rui (cotton), Nimak (salt), Loha (iron), and Gurhái (sugar) mandis or markets ; Panseribatta or druggists' quarter ; Bazáza (cloth-merchants), Halwái (confectioners), and Bisáti (pedlars) muhallas or wards, and the Chauk Daulat Rám, where two roads cross. The names of these divisions show the thoroughly commercial character of the town. There are more brick-built and stone-fronted houses than mud huts, and this gives the town an appearance of solidity and prosperity which it also really possesses. The fostering care of successive Collectors is shown throughout. The streets and lanes are level, well-drained, and metalled. In 1824 Mr. W. J. Harding established Hardingganj, and in 1821 he inaugurated the existing drainage scheme, widened the streets, and repaired the wells. Mr. E. F. Tyler, in 1851-52, improved the town and the markets. The outskirts to the north along the circular road are being built over, and on the west the same improvement is going on. To the east of the town are the remains of Daya Rám's fort, consisting of a broken mound of earth-work and four corner bastions of great size, surrounded by a ditch fully forty yards wide on the town side.. An old temple in the fort still bears traces of the furious cannonade which was thought necessary for the reduction of the place in 1817. The buildings which were left undestroyed are now used as a tahsíli. On the north-western outskirt a large and unsightly excavation is being gradually converted into a square tank with masonry steps, and on one side stands the municipal hall, and to the south a school-house with a clock tower, containing a chiming clock, has been built. Besides an ugly temple which was commenced as a dwelling-place there is no striking edifice in the town, which throughout shows nothing but devotion to the acquisition of money. The Hindús feel the want of water for bathing purposes and it is intended to supply the new tank with water from the canal, which runs at a distance of some ten miles off. A dispensary was built in 1868, and a post-office was finished in 1871. There is a munsif of the first class resident here, who has civil jurisdiction over the tahsíl. The only point requiring future attention is the unfinished state of the old excavation forming the city ditch to the west and south of the site. This has, of late years, come to be a receptacle for stagnant water and impurities, and could easily be filled up from the excess of earth on the fort mound. The water supply is not good. As a rule, the water of the old wells is brackish, but the water of the Naya bazár and the outskirts tastes well. The water in the wells stands at about 40 to 45 feet from the surface. The Banjáras are said to have built, in early times, a stone cenotaph and a well in Háthras.

Háthras lies on the route from Agra to Aligarh,—8¼ miles from Sadabad station towards Agra, and the same distance from Sásni, the station between it and Aligarh. The road all through is metalled and bridged. Between Sadabad and Háthras, five nálás are crossed. The country is open and well cultivated. The road passes Bisána at 2½ miles, Chandpa at 5 miles, and Mitái at 7¼ miles. On to Sásni the road passes Háthras at ¾ mile from the encamping-ground, which lies to the south of the town ; road to Muttra (distant two marches, or 22 miles) at 1¾ ; Rohari at 4¼, and Barsa at 7 miles. To Budaon the road (metalled and bridged) passes by Salímpur (q. v.). It is intended to construct both a broad gauge railway between the town and the Háthras Station of the East Indian Railway, now 5½ miles distant from it.

The Municipal Act has been in force in Háthras since 1865, and the affairs of the town are now administered by a committee of nine members, of whom three hold office *ex-officio* and six are elected by the tax-payers. The limits of the municipality have been carefully demarcated by means of stone pillars, and there are seven octroi stations and five police-stations, all built of brick and kunkur. The conservancy of the town is fully provided for by the entertainment of a large staff of sweepers and by the construction of numerous latrines. The Municipal Committee have completed nearly all the important works which are likely to be required for some time.

The octroi in 1873-74 fell at Re. 1-1-4 per head of the population. The following statement shows the income and expenditure for three years :—

Receipts.	1871-72.	1872-73.	1873-74.	Expenditure.	1871-72.	1872-73.	1873-74.
	Rs.	Rs.	Rs.		Rs.	Rs.	Rs.
Opening balance ...	6,553	12,380	26,075	Collections ...	5,194	4,716	3,911
Class I.—Food and drink.	31,419	50,690	30,560	Head-office ...	466	535	494
„ II.—Animals for slaughter.	114	88	15	a. Original works ...	13,481	21,152	17,661
„ III.—Fuel, &c. ...	2,461	1,914	1,269	b. Supervision ...	776	424	578
„ IV.—Building materials.	1,915	4,582	1,367	c. Repairs ...	5,185	4,019	...
„ V.—Drugs, spices,	5,294	4,491	...	Purchase of land ...	...	714	1,610
„ VI.—Tobacco ...	1,705	4,633	5,107	Compensation	30	...	5,560
„ VII.—Textile fabrics	...	10,119	4,993	Police	5,703	5,738	5,699
Metals ...	...	1,996	...	Education	3,509	3,345	3,485
				Charitable grants	500	490	533
Total octroi ...	42,908	78,758	43,311	Conservancy	2,267	2,239	2,972
				Road-watering	167	227	226
Rents ...	559	367	957	Lighting	1,713	2,229	1,590
Fines	431	315	18	Gardens	8	37	562
Pounds ...	...	199	193	Extraordinary	360	360	7,161
Extraordinary	225	7,401	23,656	Miscellaneous	481	27,794	8,752
Miscellaneous ...	1,542	675	1,157				
Total ...	52,218	1,00,095	95,367	Total ...	39,840	74,019	60,794

The following statement gives the net imports for the last two years after deducting the goods in transit on which refunds were given, and also the supposed consumption per head of the population :—

Articles.	1872-73.			1873-74.		
	Net quantity imported in 1872-73.	Net value imported in 1872-73.	Average consumption or expenditure.	Net quantity imported in 1873-74.	Net value imported in 1873-74.	Average consumption or expenditure.
	Mds.	Rs.	M. s. c.	Mds.	Rs.	M. s. c.
Grain of sorts ...	267,668	5,35,324	8 11 7	339,365	7,30,052	10 20 4
Ghi ...	14,691	2,91,820	0 18 1	8,775	2,08,728	0 10 13
Rice ...	59,200	1,77,600	1 33 5	61,625	2,00,024	1 36 5
Vegetables ...	18,557	60,890	...	1,362	2,813	
Country fruits ...	1,139	6,041	...	...	...	Exempted
Fodder ...	21,523	10,373	...	4,198	1,923	from 4th
Foreign and dried fruits.	1,082	10,882	...	...	...	June, 1873.
Betel and pán ...	8,667 bundles	2,467	...	...	343	
Sugar refined, ...	19,915	2,38,980	0 24 10	53,069	5,14,360	1 25 11½
Do., coarse ...	147,591	5,89,360	4 22 12	206,685	5,86,719	6 15 15¼
Animals for slaughter.	1,657 in number,	1,997	...	264	...	
Oil ...	6,877	68,771	0 8 8	5,214	37,654	0 6 7

Articles.	1872-73.			1873-74.		
	Net quantity imported in 1872-73.	Net value imported in 1872-73.	Average consumption or expenditure.	Net quantity imported in 1873-74.	Net value imported in 1873-74.	Average consumption or expenditure.
	Mds.	Rs.	M. s. c.	Mds.	Rs.	M. a. c.
Oil-seeds ...	32,948	58,667	1 0 13	38,358	93,107	1 7 8
Soda and rtta ...	1,294	4,520	0 1 9	...	...	} Exempted
Fuel ...	117,261	15,527	...	12,850	3,644	} from 4th
Soap and reh ...	245	151	0 0 5	56	9	} June, 1873.
						Rs. a. p.
Building materials,	71,081	46,455	...	22,808	16,208	0 8 0
Iron for building ...	7,194	57,624	0 0 14			
Drugs, gums, spices, &c.,	50,082	2,00,466	1 21 3	...	...	Exempted.
						M. s. c.
Tobacco ...	7,899	22,846	0 9 8	12,637	93,387	0 15 10¼
			Rs. a. p.			Rs. a. p.
Cloth ...	...	14,21,686	14 0 2	391,271¼ number	16,75,447	51 13 11
					...	Exempted.
Metals ...	28,949	2,35,230	7 4 6	...		
Bambus, &c., ...	56,312 in number,	21,711				

There are no manufactures deserving notice, the importance of the town entirely depending on its trade, which is immense. Even

Trade.

after exempting drugs, spices, vegetables, gums, metals and other similar articles from taxation, and lowering the tax on other goods, the incidence is still abnormally high. The refunds on exports in 1872-73 amounted to Rs. 26,846, and in 1873-74 to Rs. 8,343. The duty on grain has now been reduced to an all-round rate of three pie per maund, whilst sugar has been entirely exempted, for any tax, however small, seems to turn into a mere transit due owing to the great importance of the trade. The exports of coarse sugar in 1872-73 amounted to 87,000 maunds, and in the following year to 84,000, whilst the exports of refined sugar would appear almost to have been to the same amount. Grain of all sorts, oil-seeds, cotton, sugar and ghi are the staple exports, and the imports consist of iron for building purposes, metal vessels of all kinds, cloths both European and native, drugs and spices of all kinds, pedlar's wares, and in fact every article of local consumption in these provinces which are distributed from Háthras, as the great centre of the supply trade, to all the marts throughout the upper Duáb, Rohilkhand, and the neighbouring districts of the Panjáb. Even with the reduced schedule of duty the income will still be quite sufficient for all ordinary expenditure, whilst the check to trade caused by imposts which are vexatious where unnecessary has been practically removed. The opening of the new line of rail to Muttra, in which the municipality has invested a considerable portion of its surplus funds, and the broad guage line connecting the business portion of the town with the East Indian Railway, must give a considerable impetus to the trade of this town, which, next to Cawnpore, is already the most important commercial centre in the Duáb. It is also proposed to carry on the light line of railway by Kásganj to Farukhabad.

The history of Háthras is the history of the Ját family of Háthras which has already been given in the district notice. From 1803 to 1817 it was held by Daya Rám. On the occasion of Holkar's invasion, as well as at other times, Daya Rám acted with hostility toward the British, and at length his assumption of independence was found so mischievous and alarming, especially in the threatening state of affairs at the commencement of the Marhatta war in 1817, that it was found necessary to dislodge him. Daya Rám was summoned to surrender his fort and allow it to be dismantled, but trusting in his defences, which were modelled on those of Aligarh, he refused compliance. The town was invested, and on the 23rd of February, 1817, the town-wall was breached and evacuated, and on the 1st of March fire was opened on the fort from forty-five mortars and three breaching batteries. At the close of the same day a magazine in the fort was exploded and caused such destruction of the garrison and buildings that Daya Rám fled during the night, and Háthras and the neighbouring fort of Mursán were forthwith dismantled. Háthras remained tranquil during the mutiny of 1857 through the exertions of Chaube Ghansám Dás, a blind pensioned tahsildár, who was afterwards murdered by the rebels at Kásganj. After the mutiny of the troops at Aligarh the Europeans fled to Háthras, and thence, about the 2nd of July, to Agra. It was one of the first places recovered, and owing to the services of Gobind Singh, son of Daya Rám, who, for his conduct on this occasion and during the operations against the Koil rebels, was rewarded with the grant of several villages and the proprietary right to Koil itself.

HÁTHRAS, a parganah of the Aligarh district, is bounded on the north by parganahs Koil and Akrabad ; on the west by parganahs Gorai, Hasangarh, and Mursán; on the south by the Muttra District, and on the east by Akrabad and Sikandra Rao. According to the census of 1872 this parganah had then a total area of 218 square miles and 67 acres, of which 180 square miles were under cultivation. The area assessed to Government revenue during the same year was 212 square miles, of which 174 square miles were cultivated, 3 square miles were culturable, and 35 square miles were barren. This parganah lies near the watershed of the Duáb, and may be described as one wide level plain of loam, with no elevations, and not more depressions than are required by the natural drainage of the country. With the exception of a few villages towards Mursán and Gorai, there is little sandy soil, and no tract of sand as in other parganahs. Here and there are a few fields of gently rising ground, and in a few villages, a light soil may prevail, but as a rule the whole is composed of rich, easily workable loam. The Sengar flows through the eastern portion of the parganah, and is used as a canal escape and as a distributary. A considerable area is irrigated in this manner along its banks. There are no other streams in the parganah, and no jhíls larger than ponds.

The previous history of the parganah has been given under that of the Ját talukadárs in the notice of the district, and in compar-

Fiscal history.

ing it with the present settlement statistics note should be taken of the changes in area that have taken place between 1839 and 1868, and which are mentioned hereafter. The net gain to the parganah amounts to 13 villages, but the actual area gained is not ascertainable. The parganah as settled by Mr. Thornton in 1838 contained 206 parent villages and 107 hamlets, including talukas Mendu, Káras, Karíl, Shahzádpur, Gubrári, Samardhari, and Barha. Mr. Thornton followed the same principles that he had adopted in Mursán, that whatever may have been the standing of the talukadár, provided it was evident that, from the first, he was a species of Government officer, and that no private transfer of the rights of the original proprietors had taken place in his favour, the descendants of the old proprietors had the first and most undoubted claim to be admitted to engagements on fair and equitable terms. To them also rightly belonged the title of zamíndár as then understood, " but, perhaps, it was more suitable to allow them the equivalent designation of biswadár as long as the desire of providing for the talukadár or other causes interfered with their admission to the same terms as the village zamíndárs in other places." In nearly all these propositions Mr. Thornton carried the people with him, and even the talukadárs themselves. He lowered the Government demand by ten per cent. all round. In all cases 20 per cent. was deducted from the net assets as shown in the rental and left with the biswadárs, and where the talukadárs were recorded as zamíndárs 30 per cent. was allowed to them. [1] In biswadári villages the talukadárs' allowance or malikána was fixed at 18 per cent. on the rental, giving a total reduction of 38 per cent. on the rental assets. Mr. Thornton settled all the disputes that he found to exist, and made arrangements as far as he could for clearing off the old liabilities of the landholders. His action in these matters is so different from that adopted at the present day that it deserves careful study and notice. The village communities had been so shattered and injured that in many cases he had to reconstruct them from the foundation. Before allowing that reduction of the land-revenue which he found necessary for the welfare of the village proprietary body, he examined into their liabilities, and arranged terms with the money-lenders, by which the usufruct of a certain

---

[1] See Set. Rep., I., 281, and Re. Rep., II., N. S., 49.

term of years was held sufficient to clear off the whole mortgage. As far as he, could he " rescued the village zamíndárs from their former hopeless state, and gave them the power by future prudence and industry of recovering from all their embarassments." In furtherance of this object he procured from Government a compensation to the talukadárs of Mendu and Shahzádpur in exchange for a formal release by them of all debts due from the biswadárs in their talukas. The talukadárs themselves were not forgotten in this scheme of relief. The entire debts due by them, and indeed the whole balance due from the parganah, was remitted as irrecoverable, and thus Húthras started afresh into life.

Notwithstanding all these efforts to place matters in Háthras on a more satisfactory footing, the success obtained has been very small. Certainly great difficulties had to be encountered. The former settlements were framed on the excessive assessments which had been levied by the talukadárs, but the farming system adopted by these men had already led to the total disruption of all ties connected with the village community. Many of the old proprietary body were often obliged to bid higher than the actual outturn to secure possession of their ancestral lands and prevent the intrusion of a stranger : hence the abnormally high rates of the old settlements. Mr. Thornton reduced these assessments by ten per cent.; and had to explain his reasons for this reduction by showing that even then the village zamíndars paid Rs. 3-3-6 per cultivated acre. Still these reductions were not enough. It was found necessary in 1851-53 to allow remissions amounting to Rs. 18,420, and in 1855 again Rs. 22,693 were remitted. The greater part of the changes affecting the area took place in 1840, when taluka Sásni was received from Mursán, and certain villages from Jaláli and Akrabad, all assessed at 75 per cent. of the assets. The indebtedness of the landholders is said by Mr. Wright to have amounted to not less than twelve lakhs of rupees (in 1839), of which nine were commercial debts due to the great indigo factories of Mendu, Háthras, Sásni, and Joár, and three were for arrears of land-revenue. He writes :—" The wells have gone to decay, and the utter hopelessness of the people of escaping from their creditors has caused general neglect as to their restoration, and thus the chief means of paying the revenue has failed. The present demand is not excessive, and any difficulties in the way of collecting it must be attributed to other causes than a heavy rate of assessment." Bad seasons had something to say to this state of affairs as well as of the assessment.

Taking the results of the assessment during its entire term as shown by transfers by revenue process of rights and interests in land in the parganah, the figures are as follows on a total area amounting to 130,168 acres and assessed at Rs. 3,08,344.

Transfers between 1839 and 1868.

Farmed.				Sold by auction.				Total.			
Area in acres.	Percentage on total.	Revenue.	Percentage on total.	Area.	Percentage on total.	Revenue.	Percentage on total.	Area.	Percentage on total.	Revenue.	Percentage on total.
13,052	9·5	Rs. 28,708	9·3	12,191	8·9	Rs. 34,934	10·5	25,243	18·5	Rs. 63,642	20·6

18·6 per cent. of these transfers occurred during the first ten years of Mr. Thornton's settlement, 1·59 per cent. during the second ten years, and only 0·34 per cent. between 1859 and 1868. But the voluntary sales and transfers by order of the Civil Courts show a total revolution in the proprietary body, for which it is difficult to find a parallel in these provinces. The statistics are as follows :—

			Area.	Land-revenue.	Percentage of area.	Percentage of land-revenue.
			Acres.	Rs.		
Sold privately	...	...	54,858	1,27,139	40 27	41·22
Mortgaged	...	...	52,270	1,19,909	39·38	38 88
Auction	...	...	49,666	1,13,951	36·47	36 95
Total	...	...	156,794	360,999	115·12	117 05

Nearly 60 per cent. of this changed hands during the first ten years, 31·3 per cent. during the second ten years, and 29·7 per cent. during the last decade. In the whole parganah an area exceeding the total area by 15 per cent. changed hands by voluntary or forced sale in addition to the 20·6 per cent. transferred by revenue processes. So severe was the assessment that between 1839 and 1852 land fetched only one and a half times the Government demand, and the percentage of transfers to area show that the purchasers only held the land for a short time, and gladly allowed new speculators to come in. This was especially the case during the first decade, when nearly 79 per cent. of the entire transfers took place. In Háthras 13,874 acres, or 10·1 per cent. of the total area, has been temporarily transferred from the original proprietors by mortgage, and 1,506 acres, or 1·1 per cent., by farm. The permanent alienations from the old proprietary body amount to 76,548 acres, or 56· 2 per cent. of the entire area, leaving only 44,220 acres, or 32·2 per cent. of the total area, in the hands of those whose families possessed it in 1838. Rajpúts, Játs, Brahmans, and Kírárs have been the principal losers, and the money-lenders of Háthras, Sásni, and Koil have stepped into their places. It would appear that the benevolent

Intentions of Mr. Thornton were frustrated by their very character. His arrangements gave a heritable and transferable value to the land which it never had before. The progress of the settlement and its duration combined with the increase of population, the rise in prices and the introduction of the canal, enhanced this value. Old debts, especially those due to the indigo factories, and which were before the settlement not worth one anna in the rupee, were eagerly bought up and enforced against the land. Taking the Rajpúts alone, they have lost 50,660 acres out of 60,537 acres held by them at the commencement of the last settlement. The Porach clan, once lords of Mendu, Háthras, and Daryapur, now have only 1,346 acres. Bháts have saved only one out of 25 villages held by them in 1838. Bangars have disappeared altogether, and Gahlots only retain 1,542 out of 11,726 acres. The Játs, amongst whom must be reckoned Raja Tíkam Singh, have retained only 61 per cent. of their old possessions. Kirárs, though very industrious, have not preserved one-half of their lands, and Brahmans have lost 65 per cent. of their old shares. Out of 242 villages 218 were held by these four castes.

The following statement will show more clearly the individual loss to each caste; the column for mortgage includes 1,115 acres belonging to Thákurs which were confiscated for rebellion and 1,526 acres farmed for arrears of revenue :—

Caste.	Area held in 1838 in acres.	Lost between 1836 and 1868 by			Remaining.	Caste.	Area held in 1838.	Lost between 1836 and 1868 by			Remaining.
		Sale.	Mortgage.	Total.				Sale.	Mortgage.	Total.	
Orh ...	289	269	...	269	...	Káyath ...	1,976	319	82	401	1,575
European,	744	744	...	744	...	Kirár ...	10,437	5,108	1,004	6,112	4,325
Ahír ...	664	644	...	644	...	Khatík ...	260	260	...	260	...
Brahman,	20,976	11,018	2,763	13,781	7,195	Lodha ...	261	149	16	165	96
Thákur...	60,537	39,839	10,821	50,660	9,877	Mewáti ...	258	151	53	204	54
Ját ...	32,128	11,365	1,102	12,474	19,654	Na u-m u s-lim.	3,857	3,086	195	3,281	576
Baniya ...	1,452	952	396	1,348	104						
Chamár...	868	823	45	868	...	Musalmán,	1,481	686	31	717	764
						Total ...	136,168	75,433	16,515	91,948	44,220

The new settlement was made in 1872 by Mr. W. H. Smith. The statistics of area then collected show that the total area amounted to 139,345 acres, of which 19,583 acres were returned as barren and 5,781 acres were held free of revenue. The distribution of the assessable area was as follows :—

Culturable.				Cultivated.			
New fallow.	Old waste.	Groves.	Total.	Irrigated.	Dry.	Total.	Grand Total.
Acres.	Acres.	Acres.	Acres.	Acres.	Acres.	Acres,	Acres.
970	4,779	515	6,264	100,161	7,556	107,717	1,13,981

The proportion of culturable land to the total area is 82 per cent., and of cultivation to the culturable area is 95 per cent., whilst irrigation reaches the enormous proportion of 93 per cent. of the cultivated area. The area available for the increase of cultivation in this parganah, even including grove-land, is only five per cent., so that here, if in any parganah in these provinces, all the conditions precedent to the grant of a permanent settlement exist. Cultivation has increased by 3·36 per cent., and irrigation by 15·9 per cent., since last settlement. The new assessment of the land-revenue amounts to Rs. 3,11,635-4-0 and the cesses to Rs. 31,163-8-0. Háthras has but 2·5 per cent. of unirrigated sand, and very little of the irrigated area is sandy. The old revenue of the parganah as it now stands was Rs. 2,96,542, which rose to Rs. 3,02,226 when the present assessment commenced, whilst the new land-revenue shows an increase of three per cent. on the expiring land-revenue of the past settlement. Of the 265 maháls or estates in the parganah in 1872, two were held free of revenue, 132 were held on a zamíndári tenure, 6 were pattidári, and 125 were bháyachára ; 18·1 per cent. of the revenue is paid by owners holding more than one village, 32·6 per cent. by villages where there are not more than six co-sharers, and 49·3 per cent. by villages in which the sharers are numerous. The rabi crops cover 47 per cent. of the total cultivated area, and amongst them wheat occupies 18 per cent., barley 12 per cent, and bejar 7 per cent. Amongst the kharíf crops, cotton occupies 15·5 per cent. of the total cultivation, joár 21·5 per cent., bájra 6 per cent., and indigo 4 per cent. 1,134 holdings are recorded as the seer of proprietors, 2,943 as held by hereditary tenants, and 5,223 by tenants-at-will, or 12·9 per cent., 31·3 per cent., and 55·7 per cent., of the total cultivated area respectively. The average area of each proprietary holding is 12·5 acres. Tenants occupy 87 per cent. of the cultivated area, and with the exception of the Raja the landowners are mostly absentees. The average rent paid by hereditary tenants is Rs. 5-1-3 per acre, and by tenants-at-will Rs. 4-12-7, or together Rs. 4-14-8. In Háthras 14,258 cultivated acres are entered seer of proprietors, 34,554 acres as held by hereditary tenants, and 61,580 acres as held by tenants-at-will.

According to the census of 1872 parganah Háthras contained 241 inhabit-

Population.

ted villages, of which 53 had less than 200 inhabitants; 93 had between 200 and 500; 62 had between 500 and 1,000; 28 had between 1,000 and 2,000; and four had between 2,000 and 3,000. The only town containing more than 5,000 inhabitants is Háthras itself. The settlement records show that there were 244 villages in 1872, distributed amongst 257 maháls or estates. The average area of each village was 576 acres. The total population in 1872 numbered 159,834 souls (74,035 females), giving 733 to the square mile. Classified according to religion, there were 145,687 Hindús, of whom 67,521 were females, and 14,147 Musalmáns, amongst whom 6,514 were females. Distributing the Hindú population amongst the four great classes, the census shows 27,531 Brahmans, of whom 12,571 were females; 17,094 Rajpúts, including 7,558 females; 11,739 Baniyas (5,585 females); whilst the great mass of the population is included in "the other castes" of the census returns, which show a total of 89,303 souls, of whom 41,787 are females. The principal Brahman subdivisions found in this parganah are the Gaur(1,344), Saraswat (905), Sanádh (3,439), and Kanaujiya. Rajpúts are of the Gahlot (1,332), Chauhán (573), Badgújar, Jádon (2,298), Janghára, Gaur, Pundír, Rathor, Panwár, Bhál, Sikharwár, Gaharwár, Jarauliya, Raikwár, Khajúri, Kirár, and Surajbansi clans; whilst Baniyas belong to the Agarwál (3,568), Chausaini, Dása, Mahesri, Bárahsaini (3,990), Khandelwál, Gurwál, Jaiswár, and Saraugi subdivisions. Amongst the other castes the following have more than one thousand members:—Ját (5,880), Sonár, Barhai (3,957), Hajjám (3,707), Kalál (2,123), Káchhi (6,103), Darzi, Kahár, Jogi, Dhobi, Koli (6,264), Chamár (30,192), Khatík, Khákrob (3,601), Kumhár, Garariya, Aheriya, Káyath, and Dhúna. The following have between one hundred and one thousand members each:—Ráj, Máli, Bhát, Gosháin, Ahír, Joshi, Bairági, Lohár, Banjára, Bharbhúnja, Lodha, Malláh, Teli, Kanjar, and Chhípi. The Musalmáns belong to the Shaikh (2,381), Sayyid (346), Mughal (78), and Pathán (1,218) subdivisions. The remainder of the Muhammadan population is entered without distinction.

The occupations of the people are shown in the statistics collected at the

Occupations.

census of 1872. From these it appears that of the male adult population (not less than fifteen years of age) 914 are employed in professional avocations, such as Government servants, priests, doctors, and the like; 7,337 in domestic service, as personal servants, water-carriers, barbers, sweepers, washermen, &c.; 4,558 in commerce, in buying, selling, keeping or lending money or goods, or the conveyance of men, animals, or goods; 19,045 in agricultural operations; 8,895 in industrial occupations, arts and mechanics, and the preparation of all classes of substances, vegetable, mineral, and animal. There were 11,983 persons returned as labourers and 1,466 as of no specified occupation. Taking the total population, irrespective of age or sex, the same returns give 3,580 as landholders, 49,278 as cultivators, and 1,06,976 as engaged in occupations unconnected with agriculture. The educational statistics, which are confessedly imperfect, show 4,112 males as able to read and write out of a total male population numbering 85,799 souls. Parganah Háthras was formed out of parganahs Sadabád, Mahában, Jalesar, and Koil during the last century, and varied in size up to 1838. It then contained 220 villages, with a cultivated area amounting to 93,104 acres and a land-revenue of Rs. 2,62,168. Between 1839 and 1868, 43 villages were transferred to Iglás, 17 to Mursán, 3 to the Muttra district, and 4 to Sikandra Rao. During the same period 28 villages (taluka Sásni) were received from Jaláli, 44 (taluka Moheriya) from Mursán, 4 from the Muttra district, and 4 from Akrabad, whilst one village (Dariyapur) was divided into twelve villages.

HÁTHRAS, a tahsíl of the Aligarh district, comprises the parganahs of Háthras and Mursán. The settlement records show a total area of 185,952 acres, of which 9,317 acres are held free of revenue and 22,097 acres were barren. The assessable area comprised 154,538 acres, of which 146,632 acres were cultivated (135,912 acres irrigated) and 7,916 acres were culturable ; of the latter 554 acres were under groves. The percentage of the culturable land to the total area is 83 per cent. ; of cultivation to the culturable area is 95 per cent., and of irrigation to cultivation is 93 per cent. The old land-revenue stood at Rs. 3,91,751, falling at Rs. 2-11-5 on the cultivation, and the new assessment is Rs. 4,18,525, falling at Rs. 2-13-8 per cultivated acre, and giving a rise of 6·8 per cent. over the initial demand of the old settlement and of 5 per cent. over its expiring demand.[1] The population in 1872 numbered 207,330 souls (95,911 females), giving 715 souls to the square mile. Excluding the city of Háthras the density is 633 souls to the square mile. There are 370 inhabited villages in the tahsíl. The total number of villages is 386, with an average area of 481 acres, or 0·751 square mile to each village. In 1872 the villages were distributed amongst 408 maháls or estates, of which 11 are held free of revenue, 208 are of the class known as zamíndári, 6 are pattídári, and 183 are bháyachára, so that, roughly speaking, one-half of the tahsíl is pretty minutely subdivided amongst cultivating village communities, and one-half is held by large proprietors. The census statistics show 534 blind persons, 34 lepers, 47 deaf and dumb, 21 idiots, and 15 insane persons in the tahsíl.

The tahsíl is remarkable for the high standard it has reached. Out of the total area 83 per cent. is culturable, and of this 95 per cent. is actually cultivated, whilst irrigation reaches 93 per cent. of the cultivated area. The proportion

---

[1] Many changes have taken place ; thus Rs. 6,000 have been alienated to the Mursán Raja for two generations, and there has been a large increase.

of culturable waste still remaining• uncultivated, even including grove-land, is only five per cent., not enough for pasture and firewood. The consequence is that a yearly increasing portion of the cultivated area is being devoted to inferior fodder crops. Irrigation and cultivation have almost reached their maximum, population is dense, labour is abundant and in great demand, and great pains are bestowed on husbandry. 86 per cent. of the cultivated area is watered from wells, in which the water is found at a depth averaging from 26 to 28 feet from the surface. The crops follow the character of the cultivation. In the year of remeasurement cotton covered 15 per cent. of the cultivated area, joár 21·5 per cent., wheat 17 per cent., and barley and bejar together 20·5 per cent. In natural capabilities Háthras is unequalled in the district.

HARDUAGANJ or Hardewaganj, a town in parganah Koil of the Aligarh district, is distant six miles east from Aligarh. The population in 1848 was 5,942, in 1853 there were 8,292 inhabitants, and in 1865 there were 6,120. In 1872 the population numbered 6,970 souls, of whom 6,353 were Hindús (3,127 females) and 617 were Musalmáns (275 females). The town site occupies 80 square acres, giving 87 souls to the acre. All persons residing beyond the limits of the municipality were excluded from the census of 1872. The residents are chiefly Baniyas engaged in trade, and who occupy the brick-built houses in the eastern quarter of the town. The town clusters around the ganj in a long and narrow strip to the east and west, and is connected with the Rámghát and Aligarh metalled road by four roads, also made and drained. The ganj is a fine open bazarway lined with fair shops built of brick, and widens out on the south into a large circular space. The ganj itself is fairly raised, but elsewhere the town site where not level is depressed, especially on the west. During the rains the water overflows the site both towards the east and the west, and flows southwards towards a great jhíl about three miles off towards the head-waters of the Sengar. The Rámpur Station of the Oudh and Rohilkhand Railway, called in the traffic tables Harduaganj, is three miles north of the town, and hitherto the rail-traffic passes by Aligarh. There is a police-station, a post-office, and a school, none of which deserve any particular notice. Nearly all the town lands are irrigated by the canal, and since its introduction the water in wells has risen from 25 feet to only 10 feet from the surface. Fevers are common.

The municipality was established in 1865, and is now managed by a committee of nine members, of whom three are official, three are elected by the tax-payers, and three are nominated by the Magistrate. The incidence of taxation in 1865 was 9 annas 9 pie per head of the population. It is the only town much affected by canal traffic. It lies just a mile from Barautha bridge, and is the nearest town of any size to the canal. The chief imports are salt, timber, and bambus, and the chief exports are cotton

Municipality.

and grain. In 1860-61 a large amount of grain was imported by the canal from Cawnpore. The following table gives the receipts and expenditure of the municipality for three years : –

Receipts.	1870-71.	1871-72.	1872-73	Expenditure.	1870-71.	1871-72.	1872-73.
	Rs.	Rs.	Rs.		Rs.	Rs.	Rs.
Opening balance ..	665	420	14	Collection ...	826	803	757
Class I —Food and drink	3,509	3,073	2,313	Head office ...	63	68	10
„ II.—Animals for slaughter.	70	16	28	Original works,	1,770	...	..
„ III.—Fuel, &c. ...	289	237	131	Repairs ...	332	1,814	477
„ IV.—Building materials.	164	215	174	Police ...	481	524	528
„ V.—Drugs, spices, &c.	194	343	99	Education ...	301	340	295
„ VI.—Tobacco ...	97	98	141	Charitable grants	43	163	242
„ VII.—Textile fabrics.	...	99	132	Conservancy ...	487	502	498
„ VIII. Metals ...	...	69	159	Lighting ...	397	395	390
Total of octroi ...	4,822	4,149	3,178	Miscellaneous ..	...	8.	96
Extraordinary ...	117	5	5	Institutes ...	...	...	60
Fines ...	5	42	15				
Miscellaneous ...	8	14	48				
Pounds ...	...	...	174				
Total ...	5,118	4,629	3,428	Total ..	4,698	4,616	3,853

The following statement gives the value of the imports for two years :—
Net imports.

Articles.	Value, 1871-72.	Value, 1872-73.	Quantity, 1872-73.	Consumption per head, 1872-73.	Articles.	Value, 1871-72.	Value, 1872-73.	Consumption per head, 1872-73.
	Rs.	Rs.	Rs.	Md. s. c.		Rs.	Rs.	Md. s. c.
Grain ...	87,795	59,710	38,065	7 12 9				
Sugar .	31,738	51,782	9,201	1 31 1	Fuel, ...	1,795	1,579	...
Ghi, ...	2,996	11,639	582	0 4 8	Building materials.	4,087	7,800	1 6 11
Vegetables,	5,765	9,994	3,737	...				
Fodder, ...	1,235	2,279	4,995	...	Spices, ...	5,491	6,341	1 3 6
Pán, ...	1,327	293	1,172 bundles.	...	Cloth, ...	9,860 Mds.	18,908	3 9 6
Oil, ...	5,710	5,791	687	0 5 4	Metals, ...	6,925	26,185	4 13 3
Oil-seeds,...	...	2,081	979	0 7 8	Tobacco,...	219	519	0 3 15

Harduaganj is said to owe its origin to Hardewa or Báláráma, the brother

History.

of Krishna, whose name is also connected with Koil and with Rámghát in the Bulandshahr district. The Yádavas of Báláráam's party were accompanied by an auxiliary force of Ahírs, whose commander, Chiman, excavated the tank in the present town of Harduaganj. On the conquest of Dehli by the Muhammadans, a colony of refugee

Chauháns took up their quarters here and got possession of the neighbouring country. There is no building and no remains of any antiquity about the town, which was plundered during the mutiny by the villagers of the neighbourhood, and property estimated to be worth four lakhs of rupees was stolen or destroyed. In the last century Harduaganj was patronised by Nawáb Sábit Khán, who improved the town very much and encouraged the settlement of traders in it.

HUSAIN, a town in parganah Sikandra of the Aligarh district, is distant 22 miles from Aligarh and 8 miles from Sikandra. The population in 1865 was 2,588, and in 1872 there were 3,164 inhabitants. The Chaukidári Act (XX. of 1856) is in force in Husain, and in 1873 supported a village police numbering nine men of all grades at an annual cost of Rs. 528. The number of the houses in the town in 1872-73 was 730, and of these 653 were assessed with a house-tax averaging Re. 1-8-1 per house and Re. 0-4-10 per head of the population per annum. The income for the same year was Rs. 1,011, including a balance of Rs. 28 from the previous year, and the expenditure was Rs. 829. Husain gave its name to a Porach taluka which has since been absorbed in parganah Sikandra Rao.

IGLÁS or Agilás, a tahsíli town in parganah and tahsíl Iglás of the Aligarh district, is situated on the Muttra road, 18 miles from Aligarh and 8 miles from Beswán. The population in 1865 was 1,310, and in 1872 there were 1,491 inhabitants. It is the head-quarters of the tahsíl, and possesses a police-station and post-office. Unconnected with the public offices, Iglás is of no importance whatever, and is a mere agricultural village. The Chaukidári Act (XX. of 1856) is in force in Iglás, and in 1873 supported a village police numbering three men of all grades at an annual cost of Rs. 162. The number of the houses in the town in 1872-73 was 289, and of these 240 were assessed with a house-tax averaging Re. 0-15-1 per house and Re. 0-2-5 per head of the population per annum. The income for the same year was Rs. 298, including a balance of Rs. 70 from the previous year, and the expenditure was Rs. 287. In 1857 the Játs of the parganah attacked the tahsíl of Iglás, which was protected by Burlton's troopers and guns from Sásni. The Játs attempted to seize the guns, but a shower of rain put out their matches (palítas), and a charge of cavalry utterly overthrew and scattered them in all directions.

IGLÁS, a tahsíl in the Aligarh district, comprises parganahs Hasangarh and Gorai. According to the settlement records the total area in 1874 contained 136,568 acres, of which 2,165 acres were held free of revenue and 9,825 acres were barren. The assessable area comprised 124,758 acres, of which 117,497 acres were cultivated and 7,081 acres were culturable. Of the cultivated area 89,522 acres were irrigated, and of the culturable area 122 acres were under groves. The proportion of culturable land to the total area is 91 per cent., of cultivation to the culturable area is 94 per cent., and of irrigation to cultivation

is 76 per cent. Six per cent. of the culturable area is untilled, and this small
margin hardly suffices for grazing purposes.   In 1872 the population numbered
114,665 souls (52,226 females), giving 586 souls to the square mile, distributed
amongst 212 inhabited villages.   The census statistics show 643 persons blind,
28 lepers, 19 deaf and dumb, 4 idiots, and 10 insane persons in the tahsíl. The
new assessment amounts to Rs. 2,87,694, and the cesses to 28,769, or a total of
Rs. 3,16,463. The incidence of the old land-revenue was Rs. 2-5-4 per acre
of cultivation, and of the new revenue is Rs. 2-7-2, giving an increase in the
land-revenue of Rs. 22,703, or 8·5 per cent.   The percentage of increase in the
different portions of the tahsíl varies very much (2 to 31 per cent.), owing to
the percentages on which the former revenue was cultivated, having varied
from 58 to 80 per cent. of the rental assets. The uniform rate of 50 per cent.
of the assets has now been applied to all villages, and the incidence of the State
demand has been thus equalised.

The only poor tract is in talukas Joár and Barha, where the sand is yellow
and rises into high ridges, and the sub-soil is not favourable to well-making.
The industrious Játs are good cultivators, and over 14 per cent. of the cultivated area is manured.   They have also increased the number of hamlets in their
villages, and thus enlarged the area of the better classes of land. Irrigation is
from wells, and three-fourths of it from earthen wells; it reaches 76 per cent. of
the cultivated area.   Of the same area 23 per cent. is under wheat, 14 per cent.
under cotton, barley 5 per cent., gram 8 per cent., bájra 8 per cent., and 17 per
cent. is under joár.   These crops show the natural fertility of the soil, and in
the whole tahsíl there is only six per cent. of the culturable area uncultivated.
The agricultural classes are chiefly Játs of the Tenwa and Thakurel gots, who are
especially good cultivators, so that there is little left to desire in the prosperity
of this tract.   At the recent settlement the malikána allowances have been reduced from 30 and 22·5 per cent. on the land-revenue to a uniform allowance
of 10 per cent., and thus though enhancement of the revenue has taken place
in many cases, the general result has been a relief to the overburdened biswadári villages.   Throughout the tahsíl, while the increase in the Government
demand has been 7 per cent. in malikána villages, the actual increase in the
payments made by the village proprietors has been only 4 per cent., owing to
the fact that they now only pay Rs. 4,984, instead of Rs. 12,671, as the talukadár's allownace. It would be well, should opportunity offer, that Government should buy out these abnormal middlemen and consolidate the malikána
and revenue as one charge on the biswadári estates.

The tract comprising the tahsíl contains no natural boundaries. It is a
long strip of varying width, running from north to south, and forms a small
portion of a section of the Duáb, which to the east is continued in the same
form in Koil and Háthras, and to the west in Muttra.   Undulating ridges of

sand may be traced in three parallel bands of irregular size and form from north to south. Between these ridges are lowlying level plains of loam, interspersed with patches of sand formed by a continuation of the main ridges in the form of spurs thrown out laterally, so that there are few villages which do not contain soils of both kinds. The Karwan Nadi runs through the centre of both parganahs and forms the drainage line. It is dry during a great portion of the year, and its bed is cultivated during the hot weather. The land on each side being low is always of the best quality, though here and there the sandy hills approach to within a few hundred feet of the bank. To the west the lowlying tract is wider than elsewhere and continues on into the Muttra district. No sandy ridges or other offshoots run into this tract from the west, and the eastern ridges are more distant than elsewhere. To the east the ridges are wider and continue on into Koil and Háthras, so that, on the whole, the eastern side of the tahsíl is of inferior fertility to the western. The soil of both tracts is good, and the loam and sand to the west are as productive as any other soils of that class in the district. The natural capabilities for irrigation are excellent. Water is found at a depth of 20 to 30 feet from the surface, and the subsoil is so firm that earthen wells will stand for years with only a brushwood frame, and for many years with a wooden frame, costing from Rs. 20 to 50. The wells are all fed from springs, not from percolation.

JALÁLI, a town in parganah and tahsíl Koil of the Aligarh district, is situated close to the East Káli Nadi on the Kásganj road, 11 miles southeast of Aligarh. The population in 1853 numbered 6,599 souls, and in 1865 there were 6,155. In 1872 there were 7,480 inhabitants, of whom 4,689 were Hindú (2,153 females) and 2,791 were Musalmáns (1,400 females). The site of the town occupies 58 square acres, giving 129 souls to the acre. The most noteworthy inhabitants are the Sayyids, descendants of one Kamál-ud-dín, who settled in the town during the reign of Ala-ud-dín Muhammad Shah (1295 A.D.) Kamál-ud-dín married the daughter of the Kázi, and during the reign of Sháhjahán his descendants were powerful enough to expel the old Pathán landholders, and thus obtained the full proprietary rights in the town which they still possess. "These rights have since become so subdivided that the individual shares are scarcely worth retaining. The reputation of the family is due to their having given so many useful subordinate officers to the British Government. Among its co-sharers the village can boast of an exceptionally numerous body of men who have obtained, or are now obtaining, distinction in both the military and civil services. On the one hand Risáldár Majors, Risáldárs, Subahdárs; on the other hand, Sadr Amíns, Munsifs, Deputy Collectors, and Tahsíldárs, besides innumerable subordinate servants of the State, abound among the members of this comparatively small proprietary community." The Sayyids are of the Shiah sect, and are noted as the leading members of that division of Muhammadans in the upper Duáb. Maulvi Mukarram Husain lives here and preaches every Friday in the principal mosque to large congregations of attentive listeners. Altogether there is no town in the district possessing such an influential and energetic colony of Musalmáns.

There is little remarkable in the situation of the town beyond its isolation.

The site.

It has no good roads, and lies between two high raised *rájbahas* of the Ganges Canal. The site also is high, and presents a curious appearance from the large number of imámbárahs interspersed amidst the houses. There are upwards of eighty of these structures devoted to Musalmán worship, of which thirty are of a good size, and one is a fine building. The ways are narrow, tortuous and unmetalled, and to the west there are several large excavations charged with water which becomes stagnant during the cold weather. To the west and south the land is low, and the road there is raised, but unmade. There is no regular bazar, and no trade. There is no Government school in the town, but there are four schools where the *Korán* is taught. The town is essentially an agricultural one, comprising a cluster of villages inhabited by landholders and cultivators, and this character is borne out by the number of cattle one sees coming into it of an evening. The well-water has risen from 42 feet from the surface to 30 feet since the opening of the canal, but its quality has not deteriorated. The Chaukidári Act (XX. of 1856) is in force, and in 1872-73 supported a village police numbering 13 men of all grades at an annual cost of Rs. 744. The number of houses in the town is 1,447, and of these 1,309 were assessed with a tax averaging Re. 1-0-5 per house and Re. 0-2-10 per head of the population per annum. The income for the year 1872-73 amounted to Rs. 1,519, including a balance of Rs. 180 from the previous year, and the expenditure was Rs. 1,279. Though a staff of four sweepers is entertained, the condition of the town is extremely filthy, and nothing appears to be done by the local committee towards improving it. On the east is a hollow called the *pokhar*, in which the rainfall collects, but its natural outfall has been cut off by the *rájbaha*, and it now overflows and causes considerable damage. What is most wanted is a good road connecting it with the Aligarh road and an enforcement of sanitary rules.

Jaláli lies on the route from Aligarh by Kásganj and Kachíla Ghát to Bu-

Communications.

daun, 14¼ miles from Aligarh and 11¼ miles from Gangíri, the next stage. From Koil to Jaláli the road is metalled and bridged. It leaves the Grand Trunk Road at Panehti (302½ miles from Allahabad), 7¼ miles ; passes Allahdádpur, 7⅞ miles, from the Ganges Canal by a bridge, 10¾ miles. The encamping-ground is about half a mile from the town of Jaláli, whence supplies are procurable after due notice. Hence to Gangíri the road is metalled as far as Kauriyaganj, 2¼ miles, and beyond that is unmetalled ; passes Shahgarh and the East Káli Nadi by a bridge at Haidarámái, 7½

miles. The country open and cultivated. Jaláli gave its name to an old parganah which was absorbed in the neighbouring parganahs in 1862-63; 32 villages belonging to parganah Jaláli were transferred to parganah Koil, 28 villages
to parganah Háthras, and 29 villages to parganah Atrauli.

Local tradition makes the foundation of Jaláli to precede that of Koil itself.
The story is given in the history of the district, and
need not be repeated here (page 484). It was then
called Nilanti. It must have fallen into ruins, for it is said to have been rebuilt by
Jalál-ud-din Firúz Sháh during the reign of Ghaias-ud-dín Balban, who erected
the *minár* at Koil. A mosque still exists here bearing an inscription dated in
665 Hijri (1266-67 A.D.) Jalál-ud-dín called the town after his own name and
settled here a colony of Patháns. Previously (in 1242 A.D.) Ulugh Khán
was obliged to lead a large force to chastise " the rebels of Jaláli and Dewali
and the Mawas of the Duáb between the Ganges and the Jumna. He fought
much against the infidels and cleared the roads and the neighbouring country
from insurgents." For a short time Jaláli formed a portion of the kingdom
of Jaunpur and was occupied by the Jaunpur troops. In the time of Sháhjahán
the Patháns were ousted by the Sayyids, who are still in possession.[1]

JARAULI, a town in parganah Akrabad of the Aligarh district, is distant
12 miles from Sikandra and 11 miles from Aligarh. In 1865 there were 2,050
inhabitants, and in 1872 there were 2,366.

JATÁRI, a town in parganah Tappal of the Aligarh district, is distant 27
miles from Aligarh and 13 miles from Khair. The population in 1865 numbered
2,011 souls, and in 1872 there were 2,281 inhabitants. The Chaukidári
Act (XX. of 1856) is in force in Jatári, and in 1873 supported a village police
numbering six men of all grades at an annual cost of Rs. 342. The number
of the houses in the town in 1872-3 was 491, and of these 451 were assessed
with a house-tax averaging Re. 1-1-4 per house and Re. 0-3-6 per head of the
population per annum. The income for the same year was Rs. 629, including a balance of Rs. 139 from the previous year, and the expenditure was
Rs. 591.

JAWA, a village in parganah Koil of the Aligarh district, is distant 14 miles
from Aligarh. The population in 1865 was 1,194, and in 1872 was 1,420. There
is a police-station and a post-office here. Jawa lies on the road by Anúpshahr to
Budaon, and is distant 9¼ miles from Aligarh and 13½ miles from Dánpur. The
road is metalled and bridged throughout, and passes Chírat at 5¾ miles from Aligarh. Hence to Dánpur crosses the Ganges Canal by a bridge at one mile,
passes Tájpur at 1¾, the district boundary at 2¾, the East Káli Nadi by a
bridge at 7½, and Naráyanpur at 11¼ miles. Jawa is a mere village, but supplies
(after notice) and water are plentiful.

---

[1] Dowson's Elliot, II., 362, V., 74, 79, 89.

KACHAURA, a town in parganah Sikandra of the Aligarh district, is distant 30 miles from Aligarh and 6 miles from Sikandra. The population in 1865 was 3,384, and in 1872 there were 3,911 inhabitants. Kachaura is noted for the defence made by the fort in 1803, when the gallant Nairn was slain in the assault. The Chaukidári Act (XX. of 1856) is in force in Kachaura, and in 1873 supported a village police numbering 10 men of all grades at an annual cost of Rs. 582. The number of the houses in the town in 1872-3 was 759, and of these 609 were assessed with a house tax averaging Rs. 1-2-7 per house and Re. 0-2-11 per head of the population per annum. The income for the same year was Rs. 764, including a balance of Rs. 56 from the previous year, and the expenditure was Rs. 763.

KAURIYAGANJ, a town in parganah Akrabad of the Aligarh district, is distant 12 miles from Aligarh and 12 miles from Sikandra. The population in 1865 was 3,607, and in 1872 there were 3,852 inhabitants. The Chaukidari Act (XX. of 1856) is in force in Kauriyaganj, and in 1873 supported a village police numbering 9 men of all grades, at an annual cost of Rs. 528. The number of the houses in the town in 1872-73 was 768, and of these 728 were assessed with a house-tax averaging Re. 0-15-9 per house and Re. 0-3-0 per head of the population per annum. The income for the same year was Rs. 918, including a balance of Rs. 198 from the previous year, and the expenditure was Rs. 765. Kauriyaganj was founded by an Amil of the Oudh Government during the last century.

KHAIR, a tahsíli town in the Aligarh district, is situated on the road to the Jumna, distant 14 miles from Aligarh. The population in 1865 was 3,339, and in 1872 was 4,850. There is a tahsíli, a police-station, a post-office, a school, and a munsifi here. The Chaukidari Act (XX. of 1856) is in force in Khair, and in 1873 supported a village police numbering 11 men of all grades at an annual cost of Rs. 612. The number of the houses in the town in 1872-73 was 1,221, and of these 947 were assessed with a house-tax averaging Re. 0-15-6 per house and Re. 0-3-0 per head of the population per annum. The income for the same year was Rs. 968, including a balance of Rs. 52 from the previous year, and the expenditure was Rs. 844. In 1857 Khair was occupied by the Chauháns under Rao Bhúpál Singh, Chauhán, who set himself up as the Rája of the parganah. On the 1st June, 1857, an expedition comprising the Agra volunteers under Mr. Watson surrounded the town and captured the rebel who was tried by court-martial and hanged. Before the end of the month the Chauháns, intent on revenge, called in the Játs and attacked Khair. The Government buildings and the houses of the wealthy Baniyas and Mahájans were plundered or destroyed. The tahsíl, a strong masonry building, might have held out longer had its defenders more heart and more gunpowder. It was besieged for several days in vain, until the tahsíldár and officials, despairing of help, withdrew in the night. It is supposed that property amounting to about three lakhs of rupees was plundered during the rule of the insurgents.

KHAIR, a parganah of the Aligarh district, is bounded on the north by the Bulandshahr district ; on the east by Koil ; on the west by Chandaus and Tappal, and on the south by Parganah Nuh of Muttra and Hasangarh of this district. According to the census of 1872 this parganah had then a total area of 154 square miles and 14 acres, of which 119 square miles were under cultivation. The area assessed to Government revenue during the same year was 153 square miles, of which 118 square miles were cultivated, 12 square miles were culturable, and 23 square miles were barren. Khair extends from the north-east corner of the tahsíl, where it touches parganah Khúrja in a south-westerly direction until it joins Tappal near the southern extremity of its eastern boundary. It is drained by the Karon Nadi, which is dry except during the rains. The line of sand-hills in Chandaus are continued on into this parganah. Water, as a rule, is found at a depth of from 18 to 30 feet from the surface, and wicker-lined wells are common and easily made, and last for from two to three years. Of the 145 estates found at the recent settlement, 71 were zamíndári, 72 were imperfect pattidári, and two were held in perfect pattidári tenure, and only 11·84 per cent. of the revenue of all these was paid by landholders possessing one village or more. The following table shows the changes that have occurred in the proprietary body between 1838 and 1868 :—

Caste.			Area held in 1838.	Area trans-ferred.	Area held in 1868.	
					Area.	Revenue.
			Acres.	Acres.	Acres.	Rs.
Ját ...	...	...	24,673	15,849	8,824	15,328
Brahman	...	...	19,453	9,866	10,087	16,612
Rajpút ...	...	...	22,569	17,257	5,332	8,557
Jádon ...	...	...	24,620	9,657	14,963	22,285
Nau-muslim	...	...	4,052	2,210	1,842	2,031
Káyath ...	...	...	998	998	...	
Carpenter	...	...	425	312	113	283
Total	...		96,810	55,649	41,161	65,098

The lands held by Játs and Jádons have, as a rule, passed into the hands of members of the same clan, whilst those possessed by Chauháns have been bought up by strangers. Parganah Khair has had seven settlements of the land-revenue including the existing one. The following statement shows the statistics of each :—

Year.		No. of villages.	Revenue.	Year.		No. of villages.	Revenue.
			Rs.				Rs.
1809-11	...	115	10,37,101	1821-29	...	115	1,18,286
1812-15	...	115	1,12,225	1830-37	...	116	1,28,681
1816-20	...	115	1,16,823	1838-68	...	124	1,56,290

During the first three settlements there were two villages held free of land-revenue, and six were at that time not in the parganah. The great majority of the villages in 1821 were settled for 16 years only. The enhancement of the fifth settlement was obtained on eleven villages, ten of which were among the former 115, but were assessed only to 1829-30, and one was a revenue-free village resumed in 1825-26. The number of villages is now 125, one having been divided into two. The settlement of 1816 was made at a time when cultivation was backward, and there have been considerable and successive enhancements since then, so that the revenue has risen about 50 per cent. In Khair 5,311 acres were farmed for arrears of revenue during the currency of the past settlement, and 2,926 acres were sold, aggregating 12 per cent. of the total area, assessed with 14 per cent. of the land-revenue. Rs. 16,182 were remitted from the revenue demand during 1860-61, but as a rule the revenue has been punctually paid in this parganah. The following statement shows the areas transferred and the average year's purchase and price per acre for each decade of the last settlement :—

Mode of transfer.	1839-48.			1849-58.			1852-66.		
	Area.	Price per acre.	Years' purchase.	Area.	Price per acre.	Years' purchase.	Area.	Price per acre.	Years' purchase.
	Acres.	Rs. a. p.	·	Acres.	Rs. a. p.		Acres.	Rs a. p.	
Private sale,	8,814	10 2 3	6·54	4,670	10 12 7	7·	13,648	13 9 3	8·16
Mortgage ...	14,388	4 10 9	3 3	11,160	12 8 8	8·	11,004	8 6 9	4·99
Auction sale,	8,011	5 13 2	3·44	2,596	7 1½ 4	3 87	11,633	6 13 7	3·98
Total ...	31,213	6 8 2	4·28	18,426	11 6 8	...	36,285	9 13 8	5·84

If a single plot has changed hands twenty times, the entry has been made twenty times in this account.

The transfers by revenue process, apart from the above, amounted to 7,454 acres during the first ten years of the expired settlement, and during the whole term of settlement 5,311 acres were farmed for arrears and 6,612 acres were sold by auction on account of arrears of revenue. The price brought at these land-auctions averaged only Rs. 3-11-0 per acre, or about two years' purchase of the land-revenue. The prices brought at private sales are, however, the true standard by which to judge of the rise in the value of land. The average price per acre at private sales during the last twelve years of the expired settlement was 51·3 per cent. higher than during the first eleven years. On the whole, 47 per cent. of the area, bearing 48 per cent. of revenue, had been permanently alienated by various processes, and 11 per cent. of the area, with the same percentage of the land-revenue, was under temporary alienation in 1868, but of 55,649 acres transferred 37,600 acres belonged to proprietors of three-fourths of a village or more. *Kharíf* crops occupy 46 per cent. of the cultivated area, and amongst them cotton covers 11 per cent. of the area, *joár* 19 per cent., *bájra* 8 per cent., and *moth* 7 per cent. In the *rabi*, wheat occupies 20 per cent. of the total cultivation, *bejar* 17 per cent., and gram 8 per cent. Only 2,500 acres, or 3 per cent. of the cultivation, is leased on payments in kind. There were 15,998 bulls and bullocks, 9,502 buffaloes, 7,653 cows, 916 horses. and 10,167 goats and sheep in the parganah in 1868 ; 1,335 holdings are held by proprietors as seer, 1,082 by hereditary tenants, and 2,660 by tenants-at-will, averaging 16·1 acres, 11·3 acres, and 15·7 acres respectively. The average rental where cash is paid is Rs. 3-14-1 per acre ; hereditary tenants pay on an average Rs. 3-8-2 per acre and tenants-at-will pay Rs. 3-15-10 per acre ; 30 per cent. of the cultivated area is held by cultivating proprietors. In 1838 only 375 holdings were recorded as in the possession of hereditary tenants, with an average area of 12·4 acres, and an average rental of Rs. 2-12-3 per acre ; whilst tenants-at-will possessed 3,247 holdings, with an average area of 15·3 acres and an average rental of Rs. 3·2 per acre. The areas held by each class at each period are as follows :—

| | 1838. | | 1868. | |
	Area.	Rent.	Area.	Rent.
	Acres.	Rs.	Acres.	Rs.
Hereditary tenants ...	4,077	12,936	12,231	42,970
Tenants-at-will ...	50,337	1,57,335	41,912	1,67,318

Taluka Somna is now included in parganah Khair and is separately mentioned in the district notice. It was separately assessed at the settlement in 1838. The new assessment was made by Mr. W. H. Smith. The statistics of the present area show a total area of 98,305 acres, of which 14,845 acres are returned as barren and 365 are held free of revenue. The assessable area is distributed as follows :—

Culturable.				Cultivated.			
New fallow.	Old waste.	Groves.	Total.	Irrigated	Dry.	Total.	Grand Total.
Acres.	Acres.	Acres.	Acres.	Acres,	Acres.	Acres.	Acres.
467	6,544	294	7,305	44,754	31,036	75,790	83,095

These figures show a proportion of culturable land to the total area amounting to 84 per cent., and of cultivation to culturable area of 91·2 per cent. Irrigation reaches only by 59·2 per cent. of the cultivated area, and the margin for increase of cultivation is only 8·8 per cent. The revenue assessed amounted to Rs. 1,74,070, and the cesses to Rs. 17,407. The new land-revenue falls at Rs. 2-4-9 on the cultivated acre, and gives an increase of 11 per cent. on the old assessment (Rs. 1,56,526). Irrigation has increased since last settlement by 30·3 per cent. and cultivation by 4·8 per cent.

According to the census of 1872 parganah Khair contained 124 inhabited

Population.   villages, of which 21 had less than 200 inhabitants ; 58 had between 200 and 500 ; 23 had between 500 and 1,000 ; 19 had between 1,000 and 2,000 ; 2 had between 2,000 and 3,000, and one had between 3,000 and 5,000. The settlement records show that in 1874 there were 144 maháls or estates in the parganah and 125 villages with an average area of 786 acres ; the largest having 3,948 acres, and the smallest having 109 acres. The total population in 1872 numbered 71,951 souls (33,320 females), giving 467 to the square mile. Classified according to religion, there were 66,890 Hindús, of whom 31,013 were females and 5,061 Musalmáns, amongst whom 2,307 were females. Distributing the Hindú population amongst the four great classes, the census shows 16,016 Brahmans, of whom 7,409 were females ; 8,419 Rajpúts, including 3,798 females ; 2,889 Baniyas (1,301 females) : whilst the great mass of the population is included in " the other castes " of the census returns, which show a total of 39,566 souls, of whom 18,505 are females. The principal Brahman subdivisions found in this parganah are the Gaur (6,011), Saraswat (1,224), and Sanádh (309). The Rajpúts are chiefly members of the Chauhán (1,575), Badgújar (224), Gahlot, Jádon (6,146), Janghára (115), and Rathor clans ; and the Baniyas are of the Agarwál (760), Dása (1,279), Chausaini, Mahesri, Bárahsaini, Guráku, and Rautgi subdivisions. Amongst the other castes, those having more than one thousand members each are the Ját (8,510), Barhai, Hajjám, Kahár (2,215), Koli (1,735), Chamár, (9,819), Khatík, Khákrob, and Gararia (1,583). Those having between 100 and 1,000 members are the Sonár, Máli, Bhát, Kalál, Káchhi, Darzi, Jogi, Bairági, Dhobi, Lohár, Kumhár, Aheriya (797), Orh, Banjára, Káyath, Bharbhúnja, Dhuniya, and Teli. Musalmáns are distributed amongst Shaikhs (100), Patháns (278), and those entered without distinction.

The occupations of the people are shown in the statistics collected at the

Occupation.   census of 1872. From these it appears that of the male adult population (not less than fifteen years of age) 266 are employed in professional avocations, such as Government servants, priests, doctors, and the like ; 2,602 in domestic service, as personal servants, water-carriers, barbers, sweepers, washermen, &c. ; 1,316 in commerce, in buying, selling, keeping or lending money or goods, or the conveyance of men, animals, or goods ; 12,355 in agricultural operations ; 2,772 in industrial occupations, arts and mechanics, and the preparation of all classes of substances, vegetable, mineral, and animal. There were 3,914 persons returned as labourers and 656 as of no specified occupation. Taking the total population, irrespective of age or sex, the same returns give 1,490 as landholders, 33,621 as cultivators, and 36,840 as engaged in occupations unconnected with agriculture. The educational statistics, which are confessedly imperfect, show 1,466 males as able to read and write out of a total male population numbering 38,631 souls. At the last settlement in 1838 the parganah comprised 125 villages, with an area of 98,585 acres, and a land-revenue amounting to Rs. 1,57,082. In 1841-42 two villages were transferred to parganah Koil and one to Chandaus, and in 1851-52 one village was transferred to Hasangarh. Between 1841 and 1852 six villages were received from Koil and one village from Tappal, leaving Khair, including taluka Somna, possessed of 124 inhabited villages. The parganah proper was formerly occupied and owned by Chauháns, but even at last settlement Játs and Jádons of the Somna family had each an equal share in the parganah, and there was a good sprinkling of Brahmans. Játs and Jádons have improved, whilst the Chauháns are gradually losing the little that has remained to them.

KHAIR, a tahsíl of the Aligarh district, comprises the parganas of Chandaus, Tappal, and Khair. According to the settlement statistics in 1874 it comprised a total area of 260,147 acres, of which 1,393 acres were held free of revenue and 36,304 acres were barren. The assessable area contained 222,450 acres, of which 186,983 acres were cultivated (99,914 acres irrigated) and 35,467 acres were culturable. Of the latter 597 acres were under groves. The culturable area is 85 per cent. of the total area, and cultivation covers 84 per cent. of the culturable area, whilst irrigation reaches 53 per cent. of the cultivation. The proportion of manured land is, as in Atrauli, only 9 per cent. The old revenue amounted to Rs. 3,55,177, and the new revenue to Rs. 4,01,050, falling at Rs. 2-2-4 per acre on cultivation, and giving an increase of Rs. 12·9 per cent. over the former demand. The population in 1872 numbered 169,459 souls (78,731 females), giving 417 souls to the square mile, distributed amongst 277 inhabited villages. The census statistics show 556 blind persons, 60 lepers, 24 deaf and dumb, 6 idiots, and 13 insane persons in the tahsíl.

The greatest length of the tahsíl, from east to west, is about 32 miles, and its greatest breadth is 22 miles, but its shape is irregular, and between these extreme distances its length and breadth varies greatly. According to the settlement records its total area is 260,159 acres, or 406·5 square miles. Khair the largest, and Chandaus the smallest of the parganahs within it, occupy the eastern and greater portion of the tahsíl, and Tappal forms the western tract. The Karon Nadi runs through Chandaus and Khair, and is dry except during the rains. The general surface of the country is level and the character of its soil uniform; but three separate lines of *bhúr* or sandhills running from north to south at varying distances from each other, undulate through Chandaus and Khair. These and the khádir of the Jumna in Tappal form the only exceptions to the uniformity of the tract. Taking the bangar portions of Tappal, the irrigating capabilities of all three parganahs are about equal and bear a fair proportion to the cultivated area.

Khair is the largest tahsil in the district, though in population it is inferior to Koil. The proportion of the culturable area to the total area is 85 per cent., and of the cultivated area to the culturable area is 84 per cent., leaving only 16 per cent. for the increase of cultivation. Khair in a great measure resembles Atrauli on the east. Both tahsíls have a considerable amount of khádir land : in both there is a large percentage of sandy soil, and water.lies deep beneath the surface. As in Atrauli, we have first a khádir, then a large strip of high raised sandy soil parallel to the course of the river, then a level stretch of good loam, which however, in Khair, is interspersed with sandhills which mingle with those of Koil and Iglás on the east. On the whole, however, Khair possesses more natural advantages. The ridge of sand bordering the Jumna, from the nature of the sub-soil, permits of the construction of wells, whilst on the ridge along the Ganges well-irrigation can hardly be said to exist. The canal too has been introduced here and has extended its operations very much of late years. Again, cultivating communities of Játs and Chauháns are the rule, and the division of produce system of rent is seldom met with, " alike the cause and sign of inferiority of produce." The tahsíl as a whole has improved very much between 1839 and 1868. During the year of re-measurement cotton and joár covered thirty per cent. of the total cultivated area and two-thirds of the kharíf area alone, and on the other hand wheat covered exactly one-third of the rabi area, and barley and bejar only a little more. These facts show a more than average fertility in the soil. At the last settlement the tahsíl consisted of 273 villages, with an area of 249,442 acres, or 390 square miles, and a land-revenue of Rs. 3,48,161. The present area has been given above.

Koil, a parganah of the Aligarh district, is bounded on the north by parganahs Barauli and Morthal; on the south by Hasangarh, Gorai, and Háthras; on the east by Atrauli and Akrabad, and on the west by Khair and Hasangarh Khúrja. According to the census of 1872 the parganah had then a total area of 274 square miles and 100 acres, of which 186 square miles were under cultivation. The area assessed to Government revenue during the same year was 268 square miles, of which 182 square miles were cultivated, 18 square miles were culturable, and 68 square miles were barren. The Koil tahsíl lies almost in the centre of the district on the watershed between the great rivers. The level is therefore high and the soil of uniform character. Vast tracts of úsar, commencing in a north-west direction, run in a more or less connected line almost parallel with the course of the canal.

Bhúr villages are found here and there, but they are few and far between, and mostly lie in the tract between the Khair and Iglás metalled roads. The soil for the most part is good loam, and the tract to the north-east, so backward at the past settlement, is now so improved by irrigation that little or no inferiority is apparent in it when compared with the remainder of the tahsil.

The settlement of parganah Koil in 1838 was made by Mr. Thornton, and after his revision there were 288 villages, with an area of 145,232 acres and a revenue of Rs. 2,25,814. The former assessment was very unequal. There appears to have been, during the last century, a very general dispossession of the original proprietors, and a great number of estates, especially those lying close to the city, fell into the hands of the Lodhas and other castes as managers. Many of the villages thus held were very heavily assessed at the previous settlements, whilst the kánúngo families and others who possessed greater influence obtained easier terms. The consequence was that there was much poverty and distress in parts of it. Mr. Thornton reduced the former assessment by Rs. 3,718, and his rates fell at Rs. 2·4 per cultivated acre. Since then numerous changes have taken place in the boundaries of the parganah, and these are noted hereafter. Out of a total area of 175,274 acres at the present settlement, 41,377 acres were found to be barren and 5,567 acres were held free of revenue. In 1838, out of a total area of 162,603 acres, 35,301 acres were entered as barren and 4,120 as free of revenue. The distribution of the assessable area at both assessments was as follows:—

Year.	Culturable.				Cultivated.			Grand Total.
	New fallow.	Old waste.	Groves.	Total.	Irrigated.	Dry.	Total.	
	Acres.	Acres.	Acres.	Acres.	Acres.	Acres.	Acres.	Acres.
1868 ...	1,041	10,283	954	12,278	91,949	24,103	116,052	128,330
1838 ...	Incorrect.		...	12,160	77,880	33,142	111,022	123,182

The culturable area is 73 per cent. of the total area and the percentage of cultivation to the culturable area is 90. The percentage of irrigated area to cultivation is 79, against 72 at the preceding settlement. Only nine per cent. of the culturable area is actually available for the extension of cultivation. The same excessive assessment seems in a great measure to have been continued by Mr. Thornton, who took 70 per cent. of the assets, so that the increase in the new assessment has not been more than 15 per cent., giving a land-revenue of Rs. 281,600 and cesses Rs. 28,160.

The following statement shows the character of the transfers made during each decade of the expired settlement :—

Mode of transfer.	1839-1848.			1849-1858.			1859-1867.		
	Area.	Average per acre.	Years' purchase.	Area.	Average per acre.	Years' purchase.	Area.	Average per acre.	Years' purchase.
	Acres.	Rs. a. p.		Acres.	Rs. a. p.		Acres.	Rs. a. p.	
Private sale,	9,527	6 8 2	4 7	13,334	10 2 0	5·8	23,318	13 13 0	8·5
Mortgage ...	15,083	5 5 11	3 3	12,156	7 6 2	4·8	11,548	14 4 2	5·4
Auction sale,	9,672	6 11 3	4·3	7,869	7 11 4	4·4	14,055	8 9 2	4·9
Total, ...	34,182	6 0 10	4·0	33,359	8 8 11	5·1	48,921	12 6 7	6·5

The settlement of the city of Koil is noticed under the description of the city : and the history of the talukas of Aisa, Manchaura, Sákráwáli, Sahibabad, and the grants held by the Derridon family, is given under the district notice. The alienations during the term of the past settlement in this parganah have been very numerous. In 234 out of 320 villages, an area of 118,650 acres, out of a total area of 164,776 acres, has been transferred : 42 per cent. of these have passed by private sale, 34 per cent. by mortgage, and 24 per cent. by order of the civil courts. It is unquestionable that the proximity of a large city brings about a rapid movement of property. The facilities for contracting loans are great and the money-lenders are ever accommodating, and in addition to these the temptations to extravagance and luxury are also very great. Hence temporary mortgages often end in private sales, " or the land is put up for sale in satisfaction of the decrees of a civil court, which is at the door of the usurious lender, and the accessibility of which encourages both fraudulent and frivolous claims." The principal losers are Thákurs, Sayyids, and Musalmán Rajpúts, and no matter how long the day may be delayed, the remainder of them must all go, sooner or later, to make room for the usurers, who are the only monied men left. Fifty-two per cent. of the estates in this parganah are held on a zamíndári tenure. In 1857 hereditary tenants paid on an average Rs. 3-7-4 per acre for their cultivation : this rate increased in 1868 to Rs. 3-9-7 ; tenants-at-will, in 1857, paid Rs. 3-4-3, which increased by 17·5 per cent., or to Rs. 3-13-5, in 1868. In Koil only 267 biswas, with an area of 7,817 acres, were farmed, and 50 biswa shares, with an area of 682 acres, were sold for arrears of land-revenue between 1838 and 1868. A few confiscations for rebellion took place after 1857.

According to the census of 1872 parganah Koil contained 269 inhabited
Population.
villages, of which 63 had less than 200 inhabitants ; 109 had between 200 and 500, 75 had between 500 and 1,000 ;

16 had between 1,000 and 2,000, and three had between 2,000 and 3,000. The towns containing more than 5,000 inhabitants were Aligarh or Koil, with 58,539 ; Harduaganj, with 6,970 ; and Jaláli, with 7,480. The settlement records show altogether 274 villages, distributed amongst 321 mahóls or estates. The average village area comprises 639 acres, the smallest containing only 96 acres. The total population in 1872 numbered 194,160 souls (89,945 females), giving 708 to the square mile. Classified according to religion, there were 161,061 Hindús, of whom 74,009 were females ; 33,061 Musalmáns, amongst whom 15,924 were females ; and 38 Christians. Distributing the Hindú population amongst the four great classes, the census shows 21,106 Brahmans, of whom 9,578 were females ; 22,675 Rajpúts, including 10,028 females; 12,016 Baniyas (5,549 females); whilst the great mass of the population is included in "the other castes" of the census returns, which show a total of 105,264 souls, of whom 48,863 are females. The principal Brahman subdivisions found in this parganah are the Gaur (1,690), Saraswát (2,078), Sanádh (1,338), Kanaujiya, and Gujráti. The Rajpúts chiefly belong to the Gahlot (115), Chauhán (2,297), Badgújar (588), Jádon (15,330), Janglára (2,332), Tomar, Pundír, Solankhi, Rathor, Panwár, Jaiswár, Bhál and Bachhal clans. The Baniyas are of the Agarwál (2,867), Chausaini (686), Dasa (841), Mahesri (1,119), Bárahsaini (5,125), Khandelwal, Gurika, Saraugi, and Lohiya subdivisions. Amongst the other castes the following have more than 1,000 members each :—Ját (3,676), Sonár (1,407), Barhai (4,368), Hajjám (3,521), Mali (2,296), Káchhi (1,444), Ahír (1,997), Darzi, Kahár (3,506), Dhobi, Koli (6,613), Chamár (31,697), Khatik, Khákrob (4,535), Kumhár (2,090), Garariya (6,021), Káyath (3,386), Lodha (9,615), and Dhuna. The following have less than 1,000 and more than one 100 members each :—Raj, Bhát, Kalál, Gosháin, Joshi, Jogi, Bairági, Lohár, Aheriya (790), Orh, Bharbhunja, Teli, Kanjar, Chhípi, and Riwari. Musalmáns are distributed amongst Shaikhs (4,496), Sayyids (1,967), Mughals (403), and Patháns (4,373). The remainder are entered without distinction.

The occupations of the people are shown in the statistics collected at the census of 1872. From these it appears that of the male adult population (not less than fifteen years of age) 1,045 are employed in professional avocations, such as Government servants, priests, doctors, and the like ; 12,585 in domestic service, as personal servants, watercarriers, barbers, sweepers, washermen, &c. ; 4,534 in commerce, in buying, selling, keeping or lending money or goods, or the conveyance of men, animals, or goods ; 21,321 in agricultural operations ; 11,424 in industrial occupations, arts and mechanics, and the preparation of all classes of substances, vegetable, mineral, and animal. There were 13,719 persons returned as labourers and 1,397 as of no specified occupation. Taking the total population, irrespective

Occupations.

of age or sex, the same returns give 7,374 as landholders, 55,880 as cultivators, and 130,906 as engaged in occupations unconnected with agriculture. The educational statistics, which are confessedly imperfect, show 5,725 males as able to read and write out of a total male population numbering 104,215 souls.

Numerous changes have taken place in the limits of the parganah since the settlement in 1838. The changes up to 1870 are shown in the following table :—

Year.	Transferred to	No. of villages.	Area.	Land-revenue.	Year.	Received from	No. of villages.	Area.	Land-revenue.
			Acres.	Rs.				Acres.	Rs.
1851-2	Khair ...	6	3,856	5,404	1851-52	Khair ...	2	1,759	2 258
	Chandaus ...	1	808	1,311	1862	Akrabad ...	23	20,375	27,516
	Morthal ...	1	540	526		Jaláli ...	32	27,079	40,443
	Hasangarh ...	5	1,486	2,889					
	Gorai ...	65	22,979	42,462					
						Total ...	57	49,213	70,217
	Total ...	78	29,669	52,592		Increase, ...	...	19,544	17,625

KOIL, a tahsíl of the Aligarh district, comprises the parganahs of Koil, Morthal, and Barauli. . The total area according to the settlement records of 1874 amounts to 227,897 acres, of which 5,575 acres are held free of revenue and 53,088 acres are barren. The assessable area amounts to 169,234 acres, of which 17,378 acres are culturable and 151,856 acres are cultivated. Of the culturable area, 1,533 acres are new fallow, 14,634 acres are old waste, and 1,111 acres are under groves. Of the cultivated area, 119,070 acres are irrigated. The new assessments amounted to Rs. 3,60,569, and the cesses to Rs. 36,055, or a total of Rs. 3,96,624. The new land-revenue gave an increase of 19 per cent. over the current revenue, and falls at Rs. 2-5-11 per cultivated acre. In 1872 the population numbered 230,669 souls (106,842 females), giving 648 souls to the square mile, distributed amongst 350 inhabited villages. The same statistics show 571 persons blind, 45 lepers, 23 deaf and dumb, 19 idiots, and 20 insane persons in the tahsíl.

This tahsíl is an old one.[1] It was known as the Hazúr tahsíl up to 1840, when the name was changed to the Koil tahsíl. It is divided into two unequal parts by the Grand Trunk Road running from the south-east corner in a north-westerly direction, and into two still more unequal portions by the Ganges Canal. Property is considerably subdivided throughout the tahsíl : 55 per cent. of the

---

[1] See Rev. Rep., V., 59.

estates are held in zamíndári tenure, 15·5 per cent. in perfect pattidári, and the remainder are bháyachára. Only 18 per cent. of the land-revenue is paid by proprietors who own more than one village, 25·5 per cent. by villages owned by less than six sharers, and 56·5 per cent. by proprietary communities. Twenty-three per cent., or nearly a quarter of the cultivated area, is recorded as the seer of proprietors. Hereditary tenants cultivate 28 per cent. of the cultivated area, or 36 per cent. of the tenants' land, and hold 42,411 acres : tenants-at-will occupy 74,240 acres, or 49 per cent. of the cultivated area, and 64 per cent. of the tenants' land. The holdings of hereditary tenants average 8·7 acres each, and of tenants-at-will 11 acres; and all tenants together, 10 acres, or 17·5 pukka bíghas, which are equivalent to 53 kuchha bíghas. The average rental per acre paid by hereditary tenants is Rs. 3-8-11, and by tenants-at-will Rs. 3-13-8, giving a general rate of Rs. 3-12-0 per acre. The papers of the revision of 1857 show a rate for hereditary tenants of Rs. 3-6-3 per acre, and a rate for tenants-at-will of Rs. 3-1-10, giving a general rate of Rs. 3-2-8 per acre, which shows a rise, during the last decade, of 4·9 per cent. in the rents paid by hereditary tenants, of 22·37 per cent. in the rents paid by tenants-at-will, and a general rise of 18·4 per cent. The greatest rise has been in Morthal, which, owing to the influence of the canal, has increased its competition rate 43·8 per cent. In Barauli the increase has been 37·2 per cent., and in Koil only 17·5 per cent. In 1857 the holdings of hereditary tenants had an average area of 12 acres, and by 1868 this had dwindled down to 8 acres : the holdings of tenants-at-will have remained the same, or 11 acres. But though the area held by each hereditary tenant has diminished, the total area held by that class of tenant has increased. In 1857 they held only 20,877 acres, and in 1868 their total holdings covered 42,411 acres, or more than double the amount of land formerly cultivated by them, and at a rate 8 per cent. below that paid by other cultivators. Here there were no powerful talukadárs, as in Atrauli, to contest and practically prohibit the growth of occupancy rights, and the result is that the old cultivators have more than held their own. The old tenants probably held better land, and so paid a higher rate in 1857, but with the introduction of the canal into the poorer lands held by the tenants-at-will, the landholders have been able to increase the rates paid by the latter class of tenants, and to extract from them a much larger proportional share of the benefits derived from irrigation than they can from their old tenants. Seventy-eight per cent. of the cultivated area at assessment was irrigated, and of this, 80,424 acres, or 66 per cent. of the total irrigation, was from wells. 10·5 per cent. of the area is unirrigated sand, and rabi crops occupy 52 per cent. of the total cultivation ; kharif crops 47 per cent. ; and miscellaneous crops, such as tobacco and the like, one per cent. In the rabi, wheat takes up 25 per cent. of the total area, barley 11 per cent., bejar 8 per cent., and gram 7 per cent. In the khárif, cotton covers 14 per cent. of the area, *joár* occupies 18 per cent, *bájra* 6 per cent, and indigo 4 per cent. Two per cent. of the area leased to tenants in Koil and 7 per cent. in the remainder of the tahsíl was paid for in kind, but only in the worst villages, where poor sandy soil prevails. The entire increase in cultivation between 1838 and 1868 amounts to only 5·5 per cent., but a very appreciable portion of the cultivated and culturable area has been taken up for the purposes of the canal, railway and roads. Twenty-six per cent. of the total area is unassessable, 9 per cent. comprises culturable waste, and one per cent. is under groves. The proportion of cultivation to the culturable area is 90 per cent., and of culturable land to the total area is 74 per cent.

MAHU, a town in parganah Háthras of the Aligarh district, is distant 12 miles from Háthras and 20 miles from Aligarh. In 1865 there were 1,473 inhabitants, and in 1872 there were 1,515.

MANDRÁK, a village in parganah Koil of the Aligarh district, is distant 7 miles from Koil on the Agra road. The population in 1865 numbered 1,496, and in 1872 there were 1,687 inhabitants. The Mandrák indigo factory was the scene of the spirited defence made by Mr. Watson and eleven Europeans against 1,000 Musalmán rebels on the 1st of July, 1857, and which has been noticed in the district history. The Chaukidári Act (XX. of 1856) is in force in Mandrák, and in 1873 supported a village police numbering four men of all grades, at an annual cost of Rs. 216. The number of the houses in the town in 1872-73 was 340, and of these 240 were assessed with a house-tax averaging Re. 1-1-10 per house and Re. 0-2-7 per head of the population per annum. The income for the same year was Rs. 330, including a balance of Rs. 62 from the previous year, and the expenditure was Rs. 296.

MENDU, a town in parganah Háthras of the Aligarh district, is distant 4 miles from Háthras and 17 miles from Aligarh. The population in 1865 was 4,194, and in 1872 there were 4,262 inhabitants. Mendu gave its name to a taluka, an account of which is given in the district notice. The Chaukidári Act (XX. of 1856) is in force in Mendu, and in 1873 supported a village police numbering nine men of all grades at an annual cost of Rs. 528. The number of the houses in the town in 1872-73 was 929, and of these 875 were assessed with a house-tax averaging Re. 0-15-7 per house and Re. 0-2-11 per head of the population per annum. The income for the same year was Rs. 1,010, including a balance of Rs. 158 from the previous year, and the expenditure was Rs. 870.

MITAI, a town in parganah Háthras of the Aligarh district, is distant 5 miles from Háthras and 26 miles from Aligarh. In 1865 there were 1,533 inhabitants, and in 1872 there were 1,619.

MORTHAL, a small parganah in tahsíl Koil of the Aligarh district, is bounded on the north by parganah Pahásu of the Bulandshahr district; on the south by Koil; on the east by Atrauli; and on the west by Koil. By the census return of 1872 the parganah had then a total area of 82 square miles and 8 acres, of which 55 square miles and 8 acres were under cultivation. The area assessed to Government revenue during the same year was 82 square miles, of which 55 square miles were cultivated, 8 square miles were culturable, and 19 square miles were barren.

The physical features of the parganah so resemble that of Koil that it is needless to repeat them here. It originally formed part of the Atrauli tahsil, but since 1852 has been included in Koil. The zamíndárs are chiefly Chauhán Rajpúts. Mr. Thornton, writing in 1838, says :—" There have been more sales by auction, and there is generally more pecuniary distress in this taluka than in any other tract of land which I know of equal size, when the revenue has been on the whole so moderate. The zamíndárs have possessed great facilities for borrowing money, in consequence of there being a large mart in the neighbourhood, named Harduaganj. The Baniyas who reside in that town generally exact *badni* engagements in return, and this is a system which, sooner or later, is sure to ruin the borrowing party. Besides the above disadvantages, the soil of this taluka is for the most part of a decidedly inferior kind. The system of cultivation is almost entirely *batái*, or by division of crops. The proportion of irrigation is 57 per cent., of which 5½ per cent. is furnished by the Káli Nadi and by tanks or jhíls, and is of less value than that which is afforded by wells. Under these circumstances, the new revenue, although higher by Rs. 104 than the old, falls only at Re. 1-13-6¼ per cultivated acre."

The new assessment was made by Mr. W. H. Smith: the statistics of area are as follow :—

		Unassesable.		Culturable.			Cultivated.			Total assessable area.	Total area.
		Barren.	Revenue-free.	Fallow.	Groves.	Total.	Irrigated.	Dry.	Total.		
Former	...	6,900	548	Incor	rect.	4,839	13,076	10,188	23,264	28,103	35,551
Present	...	6,590	8	3,660	141	3,801	21,024	4,577	25,601	29,402	36,000

Here the proportion of the cultivated to the culturable area is 87 per cent., whilst the proportion of culturable soil to the total area is 82 per cent. Irrigation covers 82 per cent. of the cultivated area, showing an increase of 62 per cent. The new assessment was made at Rs. 58,379, and the cesses stand at Rs. 5,836. The increase in the land-revenue over the old settlement amounts to 36 per cent. The changes that have occurred in Morthal from 1839 to 1868 affect 46 out of 64 villages; and 24,072 acres out of a total of 35,091 acres were transferred, forming 72 per cent. of the entire area. Nearly all this, as noted above, formerly belonged to the Chauháns. The following table shows these changes more clearly :—

Mode of trans-fer.	1839-1848.			1849-1858.			1859-1867.		
	Area.	Average per acre.	Years' purchase.	Area.	Average per acre.	Years' purchase.	Area.	Average per acre.	Years' purchase.
	Acres.	Rs. a. p.		Acres.	Rs. a. p.		Acres.	Rs. a. p.	
Private sale ..	2,677	10 12 8	14·1	2,907	10 3 11	7·7	4,706	15 9 10	12·3
Mortgage ...	501	3 13 0	3·3	3,390	8 12 11	6·0	3,822	11 5 5	9·8
Auction sale ..	2,035	8 9 5	9·3	2,237	5 15 7	4·7	432	14 10 4	13·6
Total ..	5,213	9 4 2	10·7	8,534	8 8 10	6·2	8,960	13 11 11	11·3

On the whole the Chauháns have retained but few of their old possessions, and these few are slowly but surely passing out of their hands. High prices and enhanced rents have not changed the characteristics of the clan in this district, and debt, idleness and extravagance, are still producing their natural results. One thing may be noticed here, and that is the gradual rise in the value of land. The average price per acre, though weighted by the sales of land under decrees of the civil courts, which are so low owing to incumbrances, still show a decided rise in each decade of the past settlement, and the tendency is still towards a rise. At no time was there any difficulty found in paying the late assessment, which was framed at 70 per cent. of the assets then existing, and the present light assessment should, therefore, be easily paid. Only 2 5 shares, amounting to 219 acres, were farmed for arrears of revenue between 1838 and 1868; 51 per cent. of the estates in this parganah are held on a zamíndári tenure. In 1857 hereditary tenants paid on an average Rs. 3-7-0 per acre on their cultivation; this had increased in 1868 to Rs. 3-9-2 ; tenants-at-will in 1857 paid Rs. 2-10-10 per acre, and this increased in 1868 by 42·8 per cent., or to Rs. 3-13-2 per acre.

According to the census of 1872 parganah Morthal contained 57 inhabited villages, of which 16 had less than 200 inhabitants ; 25 had between 200 and 500 ; 11 had between 500 and 1,000 ; four had beetween 1,000 and 2,000 ; and one had between 2,000 and 3,000. The settlement records show altogether 54 villages, distributed amongst 66 maháls or estates.

Population.

The total population in 1872 numbered 26,857 souls (12,342 females), giving 445 to the square mile. Classified according to religion, there were 25,153 Hindús, of whom 11,582 were females; and 1,704 Musalmáns, amongst whom 760 were females. Distributing the Hindú population amongst the four great classes, the census shows 3,406 Brahmans, of whom 1,583 were females; 2,945 Rajpúts, including 1,284 females; 960 Baniyas (450 females); whilst the great mass of the population is included in " the other castes" of the census returns, which show a total of 18,842 souls, of whom 9,265 are females. The principal Brahman subdivisions found in this parganah are the Gaur (372) and Saraswat. The Rajpúts chiefly belong to the Chauhán (1,964), Gahlot, Badgújar, Jádon (586), Janghará and Bais clans, and the Baniyas to the Agarwál, Dasa, Mahesri, and Bárahsaini subdivisions. Amongst the other castes, those which have more than 1,000 members each are the Ját (1,001), Chamár (5,756), Garariya (1,327), and Lodha (2,860) castes.

The following castes have less than 1,000 and more than 100 members :— Barhai, Hajjám, Kalál, Ahír, Káchhi, Darzi, Kahár, Dhobi, Lohár, Koli, Khatík, Khákrob, Kumhár, and Káyath. The Musalmáns comprise Shaikhs (133), Patháns (144), and a number unspecified.

The occupations of the people are shown in the statistics collected at the census of 1872. From these it appears that of the male adult population (not less than fifteen years of age) 40 are employed in professional avocations, such as Government servants, priests, doctors, and the like; 968 in domestic service, as personal servants, water-carriers, barbers, sweepers, washermen, &c.; 276 in commerce, in buying, selling, keeping or lending money or goods, or the conveyance of men, animals, or goods; 4,728 in agricultural operations; 637 in industrial occupations, arts and mechanics, and the preparation of all classes of substances, vegetable, mineral, and animal. There were 2,050 persons returned as labourers and 89 as of no specified occupation. Taking the total population, irrespective of age or sex, the same returns give 715 as landholders, 12,527 as cultivators, and 13,615 as engaged in occupations unconnected with agriculture. The educational statistics, which are confessedly imperfect, show 191 males as able to read and write out of a total male population numbering 14,515 souls.

Morthal and Barauli are mere talukas, and are practically looked upon as one parganah in the revenue records. Both of them originally formed part of Parganah Koil, and during the last century became detached as separate talukas. Morthal belonged almost entirely to a Chauhán colony, and now, though a few villages, belong to Bákir Ali Khán of Pindráwal, and a few to Mahájans, the parganah may be said to be divided between the old Chauhán

proprietors and the Musalmán Badgújar Mahmud Ali Khán of Chatári.   The
following changes took place since 1838 :—

Year.	Transferred to	Villages.	Area.	Revenue.	Year.	Received from	Villages.	Area.	Revenue.
			Acres.	Rs.				Acres	Rs.
1851-52 ...	Atranli	2	1,512	1,456	1851-52 ...	Koil ...	1	522	526
„	Bulandshahr,	18	11,137	10,378	„	Atrauli ...	.1	299	790
	Total ...	20	12,649	11,834		Total ...	2	821	1,316

MURSÁN, a town in parganah Mursán and tahsíl Háthras of the Aligarh
district, lies 24 miles from Aligarh and 7 miles from Háthras, on the Muttra
road.   The population in 1853 was 6,568, and in 1865 was 5,572.   In 1872
there were 5,998 inhabitants, of whom 5,009 were Hindús (2,223 females) and
989 were Musalmáns (442 females).   The town site occupies an area of 69
square acres, giving 87 souls to the acre.   The town is separated from the
Muttra road by an excavation, to the east and west of which run the roads from
Aligarh by Iglás, and that from the fort to the main road.   The latter forms the
principal street and bazarway, and shortly after it enters the town it branches
into two near the *ganj* and joins the Iglás road.   It is raised and drained at the
sides, but all the other ways are low, unmetalled, and ill-kept.   There are but 30 or
40 brick-built houses, and these belong to grain-merchants.   Mursán is essentially an agricultural town, and there is hardly any trade, except in country produce which eventually finds its way to Háthras.   The well-water is good and lies
at about 30 feet from the surface.   There are two schools here, a police-station,
and a post-office.   On the whole the place appears to be neglected, and neither
the Raja nor any one else takes much interest in its improvement.   The Raja
employs two native physicians to attend the people in the town, but beyond
this nothing has been done for it.   There is a sarái for travellers and an
encamping-ground for carts near the high road.   The Chaukidári Act (XX. of
1856) is in force in Mursán, and in 1873 supported a village police numbering
13 men of all grades, at an annual cost of Rs. 744.   The number of the houses
in the town in 1872-73 was 1,282, and of these 1,081 were assessed with a
house-tax averaging Re. 1-1-10 per house and Re. 0-3-2 per head of the population per annum.   The income for the same year was Rs. 1,275, including
a balance of Rs. 69 from the previous year ; and the expenditure was Rs. 1,171.

The history of Mursán is that of the Ját Rajas of the place, and this has
already been given in the district notice.   Raja Tíkam

History.

Singh, C.S.I., the present representative, is an Honorary
Magistrate.   On the capture of Daya Rám's fort of Háthras in 1817, the Mursán Raja, Bhagwant Singh, surrendered his fort, of which the bastions and

walls were dismantled by the British forces. The fort is now in ruins, and is occupied by the followers of the Raja and the house of the Raja ; but the latter chiefly resides in another house at some distance from the fort.

MURSÁN, a parganah in tahsil Háthras of the Aligarh district, is bounded on the north by Hasangarh ; on the west and south by the Muttra district; and on the east by Háthras. The census statistics of 1872 show a total area of 73 square miles and 79 acres, of which 66 square miles were under cultivation. The area assessed to Government revenue during the same year was 67 square miles, of which 61 square miles were cultivated, one square mile was culturable, and five square miles were barren.

This parganah is a continuation of tahsíl Iglás, and is marked by similar physical characteristics. The Káron Nádi runs down its centre, with a khádir of good quality and tolerably fertile. As in Iglás, however, parallel lines of sandy soil run within a short distance of each side, limited in extent on the west, and broader and more irregular on the east. These are well-defined tracts and of far greater extent and poorer capability than those in Háthras. There are no jhíls in the parganah larger than ponds, and no stream other than the Káron. This absence of rivers and tanks is however made up for by the great facilities afforded for well-irrigation. Water is found at a depth of .25 to 30 feet from the surface, fed by inexhaustible springs and the subsoil is good.

The fiscal history of the parganah is given under the Mursán family in the notice of the Aligarh district. The villages of this parganah were divided by Mr. Thornton in 1834 into *zamíndári, mukadami*, and *talukadári*. The first comprised those villages in which the Raja of Mursán was found to have proprietary rights ; the second, those settled with the village communities; and the third, those settled with the Raja on the refusal of the village communities to accept the engagements for the land-revenue. Up to Mr. Thornton's revision the total amount of revenue due from the parganah had been paid through the Raja, and the sum realisable by him in the previous settlement was Rs. 2,05,414, of which the Government land-revenue was Rs. 1,74,602. Mr. Thornton reduced the demand by 13 per cent., or to Rs. 1,52,053, of which the Raja paid Rs. 60,102 for the villages settled with him, and Rs. 91,951 for the *mukadami* villages, which paid to the Raja Rs. 118,624. The incidence of the revenue was Rs. 2-9-6 per cultivated acre. This settlement framed on the heavy assessments that had been exacted by the former talukadárs, worked very badly ; and though remissions and revisions were made, 7,269 acres, or 17·67 per cent. of the entire area, were farmed, and 2,037 acres, or 4·95 per cent. of the area, were sold for arrears of revenue during the currency of Mr. Thornton's settlement. In addition to this, 38,867 acres, or 94·52 per cent., changed hands by private sale, mortgage or forced sale. At the conclusion of the present settlement operations

Fiscal history.

in 1872, only 16,052 acres, or 39 per cent. of the total area, remained to the old proprietors, whilst 19,943 acres, or 48½ per cent., had been permanently transferred to others, and the remainder had been mortgaged. Játs, Brahmans, Gahlots, and Musalmáns have been the principal losers and money-lenders the gainers.

The following statement shows the loss to each caste :—

Caste.	Area held in 1838 in acres.	Lost between 1838 and 1868 by			Remaining.	Caste.	Area held in 1838.	Lost between 1838 and 1868 by			Remaining.
		Sale.	Mortgage.	Total.				Sale.	Mortgage.	Total.	
Albási ...	549	91	165	256	293	Ját ...	2,7323	1,2745	3,281	16,026	11,297
Sanádh ...	8,710	4,159	1,167	5,326	3,384	Káyath ...	6	...	...	...	6
Agarwála	42	...	...	...	42	Gosháin ...	34	...	...	...	34
Gahlot ...	4,037	2,680	414	3,094	943	Nau-muslim	399	268	78	346	53

Between 1838 and 1869 the parganah has been reduced by the transfer of 66 villages to other parganahs. Originally the parganah was formed on purely historical considerations, and the recent changes have been made to form a compact area for administrative purposes ; any minute comparison therefore with previous areas is out of the question.

The new assessment of the land-revenue has been made by Mr. W. H. Smith. The statistics of area show a total area of 46,607 acres, of which 2,514 acres are returned as barren, and 3,536 acres are held free of revenue. The distribution of the assessable area is as follows :—

Culturable.				Cultivated.			Grand Total.
New fallow.	Old waste.	Groves.	Total.	Irrigated.	Dry.	Total.	
Acres.	Acres.	Acres.	Acres.	Acres.	Acres.	Acres.	Acres.
150	1,463	39	1,652	35,751	3,154	38,905	40,557

The proportion of culturable land to the total area is 87 per cent. ; and here also cultivation is very high, being 96 per cent. of the culturable area. Irrigation, too, reaches 92 per cent. of the entire cultivated area, and only four per cent. of the culturable area, including land under groves, has not yet been brought under the plough. Cultivation has increased by 9·18 per cent., and irrigation by 9·8 per cent. since last settlement. The new assessment amounts to Rs. 1,06,890-8-0, and the cesses to Rs. 10,869. Mursán is undoubtedly inferior to Háthras in its soil : it contains 6 per cent. of dry *bhúr,* and a large proportion of the irrigated area is of the same character. The old land-revenue at the commencement of the past settlement stood at Rs. 95,209, which rose to Rs. 95,848 when the new settlement commenced. The increase shown at the new assessment amounts to 11 per cent. Out of 143 maháls or estates in 1872, nine were held free of revenue, 76 were zamíndári, and 58 were bháyachára.[1] 59·6 per cent. of the total area is held by numerous sharers, 7 per cent. by a few, and the remainder almost entirely by the Raja of Mursán. The *kharíf* occupies 55 per cent. of the cultivated area, and in it cotton covers 13·5 per cent. of the total cultivated area, *joár* 21·5 per cent., and *bájra* 7·5 per cent. Amongst the *rabi* crops, wheat occupies 14 per cent. of the entire cultivation, barley 15 per cent., and *bajra* 9 per cent. 703 holdings are in the possession of cultivating proprietors as seer, 1,071 holdings are held by hereditary cultivators, and 2,130 holdings by tenants-at-will, or 18·6 per cent., 30·5 per cent., and 50·9 per cent. respectively of the total cultivated area. The area of each proprietary holding averages 10·6 acres. Thus, tenants who were formerly for the most part proprietors occupy 81·4 per cent. of the cultivated area, and the landowners are nearly all absentees. The average rental is Rs. 4-15-0 per acre; hereditary tenants pay, on an average, Rs. 4-13-4 per acre, whilst tenants-at-will pay Rs. 5-0-2 per acre. Though inferior to Háthras, the general rent-rate in this parganah is slightly in excess. In Mursán 7,515 cultivated acres are recorded as seer, 12,302 acres as held by hereditary tenants, and 20,526 acres as held by tenants-at-will.

According to the census of 1872, parganah Mursán contained 129 inhabited villages, of which 51 had less than 200 inhabit-

Population.

ants, 53 had between 200 and 500, 19 had between 500 and 1,000, and 5 had between 1,000 and 2,000. The only town containing more than 5,000 inhabitants is Mursán itself. The settlement records show that there were 142 villages in the parganah in 1872, distributed amongst 143 maháls or estates. The average area of each village was 328 acres. The total population in 1872 numbered 47,496 souls (21,876 females), giving 651 to the square mile. Classified according to religion, there were 44,049 Hindús, of whom 20,269 were females; 3,447 Musalmáns, amongst whom 1,607 were females. Distributing the Hindú population amongst the four great classes, the census shows 9,908 Brahmans, of whom 4,572 were females ; 973 Rajpúts, including 444 females; 1,775 Baniyas (824 females); whilst the great mass of the population is included in " the other castes " of the census returns, which show a total of 31,393 souls, of whom 14,429 are females. The principal Brahman subdivisions found in this parganah are the Gaur (558), Sanádh (1,136), and

---

[1] For further details as to the fiscal history of this parganah, see Sett. Rep. I , 247, and Rev., Rep. II., N. S., 49.

Saraswat (54). Rajpúts belong to the Gahlot (566), Chauhán, and Badgújar clans, and the Baniyas to the Agarwál (1,104), Mahesri (241), Bárahsaini (112), Dasa, and Chausaini subdivisions. The following, amongst the other castes, have more than 1,000 members each:—Ját (8,849), Barhai, Hajjám, Koli (2,031), and Chamár (18,625). The following have less than 1,000, but more than 100 members each:- Sonár, Bhút, Kalál, Ahir, Káchhi, Darzi, Jógi, Kahár, Bairági, Dhobi, Khatík, Khákrob, Kumhár, Garariya, Aheriya, Káyath, and Mallah. The Musalmáns are distributed amongst Shaikhs (803), Sayyids (101), and Patháns (460); the remainder of the Muhammadan population is entered without distinction.

The occupations of the people are shown in the statistics collected at the census of 1872. From these it appears that of the male adult

Occupations.

population (not less than fifteen years of age) 205 are employed in professional avocations, such as Government servants, priests, doctors, and the like; 2,090 in domestic service, as personal servants, water-carriers, barbers, sweepers, washermen, &c.; 1,031 in commerce, in buying, selling, keeping or lending money or goods, or the conveyance of men, animals, or goods; 6,560 in agricultural operations; 2,324 in industrial occupations, arts and mechanics, and the preparation of all classes of substances, vegetable, mineral, and animal. There were 3,585 persons returned as labourers and 419 as of no specified occupation. Taking the total population, irrespective of age or sex, the same returns give 954 as landholders, 17,425 as cultivators, and 29,117 as engaged in occupations unconnected with agriculture. The educational statistics, which are confessedly imperfect, show 935 males as able to read and write out of a total male population numbering 25,620 souls. Mursán originally formed a portion of parganahs Jalesar and Koil. In 1838 it contained 208 villages, with a cultivated area amounting to 58,621 acres and a land-revenue of Rs. 1,52,053. Between 1839 and 1868, 17 villages were received from Háthras, and 33 villages were transferred to parganah Mahában of the Muttra district, 44 villages to Háthras, and 6 to Iglás.

PILKHANA, a town in parganah Akrabad of the Aligarh district, is distant 11 miles from Aligarh and 12 miles from Sikandra. In 1865 there were 3,809 inhabitants, and in 1872 there were 4,500. The town is a very old one, and gave its name to a taluka which was farmed to Daya Rám at the commencement of the British rule. In 1817 the taluka was broken up, and the villages were settled with the original proprietors. The Chaukidari Act (XX. of 1856) is in force in Pilkhana, and in 1873 supported a village police numbering 9 men of all grades at an annual cost of Rs. 528. The number of the houses in the town in 1872-73 was 798; and of these 750 were assessed with a house-tax averaging Re. 1-4-4 per house and Re. 0-3-5 per head of the population per annum. The income for the same year was Rs. 1,043, including a balance of Rs. 88 from the previous year, and the expenditure was Rs. 894.

Pisáwa, a village of parganah Chandaus in the Aligarh district, is distant 26 miles from Aligarh and 6 miles from Chandaus. The population in 1865 numbered 2,426 souls, and in 1872 there were 2,668 inhabitants. Pisáwa gives its name to a taluka held by Játs, an account of whom is given under the district notice. In the neighbourhood there is the only jungle deserving the name in the district.

Purdilnagar, a town in parganah and tahsíli Sikandra of the Aligarh district, is 26 miles from Aligarh and 2 miles from Sikandra Rao. The population in 1865 was 3,967, and in 1872 was 4,123. There is a police-station and a post-office. The Chaukidari Act (XX. of 1856) is in force in Purdilnagar, and in 1873 supported a village police numbering 11 men of all grades, at an annual cost of Rs. 636. The number of the houses in the town in 1872-73 was 873 ; and of these, 811 were assessed with a house-tax averaging Re. 1-2-9 per house and Re. 0-3-9 per head of the population per annum. The income for the same year was Rs. 1,028, including a balance of Rs. 79 from the previous year ; and the expenditure was Rs. 915. The Ganges Canal passes close to the town which is named after Nawáb Purdil Khán of Sikandra Rao.

Salímpur, a village in parganah and tahsíl Háthras, is distant 11 miles from Háthras and 20 miles from Aligarh. The population in 1865 was 1,285, and in 1872 was 1,356. There is a police-station here. Salímpur lies on the route between Háthras and Budaun, distant 10¾ miles from Háthras and 10½ miles from Sikandra Rao, the next stage. The road throughout is metalled and bridged, and the country open and well cultivated. From Háthras, Sokhnár is passed at two miles, the railway at six, and Kailora at 7½ miles. To Sikandra Rao, the Ganges Canal is crossed by a bridge at 6 and 10½ miles. Salímpur is a mere village, and supplies can only be had after due notice. Water is, however, plentiful.

Sásni, a town in parganah and tahsíl Háthras in the Aligarh district, is distant 14 miles from Aligarh on the Agra road, and 7 miles from Háthras. The population in 1853 numbered 5,484 souls, in 1865 there were 4,994 inhabitants, and in 1872 there were 4,208. The town is steadily declining in importance. There is a police-station and a district post-office here. Sásni lies on the route from Agra to Aligarh, 8⅝ miles from Háthras and 14½ miles from Aligarh. The encamping-ground for troops is to the west of the town. The road all through is metalled and bridged, and supplies and water are abundant. From Háthras you pass the Muttra road (Muttra distant 22 miles) at 1¾, Rohari at 4¼, and Barsa at 7 miles. To Aligarh, pass Susáhat at 4 miles, Mandrák at 6¾, Parháwali at 10, road to Muttra at 12, and join the Grand Trunk Road at 12½ miles, after which pass to the east of the town of Koil, to the encamping-ground. The fort, of which the remains exist, was built by the Ját Raja Phup Singh of the Mursán family. Tradition makes him out to have been a person of a very arbitrary disposition. It is said that he was specially proud of his palace garden ; and once, when one of his young sons had broken a twig or a leaf from some favourite tree the Raja ordered the lad's arm to be cut off. The Raja's followers however interceded, and the youth was punished by being forced to go about for several days with his sleeves cut short and his arms bare. On another occasion the Raja saw a peasant woman on the road break off the leaf of an overhanging tree to cover the mouth of a pot of ghi she was carrying ; whereupon he made her empty the whole pot over the tree, " to heal," as he said, " the wound she had inflicted."

Sásni, Akrabad, Jaláli, and Sikandra Rao, at the beginning of this century, were included in the dominions of the Nawáb Wazír of Oudh. They were ceded by treaty in 1802. Raja Bhagwant Singh then held Sásni and Bijaigarh, and Thákur Harkishan held Kachaura in Sikandra. The then Lieutenant-Governor (Hon'ble Gerald Wellesley) forbade these chiefs to collect transit duties, and offered them a nankár allowance as compensation. They disobeyed, and a force was sent to reduce them. Thereupon the Sásni chief offered to surrender, but secretly made preparations to destroy by treachery the small force (commanded by Colonel Blair) which was sent to occupy the fort. General St. John was then sent against Sásni with a strong force in the winter of 1802, but the place held out until some time in 1803, when it was taken by Lord Lake in person, not without considerable loss. At Sásni are the remains of the monuments erected in memory of Lieutenant Blair and other officers who were killed in the attack on that fort. A great portion of the materials of the fort was used in the building of the Sásni indigo factories in 1806.

The Chaukidári Act (XX. of 1856) is in force in Sásni, and in 1873 supported a village police numbering 13 men of all grades at an annual cost of Rs. 720. The number of houses in the town in 1872-73 was 1,265, and of these 1,126 were assessed with a house-tax averaging Re. 0-15-10 per house and Re. 0-3-9 per head of the population per annum. The income for the same year was Rs. 1,166, including a balance of Rs. 48 from the previous year, and the expenditure was Rs. 1,047.

SIKANDRA RAO, a town in the parganah of the same-name in the Aligarh
district, is situated on the Cawnpore road, 23 miles
south-east-by-east of Koil. The population in 1847 numbered 7,195, in 1853 it was 12,873, and in 1865 there were 12,451 inhabitants. The site of the town has an area of 140 square acres, giving 96 souls to the acre. According to the census of 1872 there were 12,642 inhabitants, of whom 7,598 were Hindús (3,401 females) and 5,044 were Musalmáns (2,573 females). Distributing the population amongst the rural and urban classes, the

returns show 321 landholders, 1,499 cultivators, and 10,822 persons pursuing occupations unconnected with agriculture. The number of enclosures in 1872 was 1,516, of which 679 were occupied by Musalmáns. The number of houses during the same year was 2,556, of which 493 were built with skilled labour, and of these 197 were occupied by Musalmáns. Of the 2,063 mud huts in the town, 815 were owned by Musalmáns. Taking the male adult population, 4,084 (not less than fifteen years of age), we find the following occupations pursued by more than fifty males :—Barbers, 61 ; beggars, 51 ; butchers, 143 ; cultivators, 539 ; inn-keepers, 57 ; labourers, 647 ; landowners, 113 ; letters of vehicles, 181 ; merchants, 77 ; oil-makers, 61 ; servants, 962 ; shop-keepers, 317 ; sweepers, 103 ; water-carriers, 213 ; weavers 213.

Sikandra Rao is rather a squalid, poor looking town, badly situated in low
Site.
ground, the drainage of which is both difficult and inefficient. To the north there is a high portion, but the south is very low, and on the east there is a great jhíl about 600 yards long and 500 yards wide in the cold-weather. In the rains this lake extends fully four miles, and forms one of the sources of the Isan Nadi. It has a considerable depth and abounds with fish. Two ways connect the town with the Grand Trunk Road, one of which, to the north, leads to the tahsíli, and the other, to the south, forms the bazarway and the entrance to the business portion of the town. Both are metalled, but are very winding. There are many ruinous houses in the town, expecially in the Pathán quarter, but many new houses are also springing up, especially those belonging to the money-lending classes. The Ganges Canal passes the town about 1¼ miles to the west, and has resulted in a greater accumulation of water than ever around the town. The water in the wells is, as a rule, brackish, but in a few wells it is fairly sweet. Since the canal was opened the water level has risen by about twelve feet. Fever prevails, and many die of it every year. Out of a total number of deaths from all causes in 1871, amounting to 287, or 23·08 per thousand of the population, 247 were set down to fever alone. The greater portion of the town lands are also irrigated from the canal, and in the rains the low portion of the site is so subject to flooding that the Grand Trunk Road is the only way always free from water in the neighbourhood. There is a tahsíli, police-station, post-office, school, and dispensary here. The tahsíli is an enclosed building in the upper portion of the town with the usual public offices. The school and dispensary are poor places. There are four saráis—one inside the town and three on the Grand Trunk Road.

Sikandra Rao lies on the route from Háthras to Budaon, 10¼ miles from
Communications.
Salímpur, the previous stage, and 10 miles from Mohanpur in Eta, the next stage. The road is metalled and bridged throughout, and from Salímpur crosses the Ganges Canal by bridges at the 6th and 10½ miles. To Mohanpur, the village of Rámpur is passed at

3½ miles, Agsoli at 6¾ miles, and the district boundary at 8½ miles. The country throughout is level, open, and cultivated. The encamping-ground at Sikandra Rao is large and spacious, and supplies and water are abundant. Both the Grand Trunk Road and the road from Háthras by Kásganj to Soron are used by numbers of pilgrims from Muttra.

Sikandra Rao possesses a municipality which is now managed by a committee of nine members, of whom three are official,
Municipality.
three are elected by the tax-payers, and three are nominated by the Magistrate. The incidence of taxation in 1872-73 was eight annas and one pie per head of the population. The system has been in force since 1865, and has resulted in much local improvement; in fact, whatever has been done is almost entirely due to the municipality. The following statement shows the revenue and expenditure for three years :—

Receipts.	1870-71.	1871-72.	1872-73	Expenditure.	1870-71.	1871-72	1872-73.
	Rs.	Rs.	Bs.		Rs.	Rs.	Rs.
Opening balance...	154	3	1,038	Collection ...	769	921	1,042
Class I.—Food and drink.	2,363	3,130	4,330	Head-office ...	...	83	122
" II.—Animals for slaughter.	90	197	500	a. Original works,	...	71	1,531
				b. Repairs, &c. ...	877	355	528
" III.—Fuel, &c.	151	232	180	Police ...	1,111	1,273	1,284
" IV.—Building materials.	425	224	332	Education ...	250	275	300
				Conservancy ...	522	515	514
" V.—Drugs, spices.	154	346	165	Charitable grants,	40	100	152
" VI.—Tobacco,	325	149	275	Lighting ...	233	263	282
" VII.—Textile fabrics.	...	559	492	Miscellaneous ...	13	181	247
" VIII.—Metals...	...	53	56	Extraordinary ...	...	...	60
				Total ...	3,815	4,018	6,073
Total of octroi ...	3,473	4,890	6,330				
Extraordinary ...	137	...	25				
Fines ...	41	75	200				
Miscellaneous ...	13	89	64				
Pounds ...	...	...	368				
Total ...	3,818	5,056	8,024				

The following statement shows the imports for two years of the articles paying octroi, and gives a fair idea of the general trade of the town :—

Imports.

Articles.	Quantity imported in		Consumption per head in		Articles.	Value of imports in		Consumption per head in	
	1871-72.	1872-73.	1871-72.	1872-73.		1871-72.	1872-73.	1871-72.	1872-73.
	Mds.	Mds.	M. s. c.	M. s. c.		Rs.	Rs.	Rs. a. p.	Rs. a. p.
Grain ...	75,951	67,994	6 13 7	5 17 0	Rice ...	13,429	...	1 1 11	...
Ghi ...	428	878	0 0 7	0 2 13	Vegetables and fruit.	10,231	28,596	...	...
Sugar, coarse,	3,803	8,969	} 0 34 2	0 33 3	Milk ..	1,142	...	...	...
Do., fine ...	5,022	2,106			Fodder	5,784	4,855	...	...
Shíra ...	1,418	...			Oil-seeds ...	5,438	2,61?	...	...
Oil ...	48	226	...	0 0 12	Building materials.	11,186	15,061	0 14 11	...
Fuel ...	5,751	13,354	...		Spices, &c.	11,143	19,378	0 14 10	1 2 7
Tobacco ...	795	674	0 2 10	0 2 2	Cloth ...	55,861	62,993	4 10 6	4 12 8
Oil-seeds ...	...	5,253	...	0 16 14	Metals ...	5,296	7,137	0 7 0	0 6 7

History.

Sikandra is said to have been founded by the emperor Sikandar Lodi (1488-1517 A.D.), after whom it was called Sikandarpur. It was afterwards given in *jágír* to one Rao Khán, Afghán, and became known as Rao-ke-Sikandra, or Sikandra Rao. The town is divided into two shares, Kasba Naukhel and Kasba Afghánan. The latter contains four pattis, *viz.*, Umda Begam, Muhammad Núr Khán, Jamáyat Khán, and Míran Khán. During the mutiny of 1857 Ghaus Khán of Sikandra was one of the principal rebel leaders, and for a long time held Koil itself as deputy of Walidád Khán of Málágarh in the Bulandshahr district. Kundan Singh, a Pundír Rajpút of Nái, did good service on the British side, and for some time held the parganah in their behalf as Názim. He was rewarded for his services, and Debi Dás, Baniya, also received the thanks of the district authorities for the assistance that he was able to afford. A mosque dating from Akbar's time was built by the Governor Shahdil Khán, and a ruined house in the town was formerly the residence of another governor, Purdil Khán, who founded Purdilnagar.

SIKANDRA RAO, a parganah in the tahsil of the same name in the Aligarh district, is bounded on the north by parganas Gangíri and Akrabad ; on the west by Akrabad and Háthras ; on the south by parganah Jalesar in the Agra district, and on the east by parganahs Maráhra and Bilrám of the Eta district.

This parganah, according to the statistics of 1872, had then a total area of 141,586 acres, of which 38,473 acres were barren and 1,084 acres were held free of revenue. The assessable area during the same year amounted to 102,029 acres. The changes in area since the last settlement have been great. There are now 164 villages,—an increase due to the absorption of the whole of taluka Husain and a few villages from Háthras and parganah Maráhra of the Eta district. The last settlement of Sikandra Rao proper was made by Mr. Rose in 1838, and as the parganah then stood, the revenue fell at Rs. 2-1-0 on the cultivated acre, the irrigation being 62 per cent.[1] Mr. W. H. Smith made the existing settlement. The statistics of the assessable area are as follows :—

Culturable.				Cultivated.			
New fallow.	Old waste	Groves.	Total.	Irrigated.	Dry.	Total.	Grand Total.
Acres.	Acres.	Acres.	Acres.	Acres.	Acres.	Acres.	Acres.
621	6,192	1,149	7,972	85,356	8,701	94,057	102 029

These figures show a proportion of culturable land to the total area of 72 per
cent., but the proportion of cultivation to the cultur-
Distribution of area. able area is as high as 92 per cent., and only 9 per
cent. of the cultivation is unirrigated. The margin of waste, including groves, left for the plough is only 8 per cent. of the culturable area. The new assessment amounts to Rs. 2,56,340, and the cesses to Rs. 25,634. The new revenue falls at a rate of Rs. 2-11-0 per cultivated acre. Irrigation has increased immensely since the last settlement. Formerly there were only wells and a few lowlying fields in the valley of the Káli watered from that river ; now the canal commands the entire parganah, but not without certain disadvantages as far as the efflorescence of reh is concerned (see the Tahsíl notice).

Mr. Rose's assessment was far less severe than that of Mr. Thornton. The
soil throughout the parganah is good, and Mr. Rose's
Transfers. revision only added eight per cent. to the revenue,
whilst the new assessment shows a rise of 37 cent. above the settlement of 1838. The working of the past settlement resulted in the sale by revenue process of 673 acres and the farm of 6,817 acres. The changes by voluntary transfers and the orders of the Civil Courts were as follows :—

				Area in acres.	Revenue.	Price per acre.	Years' purchase.
					Rs.	Rs a. p.	
Private sale	...	...	...	23,496	34,571	9 4 10	6·3
Mortgage	...	...	...	66,971	88,940	5 9 1	4·0
Auction	...	...	...	26,205	36,835	3 13 10	2·7
		Total,	...	116,672	1,60,346	5 15 10	4·3

[1] I.,Sett.Rep. 380 ; II., Rev. Rep, N. S., 105.

The sales for arrears took place very shortly after the settlement in 1838, and the value of land increased after the first ten years, when it was 2·6 years' purchase in cases of private sale, to 5·5 years' purchase in the second decade, and 11·3 years purchase in the third decade. Twenty-four per cent. of the area has been permanently transferred from the original proprietors, and 30 per cent. has been mortaged. These figures include the whole of the Husain villages formerly settled with the Porach Raja. Pundír Thákurs, represented by the talukadár of Bijaigarh and the zamíndár of Nái, are now the most important clan in the two parganahs of Akrabad and Sikandra. But Thákurs as a whole have lost 57 per cent. of their old possessions, which covered 165 out of the 252 villages in the tahsíl, and 147,760 out of 218,975 acres. Musalmáns still hold 13,499 acres in the tahsil, or 47 per cent. of their ancestral lands. The changes however are chiefly from a caste to their fellow-castemen, and not to the money-lendersas in Háthras.

Large owners have been more affected by these transfers than small owners,

Castes of owners. and the conclusion is that it is the tendency of small cultivating proprietors to hold their land where the non-cultivating landholder on a larger scale will be compelled to part with his possessions, and that an assessment which will crush the latter will leave the former comparatively uninjured. The practice of the old settlement officers in sparing the large owners and pressing heavily on the more industrious cultivating communities, if strictly speaking inequitable, was at least based on a sound knowledge of who could and who would not be likely to pay the demand. In this parganah, out of the 79,299 acres transferred, 57,744 acres belonged to individuals owning three-fourths or more of an estate, and similarly all through the district, the smaller proprietary bodies have come well out of the troubles of the past half century. The following statement shows more clearly the nature of the changes in each case :—

Caste.	Area held in 1838 in acres.	Lost between 1838 and 1868 by			Remaining.	Caste.	Area held in 1838.	Lost between 1838 and 1861 by			Remaining.
		Sale.	Mort-gage, &c.	Total.				Sale.	Mort-gage, &o.	Total.	
Brahman ...	6,393	1,279	714	1,993	4,400	Riwári ...	490	490	...	490	...
Baniya ...	2,522	363	229	592	1,930	Garariya ...	890	698	...	698	192
Kayath ...	2,217	1,216	483	1,699	518	Aheriya ...	355	44	266	310	45
Rajpút ...	96,199	22 039	32,747	55,380	40,819	Abír ...	1,188	196	402	598	590
Dhusar ...	2,626	1,115	...	1, 15	1,511	European...	7,666	...	3,664	3 664	4,092
Ját ...	891	891	...	891	...	Musalmán,	21,584	4,111	7,758	11,869	9,715

Of the 204 maháls or estates returned as in the parganah at the recent revision of settlement, 129 were zamindári, 31 were held on a perfect pattidári tenure, and 44 were imperfect pattidári. One-quarter of the area was held by proprietors possessing more than one village, 28 per cent. by proprietors who were less than six sharers and possessed up to one village, and 47 per cent. by proprietors who were more than six sharers. The percentage of the land-revenue paid by each of these classes is 26, 28·5, and 45·5 per cent. respectively.

Kharíf crops occupied during the year of measurement (1871) 45,648 acres,

Crops. and *rabi* crops 48,409 acres, 12,443 acres were under cotton, 16,204 acres under *joár*, and 10,559 acres under indigo in the *kharíf*, and in the *rabi* 23,873 acres were under wheat, 10,099 acres under barley, and 6,364 under *bejar*. A summary of the prices is given under the district notice for the whole district, where also communications are fully described. 1,148 holdings are held by proprietors as seer, 6,193 by tenants with a right of occupancy, and 2,938 by tenants-at-will. Only 515 acres out of 83,560 acres are paid for in kind, and the average rental per acre at cash rates is Rs. 4-8-8, *viz.*, tenants with a right of occupancy Rs. 4-4-4, and tenants-at-will Rs. 5-1-11 per acre. Twenty-three per cent. of the cultivated area is held as seer by proprietors, 53 per cent. is cultivated by hereditary tenants, and 24 per cent. by tenants-at-will, and the average area of their holding is 18 acres, 8 acres, and 7·8 acres respectively. In 1855 hereditary tenants possessed 4,868 holdings, averaging 8·4 acres each, and tenants-at-will had 3,784 holdings, averaging 8·6 acres each; whilst the rentals showed Rs. 3-13-3 and Rs. 4-15-5 per acre respectively. Rentals have risen, and the size of the holdings has decreased in all cases. In the above remarks taluka Husain is included and the parganah as it now stands.

The Porach taluka of Husain, now included in this parganah, and in the

Husain. possession of the Jádon money-lender of Awa Mísa, has been noticed in the accounts of the old families of the district. At the revision in 1836 Mr. Thornton followed the same principles that he adopted in other talukas.[1] He found 43 villages in the Raja's name, including three formerly held free of revenue. From 1786 to 1803 the taluka had formed a portion of the *jáedád* of the Marhatta occupants of the fort of Aligarh, and they collected direct from the village occupants, and neither the Raja nor his family retained more than the three revenue-free villages mentioned above. On the arrival of the British, Mitrsen assumed such a position that in the confusion of the time he was recognized as sudder malguzar and admitted to engagements for 1211 *fasli* (1803-04 A.D.), at a revenue of Rs. 32,600, and again for 1212 *fasli* at a revenue of Rs. 30,031, and the same terms were allowed up to the end of 1215. In the beginning of 1216 *fasli* (1808-09) Mr. Elliott made a revision of the settlement and drew up a proceeding in which the Raja is recorded to have promised to permit the old proprietors to retain possession of their lands

---

[1] Set. Rep., I., 333.

at a reasonable revenue. The names of the proprietors, where ascertainable, were entered in the record, and the Raja was styled " talukadár mustájir," at a revenue of Rs. 31,001, rising to Rs. 37,001 in the third year. This assessment was continued until 1222 *fasli*. A money-lender then obtained possession of the estate and held it from 1223 to 1227 at a revenue of Rs. 44,000, and was succeeded by Jaswant Singh, and finally by Naráyan Singh, who was alive in 1836. The arrangements made by Mr. Elliott seem never to have been acted on, and the only enquiries subsequently set on foot were made with the object of extracting as much as possible from the villages, to prop up the declining fortunes of the Rája's house and to support him in his extravagance.

In applying the principles adopted in the case of Mursán to Husain, Mr. Thornton found that the Raja had never by any valid or

Mr. Thornton on taluka Husain. sufficient means acquired any proprietary rights in the taluka. His position rested neither upon a grant from Government nor upon any private and voluntary transfer on the part of the people themselves. Originally without any possessions in the taluka, he received a farm from an agent of one of the short-lived governments of the time, and remained in possession for only seventeen years. This was followed by a time of deprivation for a similar period, so that the reinstatement of Mitrsen in 1803-04 must be considered to have been merely conditional and temporary, and five years after it was distinctly stated to be so when he was allowed to renew his engagement. Mr. Thornton then began his inquiry into the history of each village, and his account throws such light upon the history of village colonisation that I quote him here :—" I was enabled, with few exceptions, to discover with great certainty to what tribe and family each village originally belonged. In many cases I could trace that gradual spread of cultivation from a central point, and consequent formation of new villages as offsets from the one first established, which affords such undeniable proof of the rights of those who in times past thus appropriated and parcelled out the soil. I had also procured from several distinct and unconnected sources a number of old records, which showed the names of the malguzars by whom each village had been held under the former Government, together with the title then assigned to them. The *muáfi* records furnished further evidence, as the numerous holders of these small rent-free portions of land, which are almost entirely the gift of the zámíndárs, had been called upon some years ago to state the date of the grant with the name of the giver. It was thus frequently made evident that the ancestors of those who now claimed in opposition to the Raja had held as zamindárs before the taluka was made over to Ratan Singh, as well as afterwards during Mitrsen's dispossession. The results of all this evidence were further corroborated by the papers given in by the kánúngoes in 1216 *fasli*, as well as by the unanimous and uncontradicted testimony of the surrounding inhabitants." Though the above-investigation showed the communities to which the soil belonged, the descendants of those old proprietors were not forthcoming in many instances, and in others were too long out of possession to admit of their being reinstated. In seventeen only of the forty-three estates in the taluka were the old proprietors restored, and the remainder were settled with the Raja as zamíndár. " The continuance of the Raja in this position," writes Mr. Thornton, " must be considered a matter of favour on the part of Government rather than of actual right on the part of the Raja, but his ancient descent and the former condition of his family confer upon him a title to consideration. It so happens, moreover, that if the taluka-dári allowance be granted for the life of the present incumbent, its future diminution or entire cessation will be felt much less severely than if it took place at present." The entire Government demand was lowered from Rs. 44,000 to Rs. 41,558, falling at a rate of Rs. 2-6-7 on the cultivated acre, with 62 per cent. of irrigation. After much litigation the whole of the taluka has fallen into the hands of the Muttra Jádons, and the only representative of the old family, now, is a childless widow. The biswadári villages formerly paid Rs. 15,950 plus *malikána*, Rs. 4,627, or a total of Rs. 20,577, and the revenue of the other villages was Rs. 25,608. The present settlement shows an assessment of Rs. 21,990 on the biswadári villages, or an increase of 37 per cent. *plus* Rs. 2,199 as *malikána*, which has been reduced from 22·5 per cent. on the revenue to 10 per cent., so that the whole increase now amounts to only 17 per cent. on the biswadári village. The zamíndári villages are now assessed at Rs. 23,684, or by 18 per cent., and the whole increase in revenue is therefore 25 per cent., and the incidence on cultivation is Rs. 2-13-9 per acre. The villages composing the taluka are among the richest in quality and the most carefully cultivated in the parganah ; rents too have been gradually raised to a high pitch by the farming system adopted by the present owner.

According to the census of 1872 pargarah Sikandra Rao contained 160 inhabited villages, of which 22 had less than 200 inhabitants ; 60 had between 200 and 500 ; 40 had between 500 and 1,000 ; 29 had between 1,000 and 2,000 ; 3 had between 2,000 and 3,000; and 5 had between 3,000 and 5,000.

Population.

The settlement records show that there were 100 maháls or estates in this parganah in 1874, and 164 villages, having an average area of 863 acres each. The total population in 1872 numbered 128,864 souls (58,829 females), giving 566 to the square mile. Classified according to religion, there were 115,473 Hindús, of whom 52,383 were females ; 13,364 Musalmáns, amongst whom 6,432 were females ; and 27 Christians. Distributing the Hindú population amongst the four great classes, the census shows 10,859 Brahmans, of whom 4,729 were females ; 15,812 Rajpúts, including 6,767 females ; 5,543 Baniyas (2,547 females) ; whilst the great mass of the population is included in "the other castes" of the census returns, which show a total of 83,259 souls, of whom 38,340 are females. The principal Brahman subdivisions found in this parganah are the Gaur (190), Saraswat (80), Sanádh (1,452), and Kanaujiya. The Rajpúts belong to the Gahlot (656), Chauhán (4,109), Badgújar (380), Jádon (4,052), Janghára (166), Pundír (4,136), Gaharwár (319), Bais Gaur, Tomar, Solankhi, Rathor, Panwár, Jaiswár, Sikharwár, Bangar, Kirár, and Surajbansi clans ; and the Baniyas to the Agarwál (1,023), Dasa, Chausaïni (246), Mahesri (452), Bárahsaini (840), Garwál, Jaiswár, Saraugi, and Lohiya. Amongst the other castes the following show more than 1,000 members each :—Barhai (2,773), Hajjám, Kalál (2,976), Ahír (9,010), Káchhi (3,635), Kahár (3,561), Koli (3,622), Chamár (25,545), Khákrob, Kumhár, Garariya (8,299), Aheriya (1,369), Káyath and Lodha (5,007). The following have less than 1,000 and more than 100 members :—Ját, Sonár, Ráj, Máli, Bhát, Gosháin, Joshi, Darzi, Jogi, Bairági, Dhobi, Khatík, Banjárá, Dhúna, Bharbhúnja, Malláh, Teli, Kanjar, and Ghosi. The Musalmáns are distributed amongst Shaikhs (2,210), Sayyids (310), Mughals (289), Patháns (1,775), and unspecified beyond religion.

The occupations of the people are shown in the statistics collected at the census

Occupations.

of 1872. From these it appears that of the male adult population (not less than fifteen years of age) 410 are employed in professional avocations, such as Government servants, priests, doctors, and the like ; 5,191 in domestic service, as personal servants, water-carriers, barbers, sweepers, washermen, &c.; 2,057 in commerce, in buying, selling, keeping or lending money or goods, or the conveyance of men, animals or goods ; 19,795 in agricultural operations ; 5,438 in industrial occupations, arts and mechanics, and the preparation of all classes of substances, vegetable, mineral, and animal. There were 8,391 persons returned as labourers and 874 as of no specified occupation. Taking the total population, irrespective of age or sex, the same returns give 3,298 as landholders, 54,745 as cultivators, and 70,821 as engaged in occupations unconnected with agriculture. The educational statistics, which are confessedly imperfect, show 2,278 males as able to read and write out of a total male population numbering 70,035 souls. Parganah Sikandra now includes taluka Husain.

SIKANDRA RAO, a tahsíl of the Aligarh district, comprises parganahs Sikandra Rao and Akrabad. The total area according to the settlement records is 215,812 acres, of which 1,237 acres are held free of revenue and 57,642 acres are barren. The assessable area comprises 156,933 acres, of which 143,909 acres are cultivated (130,991 acres irrigated) and 13,024 acres are culturable. Of the latter 1,629 acres are under groves. The amount of barren land is larger than in any other tahsíl in the district. The percentage of culturable land to the total area is only 73, but the area under cultivation is 93 per cent. of the culturable area, and irrigation reaches 91 per cent. of the cultivated area. There is very little land left either unirrigated or uncultivated in this tahsíl. Fifteen per cent. of the cultivation is manured, and there is only 4 per cent. of poor unirrigated sandy land in the tahsíl. The population in 1872 numbered 193,611 souls (88,560 females), giving 566 souls to the square mile, distributed amongst 247 inhabited villages. The old revenue demand amounted to Rs. 2,80,587; the new assessment gives a land-revenue of Rs. 3,87,320, falling at a rate of Rs. 2-11-0 on the cultivated acre, or Rs. 2-11-7 for Sikandra and Rs. 2-10-0 in Akrabad, as compared with a former incidence of Rs. 2-1-0 and Re. 1-14-11 per acre respectively. The census statistics show 471 persons blind, 39 lepers, 26 deaf and dumb, 4 idiots, and 10 insane persons in the tahsíl

The division into parganahs is purely nominal : neither has preserved its

General appearance.

ancient limits, and both are wholly alike in general character, and have been subject to the same influences during the past settlement. Mr. Smith thus describes the present character of the subdivision :—" The tahsíl lies exactly[1] on the watershed of the Duáb, and the soil is almost uniformly good loam. Two small tracts form the only exceptions of any importance : one the rising ground above the lowlands of the Káli Nadi, which for the breadth of, perhaps, from a quarter to half a mile is generally composed of *bhúr* or sand; the other a sandy ridge running from Husain due south into Jalesar. Elsewhere, in a few villages only is there any *bhúr* at all, and then over only limited areas. The proportion of sand throughout the subdivision is very small indeed, and the soils as a whole may be considered a rich and fertile loam.

The Cawnpore and Etáwa branches of the Ganges Canal run along its highest level. These two lines branch out from the main canal at Nánu, close to the Koil boundary, and flow through the tahsíl at a distance of about four miles apart. Distributaries from the upper canal, as well as from the two lower branches, command the vast majority of the villages in both parganahs, and no part of the district, Háthras alone excepted, is so amply supplied with every capability for easy irrigation. Of the whole irrigated area rather more than half is watered from the canal. A great change has thus been worked in the character of this tract of country. At last settlement there was, on the whole, indeed, a fair amount of irrigation. Of the cultivated area, 61 per cent. was irrigated from masonry and temporary wells; but facilities for obtaining water were unequally distributed. As remarked by Mr. Hutchinson, numbers of the estates were of such a nature that the formation of kuchcha wells was impracticable; masonry wells were necessary over much of the area, and the general expense of irrigation was consequently heavy. At the present time nearly every village obtains an adequate amount of water. Masonry wells are still

---

[1] See Rev. Rep., N. S., II., 105.

in use, though few new ones are constructed. Where kuchcha wells were formerly sunk at will canal-water is generally substituted: and villages where there was originally no irrigation at all are now covered with a net-work of canal-feeders. The productive power of the soil has been largely increased. In one tract, however, considerable damage has been done by the canal. Throughout the tahsíl *úsar* plains form 21 per cent. of the entire area, and since the introduction of the canal their character has changed very much, while *reh*, which formerly never exuded to any appreciable extent, has effloresced extensively and covered the ground with a brittle crust, looking like snow in the distance. This *reh*, which had previously confined itself to the *úsar* alone, has now cropped up on cultivated as well as barren lands, and is yearly throwing numerous fields out of cultivation. More than one hamlet has become wholly

Injurious efflorescence of *reh*.

waste, and has been deserted by its former residents; and fields which three years ago (1871) were surveyed as cultivated were at the time of inspection covered with white soda exudations. As yet this damage is compensated on the whole by the extra irrigation supplied by the canal to the soil which still remains unaffected, and the recorded rent-rolls show that the people, complain as they may, have, as a rule, suffered no sensible loss. But this state of things cannot last: the *reh* will increase, and in the end, though probable after many years, a great part of this tract must, in the opinion of the Settlement Officer, become waste. The efflorescence of *reh* may be due to the stoppage of the natural drainage of the country, or it may arise from the water-logging of the soil from percolation between the canals or excessive canal irrigation. The popular idea is that the canal-water collects *reh* in solution during its course and deposits it over the cultivation, and that during the rainy reason the rains have the same effect. In this district *reh* is never found except in a certain proximity to *úsar* plains, and (it may therefore be assumed) where *reh* already exists somewhere in the soil. Again, it exudes in profusion where the soil is moist and swampy; as, for instance, on the lowlands along the side of the Rind, where scarcely a field has been left uninjured. The weed *baisurái* is found in a small portion of Husain near the borders of Háthras and Jalesar, and does not appear to affect the cultivation. All other particulars regarding this tahsíl will be found under the parganah notices or in the district notice.

SOMNA, a town in parganah and tahsíli Khair of the Aligarh district, is distant on the Grand Trunk Road 14 miles from Aligarh and 11 miles from Khair. The population in 1865 was 1832, and in 1872 was 2,033. There is a police-station here and a post-office, also a station of the East Indian Railway. The elevation above the sea is 752 feet. Somna lies on the route by Khúrja from Aligarh to Dehli, distant 14¼ miles from Aligarh and 12½ miles

from Khúrja. The road is metalled throughout and bridged. From Aligarh
the road passes Bhánkri at 6 miles and Chúharpur 11 miles. Hence to Khúrja
it passes the Aligarh district at 2¼ miles ; Kirauta (59th milestone from Dehli),
6 miles ; Dasara (56th milestone), 9 miles ; Meerut road within half a mile of
Khúrja (Meerut distant 53¾ miles, or five marches) Railway Station, 3½ miles
from Khúrja.. The Chaukidári Act (XX. of 1856) is in force in Somna, and
in 1873 supported a village police numbering five men of all grades, at an
annual cost of Rs. 288. The number of the houses in the town in 1872-73
was 442, and of these 417 were assessed with a house-tax averaging Re. 1-4-5
per house and Re. 0-4-0 per head of the population per annum. The income
for the same year was Rs. 593, including a balance of Rs. 60 from the previous
year, and the expenditure was Rs. 582.

TAPPAL, a town in parganah Tappal and tahsíli Khair of the Aligarh district, is situated near the Jumna, 32 miles from Aligarh and 18 miles from
Khair. The population in 1853 was 5,941, and in 1845 was 5,744. In 1872
there were 6,023 inhabitants, of whom 4,057 were Hindús (1,998 females) and
1,966 were Musalmáns (1,067 females). The town site occupies 89 square acres,
giving 68 souls to the acre. The town is built on the old high bank of the
Jumna, which now runs four miles to the west. The inhabitants are chiefly
Rajpúts, Musalmáns, and Brahmans. The ways are unmetalled, and, with the
exception of about fifty houses, the buildings are ruinous and neglected. The
town is entered on the north-east by a low sandy road, which, as it rises with
the rising site, divides into two branches, circling round to rejoin in the midst of
the town. Where they meet is the bazar with a few poor-looking shops. The
whole town is a decaying one with no trade, and only occasionally used by carts
passing to the ghát on the Jumna. There is a school, a police-station, and a
post-office. The well water stands at 35 feet from the surface and is remarkably
good. The Chaukidári Act (XX. of 1856) is in force in Tappal, and in 1873
supported a village police numbering 11 men of all grades at an annual cost of
Rs. 636. The number of the houses in the town in 1872-73 was 1,279, and of
these 1,149 were assessed with a house-tax averaging Re. 1-2-10 per house and
Re. 0-3-7 per head of the population per annum. The income for the same
year was Rs. 1,493, including a balance of Rs. 140 from the previous year, and
the expenditure was Rs. 1,278. Tappal in former days was a place of some
note. Towards the edge of the high land separating it from the khádir of the

History.

Jumna are the remains of a very large old fort said
to have been built some eight hundred years ago, and
to the north-east of the town, where the police-station now stands, are the
remains of another fort which formerly belonged to Begam Sumru, the jágírdár
of parganah Tappal, and was the residence of her amil. In the early days
of British rule the town was the residence of a tahsíldár, but the collecting

establishment now reside at Khair, and since then the town has steadily declined in importance.

TAPPAL, a parganah in tahsíl Khair of the Aligarh district, is bounded on the north by the Bulandshahr district ; on the south by the Muttra district ; on the east by Chandaus and Khair of this district ; and on the west by the Jumna, which separates it from the Panjab. According to the census of 1872 this parganah had then a total area of 149 square miles and 29 acres, of which 106 square miles and 29 acres were under cultivation. The area assessed to Government revenue during the same year was 149 square miles, of which 106 square miles were cultivated, 30 square miles were culturable, and 13 square miles were barren.

The Jumna khádir in this parganah varies in breadth from two to seven miles. Formerly subject to constant inundation, it

Appearance.

now lies high above the river-bed, and even the lower portions are, now, submerged only in seasons of unusual flood. Close to the river's edge changes occasionally occur from diluvion or alluvion, but the newly formed soil is fertile, and the crops on it are certain. The old soil is hard and firm, and only its purely recent formation differs from the uplands. It requires the same care and skill in cultivation as the dry upland. Parallel with the khádir and along the extreme edge of the uplands there is a narrow strip of poor sandy soil, and beyond it commences the large loamy tract of the Duáb. Whilst on the Ganges side the khádir is usually rich and moist, and the *bhúr* above is remarkably poor and of a considerable extent, by the Jumna the khádir is very inferior, and the sandy upland small in quantity and comparatively fertile. The depth of water from the surface in the uplands is from 35 to 60 feet, and the substratum is so sandy that wells, if not of masonry, can only be made, as a general rule, with stages of wooden frames. These are expensive, but they last for many years. In the khádir water throughout is close to the surface, but the substratum is composed of such loose sandy soil that any but pukka wells are almost useless. The *dhenkli* or lever is used here in dry seasons, but the small wells fall in so soon and irrigate so small an area that they are little used. The new formation on the edge of the river-bed seldom requires artificial irrigation, and, when necessary, small percolation wells are dug.

The existing settlement of Tappal was made by Mr. W. H. Smith. The statistics of area show a total area of 95,499 acres, of which 8,077 acres are recorded as unculturable. Of the assessable area the distribution is as follows :—

Culturable.				Cultivated.			
New fallow	Old waste.	Groves.	Total.	Irrigated.	Dry.	Total.	Grand Total.
Acres.	Acres.	Acres.	Acres.	Acres.	Acres.	Acres.	Acres.
541	18,569	146	19,256	31,377	36,789	68,166	87,422

The proportion of culturable land to the total area is 91 per cent., but the

Fiscal statistics.

proportion of cultivation to the culturable area is only 78 per cent., showing a very large margin of waste land not yet brought under the plough (22 per cent.), but much of this is the hard old waste of the khádir now under thatching grass and scarcely culturable. Irrigation reaches only 46 per cent. of the cultivated area. The land-revenue as now assessed amounts to Rs. 1,36,090, and the cesses to Rs. 13,609. The new land-revenue falls at Re. 1-15-11 per cultivated acre, and gives a rise of 14 per cent. on the old revenue (Rs. 1,19,343). Irrigation has increased by 78·7 per cent., and cultivation by 18·8 per cent., since last settlement. Of the 99 estates existing at the recent settlement, 24 were held in zamindári tenure, 73 in imperfect pattidári, and 2 in perfect pattidári, and of. all these only 2·34 per cent. of the revenue was paid by landholders possessing one or more villages. The following table shows the losses that have fallen upon the proprietary body as it stood in 1838 between that date and 1868 :—

Caste.	Area held in 1838.	Area transferred.	Area held in 1868.		Caste.	Area held in 1838.	Area transferred.	Area held in 1868.	
			Area.	Revenue.				Area.	Revenue.
	Acres.	Acres.	Acres.	Rs.		Acres	Acres.	Acres.	Rs.
Ját ...	63,468	15,464	48,004	65,414	Chamar and Baniya.	290	290	...	...
Brahman ...	3,770	2,083	1,687	2,149	Orh ...	281	281	...	...
Rajpút ...	10,139	6,248	3,851	5,728	Musalmáns ..	10,034	8,230	1,804	1,181

The lands held by Játs and Jádons have usually passed to members of the same clans, whilst those lost by Chauháns have, as a rule, passed into the hands of strangers.

Tappal, up to 1836, formed a portion of Begam Sumru's jágír. It was resumed on her death and was summarily settled by Mr. Thornton, who reduced the demand from Rs. 1,34,625 to Rs. 1,15,489. The first regular settlement was made in 1840 by Mr. Wright, who raised the revenue to Rs. 1,18,206. Since then the boundaries have been changed, and on the expiration of the old settlement the revenue stood at Rs. 1,19,064. The revenue of the villages now constituting the parganah was from 1835-36 to 1839-40 fixed at Rs. 1,18,254, and in the following year the assessment was fixed at Rs. 1,19,343. "The change from the lax and variable character of the Begam's management," writes Mr. Smith, "to the rigidity of our system excited a dangerous and what, in these times, would have been a fatal influence on the fortunes of the Ját proprietors.

Accustomed to annual remissions when they could obtain them, or temporary flight and evasion of payment when the jágírdár's collections were obdurate,

Effect of past settlement. they soon fell into arrears under the regular demands of their new masters. More than one-third of the parganah was either sold for arrears of revenue or farmed during the first ten years (1838-39 to 1847-48) of the regular settlement, and this was purely revenue process, and is apart from all consideration of private sales or mortgages and the action of the civil courts. Out of a total area of 87,982 acres 33,657 were thus treated, and the sales at auction involving 21,405 acres only fetched an average price of 10 annas 5 pie per acre. Fortunately the very magnitude of the evil seems to have been its own cure. Outsiders either considered the property in the parganah worthless, or they were afraid to enter so close a borough as the Ját clans of Tappal. Government was compelled itself to purchase some of the estates at the nominal price of a rupee; others were bought at almost equally nominal prices by the near relations of the defaulters; others, the defaulters themselves, purchased under false names. Those which were bought by Government were farmed out in some cases to the connections of the recusant owners, in others to individuals of the defaulting community. In some way or other all, or nearly all, these estates came back to the original owners or to their close relations. By the second decade of the settlement there was no difference between the fiscal condition of Tappal and that of the neighbouring parganahs, except that in the former the proportion of transfers was small and the circumstances of the proprietors comparatively prosperous. Only 2,977 acres were farmed and 998 sold for arrears of revenue between 1256 and 1265 fasli, and the price obtained per acre (Rs. 6-13-2) was fair for the time. Since the last date there have been no revenue sales, and 5,840 acres only have been farmed. Singular enough, in no parganah in the district were there within so short a period so many coercive revenue processes, and in no other parganah has so much property in the end been found to remain in the hands of its original owners. Out of 69 villages held by Játs at the commencement of the expiring settlement, three only have been invaded by intruders of other castes; 66 are still held solely by Játs, and in the remaining three the same caste still holds shares. Not one estate has been wholly lost. Had the parganah been well known to the neighbouring capitalists, or had the value of the land been recognized, as it is now, large communities of the most deserving and industrious cultivating proprietors that we possess would have been reduced to the condition of mere tenants-at-will. Fortunately for their preservation the money-lenders of adjoining districts were too suspicious to speculate, and at that time the ownership of land was a thing of small consideration to outsiders. The Játs therefore still remain and still hold three-fourths of the parganah. The remissions found necessary during the 32 years amount to the small sum of Rs. 6,143 only. In 1855-56 the crops were terribly damaged by a violent hailstorm, and Rs. 4,505 were remitted. The remission of Rs. 1,637 is due to the famine of 1860-61."

The following statement shows the mode of transfer, the average price per acre, and the average number of years' purchase of the land-revenue brought by the areas transferred between 1838 and 1868. It is to be noted that if a single plot or estate has changed hands ten times, ten entries have been made in this account :—

Alienations.

Mode of transfer.	1839-48.			1849-58.			1859-68.		
	Area.	Price per acre.	Years' purchase.	Area.	Price per acre.	Years' purchase.	Area.	Price per acre.	Years' purchase.
	Acres.	Rs. a. p.		Acres	Rs. a. p.		Acres.	Rs. a. p.	
Private sale ...	718	2 14 8	2·69	4,758	4 13 3	4·18	12,429	6 15 11	5 41
Mortgage ...	6,570	4 7 5	3·21	2,690	8 3 10	4·23	4,312	8 12 9	5·9
Auction sale ...	1,803	4 3 10	2·64	2,018	8 15 1	4·91	2,343	8 3 8	4·35
Total ...	9,091	4 4 9	3·8	9,466	6 10 9	4 38	19,084	7 8 11	5 35

The average price per acre during the last twelve years of the expired settlement has been 75·8 per cent. higher than during the first eleven years. It was only in the last decade that the value of land in this parganah began to be properly estimated. Altogether 62 per cent. of the area bearing the same percentage of the land-revenue had been permanently alienated in 1869, and 5 per cent. of the area bearing the same percentage of the revenue was mortgaged. Out of 32,596 acres transferred, 20,940 acres belonged to proprietors of three-fourths or more of a village, whilst the smaller proprietors have escaped. Forty-six per cent. of the cultivated area is occupied by kharíf crops, and amongst these joár covers 21 per cent. of the total cultivated area, cotton 12 per cent., bájra 7 per cent., and moth 5 per cent. Amongst the rabi crops, wheat occupies 16 per cent. of the total cultivated area, bejar 24 per cent., and barley 4 per cent. 7,258 acres, or 10 per cent. of the cultivation, are leased on payments in kind. The system is confined to small, and generally the worst, portions of poor villages and on the lowlands of the Jumna, and, except in a few instances, to soil newly broken up for cultivation, where the returns are very uncertain. Very little irrigated land is held on division of produce, and here, as elsewhere in the district, the system is gradually dying out. There were 12,741 bulls and bullocks, 9,115 buffaloes, 9,206 cows, 852 horses, and 9,970 sheep and goats in the parganah in 1869. 2,082 holdings are entered as the seer of proprietors, 1,263 are held by hereditary tenants, and 2,841 by tenants-at-will, with an average area of 14·6 acres, 15 acres, and 9·5 acres respectively. The average rental where cash is paid amounts to Rs. 3-4-3 per acre; hereditary tenants pay on an average Rs. 3-2-9 per acre, whilst tenants-at-will pay Rs. 3-4-10 per acre. Altogether 45 per cent. of the cultivated area is held by cultivating proprietors. At the commencement of the expired settlement there were only 120 holdings possessed by hereditary tenants, with an average area of 14·2 acres and an average rental of Rs. 2-1-6 per acre, whilst tenants-at-will held 3,090 holdings, with an average area of 12·2 acres and an average rental of Rs. 2-5-8 per acre. The areas possessed by each class in 1839 and 1869 were as follows:—

	1839.		1869.	
	Area.	Rent.	Area.	Rent.
	Acres.	Rs.	Acres.	Rs.
Hereditary tenants	1,707	3,581	10,167	32,296
Tenants-at-will	37,771	89,006	27,072	89,445

According to the census of 1872 parganah Tappal contained 89 inhabited villages, of which 16 had less than 200 inhabitants; 34 had between 200 and 500; 25 had between 500 and 1,000; 9 had between 1,000 and 2,000; and 4 had between 2,000 and 3,000. The settlement records show that there were 100 maháls or estates in the parganah in 1874, and 91 villages, with an average area of 1,049 acres; the largest having 6,305 acres, and the smallest having 84 acres. The average area is here increased by the great size of the khádir villages. The total population in 1872 numbered 58,809 souls (27,378 females), giving 395 to the square mile. Classified according to religion, there were 54,251 Hindús, of whom 25,130 were females; 4,558 Musalmáns, amongst whom 2,248 were females. Distributing the Hindú population amongst the four great classes, the census shows 8,410 Brahmans, of whom 3,857 were females; 1,312 Rajpúts, including 603 females; 2,618 Baniyas (1,254 females); whilst the great mass of the population is included in "the other castes" of the census returns, which show a total of 41,911 souls, of whom 19,416 are females. The principal Brahman subdivisions found in this parganah are the Gaur (7,946), Saraswát (12). The Rajpúts are chiefly of the Chauhán (697), Badgújar (72), Gahlot, Janghára, Jádon, and Panwár clans, and the Baniyas belong to the Dasa (636), Agarwál (1,346), and Guráku subdivisions. Amongst the other castes the following have more than 1,000 members each:—Ját (16,900), Barhai, Hajjám, Koli (1,382), Chamár (9,160),

Khatík (2,381), and Khákrob (1,627). The following have more than 100 members each :—Sonár, Máli, Bhat, Kalál, Darzi, Kahár, Jogi, Bairági, Dhobi, Lohár, Kumhár, Gararíya, Orh, Dhuna, Malláh, and Teli. The Musalmáns are entered as Shaikhs (384) and Patháns (327). The remainder is shown without distinction.

The occupations of the people are shown in the statistics collected at the

Occupations.

census of 1872. From these it appears that of the male adult population (not less than fifteen years of age) 172 are employed in professional avocations, such as Government servants, priests, doctors, and the like; 1,658 in domestic service, as personal servants, water-carriers, barbers, sweepers, washermen, &c.; 1,139 in commerce, in buying, selling, keeping or lending money or goods, or the conveyance of men, animals, or goods; 10,853 in agricultural operations; 2,059 in industrial occupations, arts and mechanics, and the preparation of all classes of substances, vegetable, mineral, and animal. There were 2,389 persons returned as labourers, and 585 as of no specified occupation. Taking the total population, irrespective of age or sex, the same returns give 938 as landholders, 31,855 as cultivators, and 26,016 as engaged in occupations unconnected with agriculture. The educational statistics, which are confessedly imperfect, show 1,237 males as able to read and write out of a total male population numbering 31,431 souls.

The boundaries of Tappal have seen many changes. In 1838 the parganah comprised 90 villages, with an area of 90,416 acres and a land-revenue of Rs. 1,17,913. In 1840-41, 13 villages were transferred to parganah Jewar in the Bulandshahr district, and in 1851-52 one village was handed over to Khair. In 1840-41, 15 villages were received from parganah Jewar, leaving Tappal possessed of 91 villages. Tappal has been the residence of a Ját colony for many centuries. Originally settling in Khandiya, they have spread over all this parganah, and though, at first, the action of the past settlement threatened to overwhelm them, they are now more flourishing than ever.

GLOSSARY OF VERNACULAR TERMS USED IN THIS VOLUME.

A.

Abi, irrigated from tanks and rivers, 379.

Abwábs, cesses, 33.

Adhahal, a pl.ugh with one pair of bullocks (S'pur), 161.

Adh-kumbh, the festival held every sixth year at Hindu places of pilgrimage like Prayág, Hardwár, 287.

Ajár, wells lined with wicker-work to support the sides, 381.

Amaltás, the *cassia fistula*.

Amáni, a revenue term, 208.

Angasht, a digit, 478.

Anwári, the fish known as the Indian mullet (*mugil corsula*).

Aphara, windy colic, 506.

Argha, an offering, 66 (note).

Arhar, the edible grain, *cajanus bicolor*.

Asámi, a cultivator.

Asárh, the Hindu month corresponding to June—July.

Asli mauza, parent village, 427.

Aswamedha, a horse-sacrifice, 69.

Awartha, a name of Hardwár.

B.

Babúl, the *Acacia Arabica*.

Báchh, a mode of distributing the revenue, 200.

Badni, advances for produce, 475.

Bádan, dysentery in cattle.

Báhan, fallow.

Baisurái, a noxious weed, 387.

Bájra, the edible grain, *penicillaria spicata*.

Bákli, the *pentaptera tomentosa*.

Báki, arrears.

Bángar, the uplands of the Duáb.

Baoni, a cluster cf 52 villages.

Bára, lands adjoining the village site, 352.

Buráha, the boar-avatár of Vishnu.

Bardáshtkhána, a rest and supply house for troops.

Barha, outlying lands, 352.

Batái, division of produce as rent, 585.

Báwan, a cluster of 52 villages.

Bejar, mixed crops of wheat and barley or wheat and gram.

Bel, the *Ægle marmelos*.

Ber, the *Zizyphus jujuba*.

Bhayachára, a tenure of land, 222.

Bhím Sen ke gada, certain monoliths found in Eastern India, 243

Bhúa, a bad sandy soil, 143.

Bhúda, a bad sandy soil, 143.

Bhumiyas, landholders, 451.

Bhúr, a sandy soil.

Bhúsa, chaff.

Bigha, a measure of land, 478.

Biswa, a measure of land, 478.

Biswadárs, a class of under proprietors, 435.

Biswánsi, a measure of land, 478.

C.

Cháht, irrigated from wells.

Cháhkun, a well-digger.

Chaina, an edible grain (*P. miliaceum*).

Chakra, discus.

Chalísa, the name by which the famine of Sambat 1840 is known.

Charan, foot-marks of Vishnu at Hardwár, 286.

Charas, a preparation of hemp (*cannabis sativa*).

Chauk, a central space in a town, generally used as a market-place.

Chauránawe, the name by which the famine of 1894 Sambat is known.

Chauránawe kál, the same.

Chaurási, a group of 84 villages.

Chausinga, a species of deer (*tetraceros quadricornis*).

Chauwan, a group of 54 villages.

Chhatáh, a weight, the sixteenth part of a *ser*.

Chiknot, a kind of soil, 352.

Chilka, a species of fish.

Chilwa, a small fish (*aspidoparia morar*).

Chítal, the spotted deer (*axis maculatus*).

Chokri, a female servant or slave.

Chúris, glass bangles.

D.

Dakaiti, gang robbery by more than five persons.

Dákar, a kind of soil, 143.

Dál, split pulse.

Dasáni, certain shares in Koil, 522.

Dastúr, a division of a Sirkár in Akbar's reign.

Dákhili-mauza, a hamlet belonging to a parent village.

Dand, a measure of length, 478.

Daul, an estimate.

Deorhi, interest at 50 per cent., 224.

Dhák, the *butea frondosa*.

Dhatúra, the *datura alba*.

Dhaulu, a variety of sugar-cane, 307.

Dhenkli, a lever-well, 607.

Dhoti, a waist-cloth.

Dofasli, extra crops grown on land which has already borne one crop in the same year.

Dor, a species of fish.

Dúa, a species of mustard plant.

Duhur, low marsh lands.

Dúmat, a species of soil, 352.

F.

Farás, the tamarisk.

Farmáns, orders of the Emperors of Dehli.

Fasli, the Hindu agricultural year.

Fatwah, legal opinion of Muhammadan law officers.

Faujdárt, criminal court.

Faujdárí, criminal court.

G.

Gabrs, the defenders of Meerut against Tímúr, 247.
Gahla, a slave girl, 394.
Gand, native indigo.
Gaon, a village.
Gára, a kind of cloth.
Gardwari, a kind of well, 384.
Gariyál, the long-nosed alligator.
Gárna, to bury.
Ganj, a market,
Galta, a measure of length, 478.
Gaz, a yard-measure, 478.
Ghár, a kind of soil, 143.
Gira, a measure of length, 478.
Gojai, a mixture of wheat and barley, 377.
Got, a subdivision of a clan.
Gozan, an elk, 246,
Gúl, a small water-course.
Gumban, a kind of brick, 388.
Gúnchi, a species of fish.
Gúr, a preparation of sugar.
Gúral, the Himálayan chamois (*nemorhœdus goral*).
Guru, a Hindu spiritual preceptor.

H.

Hakím, a Musalmán physician.
Harat, a Persian wheel.
Hari-ki-charan, footprints of Vishnu at Hardwár.
Hari-ki-pairi, the same.
Háth, a measure of length, 478.
Henga, a harrow,
Hijri, the Musalmán era.
Hiran, a deer, usually the antelope (*Antelope bezoartica*).
Homa, a Hindu sacrifice.

I.

Ikta, a subdivision of a Sirkár.
Imli, the *Tamarindus Indica*.
Inámi, a grantee.
Istimrári, applied to tenures, one held on a fixed revenue.

J.

Jaedád, a grant on condition of military service.
Jágír, a grant of land.
Jáman, the *engenia jambolanum*.
Jaribigaz, a measure of length, 478.
Jhábar, the sloth-bear, 157 (*ursus labiatus*).
Jhíls, natural reservoirs of water.
Jhínga, a prawn.
Jítal, a coin.
Joár, the edible grain, *holcus sorghum*.

K.

Káns, a noxious weed (*S. spontaneum*).
Karait, a poisonous snake.
Kark, a rhinoceros, 246.
Kárkhána, a workshop.

Karol, a species of fish.
Katkina, a lease.
Katra, a market-place.
Kazáki, highway robbery.
Kazáks, robbers.
Khádir, the bed of a river.
Khádir matti, alluvial soil.
Kkákar, barking-deer (*cervulus aureus*).
Kháhi, unirrigated.
Kharíf, rain-crops.
Khána khdki, a revenue term, 200.
Khánsámah, a table-servant.
Khás, as a revenue term, direct management.
Khasrah kankút, lists of appraisement of produce.
Kheras, mounds, usually the ruined sites of towns.
Khidmat zamíndári, a revenue term, 428.
Khunti, second crop of indigo.
Khush kharíd, purchase in open market.
Kikar, the *Acacia Arabica*.
Kismat, fate.
Kitkinadars, lease-holders.
Koh-payah, foot of the hills.
Kos, a measure of length, close on two miles.
Kotila, a house.
Kotwál, a police officer of a town.
Kuchcha bígha, a local superficial measure.
Kuchwánsi, a division of a bígha, 478.
Kuri, a measure of length, 478.
Kumbh-mela, festival held every twelfth year at Hardwár.
Kusum, safflower (*carthamus tinctorius*).

L.

Láchi, a species of fish.
Lát, a monolith.
Lakhabagha, the tree-tiger (*Felis pardus*, var.)
Langúr, the grey monkey of the hills (*Presbytis schistaceus*).

M.

Machcha sím, the deep stream of a river, 166.
Madár, the *calatropis gigantea*.
Magar, the snub-nosed alligator.
Mahd or jarau, a species of deer, 187 (*Rusa Aristotelis*).
Maháser, a fish (*barbus tor*).
Mahúa, the *bassia latifolia*.
Malikána, allowance to superior proprietors.
Manjha, a class of soil, 322.
Mantras, charms.
Manwantaras, periods of time, 61.
Másha, a measure of weight, 478.
Másh or urd, an edible grain (*Phaseolus Roxburghii*).
Masjid, a mosque.
Masúr, an edible grain (*ervum lens*).
Math, the residence of Hindu celibates (religious).
Mattiyár, a species of soil, 352.
Maurúsi, hereditary.
Mayúra, a peacock.
Merthi, a species of sugar-cane, 299.
Mindra-i-zarín, the golden *lát* at Dehli, 243.
Misan, a class of soil, 143.
Moth, an edible grain (*phaseolus aconitifolius*.)
Mudfi bamújib mamúl, a revenue term, 417.

Muámla, a matter or subject.
Mughara, a species of fish.
Mukadam, head-man of a village.
Mukarari, applied to tenures held on a fixed revenue.
Mukararídár, the holder of a *mukarari*.
Múng, an edible grain (*phaseolus mungo*).
Múskhori, injury to crops by field mice.
Mustájirs, farmers of the revenue.

N.

Nahari, canal-irrigated.
Nankár, an allowance as maintenance, 413.
Nanwánsi, a superficial measure, 478.
Naslan bád naslan, a term in grants in perpetuity, 491.
Nílgái, the *portax pictus*.
Ním, the *Azadarachta Indica*.
Nisfi, one half.
Nukhúd, an edible grain, gram, (*cicer arietinum*).

O.

Ogal, a kind of well, 142.

P.

Pahára, the uplands.
Pajáwas, brick-kilns.
Palítas, matches for matchlock guns.
Pancha, five.
Paphri, the *pongamia glabra*.
Pára, the hog-deer (*axis porcinus*).
Patti, a sub-division of a village.
Pattidári, a revenue term.
Peta, a sweetmeat.
Píliya, a species of soil, 352.
Pípal, the *ficus religiosa*.
Pír, a Muhammadan saint.
Pokhar, a tank.
Potra, a species of fish.
Pukka, as applied to roads metalled; to buildings or wells built of masonry; generally full, complete, up to standard.
Prayága, the confluence of two rivers.
Pukka hal, a plough with two pair of oxen.

R.

Rabí, the spring crops.
Rahdárí, transit dues, 415.
Ráibandi rates are those which prevail in the neighbourhood, 434.
Ráj, a government.
Rájasuya, a royal sacrifice, 66.
Rájbahas, distributary channels on the canal.
Raiyats, tenants.
Ráki, black-mail levied by the Sikhs, 211.
Rati, a weight, 478.
Rausli, a species of soil, 143.
Reh, impure carbonate of soda, 142.
Rohu, a species of crop (*labeo rohita*).
Rotiya, a species of fish.

S.

Sál, the *shorea robusta*.
Samádh, suicide through religious motives, 103.
Sámbar, a species of deer (*Rusa Aristotelis*).
Sanad, a grant or patent.
Sanwat, the era dating from Vikramaditya, 57 B.C.
Sarkár-ka-raiyat, the tenant of Government.
Sarson, a species of mustard.
Sati, suicide by a wife on her husband's funeral pyre.
Saur, a species of fish
Sáwan, the Hindu month corresponding to July—August.
Ser, a weight equal to 2·057 lbs. avoirdupois, 479.
Seraglio, a harem.
Shajrah, a field-map.
Sharáb, intoxicating liquor.
Shasháni, a species of tenure in Koil, 522.
Shikk, a subdivision of a Subah.
Shíra, preparation of sugar.
Sherdárhidár, a tiger (*felis tigris*).
Sherguldár, a leopard (*felis pardus*).
Shísham, the *Dalbergia sissoo*.
Singi, a species of fish.
Siras, the *Albizzia speciosa*.
Sirsi, a timber-tree.
Sisú, the *Dalbergia sissoo*.
Siwái, interest at 25 per cent., 224.
Sol, a species of fish.
Soteliya, a species of fish.
Sudder málguzár, the principal person who engages for the land-revenue on behalf of the village community.
Súta, a charioteer, 64.
Swayamvara, an ancient Hindu ceremony, 65.

T.

Taka, two pice.
Takkávi, agricultural advances.
Talukadár mustájir, a revenue term, 601.
Talukadári, the holding of a talukadár.
Tank, a measure of weight, 478.
Tarái, low-lying land along a river.
Tasu, a measure of length, 478.
Thagi, the offence of murder by strangling.
Thok, a subdivision of a village.
Tola, a weight, 478.
Trisúl, a trident.
Tulsi, the *ocymum sanctum*.
Tún, the *cedrela toona*.
Tyágdena, to abandon.

U.

Urs, a Musalmán religious festival.
Urd, an edible grain (*phaseolus radiatus*).
Usar, a barren, unculturable soil, 142.

Z.

Zamíndári, the holding of a zamíndár.
Zamíndárs, landholders.

NOMINAL INDEX.

This index gives the names of the principal places mentioned in this volume under both the authorized and popular forms of spelling. The form under which the name will be found in the alphabetical arrangement, when differing from the popular form, is given in parentheses. Thus Agowta will be found under Agauta.

A.

ABBA.
Abdoollahpoor (Abdullahpur).
Abdullahpur.
Aboo (Abu).
Abu.
Achalesvara.
Acheja.
Achhnera.
Achnera (Achhnera).
Acksolee (Agsoli).
Ada.
Adah (Ada).
Adháwan.
Adháman (Adháwan).
Aeesa (Aísa).
Afghánistán.
Agauta.
Aghiána.
Agilás or Iglás.
Agouta (Agauta).
Agowta (Agauta).
Agra.
Agroha.
Agsoli.
Agwáubera.
Ahan.
Ahár.
Ahár Malikpur.
Ahmadganj.
Ahmadgarh.
Ahmadnagar.
Ahmadpur
Ahmedgurh (Ahmadgarh).
Ahmednuggur (Ahmadnagar).
Ahmednuggur (Ahmadnagar).
Ahmedpoor (Ahmadpur).
Ahneya (Abniya).
Ahniya.
Ahri.
Aikree (Ikri).
Aísa.
Ajajoo (Ajaju).
Ajaju.
Ajanta Ghát.
Ajeetpoor (Ajítpur).
Ajítpur.
Ajmer.
Ajmeer (Ajmer).
Ajmere (Ajmer).
Ajoodhiya (Ajudhiya).
Ajudhiya.
Ajunta (Ajanta).

Akarabad (Akrabad
Akbarabad (Akrabad).
Akrabad.
Aksolee (Aksoli).
Aksoli.
Alam.
Alampur.
Alawalpur.
Alee (Ali).
Aleeghur (Aligarh).
Aleegurh (Aligarh).
Ali.
Aligarh.
Alighur (Aligarh).
Allahábad.
Allahdádpur.
Allahdadpoor (Allahdádpur).
Almora.
Almorah (Almora).
Alum (Alam).
Alumpoor (Alampur).
Alwar.
Ambahta.
Ambála.
Amercot (Amrkot).
Amritsar.
Amrkot.
Anantmau.
Andauli.
Andowlie (Andauli).
Anoopshuhur (Anúpshahr).
Anuntmow (Anantmau).
Anúpshahr.
Ar.
Ara (Ada).
Aravali.
Aravally (Aravali).
Areend (Arind).
Arifpoor (Arífpur).
Arífpur.
Arind.
Arrah.
Asafgarh.
Asafnagar.
Asái.
Asophghur (Asaígarh).
Asophnuggur (Asafnagar).
Assam.
Assaye.
Atrauli.
Atrowlie (Atrauli).
Attock (Attak).
Aulum (Alam).

Nanoo (Nánu).
Naraanpoor (Naráyánpur).
Náráyanpur.
Narbada.
Nárnol (Nárnaul).
Narora.
Naroura (Narora).
Naseerpoor (Nasírpur).
Nasírpur.
Náthábarah.
Naugang.
- Naukhail.
Nawábganj.
Nayáshahr.
Neem (Ním).
Neemuch (Nímach).
Neetee (Niti).
Nepál.
Nerbudda (Narbada).
Niamu.
Nidhauli.
Nidhowlie (Nidhauli).
Nigámbodh Ghát.
Nilanti (Jaláli).
Nildhara.
Ním.
Nímach.
Niti.
Noh Jhíl.
Noh Mahal.
Nojli.
Noon (Nún).
Noornuggur (Núrnagar).
Nowgong (Naugang).
Nowkhel (Naukhail).
Nuh.
Nujuffghur (Najafgarh).
Nujeebabad (Najíbabad).
Nún.
Núrnagar.
Nynee Tal (Naini Tál).

O.

Odeypoor (Udepur).
Ogeepoor (Oghipur).
Oghiana (Aghiana).
Oghipur.
Ohun (Ahan).
Orissa.
Oudh.

P.

Pachláṇa.
Padshahpoor (Bádsháhpur).
Páhal.
Pahásu.
Pahul (Páhal).
Pahasoo (Pahásu).
Pailee Poroo (Paili Paráo).
Paili Parao.
Pákpatan.
Palee (Páli).
Páli.
Palra.
Palwal.
Pandhoi.

Panchála.
Pándu.
Panelti,
Pánípat.
Paniyála.
Panjáb.
Paota.
Pardúni.
Parháwali.
Parthia.
Pútan Tanwar.
Pathar.
Pathargarh.
Pathari.
Patiáli (Eta).
Patiyála.
Pátli Dún.
Patna.
Pattialee (Patiáli).
Patti Umda Begam (Sikandra Rao).
Payama.
Peeleebheet (Pílíbhít).
Peepur (Pípar.)
Peeran (Píran).
Peetampoor (Pítampur).
Pesh*war.
Phandpuri (Rahmánpur).
Phoora (Phúra).
Phúra.
Pilcunna (Pilkhána).
Pílíbhít.
Pilkhána.
Pindráwal.
Pípar.
Píran Kaliyar.
Pisáwa.
Pítampur.
Poona.
Poor (Púr).
Poordilnagger (Purdilnagar).
Pooth (Púth).
Pora.
Pouth (Púth).
Pratisthána.
Puchlana (Pachlána).
Pulwal (Palwal).
Pundír.
Púr.
Purdilnagar.
Purdonee (Pardúni).
Puteni.
Púth.
Puttee (Patti).

R.

Radaur.
Radawar (Radaur).
Raghunáthpur.
Rahatpur.
Rahmánpur.
Ráipur.
Ráipur Tátár.
Ráiwála.
Rájdhan.
Rájghát.
Rájpur.
Rájputána.

GENERAL INDEX.

C.

D.

ERRATA.

A full table of errata to the first three volumes will be published with the fourth volume. The following errors should be corrected in this volume :—

Page 30, line 5 from bottom, *for* "through" *read* "though."

,, 33 ,, 6 from top, *for* "Sewálik" *read* "Siwálik."

,, 46 ,, 6 from bottom and elsewhere, *for* "Sahárunpur" *read* "Saháran-pur."

,, 67 ,, 12 from bottom, *for* "Kurakshetra" *read* "Kurukshetra."

,, 68 ,, 13 from top, *for* "Drishtadyumna" *read* "Dhristadyumna."

,, 81 ,, 4 from below, *for* "Jahándár Shah" *read* "Farrukhíyár."

,, 112, 1st line, *for* "Jaudhpur" *read* "Jodhpur."

,, 178, in heading of paragraph 2, *for* "census 1874" *read* "census 1872."

,, 191, line 5 from top, *for* "Gurhwal" *read* "Garhwál."

,, 287, ,, 18 from bottom, *for* "1882" *read* "1879."

,, 307 ,, 8 from top, *for* "Saisara" and "Barsara" *read* "Saisana" and "Barsana."

,, 322 ,, 1, *for* "Landaur" *read* "Landour."

,, 329 ,, 5 from below, *for* "Damaula" *read* "Dumaula."

,, 331. In total of fourth column of receipts, *for* "36,637" *read* "47,480."

,, 347, line 3 from bottom, *for* "Rs. 26,906,474" or "26,90,647" *read* "Rs. 26,90,647" or "2,69,064."

,, 353. In the column of total irrigated, opposite Barauli, *for* "6,397" *read* "6,037 ;" and at bottom of column, *for* "6,49,115" *read* "6,48,815."

,, 370, *for* "Hatísa" *read* "Hathísa."

,, 386, *dele* the average.

,, 405, line 7 from top, *for* "Aksoli" *read* "Agsoli."

,, 409 ,, 23 from top, *for* "Bharáich" *read* "Bahráich."

,, 449 ,, 10 from below, *for* "Sukrawáli" *read* "Sakrawáli."

,, 525 ,, 3 from top, *for* "Budaon" *read* "Budaun."